Visual J++ 1.0 Publishers Edition

Microsoft® Corp Visual J++™ Publishers Edition included on the accompanying CD allows you to create your own Visual J++™ programs without purchasing the commercial version. The Publishers Edition does differ from the commercial version in some ways. These include: No Database support for SQL and ODBC databases through Data Access Objects (DAO) and Remote Data Objects (RDO). No JET engine for creating programs that work with Access and other DAO databases. No Zoomin and WinDiff Tools. No Third party tools and libraries that integrate with Visual J++™. No redistribution of Java Virtual Machine and Internet Explorer. No code samples. No Microsoft technical support. No free or discounted upgrades to later versions of Visual J++™ Professional Edition.

Microsoft Corp Visual J++™ Publishers Edition requires the following to operate:

- Personal computer with a 486 or higher processor running MS Windows® 95 or Windows NT® Workstation version 3.51 or later operation systems
- 8MB of memory (12 MB recommended) if running Windows 95; 16MB (20 recommended) if running Windows NT Workstation
- Hard-disk space:

  Typical installation: 20 MB

  Minimum installation: 14 MB

  CD-ROM installation (tools run from the CD): 50 MB
- A CD-ROM drive
- VGA or higher resolution monitor (super VGA recommended)
- Microsoft Mouse or compatible point device

The system requirements incorrectly state that the product will operate under Windows NT Workstation version 3.51 or later. This should read, "**Windows NT Workstation version 4.0 or later.**" We apologize for any inconvenience this may have caused you.

Web Programming

Bob Breedlove, et al.

sams
net

201 West 103rd Street
Indianapolis, IN 46290

UNLEASHED

Copyright © 1996 by Sams.net Publishing

FIRST EDITION

International Standard Book Number: 1-57521-117-3

Library of Congress Catalog Card Number: 96-68248

99 98 97 96   4 3 2 1

Interpretation of the printing code: the rightmost double-digit number is the year of the book's printing; the rightmost single-digit, the number of the book's printing. For example, a printing code of 96-1 shows that the first printing of the book occurred in 1996.

Composed in AGaramond and MCPdigital by Macmillan Computer Publishing

Printed in the United States of America

President, Sams Publishing: *Richard K. Swadley*

Publishing Team Leader: *Greg Wiegand*

Managing Editor: *Cindy Morrow*

Director of Marketing: *John Pierce*

Assistant Marketing Managers: *Kristina Perry,*
Rachel Wolfe

Acquisitions Editor
Sharon Cox

Development Editor
Anthony Amico

Software Development Specialist
Brad Myers

Production Editors
Tonya Simpson
Ryan Rader

Copy Editors
Miriam Bishop, Robin Drake, Kris Simmons, Robert Temple, June Waldman

Indexers
Johnna VanHoose, Christine Nelsen, Benjamin Slen

Technical Reviewers
Angela Allen, Kyle Amon, Sue Charlesworth, Raj Mangal, Jay Myers, Dennis Teague

Editorial Coordinator
Bill Whitmer

Technical Edit Coordinator
Lynette Quinn

Resource Coordinator
Deborah Frisby

Editorial Assistants
Carol Ackerman, Andi Richter, Rhonda Tinch-Mize

Cover Designer
Tim Amrhein

Book Designer
Gary Adair

Copy Writer
Peter Fuller

Production Team Supervisor
Brad Chinn

Production
Betsy Deeter, Jennifer Dierdorff, Mike Henry, Brad Lenser, Janet Seib, Ian Smith

Contents

Part II Internet Programming Languages

5 Java and the Internet   117

6 Java Development Environments   129

Dedication

This work is dedicated to my family—my wife, Madeline, for being patient and allowing me the time, and my children, Delenn, Duncan, and Diego, for keeping my life in perspective.

—Bob Breedlove

About the Authors

Robert F. Breedlove

Robert Breedlove is a senior systems engineer with EDS. He has over 20 years of experience in data processing, including extensive client/server, UNIX, intranet, and Internet experience. He can be reached at

breedlov@netcom.com

or at his home page

http://www.channel1.com/users/rbreed01/

William F. (Bill) Anderson

Upon graduation from the University of Idaho in 1968, Bill Anderson joined the U.S. Air Force as a communications officer and worked on several computer networking projects including AUTODIN. After leaving the service, he worked on several online banking systems and online railroad systems. In 1979, he started working with UNIX and in 1983, he joined Destek to write its Ethernet driver. This marked the beginning of a career in TCP/IP networking and the Internet, including a stint as the Technical Manager for NetMedia in Israel. In 1995, Bill Anderson returned to the United States and now teaches courses on networking, client/server, HTML, Java, network security, and system administration. He is the author of *Source File Management with SCCS* (Prentice Hall, 1992) and *Building UNIX System V Software* (Prentice Hall, 1994).

Billy Barron

Billy Barron just started a new job as a Senior Software Engineer programming mostly in Java at the Bruton Center for the University of Texas at Dallas. Previously, he worked for almost 10 years as a systems/Internet adminstrator and has an MS in Computer Science from the University of North Texas. He has co-authored and tech edited numerous books, including *Netscape 3 Unleashed, Creating Web Applets with Java,* and *Tricks of the Java Programming Gurus.* You can reach Billy at

billy@metronet.com

or

http://www.utdallas.edu/~billy

Mark Bishop

Mark Bishop writes from Southern California and specializes in setting up new companies on the Internet. He's the author of *The Internet Times*, a weekly online publication, and other various Internet articles. He can be reached at

```
mark.bishop@pobox.com
```

or visit his home page at

```
http://home1.gte.net/showcase/index.htm
```

Keith Brophy

Keith Brophy has many years of experience in the design, development, and testing of software systems. He is currently a software release coordinator for X-Rite, Incorporated, a leading world-wide provider of color and appearance quality control software and instrumentation in Grandville, Michigan. Before that, he was a lead software developer for IBM's System Integration and Federal Systems divisions in the Washington, D.C. area and worked on a wide variety of systems. His experience includes building Internet systems in the "pre-Web" era. During this time, he also was responsible for various operating systems, performance, and graphical user interface research and development projects. He has taught in various venues, including Northern Virginia Community College and as the advanced Visual Basic adjunct faculty member at Grand Rapids Community College.

Mr. Brophy, along with Mr. Koets, co-authored *Visual Basic 4 Performance Tuning and Optimization* (Sams 1996) and was a contributing author for *Visual Basic 4.0 Unleashed* (Sams 1995). He also served as technical editor on *Real-World Programming with Visual Basic* (Sams 1995) and the revised edition of *Teach Yourself Visual Basic 4 in 21 Days* (Sams 1995). He has a B.S. in computer science from the University of Michigan in Ann Arbor and an M.S. in information systems from Strayer College in Washington, D.C. Mr. Brophy is the founder of DoubleBlaze Software Consortium (`www.DoubleBlaze.com`), an ActiveX Internet research and development company involved in endeavors such as research for this book.

António Miguel Ferreira

António Miguel Ferreira is one of the founders and the Web expert of Esoterica S.A., an Internet Service Provider in Portugal. He graduated in Computer Science and Engineering in INSA Lyon, France. He has developed financial-analysis software and currently manages several corporate Web sites for different kinds of clients based on different hardware and software platforms. He has authored technical articles in several magazines, and his other books include *CGI Programming Unleashed* (Sams.net) and *Searching for Gold in The Internet*. For additional information, contact him via e-mail at

```
amcf@esoterica.pt
```

or at his home page

```
http://homepage.esoterica.pt/~amcf/
```

Edward Hooban

Edward Hooban is a programmer with enterWorks.com, a company that provides software for intranets, including Virtual DB, NetSeer, and NetFlow. Mr. Hoooban has been involved with the electronic publishing field for over four years. He has worked as a programmer or analyst for companies such as Ernst & Young LLP, MCI, Jet Propulsion Labs, and Thomson Technology. He loves to write business plans in his spare time.

Daniel I. Joshi

Daniel I. Joshi is the managing partner of a Microsoft Solution Provider consulting company, The Joshi Group, which provides consulting services to Fortune 500 companies in the Los Angeles, California area. Before becoming a full-time author, his corporate consulting background included work for Fortune 500 companies. As a published technical author he is a contributor to *Java Developer's Reference* (ISBN: 1-57521-129-7), and the leading author of *Teach Yourself Café in 21 Days* (ISBN: 1-57521-157-2) both with Sams Publishing.

Timothy Koets

Timothy Koets is a software engineer at X-Rite, Incorporated, a leading worldwide provider of color and appearance quality control software and instrumentation in Grandville, Michigan. Before this, Mr. Koets was a computer systems engineer in the Systems Engineering and Integration division of Martin Marietta in the Washington, D.C., area. In addition to developing Visual Basic applications, Mr. Koets has experience in many other areas including Visual C++, computer networking, client/server applications design, parallel processing and performance analysis. He, too, has previous experience building pre-Web systems that were Internet aware. Mr. Koets is an adjunct faculty member at Grand Rapids Community college, where he teaches advanced Visual Basic, and has prior teaching experience ranging from computer programming and engineering laboratory classes to Lotus Notes training courses.

Mr. Koets, along with Mr. Brophy, co-authored *Visual Basic 4 Performance Tuning and Optimization* (Sams 1996) and was a contributing author for *Visual Basic 4.0 Unleashed* (Sams 1995). He has a B.S. and an M.S. in electrical engineering from Michigan Technological University in Houghton, Michigan. Mr. Koets is the founder of Cockatiel Software, an Internet research and development company that is an affiliate of DoubleBlaze Software Consortium (www.DoubleBlaze.com).

Bryan Morgan

Bryan Morgan is a software engineer with TASC, Inc. in Fort Walton Beach, Florida. He holds a Bachelor's degree in electrical engineering from Clemson University and has also authored material for several other books by Sams.net, including *Java Developer's Reference*. Bryan and his wife, Becky, are anxiously awaiting the arrival of their first child in November, 1996.

Rob McGregor

Fascinated by computers since he can remember, Rob McGregor began exploring computer programming in BASIC as a teenager in 1978. Since then, Rob has worked as a programmer, software consultant, and 3D computer artist, and he has written a variety of programs for Microsoft and numerous other companies. In 1992 he founded Screaming Tiki Interactive, a software development company that specializes in interactive graphics and multimedia applications for Microsoft Windows. Rob lives in Rockledge, Florida, and in his free time enjoys ray tracing, reading, writing, and playing classical and electric guitar. You can contact Rob via e-mail at

```
rob_mcgregor@compuserve.com
```

Zan Oliphant

Zan Oliphant is part of a rebel group of software consultants in south Florida who specialize in Internet applications and multimedia device drivers. He has 10 years of experience in writing device drivers and applications for Windows, DOS, OS/2, Macintosh, and UNIX. Zan and his fellow PC programming cronies (left over from IBM's personal computer glory days in the Boca Raton, Florida, area) are always looking for interesting opportunities. Contact Zan at `zan@gate.net` if you have a cool project for them.

Stig Erik Sando

Stig Erik Sando studies Algorithm Analysis and Software Development at the University of Bergen, Norway. He is currently working on a multi-platform research tool for art history and a full software development system, both fully available on the Web. He spends much of his spare time experimenting with the Web, and the result is a full-fledged virtual fantasy Web site run by a large number of experimental programs to provide a truly exceptional experience. You can contact Stig at

```
<stig@ii.uib.no>
```

Dave Taylor

Dave Taylor is president of the interface design firm Intuitive Systems (`http:// www.intuitive.com`) and has been exploring UNIX and the Internet for 16 years. His online electronic mailbox is

```
taylor@intuitive.com
```

Rick Tracewell

Rick Tracewell, author of *A Web Author's Handbook* (Peachpit Press), is a columnist ("Real World Internet") and a contributor to magazines such as *MacWEEK.* He owns and operates TNT Media, an Internet and Intranet design and marketing firm. He has over 10 years experience as a marketing/advertising consultant and has been designing and marketing World Wide Web pages since early 1994. Rick, his wife Donna, and their two children, Kelsey and Nico, live in beautiful Scotts Valley, California.

Richard Wainess

Richard Wainess is a multimedia consultant and owner of Digital Visionaries, a new media company specializing in Web site design, multimedia, video production, and 3D animation. With almost two decades of experience in the evolving media arena, his clients have included corporations in air transportation, insurance, medicine, entertainment, and aerospace. He has written and produced instructional video media, training pamphlets, and numerous articles on media design. As an Authorized Macromedia Developer, he currently teaches multimedia authoring at InfoDirect (an authorized Macromedia Training Center). Richard holds a Bachelor of Arts degree in Media Management from the Radio-Television-Film department at California State University, Northridge.

Tell Us What You Think!

As a reader, you are the most important critic and commentator of our books. We value your opinion and want to know what we're doing right, what we could do better, what areas you'd like to see us publish in, and any other words of wisdom you're willing to pass our way. You can help us make strong books that meet your needs and give you the computer guidance you require.

Do you have access to CompuServe or the World Wide Web? Then check out our CompuServe forum by typing GO SAMS at any prompt. If you prefer the World Wide Web, check out our site at http://www.mcp.com.

> **NOTE**
>
> If you have a technical question about this book, call the technical support line at (800) 571-5840, ext. 3668.

As the team leader of the group that created this book, I welcome your comments. You can fax, e-mail, or write me directly to let me know what you did or didn't like about this book—as well as what we can do to make our books stronger. Here's the information:

FAX: 317/581-4669

E-mail: programming_mgr@sams.mcp.com

Mail: Greg Wiegand
          Comments Department
          Sams Publishing
          201 W. 103rd Street
          Indianapolis, IN 46290

IN THIS PART

Foundations for Internet Programming

PART

I

An Overview of Internet Programming

by Bill Anderson

CHAPTER 1

IN THIS CHAPTER

Today, the Internet and intranets are exploding like wildfire. The article, "VISA Moves to Intranet System," in the January 29, 1996, issue of *Information Week* states that "two thirds of all large companies either have an internal Web server installed or are thinking about it, and industry analysts believe that soon internal Web servers will outnumber external servers by a margin of 10 to 1. Forrester Research predicts the intranet server business will hit $1 billion by the year 2000." The daily announcements about new venture agreements, new application products, and new technology validate this prediction. In the nearly 30 years that I have worked in the computer industry, I cannot remember such an explosive period.

With all the excitement, one tends to forget that individuals laid the foundation for today's events in the late 1960s. The next three sections of this chapter look at the history, future, and fundamentals of the Internet, networks, and intranets. Then we devote four sections to the basics of TCP/IP networking. The chapter ends with a brief discussion of various applications, plug-ins, and applets.

A Short History of the Internet

Most historical reviews of the Internet imply that networking began with ARPAnet. In a sense, digital transmission of data began when Samuel B. Morse publicly demonstrated the telegraph in 1844. In 1874, Thomas Edison invented the idea of multiplexing two signals in each direction over a single wire. With higher speeds and multiplexing, Edison's teletype replaced Morse's manual system; and a few teletype installations still exist today.

> **NOTE**
>
> In 1837 both Sir Charles Wheatstone in Great Britain and Samuel B. Morse in the United States announced their telegraphic inventions.

The early telegraph systems were, in modern terms, point-to-point links. As the industry grew, switching centers acted as relay stations and paper tape was the medium that the human routers used to relay information from one link to another. Figure 1.1 illustrates a simple single-layer telegraphic network configuration. Figure 1.2 shows a more complex multilayered network.

The links of these networks were point-to-point asynchronous serial connections. For a paper tape network, the incoming information was punched on paper tape by high-speed paper tape punches and was then manually loaded on an outgoing paper tape reader.

Although this activity might seem like ancient history to younger readers, let us put this story into a more understandable framework. In early 1962, I built my first "computer"—a vacuum tube calculator—and spent the following summer reading the latest book on designing transistorized computers. At the same time, Paul Baran and his colleagues at the Rand Corporation were tackling the problem of how to build a computer network that would survive a nuclear

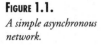

war. Yet when I joined the United States Air Force in 1968, I became an Automatic Digital Network (AUTODIN) programmer. At that time, the network was only a few years old. In essence, AUTODIN replaced the human routers with computers without changing the network model of the paper tape network.

The year 1969 was a year of milestones. Not only did NASA place the first astronauts on the

FIGURE 1.1.

A simple asynchronous network.

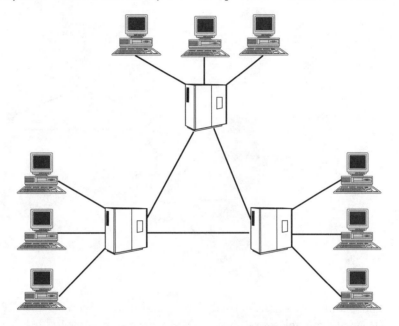

moon but also, and with much less fanfare, Department of Defense's Advanced Research Projects Agency (ARPA) contracted with Bolt, Baranek, and Newman (BBN) to develop a packet-switched network based on Paul Baran's ideas. The initial project linked computers at the University of California at Los Angeles (UCLA), Stanford Research Institute (SRI) in Menlo Park, California, and University of Utah in Salt Lake City, Nevada. The birth of ARPA is permanently engraved in my mind, because, as a young second lieutenant, I presented a briefing on the future of the ARPAnet to a group of colonels and generals. Looking back, my briefing was definitely short on vision. On the other side of the continent from the ARPAnet action, Brian W. Kernighan and Dennis M. Ritchie brought UNIX to life at Bell Labs (now Lucent Technologies) in Murray Hills, New Jersey.

Even though message switching was well known, the original ARPAnet provided only three services: remote login (telnet), file transfer, and remote printing. In 1972, when ARPAnet consisted of 37 sites, e-mail joined the ranks of ARPAnet services. In October 1972 ARPAnet was demonstrated to the public at the International Conference on Computer Communications in Washington, D.C. In the following year, TCP/IP was proposed as a standard for ARPAnet.

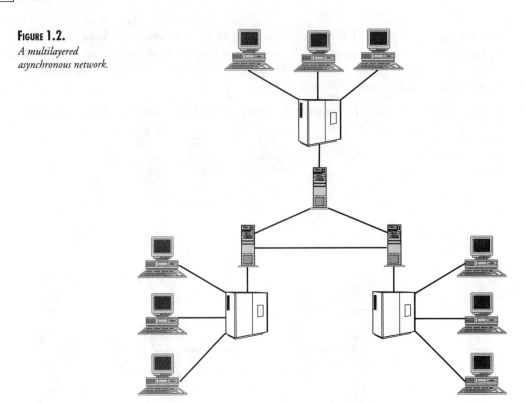

FIGURE 1.2.
A multilayered asynchronous network.

The amount of military-related traffic continued to increase on ARPAnet. In 1975 the Defense Communications Agency (DCA) changed its name to DARPA (Defense Advanced Research Projects Agency) and took control of ARPAnet. Many non-government organizations wanted to connect to ARPAnet, but DARPA limited private sector connections to defense-related organizations. This policy led to the formation of other networks such as BBN's commercial network Telenet.

The year 1975 marked the beginning of the personal computer industry's rapid growth. In February 1975, about seven months after Altair announced its microcomputer, I purchased an IMSAI 8080 (serial number 25). In those days when you bought a microcomputer, you received bags of parts that you then assembled. Assembling a computer was a lot of work, for a simple 8KB memory card required over 1,000 solder connections. Only serious electronic hobbyists, such as those who attended the Home Brew computer club meetings at the Stanford Linear Accelerator Laboratories on Wednesday nights, built computers. (I saw a demonstration of Apple I at one of those meetings.) Since that first computer, which still works, I have changed microcomputers more often than I have changed cars. From their experiences with the Altair, Paul Allen and Bill Gates founded Microsoft to develop BASIC for the new PC world.

In 1976, four years after the initial public announcement that ARPAnet would use packet-switching technology, telephone companies from around the world through the auspices of CCITT (Consultative Committee for International Telegraphy and Telephony) announced the X.25 standard. Although both ARPAnet and X.25 used packet switching, there was a crucial difference in the implementations. As the precursor of TCP/IP, the ARPAnet protocol was based on the end-to-end principle; that is, only the ends are trusted and the carrier is considered unreliable (the section on TCP/IP later in this chapter covers this technology in more detail).

On the other hand, the telephone companies preferred a more controllable protocol. They wanted to build packet-switched networks that used a trusted carrier, and they (the phone companies) wanted to control the input of network traffic. Therefore, CCITT based the X.25 protocol on the hop-to-hop principle in which each hop verified that it received the packet correctly. CCITT also reduced the packet size by creating virtual circuits.

In contrast to ARPAnet, in which every packet contained enough information to take its own path, with the X.25 protocol the first packet contains the path information and establishes a virtual circuit. After the initial packet, every other packet follows the same virtual circuit. Although this optimizes the flow of traffic over slow links, it means that the connection depends on the continued existence of the virtual circuit.

CCITT regulated input into the network by enabling transmission only when the sender received a credit packet, thereby controlling the overall traffic throughout the network. Although X.25 is now a dying protocol, it played a very important role in the development of enterprise networks.

Therefore, the end-to-end principle of TCP/IP and the hop-to-hop principle of X.25 represent opposing views of the data transfer process between the source and destination. TCP/IP assumes that the carrier is unreliable and that every packet takes a different route to the destination, and does not worry about the amount of traffic flowing through the various paths to the destination. On the other hand, X.25 corrects errors at every hop to the destination, creates a single virtual path for all packets, and regulates the amount of traffic a device sends to the X.25 network.

The year 1979 was another milestone year for the future of the Internet. Computer scientists from all over the world met to establish a research computer network called Usenet. Usenet was a dial-up network using UUCP (UNIX-to-UNIX copy). It offered Usenet News and mail servers. The mail service required a user to enter the entire path to the destination machine using the UUCP bang addressing wherein the names of the different machines were separated by exclamation marks (bangs). Even though I sent mail on a regular basis, I always had problems getting the address right. Only a few UUCP networks are left today, but Usenet News continues as NetNews. Also in 1979, Onyx Systems released the first commercial version of UNIX on a microcomputer. As one of the consultants who worked with Onyx, I received one of the first machines off the production line, and thus began my UNIX career. I learned UNIX from a programmer who held to the old-time UNIX rule that if you don't know the answer, look it up in the source code. The only problem was that the UNIX source code lacked comments, which meant that I had to become a master at reading sometimes cryptic C code.

The traveler in me took me to a project in Nigeria for the next three years. I met many wonderful people there, but moving to Nigeria was a major technology shock. I went from delivering messages by e-mail to delivering messages via a human messenger, because that was the only reliable way to deliver messages from one site to another. When I had to make one particularly dangerous trip, the local priest sacrificed a goat in order to protect me from evil spirits. Upon returning to the United States in 1983, I warped back into a world of BITNET (But It's Time Network), CSNET (Computer Science Network), and many others.

The most crucial event for TCP/IP occurred on January 1, 1983, when TCP/IP became the standard protocol for ARPAnet, which provided connections to 500 sites. On that day the Internet was born. Since the late 1970s, many government, research, and academic networks had been using TCP/IP; but with the final conversion of ARPAnet, the various TCP/IP networks had a protocol that facilitated internetworking. In the same year, the military part of ARPAnet split off to form MILNET. As the result of funding from DARPA, the University of California's Berkeley Software Distribution released BSD 4.2 UNIX with a TCP/IP stack. In addition, Novell released NetWare based on the XNS protocol developed at Xerox Park, Proteon shipped a software base router using the PDP-11, and C++ was transformed from an idea to a viable language.

During this period, I took a job with a new company called DESTEK to develop the drivers for its new Ethernet card. As an employee of a true leading-edge company, I finished making some patches to the drivers in my hotel room the night before the 1983 Comdex show opened. That was the year in which the idea of building local-area networks (LANs) was new and hot. With the introduction of LANs, the topology of networks changed from the representation shown in Figure 1.2, which ties legacy systems together, to that shown in Figure 1.3, which ties LANs together.

With the growth in number of organizations connecting to ARPAnet and the increasing number of LANs connected to ARPAnet, another problem surfaced. TCP/IP routes traffic according to the destination's IP address. The IP address is a 32-bit number divided into four octets for the sake of human readability. Whereas computers work with numbers, humans remember names better than numbers. When ARPAnet was small, systems used the host file (in UNIX the file is /etc/hosts) to resolve names to Internet Protocol (IP) addresses. The Network Information Center (NIC) maintained the master file, and individual sites periodically downloaded the file. As the size of the ARPAnet grew, this arrangement became unmanageable in a fast-growing and dynamic network.

In 1984 the domain name system (DNS) replaced downloading the host file from NIC (the section "IP Addresses and Domain Names" discusses the relationship between the two in more detail). With the implementation of DNS, the management of mapping names to addresses moved out to the sites themselves. During this time I moved to Fortune Systems and took over the project management of a new token ring product. Part of this new product included adding the Berkeley sockets technology to ForPro (Fortune's version of UNIX). With the introduction of Sun Microsystem's UNIX-based workstations in the same year, all the pieces of the technology needed to develop the Internet of today were in place.

FIGURE 1.3.

*A LAN-based model for
internetworks.*

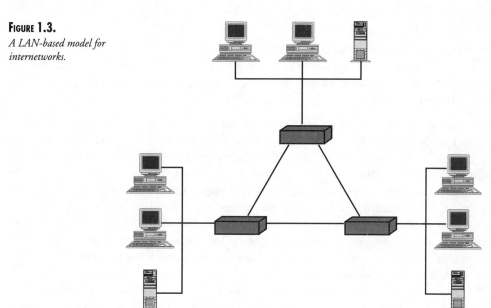

For the next seven years, the Internet entered a growth phase. In 1987 the National Science Foundation created NFSNET to link super-computing centers via a high-speed backbone (56Kbps). Although NFSNET was strictly noncommercial, it enabled organizations to obtain an Internet connection without having to meet ARPAnet's defense-oriented policy. By 1990 organizations connected to ARPAnet completed their move to NSFNET, and ARPAnet ceased to exist. NSFNET closed its doors five years later, and commercial providers took over the Internet world.

Until 1990 the primary Internet applications were e-mail, listserv, telnet, and FTP. In 1990, McGill University introduced Archie, an FTP search tool for the Internet. In 1991, the University of Minnesota released Gopher. Gopher's hierarchical menu structure helped users organize documents for presentation over the Internet. Gopher servers became so popular that by 1993 thousands of Gopher servers contained over a million documents. To find these documents, a person used the Gopher search tool Veronica (very easy rodent-oriented netwide index to computerized archives). These search tools are important, but they are not the ones that sparked the Internet explosion.

In 1992 Tim Berners-Lee, a physicist at CERN in Geneva, Switzerland, developed the protocols for the World Wide Web (WWW). Seeking a way to link scientific documents together, he created the Hypertext Markup Language (HTML), which is a subset of the Standard Generalized Markup Language (SGML). In developing the WWW, he drew from the 1965 work of Ted Nelson, who coined the word *hypertext*. However, the event that really fueled the Internet explosion was the release of Mosaic by the National Center for Supercomputing (NCSA) in 1993.

From a standard for textual documents, HTML now includes images, sound, video, and interactive screens via the common gateway interface (CGI), Microsoft's ActiveX (previously called *control OLE*), and Sun Microsystem's Java. The changes occur so fast that the standards lag behind the market.

How large is the Internet today? That is a good question. We could measure the size of the Internet by the number of network addresses granted by InterNIC, but these addresses can be "subnetted," so the number of networks is much larger than InterNIC figures suggest. We could measure the size of the Internet by the number of domain names, yet some of these names are vanity names (a domain name assigned to an organization, but supported by servers that support multiple domain names) and other aliases. Vanity names and aliases result in a higher name count than the number of IP addresses, because multiple names point to the same IP address. Ultimately, the only way to measure the size of the Internet is by the number of accounts. In my opinion, a reliable study on the number of accounts does not exist. On the other hand, one change indicates an important perceptual change by the general public. Starting in the fall of 1995, companies and organizations began to include their uniform resources locator (URL), along with their street address, telephone number, and fax number, in television ads, newspaper ads, and consumer newsletters. Therefore, a company's presence on the Internet, as represent by its Web address (the URL), reached a new level of general acceptance. The Internet emerged from academia to become a household word. Even those not connected to the Internet now know of its existence.

The question arises as to where all this technology is going. Because my crystal ball is broken, please don't hold me to what I say. The one technology that I have not mentioned yet is virtual reality. The documents and images seen on the Web are only two-dimensional and have limited interaction. The Virtual Reality Modeling Language (VRML) attempts to bring a three-dimensional image to our two-dimensional systems. One of these days, we will have three-dimensional devices and will be able to enter a three-dimensional virtual world. In his 1984 science fiction novel *Neuromancer*, William Gibson coined the words *cyperspace* and *cyperpunk*. He defined *cyperspace* as a "consensual hallucination experienced daily by legitimate operators." How the future plays out depends on you, the reader, who develops the software of the future.

The TCP/IP Protocol Model

Many works on TCP/IP networking begin with a discussion of the seven-layer Open Systems Interconnection (OSI) model and then map the TCP/IP model to the OSI model. This

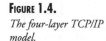

approach fails because TCP/IP does not neatly map into the OSI model and because many application models do not map to the OSI application layers. If the OSI model fails to correctly reflect the nature of TCP/IP, what is the best model? Over the years, different authors have described TCP/IP with three-, four-, and five-layer models. Because it most accurately reflects the nature of TCP/IP, the following discussion of TCP/IP uses the four-layer model as depicted in Figure 1.4.

FIGURE 1.4.

The four-layer TCP/IP model.

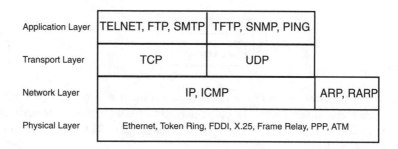

Application Layer	TELNET, FTP, SMTP	TFTP, SNMP, PING
Transport Layer	TCP	UDP
Network Layer	IP, ICMP	ARP, RARP
Physical Layer	Ethernet, Token Ring, FDDI, X.25, Frame Relay, PPP, ATM	

The TCP/IP protocols have their roots in the Network Control Program (NCP) protocol of the early ARPAnet. In the early 1970s, the Transmission Control Protocol (TCP) emerged without the IP layer. Thus the three-layer model, consisting of the physical layer, transport layer, and application layer, was created. By the time OSI published its seven-layer model in 1977, IP was a separate layer, the Network layer. Some publications add a Data Link layer between the Network layer and Physical layer. However, such an expansion is not necessary because the TCP/IP model treats the Physical and Application layers as open-ended, thereby enabling each layer to have several different models. The following sections explore the layers of the TCP/IP model in more depth.

In addition to describing the flow of information, the four-layer model (physical, network, transport, and application) also organizes the large number of protocols into a structure that makes them easier to understand. In Internet jargon, the Request For Comment (RFC) describes a protocol. Today, more than 1,900 RFCs describe protocols, provide information, or are tutorials. In part, the success of the Internet is a result of the open nature of its organization. The Internet Activities Board (IAB) provides overall direction and management (see Figure 1.5 for the organizational chart), and task forces manage the development of new protocols. The Internet Research Task Force (IRTF) deals with the long-term direction of the Internet, and the Internet Engineering Task Force (IETF) handles implementation and engineering problems. The Internet Engineering Steering Group (IESG) coordinates the activities of the many working groups. Membership is not controlled by any organization; instead, anyone who so desires can participate. Anyone can submit an RFC, and anyone can participate in a workgroup. In many ways, the Internet is a grassroots organization that is beyond the control of any organization or government.

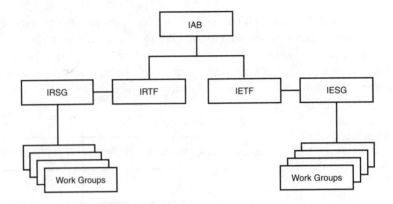

FIGURE 1.5.

The organization of the Internet Activities Board.

To get the latest status of the Internet or to obtain a copy of an RFC, the fastest route is via `http://www.internic.net`. In particular, RFC 1920 (or its replacement) describes the organization of the IAB in more detail, provides the status of RFCs, and gives instructions on how to submit an RFC.

The Physical Layer

As the lowest layer in the stack, the Physical layer has the task of transmitting the IP datagram over the physical media. Unlike the other layers, this layer has specific knowledge of the underlying network. As a result, detailed models of this layer depend on the transmission protocol being used. The sections "LAN Topologies" and "Internetworking—Linking LANs Together" explain these protocols in more detail.

In general, the Physical layer

- Encapsulates the IP datagram into the frames that are transmitted by the network
- Maps IP addresses to the physical addresses used by the network (the MAC address for Ethernet, token ring, and FDDI)
- Performs the operations necessary to transmit the frame over a particular media (such as thick cable, thin cable, telephone wire, or optical fiber)

The Network Layer

The Network layer is sometimes called the Internetworking layer, which is a more descriptive term for this layer's main function. Three protocols are defined in this layer: the Internet Protocol, Internet Control Message Protocol (ICMP), and the Address Resolution Protocol (ARP). Of these, IP is the most important protocol.

Internet Protocol

RFC 791 defines IP as a connectionless and unreliable protocol. It is connectionless because a connection to the destination host does not have to be made prior to sending an IP datagram.

The header of the IP datagram contains sufficient information for it to be transported to its destination over either connectionless or connection-oriented transmission protocols. It is an unreliable protocol because it does not perform any error checking. All error checking, if required, is the responsibility of a higher layer protocol.

What then is the purpose of IP? As the heart of the Internet, the functions of IP include

- Creating a virtual network for the user
- Performing fragmentation and reassembly of datagrams
- Routing datagrams

By creating a virtual network, IP hides the Physical layer and its underlying subnetwork from the end user. The user application needs to know only the destination IP address; IP hides the mechanics of delivery. It does this by fragmenting the packet received from the Transport layer to fit the Protocol Data Unit (PDU) of the transmission protocol. For example, the PDU for Ethernet is 1,500 octets; for SNAP, it is 1,492 octets; for X.25, it is 128 to 256 octets. For each transmission protocol encountered on a datagram's journey to the destination host, IP makes the fragmentation decision until IP reassembles the packet for the Transport layer at its final destination.

IP also handles routing of the datagram to its destination. IP accomplishes this by passing to the Physical layer the IP address of the next hop, where a hop is the distance between a device and a gateway or the distance between two gateways. The following are the rules IP uses for determining the next hop:

- For IP addresses on a local network, send the datagram directly to the host.
- For other addresses, check the routing table for the gateway IP address toward the destination network.
- For all other addresses, send the datagram to the default gateway.

A *gateway* is any device that connects to two or more networks. The gateway then follows the same rules to make a routing decision. Because gateways make the routing decisions, the movement of the datagram from source to destination is independent of any transmission protocol. In addition, each datagram contains sufficient information to enable it to follow a separate path to the destination.

Internet Control Message Protocol (ICMP)

ICMP (RFC 792) performs the error reporting, flow control, and informational functions for IP. Following are the major characteristics of ICMP:

- ICMP data units are encapsulated by IP for submission to the Physical layer.
- ICMP is a required protocol.
- ICMP does not make IP reliable, because it only reports errors.

■ ICMP reports errors on IP datagrams but not on ICMP data units.

■ ICMP reports an error only on the first IP datagram if the IP datagram is fragmented.

■ ICMP is not required to report errors on datagrams.

ICMP reports the following types of messages:

■ ICMP sends a source quench message to the host or gateway to indicate that the IP buffers are full. However, if the message flows through a gateway, the originating host does not receive the message. This ICMP message goes only to the gateway that is one hop away.

■ ICMP sends a destination unreachable message to the originating host when the network is unreachable, the host is unreachable, the protocol is unavailable, or the port is unavailable. (See the section, "The Transport Layer," for an explanation of ports.)

■ A gateway sends a redirection message to the originating host to tell it to use another gateway.

■ An echo request message can be sent to an IP address to verify that IP is running. The destination responds with an echo reply message. The Ping command uses this type of ICMP message.

Address Resolution Protocol

Address Resolution Protocol (ARP) and Reverse Address Resolution Protocol (RARP) present an interesting problem regarding which layer to assign these protocols to. Because they are used only by the multinode transmission protocols (Ethernet, token ring, and FDDI), ARP and RARP belong to the Physical layer. However, because the transmission protocol encapsulates their packets, they belong to the Network layer. To keep the encapsulation boundary clear, I have included them in the discussion on the Network layer.

ARP (RFC 826) resolves IP addresses to MAC addresses (the "Ethernet LANs" section provides additional information about the MAC address) by broadcasting an ARP request to the attached LAN. The device that recognizes the IP address as its own returns an ARP reply along with its MAC address. The result is stored in the ARP cache. On subsequent requests, the transmission protocol needs to check only the ARP cache. To allow for the dynamic nature of networks, the system removes any ARP entry in the cache that has not been used in the last 20 minutes.

RARP (RFC 903) performs a totally different function. If a device does not know its IP address (such as a diskless workstation), it broadcasts a RARP request asking for an IP address. A RARP server responds with the IP address.

The Transport Layer

The Transport layer provides two protocols that link the Application layer with the IP layer. The TCP provides reliable data delivery service with end-to-end error detection and correction. The User Datagram Protocol (UDP), on the other hand, provides an application with a connectionless datagram delivery service.

NOTE

Applications can use TCP, UDP, or both. The needs of the application determine the choice of protocols.

For both TCP and UDP, the port number defines the interface between the Transport layer and the Application layer. The port number is a 16-bit value that identifies a particular application. The *services* file, in UNIX /etc/services, connects application names with the port numbers and the associated protocol. Following is a sample of the contents of the services file:

```
# Format:
#
# <service name>      <port number>/<protocol>
#
echo        7/udp
echo        7/tcp
systat      11/tcp
netstat     15/tcp
ftp-data    20/tcp
fdp         21/tcp
telnet      23/tcp
smtp        25/tcp
time        37/tcp
time        37/udp
```

Port numbers between 1 and 255 are the "well-known services," which represent the port numbers to common application protocols. The Internet Assigned Numbers Authority assigns the numbers for the well-known services, and RFC 1700 contains the current list of assigned numbers. Port numbers between 256 and 1024 previously referred to UNIX applications, although a number of these now exist on other platforms. BSD UNIX specifies that the numbers below 1024 require root permission. The remaining numbers are assigned to experimental applications and to user-developed applications. The packets sent by TCP and UDP contain both the source port number and the destination port number in the packet header. The section "Sockets and Socket APIs" covers the use of port numbers in more detail.

The Transport layer is stream-oriented and not block-oriented. The Applications layer sends data to the Transport layer byte-by-byte. The Transport layer assembles the bytes into segments and then passes the segments to the Network layer. TCP and UDP use different methods to determine the segment size as explained in the following sections.

Transmission Control Protocol (TCP)

The key to understanding TCP lies in the end-to-end principle. In a nutshell, the principle says that only the ends can be trusted because the carrier is unreliable. The ends, in this case, are the TCP protocol of the source and the destination hosts. Thus any error checking performed by the Physical layer is redundant.

> **NOTE**
>
> Use TCP when an application must have reliable data delivery.

TCP uses a technique called positive acknowledgment and re-transmission (PAR) to ensure reliability. After waiting for a time-out, the sending host (or source host) retransmits a segment (the name for a TCP packet) unless it receives an acknowledgment from the destination host. The destination host acknowledges only segments that are error free and discards any segments that contain errors. Because an acknowledgment can arrive after the host resends the segment, the receiving host must discard duplicate segments. Also, because segments can arrive out of sequence (because each IP datagram can take a different route between the sending host and destination host) the destination host must resequence the segments.

> **NOTE**
>
> The stream-oriented nature of TCP means that the responsibility for management of blocks, frames, or records lies in the application.

TCP sequentially numbers each byte in the input data stream and uses this sequence number to track the acknowledgments of data received by the destination host. To initiate the connection and establish the initial sequence number, the source host sends a sync packet to the destination host. The destination host responds with a sync acknowledgment that also contains the initial window size and, optionally, the maximum segment size. The window size represents the maximum amount of data that can be sent before receiving an acknowledgment. Because each acknowledgment contains the window size, the destination controls the flow of information. This form of flow control is separate from the flow control mentioned in the ICMP section. ICMP refers to IP buffers, whereas window size refers to TCP buffers. ICMP flow control affects the device one hop away (which may be a gateway or the source host); window size affects only the source host.

The acknowledgment message contains the highest consecutive octet received as well as the new window size. The destination host does not acknowledge out-of-sequence segments until it receives the intervening segments. After the time-out period elapses, the source host retransmits the unacknowledged portion of the window. This sliding window provides for end-to-end flow control and minimizes IP traffic by acknowledging more than one segment.

Figure 1.6 illustrates the principle of the sliding window. For the sake of simplicity, the segment size used in Figure 1.6 is 1,000 octets. The initial window size is 5,000 octets, as specified in the sync acknowledgment message. The source host transmits segments until the window size is reached. The destination host acknowledges receiving 2,000 contiguous octets and returns a new window size of 5,000, which enables the source host to send another 2,000 octets. Should the time-out period expire before the source host receives another acknowledgment, the source host retransmits the entire 5,000 octets remaining in the window. Upon receiving the duplicate segments, the destination host trashes these duplicates.

FIGURE 1.6.

TCP sliding window.

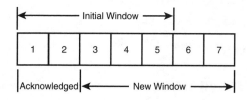

Upon receiving segments, the destination host passes the acknowledged segments to the receiving port number as a stream of octets. The application on the receiving host has the job of turning this stream into a format required by the application.

Just as the process to open a connection involves a three-way handshake, the closing process (fin) uses a three-way handshake. Upon receiving a close request from the application, the source host sends a fin request to the destination host, with the sequence number set to that of the next segment. To actually close the connection requires the acknowledgment of all segments sent and a fin acknowledgment from the destination host. The source host acknowledges the fin acknowledgment and notifies the application of the closure.

As I explained, the PAR method used by TCP minimizes the IP traffic over the connection. Furthermore, it does not depend on the reliability of the carrier. On the contrary, a carrier that spends too much time achieving reliability causes TCP to time out segments. For TCP/IP, a well-behaved transmission protocol trashes, rather than corrects, bad datagrams.

User Datagram Protocol (UDP)

UDP (RFC 768) provides an application interface for connectionless, unreliable datagram protocol. As mentioned at the beginning of "The Transport Layer" section, the protocol does not provide a mechanism for determining if the destination received the datagram or if it contained errors.

> **NOTE**
>
> Because UDP has very little overhead, applications not requiring a connection-oriented, reliable delivery service should use UDP instead of TCP. Such applications include those that are message oriented.

The UDP packet reflects its simplicity as a protocol. The UDP packet contains only the beginning and destination port number, the length of the packet, a checksum, and the data. It needs nothing else because UDP treats every packet as an individual entity.

Applications that use UDP include applications that

- Provide their own mechanism for connections, flow control, and error checking
- Produce less retransmission overhead
- Use a query/response model

For each type of application, UDP eliminates unnecessary overhead.

The Application Layer

The Application layer is the richest layer in terms of the number of protocols. This section covers the most popular protocols. The "Routing in an Internetwork" section covers the routing protocols, and "The Client/Server Model" section examines various models for application protocols. Despite this broad coverage, this chapter considers only a sampling of the many application protocols that have an RFC. An even greater number of intranet applications do not have an RFC. Applications need only follow the rules for interfacing to the Transport layer, and the socket APIs (covered in the "Sockets and Socket APIs" section) hide from the programmer the details of this interface.

It is important to remember that every TCP/IP application is a client/server application. When it comes to the well-known applications discussed in the following sections, the server side exists on every major hardware platform. Except for revisions to old application protocols and the development of new application protocols, much of the work in software development for the well-known protocols centers around the client side of the equation. This situation applies even to the wild world of HTTP. The once light Web browser now performs many tasks that once required the support of the server. Client-side image mapping, Java applets, and scripting languages such as JavaScript and Visual Basic make the Web browser the work horse. This transfer of processing to the client side leaves the server free to respond to more requests.

Telnet

Telnet is one of the oldest and most complicated of the application protocols. Telnet provides network terminal emulation capabilities. Although telnet standards support a wide variety of terminals, the most common emulation used in the Internet is the vt100 emulation. Besides terminal emulation, telnet includes standards for a remote login protocol, which is not the same as the Berkeley rlogin protocol. The full telnet specification encompasses 40 separate RFCs. The Internet Official Protocol Standards RFC (RFC 1920 as of this writing) contains a separate section that lists all current telnet RFCs. However, telnet clients usually implement a subset of these RFCs.

Telnet remains the primary protocol for remotely logging into a host. Although the terminal emulation features are important, other protocols use the remote login portion of the standard to provide authentication services to the remote host. In addition to the traditional remote login standard, some telnet clients and servers support Kerberos (the security method developed by the MIT Athena Project and used in DCE) to provide a secure login capability.

File Transfer Protocol (FTP)

FTP (RFC 959) is another old-time protocol. It is unusual in that it maintains two simultaneous connections. The first connection uses the telnet remote login protocol to log the client into an account and process commands via the *protocol interpreter*. The second connection is used for the *data transfer process*. Whereas the first connection is maintained throughout the FTP session, the second connection is opened and closed for each file transfer. The FTP protocol also enables an FTP client to establish connections with two servers and to act as the third-party agent in transferring files between the two servers.

FTP servers rarely change, but new FTP clients appear on a regular basis. These clients vary widely in the number of FTP commands they implement. Very few clients implement the third-party transfer feature, and most of the PC clients implement only a small subset of the FTP commands. Although FTP is a command-line oriented protocol, the new generation of FTP clients hides this orientation under a GUI environment.

Trivial File Transfer Protocol (TFTP)

The *trivial* part of the name refers not to the protocol itself, but to the small amount of code required to implement the protocol. Because TFTP does not include an authentication procedure, it is limited to reading and writing publicly accessible files. Consequently, TFTP is a security risk and must never be used to transfer data through a firewall.

TFTP uses the flip-flop protocol to transfer data. In other words, it sends a block of data and then waits for an acknowledgment before sending the next block. It uses UDP and therefore performs its own integrity checks and establishes a very minimal connection. In contrast to the richness of FTP, TFTP defines only five types of packets: read request, write request, data, acknowledgment, and error. Because TFTP is so limited, only a few applications (such as router management software and X-terminal software) use it.

Simple Mail Transfer Protocol (SMTP)

The word *simple* in Simple Mail Transfer Protocol refers to the protocol and definitely not to the software required to implement the protocol. Like telnet, many RFCs define SMTP. The two core RFCs are 821 and 822. RFC 821 defines the protocol for transfer of mail between two machines. RFC 822 defines the structure of the mail message. The mail handling system (MHS) model describes the components needed to support e-mail. As shown in Figure 1.7, the MHS consists of the mail transfer agent (MTA), the mail store (MS or mailbox), and the user agent (UA).

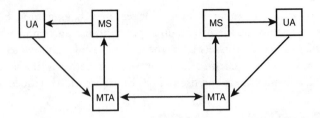

FIGURE 1.7.

Components of a mail handling system.

The MTA (such as sendmail) receives mail from the UA and forwards it to another MTA. Because the MTA for SMTP receives all mail through port number 25, it makes no distinction between mail arriving from another MTA or from a UA. The MS stores all mail destined for the MTA. The UA reads mail from the MS and sends mail to the MTA.

A UA executing on the MTA host needs only to read the MS as a regular file. However, the network UA requires a protocol to read and manage the MS. The most popular protocol for reading remote mail is the post office protocol version 3 (POP-3) as defined by RFC 1725, which makes RFC 1460 obsolete. So as to enhance the security of POP-3, RFC 1734 describes an optional authentication extension to POP-3. POP-3 transfers all of the mail to the UA and enables the mailbox to be kept or cleared. Because keeping the mail in the MS means that it is downloaded every time, most users choose the clear mailbox option. This option works when you have only one client workstation that always reads the mail. Users who need a more sophisticated approach to mail management should consider the Internet Mail Access Protocol (IMAP). RFC 1732 describes the specifications for version 4 of IMAP. With IMAP, the mail server becomes the mail database manager. This method enables a user to read mail from various workstations and still see one mail database that is maintained on the mail server.

Network News Transfer Protocol (NNTP)

In 1986, the year that Brian Kantor and Phil Lapsley wrote the Network News Transfer Protocol (NNTP) standard (RFC 977), ARPAnet used list servers for news distributions, and Usenet was still a separate UUCP network. With this standard, the door opened to establish Usenet news groups on ARPAnet. The NNTP standard provides for a new server that maintains a news database. The news clients use NNTP to read and send mail to the news server. In addition, the news server communicates with other news servers via NNTP.

Gopher Protocol

The popularity of the Gopher protocol is without question. Because it provides a simple mechanism for presenting textual documents on the Internet, Gopher servers provide access to over one million documents. Nevertheless, RFC 1436, the only Gopher protocol RFC, is an informational RFC.

Gopher uses a hierarchical menu system, which resembles a UNIX file system, to store documents. The Gopher client enables the user to negotiate this menu system and to display or download stored documents. Before the popularity of the Web browser, Gopher clients, as separate applications, were popular. Today, the Web browser is the most common client used to display Gopher documents.

HyperText Transfer Protocol

Although HTTP dates back to 1990, it still doesn't have an RFC. However, several Internet drafts reflect the "work in progress." Although the Web uses HTTP, HTTP's potential uses include name servers and distributed object management systems. HTTP achieves this flexibility by being a generic, stateless, object-oriented protocol. It is generic because it merely transfers data according to the URL and handles different Multipurpose Internet Mail Extension (MIME) types (see the following section for details about MIME types). Because it treats every request as an isolated event, HTTP is stateless.

Although an HTTP server is small and efficient, the client bears the burden of the work. The client processes the HTML-encoded document and manages all the tasks involved in retrieval and presentation of the retrieved objects. The URL and MIME open the doors to a degree of flexibility not found in any other document retrieval protocol.

Multipurpose Internet Mail Extension

The original MIME standard set out to resolve the limitations of the ASCII text messages defined in RFC 822. Using the content header standard (RFC 1049), the MIME standard defines the general content type with a subtype to define a particular message format. MIME is an extensible standard, and RFC 1896 describes the latest extensions. Once again, the client (the UA for an MHS) must take care of building and displaying MIME attachments to mail messages.

The simplicity and extensibility of the MIME standard led it to being used to extend the content of other protocols beyond the limits of ASCII text. The notable uses are in the Gopher protocol and HTTP.

LAN Topologies

Although serial and parallel links between computers had existed for some time, multinode networks did not become a serious commercial presence until the early 1980s. The growth of LANs came from two different directions. On the one hand, the corporate need to share files and resources (printers, plotters, and so on) among their PCs encouraged companies such as Novell, Banyan, and Microsoft to develop PC networks. On the other hand, the development of workstations meant that part of the workload could be moved from the server to the workstation. These contrasting developments led to the distinction between server-based LANs and peer-to-peer LANs. (See "The Client/Server Model" section for more details.)

The physical topology of a LAN refers to the networking cabling layout of which there are three types: bus (see Figure 1.8), ring (see Figure 1.9), and star (see Figure 1.10). However, there are only two types of logical topologies: bus (Ethernet) and ring (token ring).

FIGURE 1.8.

An example of a bus topology.

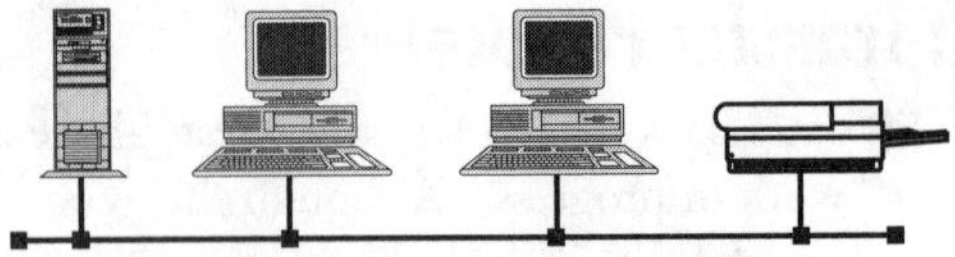

FIGURE 1.9.

An example of a ring topology.

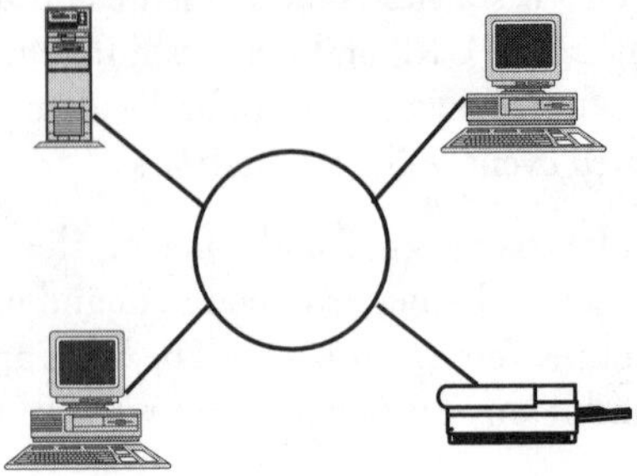

FIGURE 1.10.

An example of a star topology.

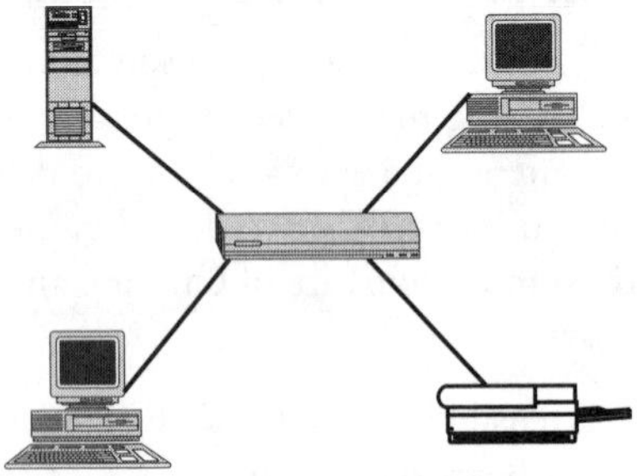

Ethernet LANs

The key difference between Ethernet and token ring is the method used to control access to the cable in a multinode network. Ethernet uses Carrier Sense Multiple Access/Collision Detection (CSMA/CD), which translates to "listen first, then send, and monitor for collisions." When a packet is placed on the cable, every node listens to determine whether the packet is addressed to it. If a collision occurs, the packet on the cable appears as garbage. The first node to hear the collision sends a jam packet, which forces the transmitting nodes to randomly set a delay before attempting to transmit again. As the amount of network traffic increases, the probability of a collision increases. In general, a traffic load between 20 and 40 percent of the bandwidth brings the network to a halt as it tries to resolve collisions.

The address used at this level is the MAC address and is not the same as the IP address. The MAC address is a 48-bit address that the manufacturer programs into each network card. To ensure against duplicates, each manufacturer is assigned a block of address by IEEE. As a media address, the MAC address applies only to LAN addressing. On the other hand, the IP address is a logical address that is independent of the media used in a particular network.

The multiplicity of Ethernet protocols confuses many newcomers trying to understand Ethernet LANs. Two Ethernet protocols are in use today: Ethernet (also called Ethernet II or DIX Ethernet) and IEEE 802.3. Although IEEE made many changes to the Ethernet II format, its change of the type field to the length field created a problem for TCP/IP, which uses the type field to define the type of IP packet. To get around this problem, IEEE 802.2 defines the Sub Network Access Protocol (SNAP), which once again includes the type field. Figure 1.11 illustrates the difference between Ethernet II and SNAP.

NOTE

DIX is an acronym for the three companies that defined the standard—Digital, Intel, and Xerox.

FIGURE 1.11.

Comparison of Ethernet II and SNAP protocols.

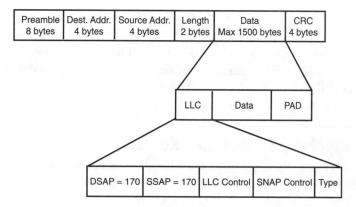

Ethernet II

Preamble 8 bytes	Dest. Addr. 4 bytes	Source Addr. 4 bytes	Type 2 bytes	Data Max 1500 bytes	CRC 4 bytes

SNAP

Preamble 8 bytes	Dest. Addr. 4 bytes	Source Addr. 4 bytes	Length 2 bytes	Data Max 1500 bytes	CRC 4 bytes

LLC	Data	PAD

DSAP = 170	SSAP = 170	LLC Control	SNAP Control	Type

Although Ethernet LANs support mixing these variations on a single network, two nodes must use the same protocol to communicate with each other. Therefore, every node on a TCP/IP network uses either Ethernet II or SNAP, but not both on the same network.

The 10Mbps bandwidth of Ethernet was fast 12 years ago; but with the increased use of multimedia in user interfaces, it no longer meets the demands of modern LANs. Fast Ethernet (100Mbps) offers one alternative, but a number of new hubs use a full-duplex technology to increase the effective utilization of bandwidth.

Token Ring Topology

Instead of CSMA/CD, the token ring network passes a token from node to node. A node transmits only when it has the token. The transmitting node marks the token as in use and then transmits a data packet with the token attached. The receiving node acknowledges the receipt and passes the token back to the sender, which then marks the token as free and passes to the next node. This deterministic process ensures that each node receives equal access to the network under all load conditions.

Although the IEEE 802.5 standard defines the token ring architecture, IBM developed a revised standard to which most token ring networks adhere. Although the topology defined by the standards is a physical star, the logical topology is still a ring topology. The multistation access unit (MAU) acts much like an Ethernet hub except that the MAUs are connected in a ring (refer to Figure 1.9).

Throughout the 1980s, token ring topology seemed poised to replace Ethernet. However, several factors prevented this from happening. The token ring hardware and software were more expensive than Ethernet components, but token ring cabling was cheaper. (Token ring uses unshielded telephone cable.) The introduction of the Ethernet hub in the late 1980s erased token ring's price advantage. In addition, even though token ring offered a 16-Mbps bandwidth (older versions used 4Mbps), the lack of standards for cabling led to vendor-dependent solutions.

Fiber Distributed Data Interface (FDDI) also uses the token ring topology. Although the ANSI X3T9.5 committee started to define the FDDI standard in 1984, the standard did not stabilize until 1990. The frame format is similar to IEEE 802.5 standard for token rings, but operates at 100Mbps. Because of the high cost of fiber, FDDI networks often form the backbone to connect lower-speed networks (see Figure 1.12).

Repeaters, Bridges, and Routers

Repeaters, bridges, and routers perform their own unique functions in networking. The simplest device is the repeater, which sole function is to link LAN segments to form a longer cable. It passes on everything that it receives so that all the packets seen on one side of the repeater are repeated on the second side. Figure 1.13 illustrates the operation of a repeater.

FIGURE 1.12.
Example of LANs connected by an FDDI backbone.

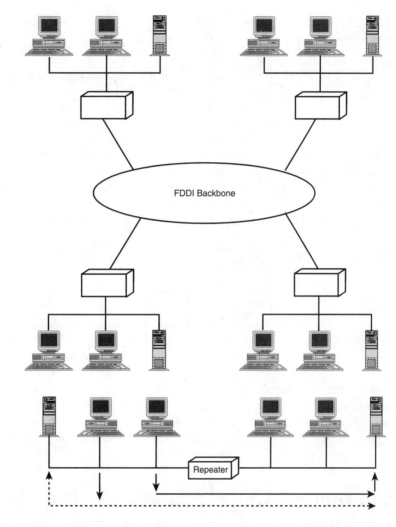

FIGURE 1.13.
Illustration of a repeater in a LAN.

Bridges are, in a sense, intelligent repeaters. Instead of passing all traffic from one side to the other, bridges pass only traffic that is addressed to a node on the other side. The bridge accomplishes this task by looking at the MAC address of the frame in question. Because the bridge does not alter the frame, the LAN segments must use the same topology (Ethernet to Ethernet; token ring to token ring) on both sides of the bridge. Figure 1.14 shows a transparent bridge in an Ethernet network.

The transparent bridge looks at the frame, but does not modify it. On the other hand, a translation bridge removes the frame encapsulation and then encapsulates the datagram with the frame protocol of the destination network. Multiport bridges route traffic according to the MAC addresses on each LAN segment. Yet even these more exotic bridges tie together only segments of a single network.

FIGURE 1.14.

*A transparent
Ethernet bridge.*

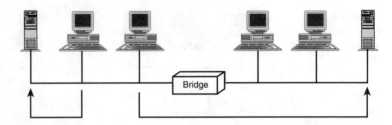

A router, on the other hand, routes traffic between separate networks. This capability earns a router the title of gateway, which is any device with two or more network interfaces. To accomplish its task, the router extracts the IP datagram from the frame, looks at the destination IP address, determines where to route the packet, and then encapsulates the packet with the frame of the next transmission protocol. Figure 1.15 illustrates the actions of a router.

FIGURE 1.15.

*A model for routing IP
datagrams.*

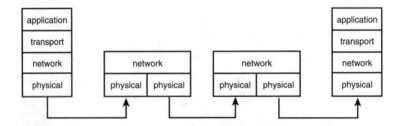

The routing decision rules are the same as the Internet Protocol rules described earlier in the chapter. If the MTU of the next transmission protocol is smaller than the size of the IP datagram, the router fragments the IP datagram to fit the new MTU. Therefore, the destination host can receive many more IP datagrams than the originating host created. The end of the next section covers the routing protocols used to build the routing table.

Internetworking—Linking LANs Together

The original ARPAnet was a wide-area network (WAN), but it was not an internetwork, at least in today's understanding of this term—LANs as we know them did not become popular until the 1980s. The connection of LANs marked the true birth of internetworking, for then individual LANs could connect to form an even larger network—an intranet. When LANs connect to the global network, they form the Internet. This section looks at the technology that makes this connection happen.

Point-to-Point Links

The most basic link between two networks is a point-to-point line between them. The telephone companies in the United States and Japan market these lines as T1, fractional T1, T3, and T4. A T1 line consists of 24 channels, each with a 64Kbps bandwidth (actually 56Kbps, because 8Kbps of the channel is for control signals) for a total bandwidth of 1.544Mbps. This scheme derives not from the needs of digital signals, but from the need to stretch copper wire by multiplexing voice channels. Thus, a fraction T1 line consists of one or more channels from a full T1 line. Going in the other direction, multiplexing 28 T1 lines forms a T3 (44.736Mbps) and six T3s make up a T4 (274.276Mpbs). In the rest of the world, the E1 line contains 32 channels with a bandwidth of 64Kbps for a total bandwidth of 2.048Mbps.

As delivered by a telephone company, these lines are devoid of any Physical layer protocol. Companies use three methods to transfer data between two routers:

- Proprietary protocols
- Serial Line Interface Protocol (SLIP)
- Point-to-Point Protocol (PPP)

To avoid depending on a single vendor for all your equipment, the preferred protocol is PPP. If PPP is not available, SLIP becomes a good second choice.

SLIP and PPP

SLIP (RFC 1055) is an IP datagram encapsulation protocol that enables IP datagrams to be transmitted over an asynchronous serial line. SLIP works on both dial-up lines or leased lines. SLIP is a simple but crude protocol that works well with TCP. However, for protocols such as NFS that use UDP without having an error correction mechanism, SLIP is a poor choice.

Originally, serial links were synchronous links using the high-level data link control (HDLC) protocol. What PPP provides is an HDLC format over asynchronous serial lines. PPP offers many advantages over SLIP in that PPP

- Provides interoperability between products from different vendors
- Supports datagrams from different protocol stacks (such as IP, IPX, and DECnet)
- Provides monitoring of the link through the link quality monitoring (LQM)
- Provides an authentication mechanism through Password Authentication Protocol (PAP)

PPP establishes a connection in two stages:

1. The two sides of the link exchange Link Control Protocol (LCP) packets to establish the link and ensure quality via LQM.
2. They then exchange Network Control Protocol (packets) for each configured protocol stack.

PPP encapsulates the datagrams using a modified HDLC format. On a periodic basis, the two sides exchange LQM packets to monitor the line quality. The network administrator configures the acceptable quality levels. Because of its strengths, PPP is superior to SLIP or other proprietary protocols.

X.25 Links

Although ARPAnet publicly demonstrated the effectiveness of packet-switched networks in 1972, CCITT did not define the X.25 standard until 1976. The X.25 standard takes a different approach to reliability. Instead of depending on higher level protocols, X.25 uses hop-to-hop verification of a packet. The standard's intent was to provide reliable delivery over lines with high error rates.

X.25 is connection oriented in that the sending party must initiate a connection to the receiving party. This connection establishes a virtual circuit that remains throughout the session. Because the virtual circuit is established at the time of connection, it is a switched virtual circuit (SVC). X.25 allows up to a maximum of 32 SVCs at the same time, of which four can be to the same destination gateway. Figure 1.16 illustrates the workings of an X.25 "cloud."

FIGURE 1.16.

An X.25 WAN.

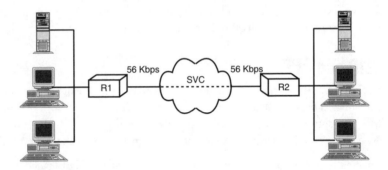

As Figure 1.16 illustrates, a WAN consists of a line, usually 56Kbps for IP, to the cloud, the SVC within the cloud, and another line to the destination gateway. Because multiple users share the lines within the cloud, X.25 regulates traffic via a credit mechanism. The sender cannot send data unless it has a credit. X.25 is not an ideal WAN protocol for TCP/IP networks for the following reasons:

- The small MTU of 128 to 256 octets increases the amount of IP fragmentation.
- The hop-to-hop approach creates redundant error checking.
- The credit system for regulating traffic results in time-outs and extra retransmission of datagrams.

Frame Relay Links

In 1990, frame relay was the hottest new WAN protocol. Instead of an SVC, frame relay uses a permanent virtual circuit (PVC). To identify each PVC, frame relay uses a data link connection identifier (DLCI). As with X.25, frame relay requires a line to the cloud. The PVC exists within the cloud itself. Figure 1.17 shows a typical frame relay setup.

FIGURE 1.17.
Example of a WAN using frame relay.

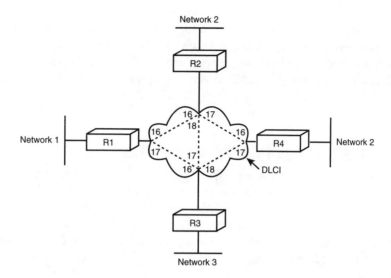

Two factors determine the speed of frame relay connections: the bandwidth of the line into the cloud and the committed information rate (CIR). The bandwidth of the line into the cloud sets the maximum total bandwidth for all PVCs assigned to the line. The CIR sets the guaranteed bandwidth within the cloud. If the rate of transmission for a PVC exceeds the CIR, the excess frames are subject to being trashed if the cloud needs the extra bandwidth to meet its committed rates, which is how frame relay regulates traffic in the cloud. This method fits with TCP's end-to-end principle. In addition, frame relay supports an MTU of 4,500 octets, which eliminates fragmentation.

Integrated Digital Service Network (ISDN) Links

After years of standards and more standards, ISDN is hot news. But despite all the media attention, is ISDN really a viable technology for building intranets or connecting to the Internet? Telephone companies offer ISDN as either a basic rate interface (BRI) or a primary rate interface (PRI). BRI consist of two 64Kbps channels (referred to as B channels) and one control channel (called a D channel) or 2B+D. The rarely used PRI consisted of 23 B channels plus a control channel (23B+D). ISDN is a dial-up service that enables one site to connect to another ISDN site. However, because it has only one D channel, the B channels cannot be connected to different sites.

Normally, the consumer pays a low monthly fee plus, in some states, a connect time charge. The cost of an ISDN connection is lower than the packet charges for X.25. However, when compared to the fixed monthly charge for frame relay, the cost for a heavily used ISDN connection is higher.

Although the number of ISDN equipment providers is increasing, ISDN still suffers from problems with interoperability. Problems of interoperability apply not only to the equipment but also to the transmission protocols used to carry the IP datagrams. Some vendors push asynchronous transfer mode (ATM) as the best protocol, while others use PPP. In general, ISDN is not the best solution for primary WAN connections, but is an alternative for backup lines and for high-speed dial-up connections.

Asynchronous Transfer Mode Links

Media announcements bill ATM as the technology of the future. Does it really deserve such intense hype or is it on the road to becoming another ISDN? While the development of ATM standards proceeds toward a full definition of ATM, manufacturers are busy producing ATM equipment. At this point in time, we face conflicting protocols for defining IP over ATM. RFC 1932 discusses this problem and summarizes the issues facing the ATM Working Group. Yet, IP over ATM is only the first step. Standards for ATM as a transport protocol are still in the works.

Following along the lines of X.25, ATM networks are connection-oriented, SVC networks. By using a small packet (called a *cell* in ATM terminology), ATM evenly multiplexes cells that contain data, voice, or video information. However, the small cell size increases the overhead and increases fragmentation. Until ATM standards stabilize, the question of the viability of ATM remains open.

Routing in an Internetwork

The previous section on routers covered how routers direct IP datagrams between networks and how routers connect networks that use different transmission protocols. This section deals with building the routing table that IP uses to make routing decisions.

The network administrator has the option to manually define static routes. However, in a large and dynamic network, this process is both tedious and prone to error. On the other hand, routing protocols automatically discover networks and the paths to the networks. However, like everything else in the Internet, routing protocols evolved over the years to meet new network demands.

Routing Information Protocol (RIP) was the first route discovery protocol defined by IETF. Because part of the job of a route discovery protocol is to find alternative paths between networks, RIP uses the *distance-vector* method to accomplish this task. In brief, the distance-vector method determines the "cost" of a path by the number of hops required to reach a network. The path with the lowest cost is stored in the routing table. Periodically, RIP rediscovers the network to find any changes. One problem with RIP is that the lowest cost path might not be the fastest path. Although many routing protocols exist, the open shortest path first (OSPF) protocol is the best solution to route discovery. Instead of using the distance-vector method, OSPF uses the link-state metric approach. OSPF adapts more quickly to changes in the network than does RIP.

As the size of the Internet increased, route discovery protocols created two problems: the routing tables became massive, and route discovery protocols consumed too much of the network bandwidth. The solution was to divide the Internet into autonomous systems (AS). Within an AS, the interior gateway protocols (IGPs), such as RIP and OSPF, dynamically discovered the network. Between autonomous systems, an exterior gateway protocol (EGP), such as the exterior gateway protocol (EGP) or the border gateway protocol (BGP), shared information between neighboring autonomous systems. Today, BGP version 4 (BGP-4) is the standard Internet EGP. However, as the number of routers connecting to the Internet continue to increase, the IETF continues to work on ways to reduce the amount of route discovery traffic. In the early 1990s, InterNIC began distributing class C addresses in classless interdomain routing (CIDR) blocks. CIDR permits the routing of class C addresses as a block rather than as individual networks. However, even CIDR is but a short-term fix to a growing problem.

IP Addresses and Domain Names

Internetworking routes IP datagrams according to the IP address, but humans find names easier to remember. This section briefly reviews the principles of IP addresses and provides an overview of how names are resolved to addresses.

What Is an IP Address?

Perhaps the easiest way to understand IP addresses is to look at the Internet as a global network. All networks that comprise the global network are just subnets. InterNIC provides the first level of subnetworking by dividing the global address space into classes that are assigned to organizations. The organizations are then responsible for subdividing their assigned address space to meet their network needs.

The IP address is a 32-bit number. To simplify the notation of addresses, divide this number into four octets and write the octets in a dotted-decimal format. Three types of IP addresses exist: network address, host address, and broadcast address. Because every host is part of a network, you divide the IP address into a network portion and a local host portion. When the local host portion is all zeros, it is a network address; all ones is a broadcast address. Anything else is a host address. However, the IP address itself contains no information about what constitutes the network portion versus the local host portion. The subnet mask provides this information. By convention, binary ones define the network portion, and zeros define the local host portion. Again, by convention, the ones must be contiguous to the left, and the remainder is zeros. Figure 1.18 illustrates this scheme.

As mentioned previously, InterNIC splits the global address space into classes and then assigns the network address according to these divisions. Table 1.1 shows the breakdown of the address space.

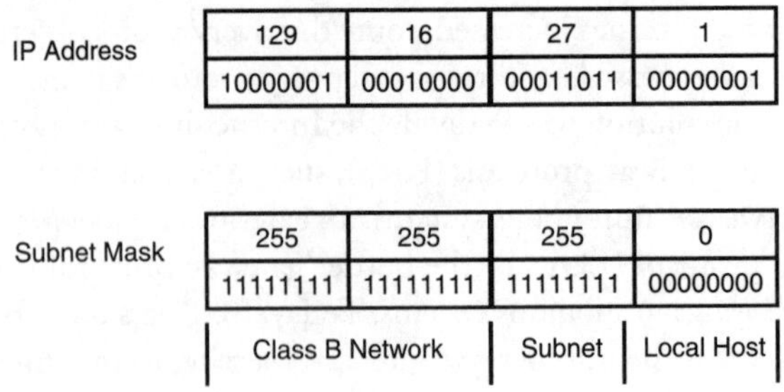

FIGURE 1.18.

IP addresses and subnet masks.

IP Address	129	16	27	1
	10000001	00010000	00011011	00000001

Subnet Mask	255	255	255	0
	11111111	11111111	11111111	00000000
	Class B Network		Subnet	Local Host

Table 1.1. IP address classes.

Table Class	Network Address	Subnet Mask	No. of Networks
table A	1-126	255.0.0.0	126
table B	128-191	255.255.0.0	16,384
table C	192-223	255.255.255.0	2,097,152
table D	224-254	255.255.255.0	(experimental)

As mentioned before, the designations shown in Table 1.1 represent assigned network addresses. The network manager for an organization is then responsible for additional subnetting, according to the requirements of their individual networks.

Special IP Addresses

Several special IP addresses also exist. For an Internet programmer, the most important special addresses are the local loopback address and the broadcast address. For the network administrator, the most important special addresses are those set aside for networks not connected to the Internet.

The local loopback address (127.0.0.1) enables a client application to address a server on the same machine without knowing the address of the host. This address is often called the *local host address*. In terms of the TCP/IP protocol stack, the flow of information goes to the Network layer, where the IP protocol routes it back up through the stack. This procedure hides the distinction between local and remote connections.

Broadcast addresses enable an application to send a datagram to more than one host. The special address 255.255.255.255 sends a "limited broadcast" to all hosts on this network. A "direct broadcast" uses the address form A.255.255.255, B.B.255.255, or C.C.C.255 to send messages to all hosts on a particular class A, B, or C network. Finally, a broadcast to a particular subnet is to the address with all local host bits set to one.

RFC 1918 specifies an Internet "best current practice" for address allocation on private internets (intranets). For a network not connected to the Internet, or a network where all Internet traffic passes through a proxy server, the Internet Assigned Numbers Authority (IANA) reserved three blocks of IP address space: 10.0.0.0 to 10.255.255.255, 172.16.0.0 to 172.31.255.255, and 192.168.0.0 to 192.168.255.255. This block is equivalent to one class A address, 16 class B addresses, and 256 class C addresses.

Resolving Names to Addresses

In the early days of ARPAnet, a system resolved names to addresses using the *hosts* file. The Stanford Research International (SRI) maintained the hosts file, and each site periodically downloaded an updated copy of the file. As the number of sites connected to ARPAnet increased, this method proved too hard to maintain and placed an increasing burden on the network. In 1984 Paul Mockapetris, of University of Southern California's Information Sciences Institute, released RFCs (882 and 883) that describe the domain name system. Today, DNS is the standard for resolving names to addresses. However, the hosts file still plays a role in name resolution during the booting of a system and as a means to provide LAN resolution when DNS is down.

In a nutshell, DNS is a distributed database whose structure looks like the UNIX file system. DNS is a client/server system in which the resolvers query name servers to find an address record for a domain name. The query process begins with the root name servers. If the root name server does not know the answer, it returns the address of a name server that knows more details about the domain name. The resolver then queries the new name server. This iterative process continues until a name server responds with the address for the domain name. Figure 1.19 illustrates the structure of DNS.

FIGURE 1.19.
The hierarchical structure of DNS.

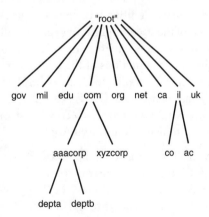

The resolver maintains the retrieved information in a cache until the designated time to live (TTL) for the record expires. This approach reduces the number of queries and, at the same time, responds to the dynamic nature of networks. By distributing the database across the Internet, the site responsible for the information maintains the information.

The Client/Server Model

By definition, every TCP/IP application is a client/server application. In this scenario the client makes requests of a server. That request flows down the TCP/IP protocol stack, across the network, and up the stack on the destination host. Whether the server exists on the same host, another host of the same LAN, or on a host located on another network, the information always flows through the protocol stack.

From the information presented to this point, the client/server model has some general characteristics:

- The server provides services and the client consumes services.
- The relationship between the client and the server is machine-independent.
- A server services many clients and regulates their access to resources.
- The client and server can exist on different hardware platforms.
- The exchange between client and server is a message-based interaction.
- The server's methodology is not important to the client.
- The client carries the bulk of the processing workload so that the server is free to serve a large number of clients.
- The server becomes a client to another server when it needs information beyond that which it manages.

By specifying only the interface between the Application layer and the Transport layer, the TCP/IP Application layer permits various Application layer models. This open-ended approach to the Application layer makes it difficult to draw a single model that illustrates all TCP/IP applications. On one end of the scale, applications run as shell-level commands; on the other, applications run in various window environments. For example, the traditional telnet is run from the shell. Yet, some implementations of the telnet client take advantage of windows technology. To make life more complicated, telnet implementations are also available for the distributed computing environment (DCE). C++ client/server applications use the Object Management Group's (OMG) Common Object Request Broker Architecture (CORBA) model. Consequently, trying to define a universal Application layer model is an exercise in futility.

However, even with all the variations, the Web browser continues to grow as a popular Windows environment for the implementation of the client side of the equation. By using a common windowing environment, users access the Web, connect to remote with telnet, download files, read mail, and access Usenet through one interface. Although browsers implement this interface in a variety of ways, the direction is toward using the browser as an interface to Internet applications.

Sockets and Socket APIs

As mentioned earlier in the chapter, the port number is an application identifier that links the Application layer to the Transport layer. However, because multiple users can run the same application, the identification of a unique connection requires additional information. The Transport layer creates a unique connection via a *socket*, which is the port number plus the IP address. The combination of the sending socket plus the receiving socket provides a unique identification for every connection.

However, if both the sending host and receiving host use the port number defined in the services file, then multiple connections between two hosts for the same application (for example, two FTP connections) results in identical socket pairs. To solve this problem, the source port number is some unique number not related to the services file. This number depends on the particular implementation. For example, UNIX-based TCP/IP uses the process number for the source port number because the process number is always unique. This scheme guarantees the uniqueness of any socket pair. Figure 1.20 illustrates how sockets work.

FIGURE 1.20.

A session established using sockets.

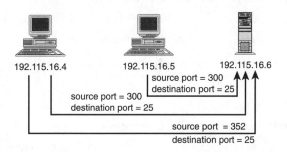

The Transport layer keeps track of these socket pairs by storing them in a *port table*. Although this device solves the technical problems, the use of socket APIs hides the details of the interface from the programmer.

In 1981, BSD introduced UNIX BSD 4.2, which contained a generic socket interface for UNIX-to-UNIX communications over networks. In 1986, AT&T introduced the Transport Layer Interface (TLI), which provides a stack-independent interface. UNIX SVR4 provides both TLI and the Berkeley socket interface. For Microsoft Windows, the WinSock is the socket API and follows the Berkeley socket interface standard. Novell adopted TLI as the standard interface to the Transport layer, although NetWare also supports NetBIOS, Named Pipes, and sockets. As part of the revised SNA standard, IBM introduced the Common Programming Interface for Communications (CPI-C) as another API standard for network communications. With different APIs on different platforms, true portability of software is still an elusive goal. Nevertheless, using an API simplifies the task of writing network software.

Applications, Plug-Ins, and Applets

Not too long ago, programmers developed applications; now they develop applications, plug-ins, and applets. Although a program is a program, the name attached to it tells us something about the nature of the program. Alas, there are more gray zones than black and white ones. In spite of this overlap, some well-defined characteristics separate applications, plug-ins, and applets.

Starting with an application, the common characteristics are that:

- It is a standalone program.
- A desktop program, including Web browsers, invokes an application in a separate window.
- An application normally implements a specific application protocol such as FTP, telnet, or SMTP.

On the other hand, a plug-in's characteristics are that:

- It represents an extension to a Web browser.
- It implements a specific MIME type in an HTML document.
- It normally operates within the browser window.

And then we have the Java applet. Is it a "small application," or is it something else? A Java applet

- Is written in the Java language and compiled by a Java compiler
- Can be included in an HTML document
- Is downloaded and executed when the HTML document is viewed
- Requires the Java runtime to execute

Whereas applications and plug-ins must be ported to each hardware platform, applets run on any platform that has a Java runtime. Thus, applets provide an object-oriented, multiplatform environment for the development of applications.

Summary

This chapter provided

- An overview of the major events in the history of the Internet, networks, and intranetworks
- A review of the TCP/IP protocol stack and the most important protocols
- A brief look at Ethernet and token ring networks and the associated LAN technology
- A survey of current intranetworking protocols and an introduction to the principles of routing

■ A short synopsis of the characteristics of client/server architecture and its relationship to TCP/IP

■ A thumbnail sketch of sockets and a summary of the major socket APIs

■ A list of features that distinguish applications, plug-ins, and applets

WWW Design Issues

by Bob Breedlove

CHAPTER 2

Masses of people worldwide are tapping into the World Wide Web (abbreviated *WWW* or simply *the Web*), lured by graphic interfaces and relatively inexpensive access to unlimited information. Many companies see these Web residents as a ready-made pool of potential customers and are turning to the Web as the next great untapped market.

The Web can be an excellent infrastructure for your application. By infrastructure, I mean that the Internet can provide a common transport mechanism and, through the Web browser interface, provide a well-known and familiar interface to your application. This is especially true if you need to build an application that can do the following:

■ Enable your customers to place orders with you from remote locations via an online catalog

■ Provide customer service support for your products

■ Give your geographically diverse sales staff instant access to pricing information

■ Open your products to an international market

■ Enable your remote offices to access catalog information immediately and place orders with your home office

Any of these requirements need telecommunications to achieve their goals. Most require that you program a graphical user interface (GUI). And some, like online catalogs, require that you display pictures of your products. Before jumping on the Web just because it's the hottest thing going, you might examine traditional alternatives for your application, such as the following:

■ Distribution of catalog and other materials in hard copy via express services

■ Customer service operations with human personnel answering questions via toll-free numbers

■ Dedicated networks running custom or off-the-shelf client/server applications

■ Dial-up operations, such as publicly accessible bulletin boards

■ Distribution (via express services) of materials such as floppy disks or CD-ROMs containing your catalogs

The Internet and the capabilities that it supports, such as the Web, offer advantages in ease of use, cost savings, and immediacy of information. But before you rush off to get your company a set of Web pages, read on.

The public Internet can be a good choice for the infrastructure for all or part of your application, but when you program for the public Internet, you face design issues beyond those for an application on a single computer or a dedicated network. This chapter discusses these design issues and offers some guidance to help you produce viable Internet applications, whether you're performing custom programming or programming for commercial Web browsers.

You Don't Own the Resources

Designing applications for the Internet is challenging, first of all because you are designing client/server applications. These types of applications are always challenging, but using the public Internet adds to this challenge primarily because you don't control most of the infrastructure over which your application runs. To understand this issue, review the following sections for a brief look at the Internet.

The Internet—More Concept than Reality

The Internet as we know it today is more a concept than a reality. Strictly speaking, the Internet really doesn't exist. This statement might sound radical; after all, for something that's more concept than reality, a tremendous amount of activity exists on it. To understand this statement, you have to look at what the Internet is—or, more precisely, what it isn't.

The Internet is not a centrally owned or managed resource. There is no "Internet Committee," "Internet Administrator," or "Internet Help Desk." As you see later in this chapter, naming and addressing are centrally controlled of necessity, but that's about the extent of central control. So, if the Internet doesn't exist, how are all these people doing business on it? What is it?

The Internet (with a capital *I*) is a network of networks (an internetwork, or internet—small *i*). In the most simple terms, the Internet is a router-based TCP/IP wide area network (WAN) formed by the cooperation of independent organizations. These organizations include

- Public agencies such as the Defense Advanced Research Projects Agency (DARPA) in the United States, and central government agencies in other countries
- Network companies such as MCI, SPRINT, and AT&T
- Public, for-profit companies such as IBM and Microsoft
- Private, nonprofit organizations such as universities and colleges
- Other organizations

These entities cooperate with each other by allowing "public" TCP/IP packets to pass through their resources (cables, routers, bridges, computers) for the benefit of all concerned. These packets carry the information for your application across the Internet. The whole thing is held together by router tables, as described in the following section.

Router Tables: The Internet "Glue"

Routers and bridges (generally called *gateways*) make an internetwork function. These devices are specialized computers that use tables of addresses ("router tables") to tell how to get packets of information from one network to another. These tables are maintained by some automatic processes (caching) and by human beings. Invalid router tables can be one of the causes of failed transactions. Look at an example of how they work to get information around the Internet.

My workstation is located on the local area network (LAN) at our building. When my company decided to become linked to the Internet, the company's network naming group contacted the Network Information Center (NIC) to request a block of addresses. They were assigned the address 198.132.0.0. Later, when our LAN was installed, we requested a TCP/IP address from the corporate naming group and were assigned the address 198.132.57.0. When my machine was added to the LAN, it was assigned this address: 198.142.57.4. TCP addresses are defined by a set of 4 numbers separated by periods. Each number can have a value between 0 and 254. There are various classes of addresses that define the meaning of the numbers. For your address class, the first three nodes of the address define the network. (That is, given the address 111.222.333.444, 111.222.333 defines the network. The last number, 444, identifies the particular device on that network.)

When my Web browser needs to communicate with another computer, it uses the address of the computer to establish a connection (socket) for communication. Suppose that I want to talk to a computer at 144.44.44.4. Because the address isn't on my LAN, the request is routed to the LAN "gateway." This "router" has tables listing LANs about which it knows. If it doesn't know about the specified LAN, it sends it to a default "gateway," and so it goes until it finds the address. After the packets reach the gateway on 144.44.44.0, the router there routes the packets to the machine whose address is 144.44.44.4.

Domain Name Service: Helping the Humans Understand

The Internet could operate entirely from these addresses; however, for humans, it's better to use names that are meaningful. (It's the same reason that companies try for phone numbers that can be rendered as meaningful words.) For example, www.microsoft.com is much easier and more meaningful than 198.105.232.6. These names are often referred to as domain names. Internet addresses are divided into domains. For example, this address is in the com (commercial) domain.

It's also easier on network administrators to use names. If the administrator has to physically move the machine hosting your Web pages to another network or has to relocate the Web server to another machine, all he has to do is change the name mapping after the machine or service has been relocated, and the machine is logically moved. Incidentally, if you look up www.microsoft.com, you'll actually get three addresses—another benefit of domain names. Domain name servers (DNS) provide these services based on naming standards and protocols that make this possible.

In simplified terms, when you type in an address like this, the browser extracts the www.microsoft.com portion of the address and formats a name request for the designated name server:

```
http://www.microsoft.com
```

The request causes the name server to return the correct dot-notation address (xxx.xxx.xxx.xxx) for Microsoft's Web server. The browser then contacts the server on the designated port using the HTTP protocol and establishes a socket connection to pass information. (Even www is probably an alias for the actual machine name. This system enables the administrator to change the machine or map the name to additional machines—without having to notify millions of Net residents that the name has changed.)

Client/Server Tools

When most of us think of the Internet, what we really think about are the *tools* that we use over the Internet—Web browsers, Telnet programs, File Transfer Protocol (FTP) modules, news and mail readers, and others. As you will see, these tools are client/server tools. That is, they consist of a piece of software on your workstation that requests services of another piece of software on a computer in another location. These tools are made possible by wide adoption of standards and protocols including the following:

- Transmission Control Protocol (TCP)
- Internet Protocol (IP)
- File Transfer Protocol (FTP)
- Hypertext Transport Protocol (HTTP)
- Simple Network Management Protocol (SNMP)
- Simple Mail Transport Protocol (SMTP)
- Domain Name Service (DNS)

Thus, when you "surf the Net," you really aren't connecting with some monolithic "Internet program." What you're really doing is using a set of client/server programs to return *pages* of information from a server (the HTTP daemon) to a client (the Web browser).

When you design an application for use over the Internet, you design a client/server application. Your custom software can provide both the client and server portions of the application, or you can choose to use standard software for either or both ends of the application. For example, you can choose to write the host (server) portion of the application to be a Web server that can take advantage of any commercial Web browser available on the market. On the other hand, you can choose to implement the host portion of your application as a Common Gateway Interface (CGI) module, and use a commercial Web server to provide the routing to a commercial Web browser. In another example, you can design an application using Java or another plug-in scripting language that utilizes commercial Web browsers and hosts.

Whatever your application, you must be connected to the Internet to make it work. Figure 2.1 illustrates some typical Internet connections.

FIGURE 2.1.

*Typical Internet
connections.*

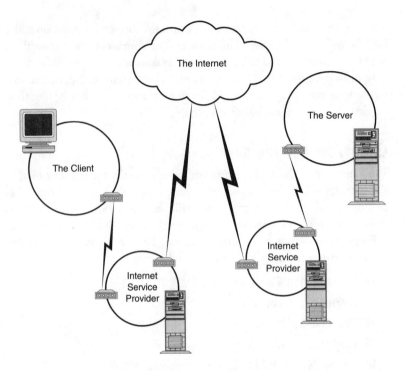

Many variations on this theme exist but, to simplify matters for discussion, assume that the client has a connection to the Internet through an Internet service provider (ISP) from a local area network (LAN). The server (host) also has a direct connection from its LAN to its ISP.

The most typical variation on this setup is for the client to have a dial-up connection over asynchronous modem to the ISP. In essence, once connected, this variation is the same as the dedicated connection. However, it's usually much slower than the dedicated connection—typically 9,600 to 28,800 baud versus 56Kb and up.

Whatever the connection, when you fire up your Web browser to access some information on the host, here—in simplified form—is what happens.

You enter a particular address (a Universal Resource Locator or URL) into your Web browser. Your browser makes a connection to your domain name service (DNS) to request a translation of the human-readable URL to a dot-notation IP address for the host. Your DNS might have to request the address from other domain name servers to fulfill your request, but assume that it returns the address successfully. (Of course, if this is your application and not a Web browser, it has to deal with the case in which the address is not returned successfully.)

Your browser "client" requests a socket connection to the HTTP "host." This request passes through your router to the ISP, and through its router(s) onto the Internet. Here it can pass through several other machines before it reaches the host's ISP and eventually the host.

Assuming that the host has the capacity, the socket connection is established between your browser and the HTTP daemon running on the host. (A *daemon* is a program that runs continually on a host. In the case of an HTTP daemon, it's looking for socket requests on a particular port—typically port 80).

Your browser then communicates with the host, using the HyperText Transport Protocol (HTTP). The actual requests and pages are created using the Hypertext Markup Language (HTML). The browser requests the particular page, which is returned by the daemon. After the page has been returned, the socket connection is broken, and your browser translates the HTML into the page layout that you see.

It is important to note that the connection is broken. That is, unless some mechanism is designed to retain information either at the client (Web browser) or the server (Web server), the information is lost. The next time your client application communicates with the server, it will be as if it had never communicated with that server before. Designers often use *cookies*, which are stored on the client machine, or *database records*, which are stored on the server and keyed by some information passed by the client, to track necessary information.

> **TIP**
>
> The fact that the socket connection isn't maintained throughout the "conversation" is an important consideration in programming for the Web.

Internet Design Considerations

Because Internet protocol (IP) addresses are used in the packet routing process that is at the heart of the Internet, they can't be allocated in a random fashion. Network naming and addressing is controlled by the Network Information Center (NIC), but it's really the only thing that is centrally controlled.

> **NOTE**
>
> The NIC is currently managed by Network Solutions, Inc., located in Chantilly, Virginia. To download information, access ftp://rs.internic.net/ via anonymous FTP.

Each segment of the Internet is controlled by the organization that owns the resources. That organization makes the rules for that segment. Each organization makes bandwidth available to pass IP packets through their routers and along their network. They can place restrictions on the use of these resources. Your packets will potentially pass through several machines, routers, and other devices that are owned and controlled by someone else.

You Don't Make the Rules

As stated earlier, you don't own most of the resources over which your application will operate. Because you don't own the resources, you don't make the rules. This means that you have to abide by the rules established by others—for completely different reasons than the objectives of your application. This situation can result in such unwanted results as finding that the user's ISP restricts the size of messages it forwards, or that your customers can't reach your home page because a name server is down for maintenance.

The point is that, when you run your application over the Internet, you can't complain to some central authority when something goes wrong. Of course, you *can* complain to your network administrator about your local resources or to your ISP about your Internet connection. But, aside from that, you have to take what you get.

In fact, sometimes the problem is finding out what the rules are. When a transaction fails, often there is no indication of the reason. Luckily, organizations supporting the Internet operate within broad guidelines and standards.

Despite this problem, the whole thing seems to operate pretty well for the most part. However, you should keep in mind the points in the following sections as you design your application.

The Resources Can Be Unreliable

You might design, develop, and test your application over one path that exists because of some organization's resources. The application runs great. Then you find out that the organization has gone out of business or decided not to carry Internet traffic, and your path to your end user suddenly changes—with negative results for your application.

You might also find that resources are temporarily unavailable. A domain name server might be unavailable during a critical period of time for your business, like month end, because the host machine is undergoing maintenance during that period. A particular host can be overloaded on Fridays or at the end of the month because it's carrying traffic from its organization's month-end processing.

It's critical to remember that the owners of resources can do anything they want with their resources. They can change their maintenance schedules, move domain name servers, modify bandwidth, and more—all without consideration for your application. After all, they run their systems primarily for their benefit. They make decisions based on their business plan and system designs, not yours. Later in this chapter, you see how to design your application to take all of these factors into account.

Transaction Timing Is Unpredictable

Because you can't control the resources on the Internet, you can't guarantee the timing of your transactions. An interaction that completes in a matter of seconds one time can take several minutes the next time—the next day, your application might not even be able to make the connection. For this reason, timing-critical transactions should not be placed on the public Internet.

> **CAUTION**
>
> Don't place timing-critical applications on the Internet.

Designing Your Application

To this point, this chapter has discussed several issues facing applications intended for the public Internet. It probably seems that you're at the mercy of other organizations and the whole thing is unreliable enough that you might as well give up. Perhaps you are and perhaps it is, but applications are running successfully on the Internet. And the capability to reach a whole world of potential customers is driving Internet development at a staggering pace.

> **TIP**
>
> Good system design and development techniques still hold for Internet applications. Planning is the key to a successful application.

The key is to plan for the Internet environment just as you would if you were designing this application for your own network or private TCP/IP network (intranet). As you see later in this chapter, good system design and development techniques still hold for Internet applications. You just have to plan for some of the idiosyncrasies of the medium. The remainder of this chapter examines what you can do to design your application for the Internet.

Design the Complete Application

Following a good system development methodology is still the best way to design for the Internet. Starting with requirements definition, through business design and into detailed technical design, construction, and testing, the Internet portion of your application must be designed just as you would design any other modules in your application.

The decision to use the public Internet for your application must be made based on business reasons. After all, alternatives to the Internet do exist:

- Build/use a private network (intranet)
- Allow direct dial-up access
- Use an existing online service, such as CompuServe or America Online

Each of these options has advantages and disadvantages that must be considered. Private networks are reliable and secure, but very expensive. Direct dial-up access provides an alternative for users who don't require full-time access to your application. Online services can provide easy access for users who might already be members of the service, but they can be expensive for your users and are not as secure as private networks.

And, of course, some applications aren't appropriate for the Internet, or simply won't run over the Internet. For example, applications requiring results in real time aren't appropriate, and applications requiring extra security (such as personnel applications) are probably inappropriate because of security concerns.

If you consider the use of the public Internet from the beginning of your project, you won't be caught by the surprises that can result from use of the public Internet. Many of these considerations can be complex and can take a good deal of planning or preparation to integrate into your application.

For example, if you plan to have a special domain name for the public to access your application, you must request it from the NIC. This process can take some time. You might have to reconfigure your routing tables to accommodate the machines on which your application will run. You might have to deal with corporate firewalls (special-purpose computers that isolate corporate networks from the general Internet) and other corporate standards to implement your application. The time that these issues take needs to be integrated into your development plan. (See Chapter 4, "Developing Intranet Applications," for more details about dealing with intranet considerations.)

Determine Which Components Will Be Internet-Based

Not all components of your application can be Internet-based. Early in your application design, you need to determine which modules of your application will be Internet-based. Because the timing and security are major issues of using the Internet, modules requiring strict security or where timing is critical should not be implemented on the Internet.

The remainder of this section examines modules that might be considered for Internet implementation.

Public Interface Components

Modules of your application permitting public access are natural candidates for the Internet, for several reasons.

By designing an interface that enables your users to take advantage of tools they already know, you can avoid the training issues that could result from requiring users to learn proprietary programs and new interfaces. The users of your system probably already know how to access the Internet by using their Web browsers, mail and news readers, and File Transfer Protocol (FTP) clients. Introducing your new screens, new addresses, and new filenames is an incremental change in known procedures for your potential users. This setup can make your system less intimidating for potential users and can be especially important if you are designing an online ordering or customer service application.

Multiple End-User Platform Requirements

Applications are often implemented into existing infrastructures. To avoid excessive costs, you might have to accommodate existing end-user platforms. In many companies, this is a mix of PC, Macintosh, and UNIX workstations. You also might want to accommodate customers' equipment and software. Internet tools enable you to reach a wide variety of customers using any type of equipment.

For example, a Web browser is an excellent choice for a client/server application over the Internet. When you write for Web browsers, you can eliminate the need to consider the hardware platforms on which they're located. The Netscape browser, for example, runs on PCs running Microsoft Windows, on the Apple Macintosh, and on various UNIX platforms running X-Windows. Other Web browsers are also available, such as lynx, a text-based browser, the Microsoft Internet Explorer, and browsers supplied by online services such as CompuServe and America Online (AOL).

Writing applications that create Web pages (generate HTML) is relatively simple. Formatting forms (screens) is also relatively simple. However, you need to take the points in the following sections into account.

Choosing a Browser Versus Writing for All Browsers

Hypertext Markup Language (HTML) is derived from Standard Generalized Markup Language (SGML, formally called ISO 88791) used in the publishing industry. HTML, together with URLs (Universal Resource Locators) and HTTP, is one of the foundations of the World Wide Web. There have been two revisions of the HTML standard (1.0 and 2.0). However, two major players in the Web browser marketplace—Netscape and Microsoft—have defined extensions to this standard that have become very popular. Netscape's version 2.0 browser, in particular, implemented several very desirable features that other browsers don't support. Since then, Microsoft and Netscape have both released version 3.0 of their respective browsers, which have further diverged from each other. Because of the installed bases of these browsers, the extensions they have implemented are a *de facto* standard when writing HTML.

Other browsers used on alternative platforms and through various online services might not implement these extensions. Still other browsers are text-based, and don't support many of the graphics that have become so popular on the Internet. Lynx is one of these browsers, implemented for UNIX shell accounts for many Internet service providers, because they provide only a text interface for the user.

To use browsers at the desktop (client), you are faced with a choice in designing your application: You can write for a particular browser, such as the Netscape or Microsoft browser, or a set of browsers that implements a particular standard or pseudo-standard. Or you can write your application so that a wide range of browsers can take advantage of the application. These are the issues involved in making the choice:

■ If you choose to write for a particular browser, be aware that you are potentially limiting the market for your application and whatever profits are attached to that application.

■ If your application requires the use of special features of a particular browser—for example, the frame capability of the Netscape 2.0 browser, or the Java applets implemented in a number of browsers—you must write for that browser.

■ You can choose to write for a particular browser if you have control of both ends of the application. For example, if you are building an application for your field sales force, you will probably provide them with a standard browser, even if they are running on different platforms.

■ If your application needs to reach the widest possible audience, you probably should choose either the HTML 1.0 or HTML 2.0 standard and stick with it in designing your pages.

■ When you are using an HTML standard, keep in mind that some of your audience might be using text-based browsers or have graphics turned off. You might want to provide text-only versions of the pages you design, and you should always provide alternatives to image maps. Graphics used as links should use the ALT keyword to provide a non-graphic alternative to determine where the link leads. For example, you can provide a set of arrow buttons to go from page to page in your application. A person with a text-only browser or with graphics turned off wouldn't have the slightest idea what these buttons meant. To avoid this problem, code the following:

```
<IMG SRC="..." ALT="[INDEX]">
<IMG SRC="..." ALT="[NEXT]">
<IMG SRC="..." ALT="[PREVIOUS]">
```

Although the image source (SRC) can be an icon with an arrow, text-based browsers will ignore it, and it won't be visible if graphics are turned off. The alternate keyword (ALT) displays text in place of the graphic to enable users without graphics to continue to use your screens.

■ Not all browsers support forms. If you are taking orders via the Internet, you might want to provide an alternative method such as mail for those customers with browsers that don't support forms.

More WYSYMNG than WYSIWYG

WYSYMNG stands for *What you see, you might not get.* Programming for a Web browser is much like programming for X-Windows. That is, you can "suggest" what the screen will look like by programming HTML directives such as bold (`<B>`) or heading 1 (`<H1>`), but you really don't have control over the total look of the final product on a particular user's browser.

You can spend a lot of time on page design to make your application user-friendly and appealing to your clients, but differing equipment and software can cause the best page to look ugly and sometimes become just barely usable.

Also, remember that the Internet is a public medium. If your application will be used by consumers, they have a lot of really "cool" pages with which to compare it. You have a lot of competition; your pages have to look their best to attract and keep the attention of the customer.

Your pages might not turn out as you planned, for several reasons:

- Users can define the type styles to be used on their browsers. One user might define 10-point Helvetica; another prefers 12-point Arial or Courier.
- Aspect ratios of screens on various platforms differ. Your screen will look different on a 640×480 Windows screen than on a 1760×1280 X Window screen or on a Macintosh.
- The number of colors supported by the user's equipment can affect the look of your page. Not everyone has equipment that supports thousands or millions of colors.
- A feature supported by one browser can look terrible when viewed with another browser.
- In addition to what's in the foreground, consider the backgrounds and choice of colors. Colors that appear reasonable on one platform can be garish on another. Also, some colors might become unreadable if you place your logo as the background of a page.

Testing is the key. Test your pages on a reasonable number of configurations. If you're writing for commercial Web browsers at the client end, test for the major programs, at least. This means that you will probably test with Netscape Navigator and Microsoft Internet Explorer. Also test with the various hardware platforms that you anticipate.

A good pilot or beta program can help you flush out any difficulties resulting from the differences in equipment and software. Encourage your testers to go a little wild with their settings and get as many varied looks at your final product as you can.

You should also design your pages so that they appear reasonable on a large number of screens. Choose a standard aspect ratio and design for that. For example, you might choose 640×480 as your typical screen size. This is a reasonable setting if your application will be accessed by the general public, because it's the smallest of the ratios you need to consider.

If your application sends graphics—and what self-respecting Web page doesn't?—don't use graphics that span the full screen width. Remember, you also need to contend with scrollbars and the fact that your user might not run his or her browser on the full screen. A general rule of thumb is to keep graphics to 480 wide (about 75 percent of the screen width) at the most. Of course, if you're programming for standard, known equipment and software, you'll know a set number of screen sizes.

Another problem with large graphics is their transmission time. The old adage "a picture is worth a thousand words" applies here. In the English language 1,000 words is about 6,000 characters. At 14,400 baud, these words would take a little more than four seconds to transmit. If you substitute a graphic that is, say, 24,000 bytes, it could take about 17 seconds. This length of time can turn off some potential customers. You might want to consider the value of the graphic and, perhaps, reduce its size or substitute words.

Text paragraphs are relatively unaffected by the size of the screen. However, remember that HTML paragraphs wrap at the borders of the browser screen or the table. You have no control over that aspect of your application. Also, text positioned by graphics using the LEFT, RIGHT, and CENTER directives can appear different (or wrong) with some screen sizes. Be sure to check the graphics on different screens to make sure that your layout isn't affected.

Maintaining Information Across Transactions

One important aspect of writing for the Web is that information about total transaction between the client and host—the "conversation"—isn't maintained across parts of the conversation. In a client/server application across a dedicated network, a socket connection is established at the beginning of the conversation and continues until the work is completed. The client and host track the information (often in memory) while the connection is in progress, because they're dealing with a known entity at the other end of the socket connection the entire time.

This isn't the case for Web transactions. Socket connections are maintained only for the length of a single send/receive exchange (transaction). That is, when the client sends information to the server (say a URL) and the server responds with information (a Web page), a socket connection is established and then broken. Information regarding the transaction is not maintained for the next send/receive transaction unless you specifically program for it.

This process is a lot like having a conversation with someone with a very short memory. You say something to him and he responds, but the next time you say something to him, he doesn't remember your first exchange. You have to keep filling in the details from previous exchanges to keep your partner up to date. In addition to this problem, the host might be carrying on thousands of transactions with other clients simultaneously. The point to remember is that you have to carry all information about the conversation with you. A couple of methods are available.

First, you can hide information on the screen (page) sent to the client. HTML provides an input type for this—hidden. Hidden information doesn't appear on the page, but is returned like any other input field. You might want to hide sequence information or other identifying information that will be used by your application to retrieve data records. Hiding information on-screen is risky, especially if it's confidential. Most browsers support the capability to examine the source code for the page. Any user taking advantage of this feature can see your hidden information. You might want to encrypt sensitive hidden information.

An alternative is to save the conversation information at the server. Send a "key" to the client, either as a display element on your page or as hidden text. When the client returns the form, use the key to retrieve information about the conversation. This alternative is more secure, but has the disadvantage of leaving information on the server for transactions that aren't completed. For this reason, you might need to devise a cleanup routine that can run periodically to eliminate these incomplete transaction segments.

Some Web browsers implement information packets called *cookies* as a mechanism to store information about a host directory tree. Cookies can be used to store key information that can later be used to retrieve information stored on the host. See the later section called "Security" for details about cookies.

Timing Issues

As mentioned, timing can be a problem on the Internet. You don't know from one time to the next whether completing the transaction will take several seconds or much, much longer. For this reason, timing-critical portions of your application should not be Internet-based.

Consider timing not only in terms of programs, but also in terms of the tolerance of human beings to timing issues. For example, you might not want to rely on the Internet for a customer service system where your customer service personnel are on the phone with disgruntled customers. The response time of the Internet is, at best, unreliable. A Web page can take one second to display one time and several minutes another time. You don't want your disgruntled customer hanging on the phone while your customer service personnel are waiting for the page in the later case.

Detecting and Recovering from Failed Transactions

If your Web browser doesn't receive a response from the Web server in a specified length of time, it will time out and notify you that the server is unavailable. Timeouts are difficult to manage in client/server applications across your own infrastructure; they're more difficult when you are dealing with the Internet. You must include code to determine that the transaction has failed and recover from this condition. Because of the unpredictability of transaction durations over the Internet, you can't reliably test the expected duration of a particular exchange. The question is, how much time is too much time? When can you determine that your application has failed?

The design of your application affects the way in which you determine timeouts. If your custom programs run each end of the client/server connection, you can control timeouts and recovery more precisely. If you are using commercial products for one or both ends of the connection, however, things are more difficult.

Commercial Web browsers have timeout settings built in. If your client is using one of these programs, it will time out after a length of time, but it will time out on the basis of the manufacturer's standards—not yours.

Handling Retransmissions Caused by the Back Button

One problem you face related to timeouts is the use of the "Back" button and retransmission of the same transaction to the host. If your client is using a browser, you can't control this occurrence. The user can go back to your screen and resubmit it as many times as he wants. He really doesn't intend to submit multiple transactions; if he's impatient or doesn't receive a "reasonable" response, he just feels that the transaction has somehow failed and attempts to resubmit it.

You help prevent the problems caused by these multiple transactions in several ways. First, provide meaningful feedback to your client. Make sure that the screen you return contains enough meaningful information to assure the client that he has successfully completed the transaction. Also, give the client a button to take him somewhere, such as to your home page or to another logical page. This option gives him an alternative to the Back button and can go a long way to mitigating this problem. Some browsers now support page refresh generated by the server. Using this option can be effective for a long-running transaction, but it limits the choice of target browsers.

Also, you can serialize your forms by using the TYPE=HIDDEN parameter of the INPUT field type. As the server program receives a transaction, it records the serial number and prevents another transaction with the same serial number from being posted. If the client submits a second transaction with the same serial number, use a gentle reminder screen to tell him that you've already received and posted the original transaction.

Connectionless Protocols: E-Mail

Some protocols are unreliable. A major example of this is e-mail. E-mail is ubiquitous, and is thus an excellent choice for some types of applications where universal access to your customers, employees, and other resources is a consideration.

With very few exceptions, everyone who is on the Internet has e-mail. And through connections to other networks, the use of uucp (UNIX-to-UNIX Copy), and interfaces to other mail systems such as corporate mail systems, you can reach even people who are not on the Internet.

There are many examples of the use of e-mail in applications:

- A mailing list to send out bulletins or product information to your registered customers
- E-mail access to your help desk personnel

- Automatic response systems to product inquiries
- Verification of order entry can be by e-mail
- Automated notification by e-mail of some update event in your application

But there is one major consideration in the use of e-mail. Because e-mail is a "store and forward" protocol, you aren't guaranteed delivery. Here's how it works. You send e-mail to a customer. The message is stored on your computer. The mail system examines the address and determines that it is not local. The message is then forwarded to another computer indicated as a mail forwarder in the local mail configuration. That machine repeats the process and passes on the message if it is not for its local mail system. The process continues from machine to machine until the message is delivered or some "fatal" error is encountered. This process can take seconds or days. In some instances, the mail cannot be delivered and it is returned to you.

Your application must be able to deal with this returned mail. First, it must be able to identify it, and then it must be able to do something with it. One consideration is that this mail can take several days to return to the system. Because handling this mail can be tricky, the most typical action is to forward the mail to some human's mailbox for him or her to deal with.

One problem can be a loop created in automated mailing lists when a message is returned to the list mailbox and interpreted as a new request, to which the original information is returned, which is then rejected and returned to the mailbox and interpreted again, and so on. You get the idea. This can be avoided by adding a return address that is not the address of the mailing list. For example, make the return address some human's mailbox and let that person deal with the complexities of this situation.

The Internet Can Be Unreliable and Can Change Without Notice

A program designed for a single computer or for use on a local area network (LAN) or dedicated wide area network (WAN) is guaranteed some specific set of resources (bandwidth, central processor usage, and so on), which results in reliable operation. With some certainty, in these situations, your application will operate much the same in terms of response time from day to day.

This is not necessarily the case with the Internet. Because there is no central control of the public Internet, it can be unreliable. Machines can be pulled out of service, networks can be reconfigured, addresses can be changed, and more, without notice. In addition, the number of people "surfing" the Net is increasing exponentially, causing delays and even failures of some parts of the Net. The time of day and day of the week can be a factor. Also, the use of automated programs such as "spiders," which search the Net in a much more intense way than humans, and the introduction of poorly designed programs that consume way too much network resources add to the situation.

How do you predict what the impact of Internet use will be on your application? Of course, the best way is to test a prototype of your application at all the times you expect it to be used. A wide area, public beta test can tell you something about timing and reliability, but predicting all the problems you will face is probably impossible. Short of this, here are some thoughts.

Make sure that your application is hosted on a machine that won't be overburdened. Also, make sure that the connection between the machine and the Internet is sufficiently fast to permit reasonable access and response times. For most commercial applications permitting public access, a T1 connection is recommended. Note, however, that T1 connections might be prohibitively expensive for many small businesses. In this case, you might want to consider renting space for your Web application on a machine at an Internet service provider (ISP) with adequate bandwidth to support your application. Depending on your area, you might also have access to ISDN phone lines. These can be a viable alternative to the faster T1 connections. However, even these can be expensive.

Design an Alternative Delivery Mechanism

If you're placing part of your business on the Internet, designing an alternative to your Internet-based application can be critical. This factor can be especially important if the application is designed to secure sales for your business. When you place a sales application on the Internet, you place at least a part of your profits at risk of the unreliable nature of the transport medium. Here are a couple of considerations:

- You also risk at least part of your business if you design your application to be accessed by your (potential) customers. If you allow customers to order your products online, or you base part of your customer service strategy on an online application, you take the chance that your customers will get a bad impression of your business from a failure of the Internet.

- You also risk part of your business if you design an Internet application to be used by your sales or field support staff. Imagine a sales representative at an important customer's site, unable to reach your Internet Web page to show your product.

To avoid losing sales from these situations, design alternative methods for your customers and field staff to access information, place orders, or obtain customer service response. Here are some ideas:

- In your media advertising (print, radio, television, direct-mail) include all sources for ordering your products.

- Provide customers with a toll-free order number that allows customers to order the same products found on your Web page.

- Provide fax-back service that allows customers to receive your catalog pages in hard copy form.

- Provide a telephone number for your remote staff to dial in to your server directly via SLIP or PPP.
- Provide a CD-ROM version of your online catalog for your sales staff.

In short, don't leave your customers with no way to place an order or get support except the Internet. Because you don't control the Internet resources, you can't guarantee delivery.

Detecting and Reporting Failures

So when does your application decide that a particular transaction has failed? This depends a great deal on whether you control both ends of the transaction. Let's look at a typical situation.

Figure 2.2 depicts a scenario in which you don't control the timeout at the client (browser) end. The browser will implement some timeout function and will usually return some standard error to your user, but how does the host determine that a transaction has failed? In addition, your host application might never respond to the customer. This can be for one of many reasons, including failure of your application, failure of the network, or an error on the part of your customer in operating his browser. To your customer, these errors all appear the same—as a failure of your application. Whatever the reason for the timeout, you need to deal with the consequences in your application. You do not want to compound the problem by sending the customer something he did not want. For this reason, you might want to implement some confirmation into your application as shown in Figure 2.2.

FIGURE 2.2.

Your host program with output to a Web browser.

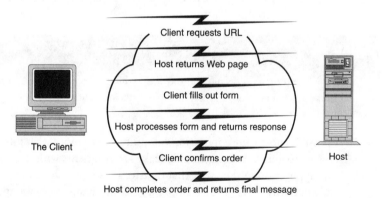

The Client

Client requests URL

Host returns Web page

Client fills out form

Host processes form and returns response

Client confirms order

Host

Host completes order and returns final message

In this example, your customer is ordering online. To make sure that the transaction has completed successfully, you might want to have one final confirmation after the order has been placed. That is, your customer fills out the order form and transmits it to the host. The host processes the order and sends a confirmation back to the client with total cost and a confirmation number. The client is required to confirm the order. When the host receives this confirmation, the transaction is complete and the customer is sent one final message.

2

WWW DESIGN ISSUES

This scenario will vary when you have custom programs at each end of the transaction or create a transaction using Java applets. However, the principle of confirming that a transaction was received still applies.

Dealing with Disasters

All systems need disaster recovery plans, but when you design a system for the Internet, the fact that you don't have control over most of the Internet's resources makes recovery more difficult. Disasters can range from simple power outages to parts of the Internet being out of service due to natural disasters such as floods, hurricanes, and so on. Your disaster recovery plan must deal with the fact that you might have no control over the recovery of Internet resources. Your application is completely dependent on some other organization, and while that organization is dealing with the problem, you can be out of business.

Of course, if your resources are the ones that are involved in the disaster, you need to have plans for an alternative infrastructure. Here are a couple of ideas for designing your application that can help when you lose all or part of your local infrastructure:

■ Use an alias to name the machine on which your server is located. For example, most Web servers are named www.something (even though the machine really isn't named www). With this strategy, if you lose this server or have to relocate your application you can restore the application on another machine, set that machine's nickname to www, update your domain name server, and you're back in business. Your domain administrator can set up this alias for you.

NOTE

Machine "nicknames" can also be a good technique to enable you to switch your application to a new machine or run it on multiple machines during standard operation.

■ If possible, host your application on multiple machines with different Internet service providers. At a minimum, make arrangements with a service provider to host your application in the event that disaster strikes your base machine. Also, plan how you will notify users of the (temporary) name change for your application *before* you need it.

Security

Security is a major issue with the Internet because it is public domain. The public nature of the Internet can cause security concerns that don't exist for private intranet or dial-up applications. Because packets pass through machines over which you have no control, someone can potentially see confidential information. Any hacker with a network datascope can get credit card numbers, Social Security numbers, and other confidential information from your transmissions. You need to design for these potential security leaks.

Passing Through Multiple Machines

Your transactions have the potential to pass through many computers and other devices on their way between the client and the host. On most UNIX systems, you can issue the `traceroute` command to see this routing. Most of these machines are acting only as routers, but they're points where your signal can be intercepted and decoded. Here's a look at the number of "jumps" that it takes to get from my account on Netcom to another computer run by the Channel 1 BBS. (The command issued was `traceroute user1.channel1.com`.)

```
traceroute to user1.channel1.com (199.1.13.9), 30 hops max, 40 byte packets
 1   netcomgw.netcom.com (192.100.81.254)
 2   f0-0.netcomgw.netcom.net (163.179.1.1)
 3   t3-1.scl-ca-gw3.netcom.net (163.179.220.194)
 4   sl-mae-w-F0/0.sprintlink.net (198.32.136.11)
 5   sl-stk-6-H3/0-T3.sprintlink.net (144.228.10.45)
 6   sl-ana-2-H4/0-T3.sprintlink.net (144.228.10.26)
 7   sl-ana-1-F0/0.sprintlink.net (144.228.70.1)
 8   sl-fw-6-H2/0-T3.sprintlink.net (144.228.10.29)
 9   sl-fw-3-F0/0.sprintlink.net (144.228.30.3)
10   sl-channel1-1-S0-T1.sprintlink.net (144.228.33.34)
11   user1.channel1.com (199.1.13.9)
```

Don't worry about the format of this display. The important point is not the details, but the fact that my information passed through ten devices other than the originating machine (not shown on this route printout) and the destination machine (`user1.channel1.com`). If you are at all concerned about security in your application, this situation should concern you.

Anyone with a Scope

Anyone with a scope on any of the devices through which your information passes can trap that information. Things like Social Security numbers (999-99-9999) and credit card numbers have patterns that can be detected by automated search programs. An unscrupulous person can place one of these programs on a device routing packets along the Internet, let it work for a period of time, and then take a leisurely look at the data that it traps.

E-Mail Example

E-mail can be even more vulnerable to this type of piracy, because mail travels as plain text in a format that's easy to read, and the full messages are stored and forwarded by post office machines. Although most of us don't like to look at them, and many mail readers filter them, mail headers can tell you a lot about the machines on which your mail rests. Take a look at a message header:

```
Received: from ns2.eds.com by mail5.netcom.com (8.6.12/Netcom)
 id NAA01582; Wed, 24 Jan 1996 13:21:17 -0800
Received: by ns2.eds.com (hello)
 id QAA07685; Wed, 24 Jan 1996 16:21:40 -0500
Received: by nnsp.eds.com (hello)
 id QAA26247; Wed, 24 Jan 1996 16:19:58 -0500
Received: from target2.sssc.slg.eds.com by dsscsun1.dssc.slg.eds.com
       (5.0/SMI-SVR4)
 id AA00143; Wed, 24 Jan 1996 15:18:57 -0600
Received: from rfbpc (rfbpc.sssc.slg.eds.com [198.132.57.4])
       by target2.sssc.slg.eds.com
```

Like the `traceroute` information presented earlier, the details of this heading information isn't important for this discussion. The important thing is the fact that this piece of mail rested on four machines not under our control. At each of these points, your message is simply part of a larger text file. Anyone with the proper security clearance (or anyone who can hack into that machine and obtain that clearance) can read your message. The headings are read from the bottom to the top:

- The mail originated on my PC (`rfbpc`).
- The mail was passed to the post office machine on our LAN (`target2`).
- The mail was forwarded by our post office to our division's mail handler (`dsscsun1`).
- The division mail post office passed the mail to our corporate firewall (`nnsp`).
- The mail passed to the corporate post office outside the firewall (`ns2`).
- Finally, the mail was delivered to the post office on the Internet service provider (`mail5`).

Incidentally, the mail passed through several machines that aren't listed in this heading. Remember that `traceroute`? Mail packets have to pass through several machines on which they don't rest, making them vulnerable to snooping.

What does this mean to your application? If you're passing sensitive, private, or confidential information, consider encryption for your application.

Encryption

Many types of encryption can be used to protect your transactions. Several Web browsers and hosts are "secure" in that they encrypt information passing between them. The extent to which you want to use encryption in your application will depend on the sensitivity of the information and the cost of encryption.

Of course, if you are writing your own application in which you will provide both the client and server modules, you can provide your own custom encryption schemes.

> **CAUTION**
>
> One caution about using encryption such as that used by products like Pretty Good Privacy. These schemes are controlled by the U.S. Federal Government, which has some restrictions against exporting encryption technology overseas. Be sure to check out this issue before committing your application to specific technology or standards.

Secure Web Servers

If you are designing an application that will be hosted by a Web server, consider placing the application on a secure Web server. These servers establish a secure connection with the client browser and encrypt all information that passes between them. The Netscape Commerce Server, for example, uses Secure Sockets Layer (SSL) to encrypt pages during transmission.

Encrypting Sensitive Information

Even if you choose not to encrypt entire transmissions, never send an unencrypted password, Social Security number, credit card number, or other sensitive information over the Internet. This data can be encrypted easily by the host CGI interface program, even if you implement your program using a commercial Web hosting program. Implementing encryption at the client end of the application is more difficult if you don't rely on the encryption capabilities of the commercial server/client. Java or some other plug-in application needs to be used to encrypt the sensitive information prior to transmission.

Encrypting or Password-Protecting Documents

If you are going to transmit documents over the Internet, such as word processing documents, you can use the capabilities of the applications that create the documents to encrypt or password-protect the documents. For example, both Microsoft Word for Windows and Microsoft Excel can provide file-sharing passwords that must be entered before a document can be accessed.

You might also want to use the capacity of compression programs such as PKZIP to password-protect files they have compressed. With this system, even if some hacker manages to intercept a file, she will have to work hard to read it.

Following are some thoughts about using passwords:

- Use the longest password you can to protect your documents.
- Don't use common words or phrases. They are easier to remember, but also easier to crack. Random combinations of letters and numbers are best.

■ Change passwords periodically. That is, if you send several documents over a period of time, make sure that you change the password at least every 30–60 days. This strategy lessens the chance that the password will be compromised.

■ Don't send passwords over the Internet; transmit them via a secure means.

Unsecure Request, Secure Response

In the case of especially sensitive information, you can allow requests to come to your application via the public Internet. However, you might want to return the requested information via a secure medium. For example, you could allow customers to request information via the Internet and then use fax-back facilities to fax the information to their machines.

Verifying the Correct Client

Another difficulty in dealing with connectionless protocols is that you might need to verify that the client you are talking to is the one you think it is. Luckily, some techniques are available, as described in the following sections.

Trusted Addresses

Your application might accept socket connections only from "trusted" TCP/IP addresses. Web browsers send the name of the machine in the SERVER_NAME field and the address of the remote in the REMOTE_ADDRESS field. Be aware that these fields can be faked, but they can be used in combination with user IDs and passwords to provide additional security.

User IDs and Passwords

Your application might ask the client for a user ID and password. For applications with custom clients, the user ID can be programmed into the client before distribution and the user can be required to enter a specific password to verify her identity. In addition, you can limit user IDs to specific TCP/IP addresses and refuse to serve ID/address pairs that don't match.

Cookies

If your application uses commercial browsers, you can take advantage of the capacity of some browsers—for example, Netscape or Microsoft's Internet Explorer—to store information on the client machine; that information can be returned to the server when a specific host path is requested.

CGI scripts can set data at the client's browser; this information is called a *magic cookie*. When a browser makes a request for a page, it sends its cookie (if it has one set) to the server along with the request. If this is the first time that this particular machine has been used to access your application, it will need to set default configurations or provide a form on which the customer can provide required information.

A magic cookie is made up of several parts:

- URLS for which the cookie will be sent
- PATH for which the cookie will be sent in the above host domain
- DATE when the browser will delete its cookie
- SECURE flag that tells the browser to send its cookie only if it has a secure connection to the server

> **TIP**
>
> Cookies can also be a convenient way to customize your application for a particular client; for example, when you are transmitting a page in a foreign language for international clients. Once a customer has visited your site, you can recognize the customer from his cookie, and automatically customize the page returned to him.

Using this capability, you could transmit a user ID to the client and then retrieve it on subsequent visits by this client. You can match the returned cookie to security information entered by the human being on-screen as an additional security precaution.

International Considerations

When you place your application on the Internet, the potential audience for your application becomes an international one. You must consider the implications of this fact, especially if you are designing an application for public access.

I Don't Think We're in Kansas Anymore

Your audience might speak a different language and come from a different culture. Even if you program your application in English, if the application will be used by someone in another country, you will have some linguistic and cultural considerations. The title of this section is a good example. For anyone who has seen the movie *The Wizard of Oz*, the meaning of the phrase "I don't think we're in Kansas anymore" is evident. For those who have never seen the movie, the meaning is blurred. In this case, the heading means that you can't assume that the rest of the world operates by the same conventions that you do in your part of the world. Be careful and always consider that the Internet is an international medium, especially if you are expecting business from international clients.

Non-English Speakers

English has become the international language of business, but your application is likely to be visited by potential customers who don't speak English or speak it as a second language. In designing your pages, avoid idioms that are likely to be misunderstood by foreign English speakers.

> **NOTE**
>
> Pages in a foreign language can be important if you are targeting your application to a specific country or culture. Be sure to use a standard form of the language and avoid idioms that can be confusing in a different country.

> **NOTE**
>
> If you expect a large number of customers, you might want to provide alternative language versions of your pages. When you do, remember that some languages are more wordy than others to express the same thought. Here's an example from my wristwatch instructions:
>
> | English | Spanish |
> | --- | --- |
> | The alarm time is set on a 12-hour basis and indicated by the alarm hour and minute hands that move independently of the main time hands. | La hora de alarma se fija en la indicación de 12 horas y es indicada por las manecillas de horario y minutero de alarma que se nueven independientemente de las manecillas de hora principal. |

These differences in the number of words required to express the same idea can affect formatting of your carefully designed screens. Be sure to account for this problem if you choose to support multiple languages.

Also, make sure that you have your pages translated by a professional translator or, at the very least, a native speaker of the language. Don't rely on automated translation programs. Often, the direct word-for-word translations aren't accurate and will not be understood.

TIP

Remember the discussion of magic cookies in the "Security" section? Cookies can also be used to store language information. That way, when a customer returns to your pages, he is automatically routed to the correct language version.

Languages vary by country. For example, the Spanish spoken in Mexico varies somewhat from the Spanish spoken in Spain. They use different words, tenses, and idioms to express the same thoughts. Spelling also differs from country to country, even in English. *Meter* and *civilization* in the USA are *metre* and *civilisation* in England. So what should you do?

- Choose a standard version of the language, but be aware that some of the words used can differ by country.

- Don't depend on automated translations by programs; have a professional translator or native speaker of the language perform the translation.

- If the language supports a formal and informal mode of conversation, choose the formal mode.

- Avoid slang and other local idioms that are a part of every language.

- If you have any doubt that an expression will be understood, try for something more standard.

- Be consistent in your use of language.

Other Cultures

When you are dealing with an international audience, you can't assume that they will have the same frame of reference as you do in your country. Even if they speak your language, they might not understand local references or idioms that might be common in your county—or even your part of the country.

Something else to consider is your use of graphics, icons, and colors. In Islamic cultures, it's inappropriate to depict human figures in certain ways, so be careful with your representations of the human form. In a number of cultures, the left hand symbolizes vulgar functions, so depicting a left hand on a button could be insulting. In some cultures, white is the color of mourning after death. The list goes on.

Be cognizant of and try to avoid these situations. Watch for them as you design your pages.

Addresses and Phone Numbers

Always use the area code and perhaps include the country code for all phone numbers. Also, don't assume that the visitor knows where you are located. Always include the full address for your company if you choose to give it. Include the country. It's arrogant to assume that all your visitors will know which country you are in by the use of a state or province.

Even things as simple as the address and phone number differ from country to country. If you will be capturing this information in your application, you need to provide forms with fields that will accommodate the differences.

Also consider edits. For example, U.S. ZIP codes are all numeric, but, if you edit for this, your customers in Canada will not be able to enter their postal codes, which include letters.

Dates and Number Formatting

On the Internet, you are addressing an international audience. Remember that numbers and dates aren't formatted the same way in all cultures. For example, 11/12/96 is November 11, 1996, in the United States and December 11, 1996 in many countries of Europe. To avoid confusion, format dates as "dd-mon-yy," for example, 11-Dec-96.

Most countries support a.m. for times before noon and p.m. for times after noon. However, you might want to use a 24-hour time reference just to be safe. Thus, 1:30 in the afternoon could be displayed as 1:30 p.m. (13:30) or just 13:30.

Numbers also have different formats in different countries. In the U.S., one million is 1,000,000.00, while in Spain it's 1.000.000,00. But digits aren't the only problem. One billion in the United States is one-thousand million (1,000,000,000), while one billion in England is one million million (1,000,000,000,000). So you have to be careful even if you use the words and not the numbers.

And speaking of numbers, your prices are important. If you are quoting prices, be sure that your audience knows what currency you are using. For example, both Canada and the United States use the dollar, but $50.00 (Canadian) is less than $50.00 (US). Be sure to specify that amounts be sent in the currency that you want.

Time Zones

The Internet has expanded the concept of the 24-hour/7-day application. When you write an application for the Internet, you need to be aware that while you are sleeping in the U.S., someone in Spain is starting their workday and people in Australia are already worried about tomorrow. If you're going to serve an international audience, the day really starts by convention at the International Dateline, not in your particular time zone.

This consideration can be especially crucial for applications that have to do things for the customer based on time of day, or that rely on information from other processes that run periodically (typically mainframe batch processing cycles). In the latter case, the question to answer is this: Can your application be unavailable during the period when the information is being processed?

To illustrate the former situation, let's look at a small application that will mail reminders daily to customers. You'd like to have these reminders arrive in their mailboxes for the start of the workday, so you decide to send them out at midnight—but midnight where?

Assume that you're in the U.S. Pacific time zone, say in California. That's -8 hours from Greenwich Mean Time (GMT). By the time it's midnight in California, it's 11 a.m. the next day in Australia. If you send out the notices at midnight California time, you will certainly miss the notice to your customers down under.

The answer, of course, is to keep time zone information with the messages. Then arrange your programs to execute once per hour and process the messages for the appropriate time zone. Thus, you would process those messages for Australia at about 1 p.m. the previous day, Pacific Time, so that they arrive in Australia in time for the start of the correct business day.

Summary

Given the discussions in this chapter, you might be discouraged about writing your application for the Internet. Designing an application for the Internet does add challenges to the basic client/server application, but none are insurmountable.

New solutions are coming to the market every day. Design your application for the Internet from the start. Rely on solid programming design methodologies and practices. Be aware of the pitfalls and provide solutions for them, and test your application thoroughly under all conditions. If you do this, you will create a successful application and join the thousands who are taking advantage of this marvelous medium.

This chapter covered issues related to writing an application for the Internet. You learned that you do not have control over the infrastructure and resources upon which your application will depend. You saw techniques that can be used in your application to deal with problems of the unreliable nature of the Internet, security and confidentiality issues, and the international nature of the Internet.

Security and Encryption

by Billy Barron

CHAPTER

3

This chapter touches on a variety of issues and technologies to help you maintain security and privacy for yourself and your clients while programming. You learn what to watch out for when writing your Internet programs. Additionally, the chapter provides some background material on security and data encryption. You don't learn specific details of how to deal with every security and encryption issue. It would be impossible to cover everything in a single chapter; whole books have been written about firewalls and encryption alone. I attempt to refer you to other resources, such as other books or Web sites, to get more information.

Security

When you are programming on the Internet, never skip security. People really do crack Internet systems. If you are on the Internet long enough, someone will try to break into your system. Even the U.S. Department of Justice has had its Web site broken into. By taking appropriate steps to secure your systems and your programs, you (hopefully) will be able to avoid break-ins. Take the word of experience: The time spent up front is well worth it. A single security incident can easily eat up weeks of your time and potentially even millions of dollars if your systems are critical or have confidential information.

If setting up security is going to take an insane amount of time and money, you need to do a risk assessment to determine whether you should go ahead and do it. In a risk assessment, you look at the likelihood of a security breach and the cost of such a breach to your organization—remembering to include indirect factors such as loss of trust by your clients and related lost business—versus the cost of securing your system. Often, this analysis makes the answer obvious.

> **NOTE**
>
> No security system is ever 100 percent secure. This doesn't mean that you should just give up on security. Your goal is to secure your system by spending less money on security than a break-in would cost to fix.

People might try to break into your system or program for a variety of reasons. Some do it for fun. Others, unfortunately, do it to steal information or damage your machines. Therefore, security is almost always important. This is especially true of your Internet programs. Because they are likely one of the first things that will be attacked, spend some time thinking about the security implications of any code you are going to deploy. If you are an Internet novice, show your design and code to an Internet expert to have him verify that your program appears to be secure.

> **NOTE**
>
> Although this chapter focuses on Internet security, you need to remember that your Internet programs should try to deal with security on other fronts. In particular, do your best to defend against attacks from the other employees at your workplace. More security breaches are caused by employees than by crackers out on the Internet. Though you think you can trust your coworkers, keep the number of people who have access to bypass the security mechanisms to an absolute minimum. This strategy improves security and account-ability.

General Internet Security

When you look at Internet security, you must look from the bottom of the protocol stack (the physical wire) all the way up to end-user applications. Any level can be attacked; therefore, every level needs some security mechanisms in place. This section mainly covers the potential weaknesses of the security mechanisms, so that you can be expecting them and possibly can deal with them in your Internet programs.

One common kind of Internet attack is to eavesdrop on packets as they cross the network, whether on the Internet or your local LAN. Networking people use the term *sniffing* instead of *eavesdropping*, however. Just about any computer can be turned into a sniffing device. The scariest thing is that any cracker who becomes root on your UNIX systems can use your UNIX box from her remote cracking site to see packets on your network. By doing this, she can gain more passwords to get into even more machines.

3

SECURITY AND ENCRYPTION

> **NOTE**
>
> Throughout this chapter, you will notice that the word *cracker* is used instead of *hacker*. The term *hacker* has two meanings. Originally, it was (and still is in many circles) a positive term, meaning "someone who plays with the internal workings of a system." The media then came along and twisted it to mean "someone who breaks into computer systems." Many people have recommended the term *cracker* for the second definition. It's a good fit, as a safe cracker is comparable to a computer cracker.

Besides preventing the cracker from getting root on your system, you can do a few things to minimize the threat of this attack:

■ Don't use Ethernet networks for your LAN if security is your number one goal because eavesdropping on an Ethernet is easy to do. However, Ethernet is a very good, inexpensive technology for LANs in general.

- If you do use Ethernet, the best thing to do from a security standpoint is to use switching hubs instead of repeated hubs. The advantage is that a single machine on a switched hub doesn't see traffic on the network that isn't supposed to go to that machine.

- The final approach is to encrypt traffic as it goes across your LAN or the Internet. This is very labor-intensive and shouldn't be done lightly. (You will learn much more about encryption later in this chapter.)

One organization that can potentially help you is *CERT* (*Computer Emergency Response Team*). CERT makes announcements about what bugs exist in Internet-related software and where to acquire patches to solve the bug problems. If patches aren't available, it usually at least suggests some workarounds. It also maintains some security tools on its FTP site. You might want to take a look before starting on Internet programming to make sure that the tools you use in your development are secure. Its URL is `http://www.cert.org/`.

Web Security

The Web can be fairly secure, completely insecure, or anywhere in between, depending on how it's configured. Because different Web servers have different security mechanisms, the types of Web security available can range widely from system to system. Most of the popular Web servers (for example, NCSA, Apache, and Netscape Communications/Commerce Server) offer reasonably good security if configured correctly.

One of the security options controls whether someone can upload files via the PUT command. I strongly recommend turning off PUT unless you absolutely need it and fully understand what it's doing. You can still get information via the Common Gateway Interface (CGI). CGI is another optional feature to which you might want to restrict access on the server. Poorly written CGI programs can create large security holes, as discussed later in this chapter.

If you need advanced security, you can run one of the Web servers that offers encryption capabilities, such as the Apache/SSL, Open Market Secure Web Server, NCSA, or Netscape FastTrack Server. It won't solve all of your security problems, but it definitely can help, especially against packet sniffing attacks.

General Programming Security

Over the 20-plus years that the Internet has been in existence, many security bugs have arisen in Internet programs. The same types of security bugs, however, tend to crop up over and over again. For example, the same kind of security bug has shown up in the `finger` daemon, `sendmail`, Gopher, and the NCSA Web server. Another set of similar bugs has appeared in `sendmail`, Gopher, and many CGI scripts. In other words, in Internet programming, history does repeat itself.

Preventing Buffer Overflow

The most common bug in Internet programs involves buffers. Internet programs must be prepared to accept input of any length; the mistake that programmers commonly make is to assume that the input has a maximum length and then write it into a fixed-length buffer when the input exceeds that maximum length. Even this can be stopped automatically if your compiler inserts code into the executable to make sure that the buffer (array) boundaries aren't crossed. However, in C, the traditional Internet programming language, array boundaries aren't checked.

A cracker can exploit this problem by overwriting the buffer. The excess input then can overwrite the program that exists beyond the end of the buffer. By this overwriting, the cracker then can have the target system execute his own code. The hard part of this attack for the cracker is that he must change his attack for every different type of machine, if not every version of a particular operating system.

To prevent this problem, you must make sure that your buffers don't overflow under any circumstance. The first solution is to always dynamically allocate your buffers as needed. Some languages (for example, Perl) can automatically do this for you. Another approach is to look at the size of the input; if it's too long, you treat it as an error or you truncate it. Each of these methods works if implemented correctly, but you need to decide which is the best method for your application.

Preventing Shell Command Attacks

Another common mistake is to allow a cracker to send commands to a shell. This problem occurs when the program accepts some input and then uses it in a shell command without performing adequate checking. On UNIX, it's absolutely critical to eliminate some special characters, such as backticks (`) and quotes ("). The characters in UNIX that are safe to pass to a shell are all alphanumeric: underscore (_), minus (–), plus (+), space, tab, forward slash (/), at (@), and percent (%). For DOS and other systems, a different set of characters might be valid. In the CGI section of this chapter, I come back to this security problem and explain some ways to solve it for CGI programs.

Changing the Root Directory

One way to minimize all Internet security programming problems is to use a chrooted environment on a UNIX system to run the server program. If you are not on UNIX, this method is not possible and you might want to go on to the next section. The name comes from the chroot (change root) command in UNIX, which changes the root directory for the program. Setting up this kind of environment correctly is somewhat troublesome, but the security benefits can be huge if security is critical for your program. If a cracker does break through your program's security, he will be in a "rubber room" environment on your system—without access to the real operating system files or anything else you don't want to expose. This isolation will enormously reduce his ability to cause damage.

If your program works with confidential or sensitive information, it's critical that your Internet programs can keep that information out of the hands of people who shouldn't see it. Beyond your program's security, you need to protect the data from access outside of your program. For example, you might have a program that receives credit card numbers. If a cracker breaks into your system and becomes root, he then can look at the file where you have stored the credit card numbers. A solution to this problem is to keep all this data encrypted whenever you store it. (Before you ignore this occurrence as being unlikely, you should know that it has already happened to a major Internet service provider.)

It is a good idea to have your program demand absolute security by keeping an audit trail; sending this audit trail to a different machine (possibly via syslog) also is advisable. With this method, if the machine that runs your program is compromised, you still have the audit trail from which to recover (as well as a backup, hopefully). Audit trails also are good for finding program bugs and abnormal use patterns, which are often a sign of compromise or attempted compromise. On the negative side, some audit trails can use an enormous amount of disk space and are hard to find useful information from.

Java Security

Java is probably the most secure of all of the Internet programming languages in existence; Java was built from the ground up to be ultra-secure. The Java security model is somewhat complex, but it incorporates security on several levels. If it were bug-free, it would be an extremely strong security mechanism that would greatly reduce worries about the security of running programs on the Internet. Unfortunately, so far a couple of bugs have been found in the security protection of the language, which would enable people to circumvent the security. The good news is that they are just bugs, not fundamental flaws in the design, and Sun is quickly addressing them. The other good news is that the bugs haven't been exploited to cause damage.

Byte Code Verifier

The lowest level of security is the byte code verifier in the Java Interpreter, which implements the Java Virtual Machine. The byte code verifier makes sure that a Java program is valid and doesn't perform any operations that might enable the program access to the machine underlying the interpreter. Checks performed include checking for code that will overflow or underflow the stack and code that tries to access objects that it isn't allowed to access.

Sun is trying hard to make sure that its byte code verifier is totally secure. When other vendors release their implementations of the Java Virtual Machine, can you trust their byte code verifiers? I don't have the answer to this question, but it's something worth paying attention to.

The byte code verifier is invoked by the class loader (java.lang.ClassLoader). The class loader is responsible for loading classes from whatever source it needs, whether the local disk or across the network. The class loader protects a class from being replaced by another class from a less-secure source.

Security Manager

One level above the Class Loader is the Security Manager. The Security Manager implements the security policy for the running Java programs. Stand-alone Java applications can set their own security policy by overriding the Security Manager and instantiating it. Web browsers instantiate their own Security Managers, and applets aren't allowed to modify them. Netscape Navigator, in particular, implements a very strict Security Manager. For example, accessing the local disk is impossible from any class loaded from the network. With HotJava and AppletViewer, accessing the local disk is possible for a class loaded off the network, if the user allows it.

By modifying the Security Manager, you can change the way security is handled in your applications. With the Security Manager, you can control file access. You can control where network connections can be made. You even can control access to threads through the Security Manager.

Writing your own Security Manager is a very advanced topic, worthy of a book in its own right. Needless to say, I won't cover it here. If you need some material on writing a Security Manager, the book *Tricks of the Java Programming Gurus* by Sams Publishing has several chapters on how to do it.

Many people are now talking about putting digital signatures on applets (digital signatures are covered later in this chapter). With this system, you will be able to know who wrote a particular applet. Then, if you trust the author, you can relax the limits that the Security Manager imposes. Watch for this technology; it will be important to you, because you probably will need to sign your applets at some point in the future.

JavaScript Security

Although *JavaScript* has the word *Java* in it, don't expect the same level of security from it as from Java. JavaScript originally was called *LiveScript* and had nothing to do with Java. The name change was almost strictly a marketing ploy on the part of Netscape.

Java offers a multilevel security model that protects Java code from doing dangerous things, but JavaScript does nothing of the sort. Netscape just tried to design a language with no dangerous commands. In Java, it's possible to control the level of security by overwriting the Security Manager. JavaScript offers no such flexibility.

Apparently JavaScript wasn't designed with security and privacy as primary design principles. If they were primary design principles, they were poorly implemented. People already have managed to exploit features in the language to do things such as steal URL history and forge e-mail. Netscape is gradually trying to address these problems.

To be honest, many people doubt that JavaScript will ever be completely secure because of its design. In fact, I don't feel comfortable with it personally, and I have disabled it in my copy of Netscape Navigator.

VBScript Security

When Java and, to a lesser extent, JavaScript, burst on the scene, Microsoft had to strike back. It did so with *Visual Basic Script* (*VBScript*). Visual Basic Script is nothing more than Visual Basic with the parts that Microsoft saw as being potentially dangerous ripped out of the language. The end result is another language—from a security point of view—that's similar to JavaScript. Whether it's secure is somewhat of a mystery at this time, because it hasn't been widely deployed on the Internet. Many systems seem secure until enough people try to break them. We will just have to see how VBScript holds up.

CGI Security

You can look at CGI security from several angles. I'll cover some of the specific programming problems first and then get around to some of the more global issues related to CGI scripts later.

Handling Input to a Shell

First, go back to the passing-commands-to-a-shell problem discussed earlier. Because Perl is the most commonly used language for CGI programs, let's look at how to fix this problem in Perl. If the input should never be used in a shell command in any way, the version of Perl known as taintperl should be used instead of normal Perl. taintperl is included with the standard Perl distribution and doesn't enable any input to be used in a shell command unless you go through a troublesome process of *untainting* it first.

However, in many cases you need to use some of the input as part of a shell command. You have two choices:

- You can write your own error-checking routines. If you do so, I would strongly recommend that you look for characters you know you can trust and then assume that anything else is an error.

- Looking for characters you can trust is a much safer method than the second alternative—looking specifically for characters you know you can't trust. This method isn't as safe because you might miss one.

If you think this is too much trouble, you're right—but you have an easy alternative. Libraries are available that check the input for you automatically, as well as parsing it into an easy-to-use format. For Perl 4, CGI-LIB is an excellent library. It's available at the following address:

```
ftp://ftp.ncsa.uiuc.edu/Web/httpd/Unix/ncsa_httpd/cgi/cgi-lib.pl.Z
```

Don't be confused by the fact that it's included with the NCSA httpd distribution. It should work with any UNIX-based Web server and possibly any Web server supporting CGI on any platform that has Perl. For Perl 5, you can get CGI.pm at the following address:

```
ftp://ftp.ncsa.uiuc.edu/Web/httpd/Unix/ncsa_httpd/cgi/CGI.pm-1.53.tar.Z
```

CGI Scripts and `userid`

If you are writing CGI programs and they don't run, the problem might be due to the security setup on your Web server. Many system administrators allow only specific people to execute CGI scripts for certain directories, to minimize the security exposure. The reason for this is that CGI scripts typically run as the `userid` of the Web server. A poorly written program (by any user) that can create files on the Web can cause damage to the Web server. If the Web server runs as `root` on UNIX or `administrator` on Windows NT, the damage could be even greater. It is never a good idea to run a Web server as either of these two user IDs. Anyway, if your script doesn't run at all, talk to your Web administrator.

To solve the problem just discussed, many Web administrators install a program called *CGI-WRAP*. CGI-WRAP runs on a UNIX Web server and is a `setuid` program that performs a variety of beneficial tasks:

- First, it runs user-written CGI scripts as that user. This scheme protects the Web server from these programs.

- Second, it eliminates all the dangerous characters previously discussed—before the CGI script ever runs—so that the system administrator doesn't need to worry about whether users are writing scripts in a secure fashion.

- It also has an option to automatically kill off CGI scripts if they use too much CPU time.

If you are on a system using CGI-WRAP, you need to use different URLs, and you might need to modify your program slightly. Find some local document or talk to your Web administrator to find out how.

> **NOTE**
>
> A common and deadly mistake that many Web administrators and programmers alike have been making recently is to place a copy of Perl itself in a directory where CGI programs can execute. A knowledgeable cracker can use this mistake to do just about anything he wants to your system. The best strategy is to always keep Perl outside any directory from which the Web server can read.

Firewalls

A *firewall* is a critical part of the security of any Internet site. Basically, a firewall improves the security of a site by limiting the access of that site to an absolute minimum. It's important to remember that although a firewall doesn't solve all Internet security problems, no Internet site should be without a firewall. This section covers only the basics of firewalls and how they affect Internet programming. If you need more detailed information, the book *Building Internet Firewalls* by O'Reily & Associates, Inc., is an excellent source.

Types of Firewalls

Three basic types of firewalls exist: the *bastion host*, the *packet filter*, and the *proxy gateway*. Before you do any Internet programming, you need to find out which kind of firewall you have. Each kind affects Internet programming in different ways. Also, your site's particular implementation factors into the programming picture. A firewall can be completely transparent to your program in some cases. In other cases, it might make your program impossible to write. If this is the case, you need to ask yourself and the security people at your site whether a way exists to relax the restrictions your firewall imposes, without compromising the security of your site. Sometimes the answer to this question is no, and you just have to give up on your project.

It's also possible to combine or modify the three basic firewall types to make more complex security setups. If this is done correctly, you can get exactly the security you want. The variations are endless and each has its own effect on Internet programming. Therefore, I cover only the effects of the basic types. If you have a more complex setup, extrapolate the information here into your own environment.

Building Your Own Firewall

You can either buy a firewall or design your own if you don't have one. Internet routers, such as Cisco or Bay Networks, offer all the packet-filtering options you could want. Because you need a router to connect to the Internet anyway, this is a good, inexpensive option. The only negative is that these devices can be hard to configure. You can purchase a variety of products, such as Firewall-1, Gauntlet, CheckPoint, and Sidewinder. These products offer advanced firewall configurations but are very expensive.

If you build your own firewall, take a look at Trusted Information Systems' (TIS) Firewall Toolkit as a base on which to build. Building your own firewall can be relatively inexpensive until you factor in personnel costs, but it probably won't be as high-quality. The good news about building your own firewall is that you can customize it highly to meet the needs of your programs.

Bastion Hosts

The *bastion host* firewall scheme is usually simple to implement, but it is very noticeable and cumbersome to users and programmers alike. The bastion host sits between the Internet and the internal network (see Figure 3.1). The Internet can talk to the bastion host. The internal network can talk to the bastion host. However, the Internet and the internal network can't talk directly to each other.

For any communication to occur between the Internet and the internal network, a login must exist to the bastion host. In the old days of the Internet, this kind of firewall was potentially very secure and the loss of functionality was acceptable in many cases. Over time, though, the network has changed—with the explosion of the Web and PCs with Internet access. In today's world, a true bastion host would make using a graphical Web browser on a PC impossible without going to extreme lengths.

FIGURE 3.1.
The bastion host.

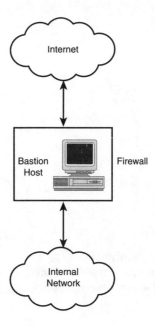

Any services your site plans to make available to the Internet must reside on the bastion host. This includes your e-mail routing server and your Web server. But these services can be too much load for one machine; you might need to have multiple bastion hosts to handle all the servers.

For Internet programmers, the bastion host can stop many programming projects cold. Basically, your programs must reside on the bastion host itself, or they won't be able to talk to the Internet at all. One trick is to have a program on the bastion host that relays information between the Internet and your main program running on the internal network. If you do this, however, you no longer have a true bastion host; you have created a proxy gateway. Proxy gateways are covered in their own section later in this chapter.

Packet Filters

Instead of trying to force all traffic between the Internet and the internal network to be authenticated through one host, like the bastion host system, the *packet filter* tries to screen out harmful traffic between the Internet and the internal network. In addition, the packet filter allows traffic directly between the Internet and the internal network (see Figure 3.2).

FIGURE 3.2.

A packet filter.

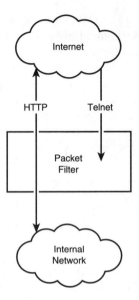

Packet filters often are implemented as part of the router that ties together the Internet and the internal network. Less often, you'll find them implemented in a host computer. Packet filters are implemented differently at every site. Their security can range from dangerously lax to incredibly strict.

With a packet filter, you can almost always restrict access on protocol and IP addresses (both source and destination addresses). With this level of control, it's possible to allow another company you work with often to have more access to your systems, while not giving any access to the rest of the Internet. Some packet filters will even look inside packets and only forward packets based on some content inside the packet.

In terms of how the firewall will affect your programs, some sites might have access to your running code, while others don't. This scheme can be helpful to you at times to help manage program security.

Proxy Gateways

A *proxy gateway* is similar to a bastion host except for one major difference. The proxy gateway has a program or a set of programs running on it to relay packets between the Internet and the internal network.

The idea is basically a game of smoke-and-mirrors, giving the user the perception that she's directly connected to services on the other side of the firewall, when in reality she isn't (see Figure 3.3).

Figure 3.3.

A proxy gateway.

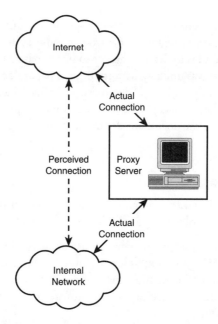

Proxies are very good security mechanisms and are great at logging Internet activity. The bad news is that they're a lot of extra work. Your client and server programs must normally be modified to be able to deal with the proxy. The good news is that the major Web browsers already support proxying, so they won't need modification.

Another problem with proxies is that the proxies have to be written for almost every different protocol. They're already written for almost every protocol currently in wide use on the Internet, but new releases of protocols can break proxies, and they might need to be rewritten. Also, for a few protocols (for example, talk), no proxy has been written, and writing one might even be impossible.

Encryption and Digital Signatures

Encryption, in one form or another, has been around since almost the dawn of civilization. Computers and networks have made advanced forms of encryption possible. The kinds of encryption historically used (for example, secret decoder rings or German Enigma machines) are trivial to break on a computer, taking only seconds. Almost all versions of UNIX come with a program called crypt, which is a software implementation of the German Enigma machine used in World War II. A program exists on the Internet that breaks this code in seconds. Therefore, when dealing with encryption, always insist on using high-quality algorithms; weak ones can be broken easily.

3

SECURITY AND ENCRYPTION

Digital signatures are a way of securely signing documents. This strategy is useful for two reasons. The first is like a regular signature—to indicate that you agree with the terms of the document. The second is to detect whether someone has changed the document after you signed it (something that was unlikely with traditional paper documents). Digital signatures are implemented by making a digest of the message, using an algorithm such as MD5. This digest is encrypted by the user's key. The recipient can decrypt the encrypted digest and compare it to the document. If the document doesn't match, it has been tampered with or has a forged signature.

Legal Issues

When writing Internet programs that involve encryption, it's very important to be aware of the legal issues involved. If you don't, you could end up in prison on felony charges.

First, some countries ban outright any use of encryption. France and Iran are two notable examples. Therefore, you shouldn't write any encryption code, import any encryption programs, or even use encryption in these two countries. Other countries might have such laws on the books. I recommend checking with an attorney unless you are absolutely sure of the legal status in your country.

The United States is another country with strange laws about encryption. No problem exists with using any form of encryption you want—within the country. The trouble starts when you want to write a piece of encryption software in the United States and then export it to another country (except possibly Canada) in electronic form. The U.S. government has labeled certain types of encryption software as munitions—just as if these programs were missiles or something. The law is known as *ITAR* (*International Traffic in Arms Regulations*).

It's possible to write certain types of weaker encryption programs for export. You then have to request an exemption from the export law from the U.S. government. The level of encryption allowed is strong enough to be time-consuming for a cracker to break the code, but it can be done in a few months on some machines. For public key algorithms, covered in the section "Public Key Encryption," the Software Publishers Association (SPA) and the government agreed to give quicker approval to algorithms using 40-bit keys or less. A message encrypted with a 40-bit key takes only about 200 MIPS/year of CPU time (that is, a 200 MIPS computer would take one year to crack it). Therefore, any highly secure, non-time-sensitive communication is potentially at risk. Keep this fact in mind.

A few ways exist to get around this law. The best is to just write your software outside the U.S. Some people ask the question, "What if my machine is out of the country, but I'm in the U.S.?" or vice versa. My answer is that there's no legal precedent on this issue, so don't take chances. The other alternative is that apparently you can print out the source code (or binary) to the program and carry the printouts out of the country without violating the law. Then, in the foreign country, you can scan them back in. Again, check with your lawyer before attempting this. Another method is for you to write a U.S. version of the program that you tightly control, and then have an associate write an international version outside the U.S. This has been done with PGP (Pretty Good Privacy), which is discussed later in this chapter.

To make matters even worse, the law even precludes giving the program to people in the U.S. who are not U.S. or Canadian citizens or permanent residents. I know this part of the law is widely violated, but my recommendation, as always, is to play it safe.

Another legal issue is that the major public key encryption algorithms are all patented. The patent owners are pretty aggressive about protecting their patents; however, many of the key patents expire in the next couple of years. The release of these patents will break the stranglehold the patent holders have had on public key encryption. I predict that after the patents expire we'll see many more public key encryption implementations than we have today.

Private Key Encryption

Private key encryption is the oldest form of encryption in existence. In private key encryption, there is one key. You encrypt the message, using this key. The person decrypting the message must have the same key. It works just like the secret decoder rings you might have played with when you were a child.

The strength of private key encryption algorithms varies greatly. Some are trivial to crack; others are computationally impossible to crack, given today's computers. Some vendors, notably WordPerfect, have included some private key encryption code in their products. It turns out that many of these are almost completely useless. You can download programs from the Internet to crack the keys, run them, and have the original file back in under 15 minutes (the download is the time-consuming part, too!).

The most famous private key encryption algorithm is *DES* (*Data Encryption Standard*). It's very popular, and you can find implementations for almost any platform available today. However, DES is aging (originally published in 1975) and computers are getting faster. Attacks on DES are becoming increasingly possible. A modified version of DES known as *Triple-DES* is available and is harder to crack.

Public Key Encryption

The big problem with private key encryption is making sure that the people on both ends of the communication have the keys—without anyone else having them. The only ways to exchange keys in a secure fashion are to already have a secure communication channel available, which means that both parties already have encryption available; or both people must be in the same place without anyone else around, so that they can be sure they're not being bugged. This is very cumbersome for most people.

Public key encryption eliminates the need for a secure key-exchange mechanism. Each person has a private key, which he uses to decrypt or digitally sign messages, and a public key, which others use to send messages to him or to verify his digital signature. Each person keeps his private key private to himself. The public key is public information and can be known by anyone.

Key Length

The length of the key is a critical issue in the security of a public key encryption algorithm. The longer the key, the safer your encrypted messages but the longer it takes to encrypt or decrypt them. My advice is to go ahead and use a long key (1024 bits or more). Most people today have enough CPU horsepower to encrypt messages to you quickly, even with a long key. This isn't true when breaking messages without knowing the key, however. The longest message known to be broken had a 429-bit key. It required an international effort, involving 600 sites. The good news is that the amount of time needed with current cracking algorithms doubles with every additional 10 bits of key length. However, computer performance and algorithms to break public key encryption algorithms are improving, making cracking easier. Therefore, a long key is essential in protecting your messages for a long period of time.

Key Exchange

With public key encryption, the main implementation difficulty changes from key exchange to identity verification. If someone e-mails you her public key across the Internet, how do you know it's really from her? The answer is that you don't. The secure way is to get together with the person, in person, and exchange public keys. Well, if you do this, you almost might as well have used private key encryption and exchanged keys. Also, this model doesn't scale well. Obviously, you can't meet with every single person with whom you need to exchange public keys.

Two basic models for key exchange have been developed. The first is a hierarchical approach. At the top is a person or organization that everyone has to trust. This person/organization hands out authority to other organizations or people who can authenticate certain groups of people. These second-tier authenticators then publicly publish the public keys of the people they authenticate. This is the simplest form of this scheme. It's possible (and probably necessary) to have many more levels than this.

Organizations or individuals can issue a special document known as a "Digital Certificate" saying that they have authenticated a certain person. Then that person can show the digital certificate to others as proof of her identity on the Internet. These digital certificates are usually in a format known as X.509. One company issuing digital certificates is VeriSign (http://www.verisign.com/). To use the Netscape FastTrack Server, you have to acquire a digital certificate from VeriSign, though it should be possible to use other companies in the near future (probably by the time you are reading this).

The other model, known as the Web of Trust, doesn't depend on being able to trust these higher-level people and organizations. In the Web of Trust, you initially exchange keys with at least a few people you meet in person. Both of you can digitally sign each other's keys with your names. Then, when others later get your key over the network, they see that it's signed by the person with whom you exchanged keys in person. If they have exchanged keys in person with that person and trust that person, they then know that they can trust your key.

To make this system work well, you have to decide how much you trust other people's ability to validate and exchange keys correctly. If you exchange keys with someone you don't think validates people correctly, you can later ignore any key you get over the network that is signed by that person and not signed by someone you do trust. If you trust their validation techniques, you take any keys signed by them. You can also partially trust them with some implementations of this model. When you start thinking about scaling this model, your head will probably start to spin, but it's a powerful way for small groups of people to communicate without a lot of overhead.

Most people tend to be rather religious about which model of key exchange is the best. However, in reality, it has been proven mathematically that either model can emulate the other model with a little work. In fact, converting the Web of Trust into the hierarchical approach is almost trivial. An organization only needs to create a key and then sign the keys of people whom they can authenticate. If people know they can trust that organization, they will accept keys that are signed by the organization as being valid.

My personal belief is that both methods are flawed in some ways. Therefore, this ability to twist one model into acting like the other is essential. Sometimes you want to get keys from a central authenticated database, especially when you can't meet this person in person or can't meet someone who can meet them to handle the key exchange. At other times, you want to get a key directly from someone (or slightly indirectly, from a source you personally trust), so that you know it's absolutely correct.

Popular Public Key Packages

The most popular piece of public key encryption software on the Internet is *PGP* (*Pretty Good Privacy*). PGP is available for numerous platforms and uses the Web of Trust model of key exchange. To get around the legal restrictions, there's a U.S. version of the program and a separate international version that was written outside the U.S. Therefore, you can use PGP without worrying about the export controls. (Just don't carry a copy on your laptop from inside the U.S. to other countries!) In reality, at least two U.S. versions of PGP exist. A version for noncommercial use is freely available by signing some documents with MIT. There's also a commercial version known as *ViaCrypt PGP*.

PEM (*Privacy-Enhanced Mail*) is another algorithm for public key encryption. PEM is based on the hierarchical key exchange model. *RIPEM* (*Riodran's Internet Privacy-Enhanced Mail*) is the reference implementation, which is available from RSA Data Systems. PEM seemed destined for greatness a couple of years ago, but it really has taken a back seat to PGP in actual use.

MOSS (*MIME Object Security Services*) is intended to correct a couple of the flaws of PEM, one being that PEM's rigid hierarchies are too strict on many occasions. MOSS relaxes the restrictions somewhat. MOSS is designed to handle MIME messages, unlike PEM. MOSS has too many options, and it might be possible for two different vendors to write MOSS implementations that can't speak to each other. Some people at the Internet Engineering Task Force

(IETF) told me and others to forget PEM, and that MOSS is the algorithm for the future. However, upon researching for this chapter, I found material on the Web indicating that MOSS is a niche system and that PEM was still alive and well. I recommend watching market trends on this debate to see which side is better to use and is gaining market share.

SSL

SSL (Secure Socket Layer) is a security protocol developed by Netscape. In the protocol stack, it runs above the TCP protocol but below the application layer protocols such as NNTP, HTTP, and FTP. While I am writing this, SSL has been implemented only in uses related to HTTP.

SSL enables the client to authenticate the server. It also enables data being transmitted over the Internet to be encrypted. If you are using Netscape Navigator, you can know you are talking to an authenticated server when the key in the lower-left corner of the window is in one piece and not broken. If you have the exportable version of Netscape Navigator, it uses only the 40-bit key discussed earlier (in the section dealing with U.S. export restrictions). So, this isn't a very secure system.

The current version that is implemented is SSL 2.0. However, the SSL 3.0 specification is available; 3.0 enables the client, as well as the server, to be authenticated.

An SSL server runs on two ports. First, it runs normal, unencrypted as always. Also, it answers on a second port, 443 by default, for encrypted transactions. If your URL for unencrypted transactions is `http://www.utdallas.edu/`, for example, your URL for encrypted transactions is `https://www.utdallas.edu/`. The only difference is at the beginning of the address: `https` instead of `http`.

At the current time, SSL is implemented in the Netscape FastTrack Server, recent versions of the NCSA server, and Open Market's Secure Web Server. Patches are also available for the popular, free Apache Web server. SSL also is implemented in Netscape Navigator on the client side. For more information, see the following address:

`http://home.netscape.com/newsref/std/SSL.html`

If you need to combine SSL with a proxy-based firewall, see this address for a specification of how to do it:

`ftp://ds.internic.net/internet-drafts/draft-luotonen-ssl-tunneling-02.txt`

S-HTTP

S-HTTP (Secure HyperText Transfer Protocol) is a higher-level encryption scheme than SSL to protect Web transmission. Although S-HTTP and SSL seem to be in competition, it has been discussed that there's no reason not to use both in conjunction with each other. In fact, Open Market has implemented both in its Secure Web Server product. Netscape is considering support of S-HTTP as well as SSL in its products. URLs using S-HTTP start with `shttp://`.

The S-HTTP specification is being developed by CommerceNet and can be seen at the following addresses:

`http://www.commerce.net/internet/standards/drafts/shttp.txt`

`ftp://ds.internic.net/internet-drafts/draft-ietf-wts-shttp-01.txt`

You can find more information at `http://www.eit.com/creations/s-http/`. An S-HTTP server can be found at `http://www.commerce.net/software/Shttpd`. Patches for the CERN httpd server can also be found at these locations. There's also a version of Mosaic called *Secure Mosaic*, but it's available only to CommerceNet members.

Shen

Shen is a proposal similar in nature to S-HTTP. It hasn't received widespread support. However, it's being developed by Phillip Hallam-Baker of the W3 Consortium; and because it is one of the key players in the Web standards world, you should keep an eye on it just in case. The message format it uses is inspired by PEM but unfortunately is not compatible with it. Shen is discussed at these addresses:

`http://www.w3.org/hypertext/shen/ref/security_spec.html`

`http://www.w3.org/hypertext/WWW/Shen/ref/shen.html`

S/MIME

S/MIME (*Secure/Multipart Internet Mail Extensions*) is a standard to exchange e-mail in encrypted form. The specification can be found at `http://www.rsa.com/rsa/S-MIME`.

Like PGP, the public key encryption is just to manage key exchange; the bulk of the encryption is done with private key encryption algorithms. S/MIME is flexible and enables the use of DES, Triple-DES, and RC2 as private key encryption algorithms.

GSS-API

GSS-API (*Generic Security Service-Applications Programming Interface*) is a program interface for security that includes both client and server authentication as well as data encryption. It's "generic" because it was designed to work with any Internet service that needs security. When used with HTTP, the URLs start with `gss-http://`. GSS-API has its supporters, but hasn't been deployed much. It's an interesting approach, though. More information can be found at this address:

`ftp://ietf.cnri.reston.va.us/internet-draft/draft-ietf-wts-gssapi-00.txt`

SET

SET (*Secure Encryption Technology*) is a standard for exchanging credit card transactions across the Internet. It was developed by a group including MasterCard, Visa, Netscape, IBM, Microsoft, VeriSign, and GTE. American Express has shown support for it more recently. The major credit card companies state that they don't see encryption technology as a point of difference between them. They all agree that all transactions should be secure—whether by them or their competition.

Because SET has the backing of so many major players in the electronic commerce world, it definitely bears watching. Expect that you will see the beginning of deployment in late 1996. It also is using X.509 certificates, just like SSL.

The SET standard is documented at this location:

```
http://www.visa.com/cgi-bin/vee/sf/standard.html
```

More technical information is available at

```
http://www.visa.com/cgi-bin/vee/set/settech?2+0
```

Summary

This chapter covered a lot of security-related material. It is enough to get you started and headed in the correct direction but by no means covers all the details. If you are working in any particular area, please use the references given to get more information.

However, one thing should be apparent to you now: In all of your Internet programming work, you should never ignore security; always think about the security implications of what you are doing. It is also a good practice to discuss your approach with someone else familiar with security to make sure you do not make an oversight. If you do these things, you will eliminate 99 percent of the potential security problems in advance.

Developing Intranet Applications

by Bob Breedlove

IN THIS CHAPTER

CHAPTER 4

The explosion in use of the Internet has shaken up the traditional paradigm for application design. In the traditional view of client/server applications, custom-written application components were distributed and used to run the application. In the new paradigm, the user has a client tool—the Web browser—to which host applications are written.

The Web browser gives the end user a unified platform on which to run applications. This new paradigm can be useful to the development of intranet applications because the new paradigm enables application designers to write multiple host applications that work with a common client. Using a common client can reduce training costs and lower the learning curve for new applications by enabling the end user to use a single client for multiple applications.

Developing applications for an intranet requires many of the same considerations as developing applications for the public Internet (see Chapter 11, "CGI and the Internet"). An intranet can be viewed as a private Internet—a non-public router-based TCP/IP network. It can, however, have some exposure to the public Internet, generally through a computer that limits the types of packets which can pass between the intranet and the public Internet—a "firewall." This chapter begins with an examination of some of the things that make programming for an intranet unique.

The Purpose of Intranet Applications

The purpose, and thus the design, of applications designed to operate over an intranet vary from those designed for the Internet. A set of Web pages (referred to in this chapter as an "application") intended for the Internet is generally intended for an outside audience, for example, customers, vendors, or other companies. The look and feel of the application will generally be more "glitzy." Being "cool" and "sharp" counts, and the pages often contain attention-getting graphics and other gimmicks designed to attract an audience to the pages.

The intent of these applications is generally to promote a product or service or actually to sell a product or service over the Internet. Thus, attracting and keeping a target audience is an important aspect of Internet programming.

Intranet applications, on the other hand, are usually intended for internal audiences such as co-workers, managers, or employees. These applications are intended to provide important information or services to manage the business. As such, users want these applications to convey this information succinctly, efficiently, and in a timely manner. The same graphics and other gimmicks that are the heart of an Internet application can actually interfere with the effectiveness of an intranet application.

Much of the following discussion assumes that you are developing applications that meet these general purposes. If you need general information or if you are developing applications for external audiences, you might find it helpful to read Chapter 1, "An Overview of Internet Programming."

You Own the Resources—Or Do You?

Before you examine the actual design of applications for an intranet, look at the factors that make intranet applications a challenge to design and implement. As you will see, many of these factors affect your development time frame and implementation effort; others affect the performance of your application after it resides on your intranet.

As shown in Chapter 1, the public Internet has no central authority or controlling body for its infrastructure. The various resources over which it operates are controlled by the organizations that own them. In contrast, an intranet is usually a centrally controlled resource. Generally in large corporations, a central authority manages at least the backbone of the intranet and handles such services as these:

- Network naming and addressing
- Security
- Corporate firewalls
- Router configuration
- Capacity management

Authority for some of these functions can be delegated to divisional or regional authorities, depending on the size of the corporate domain. Control of the intranet is generally divided, however, between locally managed local-area networks (LANs) and centrally managed wide-area networks (WANs) and backbones. What this means to your project is that you will have to work with these corporate groups to get things done. Later in this chapter, we will explore in more detail how this affects your project time lines and implementation.

> **TIP**
>
> Intranet resources are usually controlled by a corporate or divisional group. You will have to deal with these organizations to implement your system.

Figure 4.1 represents a typical corporate intranet. The backbone of the intranet is usually some packet switching technology or other high-speed wide-area network technology. This and corporate resources such as corporate firewalls (A) are usually centrally controlled. LANs (B) are usually locally controlled; however, resources that connect the LAN to the intranet (routers and bridges) can be centrally controlled and managed. Intranets also often have to contend with dial-up access (C) from field sales and other off-site staff. This dial-up access can be accessed through corporate resources or locally controlled. Mainframe access (D) is also a concern for many corporate applications. Mainframes traditionally are centrally controlled and can be controlled by groups other than the intranet groups.

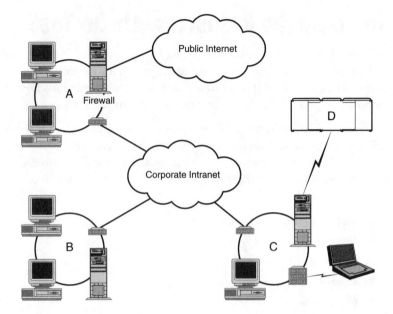

FIGURE 4.1.

A typical corporate intranet has centrally managed and locally managed resources.

In this chapter, you'll see how this control of resources can affect your system design and time lines for development. You'll learn about alternatives for your design and about development time-line considerations that you will face when working with the intranet control and management functions.

The Growth of Intranets

Most corporate intranets are a result of evolution rather than planning and design. They evolved from earlier attempts to connect LANs, WANs, and mainframes in response to the demand for greater access to information. As such, intranets are composed of a mixed bag of workstations, hosts, networks, and other devices. Intranets give users unprecedented access to corporate data resources. Dealing with the intranet itself, however, can be a major challenge in writing applications for use on this shared resource.

Application Scope

This chapter presents designing client/server applications that use some portion of the intranet infrastructure depending on the distribution of the data and applications that process it. In general terms, client/server applications can be categorized into various degrees of decentralization.

Figure 4.2 shows this continuum. From left to right in the figure, the typical configurations can be described as follows:

A.   Traditional applications with data, processing, and display/output on the same platform. These applications are typified by single-user PC applications and traditional mainframe batch applications.

B.   Data and processing on a single platform with display on a separate platform. Mainframe online transactions with video display terminals and Web server CGI applications are typical of this type of application.

C.   Data separated from processing and display. This is typified by SQL servers, which provide data from central repositories to distributed applications.

D.   Separated (three-tier) data, processing, and display, typified by applications that require processing above that provided by desktop workstations (PCs).

FIGURE 4.2.

Client/server design strategies, showing typical applications for each alternative.

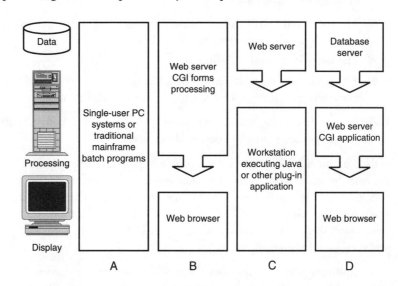

You will face different issues depending on the scope of your application. By "scope," I mean the extent to which your application will use the intranet resources. Generally, these fall into the following categories:

Application Category	Use of Intranet Resources
Single computer system	None
Local LAN-based system	None
Central processing/data access with remote display	Minimal
Central data access with remote processing/display	Moderate to heavy
Distributed data, processing, and display	Heavy

Capacity Planning

In single computer systems, the central processing unit (CPU) speed, available memory, and direct storage-device capacity and storage-device throughput are the limiting factors to system performance. With intranet applications, add to this list the network throughput. Throughput is a result of several factors:

- The load on your Web server and the machine on which it operates
- The load on your local-area network
- The bandwidth of the network segments over which the application operates and the load on those segments
- The speed and number of the routers, bridges, and other "gateway" devices through which the application operates
- The necessity to deal with firewalls
- The capacity of other servers on which your application depends, such as domain name servers, database servers, terminal servers, and so on

Each of these factors affects the operation of your application. You will have to work with corporate organizations to modify most of these factors.

If the load on your Web server is the problem, you have a few options. The first might be to increase the size of your Web server host machine, but before considering this expensive option, take a more detailed look at the capacity problem. The problem might be caused by a single page or CGI script, or it might exist only at particular times of day. The key is to determine what, specifically, is causing the load problem and when the load problem exists before you spend money on equipment.

One important point to remember about Web-based applications is that you can, within reason, place the resources anywhere on the intranet. If your current host can't handle your application, consider moving it to an existing host that can or consider splitting it between hosts to equalize the load.

Your own LAN can be the bottleneck for your application. Here you need to examine the bandwidth and the usage on the LAN. If you find that the LAN cannot provide the needed bandwidth, again, consider hosting your application on a LAN that can or increasing the capacity of the LAN. (It is unlikely that you will be able to convince your company that purchasing new LAN equipment is worthwhile, unless your application is the major one on the LAN.)

If your problems arise from the load on the LAN, consider moving your application server to a separate LAN segment. Depending on the LAN type, you might need to provide a separate network interface card for your router to accomplish this. It might relieve your application from overloading.

The need for adequate network capacity (bandwidth) is obvious. Your intranet needs the capacity to be able to handle the volume of data that your application will generate. Your application will operate, for the most part, at the speed of the slowest segment over which it operates. Unless your LAN segment is the slowest, there might be little you can do about it. Make sure that the bandwidth from your Web server to the backbone is as fast as it can be. If it isn't fast enough, consider increasing the bandwidth or moving your application to a host on a LAN that provides the bandwidth you need.

Any device through which your application's packets must travel will delay your application. This latency is built into intranets because they rely on gateways (routers and bridges) to provide packet routing. There is probably little you can do about the overall speed of the intranet.

You also should be aware of the gateway's capabilities to filter by packet type and IP address. If you find that users can't get to your application, have your network managers examine the filtering on each of the routers to determine where the packets or your IP address are being stopped. If you are running on a UNIX host, you can use the `traceroute` command to find out which devices exist between you and a specific host (see Chapter 17, "Using the Win32 Internet (WinInet) API," for an example of this command).

If you find that router filtering will be a problem, you might find that the issues are more complex than just asking router operations' personnel to remove the filter. That filter was applied for a reason. You will have to examine the business issues that caused the filter to be applied; that way you can determine whether you can remove it. If you cannot remove the filter, your alternative might be to host your application on a machine that is not filtered, duplicate your application on both intranetwork segments, or exclude that segment of the intranet from using your application.

Proper equipment such as network sniffers and cable testers can be essential in the effort to determine the actual cause of the problem. If this equipment is not supplied by some corporate resource, it might be up to your department to provide this equipment in order to determine the cause of the problem and determine the proper course to correct it.

Firewalls are placed between the intranet and the public Internet to protect corporate resources, as shown in Figure 4.1. Firewalls act as single points of entry to the corporate intranet, and often, single points where users on the intranet can gain access to the public Internet.

When we speak of a firewall, we speak of users on the corporate intranet as being "inside" the firewall and the Internet as "outside" the firewall. Generally, firewalls are configured to let all types of packets out, giving users on the intranet access to the public Internet. Firewalls are almost always configured to restrict the packets coming in, thus restricting public access to the intranet that they are installed to protect. Telnet, FTP, and HTTP packets are usually filtered from the outside, as these would enable hackers access to the resources on the intranet. Mail and news packets are often allowed to pass through the firewall freely in both directions.

At this writing, Java and other languages of its type are in their infancy. It will be interesting to see how Java transactions will be treated through a firewall. This is a potential security problem because the Java application is sent from the host *outside* the firewall but will execute on the client machine *inside* the firewall.

Although firewalls are a necessity, they can cause problems for your application, especially if users on the outside of the firewall need to access your application. Firewalls can also slow transactions and become bottlenecks for your application. For this reason, it might be best to design a distributed application with a module outside the firewall to communicate with the public Internet and an equivalent module inside the firewall for users on that side. Figure 4.3 illustrates this type of design.

FIGURE 4.3.

An application in which the main system runs inside the firewall (B) and modules run outside the firewall (A) to communicate with dial-up and Internet users.

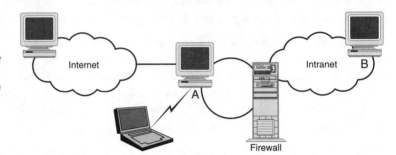

By placing some of the modules outside the firewall, you avoid having unauthorized HTTP packets passing through the firewall. By using IP address filtering, you can receive packets from your "trusted" host (A). For additional security, consider replicating data with the modules on machine "A" outside the firewall so they are completely isolated during online operation. Use FTP or another transport mechanism to gather transactions in a batch operation to integrate with the main database.

This type of "store-and-forward" operation can be effective for systems that have remote components such as hand-held field units or that send transactions such as sales order transactions that you can deal with as distinct entities. Thus, a sales representative might access the Internet to upload the day's orders and download information for the next day's sales calls at the end of his or her day.

The last consideration for using an intranet is the total load on the network. If the load is too great at critical times, your application becomes unusable. There is probably little you can do about this except design your application for some other infrastructure.

Be aware that intranet usage can vary widely by time period. Remember, most corporate intranets were not planned but evolved over time. Although capacity planners can examine the backbone of the intranet, there is often little centralized control over applications that use the intranet. When designing your application, consider other applications that will also share bandwidth with your application. This is especially important if your application performs special processing during typically busy times.

For example, if you are designing a financial application that accepts transactions that are processed in a weekly or monthly cycle, you can bet that your heavy activity will be in the period just before the cycle. If this happens to fall at the end of a week or a month, other systems can compete with your system for bandwidth, making the response times unacceptable for your user community. Be sure to test your application during these heavy periods. It might even be wise to develop a prototype early in the design cycle to assure that transaction times are acceptable during heavy load periods.

Using an existing intranet for your application offers many advantages. Capacity planning is the key to a successful intranet application. In considering capacity planning, you often must work with corporate entities. The major consideration in capacity planning is the time frame in which projections must be supplied to assure that changes can be implemented to accommodate the increased load. Lead times will vary from corporation to corporation, but they will usually require you to predict initial loads, expected loads over time, and peak loads.

Leveraging Existing Resources

An existing intranet can be a good choice for internal applications because it uses existing resources, thus saving on initial costs and start-up time. Designing for a Web browser can cut your programming efforts and, because your user already knows the technology, can reduce your training costs.

> **NOTE**
>
> Designing for a Web browser can solve the problem of programming for diverse workstation types. When designing Web pages, you write to the single HTML standard and let the browsers worry about formatting.

But running your application over an intranet that has evolved over several years can be a double-edged sword. Intranet growth is typically "organic," where workstations and network technology are purchased to answer a specific business need and then are integrated at a later date into the intranet. Because of this, the types of workstations on an intranet are likely to vary greatly. Most corporations have evolved a mix of workstations, including the following:

- Microcomputers (PCs) running Microsoft Windows
- Microcomputers running Microsoft Windows NT
- Macintosh computers
- UNIX workstations running text-based interfaces (shell accounts)
- UNIX workstations running X Window

In addition to these common workstations, your corporation can run other platforms and specialized workstations. A Web-based application is an excellent choice for applications that must accommodate these diverse platforms. By designing Web pages, you do not need to supply specialized client software. Instead, you can construct and display Web pages on the various equipment already deployed on the intranet.

As shown in Chapter 17, there are considerations when designing applications for Web browsers. There are also considerations on the Web server side of the transaction.

Hypertext Markup Language (HTML) began as a standard, but with the explosive growth of the Internet, major players in the Web browser market are racing with each other to implement new and innovative (and non-standard) features in their Web browsers. Unless your corporation has standardized a particular Web browser, your application might have to work with more than one browser.

Your application can usually detect the type of browser it services by checking a parameter passed by the browser. This parameter is not always reliable and is not passed by all browsers. If you need to support specific features or need a graphically consistent application, consider writing to a specific browser and supplying it to the users of your application.

Security

Security doesn't seem to be such a major issue on a corporate intranet as it is on the public Internet. After all, this network is not public. But business considerations can make security an important issue with which to deal.

If security on an intranet is centralized, it is usually controlled by a corporate organization. Many corporations currently do not have centralized security for their intranets, which is unfortunate as much of the hacking done today occurs on private rather than public networks.

If your corporation does have central control of intranet security, those in charge will have security standards that your application must meet before you can place it on the intranet. As with other corporate organizations, you will probably have to plan in advance to work with the corporate security department. Some intranets might even use centrally administered security for logon passwords and other security issues.

Most technicians find that security concerns often conflict with the technical considerations of their applications. Technical advances often outstrip the security department's ability to accommodate them. You might devote your time to security modules that seem overly burdensome and might find that you are unable to implement some technologies on the intranet because of security requirements and concerns. But by planning ahead, you can prepare time in your design and construction schedules to accommodate these security needs.

Protecting Confidential Material

Another concern in intranet applications is protecting confidential material. It is true that your application is operating over corporate resources, but it can pass data that should not be seen by unauthorized employees, contractors, customers, and others who have access to the intranet. Many confidentiality issues discussed in Chapter 1 for the Internet also can be applied to intranet applications. Because the intranet and Internet are both TCP/IP networks, they have the same limitations and problems when plain text is transmitted across them.

One issue that requires a balancing act is the need for confidentiality versus the availability of information for the corporate community. Security and confidentiality issues are always cost-benefit tradeoffs.

Remember also that you might have to apply local, state, and even national laws to the information in your application even though it passes over your private intranet. Personnel and financial applications are often subject to these laws. Another interesting consideration that spans political jurisdictions—states, provinces, or even countries—is that various segments of the intranet might be subject to different laws when it comes to the confidentiality of the information carried on them.

Security Versus Availability

Maintaining security and confidentiality is a juggling act. On one side is the need to keep information secure and confidential, and on the other side is the need to make information available. There are no hard-and-fast rules for managing this dilemma. You could write an entire book on security and confidentiality issues. In a single chapter, I can provide only some guidelines by which you can develop your application.

You will need to examine two things to determine the level of security that your application requires. First, determine how sensitive your data is. Some data is easy. For example, if you are developing an organization chart application that will display information about your employees such as social security numbers, home addresses, and phone numbers, you are dealing with sensitive information that should be protected from unauthorized access. Other information is more subtle. Let's say you're working on a marketing application that will enable your managers and sales representatives to share information about current and potential customers. You might think that this information doesn't need to be very tightly secured; after all, this is your internal network—your intranet. This brings us to the second consideration in the security versus availability dilemma.

Stop for a moment to consider the people who have access to your intranet. If you are part of a company of any size, you probably have all sorts of people in your intranet:

- Employees
- Temporary help
- Consultants and vendors
- Customers

Would you want all of these people to look at your data? Even subtle data can have an impact on your business. Let's say you want to put your company newsletter online. Along with those

4

DEVELOPING
INTRANET
APPLICATIONS

announcements of company activities, the local bowling league scores, and the picture of the employee of the month is an article about your marketing strategy. If consultants, vendors, or customers had access to this information, it could give them (or their other customers) a competitive advantage in the future.

If your intranet has a mix of people on it, consider giving non-employees IDs that are easily identified, perhaps with special characters in certain positions. Secure all confidential or potentially damaging information with secured Web servers. Require access via ID and password. Your application can detect the special IDs and deny access to the information.

One interesting fact is that very few corporations have implemented internal firewalls on their intranets. You might consider implementing a firewall, especially if you are designing a sensitive divisional or departmental application that needs to be isolated from other divisions or departments.

How do you decide the security issues? Only you can do so. Look at the data, and then give some thought about the people who are using your intranet. If you have any doubt, secure the information. A few tips follow.

- If you have any doubt about the security if your intranet, run your application on a secure server and pass information only to users with secure browsers to ensure that your sensitive information will not travel over your network as plain text.

- Develop a central security system that can identify the various types of users by user ID and password.

- Accept connections only from known, secure IP addresses. Make sure that machines that are accessible to unauthorized personnel cannot access your application. Use filters on your router, if appropriate, or refuse to send pages from your server to unknown IP addresses.

Change Passwords Periodically

Given a choice, most of us would select a password that was easy to remember, never change it, and use the same password everywhere. Your corporate security group probably has standards much stricter than that—for a reason. Easy passwords that never change are easy to crack, and once passwords are cracked, hackers can use them again and again.

> **TIP**
>
> Never send passwords via electronic mail unless the message is heavily encrypted. In fact, just to be safe, never send passwords through electronic mail, period!

If you must use passwords in your application, change them periodically. Once a month is typical, though your application might require more or less frequent changes. If you use the

HTTP password capability, you will want a separate process for updating passwords. One way is to use corporate security files to obtain passwords. Another suggestion is to alter the passwords periodically yourself and distribute them to your users via a secure mechanism. Never send passwords in an electronic mail message unless the message is encrypted!

Dealing with Corporate Control Organizations

As you have probably recognized, for a major part of the design and implementation effort for an intranet application, you will have to work with the corporate organizations that control the resources. Companies vary, but in this section, you'll learn some of the typical organizations. Your company can name these groups differently or roll the responsibilities into other groups, but the company will probably have some group to provide these services.

> **TIP**
>
> Working with corporate organizations can take time—plan for it in your development schedule.

Network Naming and Addressing

Probably the first place you will have to go is to network naming and addressing, especially if you are going to implement a new server for your application. This group will provide you with new TCP/IP addresses and domain names. Often in large corporations that have multiple subdomains, this responsibility is delegated for each subdomain.

It will undoubtedly take some time to get a new domain or even machine registered in a large intranet—plan accordingly. When you request addresses or names, be sure to include your development and test environments along with your production host, if they will be on different machines.

If your application will have exposure to the public Internet, you might have to work with your corporate naming and addressing organization to obtain the IP addresses and names for your hosts and register your hosts. Often corporations are assigned blocks of IP addresses and are responsible for naming their domains. In this case, your corporate group can probably supply the names and addresses that you need.

Router Operations

One frustrating aspect about intranets is router operations. Routers are the "glue" that hold the whole application together and, in a corporate intranet, are often centrally controlled. Some companies use routers as security and control mechanisms; that is, they filter specific IP addresses or groups of addresses to segregate parts of the company.

If all parts of the company must share your application, you will have to work with router operations (and possibly other corporate organizations) to resolve the issue of segregation. This can generally be a time-consuming process. The end result is usually one of three:

1. Modify the router filters to pass your particular server.
2. Host your application on a server that has access to all segments of the intranet.
3. Duplicate or split your application on servers within the intranet segments.

As you can imagine, the second and third options can raise other issues of control and access to maintain and update your application.

To test whether your application is accessible by all who require it, ask users on the various segments to attempt to retrieve pages from your server. Be sure to include all protocols—that is, FTP, SMTP, NNTP—that your application will use to ensure that packet types are not being filtered at some point in the intranet. Also, make sure that your beta testers represent all network segments that will use your application.

Corporate Standards

Unlike the public Internet, you might have to conform your application to corporate standards before you can deploy it on the corporate intranet, especially if your application will be part of a "suite" of applications, such as corporate or financial applications. You might have to conform your application to the corporate look and feel and meet performance and specific programming standards. Be sure to investigate these standards early in your design process.

LAN Groups at the Local Level

You will also have to work with the LAN administrators on the network where your server resides. Often, LANs are given naming responsibility for the domain of which the LAN is a part. These resources can help you work with corporate infrastructure. They also tend to be more accessible just because they're physically close.

Accessing Mainframe Data

Much of a corporation's data probably exists in mainframe files or databases. Often, this data is accessed through legacy mainframe systems over non-TCP/IP networks. The most common network architecture is IBM's System Network Architecture (SNA). Corporate intranets are often put into place as the infrastructure to access this data. However, converting legacy mainframe systems to client/server systems is often expensive and time consuming.

Thus, your system might have to access data on mainframes maintained by legacy systems. Typically, executive information systems (EIS) are LAN based. You can find many tools on the market that access mainframe data, but these tools tend to rely on the data being in a mainframe database or are expensive to install and maintain.

It is well beyond the scope of this chapter to talk about the various tools available for mainframe access, but I'll briefly discuss two alternatives to give you a framework for your design:

- Data mirroring on intranet-based databases
- Access through existing mainframe systems (screen scraping)

Data Mirroring

If you design a decision support system (DSS), you can choose to download data to a LAN-based database out of the mainframe system, often referred to as a data warehouse because it contains historic data, often summarized, optimized for data retrieval. Data warehouse design is a complex subject and will not be covered here.

Many tools to access intranet-based databases are coming to the market. If you choose to write your own tools, you will need to design a CGI application, which interfaces with your Web daemon through the CGI standard and the database's application programming interface (API). Figure 4.4 illustrates this design.

FIGURE 4.4.
CGI application design for CGI and LAN-based data warehouse. Mainframe data is downloaded in batch processes, summarized, and loaded.

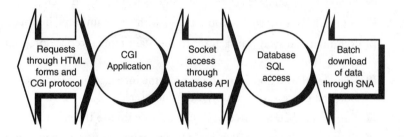

Data synchronization is an issue for this design. That is, you will have to carefully consider updating of your database and transmitting data between the mainframe database and the intranet-based database. The issues of data duplication are complex and well beyond the scope of this chapter.

Screen Scraping

Cost and time to develop client/server-based applications to meet the demands for access to corporate data are usually high. One method you can use to speed access to data at a relatively low cost is to use programs to access data from existing mainframe application screens. Figure 4.5 illustrates this application design.

There are two components in this design: a CGI application and a mainframe interface program.

CGI Application

The CGI program, the interface between the user and the mainframe interface program, receives input from the user in formats specified by the CGI standard and returns information to the user by formatting HTML pages. The program establishes a TCP/IP socket connection with the mainframe interface program and passes transactions that will be processed by the mainframe application just as if a human had typed them.

FIGURE 4.5.

A typical screen scraping system configuration using a CGI program communicating with the Web host and a mainframe interface program.

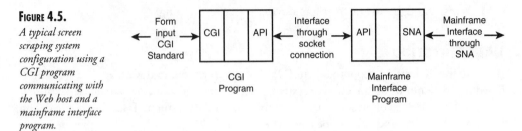

The CGI application details vary, depending on your application. However, all applications perform the following basic functions:

- Send HTML forms to request information from the end user
- Follow CGI standards to receive requests from the end user
- Establish TCP/IP socket connections with the mainframe interface program
- Reformat and send transactions to the mainframe interface program over the socket connection
- Receive information from the mainframe interface program over the socket connection and process it to return to the end user
- Format HTML screens and return information to the end user
- Store any information that must be maintained between transactions

Of course, you will have to code both the CGI application and the mainframe interface program to correctly process errors such as timeouts, unavailability of the mainframe system, and other unforeseen circumstances.

Mainframe Interface Program

This daemon program is responsible for the connections to the mainframe. It usually operates through a vendor's SNA interface API. The program varies depending on your application and the vendor's API, but programs of this type perform several basic functions:

- Sign on to the mainframe at the start of the day
- Maintain connection on lines that have an inactivity timeout
- Process transactions sent from the CGI program
- Re-establish the sessions with the mainframe in case they come down during the processing day
- Log off the mainframe at the end of processing

In addition to these basic functions, the mainframe interface program can perform other specialized functions for your application.

Because the process of signing on to the mainframe can be time consuming, the mainframe interface program signs on to the system once per day and maintains the connection until it signs off in the evening. The interface program is responsible for maintaining this connection and accommodating all security procedures to sign on to the mainframe.

The mainframe interface program receives the SNA data stream, then picks off information at specific screen locations. In doing so, the program "scrapes" information off existing application screens and thus gets the name *screen scraping*. Using existing mainframe online screens as the source of the data, you can usually implement this type of program more quickly than other types of interfaces. You can also typically use this type of screen scraping program as an interim module while more sophisticated interface modules are being developed.

NOTE

A screen scraping program can be a maintenance headache if your existing mainframe screens change frequently. Screen scrapers usually require little maintenance when interfaced to stable mainframe online screens.

One typical situation your screen scraper will face is an inactivity time-out on online applications. To deal with this, the program implements a timer that sends a dummy transaction during periods of inactivity for each monitored line. These dummy transactions can be as simple as simulating an Enter key press or can involve coding a "do nothing" transaction that can be sent periodically to the mainframe transaction monitor.

Although processing transactions will be unique to your application, the basic format for this interaction is as follows:

CGI Program	*Mainframe Interface Program*
Request socket connection	→ Establish socket with CGI program.
	← Allocate mainframe session.
Send request transaction	→ Format request for the mainframe.
	Transmit request to the mainframe.
	Receive response from the mainframe.
Format information for display	← Format and return information.
Disconnect socket	Disconnect socket.
	Deallocate mainframe session.

4

DEVELOPING
INTRANET
APPLICATIONS

Although the conversation between the modules can be much more complex, this is the basic conversation. One important point to note is that the connection between the CGI program and the mainframe interface program is broken after the conversation is complete. Also, the mainframe session established for the conversation is de-allocated after the socket connection is broken. This means that any information that needs to be carried over between conversations needs to be maintained by the CGI program, the mainframe interface program, or both.

Intranet Style Guide

As I stated at the beginning of this chapter, the purpose of intranet applications (sets of Web pages) is to convey information as succinctly, efficiently, and timely as possible. This style guide section presents some basic design elements to help you do this in your applications.

If your corporation has a style guide for intranet Web pages, use it. If not, the corporation might have a guide for Internet Web pages. If so, you look through it and keep in mind the difference between the intent of intranet versus Internet applications.

Several excellent style guides are available on the Internet. One excellent overall guide to Web page creation is the *Yale University Center for Instructional Media (CAIM) Style Guide* by Patrick J. Lynch. The address for this style guide is

```
http://info.med.yale.edu/caim/StyleManual_Top.HTML
```

Because excellent style guides are available and corporations differ greatly, I do not intend to present a complete style reference. Rather, with this section, I present suggestions for Web pages that are important to intranet applications and can apply to Internet applications as well.

Web Page Organization

Your application likely includes more than one Web page. In this case, organization and navigation are important aspects of your design. A user's perception of your application and its ease of use (navigation) are important aspects of design. To quote from the CAIM style guide, "Users need predictability and structure, with clear functional and graphic continuity between the various components and subsections of your [application]. Banner graphics, signature icons, or other graphic devices can be very useful in reinforcing domain identity within subsections of your [application]."

Although you probably won't need to reinforce "domain identity," you will have to give your users the information they require with a minimum of fuss and bother. You don't want the users' concept of your application to be a tangle of connections. The users need to have a clear picture of your organization.

If you build a set of pages, think of them as you would think of a written report or book. Organize your application into a single home page with specific submenus and pages off these menus. Figure 4.6 illustrates this organization.

FIGURE 4.6.

*A Web application
should be logically
organized to minimize
confusion.*

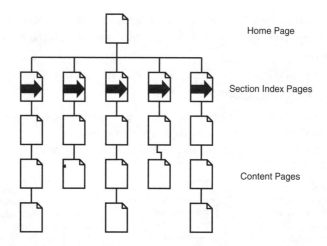

FIGURE 4.6.

*A Web application
should be logically
organized to minimize
confusion.*

Of course, don't interpret this to mean that you can't jump between content pages—quite the contrary. Logical jumps between content pages are what hypertext (the "H" in HTML) is all about. The point to remember is that your Web application should appear logical and organized, not random and disorganized.

> **TIP**
>
> You might just want to jump into producing Web pages, but organizational planning is as important to a Web application as it is to any traditional application.

If you generate screens that request, then display, information dynamically, your structure should follow in much the same way. As with any traditional application, your Web application should enhance the way users do their jobs. It should take them step by step through the required screens in a logical manner so they can achieve their goals.

Navigation

It is important to enable users to navigate through your application. If you have spent the time to plan your application's organization, you have decided on that organization for a reason.

One important point to remember is that users can drop into your application at any point. If you do not provide them with connections to navigate up and down through your application, they will not get the full benefit of it.

The minimal navigation aids that you should place on every page include the following:

```
[Previous Page][Table of Contents][Home Page][Next Page]
```

In addition to these buttons, you might want to include buttons to navigate to a next section if your application is organized into sections or to specific pages of general interest, such as a glossary.

Page Organization

Consistency and logical layout are the keys to good page organization. When you plan your Web application, design a base page template and use it whenever possible throughout your application. Figure 4.7 shows some elements you might want to consider for your template.

FIGURE 4.7.

A Web page template with HTML shows the basic elements for home pages. Actual design is not important; consistency is.

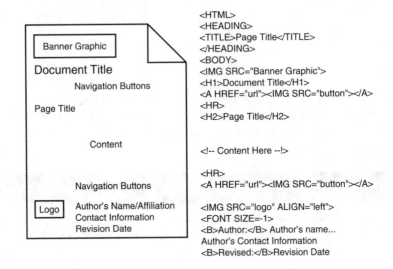

Important elements illustrated by this template include the following:

Format Element	Comment
Banner graphic	A graphic element that ties your application pages together. This element gives your pages continuity and your users a sense of a complete application even if they drop into your pages at midpoint.
Document title	The title of your application; also a strong unifying element.
Navigation buttons	Objects for the user to navigate through your pages. These buttons are important because an outside page can link to a page in the middle of your application.
Dividers	Horizontal Rule (<HR>) lines and other elements that organize your pages into logical sections.

Format Element	Comment
Page title	Element that shows the purpose of this particular page in your application. The page title and document title give users a complete sense of this page's purpose in the application.
Logo	This small element can tie related applications together. For example, you might use the same logo for all applications for a particular division or for all applications of a particular time, such as personnel applications.
Author information	This can be important information for your user. It should include both content and technical contacts, if they differ, for an application. The use of "mailto" tags can be helpful by providing a contact for further information or clarifying the use of your application or a particular page.
Revision date	In a medium like an intranet, it is important for your users to know how old the content on your page is so they can judge its value to them.

Forms

The same principles apply to HTML forms and the output they produce. If you send a series of forms, you should give them a consistent look and feel. The user should find related elements together on the form and should find similar elements on the same section of each form. If you will be integrating your forms into a larger set of Web pages, you might want to design your page template such that both informational pages and forms can appear on the same template.

Feedback

Be sure always to give your users positive and complete feedback from a form action. For example, if you store information as a result of a form submission, make sure to inform your users of that fact. Also give them somewhere to go from your feedback page without having to use their return button. You should use your standard application page template to display the feedback information if possible. This way, your users will have access to the navigation buttons that you have included in your application.

Page Design

Designing a Web application is much the same as designing a book or other publication. The same graphic design principles apply to what is essentially an electronic version of the printed page. Consistency and predictability are important to any well-designed information system.

Unlike typesetting, in which you have absolute control, on a Web page, you only suggest some of the elements. For example, you have no control over the aspect ratio of the end user's screen. You also have no control over the type face or size that they choose for their browser display. In many cases, the user can override backgrounds, turn off graphics, and do other things that lay waste to your carefully designed pages.

Enabling the user to carefully plan and extensively test your pages on different equipment with different tastes and different software can at least alert you to some of these problems. Also, design your pages so that they are best viewed on the most common equipment and software in use on your intranet. Then make sure that they are at least usable on other common types of equipment available to the intranet users. For example, you can choose to use for your main application frames that are available on some browsers but not supported by all browsers. If there are also users who must access your pages with browsers that are not capable of viewing frames, provide a non-frame version of your pages. This way, all users who must access your pages can at least get to the information they require, even if it isn't as well-organized as it might be in the frames version of the pages.

On an intranet, you might have some control over the equipment and software used if your company enforces standards for these things or purchases browser software at the corporate level. If appearance is vital to your application, you might want to consider writing for a specific browser and then distributing that browser to the users of your application.

Use of Graphics

Graphics can be the most interesting part of a Web application. If you design for the public Internet and need to attract visitors, "sharp" graphics can do so, but intranet Web applications are intended to impart specific information or perform specific functions. Graphics take a long time to send across the intranet, especially if the end user has dialed in.

To make sure that every graphic is worth the transmit bandwidth time, consider the following. "A picture is worth a thousand words" is the old adage, but the new Web-based adage should be "Is a picture worth the bandwidth?" At six characters per word, your thousand words will take up about 6,000 bytes. Graphics to display the same idea can be much larger—in the range of 10 to 60K bytes. In an intranet application, your users expect to get the job done in a minimal amount of time. The rule of thumb is use graphics only if they convey important information for your application.

Here's an example. Let's say your application creates a table of information that you want to display in a graph. You could design a program to create a graphic based on this information to display to the user. A better solution might be to design your application to create a spreadsheet that you can transmit to your user and to activate their spreadsheet program once it is transmitted. You could even include a small macro with the spreadsheet to graph the information automatically.

TIP

Evaluate each graphic for its information content. If you cannot succinctly state the purpose for this graphic in your application, consider removing it.

Look at large graphics to see whether they can be as effective if you reduce them. Also, if you use 16- or 24-bit graphics, consider converting them to eight- or even four-bit graphics. With many business graphics, such as charts and graphs, eight-bit graphics are just as effective and will greatly reduce the transmission time of the page.

If you use graphics, keep the style and placement consistent between pages. Graphics can be great devices to help users feel comfortable with your application. A small "banner" graphic can help tie pages together. This will give your users the sense that your application is unified and will help them find information on the page.

The consistent use of icons can also boost the effectiveness of your Web application. Use consistent icons across related applications. If your intranet spans national boundaries, though, remember that not all cultures share the same history. An icon that is meaningful in one culture might be completely obscure in another. If you write for an international intranet, be sure to test your icons with all cultures involved. Figure 4.8 shows a set of public domain icons that you can use in your applications.

FIGURE 4.8.

An effective set of icons can enhance your application greatly.

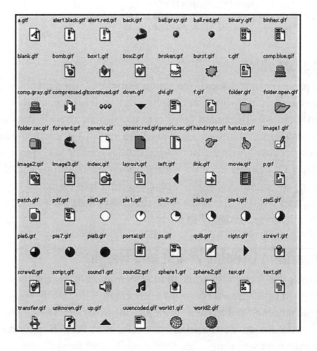

4

DEVELOPING
INTRANET
APPLICATIONS

Graphic design for a Web page is much like graphic design for a book or magazine. Many of the same design principles apply to placing graphics and using white space. The CAIM style guide has a good discussion of design principles.

The Text Alternative

When designing your Web application, always give your user a text alternative to graphics used as navigation buttons or image maps. If their time is critical, many users prefer to turn the graphics off on their Web browsers. This greatly decreases the transmission time for your application pages but can wreak havoc on your image maps or carefully crafted navigation icons.

Always code the ALT= parameter on images. This parameter should include the text version of buttons, for example:

```
<IMG SRC="nextpage.gif" ALT="[Next Page]">
```

Make sure that the text on your pages can stand alone and perhaps provide an ALT tag for graphics to give the user without graphics some sense of what they're missing.

Image maps can work as excellent graphic guides through your application if they make sense, though these large complex graphics often require a long time to download. If you provide a graphic image map for navigation, place a row of text buttons below the image to provide an alternative. For example, just below your image, you might provide

```
<A HREF="nextpage.html">[Next]</A>
<A HREF="prevpage.html">[Previous]</A>
<A HREF="homepage.html">[HomePage]</A>
```

Sizing Graphics

Often programmers make the common mistake of using graphics that are too wide to fit within the browser's default window. Graphics that spill off the screen look bad and can hide essential information. Most personal computer monitors currently display 640×480 pixels on 13- to 15-inch screens. Macintosh and Windows versions of Netscape and Mosaic both default to a window size that limits the horizontal display area of Web pages to about 500 pixels. To prevent top title banners or other wide graphics from spilling off, the graphics' horizontal measurement should not exceed 470 pixels. This leaves sufficient visual relief on both sides of the graphic and ensures that users with the most common monitor sizes will not have to scroll horizontally to see your full graphic.

Transmitting Graphic Width and Height

By transmitting the width and height information in the anchor reference to an in-line graphic, Netscape or other browsers can instantly create a bounding box for the graphic without examining the whole graphic to determine size information. Width and height statements are added just after the standard IMG in-line image tag. Web viewers that do not support this HTML language extension will simply ignore the width and height tags:

```
<IMG SRC="LARGE.GIF" WIDTH = 412 HEIGHT=137>
```

When the browser creates the image box, you can accurately place the text *before* completely transmitting the graphic. With large graphics, the user can start to read the information without interruption or having to wait for the graphic to fully transmit, making your pages appear much faster than they actually are.

Summary

An internal TCP/IP network or intranet can be a valuable infrastructure to tie an organization together. Intranet-centered applications can provide information to the organization in a common convenient format such as a Web browser. However, like applications written for the public Internet, these applications require careful planning and programming to ensure their integrity and usefulness. In this chapter, you learned several intranet programming issues and have learned several strategies and suggestions for dealing with these issues. Apply these strategies and suggestions in a structured design and programming environment and treat the intranet applications as you would any other corporate information technology resource, and your intranet applications will serve your organization well.

IN THIS PART

II

PART

Internet Programming Languages

Java and the Internet

by Dan Joshi

CHAPTER 5

This chapter gives a brief history of programming languages, from their earlier incarnations to today's modern languages, and provides a foundation of common understanding as to where Java fits in the scheme of things. This chapter is not just about the benefits of Java—it is about Java.

Java History

Structured programming was the 1960s' answer to the need for discipline in the computer programming industry, leaving spaghetti code for the history books. An excellent example of a structured programming language was Pascal, developed in 1971.

Object-oriented programming was invented to improve three things that structured programming languages lacked: the capability to "reduce, reuse, and recycle" code.

Since the birth of C++, object-oriented programming languages have become the standard by which modern programming languages are defined. Object-oriented (OO) programming languages such as C++ deal with user-defined types (UDT). UDTs are programmatic representations of objects. Programmers can reuse these objects throughout their program and in other programs.

The idea behind object-oriented programming is based on the logic of designing your code into objects and letting these objects communicate with each other through various object-based technologies. Before you can understand Java, you must understand objects; and before you can understand objects, you must understand the structured programming techniques upon which objects are founded. Object-oriented programming encompasses much more than described in this brief introduction. Many of these benefits won't be fully appreciated until you have had a chance to work with Java later in this book.

In real life we deal with objects every day. With objects we can have superobjects and subobjects. For example, a car is an object. A luxury sedan is a subobject to the object of a car, and a vehicle is a superobject to the object of a car. The concept that a car completely encapsulates the luxury sedan and that the vehicle completely encapsulates both of them helps to define what an object is. In another light, a car is a more specific representation than a vehicle, and a luxury sedan is a more specific object than a car. Thus, the car is a subobject to a vehicle and a luxury sedan is a subobject to the car. And if you can conclude that the luxury sedan is also a subobject to the vehicle, you would be correct. However, if the only vehicle you ever saw was a car, you would conclude that it would be redundant to add a subclass (that is, a more specific representation) of a car object because a car fully encompasses your definition of a vehicle.

This point brings out one of the most powerful and confusing attributes of object technology in the programming industry, which is that objects are defined. We must use our own perception of what is a subclass or superclass to another object. Even though this makes object-oriented programming difficult for most new people to understand, it is extremely powerful when you do understand it. In object-oriented programming, you get to make your own set of rules.

Before getting into more detail on the anatomy of objects, there is one other key feature of object-oriented programming to introduce. It is the capability of objects to contain both data and behavior that acts on that data. This grouping of both data (or attributes or properties) and behavior (which is represented in methods) helps to integrate your programs as opposed to conventional structured programming techniques, which separate the data-based code from the action-based code.

Objects usually contain properties. For example, the number of wheels a vehicle has is a property of the vehicle object. In order to better understand properties, let's design an acting model. The vehicle object, as defined in the preceding paragraph, is a superobject to the car object. The car object also can have properties; however, it would be inappropriate to give our car object the property of trunk size, for example, because not all cars have trunks (assuming your definition of a car includes hatchbacks). On the other hand, it would be appropriate to give the luxury sedan object a property of trunk size because all luxury sedans have some sort of trunk.

When you are assigning properties in your program, look for the highest class that would still be appropriate for the property. This follows the logic that the lower you go in a class hierarchy the more specific an object becomes. On the other hand, the higher you go in a class hierarchy the more abstract an object becomes.

Another important term used in object technology is *method*. Driving a car is an action; thus, driving could be considered, in "object jargon," a method to the car. A good way to understand a method is to think of it in terms of action. A method is always doing something. As mentioned earlier, methods can be appropriately and inappropriately placed depending on their location in the class hierarchy.

Object-oriented programming is simply another way of putting better logic into your program. Digressing into a more philosophical aspect of programming languages, here is a description of one of the most important components of the perfect programming language: Ideally, this language would be completely unrelated to computer science. The advantage of this is that anyone could sit down and use it without needing to know anything about computers and computer science. All a person would need to know to create a computer program would be his or her field of expertise. For example, an insurance broker would only need to know about his field to sit down in front of a computer and create a program that would make his job (hence his life) easier.

Unfortunately, such a language does not exist and probably won't be here any time soon. However, based on lessons learned in the history of programming languages discussed further in the next section, the object paradigm is probably one of the biggest steps toward this perfect language.

At its very core, object-oriented programming is simply a more powerful way to construct your code logically; using objects with properties and methods creates a more logical program.

Although most programming languages have many rules specific to each of them, the golden rule of all programming languages is this: Never write the same code twice. By having a more distributed program, you are more able to follow this golden rule of programming. Although most programmers would find it nearly impossible to reuse their code 100 percent of the time, object-oriented programming languages greatly improve the ability for anyone to reuse their code.

Now, imagine that you are a developer and you are writing a program called Alpha. You write this program in a structured programming language and compile it. Your program is successful, and your manager comes to you and says she wants an Alpha version 2.0.

At this point, you would usually need to modify the original program. Sometimes you can edit code that is already resident in the program. Other times you would need to write new code. Typically, you would need to do both: edit old code and write new code. However, it is also likely that, due to the nature of the changes for version 2.0, you will need to dissolve the old program and redesign it from the ground up.

Now imagine that you are an object-oriented programmer, and you are asked to write the same program called Alpha. You create the program by building objects. Your code is more logical, is easier to understand, and typically also might be smaller. Thus, you are reducing the amount of time and code you spend developing the application. Now, when your manager says she wants Alpha version 2.0, instead of going into the code of the original program, you can take your original Alpha classes and "inherit" them into new classes that have added functionality for use with version 2.0. This object technology is called *inheritance*.

With the advent of object-oriented programming like C++, Java, and SmallTalk, using inheritance you can recycle old code by taking the old objects and turning them into new ones. The key point is that in object-oriented programming you can more effectively "reduce, reuse, and recycle" your code.

Java's Place in the Object-Oriented Continuum

Java is a new object-oriented programming language that has its foundation in C++. In fact, part of the process of designing Java was taking C++ and analyzing its strengths and weaknesses. Java was the next step from C++, with a perfect fit in the Internet's multiplatformed environment. Furthermore, Java roots come from the portable electronic device industry, making it extremely portable from one device to another device, or in the case of the Net, from platform to platform.

TIP

This section includes notes on Java in terms of C/C++, helping those already familiar with C/C++ quickly learn Java.

Defining Java

Java was developed by Sun Microsystems and is a multithreaded object-oriented programming language. It is a new programming language with complete functionality like that of C++. At this point, Java's niche is on the World Wide Web. Probably the most important things that Java brings to the Web are the capacity for more interactivity on the Internet through multimedia and animation. In order to view Java applets on the Net, you must have a Java-compliant browser. The Internet Explorer (as of version 3.0) and Netscape Navigator (as of version 2.0) are two prominent browsers on the Net that support Java.

The next section defines Java applets and discusses the differences between Java and Java applets.

Java Applet Definition

Java applets are a hybrid form of Java programs to run on a Java-compliant browser on the World Wide Web. The applet is inherently embedded in an HTML document. A Web site that has one or more Java applets embedded in it is said to be "Java-powered." Java applets are portable to just about any Web site. If you would like to check out some already existing applets, go to the Gamelan home page at the following URL:

`http://www.gamelan.com`

On the same topic as Java applets is the abbreviation JARS, which stands for Java Applet Rating Service. JARS is a rating service for Java applets on the Internet. Anyone can create an applet and submit it to the JARS judges for review. Your applet then would be scored on four topics for official awards. See Table 5.1 for a breakdown of how applets are rated.

Table 5.1. Applet rating breakdown.

1	Presentation (front end)
2	AppletPerfect (programming content)
3	Function (usefulness)
4	Originality (concept, new idea)

For unofficial awards, the second topic in Table 5.1 is removed. If you would like to see some of the best Java applets on the Internet, point your browser to the JARS home page at the following URL:

`http://www.jars.com`

Because the Internet has enabled us to connect all kinds of computers from all over the world, there are major security issues that need to be addressed. Java applets have been designed with security as a top issue. Applets are specifically designed to make sure that the applet itself cannot harm the client's environment and cannot carry a downloadable virus that could infect the client's system. Unfortunately, this security benefit has a downside. On the one hand, you will have protection against potential viruses and rampaging Java applets. On the other hand, it limits Java applet potential significantly in several areas. The applet is pretty much restricted from gaining direct access to a client's system.

The Benefits of Java

As you will see in the following sections, Java benefits from serious pre-planning and design. It is a completely object-oriented programming language from the ground up and is also multithreaded, letting your programs run more smoothly. Java is platform-independent, which means one compiled Java program can be accessed by several different environments. Finally, Java handles all memory management automatically, making it an extremely powerful, useful, and versatile programming language. Let's take a closer look at each of these.

Java Is Object-Oriented

Java is an object-oriented programming language, as mentioned earlier. Instead of having to memorize a set of functions to program in Java, you have a set of classes known as the Java class library.

> **NOTE**
>
> A class library is simply a group of related classes.

The Java class library enables you to design the user interface for your Java program, access a file (if it is a Java application), or implement a thread. This helps to make Java a very functional language. Remember, though, that everything in Java deals with objects, starting from the ground up.

Java Compared to C++

Java is closely related to C++. But there are a few major discrepancies that should be noted.

Java does not use pointers. A *pointer* is a variable that contains the address of another variable's location. This form of indirectly accessing variables and UDTs has been one of the most powerful and most confusing features of C/C++. Pointers are also one of the easiest ways to crash a system. Pointers appear to be one of the major ways that seemingly non-removable bugs enter into a program. For example, simply by pointing to an area of memory where you don't belong, you can inadvertently start writing new information over the current information stored in that memory location. This is not uncommon. A pointer might point to an incorrect location. Sometimes you get lucky and write over only unused or unimportant information stored

tion that you should not be looking at. This, unfortunately, has given crackers a loophole to work with. The use of pointers was removed from Java for these reasons.

Java is based on single inheritance. C++ currently supports multiple inheritance. The major difference between multiple inheritance and single inheritance is that in C++ you can inherit more than one class into another class. So, a subclass could effectively have two or more superclasses, and each of the superclasses would completely become part of the subclass, making the subclass a more specific representation of both superclasses. In theory this was a great idea, but in practice it turned out to be much too complicated and hence more trouble than it was worth. So, Sun kept the object technology of inheritance but only allowed single inheritance; this means that a subclass can have only one superclass. This is really the best of both worlds because with single inheritance you can still inherit one class to another new one, but you can do so only once per class basis. I might add, though, that Java does have a way to support a kind of multiple inheritance; that's through the use of implementing interfaces.

Java's memory management system is greatly improved over C/C++. Java has automatic memory management and garbage collection. More information on garbage collection will be explained later in this chapter.

Some other important notes about Java are that it does support overloaded functions, but not overloaded operators; also, commands like `struct` and `union` are gone from Java's vocabulary. Another minor note on the differences between C/C++ and Java is that Java does not support the ability to change the nature of a variable implicitly. Everything must be explicitly cast in Java. In C/C++ jargon, Java does not support automatic coercion. Header files were replaced by interfaces. All functions must be wrapped with a particular class.

Finally, C/C++ does not have a native string object like Java does. Instead, you have to build it by creating an array of single-character data types or else define your own C++ based string UDT. Furthermore, character arrays in C/C++ do not do any bounds checking, so if your array of characters in C/C++ is larger than what was allocated, you are writing on memory locations that do not belong to your program, usually causing it to crash.

Java Is Multithreaded

Modern operating systems are said to be *multitasking*. This means that the operating system can process more than one thread at a time (in truth, unless you have more than one CPU, the operating system is merely fudging at handling more than one thread at any one point in time, but this statement will suffice for now). Java, on the other hand, enables the programmer to create a program that directs how the CPU will handle the thread. Probably the greatest advantage to this is shown in all of the animation- and multimedia-intensive Java applets on the Internet where the programmer has directly assigned a special thread for animation.

> A thread is merely the basic entity to which the operating system allocates CPU time.

What Multithreaded Java Brings to a Multithreaded Operating System

Before you can understand how Java improves the multithread paradigm, you need to digress a little to understand a bit about the operating system. Because operating systems vary from one platform to another, this section discusses them in a generic light as they pertain to Java.

First, let's start with an understanding of a typical operating system. When you start a program, a process is spawned.

NOTE

A process is a program loaded into memory and prepared for execution.

The process holds the code. Each process is started with a single thread, but additional independently executing threads can be created. This makes for a smoother program and environment, but it can also create conflicts such as when two or more threads attempt to access the same resource.

TIP

Thread synchronization is the answer to avoiding thread conflicts.

On a single processor system, the operating system merely gives the illusion that more than one thread is executing at one time. What is really going on is that each of the active threads receives a time slice, usually an extremely small amount of time.

NOTE

Time slices usually are measured in milliseconds.

You could think of it as a string of lights, where each of the bulbs are separate threads, blinking one at a time, but blinking so fast that to the human eye the string looks as though all the lights are on at the same time. Now if multitasking were just that simple, it would be easy to understand it.

Preemptive multitasking is the capability of the operating system to interrupt a thread (most of the time) and assign the CPU to a waiting thread. So, for example, imagine that you have a word processor and spreadsheet loaded, and in the middle of a long CPU-intensive process in the spreadsheet, you switch over to the word processor. In this scenario, you can effectively preempt the thread currently running (the spreadsheet) and give it to a thread that belongs to the word processor. This keeps the modern desktop responsive. Typically, the only time that the environment might lose its responsiveness is when too many threads are running.

The last topic to mention is the idea of thread priorities. For example, the thread that handles mouse events should have a high priority in the operation system. That way, the mouse will get more attention from the CPU, and the user will have a more responsive mouse that does not "lock up" whenever he starts a program that hogs CPU time.

With this explanation, you can pretty much tell how the operating system handles all of the threads and what they are doing. Java enables the programmer to design an application with multiple threads. You, the programmer, have control over your thread, to some extent anyway. You can create a thread and develop code to respond to various events in which the operating system handles the thread. As a Java programmer you can designate the priority of the thread in your Java applet. Also, you can directly deal with things like the synchronization of threads. Java gives you much more control over how your program will run in the user's environment. A key point is that typically you are requesting all of these things. Multithreaded environments help us deal with things in the computer in a simultaneous manner.

Java Is Dynamic

Most of the memory management technologies Java uses are based on ideas borrowed from other languages and improved. First, as object-oriented Java programmers, let's ask the question: How does Java memory management handle objects? It is all done automatically. Let's understand how.

One of the major problems with programming languages—either object-oriented or structured languages—is the idea of memory leaks. Memory leaks have been around since the structured programming days. However, take a closer look at how they occur in an object-oriented programming environment. When a program starts, it takes free memory from the environment to construct instances of objects. Next, the program runs, typically creating and destroying these objects and therefore taking and freeing memory throughout the life of the program. Finally, the program exits and destroys any remaining objects, leaving the environment with the same amount of free memory as before it was started. This is a perfect program. All of the objects constructed are destroyed; thus, all of the memory taken for the program would be released back into the environment. However, in the real world this is not the case, and in many programs the user's environment is left with less available memory than when the program was started. The key here is that in C++ typically the programmer must keep track of the allocation of memory for objects being constructed and the release of memory for objects that are no longer needed. As programs become more complicated, there is more room for error. Memory leaks are a very unwanted, yet accepted part of the program.

An excellent example of a program with memory leaks is a major application developed in C/C++: the 16-bit version of Windows. This operating system has memory leaks; to crash it, all you have to do is just use it without ever turning it off at night. Although the crash might take a week or month, eventually the system will run out of resources. To avoid such crashes, in C/C++ you have to keep track of all the objects you create and make sure that they are all properly destroyed. This is not so in Java, however. Java will take care of all the memory operations (though you do have a manual override option).

Java Is Compacted

Another important feature of Java is this: it has garbage collection. *Garbage collection* is the method Java uses to automatically handle allocating memory. Java uses two types of garbage collection tools. One is *compaction*, which is merely another word for defragmenting memory. Frankly, just as your hard disk becomes fragmented as you read and write information to it, memory also becomes fragmented. Compaction is the process of defragmenting memory.

Java Is Marked and Swept

Marking and sweeping is the other technology Java uses as part of its garbage collection tools. Marking and sweeping is a recursive process that marks objects in use; if at the end of this marking an object is not marked, it is *swept* or destroyed.

Garbage collection is not a new technology that Java just introduced; in fact, it is a fairly old one. Garbage collection has been around with languages like SmallTalk and Lisp. However, with these programming languages, particularly SmallTalk, the system grinds to a halt for a period of time whenever it is collecting garbage. Java, however, takes the idea and makes it better. Java, as you already know, has a fully functional garbage collection mechanism. And Java is a multithreaded programming environment. So, in coalescence of the two, Java runs its garbage collection on a (you guessed it) separate thread, making Java's garbage collection virtually unnoticeable. The thread is given a fairly low priority so that it will activate itself only when there is actual or anticipated idle time on the CPU. In summary, Java gives the programmer a hands-off approach to keeping track of how memory is being used and optimized.

Java Is Processor-Independent

When you write a Java program or applet, Java turns your written code into bytecodes. Bytecodes are like machine language instructions, though not quite at the level of machine language instructions. The advantage of this is that bytecodes are not processor-specific. When you compile a C/C++ program the compiler turns it directly into a set of machine codes or processor instructions. What this means is that, to take advantage of a different processor, you have to recompile the program each time. This will make a very efficient program, but it is a very tedious process every time you change processors. If you change environments, (for example, from the IBM clone to Mac, or to UNIX, and back again), you will again have to recompile your program. Not only do you have to recompile it, but also you often must rewrite the code for the specific environment you are heading toward. Java, on the other hand, takes care of "porting" the program and code to other environments.

Java is compiled and interpreted. It is compiled to bytecodes. When the program or applet is run on the client's system, the bytecodes are interpreted to the specific machine language and processor instructions of the client's system. By compiling one program in Java and turning it into bytecodes, you can use it on several environments.

Java Is Verified

Because Java uses bytecodes, it can also be verified. This makes the utilization of bytecodes a major part of Java's security model. Bytecodes can also be checked for security violations. Methods and variables are always accessed by name, instead of by numbers. This makes it easy to determine what is being used, and more important, it protects them from misuse. So, on the Internet when you are using an applet, the program is sent from the server to the client's system; then it is verified before it is interpreted.

Java Is a Multiplatform Environment

Here is more on multiple environments: In Java you can write one program and compile it once, and it will be capable of running on multiple environments. This means that Java code is 100 percent portable to all environments Java supports. Furthermore, the original source code is completely portable to any of these Java supported environments. Thus, you will only need to write the code once, and compile it once to port it to other platforms. As a result, Java is ripe for the heterogeneous environment of the Internet. Applets are interpreted by a Java-compliant browser on the client's system. By creating one applet it can run on a browser in UNIX, Mac, and the PC. This is probably one of the biggest selling points of Java and the reason for its success on the Internet.

The Negatives of Java

Java is slow. One of the newer issues that has arisen, particularly on the Internet, is that Java is relatively slow. This slowness can be explained by looking at what is going on when a Java applet is loaded on your system. First, the applet must be downloaded. Then the applet must be verified. Third, the applet is interpreted instead of executed. However, something known as a Just In Time (JIT) compiler has been released to help increase the performance of Java programs.

NOTE

Programs that are interpreted are slower than programs that are executed.

Finally, any pictures or graphics also must be downloaded. All of these steps contribute to the slowness of Java. Some things are out of the direct control of Java, such as the download time, which is pretty much up to the server, the Internet traffic at the time, and the client's connection to the Internet. Java is, however, very efficient in making the compiled classes relatively small. Pictures and graphics are up to the mercy of the programmer who decides what to use in the applet. The remaining area that causes decreased speed in Java is the verification process. Although Java has the best of both worlds by being interpreted and compiled, this still forces Java to be significantly slower than C/C++.

At this point, Java does not have a good indigenous development environment, but several development environments have been released by other software development companies. The major development environment for Java is the Java Developers Kit (JDK). Essentially, it is a command-line compiler, and if you are in the Windows environment, basically all you will have to use is an ASCII text editor. The compiler comes with the JDK. If you would like to pick up the JDK, go to the following site:

```
http://java.sun.com/download.html
```

Here is the security model for Java applets: When being downloaded from the Internet, a completely restricted environment is created for the Java applet to be placed in. This removes the capability to access files; nor can applets typically communicate with any other server than the one from where the applet came. Applets also cannot start programs on the client's system. This is a very limiting factor for Java. Probably one of the goals in future versions of Java will be finding a way to overcome these limitations without compromising security.

Summary

In this chapter, you learned what Java is and how it is part of the object-oriented programming language field. You also took a high-level look at the pros and cons of Java, including what makes it powerful and what it needs to work on for the future.

Java is still new (as far as programming languages are concerned), but has definitely established a presence in the industry.

Java Development Environments

by Dan Joshi

IN THIS CHAPTER

CHAPTER 6

This chapter explores how to write programs more effectively in Java. In the last several months, many major software development companies have been designing Java development environments for programmers to work in so that programmers would not need to have a text editor and the Java Developer's Kit. This chapter gives you an overview of several of these integrated development environments (IDE) that have greatly improved on the Java Developer's Kit (JDK).

> **NOTE**
>
> An integrated development environment is one program that contains several tools. Each of these tools (for example, a debugger and class viewer) helps you throughout the development cycle as you create or modify a program. Because integrated development environments are GUI-based, they are easy to use, and because these environments usually contain many tools, they are extremely useful.

The Java Developer's Kit is the first and probably the most wide-spread development environment currently available for Java. It is merely a set of command-line tools in which programs authored in a text editor are saved in ASCII format. These source files are compiled and debugged using command-line executables provided with the Java Developer's Kit. The Java Developer's Kit is the first topic discussed in this chapter, but you learn other environments such as the Java Workshop, Symantec Café, and some of the newer Internet-related tools from Borland. These newer programming environments are based on the integrated development environment paradigm. In these new environments, everything is designed around a GUI form. If you are a programmer new to Java, I hope that by the end of this chapter you will be able to make an informed decision about several of the major environments available. On the other hand, if you are a proficient Java programmer, you will have a better understanding of the pros and cons for each of these new environments.

> **NOTE**
>
> Throughout this chapter, there are three types of terms to describe Java-compiled classes. An "applet" is an Internet-based Java class file. A Java "program" is a stand-alone Java class file. The term "application" refers to both Java applets and programs.

Before beginning, I should point out several high-level points, particularly your knowledge of Java that is assumed in the chapter and what will be presented. First, I assume in this chapter that you have an understanding of Java and, in some cases, an understanding of C/C++. If this is true of your skill set, continue reading this chapter. If this is not true, however, review Chapter 7, "Introduction to Java," and Chapter 8, "Java Programming," and then return to Chapter 6 because those chapters give you an introduction to Java language syntax, building basic Java applets, and comparing Java to C/C++.

Java Development Environments

CHAPTER 6

131

6

JAVA
DEVELOPMENT
ENVIRONMENTS

Second, I highly recommend that you have the development environment available to follow along for each of the environments discussed in this chapter. This chapter is littered with notes, warnings, and figures on how the environments look and how they respond to various real-life programming situations. Nonetheless, in some demonstrations (for example, the Java Workshop), you actually go through the process of writing a sample applet. Finally, note that all of the environments you learn in this chapter are installed and tested for the Windows 95 and Windows NT platform, primarily because Symantec Café does not have a non-Windows version for its Java integrated development environment.

Java Development Environments

One of the most intimidating things about Java when it was first released was the fact that there were no "modern" integrated development environments with which to compile Java-related programs. For veteran programmers, that was not an issue, but for the newer programmers who might have never authored code in a text editor, it made Java appear very intimidating. As a solution, many of the major software companies started designing a kind of proprietary Java development environment to make it easier in which to code. As a result, this chapter is designed to discuss some of those major development environments.

This chapter explores the strengths and weaknesses of each of the development environments. To start off, you learn the Java Developer's Kit as an initial place to break ground. After all, every one of these new integrated development environments that is covered is based on the original Java Developer's Kit. Also, the Java Developer's Kit is what you will use in the next two chapters to design and run sample Java programs.

The Java Developer's Kit (JDK)

You use the Java Developer's Kit (also known as the JDK) in the next several chapters to test and develop all of the programs and applets for Java. The JDK was chosen primarily because most Java programs are very simple and the JDK's availability gives the greatest flexibility. The JDK contains a full copy of the Java language, including a complete set of all built-in classes used in Java. The JDK also contains all the source code for these built-in classes. Suffice it to say that when you download the JDK, you have a fully functional, object-oriented Java programming language. However, you do not have a nice front-end environment in which to develop, nor an Internet browser to test your Java-powered HTML pages. Instead you get a program called the `appletviewer` that can read information only inside the `<APPLET>` tag in an HTML page.

NOTE

For more information on using HTML tags with Java, see Chapter 8.

In fact, with the JDK, you really don't get any front end at all. All code must be written in some sort of proprietary text editor or word processor that can save to ASCII format. To do just about anything in the JDK, you must write code. In other words, with the JDK, you do not have any wizards, toolboxes, or Java code generators to point and click your way to Java computing.

The latest version of the JDK at the time of this writing is version 1.0.1. You can obtain this version for free from Sun's home page at the following site:

```
http://java.sun.com/download.html
```

The JDK is available for Windows 95, Windows NT, Sun's Solaris 2.4 or higher, and now the Macintosh. Although each of these JDK versions is extremely similar, there might be some minor differences between them. To remain consistent with the rest of the chapter, we will use the 32-bit Windows version of the JDK (that is, the JDK for Windows 95 and Windows NT). Installing the JDK for 32-bit Windows is fairly simple. Download the self-extracting file from the preceding address, run the self-extracting executable, and it will do the rest. (Let me be the first to pass my condolences to those who were expecting the InstallShield wizard.)

NOTE

InstallShield is a third-party product (from InstallShield Corp.) used to standardize the installation of a program. Its features include a completely point-and-click interface with which users can move through the installation of a program and an uninstall utility with which users can easily remove the product from their systems.

InstallShield is rapidly becoming the industry standard for software companies that use it to guide their users through installing their programs. The InstallShield is featured in the Java Workshop, Symantec Café, Borland C++ 5.0, and most likely it also will be bundled with Borland Latte when it is officially released.

When you have successfully installed the JDK, you are ready to begin. The JDK 1.0.1 compressed is about 4.4MB; after running the self-extracting executable, it should take no more than 7MB of space.

NOTE

One advantage of the JDK over all the integrated development environments is that it takes the least amount of space when it is uncompressed.

How To Use the Java Developer's Kit

Using the JDK can be pretty simple. Figure 6.1 shows the JDK directory structure after installing it on the E:\ drive.

FIGURE 6.1.

The Java Developer's Kit directory structure.

After you run the JDK, you can see that it creates a directory called `..\java`. As you can see in Figure 6.1, the first thing to notice in the `..\java` is the file `src.zip`. This file contains the zipped source code for the JDK classes.

> **NOTE**
>
> All built-in Java classes are written in Java.

Next, you learn the demos that come with the JDK. In Figure 6.1, you see the subdirectory `..\demo`. The demos located in that directory can be invaluable tools in learning about the language. Also, the JDK is set up so that a browser can locally access it. A file called `index.htm` is in the `..\java` directory. Load that HTML page in a Java-compliant browser (for example, Netscape 2.0 or later). Figure 6.2 shows `index.htm` loaded.

FIGURE 6.2.

The `index.htm` *file in the Java Developer's Kit.*

Referencing Figure 6.2 in `index.htm`, you see a link to `applet examples`. Click this link to bring up a directory listing of all the demos that come with the JDK. Click the directory `animator` to see the directory containing all the pertinent information for the animator applet. Finally, load the file `example1.htm` to load the animator applet shown in Figure 6.3.

FIGURE 6.3.

Animator example
(..\java\demo
\animator\example1.htm).

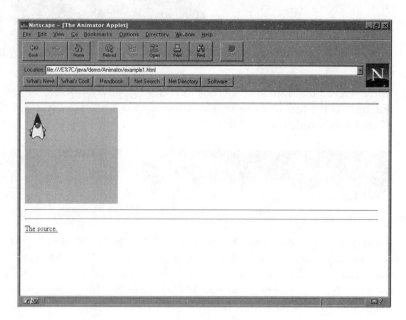

If you look at the bottom of the applet, you will see a link to the source code for this applet. In the animator example in Figure 6.3, this opens up the file `animator.java`, located in the `..\demo\animator` subdirectory, which shows the source code for this applet. Although this is not exactly a full-blown tutorial with all the bells and whistles available in the other integrated development environments that are demonstrated in this chapter, these examples give you valuable information for learning Java.

The next directory in Figure 6.1 that you learn briefly is the `..\java\lib` directory. Looking in the `..\lib` directory, the first thing to notice is the `javac.properties` file. This file is saved in a viewable format. Inside, you will see a long list of all the error messages from which the Java compiler draws during the compilation process to describe the errors it encounters when compiling your Java program. There is also a file called `javai.lib`, which is a library file used by the interpreter. The next file, `javai_g.lib`, is another copy of the `javai.lib` except that it is used to debug your Java programs. You learn more later in this section.

NOTE

Any executable with a _g at the end of its name in the JDK means that it is a nonoptimized version of the same executable designed for use with the Java debugger.

The last file is `classes.zip`. If you look at the `readme` file located in the `..\java` directory (refer to Figure 6.1), it says that you should not unzip this file. It is used by the Java compiler in this compressed form and contains the compiled class files for the built-in classes in Java.

The next and probably most significant directory for the JDK is the `..\bin` directory, which contains all of the command-line executables used to develop Java programs in the JDK.

The `..\java\bin` Directory

The `..\java\bin` directory contains all of the executable tools used in the JDK as well as the DLLs that are used by these executables. Note that some of the tools are designed specifically for advanced programming techniques and are discussed only briefly.

> **NOTE**
>
> A DLL or Dynamic Link Library is simply a compiled function that programs can call.

The `javac.exe` File

You will see many executables in the directory `..\java\bin`. The first, `javac.exe`, is probably the most important tool in the JDK because it compiles the Java source code files into Java bytecodes. You will have a chance to work with the Java compiler in the next two chapters. The source files must be named with the extension `.java` when they are compiled by `javac.exe`. By default, all files compiled will be placed in the same directory as the source file. However, you can use `javac.exe` to compile programs and place the class files in another directory by using the `-d` option:

```
javac -d e:\test c:\ABClass.java
```

In the preceding line of code, you see that by using the `-d` option on the fictitious class `ABClass.java`, it will compile the class file and place it in the `e:\test` drive. The `javac.exe` also can utilize the `-g` option, which gives you the capability of creating debugging tables.

The parameter that can be passed during compilation is the `-0` (the letter not the number) option, which can be used to optimize your compiled code.

> **NOTE**
>
> Specifically, the `-0` option optimizes your Java application by in-lining all `static`, `final`, and `private` methods. In C/C++, an in-line function is a small function whose code resides in the line of declaration (or prototype) rather than being called externally by the program. Efficiency is the advantage of in-line functions in C/C++ and Java because the application does not spend several cycles externally calling the function when the application is executed.

The next parameter I should mention is the -verbose parameter, which causes the compiler and linker to print out information about the source files being compiled, the classes being loaded, and the length of time it took to do each process.

The -nowarn parameter tells the Java compiler to skip over warnings instead of printing them out and stopping compilation.

> **NOTE**
>
> A warning is an error found by the compiler that does not merit immediate attention to run the Java program.

The last parameter is the -classpath parameter. In the compiler, this option specifies the path in which the compiler should point to reference classes in Java. The following shows a breakdown and summary of all the available compiler options in Java:

-classpath <path>	Specifies the location of class files to the compiler.
-d <directory>	Specifies the destination directory for the compiled class file.
-g	Enables the creation of debugging tables.
-nowarn	Disables warnings.
-O	Optimizes the code by in-lining static, final, and private methods.
-verbose	Displays information about the source files being compiled, the class files being loaded, and the length of time each step took.

The java.exe

The java.exe is the interpreter for compiled Java programs. The interpreter will work only with compiled class files, not the source files. Do not specify the .class extension for the class file that you want to interpret. The Java interpreter works by converting the bytecodes of the specified class file to processor-specific machine code so the client's system can execute it. An example of using the interpreter on the fictitiously created class ABClass.class follows:

```
java ABClass
```

The interpreter essentially looks for two things: the file passed containing compiled bytecodes and the location of the method main from which it can execute the body of the Java program. As in the javac.exe compiler, the interpreter also has the same functionality with the -classpath option. Also note the -debug option in the Java interpreter. This option enables the Java debugger to attach itself to this session, which is very useful in debugging programs.

Java Development Environments

CHAPTER 6

137

6

JAVA
DEVELOPMENT
ENVIRONMENTS

Another useful option is the -cs option, which actually causes the interpreter to compare the loaded class file to the loaded source file. If the source file has a more recent date, then the -cs option will recompile that file. This option can be very useful in making sure that the compiled files you are interpreting are the most up-to-date classes.

Next, note the -noasyncgc option, which toggles off the asynchronous garbage collection for this session. When this tool is activated, Java will not run a separate thread for garbage collection. In fact, Java will not run garbage collection at all unless it runs out of memory completely or the program explicitly calls to activate it. Along the same lines of garbage collection is the option -verbosegc. This parameter is very similar to the -verbose parameter mentioned with the javac.exe compiler except that it is designed to display information about the garbage collector whenever it has free memory. The following gives you a quick reference for the garbage-collection-related options with the Java interpreter:

-noasyncgc   Turns off the asynchronous garbage collection.

-verbosegc   Prints information pertaining to memory freed by the garbage collector.

NOTE

For more information on the garbage collector, see Chapter 5, "Java and the Internet."

Other parameters that are available are -verify, -noverify, and -verifyremote. These parameters all are made possible because Java utilizes bytecodes. The -verify and -noverify toggle on or off the verification of all Java code. The -verifyremote parameter, which is the default if nothing is explicitly specified, verifies only code that is loaded into the system via a special class loader. Use the following list as a quick reference to this set of parameters:

-noverify   Disables all bytecode verification.

-verifyremote   Enables bytecode verification for classes loaded into the system by a separate class loader.

-verify   Enables all bytecode verification.

Another parameter available to the Java interpreter, -version, specifies the version and build for the compiled class passed to it. This parameter is very useful in determining the version of Java in which your class file was compiled. For example, currently you are using the JDK 1.0.1 to compile your classes. The following code is an example of what to type to find the version for the class ABClass.class. The second line is an example of the output from the interpreter.

```
java -version ABClass.class
java version "1.0.1"
```

The next set of options you will learn briefly are the parameters to specify the stack and heap size for a Java session.

NOTE

A stack and heap are special regions of reserved memory in which programs can store data (usually local variables). In general, the program, operating system, and microprocessor all can have one or more stacks assigned to them. In the case of Java applications, two stacks are maintained for each thread it is running: one for the C code (referring to any native code from native methods that are used in your application) and another for the Java code.

NOTE

The data structure for a stack is organized as a LIFO (last in first out) list format. Therefore, the last data item added to the stack will be the first item used.

The following list shows the parameters pertaining to specifying the stack and for what they are used:

`-mx <number>`	Specifies the maximum size for the Java heap. The default is 16MB.
`-ms <number>`	Specifies the start-up size for the Java heap. The default is 1MB.
`-ss <number>`	Specifies the maximum C stack size for this thread that is used for any native code your Java application might contain.
`-oss <number>`	Specifies the maximum Java stack size for this thread.

NOTE

You must specify a number after each parameter when you pass values to the various stack options. The interpreter will assume that the specified number is in bytes. However, if you want to specify a larger value (that is, a value in kilobytes or megabytes), then append the letter k for kilobyte or m for megabyte to the numerical value (for example, 512k or 10m).

At this point, you have learned all of the pertinent options and syntax for the Java interpreter. Still, you can use a few more parameters with `java_g.exe` that do not come with `java.exe`. These special parameters deal specifically with debugging your Java programs. The first two are `-t` and `-tm`, which deal with printing a trace on the screen. The `-t` parameter, for example, prints out an instruction trace while `-tm` prints out a method trace. Also, `-prof` prints out profiling data about the specified session to the file `java.prof`. The last list for this JDK tool, which specifies all of the options only available to the `java_g.exe` file, follows:

-t   Enables instruction tracing.

-tm   Enables method tracing.

-prof   Prints the profiling data to a file called `java.prof`.

> **NOTE**
>
> All options introduced in `java.exe` are also available to the debugging version, `java_g.exe`.

The Java Debugger

The `jdb.exe` file is the JDK's debugging tool, which is attached to an interpreted session. This debugger is designed to attach itself to an interpreted session and execute commands. A full description of this tool is beyond the scope of this book, but it is important to note that you can use `jdb.exe` to help debug your program. Note, however, that working with `jdb.exe` has many rewards, because it can enable you to go through your program and execute one line of code at a time, enabling you to set break points to help you see exactly what your code is doing at any time. An example of how to use the default syntax for the debugger follows:

```
jdb ABClass
```

One major weakness in the JDK is that it does not have a visual debugger. Instead, it uses the command-line debugger `jbe.exe`.

javah.exe

Before we can discuss `javah.exe` and its function in the JDK, how to effectively use the `javah.exe` tool, or move forward with the discussion on the JDK, we should digress and discuss Java's native methods.

> **NOTE**
>
> Native methods are C functions used in Java.

Native methods are an advanced programming technique. If you are new to Java or have no experience with C/C++, it is a topic you might want to avoid. Native methods are more complicated than they have to be and are not really that useful except in rare cases. If this has piqued your interest, however, then continue with the following paragraphs for a quick description of native methods and using `javah.exe` to create native methods.

Native methods give you the power to link C programs to your Java programs. Of course, if computer programming were that simple, then computer programs wouldn't have bugs. Realistically, though, when you use native methods, you lose the ability to port Java programs to multiple platforms. Second, you cannot create applets with native methods because of the security risks involved. Internet browsers do not support native methods, which means that you cannot use native method technology for any kind of Internet-related solution. Third, your Java application (not applet) cannot verify the native code because the native code cannot be compiled to bytecodes.

In those few cases in which using native methods is the only solution, you will need to declare a method, place the keyword `native` in front of the declaration, and end the method with a semicolon instead of a pair of brackets.

```
public native void myMethod();
```

That's all you need to do on the Java side. On the C side, however, you must create your function to implement the method `myMethod`. This is where `javah.exe` comes in because you might need to generate C headers from your Java-compiled classes so you can work with these classes in the native environment.

```
javah ABClass
```

The last directory shown in Figure 6.1 that you have yet to learn in the JDK is the `..\java\include` subdirectory, which includes header files to help you implement your native methods. Writing native methods is not for rookies to Java. Furthermore, the programmer must have a deep understanding of C/C++ as well as Java. Frankly, native methods are so rarely used that they will not be mentioned again.

javap.exe

The `javap.exe` is a class disassembler; that is, it will take a compiled file and disassemble its bytecodes back into source code (ASCII form). The following list shows the options for this executable. Most options in the list have been discussed with the other command-line tools and a few new options are fairly self explanatory. One major problem with the Java disassembler is that in reality, it is difficult to pull source code from a compiled class file. Consequently, we won't spend much time discussing it.

`-c`	Disassembles the code (that is, prints out the public method and fields for this program).
`-classpath <path>`	Specifies the directory for `javap.exe` to look up classes.
`-p`	Prints out the private and protected methods and fields of this class.
`-verify`	Verifies the bytecodes.
`-version`	Displays the build version of this class.

Java Development Environments

CHAPTER 6

141

6

JAVA
DEVELOPMENT
ENVIRONMENTS

javadoc.exe

With `javadoc.exe`, a very useful documentary tool in the JDK, you can create HTML pages based on the proprietary classes from your source code. The `javadoc.exe` tool parses the source files of your classes. This parsing process can include specially designed comments placed in your code. You can include HTML tags in these comments and parse them to the resulting HTML page. It is very useful in creating HTML pages because it will help you and other programmers understand your code. The following is an example of parsing the source file for the fictitious class `ABClass`:

```
javadoc ABClass.java
```

If this line were executed, it would create a file called `ABClass.html`, an HTML file that you can view as a reference source in any browser. However, the following example exemplifies another powerful feature of `javadoc.exe`, in which you can pass HTML tags and comments to the HTML pages you create by writing specially designed comments in your code:

```
/**
*Below is a class I created:
* <PRE>
*      javadoc ABClass.java
* </PRE>
*
* @author John Doe
* @version 1.0
*/
```

In this example, the beginning and end of the comment is specifically designed to create a special HTML document that will comment on the method coming after it. For example, `javadoc.exe` uses the first line, `/**`, to generate the HTML page. Also, the `javadoc.exe` parser will recognize three parameters within this comment. The first is `@param`, a special setting used to place a comment just before the method in the HTML page explaining what it does; the `@return` description, which results in specifying a return for this method; and the `@exception`, which lists the available exceptions that this method can throw.

The end result is that with this new tool you will be able to generate well-documented classes on your source code. However, of all the development environments that you will learn in this chapter, the command line `javadoc.exe` is one of the most difficult to work with.

The Appletviewer

The last tool you will learn is the appletviewer. The appletviewer is used extensively in Chapter 8. Its primary function is to look for and utilize only the `<APPLET>` tag in the HTML page that is passed to it. This tool enables you to view your applets from its HTML page. The appletviewer generally has proven itself to be such a functional tool that it is incorporated into some of the other integrated development environments, such as Symantec Café.

For more information and examples on using the appletviewer, see Chapter 8.

Interestingly, when you first use the appletviewer with the JDK, it will create a directory called .hotjava, and in that directory is a file called properties (see Figure 6.4).

FIGURE 6.4.

Java Developer's Kit directory with the .hotjava *directory added by the appletviewer.*

In the .hotjava directory, you will see the file properties, where you can view and edit the properties for the appletviewer.

Currently, all Java-compliant browsers do not enable you to access the client's computer to read or write files. However, the HotJava browser and the appletviewer have an optional parameter that gives the client the capability to specify access to its system. Along these lines, you can give the HotJava browser or appletviewer access by specifying a directory for the file to have read or write access to the Java applet. You can implement this by adding the following to the properties file:

```
acl.read=/java/bin
acl.write=/home/applet/file.fle
```

Java Development Kit Closing Comments

The JDK is not the friendliest environment in which to work, but it certainly is one of the most widely used and is probably the most stable environment in which to develop. Working with the JDK is also a very cost-effective solution because it currently is available for free from Sun. If you want to learn or instruct pure Java syntax, then the JDK will be your best choice. We will reference the JDK throughout the rest of this chapter and also will use it in the following two chapters for real-life demonstrations.

Symantec Café

Symantec Café is an IDDE (integrated development and debugging environment). Café is Symantec's tool that was designed to be the next step from Symantec's previous Java development environment, Espresso.

> **NOTE**
>
> Espresso is Symantec's wrapper utility for Symantec C++ and was designed to give owners of Symantec C++ the ability to develop Java programs in Symantec C++. It is being replaced by Symantec Café, which is a stand-alone Java Integrated Development Environment.

By the end of this section, you should be able to appreciate the Symantec Café as a very powerful tool to work with in Java. With Café, you can create Java applets and embed them into Web pages. You also can link Café with your existing Web browser (if you have one installed) to view these pages or use the built-in appletviewer to view them as well. Also, Café contains the full object-oriented Java functionality to create stand-alone Java programs. Unlike the Java Workshop, about which you learn a little later, Symantec Café has provided substantial enhancements to the original JDK. However, Symantec has grounded every change it has made to focus on the JDK. Symantec has not made any changes to the built-in class libraries that also come with the JDK.

With Café, you can easily customize just about everything. Probably the most powerful feature is Symantec's version of the Java compiler, a native compiler designed to be much faster than the `javac.exe` compiler that comes with the JDK. Symantec also utilizes its own DLL for interpreting Java programs, resulting in a much faster running time.

Symantec also sports a very powerful visual debugging tool. Café is the only Java IDE currently available that has a special parser that will parse your files and create a GUI-based debugging and viewing window. With this window, you can view your classes and debug your code with your mouse.

> **NOTE**
>
> Symantec offers a tool called Visual Debugger, which is a GUI-based debugging environment that contains parsed class files from your project. Not only can you point and click your way to debugging code, you also have the ability to control and debug each and every thread in your Java program individually because the Visual Debugger was designed for Java's multithreadedness.

In the visual design environment, Symantec Café has a Visual-Basic-like design environment with a drag-and-drop toolbox to design front ends in Java. Symantec Café writes the actual code for everything on the back end.

> **NOTE**
>
> Try using both mouse buttons on anything and everything in Symantec Café to gain access to tools available to help you.

Installing Symantec Café

Installing Symantec Café is very easy because it comes in a CD and contains the standard install wizard to help you through every step of the process. During the installation process, you can choose to install various groups of tools on your hard disk. If you choose everything, Symantec Café should require about 25 to 60MB, depending on the cluster size of your hard disk.

As mentioned at the beginning of the chapter, Symantec Café currently is available only for the 32-bit Windows environment. However, Symantec also is working on another version of Café for the Macintosh environment.

> **NOTE**
>
> Symantec is working on Caffeine, a Macintosh version of its Café.

Café Desktop

The Symantec Café gives you a highly visible work environment and enables you to create customized views of your workspace that will be saved when you exit the program and automatically reloaded when you return. The Symantec Café also enables you to create customized views for your workspace that you can reference by name. You can customize different layouts with the tabbed workspaces and create your own tabs and add them to the workspace tab. You have the ability to redesign completely your view of Symantec Café.

Café Views Palette

You could probably consider the views palette to be the control center for the Symantec Café. It is located to the right of the Workspace tabs. You can activate the array of buttons by double-clicking them or use them as a drag-and-drop icon bar to edit and debug your Java programs. For example, drag the source icon from the views palette around the center of the screen, let go, and you will see a new source file created exactly where you dropped the icon with your mouse (see Figure 6.5).

FIGURE 6.5.

The views toolbar.

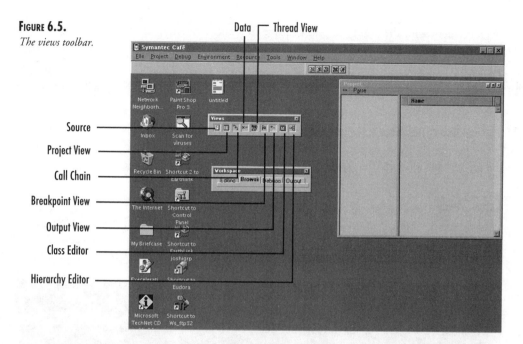

Data — Thread View

Source

Project View

Call Chain

Breakpoint View

Output View

Class Editor

Hierarchy Editor

NOTE

If you cannot find the `calendar.prj` file or the `..\samples` directory, you probably did not direct the Symantec Café to install the demos during the installation process.

The Symantec Café comes with 41 sample projects and about 85 total examples. As a demonstration of Café, you will work with one demo called `CALENDAR.PRJ`. Open `CALENDAR.PRJ` by opening the Project command on Café's main menu bar. From there, go to `..\java\café\samples\java\calendar`, which should display the project file `calendar.prj`.

NOTE

Like the Java Workshop, Symantec Café organizes its Java programs into projects controlled by files with the `.prj` extension (for example, `calendar.prj`). Unlike the Java Workshop, Symantec Café does not support the use of portfolios.

Symantec Café Express Agents

Symantec Café comes with two express agents. *Express agents* are wizard-like tools used specifically in Café. With the first express agent, called the Project Express, you can quickly create a new project using the point-and-click format. This way you can navigate your way through several screens with the ability to select source files and create new source files to begin your project.

The other express agent is the AppExpress agent, which helps you generate a new Java applet, program, or console. It will even get you started by generating some basic code based on your input.

You can access the Project Express by clicking the Project menu on Café's main menu bar and clicking New to invoke automatically the Project Express. The AppExpress can be found in the menu bar tools with the AppExpress button.

Café Studio

Possibly the most powerful tool in the Symantec Café is the Café Studio. With this very powerful visual resource editor, you can interactively create and edit menus and visual components using simple drag-and-drop techniques.

> **NOTE**
>
> For more information including a formal discussion on Java User Interface controls, see Chapter 8.

> **NOTE**
>
> With the Visual Resource Editor in the Café Studio, you can design your front end visually. The Café Studio provides methods to handle events in the front end while automatically generating the necessary source code to be placed in your project.

You can access the Café Studio by clicking Resource and New on Café's main menu bar. Symantec Café actually creates a resource file, which will be discussed later, with our sample Java program calendar.prj, which you opened earlier. In the Project View, double-click the file calendar.rc in the list and a dialog box will open, asking you if you want to open the Café Studio. Click Yes and when the Café studio loads, highlight the item Form on the right side of the new window. An item Calendar "init" on the list box below the one in which you currently are working should be displayed. Right-click that item and choose the option Edit resource. Figure 6.6 shows what you should see on the screen.

FIGURE 6.6.

Café Studio with the sample `calendar.rc` *file open.*

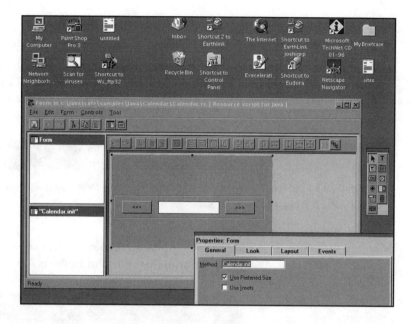

Looking at the main window in Figure 6.6, you see that you can design the form completely from the ground up. Also, looking at the properties tab window for this form, you can manipulate the general preferences for the form as well as the font types, sizes, and attributes for the objects used in this form. You can work with the layout as well as write code to handle events.

Resource Files in Symantec Café

When you save a form design using the Café Studio, it generates a proprietary resource file with the extension `.rc` (for example, `calendar.rc`). This file maintains all of the components, layout, and other pertinent information that the Café Studio used, but it is used only in Symantec Café as an intermediary to generate the Java source code for the actual designs in the Café Studio for the source files. In the end, your program will be entirely Java-based code.

NOTE

Also note that one reason that the Café Studio does not directly save information about the form designs in a Java source file is because (as you will learn in Chapter 8) in Java, you do not typically have the capability to specify exactly where all the Java controls and components are to be placed. Instead, Java uses a layout manager that follows a given format in which each object is placed relatively to each other. This is very useful in Java because the Java program can be ported to so many environments. However, this portability is not needed or wanted in the design stage of the form, which is why Symantec Café utilizes this resource file to enable you to specify more exact information of where you want to place objects.

Programmer's Editor

From just about anywhere, you can parse the Java source files and read all of the source methods imported by the project. Within the project settings, you can specify the target program type and any compile and debugging options. From the file in the project list, you can double-click a file to the open source editor with that file, and you can right-click a file to compile just the selected file.

> **NOTE**
>
> Symantec Café gives you the option of using either its native compiler, which is much faster, or the compiler bundled with the JDK.

Now look at some code in the calendar project file. Go to the Project View and double-click the file calendar.java. A window similar to that shown in Figure 6.7 should come up.

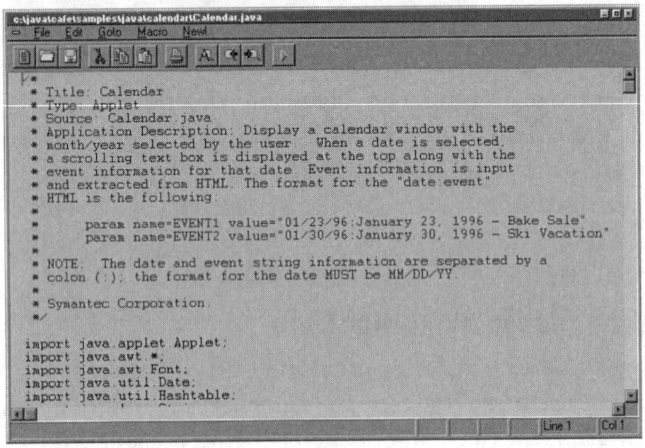

FIGURE 6.7.

Programmer's Editor example using the calendar.java *file.*

You can see that Symantec Café uses special colors to highlight various parts of the code. For example, all of the code in dark red signifies a comment and all of the code in blue is reserved for Java keywords. Café goes beyond just displaying various colors, however; Café also has linked visual tools to this code.

Symantec Café Parser

With the Symantec Café, you can have an object-oriented view of your code, especially through the use of its parsing technology and its visual class editors. Café utilizes a parser that is unrelated to the compiler. It runs on a separate thread in the background and automatically parses the changes that you make to your Java source code. This parsed code then is used by two tools in Café: the Class Editor and the Hierarchy Editor.

Class Editor

The Class Editor is a three-pane class browser that gives you a visual list of all of the classes in your program and a list of all the method and data members contained within each class. This tool is designed to focus on the abstract parts of your code, which means that it looks at your class methods and variables without displaying the actual implementation code in your Java program. As you burrow down into your classes, however, you can get to the source code to make changes in your code.

Once again, go to the Views palette and double-click the Class Editor icon. You will see three panes of information. The pane of the top left represents all of the classes in the sample project `calendar`. The top right pane shows all of the methods and variables for the selected class. The bottom pane is where the specified method's source code is displayed. You can open the source code for a given method in two ways: by right-clicking the method or variable then clicking the command Go to source or highlighting the method and double-clicking it. Open the default package as in the example in Figure 6.7 and double-click the method `Action`. The source code will open in the third pane and should look something like Figure 6.8.

FIGURE 6.8.

Class Editor example with the `calendar.prj`.

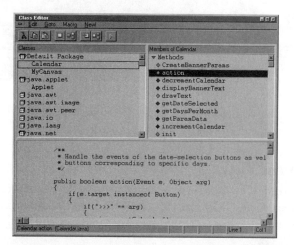

> **NOTE**
>
> Referencing Figure 6.8, the diamond colors next to each element indicate its access relationship. Green means public, yellow means protected, and red indicates that the access privilege to this element is private.

The Hierarchy Editor

The Hierarchy Editor is similar to the Class Editor except that the Hierarchy Editor is an architectural way to view your Java programs and any other classes that belong to the program.

You can directly manipulate your program's inherit structure by dragging and dropping. Also, the Hierarchy Editor enables you to double-click a particular class to activate the Class Editor with that particular object opened.

Looking at the example with the project calendar, double-click the Views Palette icon that shows the Hierarchy Editor.

FIGURE 6.9.

The Hierarchy Editor in the calendar.prj.

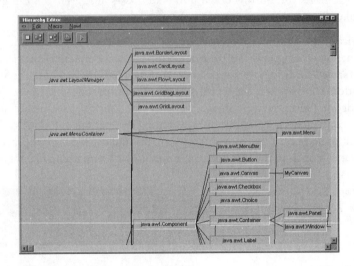

The following sections briefly discuss several tools related to the Programmer's editor in Café that help in the design and debugging process.

The Thread View

The Thread View is a very powerful feature that Symantec included in light of Java's multithreadedness. With the Thread View program, you can suspend and activate threads in a Java program.

The Call Chain

The Call Chain displays all code modules and methods executed by an individual thread and displays the current execution point as well as the return points for each called method. With the Call Chain, you can follow the execution rhythm of your program.

The Watch View

The Watch View inspects the data in variables and objects. With Watch View, you can examine the values of class members and variables. Simply drag a module from the Call Chain into the watch windows and all variables accessible to that module are displayed in the window.

Java Development Environments

CHAPTER 6

151

6

JAVA
DEVELOPMENT
ENVIRONMENTS

During the installation process, you will see that Symantec Café comes with a tutorial that demonstrates the very basics of Java as well as how to use the tools that come with the Symantec Café.

Symantec Café and the Appletviewer

Symantec Café, unlike Java Workshop, does not come with a built-in HTML viewer and does not have the Java Workshop's Web-centric focus. Instead, it is more geared toward the Symantec C++ design style for Java. The Symantec Café does come with the JDK's appletviewer built into it. It is invoked automatically when you click the command Execute Program in the Project menu bar. Let's compile the `calendar` project. Go to the Project menu and click the Build All button. Notice that the bottom window called Output will appear on the screen. The Output window displays the output of a text-mode program being compiled, parsed, or debugged. If errors are encountered during parsing, messages are displayed in the Output window. You can double-click the error message to open the source file and point to the trouble spot. At this point, build the `calendar` project (see Figure 6.10) and you should receive no errors.

FIGURE 6.10.

*The Output window
for compiling*
`calendar.prj`.

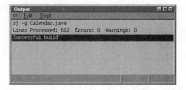

Finally, click the Project menu again and then click Execute Program to minimize Symantec Café and invoke the appletviewer with the Calendar applet loaded. When you exit the appletviewer, it will automatically restore the Symantec Café development environment (see Figure 6.11).

FIGURE 6.11.

Appletviewer of
`calendar.prj`.

Symantec Café Closing Comments

The Symantec Café is a powerful integrated development environment, no doubt aimed at serious Java development and large-scale projects. It should receive an award for bringing Java to the next level of development because it can write code for you, pinpoint Java errors with its point-and-click debugger (in half the time as the command-line debugger in the JDK), and manage large-scale development projects with its project manager. Finally, its blazingly fast compiler makes the Symantec Café definitely worth a second look.

The Borland Internet Products

Borland currently is developing several Java-related products. The first product that has been released is Borland C++ 5.0. The other project will be a unique step in a new direction for the integrated development environment. This new environment, called Borland Latte, will be Borland's Delphi look-alike for Java.

> **NOTE**
>
> Delphi is a rapid program development (RAD) environment developed by Borland. Its syntax is designed for writing programs with fewer bugs, easy to understand code, and less time spent in development. What is the price for this euphoric development language? Efficiency. In general, a RAD environment will generate less-efficient programs because it is a higher-level language. However, this efficiency versus understanding statement is valid only in environments that were designed to provide companies with quick solutions to the modern client/server topology. Because Java is such a new programming language, it will be interesting to see whether Borland Latte will follow that same paradigm or be able to develop efficient Java code.

Borland Latte

Latte will focus more on the RAD environment than all other integrated development environments discussed in this chapter. Borland Latte probably will be available by the time you read this. At this point, one feature intended for the Borland Latte is a graphical debugger. Also, as with all the other integrated development environments, Latte will have a just-in-time (JIT) compiler. Other tools, such as a form builder to point and click your way through the front-end design stage (as in Café Studio), also are planned.

Borland C++ 5.0

Borland has released several other products that also deal with Internet (more precisely, Java) development. Borland has bundled these new tools with its new version of Borland C++ (5.0). One major quality behind Borland C++ 5.0 is that it goes beyond an integrated Java development environment and seamlessly integrates developing in C++ and Java so that one project can contain both types of code. Because Java and C++ are closely related languages, it is logical to design one comprehensive set of Java-based tools.

Java Development Environments

CHAPTER 6

153

6

JAVA
DEVELOPMENT
ENVIRONMENTS

Two editions of Borland C++ 5.0 currently are available: the Borland C++ Development Suite and Borland C++ 5.0. The primary difference between the two editions (as related to Java) is that the AppExcelerator (Borland JIT compiler) is bundled only with the Development Suite edition. In the next few sections, you learn some of the other Java-related features that come with both editions of Borland C++ 5.0.

AppExpert for Java

The AppExpert for Java tool is designed to start a new Java program quickly. Just about everything in this wizard-based tool can be done with a few mouse clicks to create a custom program that will start you running. In essence, AppExpert for Java could be considered a Java code generator.

The Targetexpert Tool

The targetexpert tool lets you create Java projects with the click of a button. Because Borland has seamlessly integrated the two programming languages into one environment, this wizard-based tool will ensure that your environment is properly configured to create Java programs as well as C++.

The Borland Debugger

The key tool that Borland has designed for Java developers is the graphical debugger. This debugger is available in both editions of Borland C++ 5.0. A pre-release of the Borland Debugger, which can be downloaded and installed on top of the JDK, is also available. If you are interested in looking at the free pre-release Borland Debugger, go to the following site for more information:

```
http://www.Borland.com
```

> **NOTE**
>
> The Borland Debugger for Java is currently the only graphical Java debugger developed in Java. Therefore, it is the only graphical debugger available outside of the Windows environment.

Installing the Beta Borland Debugger

After you have downloaded the Borland Debugger, make sure that you have installed the JDK. Run the self-extracting executable in the ..\java directory in the JDK. The debugger might ask you if you want to overwrite some files; overwrite everything.

Preview of the Borland Debugger

In the Borland Debugger, you will work in one of several panes. The first pane on the left, the Call Stack pane (see (1) in Figure 6.12), shows function calls made to this point. It is interactive in that you can view details on various items by clicking them.

The second pane on the right (2) is the Source pane. This pane shows the code of that class. Use your mouse to click break points in various lines of code.

The third pane (3) is the Variable (also known as the Context) pane, which shows you all of the arguments and local variables for this function. The Context pane is in a file-manager-type design where you can expand and collapse objects and subobjects to toggle between to view the information.

The fourth pane (4), in the lower-left corner, is the Watch Point pane. Use this pane to track a variable for its entire life by dragging and dropping it into the Watch Point pane.

The fifth pane (5) is the Console pane, which gives you high-level information about what is happening during the debugging process.

FIGURE 6.12.

The Borland Debugger with numbered panes.

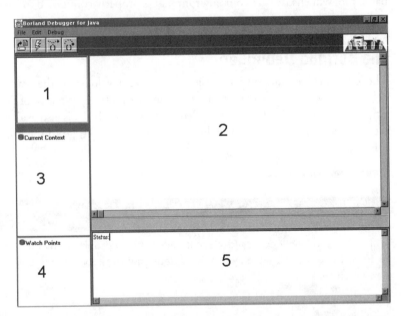

> **NOTE**
>
> The Borland Debugger has a feature called Hot Break that lets you specify break points while the program is running. Hot Break gives the programmer maximum flexibility.

is the only available Visual Debugger for Java that was written exclusively in Java, and Borland also has the only seamlessly integrated development environment for Java programming language with C++. Latte probably will be the biggest ground-breaking event in the Java-integrated development environment community coming from Borland. Latte will provide a Delphi-like development environment geared toward Java.

The last integrated development environment about which you'll learn is the Java Workshop. It, too, is completely unique with its Web-centric development environment.

The Java Workshop

The Java Workshop is Sun's addition to the Java visual development arena. It is uniquely designed as a development environment because it focuses on an Internet browser format. The Java Workshop enables you to create new applets and programs as well as author HTML pages. Hence, the Java Workshop gives you the capability to create Java-powered HTML pages all in one place. The Java Workshop also enables you to test the applets and programs in HTML pages that can be loaded in the program. One interesting feature coming to the Java Workshop is the capability to design custom HTML pages. At this point, however, that function is not supported. By the time you read this, though, the Java Workshop definitely should be officially released. At the time of this writing, the Java Workshop is in its advanced beta stage. The Java Workshop is geared specifically toward Internet/intranet development solutions. And yes, the Java Workshop was written in Java, so the Java Workshop should be available for any Java-supported environment.

Because the Java Workshop is a Web-centric development tool with added features, such as Web page authoring and applet publishing, which will be packaged with the released version, you will be able to focus the Java Workshop in an Internet/intranet solution during the development and testing process. Installing the Java Workshop should be fairly painless because it uses the InstallShield to guide you through the entire process.

> **NOTE**
>
> The InstallShield is also used with Symantec Café.

Note that the Java Workshop is a completely self-contained development environment, which means that you do not need to install the Java Workshop on top of the JDK. In fact, if you look closely you will see that the Java Workshop is actually more of a wrapper or shell around the original JDK, about which you learned earlier. If you look at the directory structure for the Java Workshop, you will see the subdirectory ..\JDK, and in there you will see the executables (for example, javac.exe) that you learned in the JDK.

Introduction to the Java Workshop

The first object to note in Figure 6.13 is the lighthouse on the right side of the window. Whenever the Java Workshop is busy (including loading HTML pages and compiling Java programs), the lighthouse will be animated just like a browser. Also, look at the icons in the panel at the bottom of the screen. Those icons represent the browser-based commands for the Java Workshop. The icons from left to right are Back, Forward, Home, Reload, and Stop. The text field at the top of the window enables you to specify a hypertext address to load an HTML page in the Java Workshop. In this sense, it is exactly like an Internet browser. However, you can tell that it is also a professional development environment by looking at the toolbar at the top of the page. In this toolbar, you can see that in this release no title represents what each of those icons means. If you glide your mouse over the icon and look at the bottom of the window however, you will see a brief explanation of what the icon represents.

FIGURE 6.13.

The Java Workshop advanced beta release main page.

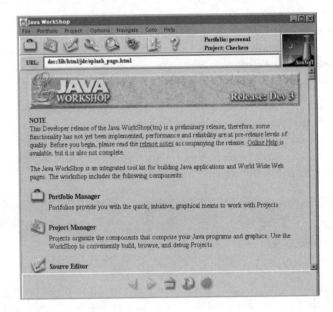

The Portfolio Manager

The first icon on the top left of the screen is a picture of a suitcase that represents the Portfolio Manager. The Java Workshop sorts its Java programs and projects into portfolios. A *portfolio* is a text file that has a .psf extension. In this text file is a list of references to a specific set of projects. Each project file has the extension .prj and contains high-level information about each project, including a list of source code files and preference information. This file is also in a text-based format. The actual source code files for each project are at the bottom of the pyramid. For a visual organizational chart of the Java Workshop, see Figure 6.14.

FIGURE 6.14.

Organizational chart for Java portfolios and projects.

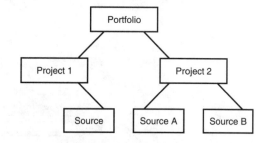

NOTE

The Java Workshop is currently the only Java-integrated development environment of all the environments you learned in this chapter that supports the use of portfolios.

Click the briefcase to open the Project Manager. Three new icons appear under the text field. From left to right are Create a New Project, Import an Existing Project, and Remove the Selected Project. In the Java Workshop, whenever you open up a manager (for example, the Portfolio Manager), a set of implementation-based icons related specifically to that manager will be displayed on a subpanel at the top. As an example of how to use the Java Workshop, you will create, test, and run a very simple Java applet. Create a new project called ButtonA by clicking the Create a New Project icon. A tab window will open, giving you several choices to create a new project. In this example, save the project in a special directory called c:\button and create a new applet called ButtonA. In this example, put it on the local drive c:\. When you are finished, it should look something like Figure 6.15. Then click Apply.

You now should have a ButtonA project icon somewhere on the screen. To begin working on the project, simply click its icon. Then click the puzzle icon next to the suitcase on the main panel at the top of the screen to open the Project Manager.

The Edit Project

Moving forward with this example, the next major icon on the top of the screen that you can double-click to open is the Edit Project (also called the Project Manager). In the Project Manager, because you are not really implementing anything, there are no secondary icons to discuss. It is through the Project Manager (see Figure 6.16) that you will be able to set various preferences for each project. In fact, think of the Project Manager as a project preference manager.

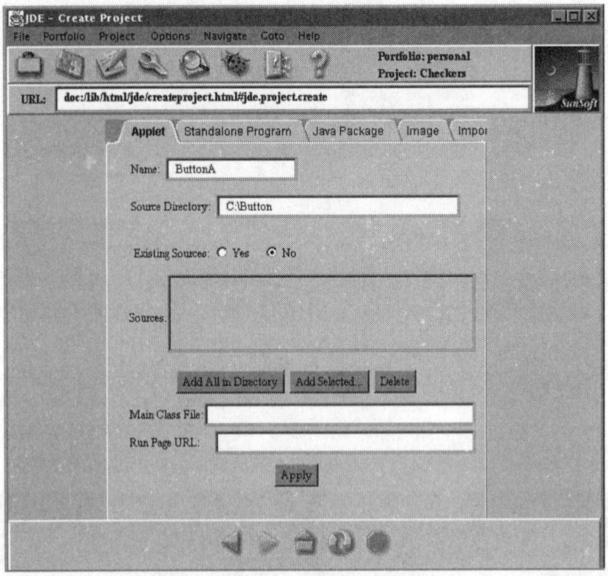

Figure 6.15.
Creating a project in the Java Workshop.

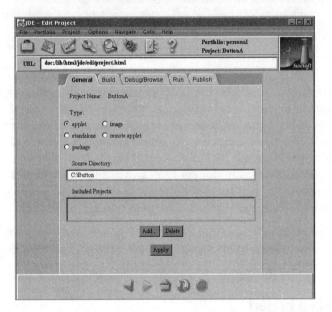

Figure 6.16.
The Project Manager.

For the ButtonA project, set the preference for this project to be an applet and place it in the directory called c:\button.

The Source Editor

The next icon, which shows a pencil writing on a notebook, is the Source Editor. Click this icon to open another window to work with your code.

6

NOTE

You can start a manager more than one way. More precisely, as you will see later in this demonstration, you can activate the Source Editor from the Build Manager and the Debug Manager as well as from the pencil and paper icon bar at the top of the main window.

The next step is to actually write the code for ButtonA (enter the code in Listing 6.1). Figure 6.17 shows the Source Editor with the code for ButtonA filled out.

FIGURE 6.17.

Java Workshop Source Editor containing the code for ButtonA.

Listing 6.1. The ButtonA.java code.

```java
// Button 1.java

import java.awt.Button;
import java.awt.Label;
import java.awt.Event;
public class ButtonA extends java.applet.Applet
    Button b

    public void init()
        b = new Button("WELCOME")
        add(b)
        show(


    public boolean action(Event e, Object obj)
        if (((Button)e.target).getLabel() == "WELCOME")
            b.setLabel("GOOD-BYE")
        } else if (((Button)e.target).getLabel() == "GOOD-BYE")
            b.setLabel("WELCOME")
```

continues

Listing 6.1. continued

```
    }
    return true;
  }
}
```

If you look carefully at the code in Listing 6.1, you might have noticed that no semicolon terminates the show() method. It is with this deliberate error that you will see how the Java Workshop responds to this pseudo-real-life situation. This takes you to the next manager.

The Build Manager

The next major icon, designated by a wrench, is the Build Manager.

> **NOTE**
>
> The buttons at the top of the toolbar are arranged from left to right so that as you develop, you use the icons from left to right.

When you open the Build Manager, you will see a new set of toolbar icons displayed in the subpanel on the main window. These icons from left to right are Go to the Previous Error, Go to the Next Error, Initiate a Build, Stop, and Build All Even if They Are Up To Date. For your example, specify the file ButtonA.java. Click the icon Build All Even if They Are Up To Date to recompile the file completely. Figure 6.18 shows the Build Manager compiling the ButtonA example.

FIGURE 6.18.

The Build Manager.

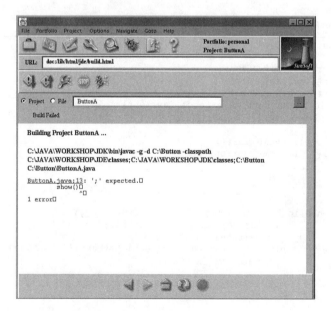

As you click the Build All Even if They Are Up To Date icon, you can see the integration of the original JDK in the Java Workshop compilation process because a DOS window opens to run the executable `javac.exe`.

The first line of text on the page actually shows the command line for the compilation of the project:

```
C:\JAVA\WORKSHOP\JDK\bin\javac -g -d C:\Button -classpath
➥C:\JAVA\WORKSHOP\JDE\classes;
➥C:\JAVA\WORKSHOP\JDK\classes;C:\Button C:\Button\ButtonA.java
```

The lines after that show the deliberate error in the typical `javac.exe` format, except that a hypertext link is here to edit the file (via the Source Editor) where the error is contained. Click that link to open the Source Editor. If you look at Figure 6.19, you will see that two new icons have appeared. These icons move between error messages. Also notice that the line of code that is offensive to the compiler is highlighted in yellow so that you can immediately see the trouble spots in your code. This is also a nice tool.

FIGURE 6.19.

Reviewing the applet in the Source Editor from the Build Manager.

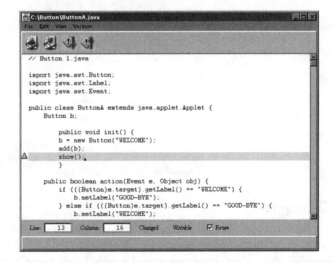

Now go ahead and put in the semicolon to terminate the end of that line, save, and close the window. You should be back in the Build Manager. Click Initiate a Build to build only the changes that were made to the original code. At this point you should see `Build Successful` printed at the bottom the subtoolbar. Your next step in using the Java Workshop in this demonstration is to take a quick look at the Source Browser.

Source Browser

In JDK language, the Source Browser translates to the graphical version for the `javadoc.exe` tool that was discussed in the JDK. If you remember, `javadoc.exe` is not very easy to use. The Source Browser has definitely improved on it, however. Here you will be able to see the big picture of the code structure because it shows all the imported as well as inherited classes and the methods used in this class. If you click specific objects, the Source Editor will open and highlight the declaration of the method on which you clicked. The Source Editor also uses a second tab to search the file to get information. This is one of the Java Workshop's strongest points because it is done automatically, giving you the programmer and anyone else who might work on your project a topographical view of what is going on. Figure 6.20 shows how the class ButtonA looks in the Source Browser Tutorial.

FIGURE 6.20.

ButtonA *in the Source Browser.*

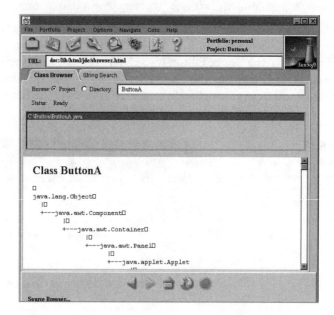

The Debugger

Debugging can be a long and tedious process. Our applet is so basic that there really is not much to debug, but you will learn some features that the Java Workshop uses. You can manipulate threads, evaluate expressions, and specify break points in your code. The Debugger provides several windows in which you can view messages as well as other objects. Debugging is an integral part of the development process, and the Java Workshop seems to have just about everything that you need for a basic visual debugging environment.

Applet Tester

The next icon, Run Applet or Stand-Alone Program, is a way of testing your applet. Your applet is quite basic; all it will display is a button labeled Welcome that will change to Good-Bye if you click it. But in the process, you have had a chance to work with the Java Workshop. If you did everything correctly, your screen should be similar to Figure 6.21.

FIGURE 6.21.

ButtonA *in the Applet Tester.*

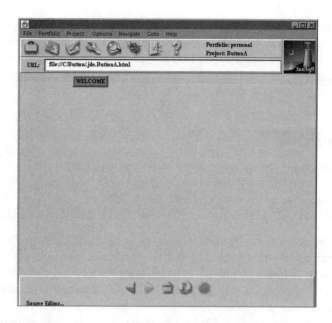

Online Help

The final icon (with the question mark) is the Help button for online help. Note that the first advanced beta version evaluated did not have a completed help file. On the surface it looked fairly good, with a table of contents as well as a help topic for every section that we covered.

> **NOTE**
>
> In any integrated development environment, note that a good help file is very important. A good help file should have complete documentation on the built-in classes, coverage of all the major errors when compiling code, a tutorial focused on introducing the user to Java as well as the integrated development environment, and information on how to use the product.

An option that was not included in this pre-release of the Java Workshop is a just-in-time (JIT) compiler. With this relatively new technology, also known as dynamic translation, you can compile very fast executables. It is an important feature that will be a very hot (no pun intended) topic for Java.

Java Workshop Closing Comments

The Java Workshop is one of the most unique development environments in which to work, especially with its Web-centric design that seems to play a major role in the environment. It is also very logically lined out—its icon bar logically reads from left to right, following each step you need to understand the environment. The premise of the Java Workshop is that it is designed to be easy to use and to help focus Java as a development solution for the Internet. This is probably going to be a good integrated development language for users new to Java who want to design Java-powered HTML pages.

Summary

In this chapter, you learned several new products, most of which are already being redesigned in their next version. There are many improvements and new tools coming out for Java almost every month. By the time you read this, Microsoft should have released its Java environment Visual J++ and Symantec should have released Visual Café (a RAD environment for Java).

At this point, the integrated development environments you have learned have their own strengths and weaknesses. The end result is that these tools all will have a place in this new industry. For example, the JDK is definitely the most cost-effective way to develop Java programs. Although the Java Workshop will no doubt focus Java solutions toward the Internet/ intranet needs, the advanced Java users will definitely benefit from Symantec Café's power tools. Users who want a more RAD-based ease of use with Java will focus on Borland Latte. For hardcore C/C++ programmers, Borland C++ 5.0 will definitely offer its users better coding integration between Java and C/C++ in one environment. While Java itself is a very new language, Java Integrated Development Environments are in their infancy. Tables 6.1, 6.2, and 6.3 give you a quick reference to compare all of the products learned in this chapter.

Table 6.1. General system requirements (requirements are for the Win95/WinNT platform).

IDE	Platform(s)	MSRP	Hard Disk	RAM
JDK	Win95/NT, Solaris, MAC	FREE	6.6MB	4MB
Café	Win95/NT	$299.95	25MB-30MB	8MB
Latte	Win95/NT, Solaris	UN	UN	UN
Borland 5.0	Win95/NT	$499.95(*)	25-200	MB(**)
Workshop	Win95/NT, Solaris	$295	45MB	16MB

NA = Not Available

UN = Unknown

(*)Borland C++ 5.0 has two editions: the regular edition and the development suite. The development suite is listed at $499.95. You can also purchase the upgrade for the development suite for $349.95. The regular edition of Borland C++ 5.0 is $349.95 and $249.95 for the upgrade.

(**)The Borland Debugger also has two editions; the size depends on how much you choose to install on your local system and how much you want to remain retrievable from the CD.

Table 6.2. Visual tools.

IDE	Web-Centric	JIT	Visual Debugger	Wizards	Visual Studio
JDK	Yes	No	No	No	No
Café	No	Yes	Yes	Yes	Yes
Latte	No	Yes	Yes	Yes	Yes
Workshop	Yes	No	Yes	No	Yes
Borland 5.0	No	Yes	Yes	Yes	Yes

Table 6.3. Other pertinent comparative information.

IDE	Native Compiler	Integrated Java	Install Shield and C++ Dev Env.
JDK	No	No	No
Café	Yes	No	Yes
Latte	UN	No	UN
Workshop	No	Yes	No
Borland 5.0	No	Yes	Yes
UN = Unknown			

Hopefully, this chapter has given you a better understanding of all the available features and where the Java Integrated Development Environments are headed. The next chapter is an introduction to pure Java. It covers all of the structured parts of Java and discusses the object technologies available to the Java language.

Introduction to Java

by Dan Joshi

CHAPTER 7

A class is Java's name for an object in the object-oriented paradigm. One of the first things you should learn is how to use Java classes. This is a logical first step because everything in Java is done through the use of classes. A major stumbling block arises for new object-oriented programmers when they try to understand the control flow stuff first and then try to apply it by writing programs. The resulting programs have major problems because of Java's reliance on objects.

Later, you will examine Java's structured environment before going on to more advanced object-oriented topics, but first your foundation should start with the basics learning objects and classes. In short, a class is the formal representation for an object in Java.

Classes, Methods, Inheritance, and Method Overriding—The Discussion

This section (as with all sections that have "The Discussion" in their headings) is designed to give you a theoretical understanding of objects, object inheritance, and method overriding. The next section gives you a workshop dealing with what was presented in this section.

Your goal in this section is to build an understanding, so don't try to compile any of the examples in the first section—they will compile but won't have the functionality to help you understand the concepts being taught in this section.

Classes

The following is an example of how a class would be declared in Java:

```
class Book {

}
```

The keyword class indicates that this is a declaration for a Java class. Classes are how Java houses objects. The brackets designate a space known as a *block*. Any code that you want to relate to the class of Book is put in that block. This is the fundamental object-oriented logic that you will use to organize all your programs. Even without putting code between the brackets, the brackets are still necessary *operators*.

Now add a variable that is related to your newly created class Book:

```
class Book {
    int NumberofPages;
}
```

The preceding code shows one format in which you can declare a variable. The int in front of the word NumberofPages tells Java that the variable NumberofPages is going to an integer of the integer data type.

Variables will be formally discussed later in the chapter, but right now let's just focus on the semicolon at the end of the declaration in that statement. One common minor mistake that programmers make is not using the semicolon to terminate the above statement. Without the semicolon, Java will give you an error message. Usually Java's compiler will catch the omission and tell you that it anticipates a semicolon where it did not find one; but sometimes it can give you 10 error messages when really only one semicolon was missing. Make a note to yourself, if you are new to semicolon languages, to make sure all the semicolons are where they belong.

Methods

A *method* is object-oriented terminology for a function. A *function* is an algorithm that can take an input, manipulate it, and return an output. The major difference between methods and functions is that a method is a function that belongs to a class.

> **NOTE**
>
> C++ programmers should note that Java does not support stand-alone methods.

The only way to employ a method is to wrap it inside a class. To avoid any confusion, the following example shows just a method declaration that is not wrapped in any class:

```
void open() {

    // algorithm to handle the method.

}
```

First, notice the word `void` in front of the word `open()`. That word `void` represents the place where a *return type* is designated for this method—just as a function (that is, an algorithm) can have a return type. Basically, when declaring a method, you use that place to declare what type of data will be returned. In this case you are using `void`, which means that no information will be returned from this method.

Second, notice the parentheses after the name `open`. This is where you can place input variables for the method. The name `open()` in this form means that you need no input variables to process the method. Once again notice that, even though you do not have an input variable yet, you still must put the parentheses around the method name. That is because the parentheses around the method are *operators* just as the brackets were operators in the earlier example of a class declaration.

The following is an example of another method—it has a return type of integer and two input integer variables that are declared values as well:

```
int AddTwoNumbers(int FirstNumber, int SecondNumber)   {
    return FirstNumber + SecondNumber;
}
```

> **NOTE**
>
> To understand what an operator does, think of a doctor (who is the *operator*) operating on the patients (who are the *operands*), producing a result.

First, notice the int before the AddTwoNumbers. That means the method will return an integer value. As you can see in the block code inside the method, you have the statement return just before the calculation. The keyword return is the method's cue to return the value of the expression immediately following it.

Going back to the first method open(), you know that Java does not support methods that are not attached to a class; so let's see how you would add open() to the class of Book:

```
class Book {
    int NumberofPages;

    void open() {
        // algorithm to handle the method.
    }
}
```

Inheritance

The next step in this lesson is to create a subclass. An important thing to understand here is how to build a subclass to extend the current class Book. Recalling the explanation of subclasses and superclasses in Chapter 5, "Java and the Internet," you will create a class named paperback. Logically, you know that not all books are paperbacks, but all paperbacks (pamphlets, leaflets, and so on excluded) are books. When you have understood the logic behind that statement, you will have mastered the relationship among classes that a programmer creates when using inheritance.

The following statement is in the *object model* of the Java programming language. In it you have created a new class called paperback. This class has its own variables and methods; but in addition, it has all the functionality (the methods and variables) of the class Book, as well.

```
class paperback extends Book {

    string NameofBook;

}
```

Looking at the preceding code, notice that the extends keyword is used to perform inheritance between the subclass paperback and the superclass Book.

There is a way, however, to prevent some variables and methods from being passed on or inherited to any other classes; that is by using the keyword private before the opening statement or declaration. Later, you will see an official definition of the keyword private and related *access modifiers,* but for now, to learn its use, you will create another class called `HardCoverBook`:

```
class HardCoverBook extends Book {

    private int EndingToTheStory;
}
```

As you can see in the preceding example, the keyword `private` is located before the *type* declaration. This position is important because it ensures that the variable will be available only to this class. The following example is a declaration for a class called `ThickHardCoverBook`. It is a subclass to `HardCoverBook`:

```
class ThickHardCoverBook extends HardCoverBook {

}
```

This class will not have access to the variable `EndingToTheStory`. Access modifiers define the accessibility of the variable or method in their own class as they relate to other classes. In the preceding example, `private` is just one of several access modifiers.

The following list shows all of the access modifiers with the most restrictive at the top:

`private`	When this is placed in front of a method or variable, that method or variable will be accessible only to the class in which it was originally declared.
`protected`	When this is placed in front of a method or variable, that method or variable will be accessible to the class it was declared in and any subclasses inherited from it.
`friendly`	This is the assumed state for a method or variable—it is what you declare a variable to be when you put nothing in front of it. Any of the classes in the package have access to it.
`public`	This access modifier is the least restrictive—it makes the method or variable accessible to everything.
`final`	This access modifier means that the current method or variable cannot be extended.
`synchronized`	This is a modifier that will lock the object while it is being used. If the method or variable is already locked, the program would wait until the method or variable becomes available before having access to it. This is useful when your program deals with multiple threads.

NOTE

A package is a group of related classes.

7

INTRODUCTION TO JAVA

Method Overriding

Java supports method overriding. Method overriding is basically replacing a method in the superclass with a method from a subclass. Here is an example of method overriding in the class Book:

```
class Book {

    int NumberofPages;

    void open() {
       // algorithm to handle the method.
    }
}
```

Now recall the inherited class paperback:

```
class paperback extends Book {

    string NameofBook;

    void open() {
       // a special algorithm specific to the class paperback.
    }
}
```

The class paperback extends Book. Remember that the same declaration for the open() method resides in paperback. The open() method in Book is now completely hidden from this class and is replaced with the implementation code of the open() method in paperback.

An easy way to think of overriding methods is as a way of replacing methods. When a subclass declares a method in exactly the same manner as a method contained in one of its superclasses, the method of the superclass is replaced by the method of the subclass. Figure 7.1 gives a topological view of the relationship between class Book and class paperback.

FIGURE 7.1.

Topology of the class Book *and class* paperback.

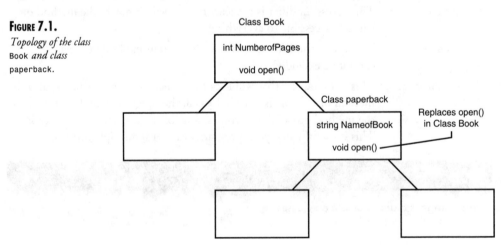

Class Book

int NumberofPages

void open()

Class paperback

string NameofBook

void open()

Replaces open() in Class Book

Just as methods and variables can have access modifiers, classes also can have modifiers. To see this, you can add an additional keyword to the class Book before the keyword class:

```
[class modifier]  class Book {

}
```

In this example, you did not add anything in front of the class Book. Does that mean that the class modifier is undefined? No. When you do not specify a modifier in front of a variable, method, or class, a default is assumed, which in this case is friendly. The following list gives class modifier keywords and a brief explanation of each one:

abstract	This means that you want this class to be a general holding tank (that is, the root of a Java class hierarchy) containing only definitions that will be implemented in a subclass down the hierarchy.
final	This means that you want this class to be the final class (for example, the root). In other words, when declaring a class final, you are specifying that the class cannot be a subclass.
public	This means that the program is accessible to any class outside of the package. However, only one public class can be put in a file, and the file must be called the same name as the class with the extension of .java.
friendly	This is the assumed class modifier for a class when nothing is declared—it is the class modifier for the class Book. This modifier will give access to any other class in the package.
synchronizable	This enables instances of a class to be made into arguments.

NOTE

You can have more than one class modifier for a particular class, as shown in this example:
```
public static void [Class Name] {
}
```

Classes, Methods, Inheritance, and Method Overriding—The Workshop

This section is a quick overview of how to compile Java programs.

To start demonstrating the material just presented, you will be using the JDK 1.0 command-line compiler to create your first Java program in a real-life scenario. If you do not have the JDK, which stands for Java Developers Kit, you can download it at the following site:

```
http://java.sun.com/download.html
```

Programs can be written in any text editor or in a proprietary development environment, although this might make it a little harder for you to follow along, because I am using the JDK 1.0. The program essentially displays the words Hello World (see Listing 7.1).

Listing 7.1. Hello World.

```
public class HelloWorld {
    public static void main( String argv[]) {
        System.out.println("Hello World");
    }
}
```

You must save the file as HelloWorld.java. Notice that the name of the file is the same as the name of the class, and that it has matching case. This is not because I am an organized programmer—it is because HelloWorld will not compile unless it is called exactly what you see in the preceding example. The reason for this is that you declared the class HelloWorld to be public. Any time you declare a class public, the file must be the same name as that class; the extension of .java is assumed. Your next step in the development cycle is to make sure you have the Java compiler and the HelloWorld.java file in the same directory, then at the DOS command line type the following:

```
javac HelloWorld.java
```

If everything runs smoothly when you compile, you will receive no error message from the compiler. You have just created a file called HelloWorld.class. The .class file is the *executable* file. The .java file is the development file and does not need to be present to run the program.

Here is exactly what to type to start the interpreter and to run your newly created class:

```
java HelloWorld
```

You will receive this statement on your screen:

```
Hello World
```

At this point you might not have understood everything that occurred at the programmatic level—that will be explained in later sections. For now let's move on by creating some more object-based classes. Take a look at Listing 7.2.

Listing 7.2. Book revision 1.

```
class Book {
    int NumberofPages;
    void ShowStuff() {
        System.out.println("The number of pages
        in this book is:   " + NumberofPages);
    }
```

```
public static void main(String args[]) {
    Book MyFirstBook = new Book();
    MyFirstBook.NumberofPages = 100;
    MyFirstBook.ShowStuff();
  }
}
```

In the code in Listing 7.2, you see that a variable called NumberofPages is declared as an integer. Then you see the method ShowStuff() declared also. Both of these are declared to be friendly, which is the default.

The statement in the fourth line of Listing 7.2 is merely a way to print things out on the screen:

```
System.out.println("The number of pages in this book is:   " + NumberofPages);
```

When you put quotes around something in this statement, it will literally be put up on the screen. That is why it is known as a *string literal*. If you do not put quotes around it, however (for example, NumberofPages does not have any quotes), Java will assume it to be a variable and will print out the value of the variable. Right now all you need to know is that it will print whatever is between the parentheses.

The next method that I want to mention is main, shown in the following example:

```
public static void main(String args[]) {
```

The method main is discussed in further detail in Chapter 8, "Java Programming." What is important here is that main will make the program run at the command prompt.

Now let's focus attention on the following line from Listing 7.2:

```
Book MyFirstBook = new Book();
```

The keyword new is known as an operator. When used as it is here, it creates another instance of the class Book. The keyword new acts as the *constructor* for a class Book named MyFirstBook. Essentially, you have created an instance of the class Book. Now let's compile this program by typing the following:

```
javac Book.java
```

If everything was typed and run correctly and you did not receive any error messages on the screen, run the program by typing

```
java Book
```

The following should be displayed on the screen:

```
The number of pages in this book is:  100
```

Here is a list of some major points that have always snagged me—especially when I was just starting out. You might want to consider copying this list and putting it near your computer as a reference every time you develop a new program. If you are having problems compiling smoothly, check for the following:

■ Make sure that the brackets are all balanced. The number of opening brackets should be equal to the number of closing brackets. Also, make sure they are in their proper places.

■ Java is a semicolon language. Make sure that you did *not* just blindly put semicolons after everything; but make sure that you *did* put them everywhere they are needed, as demonstrated in Listing 7.2.

■ Java is a case-sensitive programming language. Make sure you have typed things in the appropriate uppercase or lowercase letters.

These three troubleshooting tips will probably help about 80 percent of those having trouble with this program right now.

Now let's improve the class Book. The next revision in Listing 7.3 will unleash the power of using the operator new.

Listing 7.3. Book revision 2.

```
class Book {
    int NumberofPages;
    void ShowStuff() {
        System.out.println("The number of pages
in this book is:   " + NumberofPages);
    }

    public static void main(String args[]) {
        //Create two instances of the class Book
        Book MyFirstBook = new Book();
        Book MySecondBook = new Book();

        //specify the variable for the
        # of pages and print it out in the first book.
        MyFirstBook.NumberofPages = 100;
        MyFirstBook.ShowStuff();

        //specify the variable for the
        # of pages in the second book and print it out.
        MySecondBook.NumberofPages = 10;
        MySecondBook.ShowStuff();

    }
}
```

The // tells the compiler that everything after it on that line is a comment. It is used in the same way as ' or REM in Visual Basic.

> **NOTE**
>
> Java uses the same syntax as C/C++ for comments. Comments are a way for you to provide documentation inside your code. The single line comment is denoted by the //. The multiple line comment is shown here:
>
> ```
> /* This is an example of a multiple line comment
> in Java and C/C++ /*
> ```

After compiling and running the program shown in Listing 7.3, you will begin to see the power of *instancing* with the new operator. The output of your run should be as follows:

```
The number of pages in this book is:  100
The number of pages in this book is:
```

In this revision you have created two instances of the class Book. The first instance is named MyFirstBook and has 100 pages. The second is named MySecondBook and has 10 pages. Using the new operator and a few lines of code, you were able to create two completely separate objects of Book, each similar by design but unique by implementation, with its own special set of names and attributes. It is crucial that you understand this process of instancing, as you will be using it throughout the rest of the chapter.

You are now going to add a *string variable* into the program by declaring a *string data type* called bookTitle. You also are going to use the keyword private to limit the *access* of this variable to this class only (see Listing 7.4).

Listing 7.4. Book revision 3.

```
class Book {
   private String bookTitle;
   int NumberofPages;
   void ShowStuff() {
      System.out.println("The title of this book is:  " + bookTitle);
      System.out.println("The number of pages
      in this book is:  " + NumberofPages);
   }

   public static void main(String args[]) {
      //Create two instances of the class Book
      Book MyFirstBook = new Book();
      Book MySecondBook = new Book();

      //specify the variable for the
      # of pages and print it out in the first book.
      MyFirstBook.bookTitle = "Mathematics";
      MyFirstBook.NumberofPages = 100;
      MyFirstBook.ShowStuff();
```

continues

Listing 7.4. continued

```
    //specify the variable for the
    # of pages in the second book and print it out.
    MySecondBook.bookTitle = "Small Book";
    MySecondBook.NumberofPages = 10;
    MySecondBook.ShowStuff();


    }
}
```

> **NOTE**
>
> The consistently used indentations in your programs here are not requirements for the program to work. Java looks for semicolons and brackets to understand its structure. The indentations are simply a feature to help anyone who reads your code to make logical sense out of the program. Because you might not be the only one looking at the code you have written, it is a good idea to get into the habit of using indentation.

In Listing 7.4 you added this line to the program:

```
System.out.println("The title of this book is:  " + bookTitle);
```

Notice the plus sign between the quoted statement and the variable. This is an example of *string arithmetic*, which enables you to add a variable and a statement quite painlessly, even if the data type of the variable is not a string. Also notice that in the method main both of the instances now have their own private string variable of bookTitle, which enables you to give each of your book instances a title.

Compile and run the program once again. Your output should be as follows:

```
The title of this book is:  Mathematics
The number of pages in this book is:  100
The title of this book is:  Small Book
The number of pages in this book is:
```

> **CAUTION**
>
> Even though you might see the words *string* and *variable* in the same sentence, in Java, strings are actually objects.

Now you are going to take the paperback class discussed earlier and create a real-life version that will run at the command prompt. The class will be named paperback, which will inherit from the class Book. Open a new file called paperback.java and input the code from Listing 7.5.

Listing 7.5. paperback revision 1.

```java
class paperback extends Book {
    String colorofBook;

    public static void main(String args[]) {
        // Create an instance of paperback
        paperback MyFirstpaperback = new paperback();

        // Set the number of pages using an inherited variable
        MyFirstpaperback.NumberofPages = 120;

        // Set the color of the book
        using the String object named colorofBook in
        // this class.
        MyFirstpaperback.colorofBook = "Red";

        // Use the inherited function showStuff to display the number
        // of pages for this function.
        MyFirstpaperback.ShowStuff();
    }

}
```

Before compiling the program in Listing 7.5, notice that the following statement has the variable NumberofPages in it:

```java
MyFirstpaperback.NumberofPages = 120;
```

You did not initialize it in this class, however, so some might argue that this program might give you an error message if you tried to compile it. Remember, though, that you are extending the class Book, and Book has an integer variable called NumberofPages. Also, Book has a method ShowStuff()—these variables and methods are already built into it.

Here is one of the most unleashing powers of object-oriented programming. You can take an old class (in this case Book) and create a new class (paperback) without touching the original class. In class Book you will be able to use all of the functionality of that class and even add more functionality in the subclass paperback.

After compiling and running it, the output should be as follows:

```
The title of this book is:  null
The number of pages in this book is:  120
```

Because you did not specify what the title to your book in the class paperback should be, the variable bookTitle was made equal to null by default. Let's update the class paperback instance MyFirstpaperback by giving it a title using the variable bookTitle, which is inherited from the class Book (see Listing 7.6).

Listing 7.6. paperback revision 2.

```
class paperback extends Book {
    String colorofBook;

    public static void main(String args[]) {
        // Create an instance of paperback
        paperback MyFirstpaperback = new paperback();

        // Set the number of pages using an inherited variable
        MyFirstpaperback.NumberofPages = 120;

        // Set the color of the book using the String object named colorofBook in
        // this class.
        MyFirstpaperback.colorofBook = "Red";

        //Set the title of the book by inheriting the variable bookTitle
        //from the class Book.
        MyFirstpaperback.bookTitle = "Programming on the Net";

        // Use the inherited function ShowStuff to display the number
        // of pages for this function.
        MyFirstpaperback.ShowStuff();
    }

}
```

Compile the program in Listing 7.6. Unless you did something wrong, you should have received an error message:

```
    paperback.java:17: Variable bookTitle
in class paperback not accessible from class paperback.
        MyFirstpaperback.bookTitle = "Programming on the Net";
                        ^

1 error
```

Before explaining what this exact error message is trying to say, let's first understand the syntax of Java error messages and how to interpret them. Referencing Table 7.1, the Java compiler first displays the class where the error is located. In this case it is paperback.java. Even though you might have typed javac paperback.java, the Java compiler also checks the Book class because the Book class is referenced in the file paperback.java. If there happened to be any errors in the Book class, then even though you stated that you were compiling the paperback class, errors in the Book class would be listed as well.

The number after the word paperback.java is the line number of where the error occurred. Thus, you can go back into the code and fish out where the problem resides. After the colon, the Java compiler next gives you a brief explanation of the error; in this case it is saying:

```
Variable bookTitle in class paperback not accessible from class paperback.
```

Then, on the next line, it will display the line of code, followed underneath by a caret sign, which represents an arrow to show you where the compiler stopped when it caught the problem.

```
paperback.java:17: Variable bookTitle
in class paperback not accessible from class paperback.
        MyFirstpaperback.bookTitle = "Programming on the Net";
                        ^
1 error
```

Table 7.1. Error messages in Java.

Java error	*Explanation*
`paperback.java`	File where error occurred
`17`	Line number
`Variable bookTitle...`	Error description
`MyFirstpaperback...`	Actual line of code
`1 error`	Total number of errors and warnings

Now that you understand more about what the Java compiler is trying to tell you in its error messages, let's try to solve the problem with the program in Listing 7.6. First, you should remember that the variable `bookTitle` is not in the `paperback` class. That would not usually be a problem because the variable `bookTitle` was intended to be inherited from the `Book` class. So you should look at the `Book` class. The following is the line of code in the `Book` class in Listing 7.4, declaring the variable `bookTitle`:

```
private String bookTitle;
```

As you can see, the keyword `private` was placed in front of this variable declaration. What this means is that `bookTitle` is available only to the class `Book`. Thus, `bookTitle` is not available to the subclass of `paperback`. Logically it makes sense, but let's check the brief explanation the compiler gave you about why it could not compile the program:

```
paperback.java:17: Variable bookTitle
in class paperback not accessible from class paperback.
```

Once again this statement is telling you that the variable `bookTitle` is not accessible from the class `paperback`, which confirms the hypothesis that the access modifier keyword `private` in front of the variable `bookTitle` is causing the error. This situation also has exemplified the functionality of declaring something `private`. In this instance it seems obvious that you would receive an error message; but, when you are writing classes in the future, and you know that the variable will not be used outside of its respective class (or you don't want it accessed from outside of its respective class), you can use the above syntax to declare it `private`.

Method overriding is the final object technology for which you are going to create a real-life example. You will use method overriding in the subclass paperback to create a new method that will replace the method ShowStuff() as shown in Listing 7.7. This new method also will tell you the color of the paperback book.

Listing 7.7. paperback revision 3.

```
class paperback extends Book {
    String colorofBook;

    // Create our own string object for a title,
since the variable bookTitle is not available.
    String paperbackBookTitle;

    void ShowStuff() {
        System.out.println("The title of this paperback book is:
        " + paperbackBookTitle);
        System.out.println("The color of this book is:   " + colorofBook);
        System.out.println("The number of pages
        in this book is:   " + NumberofPages);
    }

    public static void main(String args[]) {
        // Create an instance of paperback
        paperback MyFirstpaperback = new paperback();

        // Set the number of pages using an inherited variable
        MyFirstpaperback.NumberofPages = 120;

        // Set the color of the book using the String object named colorofBook in
        // this class.
        MyFirstpaperback.colorofBook = "Red";

        //Set the title of the book by using a local variable because
        //the variable bookTitle is declared private in the superclass
        //Book.
        MyFirstpaperback.paperbackBookTitle = "Programming on the Net";

        // Instead of using the inherited function ShowStuff from
        // the class Book.  Use an overrided method display
        // information about the paperback book.
        MyFirstpaperback.ShowStuff();
    }
}
```

If the program compiled and ran smoothly, you should have received the following message:

```
The title of this paperback book is:  Programming on the Net
The color of this book is:   Red
The number of pages in this book is:   120
```

Now you can see the power of method overriding because you are able to in effect make many improvements to the original class Book without ever having to touch its code. In Listing 7.8

you will see the final revision to the paperback class. This final revision incorporates three instances of the class paperback for three separate fictitious books.

Listing 7.8. paperback revision 4.

```java
class paperback extends Book {
    String colorofBook;
    String paperbackBookTitle;

    // This is the method that will override the ShowStuff()
    // in the superclass Book
    void ShowStuff() {
System.out.println("The title of this paperback book is:
    " + paperbackBookTitle);
        System.out.println("The color of this book is:  " + colorofBook);
        System.out.println("The number of pages
in this book is:  " + NumberofPages);
    }

    public static void main(String args[]) {
        // Create three instances of paperback
        paperback MyFirstpaperback = new paperback();
        paperback MySecondpaperback = new paperback();
        paperback MyThirdpaperback = new paperback();

        // Set the number of pages using an inherited variable for the
        // three instances.
        MyFirstpaperback.NumberofPages = 120;
        MySecondpaperback.NumberofPages = 200;
        MyThirdpaperback.NumberofPages = 25;

        // Set the color for three of the books using the String
        //object named colorofBook in this class.
        MyFirstpaperback.colorofBook = "Red";
        MySecondpaperback.colorofBook = "Blue";
        MyThirdpaperback.colorofBook = "Green";

        //Set the title for the three books by using a local variable
        //because the variable bookTitle is declared private in the superclass
        //Book.
        MyFirstpaperback.paperbackBookTitle = "Programming on the Net";
        MySecondpaperback.paperbackBookTitle = "The Future of the Internet";
        MyThirdpaperback.paperbackBookTitle = "Why We Surf";


        // Use the inherited function showNumberofPages to display information
        // for the three instances
        MyFirstpaperback.ShowStuff();
        MySecondpaperback.ShowStuff();
        MyThirdpaperback.ShowStuff();

    }
}
```

7

INTRODUCTION TO JAVA

Read the comments in the code carefully to help you decipher what the program is saying. You should do the same when you create your own programs, so that other programmers looking at your code will know what you are saying. If everything in the program ran smoothly, it should have displayed the following:

```
The title of this paperback book is:  Programming on the Net
The color of this book is:  Red
The number of pages in this book is:  120
The title of this paperback book is:  The Future of the Internet
The color of this book is:  Blue
The number of pages in this book is:  200
The title of this paperback book is:  Why We Surf
The color of this book is:  Green
The number of pages in this book is:
```

This concludes the first workshop, which covered a great deal of powerful material. If you grasped all the concepts, you are well on your way toward becoming an object-oriented programmer.

Method Overloading—The Discussion

Method overloading can be used to create several functions of the same name that will perform very similar tasks, but each is designed to handle a different set of data types.

> **NOTE**
>
> In C++ it is OK for several functions with the same name to be defined with different sets of parameters. This is known as *function overloading*. C++ also supports *operator overloading*. Operator overloading is a way to customize an operator's functionality and hence its manipulation of a given expression. A major reason why operator overloading is not supported in Java is for simplicity's sake.

> **NOTE**
>
> One major discrepancy between C++ and Java is that Java does not support operator overloading.

Method Overloading—The Workshop

In both C++ and Java, it is OK for any object to have overloaded methods (in other words, methods with the same name), but they must have different arguments. In Java it is not known as function overloading; instead it is known as method overloading. Listing 7.9 shows an example of method overloading in Java.

Listing 7.9. combining revision 1.

```
class combining {
   // First method
   void combine() {
      System.out.println("You did not specify anything to combine.");
   }

   // Second method overloaded
   void combine(String firstWord) {
      System.out.println("You have only stated one word: " + firstWord);
   }
   //Third method overloaded
   void combine(String firstWord, String secondWord) {
      System.out.println("Here are your combined words:
" + firstWord + secondWord);
   }
   public static void main(String args[]) {
       //Create an instance of the class combining
       combining MyStatements = new combining();
       //Run the method combine (using the first overloaded method)
       MyStatements.combine();
       //Run the method combine (using the third overloaded method)
       MyStatements.combine("The", "End");
       //Run the method combine (using the second overloaded method)
       MyStatements.combine("Yes");
   }
}
```

Compile the program and run it. If all went well, you should have received the following as output:

```
You did not specify anything to combine.
Here are your combined words:  TheEnd
You have only stated one word: Yes
```

Using this example, you can appreciate the improved simplicity that method overloading provides. It is a very helpful way of making your program easier to understand.

Interfaces—The Discussion

`Interface` is a keyword used in Java to inherit a class of definitions, but not the implementation code contained in the methods. Because Java does not support multiple inheritance, interfaces are a solution for the functionality lost in multiple inheritance. Thus, you can also implement as many interfaces as necessary.

```
interface drive {

}
```

An interface enables you to develop a kind of multiple inheritance without making your program too complicated. Although Java officially enables only single inheritance, with classes you can add as many interfaces to your class as you want. The only catch is that with interfaces you cannot inherit implementation code. This is not really a catch—it is actually a feature. It is a means by which you can keep the best of both worlds. You can have the technology of multiple inheritance without the confusing nature that multiple inheritance is known for.

Say that you wanted to use a set of methods from each of several classes. You could create an interface and use it in each of the classes. Then you could override the method declared in the interface to carry out the method for a particular class. To demonstrate, let's create three classes called car, truck, and van:

```
class car {

}

class truck {

}

class van extends vehicle {

}
```

The classes truck and car have no superclasses. The class van is a subclass to the fictitious superclass vehicle.

Now define an interface called drive:

```
interface drive {

void firstgear();

void secondgear();

void thirdgear();
}
```

> **NOTE**
>
> Interface methods must be declared public or friendly. The default is used here, so that means it is declared friendly.

Now implement drive into the three classes:

```
class truck implements drive {
    public void firstgear() {
        // algorithm goes here to override the method
        firstgear in the interface drive.
        // the code here is specific only to truck.
```

```
    }
    public void secondgear() {
        // algorithm goes here to override the method
        in secondgear in the interface drive.
        // The code here is specific only to truck.

    }
    public void thirdgear () {
        //algorithm goes here to override the method
        in thirdgear in the interface drive.
        // The code here is specific only to truck.

    }
}
```

The power in this program might not reveal itself until you actually use it on, for example, a sample animation applet, which you will do later in Chapter 8.

If right now you are very frustrated by interfaces (as I know I was when I first worked with them), take a moment and breath deeply 10 times. Repeat to yourself "Java is cool" each time. Now let's go ahead and continue with the lesson:

```
class van extends vehicle implements drive {
    public void firstgear() {
        //algorithm goes here to override the method
        firstgear in the interface drive. With a

        // special method only for the class van.
    }
    public void secondgear() {
        //algorithm goes here to override the method
        secondgear in the interface drive.
        // with a special method only for class van.
    }
        public void thirdgear() {
        //algorithm goes here to override the method
        thirdgear in the interface drive.
        // with a special method only for class van.
    }

}
```

Here is where you will see most of the beauty of interfaces. You can use the exact same interface on several classes and in the class van. Even though van already has the class `vehicle` from which it inherits, van still can accept an interface. In fact, you can add more than one interface to a class. Here is an example implementing more than one interface:

```
class myclass extend mysuperclass implements ABC, XYZ, … {
}
```

Finishing this lesson on interfaces, you will use the exact same interface `drive` and implement it into the class car.

```
class car implements drive {

    void firstgear() {
        // algorithm goes here to override the method
        firstgear in the interface drive.
        // the code in here is specific only to the class car.
    }

    void secondgear() {
        // algorithm goes here to override the method
        in secondgear in the interface drive.
        // the code in here is specific only to the class car.

    }

    void thirdgear () {
        //algorithm goes here to override the method
        in thirdgear in the interface drive.
        // the code here is specific only to the class car.

    }
}
```

I have focused heavily on the object technology of interfaces because it is one of the more misunderstood features of Java. In fact, just about every time I am on CompuServe's Java Support Forum (GO JAVAUSER), there is someone confused by interfaces, who is leaving messages asking for help. Fortunately, friendly Java gurus are available 24 hours a day to take your call.

Interfaces—The Workshop

This section gives a real-life example of how using interfaces can help you. First, let's build two classes, adding and multiplying. The first class in Listing 7.10 is the class adding. You can start by creating a new file called adding.java and keying Listing 7.10 into it.

Listing 7.10. adding before implementation.

```
class adding {
    // Declare the three variables to hold our values
    int First;
    int Second;
    int Total;

    public static void main(String args[]) {
        // Create an instance of the class adding
        adding ad = new adding();

        // Give the first two variables a value
        ad.First = 10;
        ad.Second = 14;

    }
}
```

If you compiled the above class, you saw that it would compile and run. You did not include the statement System.out.println, however, so nothing will show up on the screen. You will add the System.out.println lines later on.

The next class you will create should be called multiplying (see Listing 7.11). Once again, create a new file and call it mutiplying.java. Then key Listing 7.11 into it.

Listing 7.11. multiplying before implementation.

```
class multiplying {
    // Declare the three variables to hold our values
    int Firstmulti;
    int Secondmulti;
    int Totalmulti;

    public static void main(String args[]) {
        // Create an instance of the class adding
 multiplying ml = new multiplying();

        // Give the first two variables a value
        ml.Firstmulti = 5;
        ml.Secondmulti = 5;

    }
}
```

These two classes need to be improved upon, because there is no code yet to actually do the adding or multiplying of the first two arguments, and because nothing is printed out on the screen to tell you the answer. The next step is to look at the interface combine in Listing 7.12. In the same directory as the last two, create a new file called combine.java; then add the code from Listing 7.12 into it.

Listing 7.12. Interface to combine and show things.

```
interface combine {
    void Combine();
    void ShowStatus();
}
```

Compile the interface class combine by typing

```
javac combine.java
```

Now you are going to use interfaces and method overriding together to make your first two classes functional. You will be using the same interface for both classes. Go back to the class adding.java and make the appropriate changes as shown in Listing 7.13.

Listing 7.13. adding after implementation.

```
class adding implements combine {
    // Declare the three variables to hold our values
    int First;
    int Second;
    int Total;
    public void Combine() {
        // Below is the overriding implementation code for the interface
        // combine
        Total = First + Second;
    }
    public void ShowStatus() {
        // Below is the overriding implementation code for the interface
        // combine
        System.out.println("The total for the class: " + Total);
    }
    public static void main(String args[]) {
        // Create an instance of the class adding
        adding ad = new adding();
        // Give the first two variables a value
        ad.First = 10;
        ad.Second = 14;
        // The method to combine the two numbers
        ad.Combine();
        // the method to combine show the numbers on the screen
        ad.ShowStatus();
    }
}
```

In Listing 7.13, notice the keyword implements in the first line of the class. This is how you inherit an interface into a class. The logic behind calling the keyword implements is that you are including the interface (in this case combine) to implement it into the class (adding). Next notice that the methods Combine() and ShowStatus() are the same methods as the ones coming from the interface combine. Finally, look at the statements of Combine() and ShowStatus(). Interface methods that are overriding with implementation code will be accessible to instances of the class adding.

Your next step is to compile and run the program. If everything runs correctly, you should receive this as the output:

```
The total for the class:
```

To exemplify the power of interfaces, you will do almost the same thing to the class multiplying. First you will implement the same interface and then override its methods as shown in Listing 7.14. Reopen multiplying.java and make the changes so that multiplying looks like Listing 7.14.

Listing 7.14. multiplying after implementation.

```
class multiplying implements combine {
   // Declare the three variables to hold our values
   int Firstmulti;
   int Secondmulti;
   int Totalmulti;
   public void Combine() {
      // Overiding implementation code.
      Totalmulti = Firstmulti * Secondmulti;
   }
   public void ShowStatus() {
      //Override the implementation code.
      System.out.println("The product of the two variables
      is:  " + Totalmulti);
   }
   public static void main(String args[]) {
      // Create an instance of the class adding
      multiplying mul = new multiplying();
      // Give the first two variables a value
      mul.Firstmulti = 5;
      mul.Secondmulti = 5;
      //invoke the method to find the product
      mul.Combine();
      //Show the result on the screen
      mul.ShowStatus();
      }
}
```

Essentially, you are doing the same thing (putting two values together), except that in the class multiplying you find the product of two numbers instead of the summation. Now compile the program, and you should receive the following message:

```
The product of the two variables is:
```

This introduction to objects in Java was meant to catch the essence of the Java object paradigm. In the next section, you will build upon your foundation by understanding other aspects of the Java language.

Introduction to Java Structure

This section gives you an overview of the structure of Java. Some of the topics include primitive data types, control flow statements, and how to handle arrays. If you are a C/C++ programmer, this section will need skimming only. However, if you are not a C/C++ programmer or if you are on shaky ground with C/C++, it will be worth your time to read through the material and try the examples.

Primitive Data Types

Although object-oriented programming languages have incorporated many improvements over structured programming languages, you do need to know structured programming in order to program objects effectively. As you go through this section, think of these structure-oriented topics as your foundation.

Booleans—The Discussion

The keyword `boolean` was named after a famous English mathematician who developed a new form of algebra based on a form of logic that is used in probably every programming language today: Boolean logic with Boolean operators. The basic data type `boolean` can have either a value of `true` or a value of `false`. Also, a boolean cannot be converted to another type (casting types will be described later in this chapter). Below is an example of declaring a `boolean`:

```
boolean here = true;
```

Data types can be assigned a value when the are declared, or you can assign them a value later on during the program in an expression or statement. An interesting point about the data type `boolean` is that, if you do not declare a value for it explicitly, it is set with a default value of `false`.

Booleans—The Workshop

Let's demonstrate how a `boolean` would work by creating a file called `ABC.java` and then coding Listing 7.15 into it.

Listing 7.15. ABC.

```
class ABC  {
   // Initialize the boolean with the default value of false.
   boolean first;

   // initialize the boolean with the value explicitly set to false.
   boolean  second = false;

   // initialize the boolean with the value explicitly set to true.
   boolean third = true;

   void ShowBools() {

   //Print out the value of each of the three booleans
   System.out.println("The value of first is " + first);
   System.out.println("The value of second is " + second);
   System.out.println("The value of third is " + third);
   }

   public static void main(String args[]) {
   public static void main(String args[]) {
//Create an instance of the class ABC
ABC abc = new ABC();
```

```
        //Change the value of third to false.
        abc.third = false;

        //Show the three booleans on the screen with their respective values.
        abc.ShowBools();
    }
}
```

Compile and run the above example; you should receive the following results:

```
The value of first is false
The value of second is false
The value of third is false
```

Integer Types

The next basic type that you are going to learn about is the subset of integer types.

Notice that there is more than one integer type in Java. The reason for this is size. It all boils down to efficiency—the larger the size of the integer you need, the more memory that must be assigned. Granted, we are only talking bits, but the more integer types your program works with, the more size will play a role in the overall performance and overhead of the program.

It is important to create your programs to be as efficient as possible.

> **NOTE**
>
> Bit is short for *binary digit*, either 1 or 0 in the binary number system. In processing any information, a bit is the smallest unit of information handled by a computer.

The smallest integer that can be declared in Java is the byte. The word byte stands for *binary term*, which is a unit of information consisting of 8 bits. The data type byte got its name because it consists of 8 bits. Because byte is the smallest, it is the most efficient to use; however, it also has the smallest range. You can only assign a byte to have a value of –128 to 127. Here is an example of declaring a byte:

```
byte myVariable;
```

As you can see, the syntax declaring primitive data types remains pretty much the same as you learned when you declared classes in Java.

The next level up is the short data type, which is also an integer, but it is 16 bits in length. Based on binary arithmetic, because its bit width is twice as long as the type byte, that will raise its range by a power of two as compared to the byte. So the short has a range of –32,768 to 32,767.

After the short comes the int, which you used in the previous section. The primary reason for using int in the previous section was because its name was similar to integer, which might be confusing; int is a 32-bit value, which equates that it is twice the size of short, which makes its range raise from short by a power of 2 as well. The range of int is –2,147,483,648 to 2,147,483,647.

The last and largest integer value you can have in Java is the data type long. As you can probably guess, long is 64 bits in length, which makes it twice the size of int. This means that it has raised int's range by a power of 2, so it would now be –9,223,372,036,854,775,808 to 9,223,372,036,854,775,807.

> **NOTE**
>
> All integer data types are initialized with a default value of zero.

No doubt long was created in case Java was ever used to compute the national debt. Use Table 7.2 as a quick reference to all of the integer types.

Table 7.2. Quick reference to integer data types.

Keyword	Size (in bits)	Low range	High range
byte	8	–128	127
short	16	–32,768	32,767
int	32	–2,147,483,648	2,147,483,647
long	64	–9,223,372,036,854,775,808	9,223,372,036,854,775,807

Character Literal

Char, which stands for *character literal,* is a character that is usually enclosed in a set of single quotes. Java characters are stored in Unicode format. To you the programmer, that means that they are 16 bits in length.

> **NOTE**
>
> *Literal* means that what was printed in the code is exactly what will be shown on the screen.

> **NOTE**
>
> Java's data type char holds 16-bit Unicode characters as opposed to ANSI C/C++'s type char, which holds the 8-bit extended ASCII character set.

Here is an example of a character being initialized with a value:

```
char X = 'J';
```

There are some characters in Java that are nonprintable. Table 7.3 shows a list of the character codes for nonprintable characters.

Table 7.3. Character codes.

Code	Description
\b	Backspace
\f	Formfeed
\n	Newline
\t	Tab
\\	Backslash
\' (Single quote)	Because you surround your character literals with single quotes, these quotes will not be printed (for example, with 'I', 'b', '$', the only things that will be printed on the screen are I, b, $). If you want to actually print a single quote, then you need to use this syntax, \'.
\" (Double quote)	String literals are basically a group of two or more characters that need to be surrounded by double quotes (for example, "This is a String literal").
\xdd	Hexadecimal
\ddd	Octal
\udddd	Unicode

Float and Double

Floating-point notation is used to handle very large numbers, very small numbers, and decimals. The following is an example of how you would declare a variable as a float or a double:

```
float myFloat;
double myDouble;
```

Floating-point numbers can be in standard or scientific notation. Here are several examples of valid floating-point values:

```
3.113   4.4e23   5.6E-40   4.2e-21
```

In Java, floating-point data types conform to the IEEE 754 standard. A `float` is known as a single-precision floating-point data type. A `double` is known obviously enough as a double-precision floating-point data type. The major difference between a `float` and a `double` is bit width. A `float` is only 32 bits long, and a `double` is 64 bits long. Because of this size differential, there is also a difference in how precise each of the two floating-point variables can be (see Table 7.4). Just like the integer types, floating-point numbers are initialized to a value of 0 as a default.

Table 7.4. Overview of Java's floating-point data type.

Keyword	Size (in bits)	Precision	Low range	High range
`float`	32	Single	3.4E –38	3.4E +38
`double`	64	Double	1.7E –308	1.7E +308

NOTE

IEEE is an abbreviation for the Institute of Electrical and Electronic Engineers. This organization is noted for setting various standards in the computer industry. One of the most famous was the IEEE 802, which set standards for the physical and data link layers of local area networks.

Casting

Casting deals with changing from one data type to another. For example, imagine that you have a `char` and you want to change it to an `int`:

```
int X;
char Y;
X = (int) Y;
```

The idea of casting is fairly basic. Referring to the preceding example, you place the name of the new data type in parentheses in front of the current data type that you want to change. If you are casting to a larger bit width data type, however, you might not need to explicitly include the parentheses of the new data type. For example, if you were to cast from a `byte` to an `int`, it could be done in an implicit manner. The overall usage of casting in real-life programs is much more complex than this, however, and data can be lost through truncation if casting is not used properly.

Another use for casting is to convert some information from one data type to another type. When casting between primitive data types, the major complication lies in size differences among the different data types. Trying to cast from one size to another can be a major cause of data loss.

Let's go over some examples of safe and unsafe casts to see exactly why there is potential for data loss. Start by declaring an integer variable called `Myshort`:

```
short Myshort = 10000;
```

Now look at the variable from the inside. Referring to Table 7.2, you see that the `short` integer type is 16 bits in length. Table 7.5 shows you the binary value for each bit. Thus, variable `MyShort` has a value of 10000.

Table 7.5. Inside the variable MyShort.

Bit #	1	2	3	4	5	6	7	8	9	10	11	12	13	14	15	16
ValueofBit	0	0	1	0	0	1	1	1	0	0	0	1	0	0	0	0

In Table 7.5, the row `ValueofBit` shows the binary representation of the number 10000. Your next step is to cast it. In this case you are going to cast it to a `byte`. Looking at Table 7.2, you see that a `byte` is only 8 bits long, so you know that somewhere along the way Java will truncate 8 bits off the variable `MyShort`. Logically and without going to the binary level, you know that, based on the definition for the range of a `byte`, that it cannot be 10000. This also confirms that there will be a problem in this cast. But Java won't throw you an error message; instead, it will return an invalid value to your new variable. The following segment of code shows the casting of a variable `MyShort` to `MyByte`:

```
byte MyByte;
MyByte = (byte) MyShort;
```

Now take the new value for `MyByte` and look at it at the binary level in Table 7.6 to find out what the value of `MyByte` will be.

Table 7.6. Truncation of MyShort to MyByte.

Bit #	1	2	3	4	5	6	7	8	9	10	11	12	13	14	15	16
ValueofBit	0	0	1	0	0	1	1	1	0	0	0	1	0	0	0	0
Truncated?	Y	Y	Y	Y	Y	Y	Y	Y	N	N	N	N	N	N	N	N

Looking at Table 7.6, you see that the first 8 bits are truncated (in other words, "blown away"). The end result is that, when you query the value `MyByte`, you will get a value of 16!

> **NOTE**
>
> In the binary number system, zeros on the left do not affect the value of the binary number.

If all of the bits truncated in Table 7.6 were zeros, you would not have had a problem. If that had been the case, the largest value the variable `MyShort` could hold would have been −128 to 127, the exact range of the `byte`. I hope this helps you understand the usefulness and dangers of truncating variables.

To end this discussion, here is a list showing casting that will be safe 100 percent of the time. Notice in the list that you are going to a larger bit size when you are casting; so at the binary level you are simply adding zeros to the left, which does not affect the value of the binary number:

- `byte` (8 bits) to `short`(16), `char`(16), `int`(32), `long`(64), `float`(32), `double`(64).
- `short` (16 bits) to `int`(32), `long`(64) , `float`(32), and `double`(64).
- `char` (16 bits) to `int`(32), `float`(32), and `double`(64).
- `int` (32 bits) to `long`(64), `float`(32), and `double`(64).
- `float` (32 bits) to `double`(64).

Casting Between Objects

Another more complex version of casting is the object technology of casting between instances of objects. For example, in Java you can implicitly cast from a superclass to a subclass without the worry of data loss, because technically the subclass is a more specific representation of the superclass. However, if you go the other way (from a subclass to a superclass), it must be done at an explicit level and can result in changes in references to instance variables.

When you cast between objects, it is practically the same as casting between data types, as mentioned earlier. For example, imagine that you had a superclass of `printer` and a subclass of `laserprinter`. The following is an example of how you would cast `laserprinter` into the superclass of `printer`:

```
printer X;
laserprinter Y;
Y = new printer();
X = (laserprinter) Y;
```

Operators

Operators are designated symbols that perform various tasks in expressions. If you have had any experience with programming, you have probably been exposed to operators. The next sections will build a common understanding of each of the groups of related operators in Java.

Once again, if you are a proficient C/C++ programmer, these sections are scanning material only.

Arithmetic Operators

The arithmetic operators are easy to understand because you were probably taught them in your first algebra classes (see Table 7.7).

Table 7.7. Arithmetic operators.

Operator	Definition	Java rep.	Algebraic rep.
+	Addition	T + 7	T +
-	Subtraction	u − v	u − v
*	Multiplication	g * m	gm
/	Division	x / y	x/y (or) x÷y
%	Modulus	I % n	I mod n

The syntax of using arithmetic operators is extremely simple. The integer variables a and b are employed in the following example with several arithmetic operators to give an idea of how to use them:

```
// Declare the values for a and b
a = 5;
b = 10;
(a + b) //Using the Addition operator to receive
        //from the expression.
( 4 - 1) //Using the Subtraction operator to receive
        //from the expression.
( 10 / 5) //Using the Division operator to receive
        //from the expression.
```

One arithmetic operator that might not be familiar to everyone is the *modulus* operator. A modulus operation returns the remainder of a division as its answer. So, for example, 25 % 8 equals 1.

NOTE

As opposed to C/C++, Java enables % operands to be non-integers.

Assignment Operators

Another set of operators in Java is the assignment operators. These also are similar to C/C++. In Table 7.8, you see a fairly self-explanatory chart of available assignment operators. Essentially, the calculation takes place before the variable is assigned a value.

Table 7.8. Assignment operators.

Operator	Java rep.	Algebraic rep.
		Assume a and b are integer variables
+=	a += b	a = a + b
-=	a -= b	a = a - b
*=	a *= b	a = a * b
/=	a /= b	a = a / b
%=	a %= b	a = a % b

Comparison, Logical, Incremental, and Decremental Operators

The terms *comparison operators* and *logical operators* refer to the relationships that values can have to each other. Later I discuss the incremental and decremental operators, which are easy to understand as well.

The logical operator focuses more on how operands relate to each other, while the comparison operator focuses on how they don't relate to each other. Table 7.9 shows a breakdown of the comparison operators in Java; Table 7.10 shows a list of the logical operators in Java. With comparison operators, if the comparison expression is true, then a boolean true is returned; and if the expression is not true, then false is returned.

Table 7.9. Comparison operators.

Operator	Definition	Example exp.	Returns
		Assume a = 5 and b =2	
==	equal to	a == 5	true
		b == 5	false
!=	not equal to	a != 5	false
		b != 5	true
<	less than	a < 5	false
		b < 5	true
>	greater than	a > 5	false
		b > 5	false
<=	less than or equal to	a <= 5	true
		b <= 5	true
>=	greater than or equal to	a >= 5	true
		b >= 5	false

Logical operators are expressions that also result in a return of `true` if the statement is true, and `false` if the statement is false. Table 7.10 shows the logical operators.

Table 7.10. Logical operators.

Operator	Definition	Example exp.	Returns
Assume a = 1 and b = 0			
& or &&	and	a && b	false
¦ or ¦¦	or	a ¦¦ b	true
^	xor	a ^ b	true
!	not	!b	true

The difference between the or (¦¦) and the xor (^) is that with the or (¦¦), one of the operands can be `true` or `false`, whereas with the xor (^) (exclusive or), one of the operands must be `true` and the other must be `false`.

Some other things to mention about the logical operators are the differences between the & and &&, and the ¦ and ¦¦. If you use the single ¦ (or &), then Java will evaluate both sides no matter what the outcome. With the &&, if the left side is false, then the compiler stops and returns `false` for the evaluation. And with ¦¦, if the left side (which also is evaluated first) is true, then the compiler stops and returns `true` for the whole statement. The ¦ and & logical operators are not available in C/C++, because C/C++ does not support this functionality.

What is the advantage of having the partial evaluation (of ¦¦ and &&) differential as opposed to the full evaluation (¦ &)? The answer: speed and efficiency.

The expressions in Listing 7.16 are very basic. Imagine that you had a 100-step process comparing a 10-step process. To squeeze as much efficiency out of a program as possible, you would use the double ¦¦ (or &&) and put the 10-instruction-step evaluation on the left. Thus, if the 10-step process returned a `false` for the && (or true for the ¦¦), then you could immediately skip the right side and continue with the program. Compound this efficiency by using the expression evaluation 10 times throughout your program and you should begin to see the advantages of having this functionality.

NOTE

C/C++ does not have an exclusive xor for logical operation. Java does, however, by using the ^ which is borrowed from the bitwise xor.

Listing 7.16 is a real-life example of using the logical operators.

Listing 7.16. Logic revision 1.

```
public class logic {
   //initial the integers
   boolean a;
   boolean b;

   void Show() {
      System.out.println("true means 1 and false means 0");
      // Logical operator and
      System.out.println("(a and b) " + (a && b));

      //Logical operator or
      System.out.println("(a or b) " + (a || b));

      //Logical operator xor (exclusive or)
      System.out.println("(a xor b) " + (a ^ b));

   }
   public static void main(String args[]) {
      logic L = new logic();

      // Declare variables for a and b. Try other values here
      L.a = true;
      L.b = false;

      // Print out the logical expressions
      L.Show();
   }
}
```

Compile and run the program. If everything went smoothly, your output should be as follows:

```
true means 1 and false means
(a and b)false
(a or b)true
(a xor b)true
```

Experiment with the values of a and b to see what other results you might receive.

The final operators that you will learn about in this section are the incremental and decremental operators. Table 7.11 shows how these relate to each other and how to use them.

Table 7.11. Incremental and decremental operators.

Operator	Definition	Algebraic rep.	Example exp.	Returns
		Assume a = 5 with each line		
++	pre-increment	a = a + 1	(++a * 2)	12 (a = 6)
	post-increment		(a++ * 2)	10 (a = 6)
--	pre-decrement	a = a - 1	(--a * 3)	12 (a = 4)
	post-decrement		(a-- * 3)	15 (a = 4)

NOTE

The difference between a pre- and post-increment/decrement operator is with pre-, the increment/decrement operation is performed first.

Bitwise Operators

Java supports the set bitwise operators. This section will give you a brief introduction.

With bitwise operators there is an easy-to-understand part and a hard-to-understand part. The easy part is that bitwise operators say exactly what they mean. Bitwise operators deal with a data type's bits. The hard part is in the implementation of these operators.

Unless you are planning to write an operating system, networking software, or diagnostic equipment program, bitwise operators are not very useful. The space and the scope of this book do not permit a detailed explanation of bitwise operators. However, if you intend to write such a system, software, or diagnostic equipment in Sun's new language, then look for an advanced C++ programming textbook. Because C/C++ and Java are similar, you should have no problem translating between the two to understand what you need to know.

Ternary Operator

One of C++'s, and now Java's, most fascinating operators is the ?. The ? operator (also known as the *ternary operator*) can be used as a control flow statement. Look at the following example of a ternary operator:

```
Expression1 ? Exp2 : Exp3
```

Using the preceding format, if Expression1 is true, then Exp1 is *fired*. Or, if Expression1 is false, then Exp3 is fired. This operator is very simple to understand and use.

Operator Precedence

As you conclude this discussion of the Java operator realm, now is a good time to mention *operator precedence*. This is another very simple form of logic that you probably learned in your first algebra classes. For example, let's look at the following mathematical statement:

```
5 + 2 * 3
```

The wrong answer for this expression is 21 (which would be derived by adding 5 and 2, then multiplying the result by 3). The correct way to find the value for the above expression is to multiply 2×3 first then add the result to 5, which yields 11. It is simple logic really—you are applying the algebraic rule that the multiplication comes before the addition. The same logic of precedence has been applied to computer programming language operators.

The following list gives an overview of operator precedence in Java. The highest precedence is first:

1. `. [] ()`
2. `++ -- !`
3. `new`
4. `* / %`
5. `+ -`
6. `< <= > >=`
7. `== !=`
8. `&`
9. `^`
10. `¦`
11. `&&`
12. `¦¦`
13. `? :`
14. `= += -=`
    `*= %= ^=`

Control Flow

The control flow stuff is a basic feature of any programming language; however, its actual syntax tends to vary between environments. Java uses almost exactly the same syntax as C/C++ control flow statements. Most of the following material on control flow statements will be discussion-based, although you will have a chance to try it in a real-life example at the end of this chapter with the bubble sort algorithm.

The **if** Conditional

The best place to start is with the **if** conditional, which is a control flow statement that will execute a piece of code if a Boolean evaluation is equal to **true**. For example, let's imagine that you are a bank and you want to create an algorithm that would print out a note to waive the monthly fee if a particular bank account's balance was over $1,000:

```
int bankaccount;
if (bankaccount > 1000) {
    System.out.println("Your service fee for this account is waived");
    }
```

If the variable **bankaccount** is over $1,000, then the Boolean expression will return **true**, and any code inside the block (contained in the brackets) will be executed. However, if the variable is not over $1,000, then the block will not be executed.

Now suppose you wanted to create this algorithm to deduct $5 from the account if the balance falls under $1,000. This can be done by implementing the keyword **else**. What you will now have is two blocks of code; if the Boolean expression is **true**, then one block will be executed, or if the expression is **false**, then the other block will be executed. Below is the implementation of using **else** in the fictitious bank account algorithm:

```
int bankaccount;
if (bankaccount > 1000) {
    System.out.println("Your service fee for this account is waived");
} else {
bankaccount -= 5;
}
```

Now if someone's account is below $1,000, then the block after **else** will be executed (in this case it will deduct 5 from the integer variable **bankaccount**).

The last scenario uses the keyword combination of **else if**. With this you can actually have more than one set of evaluations occurring in one **if** conditional statement. So, in this bank example, let's say you want to charge people $7 if their account balance is below $500; $5 if their account balance is between $500 and $1,000; and no charge if their account balance is over $1,000:

```
int bankaccount;
if (bankaccount > 1000) {
    System.out.println("Your service fee for this account is waived");
} else if (bankaccount < 500) {
        bankaccount -= 7;
} else {
bankaccount -= 5;
}
```

7

INTRODUCTION TO JAVA

The while Loops

There are two formats for the while loops. As you will see in the following example, the first of these formats is understood to execute a piece of code as long as the evaluation returns a true:

```
while (evaluation){
    //execute some code.
}
```

The other format for the while loop is the do-while loop:

```
do {
    //execute some code.
while (evaluation);
```

As shown here, this statement will do the same thing as the previous one except that it has reversed the order in which it is executing code and evaluating. Here the code will be executed first, then the evaluation will take place. Thus, code in a do-while loop will always execute at least once, but the code in a while loop might not execute at all.

The primary difference between the two while formats is the order of execution and evaluation. In the first format the evaluation will take place first, then the code will execute. In the second format the code will execute first, then the evaluation will take place.

The for Loop

The for loop is a very versatile control flow statement, mostly due to its flexibility. Essentially the for loop will *iterate* for a certain period, and with each loop it will execute a block of code. The following is an example of format in a for loop:

```
for (expression1; evaluation; expression2) {
    // execute some code
}
```

In this example's format, the for control flow statement works like this: expression1 is the starting point of the for loop. It will initialize any variables that need to be and also will initialize any other data that would be unique to the start of the loop. The evaluation is executed at every pass of the loop, each time calling expression2; and if the evaluation returns true, then the loop will continue. But if it returns false, the loop will end.

Thinking of a more practical example for the for loop, imagine that you wanted to print out the numbers from one to 100 on the screen. One way to do it would be to use the following piece of code:

```
for (int j = 1; j < 100; j++) {
    System.out.println(j);
}
```

NOTE

One thing that makes loops very useful is that you can have nested loops (in other words, a loop inside a loop). Nested loops can be double-edged swords, however, because although they do provide improved functionality, they also increase the complexity of the program. You will have a chance to work with nested loops in the example at the end of this chapter.

It is also OK to have a `for` loop that never ends (in other words, an infinite loop), though the practicality of it would be fairly unusual.

The `switch` Conditional

An easy way to think of a `switch` statement is to think of a traffic light on a busy day. In this scenario the traffic light is some sort of expression, and based on the result of the expression some lanes will stop and other lanes will go. The following shows a simple example of a `switch` statement:

```
switch (expression) {
    case const1:
    // code specific to case one goes here
    break;
    case const2:
    //code specific to case two goes here
    break;
    case const3:
    case const4:
    // specific code common to both 3 and 4 goes here
    break;
    default:
    //This is fired if none of the other cases were.
    break;
}
```

In the preceding code, notice that there is a `break` statement after every case. This tells the compiler to exit out of the case and not continue with the program. Notice with case `const3` and `const4`, however, that if either of them is chosen, it is designated to run the same code. This is useful if you have a few results that require the same code to be fired.

Scope

When you are dealing with the structured topology of any programming language, including Java, you have to deal with variable *scope*. In one light you already have dealt with scope—you have access modifiers that you can put in front of your variable declarations to affect their availability to other classes as shown in Listing 7.1. But that kind of scope is geared to situations between classes. It is crucial to note that scope does affect whether a variable declared inside a method will be accessed outside of that method.

Right now you are only going to focus on a variable's access inside its own class. When dealing with a variable, a block of code is not available outside of that block. This also means that if you declared a variable inside a block of code, you can declare another variable with exactly the same name outside the block of code, and it will be its own variable. In a sense this follows the same concept as method overriding, except that in this case it could be called variable overriding.

Create a file called scope.java and key in the code from Listing 7.17. Then compile and run it.

Listing 7.17. scope revision 1.

```
class scope {
   void Show() {
       int c = 12; //initialize a new c which hides the one in main
       System.out.println("This is the c inside of Show(): " + c);
   }

   public static void  main(String args[]) {
       int c = 10;  //initialize c in main
       scope s = new scope();  // Create a new instance of scope()
       System.out.println("This is c inside of main
before calling Show(): " + c);
       s.Show(); //This will initialize Show()
       System.out.println("This is the c inside the class
after calling Show(): " + c);

   }
}
```

The program in Listing 7.17 shows a variable c being initialized inside of the method main. Then the method Show() is called; and inside Show() is another variable c. Notice that before Show() is called, you already have a c in the method with a different value from the newer c. Also notice that after the method Show(), the original c still has the same value as before.

Now compile and run the program. You should receive the following on your screen:

```
This is c inside of main before calling Show():
This is the c inside of Show():
This is the c inside the class after calling Show():
```

Arrays—The Discussion

In C/C++ an array is a consecutive group of memory locations that all have the same data type in common. To refer to a particular location or element in the array you would specify the name of the array or the position number. In C++ there is no data type for a string variable, so a programmer would use an array's characters instead. This method is more efficient and flexible using built-in string objects (like Java has).

The reason that Java deviated from C/C++ by creating its own object was that C/C++ does no bounds checking. Hence, all you need to do is access an array that is larger than the allocated amount and presto! Instant crash. Also, because of this open-endedness, the C/C++ array of characters model gives loopholes for people to tinker with data more easily. In Java, arrays are actually objects (just as strings are objects); so when you create an array, you are actually instancing an object of an array. And that is why, when you declare an array implicitly, you use the operator new.

Look at the following example in which you are initializing an array of five integer variables called group:

```
int group[] = new int[5];
```

> **NOTE**
>
> An alternative method of declaring the array group would be to put the brackets next to the keyword int as shown here:
>
> ```
> int[] group = new int[5];
> ```

You have initialized an array of five integer variables that can be accessed by reference to the number of the location of the variable in the brackets.

> **NOTE**
>
> Just as in C/C++, the index of the array here starts with 0. So, in the example of group, the first element would be located at position group[0] and the fifth and final location would be located at group[4].

The following is an example of how you place a value in the third element in the array:

```
group[2] = 10;
```

Another way to declare arrays is by declaring all the values of the array explicitly. Thus, all the values are placed into the array up front:

```
int collection[] = {1, 13, 29, 9};
```

As you can see, the preceding example of an array has four elements. The array was initialized, and it was given a variable.

In general, arrays are a very common and basic programming technique. In Java, you can have multidimensional arrays. The following show how you would declare a two-dimensional array implicitly and explicitly:

```
int multigroups[] = new int[10][20];
int multigroups[] = {{1,2}, {2,4}, {4, 8}};
```

Arrays—The Workshop

This example is more geared toward the last several sections that dealt with control flow statements, scope, and finally arrays. In this workshop you are going to use the computer science field of sorting to exemplify an array in Java.

NOTE

Bubble sort, also known as exchange sort, is a sorting algorithm that starts at the end of a list and moves all the way through the list comparing adjacent values, and swapping them if they are not in the correct corresponding order.

The sorting algorithm is called the bubble sort. In effect, what you are going to do is take an array that has been initialized with a fairly random set of values, call the method `bubbleSort()` to sort it, and then redisplay the sorted array (see Listing 7.18). The focus of this workshop is to give you a chance to get some hands-on experience in working with array objects in Java. In addition, you will have a chance to work with some of the control flow statements that were discussed earlier in the chapter.

Listing 7.18. The sorting algorithm.

```
public class sort {

    public static void main(String args[]) {
        // Declare the array explicitly with a set of random numbers
        int nums[] = {1, 8, 5, 2, 9, 19, 3, 7};

        int size = 8;  // the number of variables in the array

        System.out.println("Original values for the array.");
        // Loop through to print out the original values
        // for the array

        for (int i = 1; i < size; i++) {
            System.out.println(nums[i]);
        }

        //The actual sort algorithm
        int temp;  // temporary holding tank for variables.
```

```
      for (int i = 1; i < size; i++) {
         for(int j = size -1; j >= i; j--) {
            if(nums[j - 1] > nums[j]) {
               //if out of order exchange
               temp = nums[j - 1];
               nums[j-1] = nums[j];
               nums[j] = temp;
            }
         }
      }

      System.out.println("Sorted values for the array");
      //loop through and display the sorted array.
      for (int i = 0; i < size; i++) {
         System.out.println(nums[i]);
      }
   }
}
```

Look at the program and study it, especially the nest algorithm. Then compile and run it. If everything ran smoothly, you should have received the output shown in Listing 7.19.

Listing 7.19. Original values for the array.

```
8
5
2
9
19
3
7
Sorted values for the array
1
2
3
5
7
8
9
19
```

Now that you have run it and seen its outcome, go back to the code to study it. Follow it, as the compiler might, through various scenarios. Then experiment with different values for the array. Also try different array sizes and see what you get. Through this experimentation, all of the techniques that were explained in the preceding sections should come together for you.

The bubble sort algorithm is not the most efficient sorting algorithm in the world, but its simplicity and relative efficiency with smaller algorithms make it an excellent tool to help you understand sorting, control flow statements, and algorithms in general.

Summary

This chapter was specifically designed to give you a foundation of common understanding of the Java programming language. None of the programs focused very much on graphics in Java or the Internet. However, this chapter was a stepping stone to understanding the next chapter, which will in effect assume that all of the concepts in this chapter are understood.

Chapter 8, "Java Programming," gives you an opportunity to focus on the applet side of Java and how to develop real-life Java applets for the Internet.

Java Programming

by Dan Joshi

What makes Java such a powerful tool for Internet development? Can Java can be used outside of the Internet? The answer to both of these questions is yes. Java is a fully functional, object-oriented programming language. With new features included in it, Java has definitely defined a niche for itself on the Internet. This chapter describes Java in the Internet environment.

Every exercise in this chapter can also be used on a Java-compliant browser (such as Netscape 2.0 or later). More important, the topics described here include tables of methods and constants available to Java applets and programs. This chapter not only gives an introduction to Java applets, it also serves as a reference as you develop new applets. Note that due to the limited space and time, the tables include only the methods most useful to the programmer. Some methods are either not used or are rarely used by the programmer; these have been removed from the tables to keep only the most useful methods at your disposal. This chapter assumes that you have a complete understanding of the HTML environment and that you have a Java-compliant Netscape browser version 2.0 or higher. It also assumes that you are familiar with the basic Java structure and objects that you learn in Chapter 7, "Introduction to Java."

Java Applets

The first level that any Java programmer (or HTML programmer) needs to understand is how to put an applet in your HTML page. This is the first and often most frustrating major challenge for most people new to the Java environment. It is so frustrating primarily because it is simple, and the browsers are very forgiving when it comes to incorrect HTML code. You might not see an error message, but your applet still won't be loaded on the screen. Your first step is to design a sample HTML page. Assume that you have a newly created Java applet called `MyClass.class`. All of the HTML attributes pertaining to a Java applet must be placed between the `<APPLET>` and `</APPLET>` tags. The following segment of HTML code shows how to put the applet on the home page:

```
<APPLET CODE=MyClass.class WIDTH=300 HEIGHT=300>
</APPLET>
```

> **NOTE**
>
> A common mistake that new programmers make is forgetting to put the `</APPLET>` tag at the end of the applet section on their HTML page. Consequently, the browser does not load the applet. It is not always correct to assume that when an applet does not show up on the HTML page, there is a problem with the applet.

Note that in this case you must have the file `MyClass.class` in the same directory as the HTML file.

Java Applet Example

Next, you will develop a sample applet to learn how to use an applet on the Internet (and more specifically, on a Netscape browser). Listing 8.1, which appears on the accompanying CD, shows the first applet you will create, which says "Hello World." Create a file called `HelloWorldC.java` and type in Listing 8.1.

Listing 8.1. The "Hello World" program.

```
import java.awt.Graphics;

public class HelloWorldC extends java.applet.Applet {
    public void paint(Graphics g) {
        g.drawString("Hello World", 5, 50);
    }
}
```

Just to refresh your memory on how to compile programs using the Java Development Kit (JDK), make sure that the Java compiler and the `HelloWorldC.java` program are in the same directory. Then type the following:

```
javac HelloWorldC.java
```

The next step is to create an HTML file called `index.html`. Listing 8.2 shows you how your `index.html` file should look.

Listing 8.2. The `index.html` program.

```
<HTML>
<APPLET CODE=HelloWorldC.class WIDTH=200 HEIGHT=100>
</APPLET>
</HTML>
```

8

JAVA PROGRAMMING

NOTE

Probably the first thing to note about the HTML code in Listing 8.2 is the attribute CODE. This attribute is not optional. It passes the name of the Java applet file that will be loaded.

The final step is to put all the files in the same directory, load Netscape, and open the file `index.html` in the browser. Figure 8.1 shows you the output on your screen.

FIGURE 8.1.

The output of your first Java program.

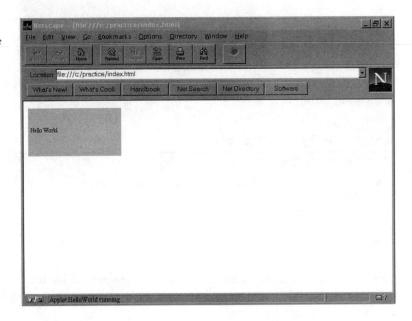

HTML Tags for Java Applets

Note that not all Internet travelers will have Java-compliant browsers, and for many professional sites it is important to have a site that will anticipate the capabilities of all the browsers that view the page. With that in mind, another HTML example with the fictitious applet MyClass.class follows. If the browser that loads this HTML page is not Java-compliant, the screen will display a comment to the users.

```
<APPLET CODE=MyClass.class WIDTH=300 HEIGHT=300>
It is time to upgrade your browser to a Java powered one. <P>
</APPLET>
```

In addition to that, an alt attribute can display a statement if the Internet surfer has a Java-compliant browser but for some other reason cannot view the applet. Technically, the alt attribute will be displayed if that browser understands the <APPLET> tag but still cannot view the applet. The following example uses alt with the applet MyClass.class:

```
<APPLET CODE=MyClass.class WIDTH=300 HEIGHT=300>
ALT= "Applet could not be loaded"
It is time to upgrade your browser to a Java powered one. <P>
</APPLET>
```

Other HTML code sets various display attributes for Java applets. Two attributes you have already used are the width and the height properties, which are fairly self-explanatory to the browser. By using these two attributes, you can set the size at which the Java applet will be displayed.

Also in this chapter, you have a chance to get hands-on experience in passing parameters from the HTML page to the Java applet. Imagine that the applet `MyClass.class` has a parameter of `color`. An example of how to pass `red` to the parameter of `color` in the HTML page follows:

```
<APPLET CODE=MyClass.class WIDTH=300 HEIGHT=300>
<PARAM NAME=Color VALUE="red">
ALT= "Applet could not be loaded"
It is time to upgrade your browser to a Java powered one. <P>
</APPLET>
```

NOTE

You can pass more than one parameter to an applet as long as the applet is programmed to accept them.

Another optional, yet very useful, attribute is `CODEBASE`. When you set the HTML site in Listing 8.2, you see that the class file and HTML file are in the same directory. In reality, Web sites with numerous files in them can become very confusing and unorganized when you throw everything into the root. You might want to create a special directory for your Java applets and use the `CODEBASE` to reference it. The `CODEBASE` accepts full and partial URLs.

NOTE

Uniform Resource Locator (URL) is what users specify to their Web browsers to connect to a particular document or resource. A Web browser can act as an FTP, Gopher, and Telnet client. Table 8.1 shows a breakdown of the URL, `http://home.netscape.com`.

Table 8.1. Anatomy of a URL.

URL part	Explanation
`http://`	Protocol
`home.`	Machine
`netscape.`	Network
`com`	Domain

The following code is an example of several possible formats for the attribute `CODEBASE`:

```
CODEBASE = "http://www.myserver.com/homepage/applets/MyClass.class"
CODEBASE = "http://www.myserver.com/homepage/applets/"
CODEBASE = "/applets/"
CODEBASE = "applet/"
```

8

JAVA
PROGRAMMING

Notice that the preceding examples point to the same relative location (www.myserver.com/ homepage/applets/MyClass.class). Extending the example of the HTML code for the fictitious class MyClass.class is another example of using CODEBASE:

```
<APPLET CODE=MyClass.class CODEBASE = "applet/" WIDTH=300 HEIGHT=300>
<PARAM NAME=Color VALUE="red">
ALT= "Applet could not be loaded"
It is time to upgrade your browser to a Java powered one. <P>
</APPLET>
```

In Netscape, you can also specify how to align the Java applet.

> **NOTE**
>
> The align attribute in the <APPLET> tag follows the same pretense as the align attribute in the <IMG> tag.

Table 8.2 shows the various states in which align can be and the meanings of those states as interpreted by the browser.

Table 8.2. Various align values.

Attribute	Explanation
align = texttop	Aligns the applet to the tallest text in the line.
align = top	Aligns to the top item in the line.
align = absmiddle	Aligns to the middle of the largest item in the line.
align = middle	Aligns the middle of the applet to the middle of the baseline.
align = baseline	Aligns with the baseline of the line.
align = bottom	Same as align = baseline.
align = absbottom	Aligns the bottom of the applet to the bottom of the line.

The last two parameters that you learn briefly are hspace, for horizontal space, and vspace, for vertical space. These attributes specify the amount of space (in pixels) between the applet and other elements in the HTML page. You will not use these attributes very often, so they aren't mentioned again in this chapter.

appletviewer

As time goes on, Java will have more proprietary environments in which to develop and test programs and applets, but this chapter uses the JDK 1.0.1 or the JDK 1.0, which is also compatible. If you do not have the JDK, you can download it from the following site:

```
http://java.sun.com/download.html
```

In Chapter 7, you used the Java interpreter (that is, `java.exe`) to work with your classes. However, the `HelloWorldC.class` applet is not designed to run through the Java interpreter because the method `main` is not defined.

> **NOTE**
>
> One major difference between Java applets and programs is that applets do not need the method `main` to load the applet on a Java-compliant browser.

The JDK comes with a program called the `appletviewer`, which lets you view Java applets. The syntax for using the `appletviewer` follows:

```
appletviewer URL
```

The URL stands for the file path and name for loading the HTML file. You use this handy tool to test and learn about the applets in the rest of this chapter. The following is an example of testing the `appletviewer` with your HTML page `index.html` from Listing 8.2:

```
appletviewer practice/index.html
```

My file `index.html` is located in the practice subdirectory of my computer, so what you type might be different if your file is in a different location. Regardless, your end result should be a window on your screen, as shown in Figure 8.2.

FIGURE 8.2.

Example of using the `appletviewer`.

Now that you have seen an introduction to the interaction between applets and browsers and the tools you will use (that is, the `appletviewer`) to test and develop your applications, you will learn about built-in classes. The first built-in class you learn is the `applet` object.

Applets (`java.applet.Applet`)

As mentioned in Chapter 5, "Java and the Internet," Java applets are slightly mutated Java programs. Now that you have enough understanding of Java and enough of an introduction to how Java interacts with the browser, you can appreciate exactly what mutations need to take place before you can call a Java program an applet. First, all applets are extended from a class called `java.applet.Applet`, which comes with the Java language.

> **NOTE**
>
> The root of every built-in Java class (and inherited user-defined Java class, for that matter) always has a root of java.*lang.Object*.

When you develop an applet, always start by extending your class from the java.applet.Applet class. Table 8.3 shows you a list of methods available to you from the Applet class.

Table 8.3. Methods of java.applet.Applet.

Method	Explanation
destroy()	A life cycle method that cleans up any resources that are still being held by the applet (the last life cycle method to be called).
getAudioClip(URL url)	Retrieves an audio clip.
getAudioClip(URL, String name)	An overloaded method that also enables you to specify the name of the audio clip you want to retrieve.
getCodeBase()	Returns a URL of where the applet resides.
getDocumentBase()	Returns the URL of the HTML page where the applet is embedded.
getImage(URL url)	Retrieves an image at the specified URL.
getImage(URL url, String name)	An overloaded method that also enables you to specify the name of the audio clip you want to retrieve.
getParameter(String name)	Returns a parameter from the HTML page in the form of a string.
getParameterInfo()	Returns an array of strings that enable you to retrieve more than one parameter to the applet.
init()	A life cycle method that initializes the object.
isActive()	Returns a Boolean response based on the evaluation of whether the applet is active.
play(URL, url)	Plays an audio clip.
play(URL url, String name)	An overloaded method that plays an audio clip.
resize(int width, int height)	Resizes the applet.
resize(Dimension d)	An overloaded method that also resizes the applet.
showStatus(String msg)	Prints a message on the appletviewer's status bar or a browser's panel.

Method	Explanation
start()	A life cycle method called to start the applet (this method is called after init()).
stop()	A life cycle method called to stop the applet.

You will not be able to work with all of the methods that are listed in Table 8.3, but this table should provide you with a reference. This section gives you a chance to work with some of the more frequently used methods in Table 8.3.

The Applet Life Cycle Discussion

Probably the easiest way to understand some of the important methods in the applet is to learn them in a little more detail and then use them in a real-life situation. First, you learn the applet life cycle (that is, the methods that constitute the applet life cycle). Figure 8.3 provides an overview of the applet life cycle.

FIGURE 8.3.
Drawing of the applet life cycle.

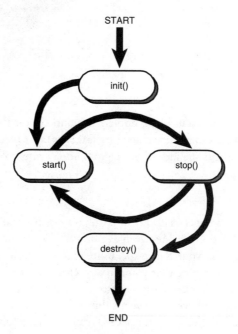

As shown in Figure 8.3, init() is the first method called when an applet is loaded. Use this method to get parameters and to initialize and prepare to officially start the applet. The next method, start(), starts the applet. The major difference between the init() and start() methods is that you can call the method start() again in the same life cycle. For example, when a client leaves the HTML page and then returns, the applet won't be discarded completely from memory, so the applet will simply restart, skipping the `init()` method and calling the `start()` method again. If the applet is completely destroyed, you will have to physically reload the applet again, which will start the life cycle all over again, initially calling `init()` again.

The `stop()` method is called when the user leaves the HTML page that contains the applet or if the applet is physically unloaded. In either case, the `stop()` method is always called. Like the relationship between `init()` and `start()`, `stop()` can be called more than once in one life cycle. The `destroy()` method is the last method called in the applet life cycle. This method causes the applet to clean up after itself by freeing any memory, resources, and so on.

When you work with the `appletviewer`, you can use the menu bar (see Figure 8.4) to perform several operations. The `appletviewer`'s menu bar has the commands Reload and Restart, which you can use to restart or reload your applet.

FIGURE 8.4.

The `appletviewer`
drop-down list of
commands.

Packaging

Now that you understand how applets live and die on the Internet continuum, let's briefly digress and discuss some new objects in `HelloWorldC.class` that you haven't officially learned. Listing 8.1 presents the idea of packaging. Look at the following line of code excerpted from Listing 8.1:

```
import java.awt.Graphics;
```

A *package* is a kind of class library in Java. Java organizes its built-in classes into packages based on common relationships between the objects. Your primary focus is to understand how to import packages to your classes (or, more precisely, how to import built-in classes that come with the JDK), but note that you can also create your own packages. In the preceding code, you import the object `Graphics` to your class. As with any type of class porting, the class itself must be declared public to receive maximum exposure to other classes. Another way you could port the class `Graphics` to your class `HelloWorldC.java` follows:

```
import java.awt.*;
```

> **NOTE**
>
> You can create your own packages by using the keyword package.

The asterisk in the preceding code has the same function as in any DOS-based environment, which means that it acts as a wildcard in Java to include all public classes and packages in this importation. At this point, you might ask yourself why you imported Graphics to the applet in the first place. The answer: Graphics is the base class for all graphic contexts in Java; you work with this abstract class in the coming sections. By importing that class, you were able to use the following method:

```
public void paint(Graphics g) {
```

You were able to use this method because it takes the object Graphics as an input object, which is why you need to import it into the program in Listing 8.1.

> **NOTE**
>
> When you use Java to display all kinds of things in your applet, the paint method is called. In order for you to paint just about anything on the screen, you need to override this method in your program. Think of it in terms of what the main method does for a Java application.

The Applet Life Cycle Workshop

Now that you have learned the applet object, its life cycles, and an introduction to drawing objects on the screen, let's compile a program to exemplify some of this material. Create a file called cycle.java and type in Listing 8.3.

> **NOTE**
>
> You are not required to override any of the life cycle methods. In fact, in Listing 8.1, the HelloWorldC.class applet did not need to use any of these methods. Later in the chapter, however, you work with animation, which gives you a chance to see these methods in action.

Listing 8.3. Applet life cycle.

```java
public class cycle extends java.applet.Applet {
    public void init() {

        // Display the this statement at the bottom of the Window
        showStatus("The applet is initializing...");

        // Pause for a period of time
        for (int i = 1; i < 1000000; i++);
    }
    public void start() {

        showStatus("The applet is starting...");

        for (int i = 1; i < 1000000; i++);
    }
    public void stop() {

        showStatus("The applet is stopping...");

        for(int i = 1; i < 1000000; i++);
    }

    public void destroy() {

        showStatus("The applet is being destroyed...");

        for(int i = 1; i < 1000000; i++);
    }
}
```

Only the showStatus method might be new to you. Table 8.3 shows that the showStatus method is located in the object java.applet.Applet, so this method is inherited from the object applet. Its primary function is to display text at the bottom of the window in the appletviewer or at the status bar on a Java-compliant browser.

In the same directory, create the HTML document cycle.html and type in Listing 8.4.

Listing 8.4. The cycle.html document listing.

```html
<applet code=cycle width=200 height=200>
</applet>
```

Now run the appletviewer and see what happens. Focus on the status bar at the bottom of the screen, which will display the stage of the applet in its life cycle. Then go to the menu bar applet, click Restart, and watch the status bar cycle through, stopping and destroying the applet. After that, click Reload and watch the status bar as the applet cycles through. Work with the Java applet in Listing 8.3 to better understand the applet life cycle.

Let's take a closer look at the method `paint` in `HelloWorldC.class` in Listing 8.1.

```java
public void paint(Graphics g) {
      g.drawString("Hello World", 5, 50);
   }
```

As you just learned, the `paint` method creates a `Graphics` object g. Therefore, for the duration of the method `paint`, you can use any of the methods from `Graphics` as long as you reference them to g. Looking at the preceding code, you see that you have done just that. Notice that `drawString` has three input parameters: The first is the string that actually will be printed, and the second and third parameters are the x and y coordinates on the applet pane where the text will be located. Figure 8.5 shows the Applet coordinate system. The origin is located at the top-left corner. In the method `drawString`, you specified the origin to be five units to the right of the y-axis origin, and, based on the third variable, you specified the origin to be 50 units down from the x-axis.

FIGURE 8.5.
The Applet coordinate system.

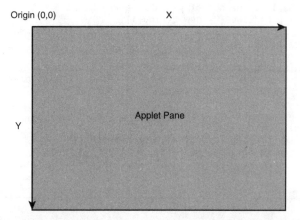

NOTE

The Java coordinate system is not similar to the Cartesian coordinate system by default (see Figure 8.4), but you can translate the origin using the method `translate` in the `java.awt.Graphics`.

The Logo Version 1.0

For the next several sections you will build and improve on a `logo` applet. Along the way you learn various methods, variables, and techniques that you can use in Java. Finally, you finish by building an applet that uses multiple threads.

Passing Parameters to the Applet

The best feature you can give to your HTML page is a logo. In this case, you will build a `logo` applet as part of the workshop, so let's discuss how to make the applet responsive to input from the browser by receiving parameters. As you remember from the previous section, you know how to build an HTML page to send a parameter to an applet. What you need to understand is how the applet can accept the parameter being passed, and you will do this by building your first version of the `logo` applet, which is shown in Listing 8.5.

Listing 8.5. The Logo version 1.0 revision 1.

```
// Logo version 1.0 rev

import java.awt.Graphics;

public class logo extends java.applet.Applet{
    // Declare the object variable array StrLine with 3 values.
    String StrLine[] = new String[1];

    public void init() {
        // Get the value for the
        String att = getParameter("Text");
        StrLine[0] = (att == null) ? "Please Enter Something
        in the parameter Text!" : att;
    }

    public void paint(Graphics g) {
        // Display the variable on the screen
        g.drawString(StrLine[0], 5, 50);
    }

}
```

As you can see in Listing 8.5, you are overriding one of the life cycle methods `init()` to accept parameters from the browser. The actual excerpted code of the overridden method follows:

```
// Get the value for the
        String att = getParameter("Text");
        StrLine[0] = (att == null) ? "Please Enter Something
in the parameter Text!" : att;
```

In the code in Listing 8.5, you see that the format to get a parameter relies on the fact that you are using a temporary variable (in this case, `att`) to accept input from the `getParameter` method that was made available to you from the class `java.applet.Applet` (see Table 8.3). The string inside the method `getParameter` specifies the default value if `att` comes back empty. The last line of code in this method exemplifies the use of the ternary operator (described in Chapter 7), and with it, you are able to test whether the `att` is `null` (that is, that no value was returned from the `getParameter` call). If the evaluation is `false`, then the default string `"Please Enter Something in the parameter Text!"` will be placed on the applet instead. If a value was returned from the call, then the evaluation will return `true`, and the value in the temporary variable will be passed on to the applet by passing it to the variable StrLine[0]. (An array is used because in later versions of this applet, you will accept more than one string.)

Referring to Listing 8.5, you see that the variable StrLine[0] is the drawString method's first input. Now the user will be able to input a variable in the HTML page and pass it to the applet (which in this case will eventually be passed to the drawString method and be printed on the applet). The advantage of passing parameters is that you can more easily customize your applet, and each time you might want to change the string, you will not need to recompile the Java applet.

> **NOTE**
>
> The format shown in Listing 8.5 for passing parameters to an applet is the standard used in some example applets that come with the JDK and is the same format that can be used to pass other types of parameters.

Your next step is to create your HTML page (see Listing 8.6) called logo.html.

Listing 8.6. The logo.html page.

```
<applet code=logo width=500 height=100>
<param name=Text value="Welcome to my Java powered page!">
</applet>
```

The last step is to run the appletviewer pointing to logo.html. If all goes well, your screen should be similar to Figure 8.6.

FIGURE 8.6.

The logo version 1.0, revision 1.

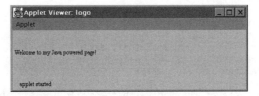

Go to the HTML page logo.html in Listing 8.6, and delete the line that passes the parameter to the applet as shown here:

```
<param name=Text value="Welcome to my Java powered page!">
```

Then execute the appletviewer again. Your screen should resemble Figure 8.7, which shows the appletviewer displaying the default string that was hard coded in your applet.

FIGURE 8.7.
The Logo *applet version
1.0, revision 1, with
the default output.*

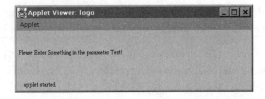

Fonts, FontMetrics, and Colors

The logo program definitely offers the customizing versatility that enables you to decide what to print in the applet. This section focuses on how to manipulate what is being printed on the screen by using Java's various font classes. To work with fonts, you need to understand the first and most basic font object in Java, the java.awt.Font class.

In the paint method, you can change the font attributes so that the Graphics object g will display your text in all shapes and sizes. Java naturally uses a Font object to handle the display and manipulation of text. For that reason, Listing 8.7 is a revised version of the Logo applet. Make the changes as shown in Listing 8.7.

Listing 8.7. The Logo version 1.0, revision 2.

```
// Logo version 1.0 rev

import java.awt.Graphics;
import java.awt.Font;

public class logo extends java.applet.Applet{
    // Declare the object variable array StrLine with 3 values.
    String StrLine[] = new String[1];

    //Declare the Font object called appFont.
    Font appFont;

    public void init() {
        // Get the value for the
        String att = getParameter("Text");
        StrLine[0] = (att == null) ? "Please Enter Something
in the parameter Text!" : att;

        //Construct the font with the following attributes:
        //                  Font        attrib      Size
        appFont = new Font("Helvetica", Font.BOLD, 28);

    }

    public void paint(Graphics g) {
        //Set the Font for object g
        g.setFont(appFont);
        // Display the variable on the screen
        g.drawString(StrLine[0], 5, 50);
    }

}
```

Listing 8.7 helps incorporate more methods in the class `java.awt.Graphics`. First notice that in Listing 8.7 you had to import the object `Font` to your class to use in this class. Also notice the following lines of code before the `init()` method:

```
//Declare the Font object called appFont.
Font appFont;
```

This declares that you can use an instance of `Font` called `appFont` by any method in the class `Logo`. The following shows the constructor of your font `appFont`:

```
//Construct the font with the following attributes:
//              Font        attrib      Size
appFont = new Font("Helvetica", Font.BOLD, 28);
```

In the preceding code, you are able to customize all the various types of fonts, sizes, and styles for your `appFont` object. The first input variable is a string with which you can specify the font you want to use. The following list shows all the fonts currently available for the `Font` object in Java:

- Dialog
- Helvetica
- TimesRoman
- Courier
- Symbol

The next input variable in the `Font` constructor is an input variable referenced by a constant (specifically, an integer). The following list shows all the available attributes for how you want the text in `appFont` displayed:

- BOLD
- ITALIC
- PLAIN

The third and final input variable is an integer that represents font size. The preceding lists, tables, and explanations can assist you in finding any font that you want to display in Java applets or programs.

Finally, the last new line of code that you should understand in Listing 8.7 follows:

```
//Set the Font for object g
g.setFont(appFont);
```

This piece of code from Listing 8.7 is located in the `paint` method and uses the built-in method of `setFont` that was given to you in `Graphics`. For the `Graphics` object g, you have set the font to the object of `appFont`. Now show your results on the screen. Compile the updated version of `Logo` in Listing 8.7. Use the same HTML page to display `Logo` that you used for the first version, located in Listing 8.6. The resulting output should look like Figure 8.8.

8

JAVA
PROGRAMMING

FIGURE 8.8.

The Logo *applet version 1.0, revision 2.*

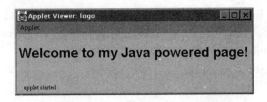

In Figure 8.8, the text in the applet stands out much more than in the original version of the Logo applet. Your next step when dealing with fonts is to introduce the class java.awt.FontMetrics. You can use this built-in class to give you information about the size attributes of the current font, and with that information you can better decide how to place text on varying sizes of windows and applets.

With java.awt.FontMetrics you can measure the current font and place it in the center of the applet. You will use the object FontMetrics in the next revision of the Logo applet.

The next class you need to learn is java.awt.Color. In Java, you can work with all colors, and as in any other development language, you have several methods strictly related to color manipulation. Because of Java's advanced object design, these variables and attributes are all housed in one object class called color. You can work with several constructors in the color object. The object color also follows the RGB format for applying color on the screen. Finally, the color class comes with a set of built-in variables with which you can specify the major colors.

Although most professional programs require exact colors (that is, you must specify an RGB value), for your program, you will use the built-in variables that define a set of standard colors. For example:

```
Color MyColor;
MyColor.red;
```

This piece of code specifies the standard color red without having to know any RGB values for the instance MyColor. The next revision to your logo class will be to create a dynamic algorithm to center the string on the screen based on the applet size (see Listing 8.8).

Listing 8.8. The Logo applet version 1.0, revision 3.

```
// Logo version 1.0 rev

import java.awt.Graphics;
import java.awt.Font;
import java.awt.FontMetrics;
import java.awt.Rectangle;
import java.awt.Color;

public class logo extends java.applet.Applet{
    // Declare the object variable array StrLine with 3 values.
    String StrLine[] = new String[1];
```

```
    //Declare the Font object called appFont.
    Font appFont;

    public void init() {
        // Get the value for the
        String att = getParameter("Text");
        StrLine[0] = (att == null) ? "Please Enter Something
in the parameter Text!" : att;

        //Construct the font with the following attributes:
        //              Font        attrib      Size
        appFont = new Font("Helvetica", Font.BOLD, 28);

    }

public void paint(Graphics g) {
        //Create an instance of the object FontMetrics called fm.
        FontMetrics fm;

        // Set the fonts metrics for the object g
        fm = g.getFontMetrics(appFont);

        // Create an instance of the object Rectangle and give it
        // the specs for the applet.
        Rectangle r = bounds();

        // Change the color of the graphics printed to red.
        g.setColor(Color.red);

        //Set the Font for object g
        g.setFont(appFont);

        // Display the variable on the screen with a dynamic setting
        // to ensure that it is centered on the applet.
        g.drawString(StrLine[0],  (r.width - fm.stringWidth(StrLine[0])) / 2,
  (r.height - fm.getHeight()) /2);
    }

}
```

The code in Listing 8.8 is the next revision for your logo applet. First, notice that you imported a few objects, some that you have not yet learned. Next, you created an instance of the FontMetrics class, and then used the instance fm to get the various specs for the font appFont:

```
// Set the fonts metrics for the object g
fm = g.getFontMetrics(appFont);
```

As you can see, you used the method getFontMetrics, which is available to you from java.awt.Graphics. With the preceding line of code, you can now use the methods contained in the class FontMetrics. With these methods, you can find the width and height of the text, which is crucial to aligning the text properly. The next line of code that you need to recognize and understand follows:

```
// Create an instance of the object Rectangle and give it
// the specs for the applet.
Rectangle r = bounds();
```

The preceding code includes a new object that you have not directly dealt with, the rectangle object. At this point, you are only using the rectangle object (more specifically, java.awt.Rectangle) to find the boundaries of your applet. Also you are using a method called bounds(), which comes from java.awt.Component, a very large object. Calling the bounds() method will retrieve the boundary of the applet in the form of a rectangle object. With that information, you can use the variables that come with the object rectangle, which are r.width and r.height (knowing the width and height of the applet is crucial to centering the text). The following is the code from Listing 8.8 that shows everything that you just learned:

```
g.drawString(StrLine[0], (r.width - fm.stringWidth(StrLine[0])) / 2,
(r.height - fm.getHeight()) /2);
```

Reviewing the preceding code, you are taking the total width of the applet (r.width) and subtracting that value from the total width of the text to be printed (fm.stringWidth(StrLine[0]), then dividing the resulting value to center the text in the applet. The text will remain in the center regardless of what size the text or applet pane becomes. The same process follows for the height, for which you use the variable r.height and the method fm.getHeight().

The final line of code you'll learn before you compile and run the program follows:

```
// Change the color of the graphics printed to red.
g.setColor(Color.red);
```

This code uses the method setColor from java.awt.Graphics. As mentioned earlier, instead of using the RGB format, you will simply use a built-in color variable that comes with the object java.awt.Color. The following list gives you all the built-in color variables:

black

blue

cyan

darkGray

gray

green

lightGray

magenta

orange

pink

red

white

yellow

Now that you have learned the new features of Logo revision 3 (see Listing 8.8), compile the applet. You will use the same HTML page that you used in Listing 8.6 to view this applet (see Figure 8.9).

FIGURE 8.9.

The Logo applet version 1.0, revision 3.

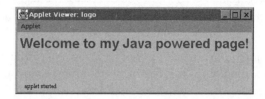

Now you will unleash the power of all that you've learned about centering text. With the applet loaded as in Figure 8.9, move your mouse to the border and the mouse pointer will change to a resize mouse icon. Change the size of the applet; the applet will call the paint method again, and the method will use the new information about the applet's size to fit the text in the middle of the applet. Figure 8.10 provides an example where the applet size was increased arbitrarily.

FIGURE 8.10.

The Logo applet version 1.0, revision 3, has been resized, yet the text still remains in the center of the applet.

8

JAVA PROGRAMMING

NOTE

If you look closely at Figures 8.9 and 8.10, you will notice that the vertical placement of the text appears to be off center. This is because the method bounds(), which was called to give the applet the boundaries, includes the menu bar and title bar as part of the height. When you measure for the height of the applet, make sure you include all elements of the page for the height.

Animation

Now that you have a well-developed background on how to display text in an applet, it is time to learn about animation and how you can take advantage of the multithreaded power of Java to build more dynamic applications. This will require a definition of animation, especially because it is one of the newest and fastest growing industries in the computer realm.

Before you jump into animating your Logo applet, start by understanding the theoretical aspects of animation. First, it is reasonable to assume that you do not have to be a film studies major to recognize the concepts behind how animation works. At a very basic level, animation is nothing more than a series of related frames (that is, pictures) that give the appearance of smooth, natural motion when shown in a particular order.

Another form of animation is moving a fixed object very slowly across a background while taking a series of pictures at regular intervals. When the pictures are played back, the object appears to be animated. No doubt these forms of animation are closely related. You already have an example of the first type of animation in the demo section of the JDK, which exemplifies how quickly you should project a series of well-timed frames to give the appearance of animation. Not only that, but you can customize the animation demo by using your own pictures. As a result, you can work with the demo applet with the JDK. Here, though, you will focus on the second form of animation. Your fixed object will be three lines of text in your Logo applet.

Animation in the PC Industry

The field of multimedia (animation in particular) is a fairly young technology. In fact, it is probably safe to say that if you were to go back about four years, the whole industry of PC multimedia would be virtually nonexistent. However, in this industry, time is definitely warped (more like warp 8), and now not only do you have full-blown multimedia, you also have completely interactive virtual worlds. One can only wonder about the future with technologies such as VRML, where Internet surfers will be able to interact with Web-based virtual worlds.

But back to animation. With the advent of multithreaded programming environments such as Java, you are bringing multimedia to a new level. In the not-too-distant past, PCs were showcased in a single-threaded environment, where running animation would stop all responsiveness from the computer as well as any other programs running in the background. Without the power of CPU, animation more than 100Mhz faced CPU time deprivation. There are two reasons for this: The CPU was simply not powerful enough to handle the computations involved, and the compression algorithms used on the animation itself were not as sophisticated as they are today (that is, not as efficient). As a result, the animation locked the system while displaying a piece of animation about one-eighth the size of the screen.

Time and technology have changed from that form of multimedia. Today, not only has animation improved, but programming languages such as Java have brought animation to the Internet.

> **NOTE**
>
> One element that makes Java such a powerful tool for programming multimedia is the fact that it is a multithreaded programming environment.

Animation Workshop

At the technical level, you will be creating an animation of text that will be displayed in an applet on the screen. One of Java's newer technologies is programming in multiple threads. (Refer to Chapter 5 for a high-level discussion on threads if you need to review.) With Java, the programmer can handle threads by using objects. More precisely, Java uses the `java.lang.Thread` object class.

In the Java programming format, you create an instance of the object `Thread` and implement the built-in interface `runnable`, resulting in overriding the method `run()`. The method `run()` is where the action code in your program will be placed. Update the `Logo` applet to incorporate the input, and use the three strings that will be animated (see Listing 8.9). Because this is a new version of the `logo` class and not just a revision, you will make a lot of changes to the original code to focus on only the topics discussed in this section. Create a new file `anilogo.java` and type in Listing 8.9.

8

JAVA PROGRAMMING

Listing 8.9. The aniLogo applet revision 1.

```
// aniLogo rev

import java.awt.*;

public class anilogo extends java.applet.Applet implements Runnable {
    Rectangle r;

    // Declare the object variable array StrLine with 3 values.
    String StrLine[] = new String[3];

    Font appFont;

    // Create a Thread object called myThread
    Thread myThread = null;

    // declare width array
    int width[] = new int[3];

    public void init() {

        // A for loop to find the three lines of text.
        for (int i = 0; i < 3; i++) {
            String att = getParameter("Text" + i);
            StrLine[i] = (att == null) ? ("Please put a parameter
in Text" + i) : att;
```

continues

Listing 8.9. continued

```java
        }

        appFont = new Font("Helvetica", Font.BOLD, 28);
        //Set r = to the bounds of the applet
        r = bounds();
    }

    // Override this method from the interface Runnable
    public void run() {
        //Set the current Threads priority.
        Thread.currentThread().setPriority(Thread.NORM_PRIORITY - 1);

        // Initialize the locations of the two lines of text to be
        // of the screen.
        width[1] = 2000;
        width[2] = 2000;
        repaint();

        // Algorithm to send the first line of Text across the screen.
        for ( int i = - 50; i < r.width/2; i += 7) {
            width[0] = i;
            repaint();
            // Rest
            Rest(1);
        }

        // Algorithm to send the second line of text across the screen.
        for (int i = r.width + 20; i > r.width/2; i -= 7) {
            width[1] = i;
            repaint();
            Rest(1);
        }

        //Algorithm to send the third line of text across the screen
        for ( int i = - 90; i < r.width/2; i += 7) {
            width[2] = i;
            repaint();
            // Rest
            Rest(1);
        }
    }

    void Rest(int r) {
        //Rest for a period of time
        try {
            myThread.sleep(100 * r);
        } catch (InterruptedException e) {
            return;
        }
    }

    public void start() {
        if (myThread == null) {
            myThread = new Thread(this);
            myThread.start();
        }
    }
```

```
    public void stop() {
        if (myThread != null) {
            myThread.stop();
            myThread = null;
        }
    }


    public void paint(Graphics g) {
        g.setColor(Color.red);

        g.setFont(appFont);

        for (int i = 0; i < 3; i++) {
            g.drawString(StrLine[i],  width[i] + (10 * i), 30 + (25 * i));
        }
    }

}
```

Listing 8.9 contains a lot of new material that you should go over. First notice that in the declaration of the applet, you are using the wildcard * to import a whole group of classes:

```
import java.awt.*;
```

Next, notice that you are implementing the interface of runnable in the applet:

```
public class anilogo extends java.applet.Applet implements Runnable {
```

As you can see in the compiled Java applet file anilogo.class in Listing 8.9, you have declared the arrays of strings to house your text. However, the line of code that is important to you is the following:

```
// Create a Thread object called myThread
    Thread myThread = null;
```

Here you declare the object myThread to be an instance of Thread, and you initialize it to be equal to null. The object myThread will be a key new feature in your applet. As you can see in the anilogo class, you made some changes to the life cycle method init(). In this version, the two important things that the method init() brings to the applet are the passing of three-string parameters from the HTML page and the specification of the rectangle r that was declared earlier to be equal to the bounds of the applet. The next excerpt of code that you learn follows:

```
// Overide this method from the interface Runnable
    public void run() {
        //Set the current Threads priority.
        Thread.currentThread().setPriority(Thread.NORM_PRIORITY - 1);
```

With the preceding code, you declare the method run() that was given to you in the interface runnable to be overridden. You will use the first lines of code inside this method to set the priority of the current object, using two methods, currentThread() and setPriority. currentThread() returns the currently running thread while with the method setPriority—which was also given to you from the class Thread—you can change the priority of the currently running thread. The priority you have set it to is NORM_PRIORITY -1. The NORM_PRIORITY constant comes with the object Thread. The following list shows the other available integer constants in addition to NORM_PRIORITY:

```
MAX_PRIORITY

MIN_PRIORITY

NORM_PRIORITY
```

By setting the currently running thread to a value of NORM_PRIORITY -1, you are one step below giving the currently running thread a normal priority. Farther along in the method, the next three for loops are used to loop through and update the integer array width. You start the applet by initializing the three values for the array to set the lines of text completely off the screen:

```
// Initialize the locations of the two lines of text to be
        // off the screen.
        width[1] = 2000;
        width[2] = 2000;
repaint();
```

The repaint() method comes from the java.awt.Component and completely clears and then repaints the screen by calling the paint method. Referencing the preceding code, you have now initialized the screen to be clear of everything. The next step is to learn the first for loop.

```
// Algorithm to send the first line of Text across the screen.
        for ( int i = - 50; i < r.width/2; i += 7) {
            width[0] = i;
            repaint();
            // Rest
            Rest(1);
        }
```

All you want to focus on right now in the preceding code is the fact that the integer i loops from -50 to the middle of the applet. Each time the integer loops, it updates the integer array width. Then it calls the repaint method, which is the program's queue to update the frame in the animation. Then the integer calls the method rest, which is a built-in method that pauses the thread for a period of time (you learn this later in the chapter). The other for loops are the same by design but different by implementation. The major difference between the first and second for loops is that the second has been reversed so that the line of text moves in from the right side of the screen. The third for loop updates the width of the third line of text; it is essentially the same as the first for loop in every other aspect. To help you tie everything together, look at the method paint.

```
public void paint(Graphics g) {
        g.setColor(Color.red);

        g.setFont(appFont);

        for (int i = 0; i < 3; i++) {
            g.drawString(StrLine[i],  width[i] + (10 * i), 30 + (25 * i));
        }
    }
```

In the preceding code, you see that the method paint has been changed from the previous version of the Logo applet by adding a for loop. This for loop will cause drawString to update all three lines of text. Each call from the repaint() method will update the three lines of text. The tricky part of the drawString method is that it has some abstruse statements for placing the x and y coordinates. Starting with the x coordinate, you have the statement width[i] + (10 * i). This code updates the location of the x coordinate for the applet. In the method run(), you have the same integer array variable width that is continually incremented with a new value. The (10 * i) gives the appearance of stepping. In other words, each line of text will be shifted a little farther to the right; in essence, that is how the animation will take place.

Exception Handling

Next, let's look at the Rest method and learn a little more about exception handling in the Java language.

```
void Rest(int r) {
        //Rest for a period of time
        try {
            myThread.sleep(100 * r);
        } catch (InterruptedException e) {
            return;
        }
    }
```

The preceding snippet of code has new keywords that deal specifically with exception handling. The method sleep will throw the exception InterrruptedException. Simply stated, when a method has a throwable exception (that is, InterrruptedException), the applet or method that calls the method must have a way to catch the exception that belongs to the method, which is done by using the keywords try and catch. Any code between try and catch will be executed. If an exception is raised during program execution of the block of code in try, the code in the block catch will be fired. In other words, the exception will be caught, and the block related to catch will handle the exception that was raised. The following is an example:

```
try {
    //Code that may throw an exception Exception
catch (Exception e) {
    //Code to handle the exception and/or display
    //messages e describing the exception that was
    //raised.
```

While you are on this topic, you need to learn about the keyword finally. The finally keyword specifies the block of code to be fired regardless of whether an exception was raised. The comments in the following code illustrates this:

```
try {
    //Code that may throw an exception Exception
catch (Exception e) {
    //Code to handle the exception and/or display
    //messages e describing the exception that was
    //raised.
```

8

JAVA
PROGRAMMING

```
finally {
    //Run some code here to clean up whether
    //an exception was raised or not
}
```

> **NOTE**
>
> You can catch only methods that have throwable exceptions declared in them (using the keyword throws). For example, in the anilogo applet in the class Thread, you use the method sleep to pause the applet. However, this method is declared to have a throwable exception InterruptedException:
>
> ```
> public static void sleep(long millisec,
> ➥int nanosec) throws InterruptedException
> ```
>
> Because this method is declared to throw InterruptedException, you are able to catch an exception with this method.

Now that you have briefly learned about exceptions in Java, let's continue with the explanation of the aniLogo code. Consider the following:

```
public void start() {
    if (myThread == null) {
        myThread = new Thread(this);
        myThread.start();
    }
}
```

In the preceding code, you have overridden another of the life cycle methods, start(). Very simply, this code performs an evaluation. If you find that the myThread thread is null, then you build a new thread by creating an instance of the thread. Part of the declaration includes a new keyword, this. The this keyword is a kind of object reference to the current thread. The keyword this is a read-only object variable. By using this special keyword, you can pass a reference of an object to itself or to another method.

The last method to discuss in the aniLogo example is the overridden life cycle method, stop, as shown in the following code:

```
public void stop() {
    if (myThread != null) {
        myThread.stop();
        myThread = null;
    }
}
```

In the stop() method, you are simply evaluating whether the object thread myThread has been made equal to null. If it has not, then you will use the method provided by Thread to stop the thread and set it equal to null.

A Summary of `anilogo`

Your final step is to update your HTML page `logo.html` (for a copy of `logo.html`, see Listing 8.6). Listing 8.10 is the updated HTML page that you will use with the `appletviewer` to exemplify your class `anilogo`.

Listing 8.10. The `logo.html` file.

```
<applet code=anilogo width=500 height=100>
<param name=Text0 value="The">
<param name=Text1 value="Widget">
<param name=Text2 value="Corp">
</applet>
```

Now that you have learned everything in the example applet, compile and run the applet. When the applet starts, nothing should be on the screen, and then the text should scroll across to the middle of the applet (see Figure 8.11).

FIGURE 8.11.

The `anilogo.java`
version 1.0, revision 1.

Optimizing Animation

In this section, you learn ways to make animation in Java more efficient. As you can tell from the applet `anilogo.class` in Listing 8.9, every time you make a change to one graphic, it repaints the entire applet pane, causing all the text (moving or not) to flicker because it is continually being redrawn. However, you can minimize the flickering that the applet undergoes every time the `repaint` method is called. So that the applet doesn't repaint the entire screen every time it needs to update the screen, you will use an overloaded method of `repaint` to enable you to input four points on the applet, specifying a rectangle. Only graphics inside that rectangle will be updated. The format for using the overloaded method `repaint` with four input variables follows:

```
//Repaints  starting point extending the length and width specified.
   repaint(int x, int y, int width, int height)
```

With that in mind, create a revision to your applet `anilogo.class` (see Listing 8.11).

Listing 8.11. The AniLogo applet, revision 2.

```java
// aniLogo rev

import java.awt.*;

public class anilogo extends java.applet.Applet implements Runnable {
    Rectangle r;
    // Declare the object variable array StrLine with 3 values.
    String StrLine[] = new String[3];

    Font appFont;

    // Create a Thread object called myThread
    Thread myThread = null;

    // declare width array
    int width[] = new int[3];

    public void init() {

        // A for loop to find the three lines of text.
        for (int i = 0; i < 3; i++) {
            String att = getParameter("Text" + i);
            StrLine[i] = (att == null) ? ("Please put a parameter in
            ➥Text" + i) : att;

        }

        appFont = new Font("Helvetica", Font.BOLD, 28);
        r = bounds();

    }

    // Overide this method from the interface Runnable
    public void run() {
        //Set the current Threads priority.
        Thread.currentThread().setPriority(Thread.NORM_PRIORITY - 1);

        // Initialize the locations of the two lines of text to be
        // off the screen.
        width[1] = 2000;
        width[2] = 2000;
        // Repaint the entire screen
        repaint();

        // Algorithm to send the first line of Text across the screen.
        for ( int i = - 50; i < r.width/2; i += 7) {
            width[0] = i;
            // repaint the entire screen since this is the first line
            // of text currently being drawn.
            repaint();
            // Rest
            Rest(1);
        }

        // Algorithm to send the second line of text across the screen.
        for (int i = r.width + 20; i > r.width/2; i -= 7) {
```

```
            width[1] = i;
            // repaint only part of the screen where line two resides
            repaint(0, 30, r.width, 35);
            Rest(1);
        }

        //Algorithm to send the third line of text across the screen
        for ( int i = - 90; i < r.width/2; i += 7) {
            width[2] = i;
            // repaint only part of the screen where line three resides
            repaint(0, 60, r.width, 30);
            // Rest
            Rest(1);
        }

    }

    void Rest(int r) {
        //Rest for a period of time
        try {
            myThread.sleep(100 * r);
        } catch (InterruptedException e) {
            return;
        }
    }

    public void start() {
        if (myThread == null) {
            myThread = new Thread(this);
            myThread.start();
        }
    }

    public void stop() {
        if (myThread != null) {
            myThread.stop();
            myThread = null;
        }
    }

    public void paint(Graphics g) {
        g.setColor(Color.red);

        g.setFont(appFont);

        for (int i = 0; i < 3; i++) {
            g.drawString(StrLine[i],  width[i] + (10 * i), 30 + (25 * i));
        }
    }

}
```

As you can see in Listing 8.11, the only changes you made were changing the repaint method in the second and third for loops. The following excerpt shows the code that was changed inside the first for loop:

```
// repaint only part of the screen where line two resides
          repaint(0, 30, r.width, 35);
```

The preceding code shows that you have specified a rectangle that is the width of the applet, only the height of the second line of text, and placed exactly where line two is located. The changes for the third line of text follow:

```
// repaint only part of the screen where line three resides
          repaint(0, 60, r.width, 30);
```

Compile this new revision of the applet `anilogo.java`, and you can use the same HTML site `logo.html` to run the new applet. The end result will look the same as Figure 8.11, but the animation will appear to be much smoother. Performing little tricks like this will make your applet better than the rest.

UI and Java

This section describes the ins and outs of designing a user interface (UI) in Java. You will be working with many built-in classes in Java, and you will have a chance to work with the functionality that comes with using Java in UI applications on the Internet. There are many figures to give you plenty of examples of front-end work in Java.

Command Buttons

No doubt the first place you need to start is with the command button. The command button is a button on the computer screen that, when pushed, will fire code. A line of code that initializes a command button in Java follows:

```
Button mycommand = new Button("OK");
```

The preceding constructor creates a command button with the label OK. Table 8.4 provides an index of all available methods for the object `java.awt.Button`. Figure 8.12 shows how a command button looks.

FIGURE 8.12.

A command button.

Table 8.4. The `java.awt.Button` methods.

Method	Explanation
getLabel()	Returns a string containing the label of the button.
setLabel(String name)	Sets the label for the button using the input variable name.

Check Boxes

Check boxes set a statement of `true` or `false`, typically based on user preference. Check boxes are best implemented when the user can toggle an option on or off. An example of how to declare a check box follows:

```
Chekbox mycheck = new Checkbox("Checkbox");
add(mycheck);
```

Table 8.5 lists all the currently available methods for the Java object `java.awt.Checkbox`. Figure 8.13 shows how a check box looks in Java.

Table 8.5. The `java.awt.Checkbox` methods.

Method	Explanation
getCheckboxGroup()	Returns the group to which this check box belongs in the form of the object CheckboxGroup.
getLabel()	Returns a string containing the label of this check box.
getState()	Returns a Boolean value representing whether the check box is checked (that is, `true` or `false`).
setCheckboxGroup(CheckboxGroup g)	Changes the CheckboxGroup to which this check box belongs to the specified CheckboxGroup.
setLabel(String)	Sets this check box's label.
setState(boolean state)	Changes the state of this check box to the specified state.

8

JAVA PROGRAMMING

NOTE

The default value for a check box is `false`.

FIGURE 8.13.
The check box.

Check Box Groups

Table 8.5 in the Checkbox class shows several of the methods that deal with the class CheckboxGroup. A CheckboxGroup is a group of check boxes that are grouped. The CheckboxGroup class enables you to associate several check boxes with only one check box that has the ability to be true (that is, checked) at any one time. For example:

```
CheckboxGroup colors = new CheckboxGroup();
```

With the constructor in the class Checkbox, you can specify the group and the state for the check box. This is good when there is a finite number of options but only one option that can be active at any one time. The following is the declaration of three colors between which you will be able to toggle:

```
Checkbox chboxRed = new Checkbox("Red", colors, false);
Checkbox chboxBlue = new Checkbox("Blue", colors, false);
Checkbox chboxGreen = new Checkbox("Green", colors, true)
add(chboxRed);
add(chboxBlue);
add(chboxGreen);
```

In the preceding code, you created three check boxes. Figure 8.14 shows how this looks in Java. Note that only one is toggled true. Also notice that their appearance is slightly different than traditional check boxes.

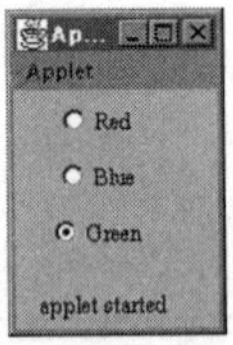

FIGURE 8.14.

Check box groups.

> ## NOTE
>
> The only two constructors (besides the default) for creating a check box follow:
>
> ```
> Checkbox chbox1 = new Checkbox("MyCheckbox");
> Checkbox chbox2 = new Checkbox("Another Checkbox", mygroup, true);
> ```
>
> If you want to create a check box that is not part of a group but would automatically toggle to true at startup, use the setState method to change the state of the check box when you construct it. Another way is to construct a check box using the second constructor format but specifying the group to be null:
>
> ```
> Checkbox chbox3 = new Checkbox("Label", null, true);
> ```
>
> This will construct a check box that is not related to any group and that will default to a value of true.

Choice

With the Choice component, also known as a combo box in other programming languages, you can create a drop-down list of items from which the user can choose. The Choice component doesn't take up as much space as a list, though, because it can hide its drop-down list. The following code illustrates the only other constructor for the Choice object:

```
Choice c = new Choice();
```

After you have created a Choice, you will need to populate it with a list of choices. A Choice cannot be populated when it is constructed; it must be populated afterward, using the method addItem in Table 8.6. An example of how to populate a Choice using the method in addItem follows:

```
c.addItem("Windows NT");
c.addItem("Windows 95");
c.addItem("Mac");
c.addItem("Unix");
add[c];
```

This code populates the Choice menu c that you constructed earlier. Figure 8.15 shows how the Choice box looks in the Java environment, based on the preceding code. The box on the right in Figure 8.15 shows the Choice open, exposing its drop-down list.

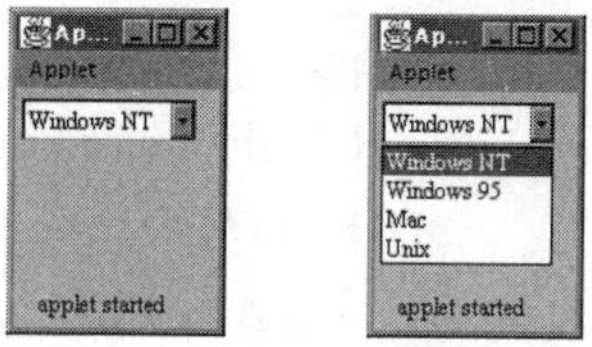

FIGURE 8.15.

The left figure shows the Choice box closed. The right figure shows the Choice box open.

Table 8.6. The java.awt.Choice methods.

Method	Explanation
addItem(String item)	Adds an item to this Choice.
countItems()	Returns the number of items in this Choice.
getItem(int index)	Returns a string that represents the specified index value in this Choice.
getSelectedIndex()	Returns an integer value representing the index of the currently selected item.
getSelectedItem()	Returns a string that represents the currently selected item in this Choice.
select(int index)	Selects the item in this Choice based on the integer value specified.
select(String value)	An overloaded method that selects the item in this Choice based on the string specified.

8

JAVA PROGRAMMING

Labels

Labels are strings of text displayed on the screen. Labels are like using the drawString method, but you can attach labels to other UI components and put them in containers, resulting in a much more versatile user interface. Two ways to construct labels follow:

```
Label l = new Label("Hello World");
Label l2 = new Label ("Hello again", Label.LEFT);
```

You can construct a label by including an input for the text that will be printed on the applet screen or by introducing another variable to accept an integer type to specify the alignment of the label, as shown in the following list:

CENTER   Specifies the center alignment (integer value of 0).

LEFT   Specifies the left alignment (integer value of 1).

RIGHT   Specifies the right alignment (integer value of 2).

Table 8.7 also lists all of the available methods for the class java.awt.Label. To see a Java label, look at Figure 8.16.

Table 8.7. The java.awt.Label methods.

Method	Explanation
getAlignment()	Returns an integer specifying the alignment for this label (see the preceding discussion of alignment options).
getText()	Returns a string specifying the label.
setAlignment(int align)	Sets the alignment for this label based on the integer value (see the preceding discussion of alignment options) for this label.
setText(String label)	Changes the text to be displayed for this label based on the specified string.

FIGURE 8.16.

*An example of a label displaying "*Hello World.*"*

Lists

Lists, also known as list boxes, are designed to display a list of items in a scrolling format. Lists function similarly to Choice, though in this case, the list always works as a drop-down menu. Although Choice takes up less space and provides the same function as the list, you can configure the list object to have more than one selection in one box. If you have a list of choices and want the user to choose more than one item at a time, implementing a list is your best bet. The following code shows the format for constructing a list:

```
List mylist = new List(5, true);
```

In this syntax, the first input variable for this constructor accepts an integer that specifies the number of rows that should be shown in this list. The second input is a Boolean value that toggles whether this list should support multiple selections. Table 8.8 breaks down the available methods for the object `java.awt.List`. Using the following code as a guide, add items to your list that correspond to the Choice using the method `addItem` in Table 8.8:

```
mylist.addItem("CD-ROM");
mylist.addItem("Sound Card");
mylist.addItem("modem");
mylist.addItem("SCSI controller");
mylist.addItem("E-IDE controller");
mylist.addItem("8 MB RAM");
mylist.addItem("16 MB RAM");
mylist.addItem("32 MB RAM");
add(mylist);
```

Figure 8.17 shows how this list would look in the Java environment.

FIGURE 8.17.

An example of `java.awt.List` *with more than one item selected.*

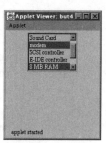

Table 8.8. The `java.awt.List` methods.

Method	Explanation
`addItem(String item)`	Adds to the end of this list the string specified.
`addItem(String item, int index)`	An overloaded method that adds the string to this list based on specifying the location and passing the integer value.
`allowsMultipleSelections()`	Returns a Boolean value representing whether this list can have multiple selections.
`clear()`	Clears the list.
`countItems()`	Returns an integer value representing the number of items in this list.

continues

Table 8.8. continued

Method	Explanation
delItem(int index)	Removes the item specified by the integer value being passed from the list.
delItems(int startIndex, int endIndex)	An overloaded method with which you can specify multiple deletions from this list.
deselect(int index)	Deselects the item at the specified location.
getItem(int index)	Returns a string representing the item that was selected based on the integer value specified.
getRows()	Returns an integer value representing the number of lines visible in this list.
getSelectedIndex()	Returns an integer value representing the selected item (-1 if no item was selected).
getSelectedIndexs()	An overloaded method that returns an array of integers representing the selected items for this list.
getSelectedItem()	Returns a string containing the selected item.
getSelectedItems()	An overloaded method that returns an array of strings that contains all of the selected items in this list.
getVisibleIndex()	Returns an integer representing the index value for the last item that was made visible by the method makeVisible.
isSelected(int index)	Returns a Boolean value based on whether the specified item is selected.
makeVisible(int index)	Makes the specified item visible.
minimumSize()	Returns the object dimension that contains the minimum dimensions needed for this list.
minimumSize(int numofRows)	An overloaded method that returns the object dimension that holds the minimum dimensions needed for a list with the specified number of items.
paramString()	Returns a string that contains the parameter of this list.
preferredSize()	Returns the object dimension that holds the preferred dimensions needed for this list.

Method	Explanation
`preferredSize(int numofRows)`	An overloaded method that returns the object dimension that holds the preferred dimensions needed for this list, with the specified number of rows.
`replaceItem(string, int)`	Replaces the item at the specified location with the specified string.
`select(int index)`	Selects the item at the specified location.
`setMulipleSelections(boolean bool)`	Changes whether this list should allow multiple selections based on the value for the Boolean value being passed.

Scrollbars

A *scrollbar* is a horizontal or vertical object that enables the user to scroll through a set of pre-determined values. The type of scrollbar talked about in this section is typically used in a stand-alone format. You can construct scrollbars in several ways; one format follows:

```
Scrollbar myscroll1 = new Scrollbar(Scrollbar.HORIZONTAL);
```

The scrollbar accepts one input value, which is an integer constant that specifies one of two states: `horizontal` or `vertical`. Another more recondite constructor for the scrollbar follows:

```
//                              orientation, default value,
paging area, min, max
Scrollbar myscroll2 = new Scrollbar(Scrollbar.VERTICAL, 50, 5, 1, 100);
```

In the preceding constructor, five integer parameters specify the following, in this order: orientation (that is, `vertical` or `horizontal`), which is the default value for the scrollbar; incremental and decremental size, for when the user clicks on the paging area (that is, the area between the thumb and arrows); and the last two input variables specify the minimum and maximum values for the entire scrollbar (1 and 100 in the preceding example). See a sample of the scrollbar in Figure 8.18. Also for reference, see Table 8.9 for a list of methods that come with `java.awt.Scrollbar`.

FIGURE 8.18.

An example of `java.awt.Scrollbar`.

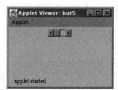

Table 8.9. The `java.awt.Scrollbar` methods.

Method	Explanation
`getLineIncrement()`	Returns an integer value for the increment of the scrollbar.
`getMaximum()`	Returns an integer that represents the maximum value for the scrollbar.
`getMinimum()`	Returns an integer that represents the minimum value for the scrollbar.
`getOrientation()`	Returns an integer value representing the scrollbar's orientation.
`getPageIncrement()`	Returns an integer value for the page increment (or decrement) of the scrollbar. This value is fired when the user clicks the area between the thumb and arrows.
`getValue()`	Returns an integer representation for the value of the scrollbar.
`getVisible()`	Returns an integer representation that represents the visible amount of the scrollbar.
`setLineIncrement(int value)`	Sets the line increment (or decrement) for the scrollbar when using the arrows.
`setPageIncrement(int value)`	Changes the page increment (or decrement) for the scrollbar. This value is fired when the user clicks the area between the thumb and arrows.
`setValue(int value)`	Sets the value of this scrollbar to the specified value.
`setValues(int value, int visible, int minimum, int maximum)`	Changes the values for the scrollbar to those specified.

Text Fields

A text field is a class that represents an area into which the user can enter data. Think of a text field as a label you can edit and design to accept data input. With a text field, you have a maximum of one row to enter information. The width of that row is determined by the number of columns you assign it, as shown in the following listing:

```
TextField myfield = new TextField(20);
TextField myfield = new TextField("This is my TextField!");
TextField myfield = new TextField ("This is my TextField!", 20);
```

As you can see in the preceding examples, you construct a TextField in three different ways. The first input specifies the number of columns that this text field can have, the second constructor example constructs a text field with the specified string as default text to be typed in it, and the third constructor shows how to implement a combination of the first two constructs for maximum extendibility. Table 8.10 shows a list of available methods for the class java.awt.TextField, and Figure 8.19 shows an example of a text field.

Table 8.10. The java.awt.TextField methods.

Method	*Explanation*
echoCharIsSet()	Returns a Boolean value based on whether the text field is set for echoing.
getColumns()	Returns an integer that represents the number of columns in the text field.
getEchoChar()	Returns the character that is echoing for the text field.
minimumSize()	Returns the object dimension that contains the minimum dimensions for the text field.
minimumSize(int cols)	An overloaded method that returns the object dimension that contains the minimum dimensions for a text field with the specified number of columns.
preferredSize()	Returns the object dimension that contains the preferred dimensions for the text field.
preferredSize(int cols)	An overloaded method that returns the object dimension that contains the dimensions for a text field with the specified number of columns.
setEchoCharacter(char c)	Changes the echo character for the text field.

NOTE

Table 8.10 lists several methods that mention echoing characters. With echoing characters, you can build TextField objects that will not show what the user prints in them. Instead, a specified character will print (or in this case, echo) to represent a placeholder for what the user really typed. Probably the most common example of an echoed TextField is the text field in which you type your password when you are at a login prompt in a Windows interface.

FIGURE 8.19.

An example of a text field.

Text Areas

A text area is another form of TextField that enables user input. The only difference is that a text area can have more than one row for inputting information. You can use three constructors to create a text area; see the following listing:

```
//First                   rows, cols
TextArea t = new TextArea(10, 50);
//Second                       String to put in TextArea
TextArea t2 = new TextArea("This is my TextArea!");
//Third                      String to put in TxtArea, rows, cols
TextArea t3 = new TextArea("This is my TextArea!", 20, 50);

add(t1);
add(t2);
add(t3);
```

With these three constructors for TextArea, you have the flexibility to create a text area best suited to your needs. In fact, the constructs for TextArea are fairly similar to those for TextField except that in a TextArea, one more input variable specifies the number of rows. Table 8.11 lists all the methods available to the object java.awt.TextArea.

Table 8.11. The java.awt.TextArea methods.

Method	Explanation
appendText(String text)	Adds the specified text to the end.
getColumns()	Returns an integer that represents the number of columns in the text area.
getRows()	Returns an integer that represents the number of rows in the text area.
insertText(String text, int pos)	Inserts the specified text at the specified point.
minimumSize()	Returns the object dimension that contains the minimum dimensions for the text area.
minimumSize(int rows, int cols)	An overloaded method that returns the object paramString().

Method	Explanation
preferredSize()	Returns the object dimension that contains the preferred dimensions for the text area.
preferredSize(int rows, int cols)	An overloaded method that returns the object dimension that contains the TextArea dimensions with the specified number of columns.
replaceText(String text, int start, int end)	Replaces text from the indicated start to end position, specifying the new text.

Figure 8.20 shows an example of a text area with the words This is my TextArea! displayed on the screen.

FIGURE 8.20.

An example of TextArea.

NOTE

All of the UI components that you have learned have a default constructor that hasn't been shown. This default constructor accepts no parameters. For example:

```
Button b = new Button();
```

Putting Components in Containers

One new feature that really helps to make Java shine is its interface called LayoutManager. With this, you can structure components relative to other components in the applet, providing the most flexibility especially because it is very hard to anticipate all the screen formats for all of the environments on which users could potentially run your applet. You can use several layouts when you develop UIs. When you are dealing with any of the UI components discussed in the last section, you will need to form some structure to define how to put them on the screen. The paradigm behind the LayoutManager is that it implements containers into which to put your UI components. In Java, you cannot specify a pixel-by-pixel coordinate to place a UI component on the screen simply because different types of screens and environments will use this same program. Instead, Java utilizes containers, which are built-in objects that hold the UI components in a relative format. You learn four containers in this section, `BorderLayout`, `CardLayout`, `FlowLayout`, and `GridLayout`.

BorderLayout

Use the first container, `BorderLayout`, as a base container for setting up user interfaces. The logic behind the `BorderLayout` format is that UI components are described in terms of geographical locations on the applet (that is, `"North"`, `"South"`, `"East"`, `"West"`, and `"Center"`). See the following listing:

```
//  Location,  constructor for UI object
add("North", new Button("OK"));
```

The end result in using `BorderLayout` is that it orients UI components on relative geographical locations in the container.

CardLayout

The second container, `CardLayout`, is different from any of the other layout objects because it is the only container that does not show all the UI components on the screen at any one time. An easy way to understand `CardLayout` is to think of a stack of cards. Only one is on top at any one time, though many others that you can call to the top (that is, show) are underneath.

FlowLayout

The `FlowLayout` container is the easiest to use. As this container displays information, it acts as a typewriter moving left to right, laying out UI components until it runs to the border of the container, and then simply continues on the left side of the next line. The `FlowLayout` wraps the UI components around the container. The following listing provides an example of how to declare and use the `FlowLayout`:

```
setLayout(new FlowLayout());
TextField f = new TextField("My Field", 20);
add(f);
```

Looking at the preceding code, the `setLayout` method is what you use to set the type of layout. The next line constructs your components (in this case, a text field), and the last line adds it using the `add()` method. Note that both `setLayout` and `add` come from the `java.awt.Component` class.

Table 8.12 shows a list of the available methods for `FlowLayout`.

Table 8.12. The java.awt.FlowLayout methods.

Method	Explanation
layoutContainer(Container)	Lays out the container.
minimumLayoutSize(Container comp)	Returns the object Dimension that contains the minimum dimensions for the container.
preferredLayoutSize(Container comp)	Returns the object Dimension that contains the preferred dimensions for the container.
toString()	Returns a string of the FlowLayout's values.

GridLayout

Only with the container GridLayout will you have the most control over placing your components. When you construct a GridLayout, you specify rows and columns in which to place your UI components. You can build a GridLayout that will have three components on each row for five rows. The following code provides one way to construct a GridLayout, where you will place two components on two lines:

```
// Construct a GridLayout with 2 cols and 2 rows.
setLayout(new GridLayout(2, 2));
// Components to be placed on the first row
add(new Label("First"));
add(new TextField(10));

// Components to be placed on the second row
add(new Button("OK"));
add(new Button("Cancel"));
```

The UI and Java Workshop, Win Version 1.0

In this section you create the first version of a UI program. Although you won't be able to build every component you learn in this section, at least you will have an opportunity to work with a few of them to appreciate the general structure of how all UI components are used in Java. Create a file called Win.java and enter the code from Listing 8.12.

Listing 8.12. Win version 1.0, revision 1.

```
// Win version 1.0 rev

import java.awt.*;

public class Win extends java.applet.Applet {
    public void init() {
        // Set the Layout to FlowLayout
        setLayout(new FlowLayout(FlowLayout.CENTER, 10, 10));
```

continues

Listing 8.12. continued

```
        // Add a Label and a Button
        add( new Label("Please press the button below:"));
        Button show = new Button("Show Window");
        add(show);
    }
}
```

Notice a couple of things about this applet, beginning with the following line of code:

```
setLayout(new FlowLayout(FlowLayout.CENTER, 10, 10));
```

This line of code centers each UI component on the screen. You can also specify two other variables, `left` and `right`. The second and third input variables will put 10 horizontal and vertical spaces between each component. Now create your HTML page, call it `Windows.html`, and type in the HTML code from Listing 8.13.

Listing 8.13. The `Windows.html` file.

```
<applet code=Win width=200 height=100>
</applet>
```

Now compile and run the applet through the `appletviewer` and you should see Figure 8.21.

However, if you click on the button in Figure 8.21, you see that nothing happens because you do not have code to handle any event for the action in this applet. Also, you do not have code under the button to create a Java window. You learn these topics as well as see an improved version of the `Win` applet in the next section.

FIGURE 8.21.

Show version 1.0.

> **NOTE**
>
> A new frame or dialog box is always invisible until you call the method `show()`.

Frames

As in any Windows-type environment, you might need to display a separate window to present information to the user. Java recognizes that need and has a built-in class that enables you to create a separate window quite painlessly. With this class, java.awt.Frame (see Table 8.13), you can create a separate window (or, more precisely, frame). Like almost everything else you have constructed in this chapter, you can create a frame by using the new operator to construct an instance of it; see the following:

```
Frame myframe = new(Frame("WELCOME TO MY JAVA WINDOW!"));
```

The preceding code constructs myFrame to have a label of "WELCOME TO MY JAVA WINDOW!".

Table 8.13. The java.awt.Frame class.

dispose()	Removes and frees any resources used by the frame.
getCursorType()	Returns an integer that represents the frame's cursor.
getIconImage()	Returns the object image that represents the icon image for the frame.
getMenuBar()	Returns the object MenuBar that represents the frame's menu bar.
getTitle()	Returns a string that represents the title for the frame.
isResizable()	Returns a Boolean value based on whether the frame is resizable.
remove(MenuComponent menu)	Removes the specified menu bar from the frame.
setCursor(int cursorType)	Sets the cursor for the frame to the specified integer constant that represents a set of predefined cursor types.
setIconImage(Image icon)	Sets the image icon for the frame.
setMenuBar(MenuBar menub)	Sets the Menubar for the frame based on the specified menu bar.
setResizable(boolean resizable)	Sets the resizablity of the frame based on the specified Boolean.
setTitle(String title)	Sets the title for the frame based on the specified string.

8

JAVA
PROGRAMMING

Figure 8.22 shows how a frame looks.

As you can see in Figure 8.22, nothing is in the frame. Also notice the yellow status bar at the bottom that displays the security level for this frame. Because Netscape has the most stringent level of security on Java, the screen displays something to the effect of "Untrusted Applet Window."

FIGURE 8.22.

An example of `java.awt.Frame.`

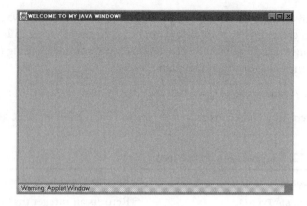

Frames Workshop

In this final workshop, you will make an improvement to the Win applet that you created earlier. First, see Listing 8.14 to make the appropriate changes to Win.java.

Listing 8.14. Win version 2.0, revision 1.

```
// Windows version 2.0 rev

import java.awt.*;

public class Win extends java.applet.Applet {
    Frame myFrame = new Frame();

    public void init() {

        // Setup for the applet
        setLayout(new FlowLayout(FlowLayout.CENTER, 10, 10));

        add( new Label("Please press the button below:"));
        Button show = new Button("Show Window");
        add(show);
        add( new Button("Close Window"));

        // Setup info for the Frame
        myFrame.setLayout(new FlowLayout(FlowLayout.LEFT, 10, 10));
        myFrame.setTitle("Welcome to My First Window!");
        myFrame.add(new Label("Please Enter your name in the test box:"));
        TextField textName = new TextField(40);
        myFrame.add(textName);
    }
```

```
    public boolean action(Event e, Object arg) {
          if (((Button)e.target).getLabel() == "Close Window") {
              myFrame.dispose();
          }   else if (((Button)e.target).getLabel() == "Show Window") {
              myFrame.show();
              myFrame.resize(300, 175);
          }
          // Return required at the end of this method
          return true;
    }
}
```

Now that you have updated your program, look at the code in Listing 8.14 to understand what changes you have made and why. First notice that you imported the object event. The action method needs the object java.awt.Event to handle events (such as a mouse click). In Java, action is a method that will be called any time one of the components (for example, text area) is the focus of an event. The following excerpt of code shows the action method:

```
public boolean action(Event e, Object arg) {
          if (((Button)e.target).getLabel() == "Close Window") {
              myFrame.dispose();
          }   else if (((Button)e.target).getLabel() == "Show Window") {
              myFrame.show();
              myFrame.resize(300, 175);
          }
          // Return required at the end of this method
          return true;
    }
```

In the preceding code, you are checking your if statement to see whether the target of any action was on a button labeled Close Window. If that statement returns true, then the code will be called to dispose the frame myFrame. The next evaluation is to see whether the Show Window button was selected. If this is true, then the frame will show, resized. Now compile this applet and, using the same HTML page, run the appletviewer on the HTML page Windows.html (see Listing 8.13). If all goes well, you should see the applet. This time, click the button Show Window and another window should pop up (see Figure 8.23).

If you click Close Window, the window will disappear because in doing so, you called the dispose method. Now click the button Show Window again, and the window should pop up. A good question to ask yourself is whether the window is being destroyed and re-created each time you click these buttons, causing the window to appear and disappear. (This question would be good to test whether someone is a true Java programmer.) Let's find out. Type your name in the text field and close the frame. Now show the frame again (that is, click the Show Window button) and look at the text field. Your name should still be in the text field. Answer yes or no, and dispose() releases all of the graphical resources held; when you call the frame to show, dispose() must reallocate them. The object textName will still exist. Note that you did not program other ways to close the window, so this is the only way you will be able to close it.

FIGURE 8.23.

Example of multiple windows.

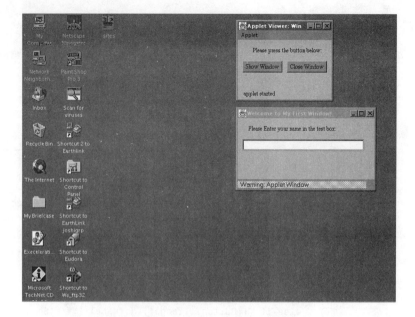

Summary

In this chapter, you have only scratched the surface of Java's built-in classes. Advanced event handling, networking, and working with streams were not covered. Hopefully, this chapter has sparked your interest in continuing to work with Java. For more on Java, reference the "JavaScript" section in this book for a chance to work with some other methods that are presented in the tables but not officially discussed. If you want to plow into newer, more exciting frontiers with Java, try the book *Teach Yourself Java in 21 Days* from Sams.net Publishing. Based on the material covered in this chapter, you should be able to skim through at least the first 10 days. After that, though, you'll get to work with some really great objects, such as streams. Finally, for an advanced look at Java programming, try *Java Unleashed* from Sams Publishing.

Although Java is in its infancy, it still has the potential of bringing more to the computer industry than was ever hoped.

Visual J++: Tools for the Internet and the Desktop

by Bryan Morgan

IN THIS CHAPTER

CHAPTER 9

Introduction To Visual J++

Visual J++ is the name of Microsoft's first Java development tool. It was originally internally dubbed Jakarta after the largest city on the island of Java, but Microsoft refrained from using yet another coffee- or Java-related name for this product. The name *Visual J++* can be taken to mean several different things:

- Visual J++ is a visual tool that uses standard GUI development techniques, such as resource builders, syntax-aware editors, and graphical debuggers.

- Visual J++ is integrated with Microsoft's "Visual" family of tools, including Visual C++ and Visual Basic.

- Visual J++ enables the developer to extend the capabilities of the Java language (that's where the ++ comes in).

At its most basic level of operation, Visual J++ provides a high-performance Java compiler, integrated development environment (with a resource editor, visual debugger, and visual editor), programming wizards, and extensive online help capabilities. Standard Java applets and applications built using the Microsoft Visual J++ tool set will run unmodified on any machine on earth that includes a copy of the Java Virtual Machine (more on this later).

Had Microsoft stopped at that point and released a tool with these capabilities, Visual J++ would be highly regarded for its excellent development environment and extremely fast compiler. Visual J++ uses the Developer Studio environment, which also is used by the Visual C++ and Fortran Powerstation products. The compiler can compile up to one million lines of Java code per second (on a standard Pentium-based computer), which should place it near the top of the heap in compilation speed. As stated earlier, had Microsoft stopped with these features, this chapter would focus primarily on the Java language and its use in the development of applets and applications (a topic that has produced over 100 books in Java's first year alone!).

However, as you probably know by now, Visual J++ is much more than a standard Java compiler. Microsoft has worked for several years to produce an object-based framework for the Windows platform with the eventual goal of making this framework *distributed* and *cross-platform.*

> **NOTE**
>
> The term *distributed* here means that objects can be shared across multiple computers. In other words, if an application were running on your local machine, it could call into objects running on machines elsewhere across the network. This enables applications to be partitioned across multiple machines for performance reasons, and improves maintenance because only one machine needs to be updated in the case of software updates.

The term *cross-platform* is used in this chapter to represent computers sharing information or programs even when the computers are running different operating systems. An example of a cross-platform environment is a network of Windows 95 and Apple Macintosh computers using programming objects stored on a UNIX server.

Microsoft's object standard is known as the Component Object Model (COM), and the implementation of this standard is personified in a group of technologies known as ActiveX. One ActiveX technology that will be familiar to Windows developers is ActiveX controls. These components (formerly known as OCX, or OLE, controls) are industry standard programming tools now used by many, if not most, Windows programmers. A partial list of products that support the use of ActiveX controls is as follows: MS Visual C++/Visual FoxPro/Visual Basic/Access, Borland C++/Delphi, Powersoft Powerbuilder, and Oracle PowerObjects.

Why is ActiveX being discussed in a section about a Java compiler? This is what separates Visual J++ from every other Java tool on the market! The Visual J++ tool set, in combination with the Microsoft Windows Virtual Machine for Java, will enable Java programmers to use ActiveX controls along with Java applets. In addition, standard Windows applications can be built using Visual J++, ActiveX, and the underlying COM. This will enable Windows developers to utilize the full power and elegance of the Java language along with the huge existing base of COM objects in which many developers already have invested.

Java + COM = First Class Citizen

What does this mean for Windows and Java programmers? First of all, it means now that these two can be one and the same. Just as there are Windows VB developers and Windows C++ developers, new projects will soon be able to choose Java as a development choice. In short, Microsoft is elevating Java from its already lofty status as a Web programming tool to that of THE Web programming tool and also a Windows programming tool. Actually, in the near future it might become inaccurate to refer to Visual J++ as simply a "Windows tool" because COM is gradually becoming a cross-platform object model (more on this later).

Had Microsoft chosen to simply make Visual J++ a graphical layer over the standard Java tools, the Visual J++ programmer could use Java to do the following:

- Develop Java applets that can run within any Java-capable Web browser
- Develop Java applications that can run on any platform containing the Java Virtual Machine
- Develop Java applications that use native methods to call existing code written in other languages such C or C++

9

VISUAL J++

With the extra capabilities that Microsoft has added to Visual J++, the Visual J++ programmer is able to

- Develop Java applets that can run within any Java-capable Web browser
- Develop Java applications that can run on any platform containing the Java Virtual Machine
- Develop Java applications that use native methods to call existing code written in other languages such C or C++
- Develop ActiveX controls in Java (in an upcoming release of Visual J++)
- Build powerful Web-based applications using a combination of Java applets and ActiveX controls that can be scripted together using any ActiveX scripting language such as JavaScript or VBScript
- Develop Windows 95 label-compliant applications in Java using the growing libraries of Java applets and the already extensive library of ActiveX controls
- Develop Windows executables that consist of true binary code that can run at native machine speeds and use the elegance of the Java language

As you can see, the first three items in this list are possible using virtually any Java tool on the market today. Despite many Java programmers' fears that Microsoft would release a proprietary tool that would somehow pollute the Java waters, these fears are unfounded. A key point is that Visual J++ is a great tool to use for non-ActiveX and ActiveX Java development. After all, despite the explosive growth and potential of the World Wide Web, it will be quite some time before the majority of applications developed are designed to run only within a Web browser.

The Java language has grown faster than any other programming language in the history of computing. Because nearly all of the Java demonstrations and press coverage of Java have focused on its use as a World Wide Web development tool, many developers might not realize that Java can be used to write stand-alone applications with advanced graphical user interfaces. Because Microsoft Windows is the most widely used operating system in the world today, and because of the vast amount of existing code already written for the Windows platform, an ideal software development tool would enable the Java developer to combine the best of the Web world with the best of the Windows world. For many developers, Visual J++ will be that tool.

Although Visual J++ will obviously be used by many for the development of standard Java applets for Web distribution, Microsoft must be credited for realizing that the Java language itself is a *great* programming language. Because of the features of the Java language and the impetus behind it, Microsoft extended Visual J++ and the Windows Virtual Machine for Java to enable Java applications to incorporate existing ActiveX controls. Using Visual J++, ActiveX controls and Java classes are identical to the Java programmer. This is possible because of the Microsoft Java Virtual Machine and the underlying similarities between Java and Microsoft's Component Object Model. The following section discusses the evolution of COM and ActiveX and concludes by showing how the Java language and COM fit together nicely. The chapter then concludes with a discussion of the benefits and weaknesses of Java and ActiveX.

Microsoft's Component Object Model (COM) and ActiveX

The next chapter focuses on using Visual J++ to develop full-featured Windows applications using Microsoft's ActiveX technologies. Many developers might wonder: Exactly what is ActiveX and where did it come from? Although it was announced by Microsoft in 1996, believe it or not, it has actually been around for several years and nearly all Windows developers have used some form of it at one time. Before diving into ActiveX, however, the history of the Component Object Model (COM) and Object Linking and Embedding (OLE) are examined.

The Birth of ActiveX: An Overview of COM and OLE

COM provides the basis for nearly all of Microsoft's new products. It is, in theory, a platform-independent, vendor-independent, and language-independent model for developing applications using intercommunication among binary objects. These objects communicate with each other using a set of predefined interfaces that each object chooses to implement.

> **NOTE**
>
> An *interface* is a set of related functions that can be implemented by an object. If an object chooses to implement an interface, all of the functions specified by that interface must be implemented.

Each object is defined by which interfaces it chooses to implement. (For example, if a developer wanted an object to be saved to disk, he or she could implement what is known as a structured storage interface.)

Note that the words *in theory* are used in the previous paragraph to describe the COM standard's cross-platform capabilities. Although a COM infrastructure could be written for any operating system, the fact remains that at the present time it is available only for the Windows family of operating systems. Microsoft recently has announced plans to assist Metrowerks in porting COM to the Apple Macintosh and currently is working with Bristol and MainSoft to port COM to UNIX. However, at the current time, developers should realize that using COM objects in an application will limit the platforms on which that application will run. This possible drawback is discussed later in the "Advantages and Disadvantages: A Close Look at Java and ActiveX" section.

COM: Specification and Implementation

COM is both a specification and an actual implementation. The COM specification specifies a binary standard for implementing the object, which is language-independent. Therefore, a

9

VISUAL J++

COM object could be written using Delphi, Visual Basic, C++, or—you guessed it—Java. All that is required is that a specific set of functions be provided by your object so that the object's provided interfaces can be queried.

The COM implementation is provided in the form of a Windows dynamic link library (DLL). This DLL exports a small number of API functions that enable the programmer to instantiate a component object using a unique class identifier known as a Class ID. What is important to realize is that COM, by itself, simply provides the "rules" for which objects can be instantiated and can intercommunicate among themselves. All of these objects can be combined to make an application. With the advent of Distributed COM (DCOM), these objects can be located anywhere across a network. This functionality is a core part of Windows NT 4.0.

Using COM Objects

Although COM is destined to be an integral part of future Microsoft operating systems, COM has never been an active topic of discussion among most Windows developers. This is because COM, by itself, does not specify any applicable, real-world objects that can be used by developers to create applications. Instead, COM is the object *model* that developers can use to integrate several objects into a working application. These objects could come from a variety of sources. Here are some examples:

- A COM object could be written in C++ and provide spell-checking if given a large string of text. A Visual Basic programmer could then instantiate the spell-check object, pass it a string of text, and reuse that functionality. Now imagine that the word processing software installed on all machines in your office was made up of a set of COM objects, one of which was a spell-check object. One nice thing about this model is that shrink-wrapped applications can in turn become programmable objects themselves; therefore, you could reuse powerful functionality already existing in desktop software products.

- A geographical information system (GIS) residing on a remote server could be used to store mapping and statistical data for your enterprise. If that GIS were built using DCOM objects, an application could be written so that users across the network could reuse these DCOM objects to display custom maps within local applications.

- COM-enabled applications such as spreadsheets and word processors could enable COM objects to be inserted directly into a document. This would enable multiple applications to be integrated together so that the document rather than the application would become the focus. This has long been a "Holy Grail" of personal computing, and COM enables this to be done today using OLE (which is discussed in the following section, "OLE 1.0").

Although it is completely possible to write from scratch COM objects that are fully compliant with the binary specification, most Windows developers have never done this. Instead, programmers who want the functionality provided by the COM object model have historically relied on a framework that lies on top of COM known as OLE. OLE stands for Object Linking and Embedding and is the parent of what is now known as ActiveX.

OLE 1.0

As the name implies, Object Linking and Embedding was originally a technology used by Microsoft to link together desktop application products. This was provided so that users could do things such as insert a Microsoft Excel spreadsheet into a Microsoft Word document. As the user scrolls through the Word document and comes upon the Excel spreadsheet, he or she could double-click the Microsoft Excel icon to launch a copy of Excel and view or edit the spreadsheet.

Although the OLE standard at this point was much simpler than what exists today, it still enabled inter-application communication and data exchange. After OLE 1.0 was developed, the methodology was well-documented and supported by Microsoft, and soon many applications appeared that enabled their application objects to be integrated together. In a short time, OLE became the standard way for applications to interoperate. Because of OLE1's success, Microsoft realized it could provide the foundation for a more generic object framework that gave the user and developer many more capabilities. At the same time, Microsoft began to aggressively position itself as an enterprise system provider using Windows NT as a network server and products such as SQL Server for database operations. In the Microsoft scheme of things, all desktop machines would be running some variant of the Windows operating system. These machines would be able to communicate among each other using a Windows NT-controlled network and could share information using products such as SQL Server and Exchange. In such a networked environment, DCOM would enable applications (or even operating systems!) to be distributed across the network for scalability and administration reasons.

As Microsoft's rapid growth in this area coincided with the development of OLE 2.0, this release of OLE became much more than a mechanism for combining documents.

OLE 2.0

OLE 2.0 was released in 1993, and some improvements were immediately visible. OLE 2.0 applications not only could embed documents created by other applications, but these documents could also be edited and updated directly within the "container" document.

If the user were to edit a Microsoft Word document that contained a chart, the application would appear to be Microsoft Word. However, if the user double-clicked the chart, OLE 2.0 enabled the application to essentially "morph" into Microsoft Excel (see Figure 9.1). The user then could operate on the chart using the Excel menus and options, and immediately switch back to the word processing functionality provided by Word after the chart had been edited.

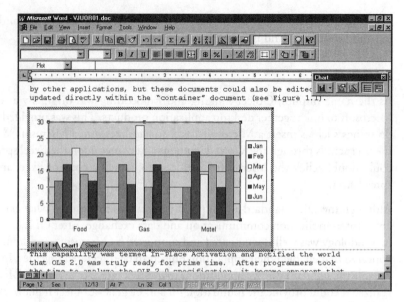

This capability was termed *in-place activation* and notified the world that OLE 2.0 was truly ready for prime time. After programmers took the time to analyze the OLE 2.0 specification, it became apparent that OLE2 was in fact a large set of advanced features that offered programmers capabilities that, in the past, would have been impossible to implement. Figure 9.2 illustrates the features provided by OLE2 and the following section explains each of these features briefly.

Features Provided by OLE 2.0

OLE 2.0 is basically a large grouping of COM-compliant objects that can be conveniently grouped into several primary categories:

- Compound documents
- Drag-and-drop
- Uniform data transfer
- Compound files
- Monikers
- OLE controls
- Automation

Each of these categories relies on the underlying Component Object Model to specify how the objects interoperate with each other.

FIGURE 9.2.

OLE 2.0 features.

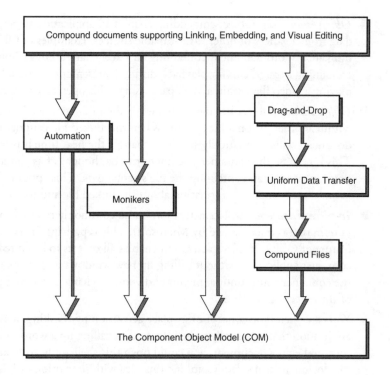

Compound Documents

The portion of OLE2 known as *compound documents* concerns itself with the linking and embedding of objects. To fully understand what a compound document is, you must first understand what it means to "link" and "embed" objects.

Objects are linked when the following steps occur:

1. A portion or all of a file's contents created by Application1 is inserted into a file created by Application2.
2. The portion of Application1's file is designated as a link within Application2.
3. When Application1's file is modified, these changes become apparent when you are viewing Application2's file.

Objects are embedded when an object created by one application is visually and physically part of a file created and displayed by another application instance. Figure 9.1 shows an example of embedding.

To give you an idea of the amount of progress made between OLE1 and OLE2, OLE1 essentially consisted of two subsets of compound documents: linking and embedding. Obviously, OLE2 was a huge leap forward! You can think of an OLE2 compound document as providing three possible features:

■ *Object embedding.* Object embedding enables an application to act as a container of data from a variety of other OLE-capable sources. Examples of OLE2 object embedding are a Word document containing an Excel chart, a PowerPoint presentation containing a sound clip for playback during a presentation, and a Web browser playing a video file within a Web page using OLE operating system components.

■ *Object linking.* Object linking occurs when the inserted object's data actually resides within another file on a file system. When this linked file is updated, the container document will automatically see these changes the next time it is opened or updated. This is because the container document can be thought of as containing a "pointer" to that file rather than containing the file's actual data. This "pointer" is known as a *moniker* and contains information about the linked file and its contents.

■ *In-place activation.* In-place activation is also commonly referred to as Visual Editing (a term that is trademarked by Microsoft). This is perhaps the coolest and most visible feature of OLE2. In-place activation enables all objects to be edited within their container application without calling up new windows to confuse the user. Instead, the container's surrounding menus and window changes to represent the application of the object being edited.

You can extend the concept of in-place activation by thinking of a generic container application that is basically a shell. Instead of calling up a word processor or spreadsheet to begin a document, you could open this shell application and add objects to the document as needed. Combine this idea with the notion of Distributed COM, and you can envision an environment in which these objects can lie anywhere across a very large network. Instead of loading huge, monolithic applications onto your hard drive, in the near future you might have the option of downloading application objects for use in document creation. With the advent of DCOM in the fall of 1996, this "app of the future" might not be as far off as you might think.

Uniform Data Transfer

All data transfers that occur among OLE2 objects use the technology known as Uniform Data Transfer. This capability provides the definition of something known as a *data object*. A data object is a single piece of code that can be used in all data transfers: DDE, OLE, drag-and-drop, and Clipboard transfers. Note that this data transfer does not necessarily take place through memory. OLE2 enables the programmer to perform data transfer using files, memory, or any other methodology that the programmer chooses. Once again, looking into the future, one can envision transfer methods such as FTP or HTTP for extending what we now think of as OLE2.

Drag-and-Drop

In most GUI environments such as Macintosh, Motif, or Windows, users have had the capability to drag and drop items within applications or from File Manager-type applications. OLE2 takes this functionality a step further by enabling any data object from any application to be dragged and dropped into any other OLE2 application that supports this feature. Essentially, any data object that can be copied to the Windows clipboard can be used with drag and drop.

Compound Files

You can think of compound files as files within files. Programmers building files using OLE2 compound files can literally create directory trees within files for storing different types of data. Compound files also can contain data created by several different applications. Because compound files are composed of a tree-like structure, you can query compound files for information such as author, modification date, and other features. An example of a compound file that is an integral part of all Windows systems now is the Windows Registry. Under Windows 95, you can examine the Registry by running REGEDIT.EXE. Under Windows NT, this file is called REGEDT32.EXE.

Monikers

Monikers are used to provide links between objects on a system (or across a distributed system). A moniker is another word for a nickname, and you can think of OLE2 monikers as a type of nickname. Monikers are basically nicknames that identify the source of data and understand how to bind an application to that data. There are many different types of monikers in OLE2, including File, Pointer, and Item monikers.

OLE Controls

OLE Controls, or OCX Controls as they are often called, carry on the spirit of the VBX controls introduced with Visual Basic 3.0. Unlike VBX controls, which are special-case 16-bit DLLs, OLE Controls can be 32-bit controls that implement a standard set of OLE2 interfaces. The result is a programming object that can be used at design-time (in a development environment such as Visual Basic or Delphi) and at runtime within an application. These controls are language-independent and have been extremely successful. At the present time, over 1,000 OLE Controls are commercially available.

Automation

OLE Automation is a technology that is included within the OLE2 umbrella. However, in many ways it is much larger than OLE2. An application can support OLE Automation by exposing its desired functionality through a set of interfaces. These interfaces can then be used to manipulate (automate) the application by another piece of code. Visual Basic is commonly used to control Microsoft Office applications through the use of OLE Automation. (In fact, there are whole books written on that topic alone!) Through the process of OLE Automation, programmers can choose the language and tool they would like to use to control other programmable objects. OLE Automation is included in most discussions of OLE2 because it uses the underlying Component Object Model as a blueprint for inter-object communication.

9

VISUAL J++

All of these technologies represent a huge investment for Microsoft. Thousands of hours and millions of dollars have been spent to build an object framework for the Windows platforms. With the advent of DCOM in the very near future, Microsoft is positioned to finally compete and interoperate with other popular object models such as Distributed Computing Environment (DCE) and Component Object Request Broker Architecture (CORBA). From Microsoft's point of view, it is clear that technologies such as the World Wide Web and Java can be used to interoperate with their existing code infrastructure. To do this, Microsoft has introduced a trimmed-down version of OLE2 known as ActiveX to truly activate the Internet.

ActiveX: Activating the Internet

The wary reader might by this point be wondering where this discussion is headed. After all, on one hand you have learned the Web and Java's use in building networked, platform-independent applications. On the other hand, you have learned OLE and its capabilities for building object-based applications on the Windows platform. Now the two technologies will be brought together using the magic of COM and Windows Virtual Machine for Java.

In 1995, all Microsoft projects were issued a well-publicized edict to Internet-enable every product if possible. The results of that request are beginning to be seen nearly a year later as Microsoft is releasing a flood of products aimed at corporate and independent Web developers. (Visual J++ is one of the products leading this charge.) While OLE2 was introduced to address the needs of desktop software developers and system integrators, in the previous section you learned many topics that could clearly be applied to networked applications. Like all other Microsoft products, OLE2 was thoroughly examined from an Internet point of view and the resulting set of transformed technologies has been named ActiveX. Many pieces of OLE2 have been completely reworked for maximum performance benefits for Web usage, while other technologies basically have been renamed and remarketed as ActiveX technologies.

Like its parent, OLE2, ActiveX cannot be summed up as one simple technology. Instead, it can be broken into several parts, all of which can be thought of collectively as Microsoft's ActiveX architecture. The following highlights the key ActiveX technologies and draws a parallel between them and their parent OLE2 technologies.

What Is ActiveX?

ActiveX is the name of a group of related technologies from Microsoft that is designed to enable developers to provide active Web content. Although at the current time ActiveX is a Windows-only technology, implementations for the Macintosh and UNIX operating systems are slated for release in the near future. When this platform independence is a reality, ActiveX will enable software developers to choose their language and tools, reuse existing inventories of objects, and develop extremely powerful distributed applications for use on a variety of operating platforms. It will do this using a variety of technologies that exist under the ActiveX umbrella, including

■ ActiveX documents
■ ActiveX controls
■ ActiveX scripting
■ ActiveX-enabled Internet protocols
■ ActiveX APIs
■ Microsoft Windows Virtual Machine for Java

ActiveX Documents

ActiveX documents can be thought of as Internet-aware OLE2 compound documents. An ActiveX-enabled Web browser such as Microsoft Internet Explorer can download a Word document from a Web browser and immediately know how to display that file through the use of ActiveX documents. This technology continues Microsoft's information-centric approach, which enables users to concentrate more on an application's content than on the application itself.

ActiveX Controls

ActiveX controls are extensions of the OLE controls mentioned earlier in this chapter. In fact, in many instances there is no difference at all between an ActiveX control and an OLE control. Microsoft simply reduced the number of interfaces that an ActiveX control is required to implement. Potentially, this enables ActiveX controls to be much smaller than their OLE counterparts. However, in many situations the same interfaces will be required to be implemented.

ActiveX Scripting

ActiveX scripting extends the concept formerly known as OLE Automation by adding scripting capabilities to Web pages, programs, or even server applications. ActiveX scripting enables scripts to be written in a variety of languages because it uses two components: a scripting host and a scripting engine. The scripting host is an application that is responsible for creating the scripting engine. The scripting engine in turn is responsible for processing and performing the script commands. Examples of scripting hosts include

■ Microsoft Internet Explorer
■ Future Microsoft Server products
■ Various Web authoring tools including Microsoft FrontPage

Scripting engines are currently available for Visual Basic for Applications (VBA), Visual Basic Scripting Edition (VBScript), and JavaScript.

ActiveX-Enabled Internet Protocols

Common Internet protocols such as FTP and HTTP can use ActiveX technologies such as monikers (equivalent to an OLE moniker). These monikers can serve as pointers to applications and can be interpreted by ActiveX server products in order to link applications to the Internet.

ActiveX APIs

An entire suite of ActiveX APIs is available through the ActiveX Software Development Kit (SDK). These APIs enable software developers to extend traditional Windows-based programs with Internet capabilities such as file transfer and Web server access.

Microsoft Windows Virtual Machine for Java

The final component of ActiveX that you will learn is the Microsoft Windows Virtual Machine for Java. This Java Virtual Machine is designed to both run standard Java applets and also expose Java applets as COM objects for their use in ActiveX applications. The Windows Virtual Machine for Java also enables Java applets to coexist with ActiveX controls because to the programmer, both are just objects composed of properties, methods, and events.

Comparing Java and COM

Visual J++ is the first product to combine two extremely popular technologies: Java and COM. This is possible because the two are extremely similar on many levels. This section summarizes the capabilities of Java and COM and discusses why they fit together very well.

Java and COM: Some Differences

From the outset, it is obvious that in some ways Java and COM are very different technologies. Most notably, Java is a programming language, and COM is an object model that specifies how objects created in any programming language must interact. However, it is fair to say that Java *objects* and COM *objects* can be compared and contrasted.

Java objects are not distributed. Although it is true that Java objects can be stored on remote servers, these objects must actually be uploaded to the client machine before they can be used to run an applet within a browser. Meanwhile, DCOM objects can be stored on a remote machine and can be called from that remote machine using a Remote Procedure Call (RPC).

Java applets are designed with specific security restrictions. These restrictions include the incapability to call code on any server other than the originating server and the incapability to make local operating system calls. COM objects have full access to the underlying operating system and rely on a completely different security model that revolves around a concept known as *code signing*.

Java classes are not required to implement interfaces (groups of related functions that can be thought of as a unit). The Java programmer can choose to implement zero or more interfaces for each Java class. COM objects are required to implement at least one interface: IUnknown. This interface then is used to determine specific information about the object and to acquire new interfaces if necessary.

Java also uses a technique known as *garbage collection* for automatic memory management. When the system knows that an object is not going to be used any longer, the Java runtime system automatically frees that object's memory. Memory management with COM produces an equivalent result to produce automatic memory management. Instead of garbage collection, however, COM tracks the *reference count*, or the number of instances using an object. When the reference count drops to zero, that object is freed in memory.

Java and COM: Surprising Similarities

Despite the differences mentioned in the previous section, the number of similarities between Java and COM is very interesting (and an excellent sign that both technologies benefit from a good design!). This is probably not surprising if one stops to really think about what both Java and COM were designed to solve. They both were intended to be

- Platform-independent
- Object-oriented
- Multi-threaded
- Dynamic

To start with, Java and COM both require a foundation underneath them to support their platform-independent claims. Java's foundation is known as the Java Virtual Machine, whereas COM requires an implementation of the Component Object Model for each specific platform. After this foundation is in place, both systems rely on objects that are created on the fly and are dynamically linked together at runtime.

Even the way that the objects are defined is similar in some respects. Java uses a .class file format that is well-documented. The class file defines the contents of the internal class and any interfaces it implements. COM uses a .tlb (type library) file to define the contents of the COM object and any interfaces it implements. A key factor in the operation of the Windows Virtual Machine is its capability to create type libraries from Java classes and likewise create Java classes from COM object's type libraries.

As you might have noticed by now, both rely heavily on the use of interfaces. Interfaces enable objects to implement a related set of functions for an object. The intent of these interfaces is generally documented, therefore the interface serves as a sort of contract between one object (the implementor of the interface) and another (the user of the interface). Java and COM both use classes (a concept familiar to object-oriented programmers) to group together related functions and data.

9

VISUAL J++

One feature of many systems and languages is *exception handling.* Exception handling enables the developer to trap errors and handle them accordingly so that the program will not simply crash. Java handles exceptions through the use of the Throwable interface. COM handles exceptions through the use of the IErrorInfo interface.

Advantages and Disadvantages: A Close Look at Java and ActiveX

Because of the excitement surrounding Java since its introduction in 1995, the software development community has enthusiastically supported Java and pushed it to the forefront of Web development. However, like all new technologies, it has some advantages as well as disadvantages. ActiveX is no different than Java in this respect. You learn these strengths and weaknesses here so that you are well aware that no technology by itself can solve every problem out there. As with all complicated undertakings, a variety of issues need to be weighed before decisions are made.

Java's greatest advantage might be that it is the most powerful, ubiquitous programming language that enables developers to create platform-independent code. Unlike most other cross-platform tools, the Java developer actually has to make an effort in order to add platform-dependent code to the application at hand. Java programmers can thank the availability of the Java Virtual Machine for this feature.

> **NOTE**
>
> Although it is true that Java is not truly platform-independent without the availability of a Java Virtual Machine, the fact is that the JVM is available now (or will be soon) on nearly every popular operating system in widespread use today.

Java is also object-oriented. This is truly an advantage because of the large effort made over the last few years to train programmers to think in terms of objects and designing systems this way. Object-oriented programming has been demonstrated repeatedly to improve productivity through a systematic approach to object design and analysis.

Java's object-oriented structure and platform independence are also enabling it to be quickly "retrofitted" to Component Object Request Brokers for use in building distributed applications. In fact, the Netscape Navigator 4.0 Web browser will include ORB client software by Visigenic for use in building distributed, object-based applications using the Netscape Open Network Environment (ONE) platform.

Even though Java was introduced by Sun Microsystems, it remains largely a vendor-neutral architecture. Sun Microsystems originally developed the JVM for Sun Solaris, Apple Macintosh, and Windows 95/NT, but JVMs have now been developed by many other corporations, including IBM, Microsoft, and Netscape. Developers deciding to develop applications using Java can choose from a broad range of tools from a variety of vendors and are not tied exclusively to Sun Microsystems' line of products.

Java also has the advantage of widespread acceptance and near-ubiquity. It is rapidly becoming the programming language of choice for Web solutions and is being used for actual product development now for things like Web server software, collaboration systems, and desktop applications. Business analysts often discuss the topics of market share and mind share. While market share is of course the universal indicator used to judge the success or failure of a product, mind share is a much more difficult and subjective indicator to measure. For developers trying to decide whether to implement a pure Java solution or an ActiveX solution, the decision becomes extremely difficult because of these two measuring sticks.

In terms of product support and existing lines of code, ActiveX is the market share leader because it effectively existed as OLE for several years already. However, developers who try to keep a finger on the pulse of the computing community realize that Java has captured an ever-increasing mind share of the programming audience. For Sun Microsystems, the maturation of Java and its role in it will determine if that mind share can be converted into market share at a future time for its software and hardware products.

A lack of existing code and experienced programmers in some ways are drawbacks to implementing standard Java applications. Although advanced class libraries, thousands of existing controls, and several excellent tools exist for the ActiveX developer, the Java programmer is often forced into the "roll-your-own" mode of development. Naturally, it is through this trial by fire that beginning Java developers turn into expert Java developers, but in some cases the business case for new Java development might be hard to sell when compared to existing partial solutions that already exist in the form of ActiveX.

For example, several ActiveX controls that enable developers to create impressive charts and graphs that appear to the user as full-featured mini-applications now exist. These controls are relatively inexpensive ($99—$299) and many employ internal object models for ease of development. To date, there is no Java applet available that approaches the sophistication of these controls, and because of Java applet's security restrictions, some features on these applets might never be implemented to compete directly with their ActiveX counterparts.

The huge interest in Java and its related technologies has also made it increasingly difficult for businesses to find truly qualified programmers. It is common to hear HTML designers who have included an applet within a Web page refer to themselves as Java programmers. The truly seasoned developer can use the Web to his or her advantage however, by publishing work samples on the Web for all to see. A well-placed URL on a resume can go a long way to quieting someone's anxiety when they examine your resume.

Perhaps Java's biggest drawbacks come in the area where it is the most visible: the Web browser client. Because rogue applets can damage a user's system, the designers of Java built it around a strict security model that treats applets extremely carefully within most Web browsers. This security model prevents applets from

- Accessing the local hard drive
- Communicating with any server other than the originating server
- Making any calls to the local operating system

Java applets also have no persistence. Because Java is object-oriented and each class can derive from another class and implement several interfaces, when an applet is uploaded to a Web browser, it can require the uploading of one, two, maybe twenty other class files with it. Because these applets are not persistent, the next time the user visits that Web site, this same group of applets will need to be reloaded all over again. In an intranet setting where users will continually upload the same Java applets over and over again, it is possible that the users could install local versions of these applets, but Java provides no "self-installation" capabilities.

One final weakness of Java that should be pointed out is that it is an interpreted language and suffers from poor performance without the existence of a Just-In-Time compiler. Just-In-Time (JIT) compilers actually compile Java code into native machine code on the fly after the applets have been downloaded so that the applets can have improved performance. This feature is included in the Netscape Navigator 3.0 browser and the Microsoft Internet Explorer 3.0 browser. Even with the existence of a JIT compiler, Java code still runs slower than comparable "C" code, and this point should be considered. A general rule of thumb is that whenever a task is I/O-bound (such as user interface operations), the slower language probably will not make a difference. However, in tasks that are CPU-bound (such as mathematical operations), the interpreted language will force your code to take a performance hit.

Native ActiveX controls are natively compiled, dynamically linked code modules that run without the aid of an interpreter. This enables them to boast a performance advantage over comparable Java applets. Although it is easy for developers to say that machines today are fast enough where performance differences probably will not matter, keep in mind that we are often writing for the lowest common denominator. I have been in many situations in which software ran just fine on my souped-up development machine only to see it suddenly crawl on a user's less-capable box.

ActiveX controls also are, for better or worse, persistent on a client's local systems after being downloaded the first time. At the present, Microsoft Internet Explorer does not automatically remove these controls when the browser exits. Instead, these controls reside indefinitely until the user deletes them. Microsoft has stated that control removal will be an option in later versions of Internet Explorer.

Some ActiveX technologies such as ActiveX controls also benefit from the large existing code base. Well over 1,000 ActiveX controls currently exist that will run within an Internet Explorer or Netscape Navigator page. This is a double-edged sword however, because the Windows platform is the only platform on which these controls can be used. Platform-dependence is without a doubt the primary drawback to implementing ActiveX Web sites. Until COM becomes available for other popular operating systems such as Macintosh and UNIX, ActiveX might remain primarily an intranet development technology. This is because within an intranet, Web designers usually are able to pinpoint exactly which machines will be using a Web-based application and can plan their design accordingly.

ActiveX controls have a truly distinct advantage: language independence. These controls can be built using a variety of popular products including Visual Basic 5.0, Visual C++, Delphi, and future versions of Visual J++. In addition, they are not simply a Web-only solution. As mentioned earlier, ActiveX controls currently are being used by Delphi, Visual Basic, C++, and even COBOL developers worldwide. This capability alone ensures that ActiveX will continue to grow in the future regardless of the success of Java and other technologies.

The lack of browser support could possibly slow the adoption of ActiveX for Web-based development. Because Netscape Navigator is the market leader (remember the discussion on market share earlier?) and because Netscape has chosen not to implement ActiveX support within its browser, users are being forced to decide between the two market leaders, Microsoft and Netscape. Although users can download an ActiveX Netscape plug-in from NCompass Labs that will enable Netscape to use ActiveX controls, very few users (relative to the total number of users) have chosen to do so. Once again, the topic of mind share versus market share is brought up. If Microsoft Internet Explorer suddenly experiences a dramatic increase in mind share among "power users," this could only help ActiveX and its related technologies. One can only hope that the end user will be the eventual winner of the browser "wars," and that the best technologies will survive in the long run.

Summary

Visual J++ is an extremely powerful development tool that can be used for a wide variety of undertakings. Java applets and applications can be created using this product making it a valuable resource for the World Wide Web programmer who decides to program using the Windows platform. In addition to these capabilities, Visual J++ is the first tool to enable Java and the Component Object Model (COM) to be combined in the application development process. The Windows Virtual Machine for Java enables Java classes to be treated as COM objects. Because of this, Java classes can be used both for interactive Web content as well as for building powerful Windows-based applications.

Visual J++ also will enable the reverse process to take place. In other words, COM objects can be used side by side with Java objects to produce the most powerful (and flexible) application possible. Capabilities within Microsoft's Internet Explorer browser enable this functionality to be carried over to the Web as well.

COM objects that act as plug-and-play programming tools are known as ActiveX controls. These controls are descendants of the popular VBX controls introduced in Visual Basic 3.0. ActiveX controls are programming objects that expose a set of properties, methods, and events that can be used by the programmer to construct applications from other's code. Because COM is a language-independent standard, ActiveX-enabled Java classes can now be used in common Windows programming environments such as Visual J++, Visual C++, Delphi, PowerBuilder, Visual Basic, Access, and many others. ActiveX-aware applications such as the Microsoft Office suite (Word, Access, Excel, and PowerPoint) can also use ActiveX controls to create powerful, custom-built applications.

In short, Visual J++ satisfies the needs of Web developers and also introduces Java to a much broader programming audience. Using this tool, Java might soon be the Windows programming language of choice as well as the unquestioned programming language of choice for the World Wide Web.

At the end of the chapter you learned the strengths and weaknesses of the Java and ActiveX technologies. Issues such as performance, platform-independence, and vendor support will apparently continue to be key factors in designers' decisions despite the early promise of the World Wide Web.

Extending Java Using ActiveX

by Bryan Morgan

IN THIS CHAPTER

CHAPTER 10

Since its introduction in 1995, Java has dominated the computer industry's discussion of client-side Web programming. Because it was the first programming language and environment introduced with the World Wide Web specifically in mind, Java is a natural fit for developers wanting to add truly interactive content to Web pages. Some of Java's chief advantages are that it is object-oriented, multithreaded, secure, and platform-independent. However, this is not to say that it does not have its disadvantages. Currently, downloaded Java applets suffer from poor performance, are not persistent on the client, and are severely restricted on the client from performing system-level tasks. Also, despite the tremendous potential of the Web, the fact remains that the vast majority of code being written today is still being written for operating-specific, stand-alone applications.

Since 1990, Microsoft has been promoting an object model (COM) that specifies how binary objects can interact and build on each other. Object Linking and Embedding (OLE) was Microsoft's implementation of an object framework using COM. OLE provides several objects that enable the user to work in a document-centric way. This means that the document on which the user is working is the real focus, not the individual applications that are used to create the document. An OLE compound document could include word processing text, graphics, spreadsheets, sound, video, or any other OLE-compliant application's output. Simply clicking any of these objects within the document could activate the application that created the object. OLE became so successful on the Windows platform that Microsoft decided to make it the basis of its distributed computing framework. Microsoft also introduced another COM-based technology that used OLE and other COM-based objects to collectively create programming objects (OLE controls or OCX controls) that could be dropped into any OLE control-aware programming environment. Environments that currently support OLE controls include Visual Basic 4, Visual C++, PowerBuilder, Borland Delphi, Borland C++, and Access.

The explosion in Internet usage forced Microsoft to rethink many of its applications and technologies, and many parts of OLE were reworked to provide better performance, smaller code size, and a different security model. These technologies were introduced to the public in 1995 as ActiveX. ActiveX technologies currently available include the programming objects known as ActiveX controls, the ActiveX scripting engine in Microsoft Internet Explorer 3.0 (used to run VBScript and JavaScript), ActiveX Documents (see Figure 10.1), and the ActiveX Server Framework, which provides security, database access, and server-side tools.

This chapter points out the strengths and weaknesses in Microsoft's ActiveX technology. A key point to remember is that with Microsoft Visual J++, the Java developer has both options to play with: pure Java and ActiveX. In other words, developers are no longer forced to choose between ActiveX and Java. Therefore, the decision is left up to the developer to pick the best tool for the job (which is the way it is supposed to be).

FIGURE 10.1.

Microsoft Internet Explorer 3.0 displays an ActiveX document.

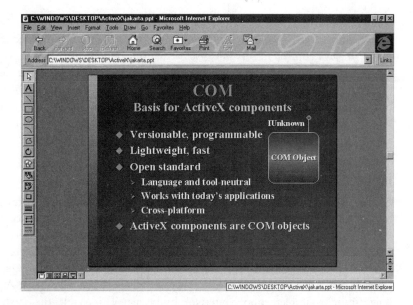

The ActiveX Advantages

In any fair discussion, nearly every new technology has a set of advantages and disadvantages. ActiveX has been praised by many and criticized by just as many others. (In general, this usually indicates that you must be at least be doing something interesting to evoke such a large amount of discussion!) Nonetheless, with the advent of the Microsoft Internet Explorer 3.0 browser, the Microsoft Virtual Machine for Java, and Visual J++, ActiveX is going to be around for quite some time. This section focuses on the advantages of ActiveX and how it can benefit the Web programmer. To begin, you learn that you can do things with ActiveX that you simply cannot do using any other technology. This, by default, gives ActiveX an advantage in many areas where it faces no competition.

High Performance

The ActiveX technologies are all *binary* technologies. This means that, unlike Java, there is no runtime interpreter that translates bytecodes into machine code. Therefore, downloaded components (ActiveX controls) are able to run at true machine speeds, which means ActiveX controls run much faster than comparable Java applets.

Persistence

Although in some instances object persistence can be a disadvantage, when ActiveX controls are initially downloaded they are installed onto the local system and remain there. (Future versions of Internet Explorer will enable the user to set defaults that control how ActiveX

10

EXTENDING JAVA
USING ACTIVEX

controls are saved.) The next time the user visits a page containing this ActiveX control, no downloading needs to be done. Instead, the ActiveX control is embedded immediately within the form. Java applets, meanwhile, are cached on the local file system only during the Web browser's current session. The next time the user visits the Web site (after closing the browser), the applet most likely will have to be downloaded again. This might not seem like a big deal, but because many applets inherit and use a wide variety of other classes, many of these additional classes also have to be downloaded. It is not unusual for a single applet to download 50 separate class files before it can be used within the Web page.

Huge Existing Code Base

Although Java is clearly an extremely exciting technology and might be the language of choice for many in the coming years, ActiveX technologies have been around since 1990. An extremely large base of code currently exists in the thousands of ActiveX controls available on the market today. Because of the COM foundation, all OLE controls available before the introduction of ActiveX can be downloaded and used within a Web browser just like ActiveX controls. The primary difference between ActiveX controls and OLE controls is that ActiveX controls are only required to implement one interface: Iunknown. This enables them to be potentially much smaller than OLE controls, although in some cases ActiveX controls are no different than their OLE counterparts.

ActiveX controls are hugely popular, and an entire industry already exists and thrives on their production and sales. Examples of ActiveX controls currently installed on my machine include

- Map Display
- Chart
- Spreadsheet
- Spellchecker
- RealAudio
- Stock Ticker
- Movie Player
- Image Viewer
- Date and Calendar
- Progress Bar

Although it is true that Java applets exist to perform some of the functionality previously mentioned, there are other operations listed here for which no Java applets exist whatsoever. In addition, many of the Java spreadsheet and chart classes available (to pick some examples) suffer from extremely poor performance and low functionality. Meanwhile, the market has pretty much sorted out the winners from the losers in the ActiveX control arena. Companies such as Sheridan, Micro-Help, and Visual Components have established excellent reputations for building high-performance, high-functionality ActiveX objects. Therefore, when components are purchased from these companies, there is some assurance that they will work as advertised.

You can build the following applications using Visual J++ and the controls listed previously:

- A Web page that contains HTML and an ActiveX control to display mapping coverages
- A Windows application written in Java to show a spreadsheet
- A Web application that contains Java applets and ActiveX controls side-by-side to plot data to a screen based on input coming from a real-time stock ticker; data from this application could be printed to a local printer in the form of customized reports (not just a mirror of the Web page sent to the printer)

The Windows Virtual Machine for Java makes all of the preceding functionality possible. You might be surprised to learn that even the Microsoft Virtual Machine itself was built as an ActiveX object. Thousands of developers have spent huge amounts of time and money investing in application development using ActiveX components. It is wishful to expect all of these developers to simply stop everything they have been doing for the past two years, retool, and begin developing Web-based Java applications. ActiveX acts as a bridge between the two technologies by enabling existing components to be reused while enabling new components to be added to applications. These components could be written in Java, Visual Basic, Delphi, C++, or any other language that supports the creation of ActiveX controls.

Language Independence

ActiveX objects also have one additional advantage: They can be written in any language and can be called from any other language.

> **NOTE**
>
> Before discussing this further, let me take a moment to define the word "any" in the world of Microsoft. Developers cannot simply sit down with a Fortran compiler and immediately start using ActiveX controls. Instead, the compiler needs to be able to support the linkages between ActiveX and standard code. Likewise, for a language to call an ActiveX object, the compiler must be "ActiveX-aware" and support the hooks necessary to dynamically link together ActiveX objects with binary code.

Under Windows 95/Windows NT, the development tools that control the lion's share of the PC software development market all support the usage of ActiveX controls. As mentioned earlier, this includes Visual Basic and C++, Delphi, PowerBuilder, FoxPro, Access, and many others. C++, Delphi, and VB 5.0 also support the creation of ActiveX controls. Therefore, an ActiveX object written in C++ could be dropped onto a Delphi form (or an HTML page for viewing in MS Internet Explorer). The word "object" is intentionally used here to mean a programming construct that encapsulates data and methods in an atomic object.

Programs written in Java, meanwhile, are limited in their capability to communicate with code written in other languages. "Native" language methods can be called through the use of *native methods*; however, once these methods are used, Java classes cannot "travel" to remote machines as they do when they are downloaded to a client browser. Native methods can also link only to static object code, so there is no way to dynamically update the linked-in code, as there is with ActiveX objects.

Distributed

With the advent of Distributed COM in Windows NT 4.0, ActiveX objects also have the capability to communicate with other objects located on remote machines. These objects can be placed on other machines for a variety of reasons:

- Maintainability—Objects can be updated once on the server, and all clients will immediately "see" the update.

- Network Performance—Each individual object does not need to be downloaded in its entirety over the network; instead, remote procedure calls (RPCs) are used to communicate between the objects.

- Scalability—DCOM enables objects to be mirrored across multiple machines to improve performance for the end user.

Much attention has been paid to the two-tier design of traditional client/server applications. In this development mode, all of the display and application logic resides on the client (the Web browser containing applets or controls, or a normal GUI application) and the database operations reside on the server. Several problems arise with this development paradigm. The biggest problem is that the display code and the application code often become so intertwined that code maintenance is extremely difficult. If you need to dramatically change a screen, a huge amount of reworking is involved before you can make the change. Breaking applications into logical portions and distributing these segments across multiple tiers (often called *n-tiers*) leads to better maintainability, performance, and scalability.

The Flip Side: ActiveX's Disadvantages

Believe it or not, despite the marketing hype surrounding ActiveX, it does have some real disadvantages to go with its advantages. These disadvantages are discussed in an unbiased manner in the following sections.

Platform-Dependent

ActiveX is advertised by Microsoft as having "cross-platform support." Although behind-the-scenes versions of ActiveX are being readied for the Macintosh and UNIX operating systems, the fact remains that ActiveX today can be used only on Microsoft's own operating system (Windows). To Microsoft's credit, the Component Object Model (COM) in no way specifies any vendor- or platform-specific implementation features. However, so far no company besides Microsoft has stepped forward and built an implementation on top of COM.

A discussion seems to continually rage in the Java newsgroup (comp.lang.java) over whether the words "cross-platform" even matter. After all, Microsoft owns a nearly 90 percent share of the personal computing operating system market, so who cares about "cross-platform"? In other words, what good does being "cross-platform" do you if all of your customers' platforms are the same? This is an extremely interesting point and, as with all good questions, there is no easy answer. In an ideal world, each individual user could choose his computing environment based on his personal preferences. That is, the software would come to the user, rather than the user being forced to go where the software is.

Java is not completely free from this discussion, either. Even though Java code might be able to run unmodified on virtually any platform, it is unable to interoperate with other parts of the operating system. In a generic Web-centric environment, the Web browser itself could act as the operating system and applet execution environment. However, this excludes all of the applications that take advantage of operating-system features to provide more value to the end user (printing, file access, inter-application data sharing, and so on).

Microsoft has announced its intention to develop ActiveX-aware versions of its Internet Explorer browser for the Macintosh and UNIX operating systems. The time frame in which these browsers are introduced, combined with the success of the Mac and UNIX ports of ActiveX, plays a key role in the success of Microsoft's "cross-platform" ActiveX strategy.

Security Model

Java was designed from the ground up to ensure that a person who used a client machine running Java code could be nearly certain that the code would not harm the local system. No matter who the developer of the Java applet is, a user can download an applet, run it, and never really think about the security implications of doing so. This is because Java applets have no capability to read or write to the local file system or to make any operating system calls (a security technique known as *sandboxing*). Although no system connected to the outside world via the Internet can ever be 100 percent secure, the Java language and runtime environment go a long way to prevent security flaws.

ActiveX controls, meanwhile, have full system privileges. After an ActiveX control is downloaded, your Windows Registry can be updated, and the component will be installed onto your local system. The ActiveX control can perform a directory search of the file system, change video resolutions, reboot your computer, or even grab files and send them over the Internet to a remote server. With these capabilities, no security model on earth will ever make users feel completely comfortable. Microsoft is trying, however, to convince the computer industry and the public in general of the virtues of its ActiveX security model. This model uses a technique known as *code signing* to verify the contents of ActiveX controls before they are downloaded.

Code signing is provided by an independent software testing facility (called Certification Authorities) that tests code to verify that it does what it says it does. When this software has been tested, the code is signed using a *digital signature.* These signatures contain information that can be examined by software that supports the Microsoft Trust Verification service (Internet Explorer, for example). Using this service, a Web browser can determine whether a control has been modified since it was assigned a digital signature. If it has been tinkered with, the Web browser can alert the user or disenable downloading.

> **CAUTION**
>
> Keep in mind that ActiveX components, unlike Java applets, do not undergo any runtime verification. Therefore, after the control is installed on a machine it is free to do whatever it wants.

ActiveX controls are not required to use code signing. In fact, Internet Explorer 3.0 offers users the ability to fully control the security level at which they want to operate (see Figure 10.2).

Figure 10.2.

The Internet Explorer Security Options dialog box.

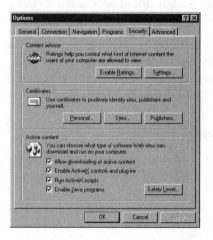

Security can mean different things to different people. Java is secure in that Java code is unable to access the local operating system when it is running within a Web browser. ActiveX security, though not as foolproof, potentially still could provide the same level of security that is expected today when users purchase shrink-wrapped software. Perhaps the biggest problem with ActiveX security is the fact that it leads the public to trust only software produced by the major software manufacturers. A tiny, brand-new software company might have difficulty convincing the public to download and run its ActiveX code, especially when a comparable product is offered by a major manufacturer such as Microsoft.

Network Performance

One other disadvantage of ActiveX controls that is often ignored is their sheer size. Going back to the partial list of ActiveX controls installed currently on my machine, the following listing shows these controls and their size. Some of the controls are OLE controls and others are actual ActiveX controls, and therefore are noticeably smaller (the Stock Ticker and RealAudio controls, in particular).

- Map Display (374KB)
- Chart (294KB)
- Spreadsheet (623KB)
- Spellchecker (84KB)
- RealAudio (114KB)
- Stock Ticker (88KB)
- Movie Player (187KB)
- Image Viewer (96KB)
- Date and Calendar (325KB and 228KB)
- Progress Bar (208KB)

In contrast, the 470 Java classes included in the Visual J++ `classes.zip` file take up a total of 804KB, or approximately 1.71KB each. Although it is true that some applets also download several additional classes in order to be interpreted and run, all of the 470 files in the Visual J++ class library will be included on the local Windows machine as part of the Microsoft Virtual Machine. (In other words, they don't need to be downloaded in that case.) Microsoft has gone a step further with the Visual J++ product and enabled developers to package all of the required class files for an applet together into a single `.CAB` file. This file is compressed on the server side, and then the individual class files are extracted from the CAB file as the Java Virtual Machine needs them. Compressing files in this way greatly reduces download time of Java classes.

Some ActiveX controls also require DLLs (dynamic link libraries) and other files to be installed along with the ActiveX control. When these controls are downloaded, an installation routine will often start and install the control onto the local machine. Although this process has to be completed only once, it still causes a long enough wait that many users might just cancel the operation altogether. Developers who have built OLE controls should obtain the ActiveX SDK and really look at converting these controls to true ActiveX controls in order to save download time.

Browser-Dependent

As you probably are well aware by now, ActiveX is supported natively only in Microsoft's Internet Explorer 3.0 browser. A Netscape plug-in that enables Netscape Navigator to display pages containing ActiveX controls can be obtained from nCompass Labs, but this product is not supported by Netscape. Through the 4.0 release of Navigator, Netscape has no plans to add ActiveX support into its browser, either. All of this means that if you were to build Web pages containing ActiveX controls or Java applets communicating with ActiveX components (as you see later in this chapter), those pages would not display correctly within any browser but Microsoft Internet Explorer.

As new ActiveX-enabled versions of Microsoft Internet Explorer become available for the Macintosh and UNIX platforms, the debate is sure to change. At that point, an overwhelming majority of operating systems would feature support for ActiveX and Java, making it likely that both technologies will continue to coexist for some time to come. However, developers interested in ActiveX should realize that there is a growing contingent of users who are worried about ActiveX's security drawbacks, as well as its platform dependence. These concerns should be taken into consideration when making development choices.

What Does This Mean for the Web Developer?

All of this jockeying for position in the Web sweepstakes has left many developers' heads spinning. Microsoft continues to release a barrage of related ActiveX technologies, with little explanation of the benefits and drawbacks inherent in each technology's usage. What's worse, because of the real-time nature of the Web, many new features and products have been reported before these features are actually fully developed. (When good developers find it difficult to keep up with new technologies, non-developing journalists can rarely be relied upon to explain these technologies.)

ActiveX and the Intranet

In the short term, the success of ActiveX will be found in the intranet setting. At the department or division level, software and hardware resources can be quantified and controlled to a much larger degree than in the entire Internet. Therefore, organizations that have already chosen Windows 95 or NT as part of their standard desktop should find implementing ActiveX solutions relatively easy. The advantages of ActiveX really show up in this situation, because the department's IS staff can continue to work with the tools with which they've been developing for the past few years. Developers can set up Web servers to provide replication, if necessary, and update objects on servers so that users see the changes in real time. In fact, they can even reuse existing OLE controls and ActiveX controls. At this point, the professional developer should look at encapsulating application logic in the form of distributed objects on servers. The user interface can be generated fairly rapidly using standard Web publishing tools. Developers can also use Java throughout development projects, in combination with ActiveX, to match the best tool with the job.

ActiveX and the Internet

On the other hand, ActiveX faces a much more daunting task before it can claim success across the World Wide Web. Because of security concerns and the fact that a large number of World Wide Web clients are non-Windows machines, ActiveX on the Internet is met with skepticism by most developers. As Microsoft demonstrates the effectiveness of its code-signing solution, and as ActiveX is ported to other platforms, ActiveX should slowly gain a larger measure of support than it currently is receiving.

In any case, to reach the lowest common denominator, pure Java is still the best choice for providing active Web applications to the greatest number of clients. Despite its flaws, the Java language and runtime environment were designed with the Web in mind (not retrofitted for the Web after the fact) and contain several advantages simply not found in any other technology on the market today. The following example illustrates the use of Java (using Microsoft Visual J++) to build a COM-aware Java applet.

Combining Java and COM Using Visual J++

No matter how you look at it, the Web developer skilled in Java and COM/ActiveX has the best of the desktop and the Internet at his or her fingertips. The Visual J++ development tool enables the Java programmer to call COM objects using Java code. These COM objects look exactly the same to the developer as every other Java class. In fact, using tools included with Visual J++, actual Java class files are generated for each COM object. These classes can then be imported and used just as if they were a standard class.

This "magic" is made possible through the use of the Microsoft Virtual Machine for Java. Microsoft has licensed the JVM spec from Sun Microsystems and has signed an agreement to build the "reference implementation" of the JVM for the Windows platform. Any additions made to the Windows JVM by Microsoft can then be given back to Sun for inclusion in the Java Virtual Machine Specification, owned by Sun Microsystems. Unlike the virtual machine included with most Web browsers, such as Netscape Navigator, the Microsoft Virtual Machine actually becomes part of the operating system after installation. This means that it is then available to all Windows applications. Because it is itself implemented as a COM object, the Microsoft Virtual Machine can be utilized by any application that supports the same COM interfaces. This enables objects created in Java to appear as COM objects to other Windows applications. In providing this, Microsoft has elevated Java to the same programming status as its other flagship languages: C++ and Visual Basic.

The javabeep example included with Visual J++ demonstrates a Java class-calling COM object (located in the beeper.dll file). This simple object is used to build a Java applet and application that will beep and print a message each time the user clicks the mouse on the application's client window.

Using the Java Type Library Wizard in Visual J++, standard Java classes are generated from the COM object's type library.

These classes provide a mapping between the variables, methods, and interfaces used in the COM object, and the variables, methods, and interfaces in the new Java class. When the Type Library Wizard is finished, two new classes will have been created for your use in the \windows\java\lib\beeper directory:

- `Beeper.class`
- `IBeeper.class`

At this point, to access these two objects (actually contained in the `beeper.dll` COM library), add the following line of code to your Java applet or application:

```
import beeper.*;
```

This will import both classes in the Beeper package. To create a new beeper object for use within your Java class, the following code is sufficient:

```
IBeeper m_Beeper = null;
...
if(m_Beeper==null)
  m_Beeper = (IBeeper) new Beeper();
```

After the object has been created, the following statement will call into the `beeper.dll` and issue a beep:

```
m_Beeper.beep();
```

Programmers with some Java experience should notice that syntactically there is nothing here but standard Java code. The real work is being done at the Virtual Machine level. Figure 10.3 shows the javabeep project running as an application.

Figure 10.4 shows the javabeep project running as an applet.

FIGURE 10.3.

A Java application calling a COM object.

FIGURE 10.4.

A Java applet calling a COM object.

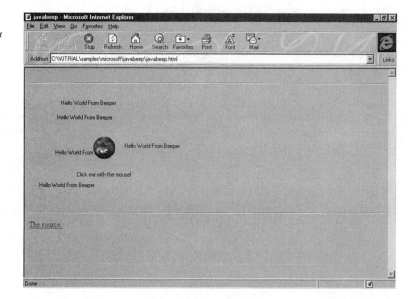

Summary

The ActiveX technologies are extremely powerful and have the potential to enable Web-based applications to do things that were previously impossible. Using ActiveX controls, ActiveX scripting, and ActiveX documents in combination with HTML and Java applets, the software developer can develop truly interactive, interesting applications using the Web browser as the operating environment. With a tool such as Visual J++, the ActiveX controls can even be built using Java, and Java applets can contain ActiveX controls. This gives the professional software developer the best technologies of the desktop, combined with the best technologies of the Internet.

ActiveX itself comes with several advantages and disadvantages. It has the advantages of being language independent, having good performance, and a large existing code base. Some of its drawbacks include its platform dependence (it can be used only on Windows at the current time), its access to the local operating system, and its level of browser support (only Internet Explorer at the current time).

10

EXTENDING JAVA
USING ACTIVEX

Microsoft is taking steps to address each of these issues and will eventually get there, but many developers are comfortable with the capabilities of Java as it currently exists. To port ActiveX to a small number of desktop operating systems requires an extensive effort, while the Java Virtual Machine already exists on nearly every operating platform in use today. ActiveX security (via code signing) requires an independent certification authority to certify and verify a control's behavior.

Tools such as Visual J++ enable Java developers to pick and choose among different Java, COM, and ActiveX objects and build applications using the best features of all three technologies. Visual J++ comes with three wizards designed to greatly enhance the productivity of the Java programmer.

- The Java Applet Wizard
- The Java Resource Wizard
- The Java Type Library Wizard

These wizards, combined with a visual debugger, online documentation, and excellent development environment, give the Java programmer an extremely flexible tool that can be used for standard Java programming, as well as ActiveX programming.

Over time, it will become more apparent whether ActiveX's strengths are enough to overcome its inherent weaknesses. Until then, it is likely that both technologies will coexist and continue to improve. If this happens, it will be to the software developer's benefit.

CGI and the Internet

by Bob Breedlove

IN THIS CHAPTER

What Is CGI and What Can It Do?

The Common Gateway Interface (CGI) is a standard for interfacing external applications with information servers, such as Web servers. A plain HTML document that the Web server retrieves is static—a text file that doesn't change. Every time you call a CGI program in real time, on the other hand, it executes and outputs dynamic information.

CGI version 1.1 started with the idea of hooking a UNIX database to the Internet. Figure 11.1 shows the simple concept of the CGI interface.

FIGURE 11.1.

The concept of CGI programs.

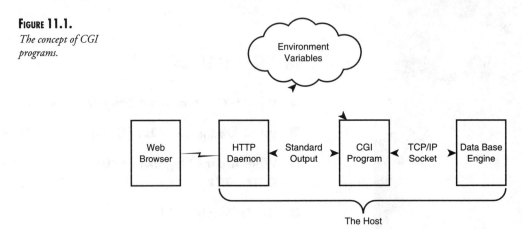

CGI began as a way to interface databases to the Web, but CGI programs provide whatever access you want to program within the limits of the server/browser.

The Web browser communicates with the host server (daemon) using HTTP. When the Web browser requests the Universal Resource Locator (URL), or address, of a CGI program, the server starts the CGI program with the daemon's standard input attached to the CGI program's standard output. The CGI program services the request and communicates with the database engine using its application program interface (API), which usually uses some form of interprocess communication, shared memory, or sockets.

The database engine retrieves the requested data and returns it to the CGI program. The CGI program formats a Web page using hypertext markup language (HTML) and returns it to the Web daemon via its standard output. The daemon returns the HTML to the browser on the client machine, which formats the page for display.

All CGI programs use this basic concept. A CGI program outputs more than an HTML page, performs all the processing itself, or accesses any type of server. Figure 11.1 shows that the basic process remains the same.

Terminology

In this chapter, many of the terms used are the same as the hypertext markup language (HTML) standards. Some terms are unique to CGI and might not match common usage.

Environment variable	A named parameter that carries information from the server to the script. It is not necessarily a variable in the operating system's environment, although that is the most common implementation.
Script	The software that is invoked by the server via this interface. It need not be a stand-alone program, but could be a dynamically loaded or shared library or even a subroutine in the server.
Server	The application program that invokes the script in order to service requests. Generally, this application runs as an independent process on the host computer. In UNIX terms, this program is referred to as a *daemon*.

What Are the Benefits of Using CGI?

HTML pages are static. That is, once you create and place them on the server, requests are transmitted in the same format each time they are requested. As Figure 11.2 shows, CGI programs run on the server in real time. With CGI programs, a user can retrieve real-time data and format dynamic pages, and the pages are different with each transmission.

FIGURE 11.2.
CGI programs access data, equipment, and other processes and return a myriad of document types.

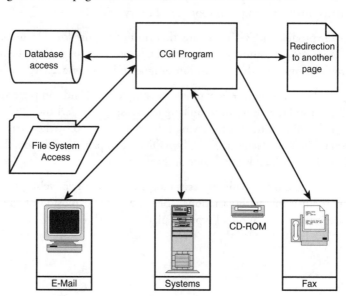

CGI programs return a myriad of document types, not just HTML pages, to the server. They send back an image, a plain-text document, or even an audio clip as well as redirect the user to other documents or CGI programs.

CGI programs can also store and retrieve information about the browser in records called cookies on the client machine. These cookies store information about the user during one session, which the browser transmits when the user next requests your pages. This typically validates a user or allows the user to set up a custom page for their own use on your system. For example, this information is used to store information about what the user has accessed during visits to the site and then is used to customize information (such as advertising) that the user sees on his or her next visit to the site.

Many different compiled languages or scripting languages can be used to write CGI programs. Some of the typical languages include

- C/C++
- Perl
- TCL
- Any UNIX shell
- Visual Basic
- AppleScript

Many people prefer to write CGI in a scripting language such as Perl or a shell rather than a compiled language. This is because scripts don't require compiling, which results in easier incremental development and debugging. The programs to interpret the scripts and their environments usually take up less room on the server.

Tools for producing CGI programs that do not require knowledge of a particular programming language are coming to the market. Choose a language or tool with which you are familiar or which supports the application programming interface (API) of your database engine.

There are hundreds of modules, sample code, and complete applications available for any of the more common languages, especially Perl and C/C++. There are also libraries of routines for retrieving information stored by the daemon and returning information to the Web daemon. The CD-ROM accompanying this book has several examples and URLs to sites with additional code and information.

Unlike Java and other evolving technologies, CGI is a relatively mature protocol. Most Web servers use it (some with variations). Because of the explosion of the Internet, many people have experience with it on all types of platforms and servers.

What Are the Negatives of Using CGI?

One of the biggest negatives of using CGI for Web programming is a security issue.

Running a CGI program is like inviting the world to run a program on your system; therefore, there are security considerations when using CGI programs. Because of the possibility of this abuse by CGI programs, most HTTP daemons limit the directories in which CGI programs reside. Most HTTP daemons require an ID that limits the program's access to other parts of the system.

Hackers can take advantage of poorly protected host systems. CGI programs, therefore, should check data before passing it on. Hackers even breach security holes in some mail systems.

Because CGI programs run entirely on the host computer, they can be a drain on host and network resources. If the user receives a form on his browser and enters information, the information, in whatever state, is transmitted to the CGI program through the HTTP host, and the CGI program edits the information. If errors are found, the information returns over the network to the user for correction. Users edit on the host computer, forcing incorrect information to transmit over the network before discovery.

New technologies, such as Java, promise the capability of editing on the client before the data is transmitted to the host. This should minimize the amount of invalid data that is transmitted over the network.

The Protocols

The basics of CGI are relatively straightforward. As seen in Figure 11.1, the server communicates with the CGI program primarily through environment variables and under some conditions through the command line.

> **NOTE**
>
> Although most CGI implementations use environment variables to transmit information from the server to the CGI program, some implementations may pass information through specific files. An example is MS-DOS where environment space can sometimes be at a premium.

The CGI program communicates with the server through standard output (`stdout`). In most instances, the programmer writes as if the CGI program communicates directly with the client browser. Most information sent by the CGI program passes unaltered by the server to the browser.

The CGI program activates when the browser receives a request for the program's Universal Resource Locator (URL). The server places information in environment variables and activates the program by piping its `stdout` the server's standard input (`stdin`).

The information passes from the server to the program in a standard format. It is the CGI program's job to read and decode this information, perform specific processing, and return information to the browser.

There is no connection maintenance between send/receive exchanges in CGI interactions. If an application requires multiple send/receive exchanges to complete its work, the CGI program is responsible for maintaining information about the conversation between exchanges.

The CGI program writes the information to files or databases on the host or passes information through cookies (which are supported by many browsers). The CGI program then stores information on the client system. This book does not include a discussion of this part of the CGI application function because it is not covered by the CGI specification.

Environment Variables

The server must pass information about the request from the browser to the CGI program. In order to do this, it uses a combination of the command line and environment variables. The following variables are passed to the CGI program for every request:

Environment variable	*Purpose/Comment*
GATEWAY_INTERFACE	The revision of the CGI specification to which this server complies. The format is `CGI`/`revision`.
SERVER_NAME	The server's host name, DNS alias, or IP address as it appears in URLs.
SERVER_SOFTWARE	The name and version of the information server software answering the request (and running the gateway). The format is `name`/`version`.

The next set of environment variables is specific to the request serviced by the CGI program.

Environment variable	*Purpose/Comment*
SERVER_PROTOCOL	The name and revision of the information protocol this request has. The format is `protocol`/`revision`.
SERVER_PORT	The port number to which the request was sent.
REQUEST_METHOD	The method with which the request was made. For HTTP, this is GET, HEAD, POST, and so on.
PATH_INFO	The client gives the extra path information. Scripts can be accessed by their virtual path names followed by extra

	information at the end of this path. The extra information is sent as PATH_INFO and if it comes from a URL, the server should decode it before passing it to the CGI script.
PATH_TRANSLATED	The server provides a translated version of PATH_INFO, which takes the path and does any virtual-to-physical mapping.
SCRIPT_NAME	A virtual path to the script being executed, used for self-referencing URLs.
QUERY_STRING	The information that follows the ? in the URL referencing this script. This is the query information. Never decode the query string in any way. This variable should always be set when there is query information, regardless of command-line decoding.
REMOTE_HOST	The host name making the request. If the server does not have this information, it should set REMOTE_ADDR and leave this unset.
REMOTE_ADDR	The IP address of the remote host making the request.
AUTH_TYPE	If the server supports user authentication and the script is protected, this is the protocol-specific authentication method used to validate the user.
REMOTE_USER	This is the authenticated user name if the server supports user authentication and the script is protected.
REMOTE_IDENT	If the HTTP server supports RFC 931 identification, this variable is set to the remote user name retrieved from the server. Usage of this variable should be limited to logging only.
CONTENT_TYPE	For queries with attached information, such as HTTP POST and PUT, this is the content type of the data.
CONTENT_LENGTH	The length of the content as given by the client.

In addition to these variables, the client supplies any header lines and places them into the environment with the prefix HTTP_ followed by the header name. Any dash characters in the header name then change to underscore characters. The server can exclude any headers that it has already processed, such as Authorization, Content-type, and Content-length. If necessary, the server can choose to exclude any or all of these headers if including them would exceed any system environment limits.

An example of these header lines is the HTTP_ACCEPT variable defined in CGI/1.0. Another example is the header User-Agent.

Environment variable	Purpose/Comment
HTTP_ACCEPT	The MIME types that the client accepts, as given by HTTP headers. Other protocols might need to obtain this information elsewhere. Separate each item in this list with commas according to the HTTP spec. The format is *type/subtype, type/subtype*.
HTTP_USER_AGENT	The browser the client uses to send the request. The general format is *software/version library/version*.

Getting Information from the Server

Every time a server receives a request for the URL of a CGI program, it executes the program in real time. Most of the program's output goes directly to the client. A CGI program does not accept command-line arguments because it uses the command line for other purposes.

CGI uses environment variables to send parameters to the program. The two major environment variables for this purpose are QUERY_STRING and PATH_INFO.

QUERY_STRING is anything that follows the first question mark (?) in the URL. For example, the URL `http://www.myhost.com/cgi-bin/myprog.cgi` activates the program `myprog.cgi` in the `/cgi-bin` directory under the document root on host `www.myhost.com`. To pass additional information to the program, the URL expands to

`http://www.myhost.com/cgi-bin/myprog.cgi?mydata is here`

Place the information in QUERY_STRING as

`QUERY_STRING=mydata+is+here`

This string is encoded in the standard URL format of changing spaces to plus signs (+) and indicating special characters with a percent sign and two-digit number (%xx). The CGI program must decode the string in order to use it.

You can add the QUERY_STRING information using either an ISINDEX document or an HTML form (with the GET action). Another way is to manually embed it into the HTML anchor, which references your gateway. This string usually is an information query—for example, what the user wants to search for in the databases or the encoded results of your feedback GET form.

If the Web daemon is not decoding results from a form, the query string decodes onto the command line. This means that each word of the query string is in a different section of ARGV. The CGI program receives, for example, the query string `my data` as

```
argv[1]="forms"
argv[2]="rule"
```

No decoding or other processing is necessary in order to use the data.

CGI enables the URL to receive extra embedded information, which transmits extra context-specific information to the scripts. The PATH_INFO information passes at the end of the URL without the server encoding any of the information.

A typical use for PATH_INFO information is to provide directory or file information for processing. Suppose that the CGI program

```
http://www.myhost.com/cgi-bin/myprog.cgi
```

needs to process information in directory /mydir. This information passes as an addition to the URL:

```
http://www.myhost.com/cgi-bin/myprog.cgi/mydir
```

> **TIP**
>
> One use of PATH_INFO is to pass configuration filenames to a CGI program. The same base CGI program can then handle multiple configurations by including the configuration file in the URL for the application.

Myprog.cgi knows the location of the document relative to the DocumentRoot via the PATH_INFO environment variable or the actual path to the document via the PATH_TRANSLATED environment variable, which the server generates. Because the first slash / passes with the PATH_INFO variable, it must be stripped if it is not needed.

Getting Form Data

Use the GET and POST methods to retrieve information from the forms. Each method returns the form information in a different manner.

<FORM ACTION=CGI URL METHOD=GET>

If the form tag includes the GET method, the CGI program receives the tags in the QUERY_STRING environment variable. This can be a method of maintaining information about a set of request/send transactions between the client and CGI program. For example, the CGI program might store information about the client by indexing a serial number key and encoding this key in the URL specified in the ACTION= option of the form tag. The URL with the additional key information returns to the program with a click of the Submit button. This allows the program to retrieve the stored information and restore its working environment.

<FORM ACTION=CGI URL METHOD=POST>

If the form tag includes the POST method, the CGI program receives the tags through stdin. Note that the server does not send an indication of end of file (EOF) at the end of data. The program must read the CONTENT_LENGTH environment variable in order to determine the length of the input to read.

Decoding Form Information

Both the GET and POST methods send URL-encoded TAG=data pairs separated by ampersands (&). Plus signs (+) replace spaces, and certain characters are encoded as %xx hexadecimal characters. A NAME tag identifies each FORM variable, and this NAME is placed in the TAG part of the data pair. For example, given the following form:

```
<FORM METHOD=POST>
<INPUT NAME="A" SIZE=5>    (Input "A B C")
<INPUT NAME="B" SIZE=5>    (Input "12345")
<INPUT NAME="C" SIZE=2>    (Input "DE")
</FORM>
```

The CGI program receives the following:

```
CONTENT_LENGTH=20
stdin: A=A+B+C&B=12345&C=DE
```

Luckily, several library routines are available for various languages to decode URL-encoded data. This makes life easier when creating CGI programs.

Returning Information to the Client

CGI programs return many document types:

- An image
- An HTML document
- A plain-text document
- An audio clip

Others types are defined by MIME type. CGI programs also can return references to other documents. The client must know what kind of document the program is sending it so it can display it accordingly. For the client to know this, the CGI program must tell the server what type of document it is returning.

To tell the server what kind of document the program is sending back, whether it is a full document or a reference to one, CGI requires the CGI program to place a short header on the output. This header is ASCII text, consisting of lines separated by either line feeds or carriage returns (or both) followed by a single blank line. The output body then follows in its native format.

A Document with MIME Type

For a full document, the CGI program must tell the server what kind of document it is delivering via a MIME type. Examples of common MIME types are text/html for HTML and text/plain for ASCII text.

Here is an example of an HTML document:

```
Content-type: text/html
<HTML>
<HEAD>
<TITLE>Title Goes Here</TITLE>
</HEAD>
<BODY>
<H1>Heading Goes Here</H1>
Body of the HTML document.
</BODY>
</HTML>
```

A Reference to a Document

Instead of sending the document, the CGI program directs the browser to a particular predefined document or has the server automatically send the new one.

An example is an application that sends existing published white papers based on information requests. In this case, the program should know the full URL of the files to reference and send something like the following:

```
Location: http://www.myserver.com/document_location<lf><lf>
```

The two line-feed characters form a blank line after the Location: line. The server acts as if the client's request was for the returned URL instead of the CGI program. It takes care of looking up the file type and sending the appropriate headers.

If you do want to reference a document that is protected by access authentication, the program must have a full URL in the Location: line. This is because the client and the server must retransact to set up access to the referenced document.

> **NOTE**
>
> If your application needs to send headers such as Content-encoding, your server must be compatible with CGI/1.1. Send the headers and Location or Content-type, and they are sent back to the client.

Using CGI in Internet Applications

by Bob Breedlove

IN THIS CHAPTER

CHAPTER 12

A Common Gateway Interface (CGI) program interfaces with the HTTP server to receive requests from the client browser, perform specific processing, and return information to the user in the form of MIME-encoded documents, most typically Hypertext Markup Language (HTML) pages.

As discussed in the previous chapter, CGI programs can perform any type of processing either directly or indirectly by accessing servers such as database servers. Whether the CGI program performs all the processing itself or is simply the input/output part of a more complex system, the basic concepts are the same.

This chapter presents a basic CGI program to illustrate CGI processing. You can write CGI programs in any number of programming languages. I chose Perl for this illustration for several reasons: It runs on several platforms, it is relatively C-like, and it is easy to modify and run for your own experimentation.

Pseudo Code

Because the actual processing performed by a CGI program depends on your application, it is difficult to define how the bulk of your CGI application will look. This little program doesn't do much useful work (you'll have to decide how to do that), but it does illustrate the basics of CGI programming. Here is the basic pseudo code for the application:

```
Initialize application
if client requests form then
        Send the client form
if client returns form then
        Determine required processing
        Format appropriate reply
        Send Reply to server
Terminate application
```

I'll examine each part of this simple application to discuss elements of CGI programming. More detailed and complex programs are presented in the sections on specific programming languages in Part III, "Internet Scripting Languages."

The CGI Program

The Perl program is called showcgi.pl. The method used to execute this program depends on your environment and server software. However, the most typical way to execute the program includes the following basic steps:

1. Copy the script to the executable directory for your server (typically cgi-bin under the HTTP base subdirectory).

2. Indicate that the program is executable and set the location of your Perl interpreter on the first line of the script.

3. Some servers might require that you change the name of the program to meet some standard.

The entire program follows:

```perl
#!/usr/bin/perl
###################################################################
# Demonstration program for CGI
###################################################################

$http_action = 'http://www.myhost.com/cgi-bin/showcgi.pl';

if ($ENV{'REQUEST_METHOD'} eq "GET") {
    print "Content-type: text/html\n\n";
    print <<EOF;
<H1>Simple Test Form</H1>
<HR>
<FORM ACTION="$http_action" METHOD=POST>
Field1: <input name="field1"><br>
Field2: <input name="field2"><br>
Check : <input type=radio name="cbx1" value="1"> Yes
<input type=radio name="cbx1" value="2"> No <P>
<input type="submit"><P>
</form>
EOF
    ;
} else {
    &ReadData();

    print "Content-type: text/html\n\n";
    print "<H1>Results</H1>";
    print "<HR>";
    print "<H2>Variables</H2>";

    print "<B>GATEWAY_INTERFACE</B>: $ENV{'GATEWAY_INTERFACE'}<BR>\n";
    print "<B>SERVER_NAME</B>: $ENV{'SERVER_NAME'}<BR>\n";
    print "<B>SERVER_SOFTWARE</B>: $ENV{'SERVER_SOFTWARE'}<P>\n";
    print "<B>SERVER_PROTOCOL</B>: $ENV{'SERVER_PROTOCOL'}<BR>\n";
    print "<B>SERVER_PORT</B>: $ENV{'SERVER_PORT'}<BR>\n";
    print "<B>PATH_INFO</B>: $ENV{'PATH_INFO'}<BR>\n";
    print "<B>PATH_TRANSLATED</B>: $ENV{'PATH_TRANSLATED'}<BR>\n";
    print "<B>SCRIPT_NAME</B>: $ENV{'SCRIPT_NAME'}<BR>\n";
    print "<B>QUERY_STRING</B>: $ENV{'QUERY_STRING'}<BR>\n";
    print "<B>REMOTE_HOST</B>: $ENV{'REMOTE_HOST'}<BR>\n";
    print "<B>AUTH_TYPE</B>: $ENV{'AUTH_TYPE'}<BR>\n";
    print "<B>REMOTE_USER</B>: $ENV{'REMOTE_USER'}<BR>\n";
    print "<B>REMOTE_IDENT</B>: $ENV{'REMOTE_IDENT'}<BR>\n";
    print "<B>CONTENT_TYPE</B>: $ENV{'CONTENT_TYPE'}<BR>\n";
    print "<B>CONTENT_LENGTH</B>: $ENV{'CONTENT_LENGTH'}<P>\n";
    print "<B>HTTP_ACCEPT</B>: $ENV{'HTTP_ACCEPT'}<BR>\n";
    print "<B>HTTP_USER_AGENT</B>: $ENV{'HTTP_USER_AGENT'}<P>\n";

    print "<HR>\n";
    print "<H2>Variables Found</H2>\n";
    print "<B>Raw Input:</B> $in<p>";
    print &PrintVariables(%in);
}
```

```perl
sub ReadData {
    local (*in) = @_ if @_;
  local ($i, $loc, $key, $val);

  # Read in text
  if ($ENV{'REQUEST_METHOD'} eq "GET") {
    $in = $ENV{'QUERY_STRING'};
  } elsif ($ENV{'REQUEST_METHOD'} eq "POST") {
    read(STDIN,$in,$ENV{'CONTENT_LENGTH'});
  }

  @in = split(/&/,$in);

  foreach $i (0 .. $#in) {
    # Convert plus's to spaces
    $in[$i] =~ s/\+/ /g;

    # Split into key and value.
    ($key, $val) = split(/=/,$in[$i],2); # splits on the first =.

    # Convert %XX from hex numbers to alphanumeric
    $key =~ s/%(..)/pack("c",hex($1))/ge;
    $val =~ s/%(..)/pack("c",hex($1))/ge;

    # Associate key and value
    $in{$key} .= "\0" if (defined($in{$key})); # \0 is the multiple separator
    $in{$key} .= $val;

  }
}

sub PrintVariables {
  local (%in) = @_;
  local ($old, $out, $output);
  $old = $*;   $* =1;
  $output .=  "<DL COMPACT>";
  foreach $key (sort keys(%in)) {
    foreach (split("\0", $in{$key})) {
      ($out = $_) =~ s/\n/<BR>/g;
      $output .=  "<DT><B>$key</B><DD><I>$out</I><BR>";
    }
  }
  $output .=  "</DL>";
  $* = $old;

  return $output;
}
```

Well, it's not much of a program. In fact, it is just slightly more complex than the classic "Hello World" program found in many C programming texts. Perl is especially suited to CGI programming because it performs excellent text processing, which is the heart of this type of programming.

NOTE

To keep with tradition, here is a Perl "Hello World" CGI program.

```perl
#!/usr/bin/perl
###################################################################
# Demonstration program for CGI
###################################################################

require '/www/cgi-bin/cgi-lib.pl';

print &PrintHeader;
print <<EOF;
<HTML>
<HEAD>
<TITLE>Hello World!</TITLE>
</HEAD>
<BODY>
Hello World!
</BODY>
</HTML>
<<EOF
;
```

This program simply produces a form and displays some information in response to the user's input. An actual CGI application would have more complex processing, but this chapter isn't about the actual programming of the application-specific logic. Instead, it's about the CGI interface side, which is relatively simple.

The program shows much of the decoding logic to illustrate the techniques. In real applications, you will probably use a precoded library for this basic processing. See the specific programming language chapters in Part III for information on these libraries.

Initialization

A CGI program is started from scratch each time the server receives a request for its URL. This means that the program must establish its processing environment each time it is called. The CGI interface does not require any specific initialization. However, your application might need to perform application-specific initialization before processing the CGI request.

Before calling the CGI program, the server places labeled information into environment variables and places other specific information on the command line. The server also communicates with the CGI program through its standard input (stdin) and output (stdout) file handles. In your specific language implementation, you might need to initialize the standard input and output before you use them. Perl does not require initialization of stdin and stdout because it writes to these by default, so only program-specific variables must be initialized at this point.

In showcgi.pl, you need only to set the variable $http_action to the script name. This practice allows the program to perform more complex processing by returning an action that includes a `QUERY_STRING` or `PATH_INFO` entry. For example, suppose your program needs to store information about the user between transactions. The program stores the information in a file whose name is a generated serial number and then passes it back on the `ACTION=` parameter of the `FORM` tag. Here is the Perl code for this type of processing:

```
$HTTP_ACTION = "http://www.myhost.com/cgi-bin/myprog.pl"
# Processing occurs here . . .

if ($ENV{'REQUEST_METHOD'} eq "GET") {
    &File = "$serialnumber"
    print <<EOF
    <HTTP>
    # more of your form here
    <FORM ACTION="$HTTP_ACTION?$File" METHOD=POST>
    # the remainder of the form
EOF
    ;
} else {
    $File = $ENV('QUERY_STRING'};
#    The remainder of POST processing here
}
# The remainder of the program here
```

When this program is first called, the URL does not contain the filename. When the user fills out the form and presses the Submit button, the file information is returned in `QUERY_STRING` and can be used to retrieve the configuration file.

Determining the Request Method

Next, the CGI program must determine what the user is requesting and perform that action. Typically, the first request to a CGI program causes the program to send a form to the user. Once the user has filled out the form, he clicks a Submit button, which returns the information from the form for the CGI program to process.

The CGI program can use several methods to identify the user's request. The most straightforward method is to check the `REQUEST_METHOD` environment variable. The default request method is `GET`. That is, if the user simply clicks the URL, the server returns the `GET` method to his program in the `REQUEST_METHOD` variable. The `POST` method is returned when the Submit button is coded with the `METHOD=POST` parameter. The code to test these is a simple `IF` statement:

```
if $ENV{'REQUEST_METHOD'} eq "GET" {
    Format and return the form
} else {
    Process the user's information
}
```

> **NOTE**
>
> Perl provides the %ENV associative array as a method to access the environment variables passed to the program. Of course, for more complex processing, you can use combinations of request methods and other techniques to distinguish among multiple processing paths.

Sending the Form

Sending a form involves writing the HTML in the correct format to the CGI program's standard output. This information is processed by the server and passed more or less intact to the browser. Remember, the program must write a short header so that the server knows what type of document it is processing. The line in a Perl program to send an HTML page is

```perl
print "Content-type: text/html\n\n";
```

Other headers are determined by the server software. Remember to return a blank line formed by two end-of-line characters (\n\n). Depending on your operating system, these are either carriage return/line feed pairs or simple line feeds.

After the program has sent the header, simply write the document to the standard output in its native format. For HTML, this format is plain ASCII text with HTML markers. The following code fragment illustrates the use of this statement:

```perl
# Program processing to this point . . .
    print "Content-type: text/html\n\n";
    print <<EOF;
<H1>Simple Test Form</H1>
<HR>
<FORM ACTION="$http_action" METHOD=POST>
Field1: <input name="field1"><br>
Field2: <input name="field2"><br>
Check : <input type=radio name="cbx1" value="1"> Yes
<input type=radio name="cbx1" value="2"> No <P>
<input type="submit"><P>
</form>
EOF
    ;
# Additional program processing below . . .
```

In this code fragment, the program prints the header and then prints all the information between the print <<EOF statement and the line containing only EOF. Note the FORM tag specifically:

```perl
<FORM ACTION="$http_action" METHOD=POST>
```

The METHOD= option specifies the method that is returned when the user clicks the Submit button. This particular form sends the POST method. Figure 12.1 shows the form produced by this simple script.

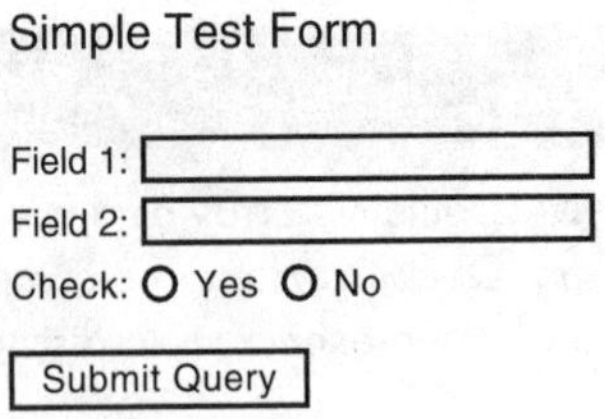

FIGURE 12.1.
The form produced by
showcgi.pl.

Simple Test Form

Field 1: [_____]
Field 2: [_____]
Check: ○ Yes ○ No

[Submit Query]

Note that the Submit button doesn't have to be labeled "Submit."

```
<input type="submit">
```

It's the TYPE= parameter that counts, not the label on the button. You can change the label to anything you want. Note, also, that a more complex screen would probably also include a reset button, which allows the user to clear the screen:

```
<input type="reset">
```

This can be useful if the user uses the Back button on his browser to clear the screen.

Receiving Information from the User

The user fills out the form you send through the server and presses the Submit Query button. This causes the browser to extract the information and send it back to the server. This time, the server sends the POST action in the REQUEST_METHOD environment variable.

The CGI program needs to process the data received with this POST request. The key to receiving this information is to parse the input string and decode it correctly. The subroutine ReadData() does this for my little program.

```perl
sub ReadData {
    local (*in) = @_ if @_;
  local ($i, $loc, $key, $val);

  # Read in text
  if ($ENV{'REQUEST_METHOD'} eq "GET") {
    $in = $ENV{'QUERY_STRING'};
  } elsif ($ENV{'REQUEST_METHOD'} eq "POST") {
    read(STDIN,$in,$ENV{'CONTENT_LENGTH'});
  }

  @in = split(/&/,$in);

  foreach $i (0 .. $#in) {
    # Convert plus's to spaces
    $in[$i] =~ s/\+/ /g;

    # Split into key and value.
    ($key, $val) = split(/=/,$in[$i],2); # splits on the first =.

    # Convert %XX from hex numbers to alphanumeric
    $key =~ s/%(..)/pack("c",hex($1))/ge;
```

```
$val =~ s/%(..)/pack("c",hex($1))/ge;

# Associate key and value
$in{$key} .= "\0" if (defined($in{$key})); # \0 is the multiple separator
$in{$key} .= $val;

    }
}
```

It is not my intention to teach Perl in this chapter. That is left for Section 4, "Perl." You can use this same technique to interpret the input in whatever language you use, so examining the process has some merit.

The first thing to do is read the text. This task varies depending on the method (GET or POST). The following short if statement accomplishes the task:

```
if ($ENV{'REQUEST_METHOD'} eq "GET") {
    $in = $ENV{'QUERY_STRING'};
  } elsif ($ENV{'REQUEST_METHOD'} eq "POST") {
    read(STDIN,$in,$ENV{'CONTENT_LENGTH'});
  }
```

If the request method is GET, the information is contained in the QUERY_STRING environment variable. Simply get the information from this variable into the local variable ($in). If the request method is POST, the process is only slightly more complex. The information is read from standard input. However, the server is not required to place an end-of-field marker of any kind on the data stream. Instead, the length of the data to read from standard input is placed in the CONTENT_LENGTH environment variable. The following line accomplishes this read:

```
read(STDIN,$in,$ENV{'CONTENT_LENGTH'});
```

You can use a similar function in C to accomplish this.

After the program has the data, it must decode it. Say that the input from your form was the following data:

```
Field 1: Field 1 Input
Field 2: Field 2 Input
Cbx1 : YES Checked
```

The input stream would look like this code:

```
field1=Field+1+input&field2=Field+2+input&cbx1=1
```

The CONTENT_LENGTH variable would contain 48.

To process this information, the program has to parse the input into VARIABLE=VALUE pairs. It then has to decode the text VALUE pairs. Finally, it places the information into program variables for processing. The following Perl code accomplishes this for my program:

```
@in = split(/&/,$in);

  foreach $i (0 .. $#in) {
    # Convert plus's to spaces
    $in[$i] =~ s/\+/ /g;
```

```
# Split into key and value.
($key, $val) = split(/=/,$in[$i],2); # splits on the first =.

# Convert %XX from hex numbers to alphanumeric
$key =~ s/%(..)/pack("c",hex($1))/ge;
$val =~ s/%(..)/pack("c",hex($1))/ge;

# Associate key and value
$in{$key} .= "\0" if (defined($in{$key})); # \0 is the multiple separator
$in{$key} .= $val;
```

I won't spend time on the Perl code, which is explained in Section 4. However, notice that Perl's arrays and powerful text-handling features make it especially adept at this type of processing.

System Processing

At this point, your instructions have been retrieved and decoded so that the function of your program is determined. Your program performs the heart of its processing at this point. My "little program" does very little, but the processing that can be done in CGI scripts is limited only by the language and the APIs available to you.

One caution is that your program shouldn't spend too much time doing its work. Browsers have time-outs and if your program takes too long, the browser will think that the transaction has failed and will return a time-out message to the user.

Sending a Reply to the User

After your program finishes processing the request, it can return the new document to the user. Again, your program can choose to send one of many document types. The process is essentially the same as sending out the original document. The following code fragment accomplishes this for my program:

```
print "Content-type: text/html\n\n";
print "<H1>Results</H1>";
print "<HR>";
print "<H2>Variables</H2>";

print "<B>GATEWAY_INTERFACE</B>: $ENV{'GATEWAY_INTERFACE'}<BR>\n";
print "<B>SERVER_NAME</B>: $ENV{'SERVER_NAME'}<BR>\n";
print "<B>SERVER_SOFTWARE</B>: $ENV{'SERVER_SOFTWARE'}<P>\n";
print "<B>SERVER_PROTOCOL</B>: $ENV{'SERVER_PROTOCOL'}<BR>\n";
print "<B>SERVER_PORT</B>: $ENV{'SERVER_PORT'}<BR>\n";
print "<B>PATH_INFO</B>: $ENV{'PATH_INFO'}<BR>\n";
print "<B>PATH_TRANSLATED</B>: $ENV{'PATH_TRANSLATED'}<BR>\n";
print "<B>SCRIPT_NAME</B>: $ENV{'SCRIPT_NAME'}<BR>\n";
print "<B>QUERY_STRING</B>: $ENV{'QUERY_STRING'}<BR>\n";
print "<B>REMOTE_HOST</B>: $ENV{'REMOTE_HOST'}<BR>\n";
print "<B>AUTH_TYPE</B>: $ENV{'AUTH_TYPE'}<BR>\n";
print "<B>REMOTE_USER</B>: $ENV{'REMOTE_USER'}<BR>\n";
```

```
print "<B>REMOTE_IDENT</B>: $ENV{'REMOTE_IDENT'}<BR>\n";
print "<B>CONTENT_TYPE</B>: $ENV{'CONTENT_TYPE'}<BR>\n";
print "<B>CONTENT_LENGTH</B>: $ENV{'CONTENT_LENGTH'}<P>\n";
print "<B>HTTP_ACCEPT</B>: $ENV{'HTTP_ACCEPT'}<BR>\n";
print "<B>HTTP_USER_AGENT</B>: $ENV{'HTTP_USER_AGENT'}<P>\n";
print "<HR>\n";
print "<H2>Variables Found</H2>\n";
print "<B>Raw Input:</B> $in<p>";
print &PrintVariables(%in);
```

As you can see, formatting an HTML page is nothing more than including a set of statements that write to standard output. The subroutine `&PrintVariables(%in)` formats the variables parsed and decoded by the ReadData subroutine to produce a "pretty" output. Figure 12.2 shows part of the page produced by these print statements.

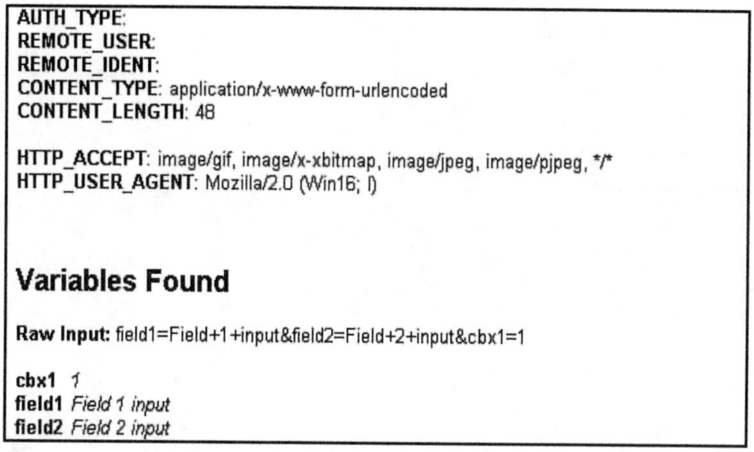

FIGURE 12.2.

Print statements to reply to the user.

```
AUTH_TYPE:
REMOTE_USER:
REMOTE_IDENT:
CONTENT_TYPE: application/x-www-form-urlencoded
CONTENT_LENGTH: 48

HTTP_ACCEPT: image/gif, image/x-xbitmap, image/jpeg, image/pjpeg, */*
HTTP_USER_AGENT: Mozilla/2.0 (Win16; I)
```

Variables Found

Raw Input: field1=Field+1+input&field2=Field+2+input&cbx1=1

cbx1 *1*
field1 *Field 1 input*
field2 *Field 2 input*

Note that you can use showcgi.pl to show the environment variables passed by the server to the CGI program. You might want to try it on your installation.

Summary

Those are the basics of CGI processing. Your programs will be more complex depending on the processing that they must do and the document types they return—but the basics will be the same, straightforward processing as presented in this chapter.

Perl and the Internet

by Bob Breedlove

IN THIS CHAPTER

The Practical Extraction and Reporting Language (Perl) might be one of the best choices for Common Gateway Interface (CGI) scripting languages among the interpreted languages. It is certainly the most popular for a number of reasons. In this chapter, I examine Perl as a language for Internet applications.

What Is Perl?

Perl is an interpreted language optimized for scanning arbitrary text files, extracting information from these files, and printing reports based on that information. It is also a good language for many system management tasks. The language is intended to be practical—easy to use, efficient, and complete—rather than beautiful—tiny, elegant, and minimal. Perl was written by Larry Wall (`lwall@sems.com`), with the help of many other folks.

Perl combines some of the best features of C, sed, awk, and sh. People familiar with these languages should have little difficulty being productive in Perl. Perl's expression syntax is very C-like. Perl uses sophisticated pattern-matching techniques to scan large amounts of data very quickly. Although optimized for scanning text, Perl also can deal with binary data. If you have a program that would ordinarily use sed or awk or sh, but it exceeds their capabilities and you don't want to write the program in a compiled language such as C, then Perl may be for you.

What Are the Benefits of Using Perl?

Perl has many advantages as a CGI scripting language, as described in the following sections.

Cost and Licensing

First, it is generally available on most server platforms, including most UNIX variants, MS-DOS, Windows NT, OS/2, and Macintosh. It also has the distinct advantage of low cost. It is often distributed free or for a small copying fee depending on the source from which you receive the package. Perl is also starting to be distributed with many operating systems or utility packages. For example, the Windows NT Resource Kit includes a copy of Perl.

Actually, Perl is distributed under the GNU CopyLeft agreement or under an "Artistic" license. These licenses have some differences in their requirements and rights assigned. But, basically, they enable you to execute Perl on your system(s), create and distribute Perl applications (scripts) and, if you want, gain access to the source code for Perl itself.

Availability

Perl is readily available from many sources, including any `comp.sources.unix` archive or comprehensive Perl archive network (CPAN) site. If you don't have it on your server or development machine, it is easy to obtain either as source code or precompiled binaries for many platforms. For those not on the Internet, Perl is available via anonymous uucp from both uunet and osu-cis. Also, it is often distributed with CD collections of utilities for UNIX platforms.

Interpreted Language

Perl is interpreted. This can be either an advantage or disadvantage, depending on your point of view. I discuss the disadvantages of interpreted languages in the next section. There are some definite advantages I should go over first.

One advantage of an interpreted language for script development is that you can perform incremental, iterative development and testing without going through a create/modify-compile-test-debug process (cycle). This can speed the development cycle drastically. An interpreted language also can be helpful if you are evolving your application by implementing it with minimal capabilities and adding advanced capabilities later.

Language Capabilities

The heart of programming CGI applications that produce Web pages is text processing. Perl is optimized for text processing, and therefore, it is very efficient at producing Web pages. For example, fields are passed to a CGI application as a string of URL-encoded (Universal Resource Locator or address) text. This means that given three variables (A, B, and C) with text values, for example, you would get something on standard input that looks like this:

```
B=value+of+variable+1&C=value+of+variable+2&C=value+of+variable+3c
```

The CONTENT_LENGTH environment variable is set to the length of this string (67). To read and decode this into variables that the program can use, the CGI application must read in the string for a length of 67, split the variable=value pairs at the & signs, and then change the + signs to spaces. Here is some Perl code to do just that:

```perl
read(STDIN,$in,$ENV{'CONTENT_LENGTH'});

@in = split(/&/,$in);

foreach $i (0 .. $#in) {
    # Convert plus's to spaces
    $in[$i] =~ s/\+/ /g;

    # Split into key and value.
    ($key, $val) = split(/=/,$in[$i],2); # splits on the first =.

    # Convert %XX from hex numbers to alphanumeric
    $key =~ s/%(..)/pack("c",hex($1))/ge;
    $val =~ s/%(..)/pack("c",hex($1))/ge;

    # Associate key and value
    $in{$key} .= "\0" if (defined($in{$key})); # \0 is the multiple separator
    $in{$key} .= $val;
```

This code ends up with an associative array that can be referenced by variable name. Thus, when the CGI program needs the value of variable A, it can refer to

```
$workfield = $in{'A'}
```

Perl is also very good at handling text files that can be used for small databases. Because Perl uses as much memory as is available, it often can hold entire small files in memory in arrays. Because Perl variables are not strongly typed, arrays can hold combinations of numeric and alphabetic information. Here is an example of Perl code to open a comma-delimited file of the type typically produced by databases or spreadsheets and read it into a set of variables:

```
open(IN, "$inFile");

while(<IN>) {
    ($name, $age, $city, $state, $telephone) = split(/,/);
    ...
}

close(IN);
```

Perl also can assign dbm databases to associative arrays. This feature can make dbm databases appear as associative arrays and make them as easy to manipulate as an associative array that is not associated with an underlying database.

The code can create a dbm file and add, update, and delete records from this file with the same commands used to manipulate simple associative arrays. Here is code to open a dbm database and manipulate the records:

```
dbmopen(%mydb,"$filename",0644);

# Add a record to the array with a key of "A"
$mydb{'A'} = 25;

# Get the value of a record with a key of "B"
$value = $mydb{'B'};

# Delete the record with a key of "C"
delete $mydb{'C'};

dbmclose(%mydb);
```

Use C Libraries

Perl can access C libraries to take advantage of much of the code written for this popular language. Utilities included with Perl distributions enable you to convert the headers for these C libraries into their Perl equivalents.

Specialized Extensions to Perl

Perl has many specialized extensions, primarily for handling specific databases such as Oracle, Ingres, and Informix. These combine the strengths of the Perl language with the access to the host database.

ftp.demon.co.uk (158.152.1.44) is the official repository for the database *<foo>*perls in the following list, which can be found in /pub/perl/db/perl4/. The site is mirrored at ftp.cis.ufl.edu (198.17.47.33) in /pub/perl/scripts/db/.

- ■ btreeperl—NDBM extensions
- ■ ctreeperl—C-Tree extensions
- ■ duaperl—X.500 Directory User Agent
- ■ ingperl—Ingres
- ■ isqlperl—Informix
- ■ interperl—INTERBASE
- ■ oraperl—Oracle 6 and 7
- ■ pgperl—POSTGRES
- ■ sybperl—SYBASE 4
- ■ uniperl—UNIFY 5.0

Socket Capability

Perl has the capability to read and write TCP/IP sockets. This gives it the capability to communicate with many servers of all types that rely on socket communication. It also enables you to write utility and "robot" programs in the Perl language. For example, you can use Perl's socket capability to write a robot program to automate site checking to verify the validity of links on your pages. This can be especially useful in keeping a site up-to-date, given the volatility of the Internet in its relative infancy.

Perl Is Relatively Easy to Learn

Unlike many programming languages, Perl is designed to be practical rather than beautiful. Programming in Perl is relatively easy, especially if you have experience in C or another C-like language. Like many scripting languages, Perl reads its programs from the first line to the last. It doesn't require complex structures to create a program. It does, however, support subroutines or functions, and version 5.0 can be object-oriented.

As an example, the "Hello World" program in C is

```
void main()
{
    printf("Hello World!");
}
```

In Perl, it is

```
print 'Hello World!';
```

Perl Has Built-In Debugging Facilities

The Perl interpreter has a built-in debugger that can help reduce the time it takes to debug applications. Because of the nature of CGI programs, however, you might not be able to use this debugger as extensively as you would with other applications.

Perl Help Is Readily Available

Because Perl is very popular as a CGI programming language, there is a lot of help out there. Newsgroup discussions are a good place to start when you require help on Perl programming. There are newsgroups devoted entirely to Perl and newsgroups devoted to Web page creation in which the majority of the discussion is about Perl. Here are some of them:

Newsgroup	Comment
comp.infosystems.www.authoring...	Information about Web page authoring in general.
comp.infosystems.www.authoring.cgi	Information about general CGI programming. Because of the popularity of Perl for CGI, a majority of questions is about the use of Perl on various platforms and with various servers.
comp.infosystems.www.authoring.html	Information about the use of HTML. Some questions require programming in order to implement.
comp.infosystems.www.authoring.misc	Miscellaneous questions about Web authoring. Not as valuable as the specific newsgroups because it carries cross postings from other groups and duplicates much of the information.
comp.infosystems.www...	Information about the specific platforms. The groups covering servers can be valuable.
comp.lang.perl...	Information about Perl in general. Much of the discussion in the specific groups covers using Perl for utility purposes and also as a CGI scripting language.
comp.lang.perl.announce	Information about new modules for Perl programming.
comp.lang.perl	The main newsgroup about Perl.
comp.lang.perl.modules	Discussions of Perl modules.
comp.lang.perl.tk	Discussions of tk use with Perl.

There are, of course, Web pages related to Perl. Check the newsgroups for announcements about these pages. Here are just a couple I have found:

URL	Comment
`http://www.perl.com/`	The Perl language home page. Links to Perl resources.
`http://www.eecs.nwu.edu/perl/perl.html`	Northwestern University's Perl page.
`http://www.yahoo.com/Computers/Languages/Perl/`	Yahoo's Perl index.
`http://www.virtualschool.edu/mon/Perl.html`	The "middle of nowhere" Perl archive (Netscape 2.0 pages).
`http://www.teleport.com/~rootbeer/perl.html`	References with a special emphasis on using Perl for Web-related programming and learning Perl.

Several Frequently Asked Questions (FAQ) lists are posted to the Perl newsgroups. One of the best to start with is the Perl Meta-FAQ produced by Neil Bowers (`neilb@khoros.unm.edu`). As you would expect, this is a FAQ about FAQs. It's available at this writing from the following sources:

HTML	`http://www.khoros.unm.edu/staff/neilb/perl/metaFAQ/metaFAQ.html`
PostScript	`ftp://ftp.khoros.unm.edu/pub/perl/metaFAQ.ps`
ASCII	`ftp://ftp.khoros.unm.edu/pub/perl/metaFAQ.txt`

There are also several excellent books on programming in the Perl language. Most of these give you a good background in the language. Here are a couple of excellent titles from Sams Publishing:

Till, David. *Teach Yourself Perl in 21 Days*. Sams Publishing. ISBN: 0-672-30586-0, $29.99.

Teach Yourself CGI Programming with Perl in a Week. Sams.net Publishing. ISBN: 1-57521-009-6, $39.99.

Perl Examples Are Readily Available

Again, because Perl is so popular as a utility language, there are lots of examples of Perl modules out there. One of the best sources is available via file transfer protocol (FTP) from one of the CPAN sites around the world.

Following are the sites available at the time of this writing. The master CPAN site is `ftp://ftp.funet.fi/` (Finland, Europe). Select the site nearest to you from the following list to get the best response time and bandwidth:

Africa	
South Africa	`ftp://ftp.is.co.za/programming/perl/CPAN/`

Asia	
Japan	`ftp://ftp.lab.kdd.co.jp/lang/perl/CPAN/`
Taiwan	`ftp://dongpo.math.ncu.edu.tw/perl/CPAN/`

Australasia	
Australia	`ftp://coombs.anu.edu.au/pub/perl/`
	`ftp://ftp.mame.mu.oz.au/pub/perl/CPAN/`
New Zealand	`ftp://ftp.tekotago.ac.nz/pub/perl/CPAN/`

Europe	
Czech Republic	`ftp://sunsite.mff.cuni.cz/Languages/Perl/CPAN/`
Finland	`ftp://ftp.funet.fi/pub/languages/perl/CPAN/`
France	`ftp://ftp.ibp.fr/pub/perl/CPAN/`
	`ftp://ftp.pasteur.fr/pub/computing/unix/perl/CPAN/`
Germany	`ftp://ftp.leo.org/pub/comp/programming/languages/perl/CPAN/`
	`ftp://ftp.rz.ruhr-uni-bochum.de/pub/CPAN/`
Netherlands	`ftp://ftp.cs.ruu.nl/pub/Perl/CPAN/`
Poland	`ftp://ftp.pk.edu.pl/pub/lang/perl/CPAN/`
Portugal	`ftp://ftp.ci.uminho.pt/pub/lang/perl/`
Slovenia	`ftp://ftp.arnes.si/software/perl/CPAN/`
Sweden	`ftp://ftp.sunet.se/pub/lang/perl/CPAN/`
Switzerland	`ftp://ftp.switch.ch/mirror/CPAN/`
U.K.	`ftp://ftp.demon.co.uk/pub/mirrors/perl/CPAN/`
	`ftp://unix.hensa.ac.uk/mirrors/perl-CPAN/`

North America	
California	`ftp://ftp.cdrom.com/pub/perl/CPAN/`
Florida	`ftp://ftp.cis.ufl.edu/pub/perl/CPAN/`
Illinois	`ftp://uiarchive.cso.uiuc.edu/pub/lang/perl/CPAN/`

Massachusetts	`ftp://ftp.delphi.com/pub/mirrors/packages/perl/CPAN/`
Oklahoma	`ftp://ftp.uoknor.edu/mirrors/CPAN/`
Texas	`ftp://ftp.sedl.org/pub/mirrors/CPAN/`
	`ftp://ftp.metronet.com/pub/perl/`
	`ftp://ftp.sterling.com/CPAN/`

If you program for Perl 5, you might want to get a copy of the Perl 5 Module list maintained by Tim Bunce (`Tim.Bunce@ig.co.uk`) and Andreas Koenig (`modules@franz.ww.tu-berlin.de`). Here's a bit about the list from its introduction:

"This document is a semi-formal list of Perl 5 Modules. The Perl 4 concept of packages has been extended in Perl 5 and a new standardized form of reusable software component has been defined the Module. Perl 5 Modules typically conform to certain guidelines which make them easier to use, reuse, integrate, and extend. The list is posted to `comp.lang.perl.announce` and `comp.answers` on a semi-regular basis. It has two key aims:

1. FOR DEVELOPERS: To change duplication of effort into cooperation.

2. FOR USERS: To quickly locate existing software which can be reused.

This list includes the Perl 5 standard modules, other completed modules, work-in-progress modules, and would-be-nice-to-have ideas for modules. It also includes guidelines for those wishing to create new modules including how to name them."

What Are the Negatives of Using Perl?

Perl has few negatives as a programming language for producing Web pages, but there are some you need to know.

Interpreted Language

Perl is interpreted. Therefore, it is not as fast as compiled languages such as C or C++. Given the speed of modern CPUs, this does not make a significant difference in all but very large or time-critical applications. In fact, the interpreted nature of the language can reduce development time significantly by eliminating the time needed to compile and debug versions of the program.

GNU CopyLeft License Agreement

The GNU license under which Perl is distributed is really pretty innocuous, but it might be a problem depending upon the type of application you are developing. If you intend to do either of the following, Perl is probably not the best language to choose:

- Sell the application as a packaged product
- Distribute an application that includes trade secrets

What Can Perl Do?

Perl is used to develop many Internet applications and their supporting utility applications. I present some examples here, but Chapters 14, "The Perl Language," and 15, "Perl in Internet Applications," give you a broader understanding of the types of Internet programming that you can perform with the language.

CGI Scripts

As mentioned throughout this chapter, Perl is one of the most popular languages for creating CGI applications. There are literally thousands of examples of dynamic CGI programming in Perl. You can use Perl to create dynamic Web pages that can change depending on different factors, including which visitor is viewing them.

One of the most common uses of Perl on the Internet is processing form input. Perl is especially adept at this chore because most of this input is textual, Perl's strength.

Mail Processing

Another popular use of Perl is the automated processing of Internet e-mail. Perl scripts have been used to filter mail based on address or content. Perl scripts also have been written to automate mailing lists. One of the most popular of these programs is Majordomo.

I have written a Perl script to automate my "What's New?" Web page. This script processes mail messages and adds them to my "What's New?" page. It also removes the entries from the page after they have been there for a specified length of time.

Automating Web Site Maintenance

You can use Perl to automate the maintenance of Web sites. Because Web pages are little more than text files in a specific format, Perl is particularly adept at processing them. You also can use Perl's socket capability to contact other sites and request information using HTTP. There has even been a Web server written in Perl.

To check the links on a site, a Perl program must parse the site's pages starting with the main page, extract the URLs, and determine that these URLs are still active.

Automating File Retrieval

Several FTP clients are written in Perl. You can use Perl to automate file retrieval via FTP. Again, this combines the socket capability of Perl with its text-processing capability.

Is Perl for You?

Only you can answer this question. The next few chapters give you a good foundation in the Perl language, which might help you decide if you want to use Perl for Internet programming. If you don't make it your main Web programming language, you might find that it becomes your utility language for the Web because of its versatility, ease of use, and popularity.

The Perl Language

by Bob Breedlove

IN THIS CHAPTER

CHAPTER 14

The goal of this chapter is to explain the Perl language so that you can use it to create Web applications. I do not attempt in this short space to cover all the capabilities of Perl. Several good books on programming Perl are available, including *Teach Yourself Perl in 21 Days* and *Perl 5 Unleashed*, both from Sams Publishing. This chapter assumes that you have at least a basic understanding of programming and programming terminology.

This chapter relies heavily on the Perl manual pages (man pages). The UNIX man facility provides online documentation from specially formatted files and is the standard for UNIX-based documentation. Implementations of Perl for other operating systems might also supply versions of this authoritative documentation. For ease of access, the Perl manual has been split up into several sections. References are made throughout this chapter using the standard naming convention for these pages as shown in the following table.

Man page	Description
perl	Perl overview (this section)
perldata	Perl data structures
perlsyn	Perl syntax
perlop	Perl operators and precedence
perlre	Perl regular expressions
perlrun	Perl execution and options
perlfunc	Perl built-in functions
perlvar	Perl predefined variables
perlsub	Perl subroutines
perlmod	Perl modules
perlref	Perl references and nested data structures
perlobj	Perl objects
perlbot	Perl object-oriented tricks and examples
perldebug	Perl debugging
perldiag	Perl diagnostic messages
perlform	Perl formats
perlipc	Perl interprocess communication
perlsec	Perl security
perltrap	Perl traps for the unwary
perlstyle	Perl style guide
perlapi	Perl application programming interface
perlguts	Perl internal functions for those doing extensions
perlcall	Perl calling conventions from C

Man page	Description
perlovl	Perl overloading semantics
perlembed	How to embed Perl in your C or C++ app
perlpod	Perl plain old documentation

One excellent version of the documentation is supplied as Adobe Acrobat files. It is available on the Web at

`http://www.perl.com/CPAN/authors/id/BMIDD/perlpdf-5.002.tar.gz`

Adobe readers are available free for many operating systems; check `http://www.adobe.com` for current availability.

The man pages are also available in HTML format as Web pages. They are available on the Internet at

`http://www.perl.com/CPAN/doc/manual/html/index.html`

or packaged in two formats at

`http://www.perl.com/CPAN/doc/manual/html/PerlDoc-beta1g-html.tar.gz`
`http://www.perl.com/CPAN/authors/id/BMIDD/perlhtml-5.002.tar.gz`

If you do not have easy access to this complete reference set with your version of Perl, you should take the time to download a copy.

At this writing, two versions of Perl are in common use. Version 4+ and version 5+ (version numbers for version 5 might vary). I cover aspects of the language common to both and only touch on the more advanced aspects of version 5+ that are directly applicable to Web applications.

After you have completed this and the next chapter, "Perl in Internet Applications," you should have a solid understanding of Perl and be able to create Web applications using this language.

About the Perl Chapters

This and the following chapters form a reference and tutorial for the Perl language in Internet programming. This chapter follows the organization of the Perl manual. I hope that the information here clarifies some aspects of Perl programming that are especially important in Internet programming.

Perl provides a number of equally good ways to accomplish a task. The best way to learn to program in Perl is to program in Perl. Because it is an interpreted language, you can develop and test small portions of a program with relative ease in a small amount of time. In the following chapter, a small application acts as a tutorial in Perl programming. You are encouraged to

14

THE PERL
LANGUAGE

enter the program code along with the chapter, to try it, and to experiment with alternative programming techniques by either modifying the samples or creating your own code based on the demonstrated techniques.

Perl varies some depending on the platform on which it is implemented and the version of the language that runs on your installation. I'll point out differences where applicable.

Writing Perl Scripts

To reiterate an important point, the best way to learn to write Perl scripts is to simply write Perl scripts. That statement isn't quite as silly as it sounds. Perl is intended to be a language in which you can get things done, and it usually gives you more than one way to accomplish a task. The scripts can be simple, straightforward, and quick-and-dirty or elegant and organized. (This ability to write either quick-and-dirty code or elegant and organized code is especially true if you are using the object-oriented aspects of Perl version 5. These aspects of the language are beyond the scope of this chapter, however.)

In keeping with the tradition of most programming texts (at least for C-like languages), here is the popular Hello World script (program) for Perl:

```
print "Hello World\n";
```

Not much of a program, is it? It is fully functional, however. Compare the Perl script with its C counterpart:

```
void main()
        printf("Hello World\n");
}
```

You'll notice differences right away. First, because Perl is a scripting language, it starts at the top of the script file and works its way to the bottom. It can take some branches, perform some loops, or execute some functions, but top-to-bottom execution is the basic rule of script programming. Perl has no main() function. Perl starts with the first executable instruction it finds and executes instructions until it executes the entire script. Note that subroutines (functions), methods, packages, and so on are not considered executable instructions for this purpose.

The Perl print statement is also less complex than its C counterpart. Perl actually supports the printf() function, but the print statement prints to the standard output just fine.

Executing Perl Scripts

The techniques used to execute Perl will vary somewhat by operating system. Generally, Perl is supplied as an executable program (file). Refer to your specific operating system manuals for instructions on how to execute programs, and refer to the documentation with Perl for your specific platform for specifics on executing Perl scripts. This section takes the simplest example of command-line operating systems such as UNIX and MS-DOS. In general, the following steps are needed to create and execute the Hello World script:

- Create a file with your favorite text editor.
- Type the line `print "Hello, world\n";`.
- Save the file under any name you want—`hello.pl` might be appropriate on many systems; `my.first.Perl.hello.program` or `the first script` also works for those of you who simply won't conform to the eight-plus-three MS-DOS naming convention, and your operating system allows long names.
- Type `Perl hello.pl`.

You should see the `Hello, world` phrase on your screen followed by a newline.

On most UNIX systems and Windows NT, the Perl interpreter can be associated with a particular file naming pattern to allow a safer execution of Perl for purposes of writing CGI programs. For example, if you had associated Perl with files ending in `.pl`, the command `hello.pl` would execute the `Hello World` script when entered on the command line.

Note that in Web programming the following construct is *very* dangerous, and you should avoid using it at all costs:

```
http://{host}/{library}/Perl?hello.pl
```

If you allow this, any Perl script can be substituted, with possible disastrous effects for your host site. Instead, if you are going to do Web programming in Perl, you should be able to execute your Perl scripts by entering only the name of the script. The exact method you use to accomplish this task depends upon your operating system.

On UNIX platforms, Perl scripts can be executed in the same way that shell scripts are executed—that is, by providing the full location of the interpreter (Perl, in this case) on your system by making the first line of the script a comment in a special format:

```
#!{interpreter location}
```

On my installation, the location is `/usr/bin/Perl`. Thus, you can modify the "Hello World" program to be

```
#!/usr/bin/Perl
print "Hello World\n";
```

Then use the `chmod` command to set the resulting script file to be executable using some variation of the command:

```
chmod +x hello.pl
```

You run the executable by simply entering its name at the command prompt (`hello.pl<enter>`).

On other systems, you might have to register the extension (`.pl`) with the operating system to run the interpreter when a file with this extension is selected. Note also that some HTTP daemons or installations require scripts with specific extensions. The installation on which my home page is located (`http://www.channel1.com/users/rbreed01/`), for example, requires that all executable scripts have an extension of `.cgi`.

Perl Style

Everyone who writes in Perl develops a personal style. Style is important when you want to change something on your script—and you *will* want to change things—sometimes months after you have implemented the script. Style and comments can help you make improvements in your script at a later date with a minimum of fuss.

Programmers can argue style until the cows come home. Larry Wall has some definite feelings about Perl style. If you're interested, check out the perlstyle man page. The important point is readability and maintainability. You have to be able to figure out what is going on and be able to make changes to your code quickly.

The following list outlines some more substantive style issues you might want to consider. For examples and other issues, see the perlstyle man page.

- Perl gives you several ways to do anything, so consider picking the most readable one.

- Just because an operator allows you to omit default arguments doesn't mean that you have to use the defaults. If you want a more maintainable program supply the argument.

- Just because Perl enables you to omit parentheses in many places doesn't mean that you should.

- Don't go through silly contortions to exit a loop at the top or the bottom when Perl provides the last operator so you can exit in the middle. Use a comment to emphasize that you are exiting the loop at that point.

- Use loop labels to enhance readability as well as allow multilevel loop breaks.

- For portability, when using features that might not be implemented on every machine, test the construct with an eval statement to see if it fails. If you know the version or patch level in which a particular feature was implemented, you can test $] ($Perl_VERSION in English) to see if it is implemented. The Config module also lets you interrogate values determined by the Configure program when Perl was installed.

- Use mnemonic identifiers. $LastDate is much more useful than $a1.

- Use underscores or capitalization to enhance readability. $MyLastName or $My_Last_Name is more readable than $mylastname. (I prefer to use capital letters because I don't like pressing the Shift key hundreds of times to get underscores into the program.)

- Use the /x modifier and put some whitespace into long, complex regular expressions to make them more readable. Don't use the slash as a delimiter when your regexp has slashes or backslashes.

- Use "here documents" (print <<LABEL) instead of repeated print() statements.

> **NOTE**
>
> Using "here documents" can actually detract from readability of indentations used for formatting in programs. You might want to include some comments and whitespace to delineate the document.

- Line up corresponding elements such as the beginning and end of blocks and commands within a block vertically, especially if you can't fit everything on one line.

- Always check the return codes of system calls. Good error messages should go to STDERR, include which program caused the problem, identify the failed system call and arguments, and (very important) contain the standard system error message for what went wrong.

- Think about reusability. Why waste brain power on a one-shot program? Consider generalizing your code. Consider writing a module or object class.

- Be consistent—not only within a program, but for all programs. If you always do things the same way, you won't have to shift mental gears when you go from script to script.

Perl Data Types

Perl has three data types:

- Scalars
- Arrays of scalars
- Associative arrays of scalars ("hashes")

Perl is not strongly typed. In fact, all data in Perl is either a scalar, an array of scalars, or a hash of scalars. You do not have to declare variables as a particular type (integer, character, or Boolean) before you use them. Variables can contain either numeric or alphanumeric data and can vary throughout the execution of the program. The following code is valid in a Perl script:

```
$a = 'some string';
...
$a = 25;
```

Because arrays are arrays of scalars, different elements of an array can contain either numeric or alphanumeric data. The following code

```
@a = (1, 2, 'buckle my shoe,', 3, 4, 'shut the door.');
print join(' ',@a), "\n";
```

works just fine and results in the following line:

```
1 2 buckle my shoe, 3 4 shut the door.
```

A scalar value is interpreted as TRUE in the Boolean sense if it is not the null string or the number 0 (or its string equivalent, 0). The Boolean context is simply a special kind of scalar context.

The two varieties of null scalars are defined and undefined. *Undefined null scalars* are returned when something doesn't have a real value, such as when an error occurs, at end of file, or when you refer to an uninitialized variable or element of an array. In Perl, variables do not have to be predefined. Therefore, an undefined null scalar may become defined the first time you use it as if it were defined (such as in an assignment statement). However, before that, you can use the defined() operator to determine whether the value is defined.

Normal arrays are indexed by number with the first element indexed at zero. Negative subscripts count from the end. Hash arrays are indexed by string.

Scalar values are always named with $, even when referring to a scalar that is part of an array:

```
$month # a simple value holding the month of the year

@month =
➥('Jan','Feb','Mar','Apr','May','Jun','Jul','Aug','Sep','Oct','Nov','Dec');
$month[0] # the first element of array @month, 'Jan'
%month = ('Jan',31,'Feb',28,'Mar',31);
$month{'Feb'} # the 'Feb' value from the associative array %month or 28
```

Entire arrays or array slices are denoted by @:

```
@month # The entire array
@value[3,4,5] # the 4th through 6th elements of the array
@things{'abc','def'}
➥# the elements indexed by 'abc' and 'def' from the associative array
```

Entire hashes are denoted by %:

```
%days # (key1, val1, key2, val2 ...)
```

Subroutines are named with an initial &:

```
if (&getValue() < 10) {
        ...
}
sub getValue {
        ...
        return $value
}
```

Perl Variable Naming Conventions

Every variable type has its own namespace. You can use the same name for a scalar variable, an array, or a hash. Therefore, $foo and @foo are two different variables, and $foo[1] is a part of @foo, not a part of $foo.

In general, Perl variable names can contain any combination of characters, underscores, and special characters. I personally prefer to use all characters and digits to avoid some of the special cases described in the following paragraphs.

Because variable and array references always start with $, @, or %, the Perl "reserved" words, which define the language constructs, aren't in fact reserved with respect to variable names. They are reserved with respect to language elements, such as labels and filehandles, however, which don't have an initial special character.

Like C, case is significant in Perl—"FOO", "Foo", and "foo" are all different names. Names that start with a letter or underscore can also contain digits and underscores.

You can use an expression that returns a reference to an object of the same type as a variable.

Names that start with a digit can only contain more digits. Names that do not start with a letter, underscore, or digit are limited to one character—for example, $% or $$. (Most one-character names have a predefined significance to Perl. For instance, $$ is the current process ID.)

Scalar Values

Numeric literals are specified in any of the customary floating-point or integer formats:

```
12345
12345.67
.23E-10
0xffff # hex
0377 # octal
4_294_967_296 # underline for legibility
```

String literals are usually delimited by either single or double quotes. Double-quoted string literals are subject to backslash and variable substitution. Single-quoted strings are not subject to these substitutions except for "" and \\. The usual UNIX backslash rules apply for making characters such as newline and tab, as well as some more exotic forms.

You can also embed newlines directly in your strings; that is, strings can end on a different line from where they begin. This feature is nice, but if you forget your trailing quote, the error is not reported until Perl finds another line containing the quote character, which might be much farther on in the script. Variable substitution inside strings is limited to scalar variables, arrays, and array slices. The following example prints the name in the line:

```
$name = 'Fred';
print "Hello, $name!\n";
```

As in some shells, you can put curly brackets around the identifier to delimit it from following alphanumerics. In fact, an identifier within such curlies is forced to be a string, as is any single identifier within a hash subscript.

```
$days{'Feb'}
```

can be written as

```
$days{Feb}
```

and the quotes are assumed automatically. Anything more complicated in the subscript is interpreted as an expression.

Note that a single-quoted string must be separated from a preceding word by a space because a single quote is a valid character in an identifier.

A word that has no other interpretation in Perl is treated as a quoted string. These words are known as *barewords*. A bareword that consists entirely of lowercase letters risks conflict with future reserved words. You might want to avoid barewords entirely or always code them in uppercase.

Perl supports a line-oriented form of quoting. Following a command, you specify a string to terminate the quoted material, and all lines following the current line down to the terminating string are the value of the item. The terminating string can be either an identifier (a word) or some quoted text. If quoted text, the type of quotes you use determines the treatment of the text, just as in regular quoting. An unquoted identifier works like double quotes. You cannot leave a space between the << and the identifier. The terminating string must appear by itself— unquoted and with no surrounding whitespace—on the terminating line.

This line-oriented format can be especially helpful in producing HTML pages. The following script prints the template for an HTML page:

```
print <<EOF;
<HTML>
<HEAD>
<TITLE>...</TITLE>
</HEAD>
<BODY>
...
</BODY>
</HTML>
EOF
        ;
```

Note that the terminating EOF is on a line by itself and a semicolon (;) is supplied on the next line.

List values are separated by commas and enclosed in parentheses. The following code

```
@myList = (1,2,3,4,5);
```

assigns the values 1–5 to the array variable @myList. Arrays assigned to other arrays lose their identity. Given the assignment above,

```
@myList2 = (@myList,6,7,8,9,10);
```

is equivalent to

```
@myList2 = (1,2,3,4,5,6,7,8,9,10);
```

You cannot identify @myList within @myList2.

The null list is represented by ().

Lists can be assigned to when the elements of the list are valid to be assigned to. This feature can be useful when splitting comma-delimited files.

```
while(<IN>) {
      chop;
      ($name, $addr, $city, @junk) = split(/,/);
      ...
}
```

The preceding script reads lines from the filehandle IN and splits them by commas, placing the first three results from the split into $name, $addr, and $city, respectively, and the remainder of the line, if any, into the array @junk. (If you aren't going to use the remainder of the line, you can leave off @junk, and the remainder of the line is not assigned.)

You can actually place an array or hash anywhere in a list, but then all remaining items are assigned to the array; any subsequent items in the list are unassigned.

When assigning values to a hash, you can use the => operator. Using the operator is just a more visible way of showing the assignment. For example, the following assignments are equivalent:

```
%stuff = ( thing1 => 'abcde',
           thing2 => 'defgh',
           thing3 => 'ijklm');

%stuff = ( thing1, 'abcde',
           thing2, 'defgh',
           thing3, 'ijklm');
```

One thing to note about hashes: The order in which a hash is initialized is not necessarily the order in which the elements are retrieved from the hash (see the description of the SORT statement).

Assigning an array to a scalar variable returns the number of items in the array. If the number returned is zero, then the array is empty.

Perl uses an internal type called a typeglob to hold an entire symbol table entry. The type prefix of a typeglob is a * because it represents all types. Typeglobs used to be the preferred way to pass arrays and hashes by reference into a function, but now that there are real references, you rarely use this technique.

One place to still use typeglobs is for passing or storing filehandles. To save a filehandle, do this:

```
$fh = *STDOUT;
```

Use the same method to create a local filehandle.

Predefined Variables

Predefined variables are names that have special meaning to Perl. Most of the punctuation names (such as $$ and $#) have reasonable mnemonics, or analogues, in one of the shells. Nevertheless, if you wish to use the long variable names, you just need to say

```
use English;
```

at the top of your program. This statement will alias all the short names to the long names in the current package (that is, the module) so that you can use the longer English names instead of the more cryptic special character names. Some of them even have medium names, generally borrowed from the UNIX pattern matching language awk.

A few of these variables are considered read-only. If you try to assign to a read-only variable, either directly or indirectly through a reference, you raise a runtime exception.

The following table describes the Perl predefined variables.

Variable	Description
$ARG	The default input and pattern-searching space.
$_	Here are the places where Perl assumes $_ even if you don't use it:
	■ Various unary functions, including functions like ord() and int(), as well as all the filetests (-f, -d) except for -t, which defaults to STDIN.
	■ Various list functions like print() and unlink().
	■ The pattern matching operations m//, s///, and tr/// when used without an =~ operator.
	■ The default iterator variable in a foreach loop if no other variable is supplied.
	■ The implicit iterator variable in the grep() and map() functions.
	■ The default place to put an input record when a C<<FH>> operation's result is tested by itself as the sole criterion of a while test. Note that outside a while test, this condition does not occur.
$<digit>	Contains the subpattern from the corresponding set of parentheses in the last pattern matched, not counting patterns matched in nested blocks that have been exited already. [*read-only*]

Variable	Description
$MATCH $&	The string matched by the last successful pattern match excluding any matches hidden within a BLOCK or eval() enclosed by the current BLOCK. [*read-only*]
$PREMATCH $'	The string preceding whatever was matched by the last successful pattern match excluding any matches hidden within a BLOCK or eval enclosed by the current BLOCK. [*read-only*]
$POSTMATCH $'	The string following whatever was matched by the last successful pattern match excluding matches hidden within a BLOCK or eval() enclosed by the current BLOCK. [*read-only*]
$LAST_PAREN_MATCH $+	The last bracket matched by the last search pattern. This variable is useful if you don't know which of a set of alternative patterns matched. [*read-only*]
$MULTILINE_MATCHING $*	Set to 1 to do multiline matching within a string, or 0 to tell Perl that it can assume that strings contain a single line for the purpose of optimizing pattern matches. Pattern matches on strings containing multiple newlines can produce confusing results when $* is 0. Default is 0. Note that this variable influences only the interpretation of ^ and $. You can search for a literal newline even when $* is 0.
input_line_number HANDLE EXPR $INPUT_LINE_NUMBER $NR $.	The current input line number of the last filehandle that was read. An explicit close on the filehandle resets the line number. Line numbers increase across ARGV files.
input_record_separator HANDLE EXPR $INPUT_RECORD_SEPARATOR	The input record separator. Set to newline by default.

continues

14

Variable	Description
$RS $/	Treats blank lines as delimiters if set to the null string. You can set the separator to a multicharacter string to match a multicharacter delimiter. Note that setting the separator to \n\n means something slightly different than setting it to "" if the file contains consecutive blank lines. Setting it to "" treats two or more consecutive blank lines as a single blank line. Setting it to \n\n blindly assumes that the next input character belongs to the next paragraph, even if it's a newline.
autoflush HANDLE EXPR $OUTPUT_AUTOFLUSH $¦	A setting of nonzero forces a flush after every write or print on the currently selected output channel. The default is 0.
output_field_separator HANDLE EXPR $OUTPUT_FIELD_SEPARATOR	The output field separator for the print operator.
$OFS $,	Ordinarily, the print operator simply prints the comma-separated fields you specify.
output_record_separator HANDLE EXPR $OUTPUT_RECORD_SEPARATOR	The output record separator for the print operator.
$ORS $\	Ordinarily, the print operator simply prints the comma-separated fields you specify with no trailing newline or record separator assumed.
$LIST_SEPARATOR $"	This separator is like $, except that it applies to array values interpolated into a double-quoted string or similar interpreted string. Default is a space.
$SUBSCRIPT_SEPARATOR $SUBSEP $;	The subscript separator for multidimensional array emulation. Default is \034. Note that if the keys contain binary data, $; might not have a safe value.
$OFMT $#	The output format for printed numbers. The initial value is %.20g.

Variable	Description

`format_page_number` HANDLE EXPR
`$FORMAT_PAGE_NUMBER`
`$%`
	The current page number of the currently selected output channel.

`format_lines_per_page` HANDLE EXPR
`$FORMAT_LINES_PER_PAGE`
`$=`
	The current page length of the currently selected output channel. Default is `60`.

`format_lines_left` HANDLE EXPR
`$FORMAT_LINES_LEFT`
`$-`
	The number of lines left on the page of the currently selected output channel.

`format_name` HANDLE EXPR `$FORMAT_NAME`	The name of the current report format for the currently selected output channel. Default is the name of the filehandle.

`format_top_name` HANDLE EXPR
`$FORMAT_TOP_NAME`
`$^`
	The name of the current top-of-page format for the currently selected output channel. Default is the name of the filehandle with `_TOP` appended.

`format_line_break_characters` HANDLE EXPR
`$FORMAT_LINE_BREAK_CHARACTERS`
`$:`
	The current set of characters after which a string can be broken to fill continuation fields (starting with `^`) in a format. Default is `\n-` to break on whitespace or hyphens.

`format_formfeed` HANDLE EXPR
`$FORMAT_FORMFEED`
`$^L`
	What the program outputs to perform a form feed. Default is `\f`.

`$ACCUMULATOR` `$^A`	The current value of the `write()` accumulator for `format()` lines. A format contains `formline()` commands that put their result into `$^A`. After calling its format, `write()` prints the contents of `$^A` and empties. You never actually see the contents of `$^A` unless you call `formline()` yourself and then look at it.

continues

14

THE PERL
LANGUAGE

Variable	Description
$CHILD_ERROR $?	The status returned by the last pipe close, backtick (```) command, or system() operator. Note that this status word is returned by the wait() system call, so the exit value of the subprocess is actually ($? > 8>). Thus, on many systems, $? & 255 specifies which signal, if any, the process died from and whether a core dump occurred.
$OS_ERROR $ERRNO $!	If used in a numeric context, $! yields the current value of errno with all the usual caveats. (That is, you shouldn't depend on the value of $! to be anything in particular unless you've gotten a specific error return indicating a system error.) If used in a string context, $! yields the corresponding system error string. You can assign a value to $! in order to set errno if, for example, you want $! to return the string for error n or you want to set the exit value for the die() operator.
$EVAL_ERROR $@	The Perl syntax error message from the last eval() command. If null, the last eval() parsed and executed correctly (although the operations you invoked might have failed in the normal fashion). Note that warning messages are not collected in this variable. You can, however, set up a routine to process warnings by setting $SIG{__WARN__} below.
$PROCESS_ID $PID $$	The process number of the Perl running this script.
$REAL_USER_ID $UID $<	The real user ID (uid) of this process.

Variable	*Description*
$EFFECTIVE_USER_ID $EUID $>	The effective user ID of this process.
$REAL_GROUP_ID $GID $(	The real group ID (gid) of this process. If you are on a machine that supports membership in multiple groups simultaneously, the variable gives a space-separated list of groups you are in. The first number is the one returned by getgid(), and the subsequent numbers are returned by getgroups(), one of which may be the same as the first number.
$EFFECTIVE_GROUP_ID $EGID $)	The effective gid of this process. If you are on a machine that supports membership in multiple groups simultaneously, it gives a space-separated list of groups you are in. The first number is the one returned by getegid(), and the subsequent numbers are returned by getgroups(), one of which may be the same as the first number.
$PROGRAM_NAME $0	Contains the name of the file containing the Perl script being executed. Assigning to $0 modifies the argument area that the ps(1) program sees.
$[	The index of the first element in an array and of the first character in a substring. The default is 0.
$Perl_VERSION $]	The string prints the version number of this Perl installation (equivalent to the command line perl -v).
$DEBUGGING $^D	The current value of the debugging flags.

continues

14

THE PERL LANGUAGE

Variable	*Description*
$SYSTEM_FD_MAX $^F	The maximum system file descriptor, ordinarily 2. System file descriptors are passed to exec()ed processes, whereas higher file descriptors are not. Also, during an open(), system file descriptors are preserved even if the open() fails. (Ordinary file descriptors are closed before the open() is attempted.) Note that the close-on-exec status of a file descriptor is decided according to the value of $^F at the time of the open, not at the time of the exec.
$INPLACE_EDIT $^I	The current value of the inplace-edit extension. Use undef to disable inplace editing.
$PERLDB $^P	The internal flag that the debugger clears so that it doesn't debug itself. You could conceivably disable debugging yourself by clearing it.
$BASETIME $^T	The time at which the script began running in seconds since the epoch (beginning of 1970). The values returned by the -M, -A, and -C filetests are based on this value.
$WARNING $^W	The current value of the warning switch, either TRUE or FALSE.
$EXECUTABLE_NAME $^X	The name that the Perl binary itself was executed as, from C's argv[0].
$ARGV	Contains the name of the current file when reading from <>.
@ARGV	The array @ARGV contains the command-line arguments. Note that $#ARGV is the number of arguments minus one because $ARGV[0] is the first argument, not the command name. See $0 for the command name.

Variable	Description
@INC	The array @INC contains the list of places to look for Perl scripts to be evaluated by the do EXPR, require, or use constructs. @INC initially consists of the arguments to any -I command-line switches, followed by the default Perl library, followed by ., to represent the current directory.
%INC	The hash %INC contains entries for each filename that has been included via do or require. The key is the filename you specified, and the value is the location of the file actually found. The require command uses this array to determine whether a given file has already been included.
$ENV{*expr*}	The hash %ENV contains your current environment. Setting a value in ENV changes the environment for child processes.
$SIG{*expr*}	The hash %SIG is used to set signal handlers for various signals.

Perl Syntax

Perl is generally a free-form language. The only elements that you need to declare are report formats and subroutines. To create a variable or other object, simply use it. All uninitialized user-created objects are assumed to start with a null or 0 value until they are defined by some explicit operation such as assignment.

The sequence of statements is executed just once. The interpreter first "compiles" the script, checking for syntax errors. With the exception of subroutines (functions), Perl executes statements from the first line of the script to the last. Of course, like any programming language, Perl supports looping and branching statements, which affect the flow of the program but generally continue execution at the next sequential statement after the statements complete their operation.

Comments—Documenting the Script

Comments are indicated by the # character and extend to the end of the line. Here are examples of comments:

```
# This is a comment which extends over the entire line
# Comments do not span lines, the "#" character must be used
# at the start of the comment on every line.
$a = 1; # Comments can be added to lines
$b = 2; # to explain usage of a particular instruction.
```

Declarations

Declarations all take effect at compile time when the script is first executed. You can put a declaration anywhere you can put a statement, but a declaration has no effect on the execution of the primary sequence of statements.

Declaring a subroutine allows a subroutine name to be used as if it were a list operator from that point forward in the program.

Simple Statements

A simple statement is an expression that is evaluated and executed by the interpreter. You must terminate every simple statement with a semicolon unless it is the final statement in a block.

Optionally, you can place a SINGLE modifier after any simple statement; the modifier goes just before the terminating semicolon (or block ending). Here are the four valid modifiers:

```
if {expression}
unless {expression}
while {expression}
until {expression}
```

The if and unless modifiers work as you might expect. The statement is executed if or unless the {expression} is true.

```
$a = 2 if $b = $c;
```

The variable $a is initialized to 2 if the variable $b is equal to the variable $c. An equivalent statement in a more traditional format is

```
if $b = $c {
      $a = 2;
}
```

The unless operator executes the statement only if the {expression} is not true. For example,

```
$a = 2 unless $b = $c;
```

sets $a equal to 2 only if $b is not equal to $c. The equivalent statement is

```
if $b != $c {
        $a = 2;
}
```

The `while` and `until` modifiers first evaluate the conditional except when they follow a `do` block.

```
$c = 0;
$c += 2 until $a + $c > 10;
```

adds 2 to `$c` until `$a` plus `$c` equals 10. If `$a` is 0 before this statement, it might execute several times. If `$a` is equal to or greater than 10 when the statement is first evaluated, it would never execute.

In the case of a `do{}` block, the block executes once before the conditional is evaluated. Therefore, you can write loops such as

```
do { $in = <STDIN>; ... } while $in ne ".\n";
```

The statements within the `do{}` block read and process at least one statement from standard input. If that statement is a period followed by an end-of-line character, the loop terminates.

Compound Statements

A series of statements that defines a scope is called a block (referenced as BLOCK throughout this chapter). Generally, a block is delimited by braces (`{}`).

You can use the following compound statements to control flow:

```
if (expression) {...}
if (expression) {...} else {...}
if (expression) {...} elsif (expression) {...} else {...}
label while (expression) {...}
label while (expression) {...} continue {...}
label for (expression; expression; expression) {...}
label foreach variable (list) {...}
label {...} continue {...}
```

Note that, unlike C and Pascal, which execute only the next statement after the conditional unless braces or `begin`/`end` pairs are used, Perl compound statements are defined in terms of BLOCKs, not statements. Consequently, the braces are *required*.

The `if` statement in Perl works the same as it does in all other languages. If you use `unless` in place of `if`, the sense of the test is reversed.

The `while` statement executes the block as long as the expression is true (not the null string or 0 or 0). The *label* is optional. If a *label* is included, it consists of an identifier followed by a colon. The *label* identifies the loop for the loop control statements `next`, `last`, and `redo`. If the *label* is omitted, the loop control statement refers to the innermost enclosing loop.

A `continue` block is always executed immediately before the conditional is about to be evaluated again, just like the third part of a `for` loop in C. Therefore, you can use a `continue` block to increment a loop variable, even when the loop has been continued via the `next` statement.

Loop Control

The following statements control looping in Perl scripts. They are generally equivalent to their C language counterparts.

next

Starts the next iteration of the loop. In the following example, the code in the `while` loop will not be executed if the line begins with a #, indicating a comment in a Perl script. (This is a convenient construct to strip comments from Perl code.)

```
LINE: while (<IN>) {
next LINE if /^#/; # strip comments
... # additional code
} #end of while loop
```

last

Immediately exits the loop. The `continue` block, if any, is *not* executed.

```
GET1: while (<IN>) {
last GET1 if /^EOF/; # exit when a line starting with EOF is encountered;
 ...
}
```

redo

Restarts the loop block without evaluating the conditional again. The `continue` block, if any, is *not* executed.

For example, when processing a file, input lines might end in a continuation character, such as the plus sign. You can use `redo` to skip ahead and get the next record.

```
while (<>) {
        chop; #remove training linefeed
        if (s/\+$//) {  # record ends in a plus sign indicating a continued line
                $_ .= <>; #append the next line to $_
                redo unless eof(); # go back and check again
        } # end of if statement
... # process the record after gathering continuation lines
} # end of while statement
```

For Loops

Perl's `for` loops are exactly like their C equivalents.

```
for ($i = 1; $i < 100; $i++) { ... }
```

You could write the same thing using a `while` loop:

```
$i =1;
while ($i < 100) {
        ...
```

```
} continue {
      $I++;
}
```

Foreach Loops

The foreach loop iterates over a normal list value and sets the variable to be each element of the list in turn. The variable is implicitly local to the loop and regains its former value upon exiting the loop.

The foreach keyword is actually a synonym for the for keyword, so you can use foreach for readability or for for brevity. If the variable is omitted, $_ is set to each value. If LIST is an actual array (as opposed to an expression returning a list value), you can modify each element of the array by modifying the variable inside the loop.

Here are some examples. The first reads the array @things, returning each value into $_ and changing the name smith to jones.

```
foreach (@things) {
      s/smith/jones/
}
```

The next example reads each element of @numbs into $num and then multiplies it by 2.

```
foreach $numb (@numbs) {
$numb *= 2;
}
```

The last example prints the keys and values in the associative array %items.

```
foreach $item (key %items) {
      print "$item = $items{$item}\n"
}
```

Blocks

A labeled or unlabeled block is equivalent to a loop that executes once. Therefore, you can use any of the loop control statements to leave or restart the block. The continue block is optional.

Unlike C, Perl does not have a switch statement. Perl does have several alternative ways to write equivalent statements. The block construct is particularly nice for doing case structures. Here's an example using a block. Note that SWITCH: is not a statement, but merely a label. Any other label would work as well. This statement tests the first character of $_ and performs the logic related to it.

```
SWITCH: {
      if (/^a/) {
            $value = 1;
            last SWITCH;
      }
      if (/^b/) {
            $value = 2;
            last SWITCH;
```

```
        }
        if (/^c/) {
                $value = 3;
                last SWITCH;
        }
        $value = 0;
}
```

Goto

Perl does support three forms of the goto statement: `goto-LABEL`, `goto-EXPR`, and `goto-&NAME`. A loop's LABEL is not a valid target for a goto; it's just the name of the loop. However, these statements could be considered bad programming form, so I advise against using them unless absolutely necessary and will not spend time on them here. These functions are described in the "Alphabetical Listing of Perl Functions."

Perl Operators

The following list outlines Perl operator associativity and precedence, from highest precedence to lowest. With very few exceptions, Perl operators operate on scalar values only, not on array values.

Left Terms and List Operators (Leftward)

left `->`

nonassoc `++` `--`

right `**`

right `!` `~` `\` and unary `+` and `-left`

`=~` `!~`

left `*` `/` `%` `x`

left `+` `-` `.`

left `<<` `>>`

Nonassoc Named Unary Operators

nonassoc `<` `>` `<=` `>=` `lt` `gt` `le` `ge`

nonassoc `==` `!=` `<=>` `eq` `ne` `cmp`

left `&`

left `¦` `^`

left `&&`

left `¦¦`

nonassoc `..`

right ?:

right = += -= *= and so on

left , =>

Nonassoc List Operators (Rightward)

left not

left and

left or xor

The following sections present the operators in precedence order.

Terms and List Operators (Leftward)

Any term (shown throughout this chapter as "TERM") is of the highest precedence of Perl. Terms include variables, quote and quote-like operators, expressions in parentheses, and functions whose arguments are parenthesized.

If any list operator (print(), for example) or any unary operator (chdir(), for example) is followed by a left parenthesis as the next token, the operator and arguments within parentheses are taken to be of highest precedence, just like a normal function call.

In the absence of parentheses, the precedence of list operators such as print, sort, or chmod is either very high or very low depending on whether you look at the left side of the operator or the right side of it. In the following example, the elements (commas) on the right of the sort are evaluated before the sort, but the commas on the left are evaluated after.

```
@ary = (1, 3, sort 4, 2);
print @ary; # prints 1324
```

List operators tend to "gobble up" all the arguments that follow them and then act like a simple TERM with regard to the preceding expression. Note that you have to be careful with parentheses. This is illustrated in the following examples.

```
# These evaluate exit before doing the print and, thus never print:
print($foo, exit); # Obviously not what you want.
print $foo, exit; # Nor is this.

# These do the print before evaluating exit:
(print $foo), exit; # This is what you want.
print($foo), exit; # Or this.
print ($foo), exit; # Or even this.
```

Also note that

```
print ($foo & 255) + 1, "\n";
```

probably doesn't do what you expect at first glance. A complete discussion of parentheses is beyond the scope of this chapter. See "Named Unary Operators" in the perlop man page for a more complete discussion of parentheses.

14

THE PERL
LANGUAGE

Also parsed as terms are the `do{}` and `eval{}` constructs, as well as subroutine and method calls and the anonymous constructors `[]` and `{}`.

The Arrow Operator

Just as in C and C++, `->` is an infix dereference operator. If the right side is either a `[...]` or `{...}` subscript, then the left side must be either a hard or symbolic reference to an array or hash (or a location capable of holding a hard reference, if it's an `lvalue`). See the `perlref` man page for a more complete explanation of its use.

Otherwise, the right side is a method name or a simple scalar variable containing the method name, and the left side must either be an object or a class name. See the `perlobj` man page for a more complete discussion.

Autoincrement and Autodecrement

`++` and `--` placed before a variable increment or decrement the variable before returning the value. Placed after, they increment or decrement the variable after returning the value.

The autoincrement operator has an extra functionality built into it. If you increment a variable that is numeric, or that has ever been used in a numeric context, you get a normal increment. If, however, the variable has been used only in string contexts since it was set and has a value that has any number of alpha characters followed by any number of numeric characters (`/^[a-zA-Z]*[0-9]*$/`), the increment is done as a string, preserving each character within its range with carry. Here are some examples:

```
print ++($foo = '99'); # prints '100'
print ++($foo = 'a0'); # prints 'a1'
print ++($foo = 'Az'); # prints 'Ba'
print ++($foo = 'zz'); # prints 'aaa'
```

The autodecrement operator does not perform this little trick in reverse.

Exponentiation

`**` is the exponentiation operator. Note that it binds even more tightly than unary minus, so `-2**4` is `-(2**4)`, not `(-2)**4`.

Symbolic Unary Operators

These are operators represented by single character symbols. Many are equivalent to their counterparts in languages like C, COBOL, or Pascal. Others have unique meaning or usage in Perl.

!	Logical negation, that is, "not."
-	Arithmetic negation if the operand is numeric. If the operand is an identifier, a string consisting of a minus sign concatenated with the identifier is returned.

Otherwise, if the string starts with a plus or minus, a string starting with the opposite sign is returned.

~ Bitwise negation (1's complement).

+ Has no effect whatsoever, even on strings.

\ Creates a reference to whatever follows it. See the `perlref` man page. Do not confuse this behavior with the behavior of a backslash within a string, although both forms do convey the notion of protecting the next thing from interpretation.

Binding Operators

Binding operators bind an expression to a pattern match.

=~ Binds a scalar expression to a pattern match. Certain operations search or modify the string `$_` by default. This operator makes that kind of operation work on some other string. The right argument is a search pattern, substitution, or translation. The left argument is what is supposed to be searched, substituted, or translated instead of the default `$_`. The return value indicates the success of the operation.

!~ Performs just like =~ except the return value is logically negated.

Perl Built-In Functions

Perl supports a rich set of built-in functions. These functions can be used as terms in an expression. The two categories of functions are

- List operators
- Named unary operators

The difference between the categories is their precedence relationship with a following comma. List operators take more than one argument, whereas unary operators can never take more than one argument.

In the syntax descriptions in Table 14.1, list operators that expect a list are shown with LIST as an argument. Such a list can consist of any combination of scalar arguments or list values; the list values are included in the list as if each individual element were entered at that point in the list, forming a longer single-dimensional list value. Elements of the LIST should be separated by commas.

You can use any function in Table 14.1 with or without parentheses around its arguments.

Perl Functions By Category

Table 14.1 shows the Perl functions by category. Some functions appear in more than one place. Not all of these functions are covered in detail in this chapter. I skip the functions that have no value in most CGI programs or that are more complex. Refer to the `perlfunc` man page or the Sams books mentioned earlier in the chapter for information about these functions.

Table 14.1. Perl functions by category.

Category	Perl function
Functions for scalars or strings	chomp, chop, chr, crypt, hex, index, lc, lcfirst, length, oct, ord, pack, q/STRING/, qq/STRING/, reverse, rindex, sprintf, substr, tr///, uc, ucfirst, y///
Regular expressions and pattern matching	m//, pos, quotemeta, s///, split, study
Numeric functions	abs, atan2, cos, exp, hex, int, log, oct, rand, sin, sqrt, srand
Real @ARRAY functions	pop, push, shift, splice, unshift
List data functions	grep, join, map, qw/STRING/, reverse, sort, unpack
Real %HASH functions	delete, each, exists, keys, values
Input and output functions	binmode, close, closedir, dbmclose, dbmopen, die, eof, fileno, flock, format, getc, print, printf, read, readdir, rewinddir, seek, seekdir, select, syscall, sysread, syswrite, tell, telldir, truncate, warn, write
Functions for fixed length data or records	pack, read, syscall, sysread, syswrite, unpack, vec
Functions for filehandles, files, or directories	-X, chdir, chmod, chown, chroot, fcntl, glob, ioctl, link, lstat, mkdir, open, opendir, readlink, rename, rmdir, stat, symlink, umask, unlink, utime
Keywords related to the control of program flow	caller, continue, die, do, dump, eval, exit, goto, last, next, redo, return, sub, wantarray
Scoping keywords	caller, import, local, my, package, use
Miscellaneous functions	defined, dump, eval, formline, local, my, reset, scalar, undef, wantarray

Category	Perl function
Functions for processes and process groups	alarm, exec, fork, getpgrp, getppid, getpriority, kill, pipe, qx/STRING/, setpgrp, setpriority, sleep, system, times, wait, waitpid
Keywords related to Perl modules	do, import, no, package, require, use
Keywords related to classes and object orientation	bless, dbmclose, dbmopen, package, ref, tie, tied, untie, use
Low-level socket functions	accept, bind, connect, getpeername, getsockname, getsockopt, listen, recv, send, setsockopt, shut-down, socket, socketpair
System V interprocess communication functions	msgctl, msgget, msgrcv, msgsnd, semctl, semget, semop, shmctl, shmget, shmread, shmwrite
Fetching user and group information	endgrent, endhostent, endnetent, endpwent, getgrent, getgrgid, getgrnam, getlogin, getpwent, getpwnam, getpwuid, setgrent, setpwent
Fetching network information	endprotoent, endservent, gethostbyaddr, gethostbyname, gethostent, getnetbyaddr, getnetbyname, getnetent, getprotobyname, getprotobynumber, getprotoent, getservbyname, getservbyport, getservent, sethostent, setnetent, setprotoent, setservent
Time functions	gmtime, localtime, time, times

Alphabetical Listing of Perl Functions

This section presents the basic Perl functions in alphabetical order as a reference. Not all functions in the language are included in detail here.

-X [[FILEHANDLE¦EXPR]]

A file test, where *x* is one of the letters in the list that follows. This unary operator takes one argument, either a filename or a filehandle, and tests the associated file to see if something is true about it. If the argument is omitted, the expression tests $_, except for -t, which tests STDIN. Unless otherwise documented, this test returns 1 for TRUE, "" for FALSE, or the undefined value if the file doesn't exist. Precedence is the same as any other named unary operator, and the argument may be parenthesized like any other unary operator. The operator may be any of the following:

-r	File is readable by effective uid/gid.
-w	File is writable by effective uid/gid.
-x	File is executable by effective uid/gid.
-o	File is owned by effective uid.
-R	File is readable by real uid/gid.
-W	File is writable by real uid/gid.
-X	File is executable by real uid/gid.
-O	File is owned by real uid.
-e	File exists.
-z	File has zero size.
-s	File has nonzero size (returns size).
-f	File is a plain file.
-d	File is a directory.
-l	File is a symbolic link.
-p	File is a named pipe (FIFO).
-S	File is a socket.
-b	File is a block special file.
-c	File is a character special file.
-t	Filehandle is opened to a tty.
-u	File has setuid bit set.
-g	File has setgid bit set.
-k	File has sticky bit set.
-T	File is a text file.
-B	File is a binary file (opposite of -T).
-M	Age of file in days when script started.
-A	Same for access time.
-C	Same for inode change time.

Note that not all of the preceding operators have meaning in all operating systems. See the Perl man pages for details of using these switches.

abs VALUE

Returns the absolute value of its argument.

accept NEWSOCKET,GENERICSOCKET

Accepts an incoming socket connection, just as the UNIX accept(2) system call does. Returns the packed address if it succeeded, FALSE otherwise.

atan2 Y,X

Returns the arctangent of Y/X in the range -PI to PI.

bind SOCKET,NAME

Binds a network address to a socket, just as the bind system call does. Returns TRUE if it succeeded, FALSE otherwise. NAME should be a packed address of the appropriate type for the socket.

binmode FILEHANDLE

The file identified by FILEHANDLE is read or written in binary mode in operating systems that distinguish between binary and text files. Files that are not in binary mode have CR LF sequences translated to LF on input and LF translated to CR LF on output.

caller [EXPR]

caller returns the context of the current subroutine call. In a scalar context, it returns TRUE if a caller exists, that is, in a subroutine or eval() or require(); otherwise, it returns FALSE. In a list context, returns

```
($package, $filename, $line) = caller;
```

With EXPR, caller returns some extra information that the debugger uses to print a stack trace. The value of EXPR indicates how many call frames to go back before the current one.

```
($package, $filename, $line, $subroutine, $hasargs, $wantargs) = caller($i);
```

chdir [EXPR]

Changes the working directory to EXPR, if possible. If EXPR is omitted, it changes the working directory to the home directory. Returns TRUE upon success; otherwise, returns FALSE.

chmod LIST

Changes the permissions of a list of files. The first element of the list must be the numerical mode, which should probably be an octal number. Returns the number of files successfully changed.

```
$cnt = chmod 0755, 'foo', 'bar';
chmod 0755, @myfiles;
```

chomp [VARIABLE¦LIST]

chomp is a slightly safer version of chop (see next entry). chomp removes any line ending that corresponds to the current value of $/ and returns the number of characters removed. It's often used to remove the newline from the end of an input record when you're worried that the final record may be missing its newline. When in paragraph mode ($/ = ""), chomp removes all trailing newlines from the string. If VARIABLE is omitted, it chomps $_.

```
while (<>) {
        chomp; # avoid \n on last field
        @array = split(/:/);
        ...
}
```

You can actually chomp anything that's an lvalue, including an assignment:

```
chomp($cwd = 'pwd');
chomp($answer = <STDIN>);
```

If you chomp a list, each element is chomped and the total number of characters removed is returned.

chop [VARIABLE¦LIST]

Chops off the last character of a string and returns the character chopped. The primary use of chop is to remove the newline from the end of an input record. It neither scans nor copies the string. If VARIABLE is omitted, it chops $_.

If you chop a list, each element is chopped. Only the value of the last chop is returned.

Note that chop returns the last character. To return all but the last character, use

```
substr($ string, 0, -1)
```

chown LIST

Changes the owner (and group) of a list of files. The first two elements of the list must be the numerical uid and gid, in that order. Returns the number of files successfully changed.

chr NUMBER

Returns the character represented by that NUMBER in the character set. For example, chr(65) is A in ASCII.

close FILEHANDLE

Closes the file or pipe associated with the filehandle, returning TRUE only if stdio successfully flushes buffers and closes the system file descriptor.

FILEHANDLE may be an expression whose value gives the real filehandle name.

closedir DIRHANDLE

Closes a directory opened by opendir().

connect SOCKET,NAME

Attempts to connect to a remote socket, just as the connect system call does. Returns TRUE if successful, FALSE otherwise. NAME should be a packed address of the appropriate type for the socket.

continue BLOCK

Actually a flow control statement rather than a function. If a continue BLOCK is attached to a BLOCK (typically in a while or foreach), the continue statement is always executed just *before* the conditional is about to be evaluated again, just like the third part of a for loop in C.

cos EXPR

Returns the cosine of EXPR (expressed in radians). If EXPR is omitted, the function takes the cosine of $_.

crypt PLAINTEXT,SALT

Encrypts a string exactly like the crypt(3) function in the C library.

defined EXPR

Returns a Boolean value saying whether EXPR has a real value or not. Many operations return the undefined value under exceptional conditions. This function allows you to distinguish between an undefined null scalar and a defined null scalar with operations that might return a real null string, such as referencing elements of an array.

See also undef.

delete EXPR

Deletes the specified value from its hash array. Returns the deleted value or the undefined value if nothing was deleted. Deleting from $ENV{} modifies the environment. Deleting from an array tied to a DBM file deletes the entry from the DBM file.

The following deletes all the values of an associative array:

```
foreach $key (keys %ARRAY) {
        delete $ARRAY{$key};
}
```

die LIST

Outside of an eval(), prints the value of LIST to STDERR and exits with the current value of $! (errno). If $! is 0, exits with the value of ($? > 8)> (backtick 'command' status). If ($? > 8)> is 0, exits with 255. Inside an eval(), the error message is stuffed into $@, and the eval() is terminated with the undefined value; this functionality makes die() the way to raise an exception in a script.

14

do BLOCK

Not really a function. Returns the value of the last command in the sequence of commands indicated by BLOCK. When modified by a loop modifier, executes the BLOCK once before testing the loop condition.

do SUBROUTINE(LIST)

A deprecated form of subroutine call. See the perlsub man page for more information on subroutines.

do EXPR

Uses the value of EXPR as a filename and executes the contents of the file as a Perl script. Its primary use is to include subroutines from a Perl subroutine library.

```
do 'stat.pl';
```

is just like

```
eval 'cat stat.pl';
```

except that it's more efficient, more concise, keeps track of the current filename for error messages, and searches all the -I libraries if the file isn't in the current directory. Both statements parse the file every time they are called.

A better way to include library modules is to use the use() and require() operators, which also do error checking and raise an exception if a problem occurs.

dump LABEL

This function causes an immediate core dump.

each ASSOC_ARRAY

Returns a two-element array consisting of the key and value for the next value of an associative array so that you can iterate over it. Entries are returned in an apparently random order. When the array is entirely read, a null array is returned. The following call to each() starts iterating again. The iterator can be reset only by reading all the elements from the array. You should not add elements to an array while you're iterating over it. Each associative array has a single iterator that all each(), keys(), and values() function calls in the program share.

eof [FILEHANDLE¦()]

Returns 1 if the next read on FILEHANDLE returns end of file or if FILEHANDLE is not open. FILEHANDLE may be an expression whose value gives the real filehandle name.

An eof without an argument uses the last file read as an argument. Empty parentheses may be used to indicate the pseudofile formed of the files listed on the command line. Use eof(ARGV) or eof without the parentheses to test each file in a while (<>) loop.

eval [EXPR¦BLOCK]

EXPR is parsed and executed as if it were a little Perl program. It is executed in the context of the current Perl program so that any variable settings, subroutines, or format definitions remain afterwards. The value returned is the value of the last expression evaluated; alternatively, a return statement may be used, just as with subroutines.

> **NOTE**
>
> Eval can be very dangerous in CGI programming. Do not automatically eval anything sent to you by a Web browser!

If a syntax error or runtime error occurs or a die() statement is executed, eval() returns an undefined value and $@ is set to the error message. If no error occurs, $@ is guaranteed to be a null string. If EXPR is omitted, eval evaluates $_. You may omit the final semicolon, if any, from the expression.

Note that because eval() traps otherwise fatal errors, it is useful for determining whether a particular feature (such as socket() or symlink()) is implemented. It is also Perl's exception-trapping mechanism, when the die operator is used to raise exceptions.

exec LIST

The exec() function executes a system command and never returns. Use the system() function if you want it to return.

exists EXPR

Returns TRUE if the specified hash key exists in its hash array even if the corresponding value is undefined.

```
print "Exists\n" if exists $array{$key};
print "Defined\n" if defined $array{$key};
print "True\n" if $array{$key};
```

A hash element can only be TRUE if it's defined, and it can be defined if it exists, but the reverse doesn't necessarily hold true.

exit [EXPR]

Evaluates EXPR and exits immediately with that value. See also die(). If EXPR is omitted, exits with 0 status.

exp [EXPR]

Returns e (the natural logarithm base) to the power of EXPR. If EXPR is omitted, gives exp($_).

fcntl FILEHANDLE,FUNCTION,SCALAR

Implements the fcntl(2) function.

fileno FILEHANDLE

Returns the file descriptor for a filehandle. This function is useful for constructing bitmaps for select(). If FILEHANDLE is an expression, the value is taken as the name of the filehandle.

flock FILEHANDLE,OPERATION

Calls flock(2) on FILEHANDLE. See the flock(2) man page for definition of OPERATION. Returns TRUE for success, FALSE for failure. This function produces a fatal error if it is used on a machine that doesn't implement either flock(2) or fcntl(2).

fork

Does a fork(2) system call. Returns the child process ID (PID) to the parent process and 0 to the child process, or returns undef if the fork is unsuccessful.

> **NOTE**
>
> Unflushed buffers remain unflushed in both processes, which means you may need to set $¦ ($AUTOFLUSH in English) or call the autoflush() filehandle method to avoid duplicate output.

getc FILEHANDLE

getc returns the next character from the input file attached to FILEHANDLE or a null string at end of file. If FILEHANDLE is omitted, reads from STDIN. This is not particularly efficient. It cannot be used to get unbuffered single characters, however.

getlogin

Returns the current login from /etc/utmp, if any. If null, use getpwuid().

getpeername SOCKET

Returns the packed sockaddr address of the other end of the SOCKET connection.

getpgrp PID

Returns the current process group for the specified PID and returns 0 for the current process. Raises an exception if used on a machine that doesn't implement getpgrp(2). If PID is omitted, the function returns the process group of the current process.

getppid
Returns the process ID of the parent process.

getpriority WHICH,WHO
Returns the current priority for a process, a process group, or a user. (See the getpriority(2) man page.) Raises a fatal exception if used on a machine that doesn't implement getpriority(2).

getpwnam NAME

getgrnam NAME

gethostbyname NAME

getnetbyname NAME

getprotobyname NAME

getpwuid UID

getgrgid GID

getservbyname NAME,PROTO

gethostbyaddr ADDR,ADDRTYPE

getnetbyaddr ADDR,ADDRTYPE

getprotobynumber NUMBER

getservbyport PORT,PROTO

getpwent

getgrent

gethostent

getnetent

getprotoent

getservent

setpwent

setgrent

sethostent STAYOPEN

setnetent STAYOPEN

setprotoent STAYOPEN

setservent STAYOPEN

endpwent

endgrent

endhostent

endnetent

endprotoent

endservent

All these routines perform the same functions as their counterparts in the system library.

getsockname SOCKET

Returns the packed `sockaddr` address of this end of the `SOCKET` connection.

```
use Socket;
$mysockaddr = getsockname(SOCK);
($port, $myaddr) = unpack_sockaddr_in($mysockaddr);
```

getsockopt SOCKET,LEVEL,OPTNAME

Returns the socket option requested or returns undefined if there is an error.

glob EXPR

Returns the value of EXPR with filename expansions such as a shell would do. This routine is the internal function implementing the `<*.*>` operator.

gmtime EXPR

Converts a time as returned by the time function to a nine-element array with the time localized for the standard Greenwich time zone. Typically used as follows:

```
($sec,$min,$hour,$mday,$mon,$year,$wday,$yday,$isdst) = gmtime(time);
```

All array elements are numeric and come straight out of a struct `tm`. Specifically, `$mon` has the range 0...11, and `$wday` has the range 0...6. If EXPR is omitted, `gmtime` performs the equivalent of gmtime(time()).

goto [LABEL¦EXPR¦&NAME]

The goto-LABEL form finds the statement labeled with LABEL and resumes execution there. It may not be used to go into any construct that requires initialization, such as a subroutine or a foreach loop, or to go into a construct that is optimized away. Although the goto-LABEL form can be used to go almost anywhere else within the dynamic scope, including out of subroutines, a better method is to use some other construct such as last or die.

The goto-EXPR form expects a label name, whose scope is resolved dynamically.

The goto-&NAME form substitutes a call to the named subroutine for the currently running subroutine. This form is used by AUTOLOAD subroutines that want to load another subroutine and then pretend that the newly loaded subroutine had been called in the first place. After the goto, not even caller() is able to tell which routine was called first.

grep [BLOCK¦EXPR], LIST

Evaluates the BLOCK or EXPR for each element of LIST (locally setting $_ to each element) and returns the list value consisting of those elements for which the expression evaluated to TRUE. In a scalar context, grep returns the number of times the expression was TRUE.

hex EXPR

Interprets EXPR as a hex string and returns the corresponding decimal value. If EXPR is omitted, the function uses $_.

index STR,SUBSTR[,POSITION]

Returns the position of the first occurrence of SUBSTR in STR at or after POSITION. If POSITION is omitted, starts searching from the beginning of the string. The return value is based at 0 (or whatever you've set the $[variable to). If the substring is not found, returns one less than the base, ordinarily -1.

int EXPR

Returns the integer portion of EXPR. If EXPR is omitted, uses $_.

ioctl FILEHANDLE,FUNCTION,SCALAR

Implements the ioctl(2) function.

join EXPR,LIST

Joins the separate strings of LIST or ARRAY into a single string, with fields separated by the value of EXPR, and returns the string. This routine can be used to create delimited records for inclusion in databases. For example, given a form that returns three variables that have been parsed into the hash %in, the following code

```
$in{'var 1'} = 'Last Name';
```

```
$in{'var 2'} = 'First Name';
$in{'var 3'} = 'Middle Name';
$dbrec = join(',', $in{'var1'}, $in{'var2'}, $in{'var3'});
```

results in

```
Last Name,First Name,Middle Name
```

See split.

keys ASSOC_ARRAY

Returns a normal array consisting of all the keys of the named associative array. (In a scalar context, returns the number of keys.) The keys are returned in an apparently random order, but it is the same order as either the values() or each() function produces.

This routine can be very useful in processing lists of key/value pairs. For example, given an associative array called %stuff, the following code prints the keys and their values:

```
foreach $key (keys %stuff) {
        print "$key = $stuff{$key}\n";
}
```

kill LIST

Sends a signal to a list of processes. The first element of the list must be the signal to send. Returns the number of processes successfully signaled.

last [LABEL]

The last command is like the break statement in C. It immediately exits the loop in question. If the LABEL is omitted, the command refers to the innermost enclosing loop. The continue block, if any, is not executed:

```
LINE: while (<STDIN>) {
        last LINE if /^$/; # exit when done with header
        ...
}
```

lc EXPR

Returns a lowercased version of EXPR.

lcfirst EXPR

Returns the value of EXPR with the first character lowercased.

length EXPR

Returns the length in characters of the value of EXPR. If EXPR is omitted, returns length of $_. Remember that unless you have reset $[, strings are zero based. Thus, length({string}) actually points one character beyond the end of the string.

link OLDFILE,NEWFILE

Creates a new filename linked to the old filename. Returns 1 for success, 0 otherwise. (Note, link might not be implemented on all operating systems.)

listen SOCKET,QUEUESIZE

Does the same thing that the listen system call does. Returns TRUE if it succeeded, FALSE otherwise.

local EXPR

A local modifies the listed variables to be local to the enclosing block, subroutine, eval{}, or do. If more than one value is listed, the list must be placed in parentheses.

localtime EXPR

Converts a time as returned by the time function to a nine-element array with the time analyzed for the local time zone. Typically used as follows:

```
($sec,$min,$hour,$mday,$mon,$year,$wday,$yday,$isdst) = localtime(time);
```

All array elements are numeric and come straight out of a struct tm. In particular, $mon has the range 0..11 and $wday has the range 0..6. If EXPR is omitted, does localtime(time).

In a scalar context, prints out the ctime(3) value:

```
$now_string = localtime; # e.g. "Thu Oct 13 04:54:34 1994"
```

log EXPR

Returns logarithm (base e) of EXPR. If EXPR is omitted, returns log of $_.

lstat [FILEHANDLE¦EXPR]

Does the same thing as the stat() function, but performs the stat function on a symbolic link instead of the file to which the symbolic link points. If symbolic links are not implemented on your system, a normal stat() occurs.

m// or //

The match operator. See the section, "Perl Regular Expressions," for more details on the match operator and its available options.

map [BLOCK LIST¦EXPR,LIST]

Evaluates the BLOCK or EXPR for each element of LIST (locally setting $_ to each element) and returns the list value composed of the results of each such evaluation. Evaluates BLOCK or EXPR in a list context, so each element of LIST may produce zero, one, or more elements in the returned value.

```
@chars = map(chr, @nums);
```

translates a list of numbers to the corresponding characters.

mkdir FILENAME,MODE

Creates the directory specified by FILENAME with permissions specified by MODE (as modified by umask). If it succeeds, mkdir returns 1; otherwise, it returns 0 and sets $! (errno). MODE varies depending on the operating system implementation.

msgctl ID,CMD,ARG

Calls the System V IPC function msgctl(2). If CMD is &IPC_STAT, then ARG must be a variable that holds the returned msqid_ds structure. Returns values like ioctl: the undefined value for error, "0 but true" for zero, or the actual return value.

msgget KEY,FLAGS

Calls the System V IPC function msgget(2). Either returns the message queue ID or returns the undefined value if an error occurs.

msgsnd ID,MSG,FLAGS

Calls the System V IPC function msgsnd to send the message MSG to the message queue ID. MSG must begin with the long integer message type, which may be created with pack("l", $type). Returns TRUE if successful; returns FALSE if an error occurs.

msgrcv ID,VAR,SIZE,TYPE,FLAGS

Calls the System V IPC function msgrcv to receive a message from message queue ID into variable VAR with a maximum message size of SIZE. If a message is received, the message type is the first thing in VAR; the maximum length of VAR is SIZE plus the size of the message type. Returns TRUE if successful or returns FALSE if an error occurs.

my EXPR

A my declares the listed variables to be local (lexically) to the enclosing block, subroutine, eval, or do/require/use file. If more than one value is listed, the list must be placed in parentheses.

next [LABEL]

The next command is like the continue statement in C; it starts the next iteration of the loop:

```
LINE: while (<STDIN>) {
        next LINE if /^#/; # discard comments
        ...
}
```

Note that if the preceding code contained a continue block, the block would be executed even on discarded lines. If the LABEL is omitted, the command refers to the innermost enclosing loop.

no Module LIST

This function is the opposite of the use function. See the use function.

oct EXPR

Interprets EXPR as an octal string and returns the corresponding decimal value. (If EXPR happens to begin with 0x, this function interprets it as a hex string instead.)

If EXPR is omitted, uses $_.

open FILEHANDLE[,EXPR]

Opens the file whose filename is given by EXPR and associates it with FILEHANDLE. If FILEHANDLE is an expression, its value is used as the name of the real filehandle wanted. If EXPR is omitted, the scalar variable of the same name as the FILEHANDLE contains the filename. The following characters have special meaning if they begin the filename:

< or nothing	Opened for input
>	Opened for output
>>	Opened for appending

You can put a + in front of the > or < to indicate that you want both read and write access to the file. Thus, +< is usually preferred for read/write updates—the +> mode would clobber the file first. These indicators correspond to the fopen(3) modes of r, r+, w, w+, a, and a+.

If the filename begins with a vertical bar (¦), the filename is interpreted as a command to which output is to be piped; and if the filename ends with a ¦, the filename is interpreted as a command from which input will be piped.

Opening - opens STDIN, and opening >- opens STDOUT. Open returns nonzero upon success and returns the undefined value otherwise. If the open involved a pipe, the return value is the process id (PID) of the subprocess.

opendir DIRHANDLE,EXPR

Opens a directory named EXPR for processing by readdir(), telldir(), seekdir(), rewinddir(), and closedir(). Returns TRUE if successful. DIRHANDLEs have their own namespaces separate from FILEHANDLEs.

ord EXPR

Returns the numeric ASCII value of the first character of EXPR. If EXPR is omitted, uses $_.

14

THE PERL LANGUAGE

pack TEMPLATE, LIST

Takes an array or list of values and packs it into a binary structure, returning the string containing the structure. The TEMPLATE is a sequence of characters that give the order and type of values, as follows:

A	ASCII string, space padded
a	ASCII string, null padded
b	Bit string, ascending bit order
B	Bit string, descending bit order
h	Hex string, low nybble first
H	Hex string, high nybble first
c	Signed char value
C	Unsigned char value
s	Signed short value
S	Unsigned short value
i	Signed integer value
I	Unsigned integer value
l	Signed long value
L	Unsigned long value
n	Short in "network" order
N	Long in "network" order
v	Short, little-endian order
V	Long, little-endian order
f	Single-precision float, native format
d	Double-precision float, native format
p	Pointer to null-terminated string
P	Pointer to a structure (fixed-length string)
u	Uuencoded string
x	Null byte
X	Back up a byte

Each letter may optionally be followed by a number that gives a repeat count. With all types except a, A, b, B, h, H, and P, the pack function gobbles up that many values from the list. A * for the repeat count means to use however many items are left. The a and A types gobble just one value but pack it as a string of length count, padding with nulls or spaces as necessary. (When unpacking, A strips trailing spaces and nulls, but a does not.) Likewise, the b and B fields pack a string that many bits long. The h and H fields pack a string that many nybbles long. The P packs a pointer to a structure of the size indicated by the length. Real numbers (floats and doubles) are in the native machine format only; because of the large number of floating formats and the lack of a standard network representation, no facility for interchange has been made. Therefore, packed floating-point data written on one machine may not be readable on another—even if both use IEEE floating-point arithmetic (as the "endian-ness" of the memory representation is not part of the IEEE specification). Note that Perl uses doubles internally for all numeric calculations, and converting from double to float and back to double again inevitably loses precision (for example, unpack("f", pack("f", $foo)) does not in general equal $foo).

You can generally use the same template in the unpack function.

package NAMESPACE
Declares the compilation unit as being in the given NAMESPACE. The scope of the package declaration is from the declaration itself through the end of the enclosing block (the same scope as the local() operator).

pipe READHANDLE,WRITEHANDLE
Opens a pair of connected pipes like the corresponding system call. Note that if you set up a loop of piped processes, deadlock can occur unless you are very careful. In addition, note that Perl's pipes use stdio buffering, so you may need to set $¦ to flush your WRITEHANDLE after each command, depending on the application.

pop ARRAY
Pops and returns the last value of the array, shortening the array by 1. If the array is empty, returns the undefined value. If ARRAY is omitted, pops the @ARGV array in the main program and the @_ array in subroutines, just like shift().

pos SCALAR
Returns the offset of where the last m//g search left off for the variable in question. (m//g searches for all occurrences of the regular expression in a line.) Can be modified to change that offset.

print [FILEHANDLE LIST¦LIST]
Prints a string or a comma-separated list of strings. Returns TRUE if successful. FILEHANDLE may be a scalar variable name, in which case the variable contains the name of or a reference to the filehandle. If FILEHANDLE is omitted, prints to standard output or to the last selected output channel. If LIST is also omitted, prints $_ to STDOUT. To set the default output channel to something other than STDOUT, use the select operation. Note that, because print takes a LIST, anything in the LIST is evaluated in a list context, and any subroutine that you call has one or more of its expressions evaluated in a list context. Also, be careful not to follow the print keyword with a left parenthesis unless you want the corresponding right parenthesis to terminate the arguments to the print.

push ARRAY,LIST

Treats ARRAY as a stack and pushes the values of LIST onto the end of ARRAY. The length of ARRAY increases by the length of LIST. Returns the new number of elements in the array.

q[q¦x¦w]/STRING/

Generalized quotes.

quotemeta EXPR

Returns the value of EXPR with all regular expression metacharacters backslashed.

rand [EXPR]

Returns a random fractional number between 0 and the value of EXPR. (EXPR should be positive.) If EXPR is omitted, returns a value between 0 and 1. This function produces repeatable sequences unless srand() is invoked. See also srand.

read FILEHANDLE,SCALAR,LENGTH[,OFFSET]

Attempts to read LENGTH bytes of data into variable SCALAR from the specified FILEHANDLE. Returns the number of bytes actually read or returns undef if an error occurs. SCALAR is grown or shrunk to the length actually read. An OFFSET may be specified to place the read data at some place other than the beginning of the string. This call is actually implemented in terms of stdio's fread call. To get a true read system call, see sysread.

readdir DIRHANDLE

Returns the next directory entry for a directory opened by opendir(). If used in a list context, returns all the rest of the entries in the directory. If there are no more entries, returns an undefined value in a scalar context or a null list in a list context.

readlink EXPR

If symbolic links are implemented, readlink returns the value of a symbolic link. If not, it gives a fatal error. If a system error occurs, readlink returns the undefined value and sets $! (errno). If EXPR is omitted, uses $_.

recv SOCKET,SCALAR,LEN,FLAGS

Receives a message on a socket. Attempts to receive LENGTH bytes of data into the variable SCALAR from the specified SOCKET filehandle. Returns the address of the sender. Returns the undefined value if an error occurs. SCALAR is grown or shrunk to the length actually read. Takes the same flags as the system call of the same name.

redo [LABEL]

The `redo` command restarts the loop block without evaluating the conditional again. The `continue` block, if any, is not executed. If the LABEL is omitted, the command refers to the innermost enclosing loop.

ref EXPR

Returns a TRUE value if EXPR is a reference, FALSE otherwise. The value returned depends on what EXPR is a reference to. The built-in types that EXPR can reference include REF, SCALAR, ARRAY, HASH, CODE, and GLOB.

rename OLDNAME, NEWNAME

Changes the name of a file. Returns 1 for success, 0 otherwise. Does not work across file system boundaries.

require [EXPR]

Demands some semantics specified by EXPR or by $_ if EXPR is not supplied. If EXPR is numeric, demands that the current version of Perl ($] or $Perl_VERSION) be equal to or greater than EXPR.

Otherwise, demands that a library file be included if it hasn't already been included.

Note that the file is not included twice under the same specified name. The file must return TRUE as the last statement to indicate successful execution of any initialization code, so it's customary to end such a file with 1;.

If EXPR is a bare word, `require` assumes a .pm extension to enable you to load standard modules without altering your namespace.

reset [EXPR]

Generally used in a `continue` block at the end of a loop to clear variables and reset `??` searches so that they work again. The expression is interpreted as a list of single characters (hyphens are allowed for ranges). All variables and arrays beginning with one of those letters are reset to their pristine state. If the expression is omitted, one-match searches (?pattern?) are reset to match again. Only resets variables or searches in the current package and always returns 1.

return LIST

Returns from a subroutine or eval with the value specified. If LIST is omitted, a subroutine or eval() automatically returns the value of the last expression evaluated.

reverse LIST

In a list context, returns a list value consisting of the elements of LIST in the opposite order. In a scalar context, returns a string value consisting of the bytes of the first element of LIST in the opposite order.

rewinddir DIRHANDLE

Sets the current position to the beginning of the directory for the readdir() routine on DIRHANDLE.

rindex STR,SUBSTR[,POSITION]

Works just like index except that it returns the position of the last occurrence of SUBSTR in STR. If POSITION is specified, returns the last occurrence at or before that position.

rmdir [FILENAME]

Deletes the directory specified by FILENAME if it is empty. If it succeeds, rmdir returns 1; otherwise, rmdir returns 0 and sets $! (errno). If FILENAME is omitted, uses $_.

s///

The substitution operator. See the section "Perl Regular Expressions" for more detail on the substitution operator and its available options.

scalar EXPR

Forces EXPR to be interpreted in a scalar context and returns the value of EXPR.

seek FILEHANDLE,POSITION,WHENCE

Randomly positions the file pointer for FILEHANDLE, just like the C fseek() call of stdio. FILEHANDLE may be an expression whose value gives the name of the filehandle. The values for WHENCE are

0	Set file pointer to POSITION
1	Set file pointer to current plus POSITION
2	Set file pointer to EOF plus offset

You can use the values SEEK_SET, SEEK_CUR, and SEEK_END for this from a POSIX module. Returns 1 on success and 0 otherwise.

seekdir DIRHANDLE,POS

Sets the current position for the readdir() routine on DIRHANDLE. POS must be a value returned by telldir().

select [FILEHANDLE]

Returns the currently selected filehandle. If FILEHANDLE is supplied, select sets the current default filehandle for output. This action has two effects. First, a write or a print without a filehandle defaults to this FILEHANDLE. Second, references to variables related to output refer to this output channel.

select RBITS,WBITS,EBITS,TIMEOUT

Calls the select(2) system call with the bit masks specified, which can be constructed using fileno() and vec().

semctl ID,SEMNUM,CMD,ARG

Calls the System V IPC function semctl. If CMD is &IPC_STAT or &GETALL, then ARG must be a variable that holds the returned semid_ds structure or semaphore value array. semctl is similar to ioctl: in that both return the undefined value for error, "0 but true" for zero, or the actual return value otherwise.

semget KEY,NSEMS,FLAGS

Calls the System V IPC function semget. Returns the semaphore ID; if an error occurs, returns the undefined value.

semop KEY,OPSTRING

Calls the System V IPC function semop to perform semaphore operations such as signaling and waiting. OPSTRING must be a packed array of semop structures. Each semop structure can be generated with pack("sss", $semnum, $semop, $semflag). The number of semaphore operations is implied by the length of OPSTRING. Returns TRUE if successful; returns FALSE if an error occurs.

send SOCKET,MSG,FLAGS[,TO]

Sends a message on a socket. Takes the same flags as the system call of the same name. On unconnected sockets, you must specify a destination to send TO, in which case send does a C sendto(). Returns the number of characters sent or the undefined value if an error occurs.

setpgrp PID,PGRP

Sets the current process group for the specified PID, 0 for the current process. Produces a fatal error if used on a machine that doesn't implement setpgrp(2).

setpriority WHICH,WHO,PRIORITY

Sets the current priority for a process, a process group, or a user. Produces a fatal error if used on a machine that doesn't implement setpriority(2).

setsockopt SOCKET,LEVEL,OPTNAME,OPTVAL

Sets the socket option requested. Returns undefined if an error occurs. OPTVAL may be specified as undef if you don't want to pass an argument.

14

THE PERL LANGUAGE

shift [ARRAY]

Shifts the first value of the array off and returns it, shortening the array by 1 and moving everything down. If the array is empty, returns the undefined value. If ARRAY is omitted, shifts the @ARGV array in the main program and the @_ array in subroutines. Shift and unshift do the same thing to the left end of an array that push and pop do to the right end.

shmctl ID,CMD,ARG

Calls the System V IPC function shmctl. If CMD is &IPC_STAT, then ARG must be a variable that holds the returned shmid_ds structure. shmctl is like ioctl: in that both return the undefined value for error, "0 but true" for zero, or the actual return value otherwise.

shmget KEY,SIZE,FLAGS

Calls the System V IPC function shmget. Returns the shared memory segment ID or returns the undefined value if an error occurs.

shmread ID,VAR,POS,SIZE

shmwrite ID,STRING,POS,SIZE

Reads or writes the System V shared memory segment ID starting at position POS for size SIZE by attaching to it, copying in/out, and detaching from it. When reading, VAR must be a variable that holds the data read. When writing, if STRING is too long, only SIZE bytes are used; if STRING is too short, nulls are written to fill out SIZE bytes. Returns TRUE if successful or FALSE if an error occurs.

shutdown SOCKET,HOW

Shuts down a socket connection in the manner indicated by HOW, which has the same interpretation as in the system call of the same name.

sin EXPR

Returns the sine of EXPR (expressed in radians). If EXPR is omitted, returns sine of $_.

sleep EXPR

sleep causes the script to sleep for EXPR seconds or forever if no EXPR is set. May be interrupted by sending the process a SIGALRM. Returns the number of seconds actually slept. sleep is not suitable for CGI programming.

socket SOCKET,DOMAIN,TYPE,PROTOCOL

Opens a socket of the specified kind and attaches it to filehandle SOCKET. DOMAIN, TYPE, and PROTOCOL are specified the same as they are for the system call of the same name. You should code use Socket; first to import the proper definitions.

socketpair SOCKET1,SOCKET2,DOMAIN,TYPE,PROTOCOL

Creates an unnamed pair of sockets in the specified domain, of the specified type. DOMAIN, TYPE, and PROTOCOL are specified the same as they are for the system call of the same name. If this function is not implemented on your computer, socketpair yields a fatal error. Returns TRUE if successful.

sort [[SUBNAME¦BLOCK]] LIST

Sorts the LIST and returns the sorted list value. Nonexistent values of arrays are stripped out. If SUBNAME or BLOCK is omitted, sort sorts in standard string comparison order. If SUBNAME is specified, sort gives the name of a subroutine that returns an integer less than, equal to, or greater than 0, depending on how the elements of the array are to be ordered. (The <=> and cmp operators are extremely useful in such routines.) SUBNAME may be a scalar variable name, in which case the value provides the name of the subroutine to use. In place of a SUBNAME, you can provide a BLOCK as an anonymous, in-line sort subroutine.

splice ARRAY,OFFSET[,LENGTH[,LIST]]

Removes the elements designated by OFFSET and LENGTH from an array, and replaces them with the elements of LIST, if any. Returns the elements removed from the array. The array grows or shrinks as necessary. If LENGTH is omitted, splice removes everything from OFFSET onward.

split [/PATTERN/[,EXPR[,LIMIT]]]

Splits a string into an array of strings and returns it. If not in a list context, split returns the number of fields found and splits into the @_ array. (In a list context, you can force the split into @_ by using ?? as the pattern delimiters, but it still returns the array value.)

If EXPR is omitted, split splits the $_ string. If PATTERN is also omitted, split splits on whitespace (after skipping any leading whitespace). Anything matching PATTERN is taken to be a delimiter separating the fields. (Note that the delimiter may be longer than one character.) If LIMIT is specified and is not negative, split splits into no more than that many fields (though it may split into fewer). If LIMIT is unspecified, trailing null fields are stripped (which potential users of pop would do well to remember). If LIMIT is negative, the LIMIT is treated as if an arbitrarily large LIMIT had been specified.

A pattern matching the null string (not to be confused with a null pattern //, which is just one member of the set of patterns matching a null string) splits the value of EXPR into separate characters at each point it matches.

sprintf FORMAT,LIST

Returns a string formatted by the usual printf conventions of the C language.

14

sqrt EXPR

Returns the square root of EXPR. If EXPR is omitted, returns the square root of $_.

srand EXPR

Sets the random number seed for the rand operator. If EXPR is omitted, sets a random number seed based on time, for example, srand(time).

stat [FILEHANDLE¦EXPR]

Returns a 13-element array giving the status information for a file, either the file opened via FILEHANDLE or the file named by EXPR. Returns a null list if the stat fails.

```
($dev,$ino,$mode,$nlink,$uid,$gid,$rdev,$size,
➡$atime,$mtime,$ctime,$blksize,$blocks) = stat($filename);
```

Not all fields are supported on all file system types. Here are the meanings of the fields:

dev	Device number of file system
ino	Inode number
mode	File mode (type and permissions)
nlink	Number of (hard) links to the file
uid	Numeric user ID of file's owner
gid	Numeric group ID of file's owner
rdev	The device identifier (special files only)
size	Total size of file in bytes
atime	Last access time since the epoch
mtime	Last modify time since the epoch
ctime	Inode change time (*not* creation type!) since the epoch
blksize	Size of each block
blocks	Number of blocks

If stat is passed the special filehandle consisting of an underline, no stat is done, but the current contents of the stat structure from the last stat or file test are returned.

sub [BLOCK¦NAME¦NAME BLOCK]

This "function" is actually a subroutine definition. With just a NAME (and possibly prototypes), sub is just a forward declaration. Without a NAME, it's an anonymous function declaration and actually returns a value: the CODE reference of the closure you just created.

substr EXPR,OFFSET[,LEN]

Extracts a substring out of EXPR and returns it. The first character is at offset 0 or at the current setting of $[. If OFFSET is negative, substr starts the offset distance from the end of the string.

If LEN is omitted, substr returns everything to the end of the string. If LEN is negative, substr leaves that many characters off the end of the string.

You can use the substr function as an lvalue, in which case EXPR must be an lvalue. If you assign something shorter than LEN, the string shrinks; and if you assign something longer than LEN, the string grows to accommodate it. To keep the string the same length, you may need to pad or chop your value using sprintf.

symlink OLDFILE,NEWFILE

Creates a new filename symbolically linked to the old filename. Returns 1 for success, 0 otherwise. On systems that don't support symbolic links, produces a fatal error at runtime.

syscall LIST

Calls the system call specified as the first element of the list, passing the remaining elements as arguments to the system call. If syscall is unimplemented, using the statement produces a fatal error. The arguments are interpreted as follows: If a given argument is numeric, the argument is passed as an int. If not, the pointer to the string value is passed. You are responsible for making sure a string is preextended long enough to receive any result that might be written into that string. If your integer arguments are not literals and have never been interpreted in a numeric context, you may need to add 0 to them to force them to look like numbers.

> **NOTE**
>
> Note that the maximum number of arguments to your system call that Perl supports is 14, which in practice should usually suffice.

sysopen FILEHANDLE,FILENAME,MODE[,PERMS]

Opens the file whose filename is given by FILENAME and associates it with FILEHANDLE. If FILEHANDLE is an expression, its value is used as the name of the real filehandle wanted. This function calls the underlying operating system's open function with the parameters FILENAME, MODE, PERMS.

The possible values and flag bits of the MODE parameter are system dependent.

sysread FILEHANDLE,SCALAR,LENGTH[,OFFSET]

Attempts to read LENGTH bytes of data into a variable SCALAR from the specified FILEHANDLE, using the system call read(2). sysread bypasses stdio, so mixing this read with other kinds of reads may cause confusion. Returns the number of bytes actually read or returns undef if an error occurs. SCALAR is grown or shrunk to the length actually read. An OFFSET may be specified to place the read data at some place other than the beginning of the string.

system LIST

system LIST does exactly the same thing as exec LIST except that system does a fork first, and the parent process waits for the child process to complete. Note that argument processing varies depending on the number of arguments. The return value is the exit status of the program as returned by the wait() call. To get the actual exit value, divide by 256. See also exec. If you want to capture the output from a command, you should merely use backticks rather than system LIST.

syswrite FILEHANDLE,SCALAR,LENGTH[,OFFSET]

Attempts to write LENGTH bytes of data from the variable SCALAR to the specified FILEHANDLE, using the system call write(2). syswrite bypasses stdio, so mixing this function with prints may cause confusion. Returns the number of bytes actually written or undef if an error occurs. An OFFSET may be specified to get the write data from some place other than the beginning of the string.

tell FILEHANDLE

tell returns the current file position for FILEHANDLE. FILEHANDLE may be an expression whose value gives the name of the actual filehandle. If FILEHANDLE is omitted, assumes the file last read.

telldir DIRHANDLE

telldir returns the current position of the readdir routines on DIRHANDLE. A value may be given to seekdir to access a particular location in a directory. telldir has the same caveats about possible directory compaction as the corresponding system library routine.

tie VARIABLE,CLASSNAME,LIST

This function binds a variable to a package class that provides the implementation for the variable. VARIABLE is the name of the variable to be bound. CLASSNAME is the name of a class implementing objects of the correct type. Any additional arguments are passed to the "new" method of the class (meaning TIESCALAR, TIEARRAY, or TIE-HASH). Typically, these arguments resemble arguments that might be passed to the dbm_open function of C. The object returned by the new method is also returned by the tie function, which is useful if you want to access other methods in CLASSNAME.

tied VARIABLE

Returns a reference to the object underlying VARIABLE (the same value that was originally returned by the tie call that bound the variable to a package). Returns the undefined value if VARIABLE isn't tied to a package.

time

Returns the number of non-leap seconds since 00:00:00 UTC, January 1, 1970. Suitable for feeding to gmtime() and localtime().

times

Returns a four-element array giving the user and system times, in seconds, for this process and the children of this process.

tr///

The translation operator. See the section, "Perl Regular Expressions," for more detail on the translation operator and its available options.

truncate [FILEHANDLE¦EXPR],LENGTH

Truncates the file opened on FILEHANDLE or named by EXPR to the specified length. Produces a fatal error if truncate isn't implemented on your system.

uc EXPR

Returns an uppercased version of EXPR. uc is the internal function implementing the \U escape in double-quoted strings. Should respect any POSIX setlocale() settings.

ucfirst EXPR

ucfirst returns the value of EXPR with the first character in uppercase. This function is the internal function implementing the \u escape in double-quoted strings. Should respect any POSIX set-locale() settings.

umask [EXPR]

Sets the umask for the process and returns the old one. If EXPR is omitted, it merely returns the current umask.

undef [EXPR]

Undefines the value of EXPR, which must be an lvalue. Use only on a scalar value, an entire array, or a subroutine name (using &). (Using undef() will probably not do what you expect on most predefined variables or DBM list values.) Always returns the undefined value. You can omit the EXPR, in which case nothing is undefined, but you still get an undefined value that you could, for instance, return from a subroutine.

unlink LIST

Deletes a list of files and returns the number of files successfully deleted.

14

THE PERL
LANGUAGE

unpack TEMPLATE,EXPR

unpack does the reverse of pack: It takes a string representing a structure and expands it into a list value, returning the array value. (In a scalar context, unpack merely returns the first value produced.) TEMPLATE has the same format as it has in the pack function.

untie VARIABLE

Breaks the binding between a variable and a package. (See tie.)

unshift ARRAY,LIST

Does the opposite of a shift (or the opposite of a push, depending on how you look at it). Prepends the list to the front of the array and returns the new number of elements in the array.

use Module [LIST]

Imports some semantics into the current package from the named module, generally by aliasing certain subroutine or variable names into your package.

utime LIST

Changes the access and modification times on each file of a list of files. The first two elements of the list must be the numerical access and modification times, in that order. Returns the number of files successfully changed.

values ASSOC_ARRAY

Returns a normal array consisting of all the values of the named associative array. (In a scalar context, returns the number of values.) The values are returned in an apparently random order, but it is the same order as either the keys or each function.

vec EXPR,OFFSET,BITS

Treats the string in EXPR as a vector of unsigned integers and returns the value of the bit field specified by OFFSET. BITS specifies the number of bits that are reserved for each entry in the bit vector and must be a power of two from 1 to 32. vec may also be assigned to by an assignment statement, in which case you must use parentheses to give the expression the correct precedence.

waitpid PID,FLAGS

Waits for a particular child process to terminate and returns the pid of the deceased process or -1 if there is no such child process. The status is returned in $?.

warn LIST

warn produces a message on the standard error stream (STDERR) just like die but doesn't exit or raise an exception.

write [[FILEHANDLE¦EXPR]]

Writes a formatted record (possibly multiline) to the specified file, using the format associated with that file. By default, the format for a file is the one with the same name as the filehandle, but the format for the current output channel (see the `select` function) may be set explicitly by assigning the name of the format to the `$~` variable.

If `FILEHANDLE` is unspecified, output goes to the current default output channel, which starts out as `STDOUT` but may be changed by the `select` operator. If the `FILEHANDLE` is an `EXPR`, then the expression is evaluated and the resulting string is used to look up the name of the `FILEHANDLE` at runtime. For more on formats, see the `perlform` man page for more information.

y///

The translation operator. See the following section for more detail on the translation operator and its available options.

Perl Regular Expressions

Perl supports powerful regular expression parsing, which can be used with the following matching operators.

`m//` (`//`)	Match operator
`s///`	Substitution operator
`tr///`	Translation operators
`y///`	

The matching operators can have various modifiers, some of which relate to the interpretation of the regular expression inside. These are

I	Perform case-insensitive pattern matching.
m	Treat the string as multiple lines.
s	Treat the string as a single line.
x	Extend your pattern's legibility with whitespace and comments.

These expressions are usually written as the `/x` modifier, even though the delimiter in question might not actually be a slash. In fact, any of these modifiers may also be embedded within the regular expression using the new `(?...)` construct described later in this section.

The `/x` modifier itself needs a little more explanation. It tells the regular expression parser to ignore whitespace that is not backslashed or within a character class. You can use the `/x` modifier to break your regular expression into (slightly) more readable parts. The # character is also treated by the expression as a metacharacter introducing a comment, just as in ordinary Perl code. Taken together, these features go a long way toward making Perl 5 a readable language. (Note that this feature is not available in Perl 4.)

Regular Expressions

The patterns used in pattern matching are regular expressions such as those supplied in the version 8 `regexp` routines.

In particular, the following metacharacters have their standard meanings from the UNIX `egrep`:

\	Quote the next metacharacter.
^	Match the beginning of the line.
.	Match any character (except newline).
$	Match the end of the line (or before newline at the end).
¦	Alternation.
( )	Grouping.
[ ]	Character class.

By default, the ^ character is guaranteed to match only at the beginning of the string, and the $ character matches only at the end (or before the newline at the end). Perl does certain optimizations with the assumption that the string contains only one line. Embedded newlines are not matched by ^ or $. However, you might want to treat a string as a multiline buffer, so that the ^ matches after any newline within the string and $ matches before any newline. At the cost of a little more overhead, you can do this matching by using the /m modifier on the pattern match operator. (Older programs did this matching by setting $*, but this practice is not encouraged in Perl 5.)

To facilitate multiline substitutions, the . character never matches a newline unless you use the /s modifier, which tells Perl to pretend the string is a single line—even if it isn't. The /s modifier also overrides the setting of $*, in case you have some (badly behaved) older code (such as that written for versions of Perl before version 5) that sets $* in another module.

The following standard quantifiers are recognized by regular expressions:

*	Match 0 or more times.
+	Match 1 or more times.
?	Match 1 or 0 times.
{n}	Match exactly *n* times.
{n,}	Match at least *n* times.
{n,m}	Match at least *n* but not more than *m* times.

If a curly bracket occurs in any other context, it is treated as a regular character. The * modifier is equivalent to {0,}, the + modifier to {1,}, and the ? modifier to {0,1}. *n* and *m* are limited to integral values less than 65,536.

By default, a quantified subpattern is "greedy"; that is, it matches as many times as possible without causing the rest of the pattern not to match. The standard quantifiers are all greedy in that they match as many occurrences as possible (given a particular starting location) without causing the pattern to fail. If you want it to match the minimum number of times possible, follow the quantifier with a ?. Note that the meanings don't change, only the "gravity":

*?	Match 0 or more times.
+?	Match 1 or more times.
??	Match 0 or 1 time.
{n}?	Match exactly n times.
{n,}?	Match at least n times.
{n,m}?	Match at least n but not more than m times.

Because patterns are processed as double-quoted strings, the following metacharacters are also expanded:

\t	Tab
\n	Newline
\r	Return
\f	Form feed
\v	Vertical tab
\a	Alarm (bell)
\e	Escape
\0nn	Octal character
\xnn	Hex character
\c[	Control character
\l	Lowercase next character
\u	Uppercase next character
\L	Lowercase until \E
\U	Uppercase until \E
\E	End case modification
\Q	Quote regexp metacharacters until \E

In addition, Perl defines the following metacharacters:

\w	Match a word character (alphanumeric plus "_").
\W	Match a non-word character.
\s	Match a whitespace character.
\S	Match a non-whitespace character.
\d	Match a digit character.
\D	Match a non-digit character.

14

Note that \w matches a single alphanumeric character, not a whole word. To match a word, you say \w+. You may use \w, \W, \s, \S, \d, and \D within character classes (although not at either end of a range).

Perl defines the following zero-width assertions:

\b	Match a word boundary.
\B	Match a non-word boundary.
\A	Match only at beginning of a string.
\Z	Match only at end of a string (or before newline at the end).
\G	Match only where previous m//g left off.

A word boundary is defined as a spot between two characters that has a \w on one side of it and a \W on the other side of it (in either order), counting the imaginary characters off the beginning and end of the string as matching a \W. (Within character classes, \b represents backspace rather than a word boundary.) The \A and \Z are just like ^ and $ except that they won't match multiple times when the /m modifier is used, whereas ^ and $ match at every internal line boundary. To match the actual end of the string, not ignoring newline, you can use \Z(?!\n).

When the bracketing construct (...) is used, \<digit> matches the \<digit>th substring. Outside of the pattern, always use $ instead of \ in front of the digit. (Although the \<digit> notation can on rare occasions work outside the current pattern, you should not depend on it. See the warning that follows.) The scope of $<digit> (and $`, $&, and $´) extends to the end of the enclosing BLOCK or eval string or to the next successful pattern match, whichever comes first. If you want to use parentheses to delimit a subpattern (for example, a set of alternatives) without saving it as a subpattern, follow the (with a ?.

You can have as many parentheses as you want. If you have more than nine substrings, the variables $10, $11, and so on refer to the corresponding substring. Within the pattern, \10, \11, and so on refer to substrings if at least that many left parentheses occurred before the back reference. Otherwise (for backward compatibility), \10 is the same as \010 (a backspace), and \11 the same as \011 (a tab) and so on. (\1 through \9 are always back references.)

$+ returns whatever the last bracket match matched. $& returns the entire matched string. (In Perl versions prior to version 5, $0 used to return the same thing, but not any more.) $` returns everything before the matched string. $´ returns everything after the matched string.

```
s/^([^ ]*) *([^ ]*)/$2 $1/; # swap first two words
if (/Time: (..):(..):(..)/) {
        $hours = $1;
        $minutes = $2;
        $seconds = $3;
}
```

You will note that all backslashed metacharacters in Perl are alphanumeric, such as \b, \w, and \n, unlike some other regular expression languages. Anything that looks like \\, \(, \), \<, \>, \{, or \} is always interpreted as a literal character, not as a metacharacter. This convention makes it simple to quote a string that you want to use for a pattern but that you are afraid might contain metacharacters. Simply quote all the nonalphanumeric characters:

```
$pattern =~ s/(\W)/\\$1/g;
```

You can also use the built-in `quotemeta` function to quote a string. An even easier way to quote metacharacters within the match operator is to say

```
/$unquoted\Q$quoted\E$unquoted/
```

Perl 5 defines a consistent extension syntax for regular expressions. The syntax is a pair of parentheses with a question mark as the first character within the parentheses (this construct produced a syntax error in Perl 4). The character after the question mark gives the function of the extension. Several extensions are already supported:

`(?#text)`	A comment. The text is ignored. If the `/x` switch is used to enable whitespace formatting, a simple # will suffice.
`(?:regexp)`	This groups things like "`()`" but doesn't make back references as "`()`" does.
`(?=regexp)`	A zero-width positive look-ahead assertion.
`(?!regexp)`	A zero-width negative look-ahead assertion.
`(?imsx)`	One or more embedded pattern-match modifiers. This modifier is particularly useful for patterns that are specified in a table somewhere, some of which want to be case-sensitive and some of which don't. The case-insensitive patterns merely need to include `(?i)` at the front of the pattern.

Perl Subroutines

Like many languages, Perl provides for user-defined subroutines. These subroutines may be located anywhere in the main program; loaded in from other files via the `do`, `require`, or `use` keywords; or even generated on-the-fly using `eval` or anonymous subroutines (closures). You can even call a function indirectly using a variable containing its name or a code reference to it, as in `$var = \&function`.

The Perl model for function calls and return values is simple: All functions are passed as parameters a single flat list of scalars, and all functions likewise return to their caller a single flat list of scalars. Any arrays or hashes in these call and return lists collapse, losing their identities—but you may always use pass-by-reference instead to avoid this situation. Both call and return lists may contain as many or as few scalar elements as you'd like.

Any arguments passed to the routine come in as the array `@_`. If you call a function with two arguments, those are stored in `$_[0]` and `$_[1]`. The array `@_` is a local array, but its values are implicit references to the actual scalar parameters. The return value of the subroutine is the value of the last expression evaluated. Alternatively, you can use a return statement to specify the returned value and exit the subroutine. If you return one or more arrays or hashes, they are flattened together into one large indistinguishable list.

Perl does not have named formal parameters, but in practice, all you do is assign a list of parameters to a my list. Any variables you use in the function that aren't declared private are global variables.

In the following example, `$max` is local to the subroutine max because it is declared in a my list:

```perl
sub max {
        my $max = shift(@_);
        foreach $foo (@_) {
                $max = $foo if $max < $foo;
        }
        return $max;
}

$bestday = max($mon,$tue,$wed,$thu,$fri);
```

In the following example, `$lookahead` is a global variable that is set both in the mainline code and in the subroutine `get_line`:

```perl
# get a line, combining continuation lines
# that start with whitespace
sub get_line {
        $thisline = $lookahead; # GLOBAL VARIABLES!!
        LINE: while ($lookahead = <STDIN>) {
                if ($lookahead =~ /^[ \t]/) {
                        $thisline .= $lookahead;
                } else {
                        last LINE;
                }
        }
        $thisline;
}

$lookahead = <STDIN>; # get first line
while ($_ = get_line()){
        ...
}
```

Use array assignment to a local list to name your formal arguments:

```perl
sub maybeset {
        my($key, $value) = @_;
        $Foo{$key} = $value unless $Foo{$key};
}
```

The technique of assigning variables using a my list also has the effect of turning call-by-reference into call-by-value because the assignment copies the values. Otherwise, a function is free to do in-place modifications of @_ and change its callers' values.

```perl
upcase_in($v1, $v2); # this changes $v1 and $v2

sub upcase_in {
```

```
        for (@_) {
                tr/a-z/A-Z/
        }
}
```

You aren't allowed to modify constants in this way, of course. If an argument were actually literal and you tried to change it, you'd take an exception.

You will, of course, be safer if you write the upcase_in() function to return a copy of its parameters instead of changing them in place.

You can call a subroutine using the & prefix. The & is optional in Perl 5 and so are the parentheses if the subroutine has been predeclared. Note, however, that the & is *not* optional when you're just naming the subroutine, such as when it's used as an argument to defined() or undef(). Nor is the & optional when you want to do an indirect subroutine call with a subroutine name or reference using the &$ subref() or &{$subref}() constructs. (See the perlref man page for more on subroutine naming.)

Subroutines can be called recursively. If a subroutine is called using the & form, the argument list is optional, and if omitted, no @_ array is set up for the subroutine. Instead, the @_ array at the time of the call is visible to the subroutine. This setting of the @_ array is an efficiency mechanism that new users might want to avoid.

Private Variables via my()

A my declares the listed variables to be confined (lexically) to the enclosing block, subroutine, eval, or do/require/use file. If more than one value is listed, the list must be placed in parentheses. All listed elements must be legal lvalues. Only alphanumeric identifiers may be lexically scoped—magical built-ins like $/ must currently be localized with local instead.

Unlike dynamic variables created by the local statement, lexical variables declared with my are totally hidden from the outside world, including any called subroutines (even if it's the same subroutine called from itself or elsewhere—every call gets its own copy).

Temporary Values via local()

A local() modifies its listed variables to be local to the enclosing block, (or subroutine, eval{}, or do) and any blocks called from within that block. A local() gives temporary values to global variables. This technique is known as *dynamic scoping. Lexical scoping* is done with my, which works more like C's auto declarations.

> **NOTE**
>
> In general, you should be using my instead of `local` because it's faster and safer. Exceptions to this include the global punctuation variables, filehandles, formats, and direct manipulation of the Perl symbol table itself. Format variables often use `local` though, as do other variables whose current value must be visible to called subroutines.

If more than one variable is given to `local()`, they must be placed in parentheses. All listed elements must be legal lvalues. This operator works by saving the current values of those variables in its argument list on a hidden stack and restoring them upon exiting the block, subroutine, or `eval`. Consequently, called subroutines can also reference the local variable, but not the global one. The argument list may be assigned if desired, which allows you to initialize your local variables. (If no initializer is given for a particular variable, it is created with an undefined value.) This technique is commonly used to name the parameters to a subroutine.

Because `local()` is a runtime command, it gets executed every time through a loop. In releases of Perl previous to 5.0, `local()` used more stack storage each time until the loop was exited. Perl now reclaims the space each time through, but declaring your variables outside the loop is still more efficient than using `local()`.

A `local` is simply a modifier on an lvalue expression. When you assign to a localized variable, the `local` stays the same regardless of whether its list is viewed as a scalar or an array.

Passing Symbol Table Entries (`typeglobs`)

Sometimes you want to pass the name of an array, rather than its value, to a subroutine so that the subroutine can modify the global copy of it rather than work with a local copy. In Perl, you can refer to all objects of a particular name by prefixing the name with * (for example, *foo). This mechanism is often known as a `typeglob` because the * on the front can be considered a wildcard match for all the funny prefix characters on variables and subroutines and such.

When evaluated, the `typeglob` produces a scalar value that represents all the objects of that name, including any filehandle, format, or subroutine. When assigned, a `typeglob` causes the name mentioned to refer to whatever * value was assigned to it.

Note that scalars are already passed by reference, so you can modify scalar arguments without using this mechanism by referring explicitly to `$_[0]`, `$_[1]`, and so on. You can modify all the elements of an array by passing all the elements as scalars, but you have to use the * mechanism (or the equivalent reference mechanism) to push, pop, or change the size of an array. It is certainly faster to pass the `typeglob` (or reference).

Pass By Reference

If you want to pass more than one array or hash into a function—or return them from a function—and have them maintain their integrity, you must use an explicit pass by reference. First, you need to understand references as detailed in the `perlref` man page.

Prototypes

As of the 5.002 release of Perl, if you declare

```
sub mypush (\@@)
```

then `mypush()` takes the same arguments that `push()` does. The declaration of the function to be called must be visible at compile time. The prototype only affects the interpretation of new-style calls to the function, where new-style is defined as not using the & character. In other words, if you call `mypush` like a built-in function, then it behaves like a built-in function. If you call `mypush` like an old-fashioned subroutine, then it behaves like an old-fashioned subroutine. From this rule, you can see that prototypes have no influence on subroutine references like `\&foo` or on indirect subroutine calls like `&{$sub-ref}`.

Overriding Built-In Functions

Although you can override many built-in functions, you should only do so occasionally and for good reason. For example, a package attempting to emulate missing built-in functionality on a non-UNIX system might override a built-in function. Discussion of this capability is beyond the scope of this chapter.

What's Next?

Chapter 15, "Perl in Internet Applications," presents a tutorial of Perl programming in the context of developing a CGI application. The programs show basic Perl programming and allow you to modify them to gain practice in coding in Perl.

Summary

You have learned a great deal of information about the Perl language in this chapter. Perl is a complex, full-featured scripting language, and a complete treatment of the language requires thousands of pages. This chapter is intended as a reference chapter to the Perl language to help you use it for Internet programming. It provides references to most of the common language elements that you would use in programming Web pages. The next chapter rounds out the explanation of Perl for Internet programming by presenting techniques and examples using many of the functions and features detailed in this chapter.

Perl in Internet Applications

by Bob Breedlove

IN THIS CHAPTER

The best way to learn to program in Perl is to program in Perl. This chapter gives you an opportunity to do just that. The application that you will develop is contained on the CD-ROM in its entirety. I encourage you to examine and modify it to meet your needs. Because there are many different ways to do things in Perl, I don't claim that the methods used in this application are best (whatever that means to you). But they do illustrate many common techniques that can be used to create Internet applications in Perl.

A CGI Shell

Before you start into the relatively complex GO application, look at a basic CGI shell. A basic CGI program is relatively simple and straightforward. Here is the basic shell:

```
#!/usr/bin/perl           #(1)

# Module which implements common CGI handling routines
require 'cgi-lib.pl';     #(2)
# Startup Code            #(3)
# Put any code here that you need to perform each time the
# program starts up.

                          #(4)
if (&MethGet()) {
#     Place the GET method code in this section
} elseif (&MethPut()) {
#     Place the PUT method code in this section

# Finalization Code       #(5)
# Place any common finalization code here

# Subroutines            #(6)

# End of Program
```

Let's take a quick look at this template program. The numbers refer to the numbers in parentheses after the comment operator (#).

1. Your operating system might require a line to allow you to execute the program by name. This construct is for the UNIX operating system and is the same for all shell-like scripting programs.

2. require/use statements are usually placed at the start of a program. The GO system uses the excellent cgi-lib.pl by Steven E. Brenner. There are several excellent packages for handling CGI basics. I recommend finding one that has the functions you require and using it.

3. Perl executes programs from start to finish. Place any common initialization code here.

4. This `if{}elsif{}` statement is the heart of the program. The GET method is the default and is usually sent to indicate that a form is to be returned. The POST method is usually returned after the form has been filled out and data needs to be passed to the module.

5. Place any common finalization code here. There might be little to do here or in the initialization section because Perl does not require variable initialization.

6. I usually place all subroutines after the main program. Technically, however, they can be placed anywhere in the program. Keeping subroutines together makes maintenance easier.

The code in each of the sections can be very complex, but this simple template is the basis of most CGI programs. To illustrate, let's construct a slightly more complex hello world program. This is the basic Perl hello world program:

```
#!/usr/bin/perl

print "Hello World\n";
```

Here's one that puts out a Web page format and prints the "Hello World" line followed by a line feed. It uses the print-to-here format to print the form:

```
print <<EOF;
Content-type: text/html

<HTML>
<HEAD>
<TITLE>Hello World!</TITLE>
</HEAD>
<BODY>
Hello World!
</BODY>
</HTML>
EOF
;
```

The "to-here" version of the `print` statement prints everything between the line

```
print <<EOF;
```

and the corresponding

```
EOF
```

Notice that the `here` label must be the same as that following the `<<` on the print line. The line must be terminated by a semicolon (;), so this is placed on the next line. For style, I like to place a Tab before the semicolon. It makes the terminating label a bit more obvious. Figure 15.1 shows the output of this simple program.

FIGURE 15.1.

The output of the "Hello World" page.

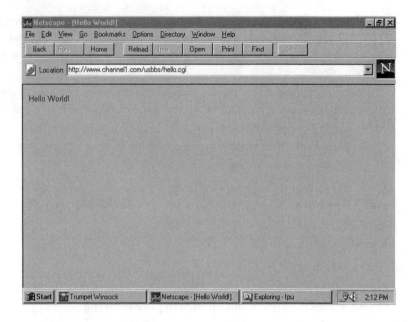

The same page can be implemented using the `cgi-lib` routines. Using a library can simplify the code in your main program. Here's the same page:

```
require 'cgi-lib.pl';

print &PrintHeader();

$title = 'Hello World!';  # Set title to be used by $HtmlTop
print &HtmlTop();

print "Hello World\n";

print &HtmlBot();
```

Let's take a quick look at each of the subroutines that make the main program easier to maintain. Each of these subroutines uses the `return` statement to return the text required to implement the function. Notice that the subroutines do not have to be typed.

```
# PrintHeader
# Returns the magic line which tells WWW that we're an HTML document
sub PrintHeader {
  return "Content-type: text/html\n\n";
}
```

The `PrintHeader` subroutine returns the `Content-type` line, which tells the Web server what type of document it should process. Notice the two line feeds (`\n\n`), which create the blank line required after the `Content-type` statement. The return sends the line back to the main program print routine for printing. It could just as easily have been returned to a routine that would write the line to a file for use later.

```
# HtmlTop
# Returns the <head> of a document and the beginning of the body
# with the title and a body <h1> header as specified by the parameter
sub HtmlTop
{
  local ($title) = @_;

  return <<END_OF_TEXT;
<html>
<head>
<title>$title</title>
</head>
<body>
<h1>$title</h1>
END_OF_TEXT
}
```

This subroutine returns the top part of the HTML template. The variable $title needs to be set prior to calling &HtmlTop. This can be done because variables, unless specified in a local() or my() statement, are global. After &HtmlTop, place statements for the body of your page.

```
# Html Bot
# Returns the </body>, </html> codes for the bottom of every HTML page

sub HtmlBot
{
    return "</body>\n</html>\n";
}
```

&HtmlBot sends the bottom of the Web page. The two line feeds are not strictly necessary, but they make the produced page more readable. This formatting can make debugging programs easier.

"Hello World" Interactive

"Hello World" will be the same each time it is run. This isn't any better than a static Web page. The whole advantage of CGI is to create dynamic Web pages. Before examining the more complex go.cgi application, let's make the "Hello World" program put out a form to get your name and then say "hello" to you by name.

Here's the entire program:

```
#!/usr/bin/perl

# Module which implements common CGI handling routines
require 'cgi-lib.cgi';

$HtmlAction = 'hello.pl';

if (&MethGet()) {          # Send the form
    print &PrintHeader();
    $title = 'Hello World Interactive';
    print &HtmlTop;
    print <<EOT;
```

```
<FORM ACTION="$HtmlAction" METHOD=POST>
Please enter your first name:
<INPUT SIZE=20 NAME="fname"><P>
<INPUT TYPE=SUBMIT>
<INPUT TYPE=RESET>
</FORM>
EOT
    ;
    print &HtmlBot();
} elsif (&MethPost()) { # Process the form
    &ReadParse();

#    Output the form including the name
    print &PrintHeader();
    $title = 'Hello World Interactive';
    print &HtmlTop;
    print "Hello, $in{'fname'}!";
    print &HtmlBot();
}

# End of Program
```

There is some minimal initialization code in this program. The single line

```
$HtmlAction = 'hello.pl';
```

sets the `$HtmlAction` variable to the program to be activated when the form is submitted. The title of the program could be placed at the point where it is used, but initializing it here allows easier maintenance if you need to change the location of your page or the name of the script.

Figure 15.2 shows the form produced by this program. Because I don't like to reinvent the world, the program used `cgi-lib.pl`. When a link is clicked for this script, the Web server activates the script (`hello.pl`) with the GET method. This causes the first branch of the if() statement to be executed.

```
if (&MethGet()) {          # Send the form
    print &PrintHeader();
    $title = 'Hello World Interactive';
    print &HtmlTop;
    print <<EOT;
<FORM ACTION="$HtmlAction" METHOD=POST>
Please enter your first name:
<INPUT SIZE=20 NAME="fname"><P>
<INPUT TYPE=SUBMIT>
<INPUT TYPE=RESET>
</FORM>
EOT
    ;
    print &HtmlBot();
```

You've seen the subroutines &PrintHeader, &HtmlTop, and &HtmlBot before. The lines in the print to-here statement produce the form. There are few frills here. Because this book includes a chapter on HTML, I won't go into details on most of the statements. However, note that the <INPUT> statement includes a NAME= clause that sets the name to fname. This name will be returned when the form is submitted.

FIGURE 15.2.

The "Hello World, Interactive" form.

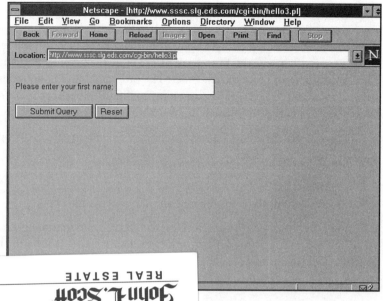

utton, the information on the form
the elsif branch of the if() state-

```
print &HtmlTop;
print "Hello, $in{'fname'}!";
print &HtmlBot();
}
```

The &ReadParse subroutine is called to parse the information received into an associative array. If no reference is passed to the subroutine, it parses the key/value pairs into %in. The page returned is much the same as the form page. However, note the line on which the name is printed:

```
print "Hello, $in{'fname'}!";
```

It uses the information from the form to get the actual name entered by the visitor. The line in the Web page is

```
<INPUT SIZE=20 NAME="fname">
```

The program matches the NAME= clause of the INPUT directive with the key for the %in associative array to return the information to the program.

I won't discuss the actual workings of &ReadParse here. You'll get into the techniques it uses in the discussion of the GO application, which follows. But before you leave this simple example to tackle the more complete GO application, you need to learn one other item. When the hello.pl script has sent the form back to the visitor, all connection with that visitor is lost. This is an important point to remember. The program does not know any information about any request sent to it unless the information is contained in the request from the visitor or can be retrieved from databases based on information received in the request.

Now that you've seen a simple example, you are able to do the following:

■ Output a form.
■ Receive information.
■ Process and display a form based on that information.

As simplistic as it sounds, this is the basis for all CGI programming. In the GO application, you'll also learn about some support/utility programs, but you have the basics for creating interactive Web pages and displaying them for your visitors using Perl. Let's move on to the more complex GO application.

Programming the GO Application

You examine the GO application in detail in this section and see how it was programmed based on the template presented earlier. You examine techniques that you can use in your CGI programming and see interfaces to mail systems (sendmail) and text file processing. Variations of Perl are able to access databases, but this topic is beyond the scope of this chapter. The techniques you learn here will be applicable to whatever data storage/retrieval system you are using.

The GO Application

Figure 15.3 illustrates the template for the execution of the GO application.

This application implements a simple index of links in various categories. It is in use as the "Been There, Done That" page of my home page (http://www.channel1.com/users/rbreed01/). It is located under the Links tab from the home page. The URL of the link page itself is http://www.channel1.com/usbbs/go.cgi/jumppts.cfg.

GO uses regular flat (text) files for its "database." It displays all entries in a category and does not do string searches. (These might be hints for enhancements to the GO application.)

The first page enables visitors to pick a category in which they are interested. The Webmaster defines categories that he wants to include on the page. Figure 15.4 shows the main screen of the application.

FIGURE 15.3.
Overview of the GO application.

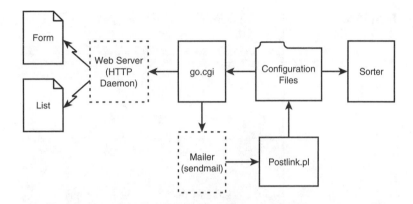

FIGURE 15.4.
The GO main category selection screen.

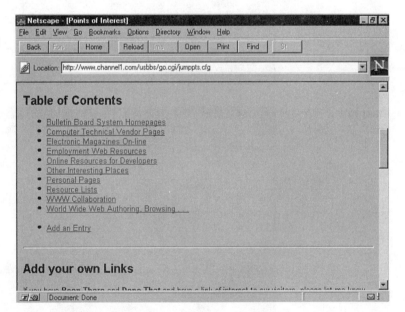

When visitors pick a category, all the links in this category are displayed for them. Figure 15.5 shows part of a link page.

This system is definitely not as sophisticated as the search engines on many pages, but it does allow links and descriptions from the home page for connections to pages of interest. In addition, GO allows visitors to request that their pages be listed under a category.

As shown in Figure 15.6, visitors can enter their link information in a form displayed on request.

15

PERL IN INTERNET APPLICATIONS

FIGURE 15.5.

A GO link page.

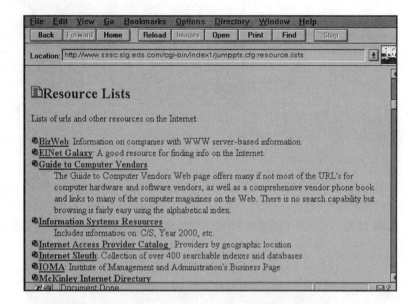

FIGURE 15.6.

The GO add-a-link form.

This information is formatted and mailed to the Webmaster. After reviewing the link request, the Webmaster can mail it back for processing by the Mail Parser and addition to the home page in the correct category.

This leads to an interesting consideration about Web programming in general. When I first designed and implemented GO, the form would post the entry immediately. I blindly thought that visitors would be responsible enough to post their links in the proper categories. This trust was misplaced. I found many duplicate entries, others posted in the wrong categories, obscene entries, and other stupidity that led to the current design, which includes screening. It is unfortunate that this is the case, but it has led me to conclude that you can't trust anyone on the Internet and should take precautions to protect your reputation and avoid wasting time.

`go.cgi`: The Heart of the GO Application

`go.cgi` is the heart of the CGI portion of the application. It displays the table of contents and the link pages, plus the input form. The program follows the basic CGI template demonstrated earlier in the "Hello World" program. Figure 15.7 shows the relationship of the major subroutines of `go.cgi` and the configuration files read by these routines.

FIGURE 15.7.

The `go.cgi` *program logic showing major subroutines and configuration files.*

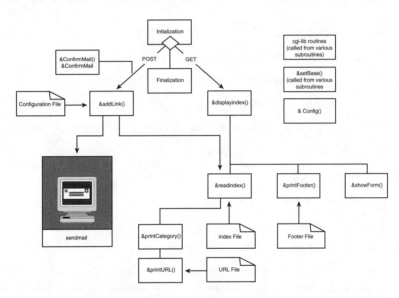

As you can see, `go.cgi` has sections that handle initialization, the Get and Post methods, and finalization as does the basic template. I'll fill in the logic of the basic CGI template by examining the code in the subroutines that actually perform the work to illustrate techniques for Internet programming in Perl as you develop the program. However, before that, I need to say a word about a couple of important concepts: comments and subroutines.

Use of Comments and Subroutines

Use comments liberally to annotate your code. Comments in Perl begin with a #, and the interpreter ignores the remainder of the line. Use comments throughout the code as a reminder of what a piece of code is doing and why it was coded a particular way. You'd be surprised at how soon you forget why you used a particular technique or what a particular subroutine is doing.

Use subroutines to organize your code. Perl code can be written in a straight line from the top of the program to the bottom. This might be the best way to do a "quick-and-dirty" utility or piece of one-use code. However, if you intend to maintain or enhance the application or reuse parts of the code in another application, some form of organization will be invaluable.

Subroutines should be logical and, in general, should perform a single function. Subroutines can also be used as organization points for logical processes by calling other subroutines. You will see subroutines used for both of these purposes throughout this chapter.

Examining the go.cgi Application

Let's examine go.cgi in detail. We start with the basic shell for a CGI script:

```
#!/usr/bin/perl
require 'cgi-lib.cgi';

# Initialization code goes here

if ($ENV{'REQUEST_METHOD'} eq 'GET') {  # Send them the form

#    GET Method code goes here

} elsif ($ENV{'REQUEST_METHOD'} eq 'POST') {  # Send them the form

#    POST Method code goes here

}    #POST

# Finalization Code goes here

# Subroutines go here

# End of Program
```

You can use the cgi-lib library to make your work easier. You might want to use another library, but cgi-lib provides all the routines for handling input/output that you will need. You'll be running this on a UNIX system, so the first line tells the shell where to find the Perl interpreter to process the script.

Because Perl starts at the top of the script, I will too. The initialization code for go.cgi, like most CGI programs, is relatively simple. Here it is in its entirety:

```
#!/usr/bin/perl
########################################################################
# Produces a page of category titles and listings
# under those categories.
#
# Requires:
#
#  - Configuration File
#  - Directory set up for the index files and category
#    files.
#  - Index files
#  - Category files
########################################################################
```

```perl
require '/www/cgi-bin/cgi-lib.pl';

print &PrintHeader();

###########################################################
# Base Directory
#
# Substituted for B+ in configurations
# Do NOT end in trailing slash!
#
# Note, this directory can be reset in the config
# file by the "Base" directive
###########################################################

$baseDir = '/www/etc';

###########################################################
# Configuration File,
#
# The file looks for things between indicators.  The
# indicators are in the format:
# <xxxx> : The start of the section
# </xxxx>: The end of the section
###########################################################
($junk,$tag) = split(/\:/,$ENV{'PATH_INFO'});

$ScriptEdition = '5.0 beta';
$ScriptDate    = '10Apr96';

# The command required to active your mailer
$sendmail = "/usr/lib/sendmail -t -n";

# Leave this here.  For the PUT, you need the Configuration file
# name unexpanded since it will be expanded below.
$script_http = "/cgi-bin/go.cgi$junk";

$cfgFile = &setBase("B+$junk"); # name of the configuration file

###########################################################
# Check the Configuration File to see if it resets
# the base directory.
###########################################################
if (&Config("$cfgFile","Base") ) {
    $baseDir = $Cfg[0];  # Name of the index file
}

###########################################################
# The Category Index file
#
# The index file contains all the categories, their
# filenames
#
# Organized:
#      file=<filename>
#      name=title
#      gif=picture to show on title line
#      defgif=picture to show on each line by default
```

```
#       text
#       <end>
#
#    Filename: is the full pathname to the index file
#    Description: printed as heading
#    Gif: if present, displayed in the heading 2 description
#    Text: If present, printed under the heading.  The
#          <end> token must be present whether the text
#          is present or not.
#######################################################
if (&Config("$cfgFile","Index") ) {
    $indexFile = &setBase($Cfg[0]);  # Name of the index file
}

&ReadParse();

$referrer = "$ENV{'HTTP_REFERER'}";

# Set up the referrer field
if ($referrer =~ /go\.cgi/) {
    $referrer = $in{'home'}};
}
```

Let's examine the components. First, add a couple of identifying variables:

```
$ScriptEdition = '5.0 beta';
$ScriptDate    = '10Apr96';
```

These variables can be displayed on the Web page as a reference for your visitors. For example, the code

```
print "GO: Version $ScriptEdition ($ScriptDate)<P>";
```

prints the following on your page:

```
GO: Version 1.0 (13Apr96)
```

This type of identification is often helpful to your visitors. When you place these variables at the top of the program, they can easily be changed as you modify the script.

You should keep the configuration files in a set of related subdirectories that might not be in the path used by your Web server. The statement

```
$baseDir = '/www/etc';
```

sets a variable that will be used to enable you to enter a simple URL and not have to provide this entire path. This technique can be used when your Internet service provider (ISP) places your directories at the end of a long path like the one that I have been assigned: /usr/homes/ www/public_html/users/rbreed01/jumppts.

Next, set the command to run your "send mail" version:

```
# The command required to activate your mailer
$sendmail = "/usr/lib/sendmail -t -n";
```

You will see how this is used later.

You want to be able to use the GO application to display more than one set of links. To accomplish this, you'll use the URL to pass in the name of the Main Configuration file. Here is the URL for the "Been There..." implementation of GO:

```
http://www.channel1.com/users/rbreed01/go.cgi/jumppts.cfg[:{tag}]
```

`/jumppts.cfg[:{tag}]` is passed to the program in the `PATH_INFO` environment variable. `:{tag}` is optional. As you'll see, it identifies a specific index category to display. The statement

```
($junk,$tag) = split(/\:/,$ENV{'PATH_INFO'});
```

processes this information. Environment variables are passed to a Perl program in the `%ENV` associative array. The names of the variables form the keys to the array.

The `split()` function divides the line at the colon (`/\:/`). The backslash (`\`) escapes the colon to assure that it is interpreted as a colon and not as a special character. The program places the parts of the string into the scalar variables `$junk` and `$tag`. Note that if there had been more than one colon in the string, the remainder of the string after the second colon would have been lost.

Next, the program sets the `$script_http` variable:

```
# Leave this here.  For the PUT, you need the Configuration file
# name unexpanded since it will be expanded below.
$script_http = "/cgi-bin/go.cgi$junk";
```

The statement itself is very straightforward. It initializes a variable that will be used in the HTML `<FORM>` statement. However, the position of the assignment statement is important. Later in the initialization section, the name will be expanded.

The next statement calls a subroutine to set the expanded name of the configuration file:

```
$cfgFile = &setBase("B+$junk"); # name of the configuration file
```

Here is the `setBase` subroutine. You'll place it after the finalization code.

```
sub setBase {
    local($n) = $_[0];
    $n =~ s/B\+/$baseDir/;
    $n;
}
```

`setBase` adds a base directory path (`$baseDir`) to the filename in `$junk` to create the full configuration filename. `setBase` is called from several points in the program.

The parameters to a subroutine are passed in the array `@_`. The `setBase` subroutine moves the first element of `@_` (`$_[0]`) to the local variable `$n`. It then uses the substitution operator (`s///`) to replace the `B+` with `$baseDir`. The subroutine returns the modified value contained in `$n`. (Note that `$n` is localized with the local statement. Thus it is available only to the code block defined by the subroutine.)

You'll use the Main Configuration file at several points throughout the program. The GO application relies on several configuration and data files. You could have chosen any number of file structures (flat files, databases, index files, hashes, and so on) for these files. However, Perl is optimized to process text, and text files make excellent configuration files. Text files do not require any special programming or utilities to maintain. They can be created or maintained with any text editor.

The Main Configuration file contains information that will allow the GO application to control several different indexes of information. Let's take a look at this file before you examine the code to access it.

The Main Configuration File

The Main Configuration file contains many of the values used by the program. The file is in the following format:

```
<label>
{value}
...
</label>
```

This format enables multiline values to be parsed from the file. The values can be parsed into an array by a subroutine.

Here is the basic configuration file for the "Been There, Done That..." implementation of go.cgi:

```
<Index>
B+/jumppts/00index
</Index>
<Title>
Points of Interest
Been There, Done That . . .
/users/rbreed01/world.gif
</Title>
<PageDesc>
Places of interest on the Internet.
<IMG SRC="/users/rbreed01/marble-g.gif"> Indicates a visitor contributed
link.
</PageDesc>
<PrintForm>
Yes
</PrintForm>
<FormIntro>
If you have <i>been there and done that</i>, and you know a link that
would be of interest to our visitors, please tell us about it.  If you
have problems with this feature, please contact
<A HREF="http://www.channel1.com/users/rbreed01/">Bob Breedlove</a>.
</FormIntro>
<UserLinkGif>
/users/rbreed01/marble-g.gif
</UserLinkGif>
<Footer>
B+/jumppts/footer
</Footer>
```

Several options could be used to access the information in this file. The most common is to read the entire file into memory in an associative array. However, to conserve memory and to illustrate the techniques, you have chosen to read the file each time the program needs a value from it. The subroutine Config() processes the file at various points in the program:

```
#
# Reads the $cfgFile and returns everything between <$_[0]> and
# </$_[0]> in the array @Cfg.
#
# NOTE: because @Cfg is kept in memory, you may wish to limit
#       the size of options!
#
sub Config {
#    Clear the array to initialize
    @Cfg = ();

#    Check to see if the configuration file exists.
    if (-e "$_[0]") {
        open(CFG, "$_[0]") || print "unable to open $cfgFile";
        while(<CFG>) {
            chop;
            last if (/<$_[1]>/);
        }        # while
        if (/<$_[1]>/) {
            while(<CFG>) {
                chop;
                last if (/<\/$_[1]>/);
                if (!/^\#/) { # skip comments
                    push(@Cfg,$_);
                }
            }    # while
        } else {
            return 0;
        }
        close(CFG);
        return 1;
    } else {
        print "Cannot find $cfgFile!<p>";
        return 0;
    }    # else
}    # Config
```

Config is called by passing the filename to read and specific topic tag to display as parameters. It sets the value of the configuration element into the array @Cfg. Remember that variables are global unless explicitly declared to be local. Config initializes the array by setting it to the empty set:

```
@Cfg = ();
```

It then checks to see whether the file exists before opening it:

```
if (-e "$_[0]") {
    ...
} else {
    print "Cannot find $cfgFile!<p>";
    return 0;
}    # else
```

You could have simply opened the file and then reacted to the open error, but the file tests are more efficient because they only have to go to the directory entries on most operating systems. Here, the logic will process normally in the TRUE branch of the if/else statement. If the file doesn't exist, you'll put out an error to the Web page and terminate the routine.

Config relies on two while{} loops to do its work. These statements use the <{filehandle}> operator to return records from the file. This operator returns the line into $_. Many operators work on $_ by default.

The first while{} loop searches for the opening tag and exits via the last statement when it finds the correct tag:

```
while(<CFG>) {
    chop;
    last if (/<$_[1]>/);
}    # while
```

The second while{} loop reads all lines until the terminating tag and stores them in the @Cfg array via the push function. If the tag is found and a value is returned, the subroutine returns 1 (TRUE). If the tag is not found for one reason or another, it returns 0 (FALSE).

Finishing Initialization

The initialization code calls the &ReadParse() routine to parse out the variables from the Web browser into the %in associative array. The variable uses many of the routines discussed here, so I won't spend much time on it.

Next, the routine sets up a variable that you will use as a link to the calling page. This is obtained from the HTTP_REFERER variable passed to the program in the %ENV array. Note that you want the last page that is *not* part of the GO application. That is the calling page for the application. Therefore, you check for the phrase go.cgi to make sure you aren't coming from one of your own pages before setting this variable. Here is the code:

```
$referrer = "$ENV{'HTTP_REFERER'}";

# Set up the referrer field
if ($referrer =~ /go\.cgi/) {
    $referrer = $in{'home'};
}
```

Note that you had to escape the period in go.cgi. When the dot (.) is used in a regular expression such as this one, it indicates that any character can be at this location. If you had not placed the back slash (\) to "escape" this character, it would have taken on its special meaning, and the program would look for go{any character}cgi.

Next, you call &PrintHeader() to put out the document type for the Web server. You do this in initialization because this program only produces HTML pages. If you were to output multiple document types, you might have placed the call in the routines that determined the type of document to send.

The Index Files

Before you start on the main logic of the program, let's take a look at the other configuration files—the index files. There are two types of files:

- The Index Directory
- Individual index files

The first value that `go.cgi` retrieves from the Main Configuration file is the name of the Index Directory for this particular implementation. This file contains information about the index files, which actually contain the information about the links in each category. The index file, too, is a text file and uses a very common format:

```
{tag}={value}
```

This format is often used for configuration files. For example, most of the `*.ini` files used by Microsoft Windows are in this format. Microsoft Windows `*.ini` files also use sections that can be located with the technique used in the `Config` subroutine mentioned earlier.

The `00index` file is a bit more complex than a simple configuration file because it must also support a text field of some length for the description. You do this using another common technique. The file uses tags in the format `<{start tag}>`, `<{end tag}`. Specifically, the `<desc>` tag on a line by itself marks the beginning of the description. The `<end>` tag on a line by itself marks the end of the entire entry. This enables the script to read everything after the line containing the `<desc>` as part of the description and stop when it reaches the `<end>` line. Note that the `<end>` tag line indicates the end of an entry whether or not it contains a long description.

Here is part of the `00index` file for the "Been there..." installation:

```
file=B+/jumppts/resource.lists
title=Resource Lists
defgif=/users/rbreed01/marble-r.gif
<end>
file=B+/jumppts/technical
title=Technical/Vendor Pages
gif=/users/rbreed01/equip.gif
defgif=/users/rbreed01/marble-r.gif
<end>
file=B+/jumppts/develop
title=Online Resources for Developers
defgif=/users/rbreed01/marble-r.gif
<end>
...
```

This file is processed by the following code in the `go.cgi` program:

```
###############################################################
# Read the index file.
###############################################################
sub readIndex {
    $producePage = $_[0];
    if (-e "$indexFile") {
        open(NDX,"$indexFile") || die "Unable to open $indexFile\n";
        %index = ();
        while (<NDX>) {
            chop;
            if  ($_ eq '' || /^\#/) {
            } elsif (/\<end\>/) {
                @desc=();
                if (-e &setBase($index{'file'})) {
                    &printCategory();
                }
            } elsif (/\<desc\>/) {
                @desc = ();
                while (<NDX>) {
                    chop;
                    if ($_ eq '<end>') {
                        last;
                    }
                    push(@desc,$_);
                }   #while
                if (-e "$index{'file'}") {
                    &printCategory();
                }
            } else {
                @F = ();
                @F = split(/\=/);
                $index{$F[0]} = $F[1];
            }   #else
        }    # while
        close(NDX);
    } else {
        print "Unable to find $indexFile!";
    }   #else
}   #readIndex
```

This code is the main "driver" logic for the Web page creation. When the program needs to produce a Web page, it first calls this routine, which calls other subroutines to display the pages. You'll examine these later for the techniques that they use.

This logic is relatively straightforward, but it does use some techniques that allow it to perform multiple duties in the program. First, this routine is called to read the Index Directory, regardless of whether or not it needs to produce a Web page. This is necessary to get the values for the category pull-down on the form. The calling routine passes a flag to this routine indicating whether or not to produce the Web page. Like all subroutines, this is passed in @_. The program assigns the first value from this array to a variable:

```
$producePage = $_[0];
```

This is more for human use than it is valuable to the program. It makes the routine more readable and thus more maintainable. Also, like C/C++, arrays in Perl are zero-based (unless you have set them otherwise). You also could have set the global variable `$producePage` and then called the routine. But, passing the element on the call makes for a more readable program.

Next the routine checks for the existence of the Index Directory. Again, you could have simply attempted to open the file, but the file tests are more efficient and make for a more readable program.

The major work of the subroutine is performed in the `while{}` loops. The Index Directory is a combination of `{tag}={value}` lines and multiline entries similar to those seen in the Main Configuration file. Let's look at the basic structure again:

```
# {comment}

{tag}={value}
...
<desc>
...
<end>
```

Each entry consists of a series of `{tag}={value}` lines optionally followed by a description section marked with a `<desc>` line and terminated with an `<end>` line. Comment lines begin with the pound sign (#), like the Perl language itself. Blank lines are also allowed in the file.

`&readIndex()` reads the entire file, accumulating information on an entry into the `%index` associative array and, optionally, the `@desc` array until it finds the `<end>` line. It then calls `&printCategory()`, which you'll look at later.

The technique of accumulating information in a `{tag}={value}` format is useful, especially if you can't be sure in what order the information will be presented. The `{tag}` becomes the key to an associative array, and the `{value}` is the data in the array. Perl's capability to store all types of information into a variable makes this possible because you don't have to be concerned about the type of data until it is used.

The logic to do this is rather unremarkable. The subroutine uses nested `while{}` statements and `if...elsif...else` statements to do its work. Note the use of the `last` statement to break out of the inner loop, which collects description information into the `@desc` array:

```
@desc = ();
while (<NDX>) {
    chop;
    if ($_ eq '<end>') {
        last;
    }
push(@desc,$_);
}    #while
```

Note also that you have used the `push()` function to put the information into the `@desc` array. Later, you'll use the corresponding `pop()` function to get the information off the array.

The `{tag}={value}` information is placed in the `%index` associative array using the following code:

```
@F = ();
@F = split(/\=/);
$index{$F[0]} = $F[1];
```

The first line clears the @F array. The second line splits the line contained in $_ into @F. And the third line sets the %index associative array using the first element of @F as the key and the second element as the value. You know that there aren't any equal signs in your data. However, if you aren't sure, you can rewrite the code like this:

```
@F = ();
($key,@F) = split(/\=/);
$index{$key} = join(/=/,@F);
```

This splits the first element on the line into the variable $key and the remainder of the line into @F. The join() function reintegrates the line, tying it together with the equal sign, which was originally removed by the split() operation.

GET Method

The GET method sends the index pages. When the program is activated with the REQUEST method environment variable set to GET, the program executes the &displayIndex() subroutine. Here it is:

```
#########################################################################
# Display the index page.  This is the main routine to display information
# for the user.
#########################################################################
sub displayIndex {
###############################################
# Categories maintains a list of categories which
# will be displayed if the user form is displayed
# it is loaded in printCategory
###############################################
%Category = ();
###############################################
# Title entry contains the title and the
# main heading for the page.  Also a GIF.
# NOTE, if you do not want a GIF, leave this entry
# blank, but include the line!
###############################################
if ( &Config("$cfgFile","Title") ) {
    $title = $Cfg[0];
    $heading = $Cfg[1];
    $mainGIF = &setBase($Cfg[2]);
} else {
    $title = "Places of Interest";
    $heading = "Been there, done that . . .";
    $mainGIF = '';
}    #else

print <<head1EOT;
<HTML>

<HEAD>

<TITLE>$title</TITLE>
```

```
</HEAD>

<H1><IMG SRC="$mainGIF">
$heading</H1>
head1EOT
    ;

#################################################################
# PageDesc: A paragraph printed for the page.  It can be
#           layed out as html and will be displayed exactly
#           as typed.
#################################################################
if (&Config("$cfgFile","PageDesc") ) {
    foreach(@Cfg) {
        print "$_ ";
    }   #foreach
}   #if

print "<hr>\n\n";

############################################
# Build the table of contents for the page.
############################################
&readIndex(0);
if ($tag eq '') {
    print "<A NAME=\"TOC\"></A>\n<H2>Table of Contents</H2>\n";
    print "<DL>\n";
    foreach $key (sort keys %Category) {
        @tagName = split(/\//,$Category{$key});
        print "<DT><IMG SRC=\"/users/rbreed01/icons/folder.gif\">
<A HREF=\"$script_http\:$tagName[$#tagName]\">$key</A>\n";
    }

    ############################################
    # look for the PrintForm option, if it is
    # Yes, then display entry for the form.
    ############################################
    if  (&Config("$cfgFile",'PrintForm')) {
        if  ($Cfg[0] eq 'Yes') {
            print "<P><DT><IMG SRC=\"/users/rbreed01/icons/image1.gif\"> ";
            print "<A HREF=\"#form\">Add an Entry</A>\n";
        }   #if
    }   #if

    print "</DL>\n<P>\n<HR>\n";
} else {
    &readIndex(1);
}

############################################
# look for the PrintForm option, if it is
# Yes, then show the form.
############################################
if  (&Config("$cfgFile",'PrintForm')) {
    if  ($Cfg[0] eq 'Yes') {
        &showForm();
    }   #if
}   #if

&printFooter();
```

```
print<<footEOT;

</BODY>
</HTML>

footEOT
    ;
}    #displayIndex
```

The routine first reads the Main Configuration file for the <Title> entry. This entry supplies the title, heading, and main image (GIF) for the pages. If it can't find this entry, it supplies default values for these page elements. This means that the visitor gets at least the skeleton of a page with meaningful elements, even if some error occurs.

The routine then prints the header for the page using the print to-here format of the print statement:

```
print <<head1EOT;
<HTML>

<HEAD>

<TITLE>$title</TITLE>

</HEAD>

<H1><IMG SRC="$mainGIF">
$heading</H1>
head1EOT
    ;
```

A couple of things should be pointed out about this statement. First, the to-here tag (head1EOT) must immediately follow the <<. Second, the line that terminates the printing must contain the tag exactly. Other than that, the lines are printed exactly as displayed with variable substitution.

Next, the routine builds and, if appropriate, prints the table of contents for the page.

```
###########################################
# Build the table of contents for the page.
###########################################
&readIndex(0);
if ($tag eq '') {
    print "<A NAME=\"TOC\"></A>\n<H2>Table of Contents</H2>\n";
    print "<DL>\n";
    foreach $key (sort keys %Category) {
        @tagName = split(/\//,$Category{$key});
        print "<DT><IMG SRC=\"/users/rbreed01/icons/folder.gif\">
<A HREF=\"$script_http\:$tagName[$#tagName]\">$key</A>\n";
    }
    print "</DL>\n<P>\n<HR>\n";
} else {
    &readIndex(1);
}
```

To build the table of contents, the routine calls `&readIndex(0)`. You'll look at the routines called by `&readIndex()` in more detail in the sections, "Printing Categories" and "Printing URLs," which follow. Note the zero (0) passed to `&readIndex()`. Perl recognizes zero as FALSE and non-zero as TRUE. This value is set into the `$producePage` variable in `&readIndex()`. Among other things, the subroutines called by `&readIndex()` produce `%Category`. This associative array contains the descriptions and keys for the categories you have defined. These are used to create the table-of-contents page and the pull-down category selection on the index form.

The routine then checks the `$tag` passed in on the URL—that is, the part after the colon. If there is no `$tag`, the program assumes that the table of contents must be printed. A `foreach` loop is used to return the keys in sorted order. Notice that you've decided to print the categories sorted by key. This will put them in alphabetical order.

Each line in the table-of-contents page creates an HTML link. The routine builds this link dynamically from the pathname information in the Index Directory file. It uses the filename to create the URL. A split function is used to isolate the filename from the full pathname into the `@tagName` array:

```
@tagName = split(/\//,$Category{$key});
```

You can't predict how many subdirectories will be in the full pathname, so the `$#tagName` variable is used to index to the last element of the array (`$tagName[$#tagName]`).

This section uses simple print statements to print this part of the page. Notice that you have placed line-feed characters (`\n`) at the end of each line. These are not needed by the HTML page, but they make debugging easier by displaying the code for the page in a more readable format.

Let's take a look at the routines called by `&readIndex()`. The first is `&printCategory()`.

Printing Categories

The `&printCategory()` subroutine is used regardless of whether the categories are to be physically printed. This is because these categories are used in the pull-down form. Remember that this routine is called each time a complete index entry is found in the Index Directory file. The values are placed in the `%index` associative array. Here is the complete subroutine:

```
######################################################################
# Print category heading
######################################################################
sub printCategory {
#
#     Build the Category pull-down entries on the fly
#
      $Category{$index{'title'}} = &setBase($index{'file'});

#
#     This same code is used if the page is to be dislayed or
#     not.
#
```

```
#    Check the file against the requested tag.
   if ($index{'file'} !~ /$tag$/) {
   } elsif ($producePage) {
       @tagName = split(/\//,$index{'file'});
       print "<A NAME=\"$tagName[$#tagName]\">";
       print "<H2>";
       if  ($index{'gif'} ne '') {
           print "<IMG SRC=\"$index{'gif'}\" >";
       }    #if
       print "$index{'title'}</H2>\n";
       foreach (@desc) {
           print "$_\n";
       }    #foreach
       &printURLs("$index{'file'}");

       print "<P><A HREF=\"$script_http\">[Table of Contents]</A>\n";

       print "<hr>";
   }    #if
   %index = ();
}    #printCategory
```

This routine builds the %Category associative array, which is used for the pull-down menu and to print the table-of-contents page. It then checks to see whether this is the requested page. If it is, it then checks to see whether the page should be produced. Here is the if{} statement that does this:

```
if ($index{'file'} !~ /$tag$/) {
} elsif ($producePage) {
```

Notice that the if{} leg of the statement performs no logic. It also uses the not-like (!~) operator to check whether this is the requested tag (/tag/). This statement looks a little strange until you realize that the first dollar sign is part of the variable name ($tag). The second dollar sign (tag$) is part of the regular expression, indicating that the tag must be at the end of the line.

The elseif leg evaluates $producePage. Remember that it is set in &readIndex, but because variables in Perl are global unless explicitly set local, you can use it here. Also note that if $producePage evaluates to zero, it is FALSE. A non-zero value is TRUE.

Most of the routine uses statements that you have seen before. Note that the foreach statement that prints the description uses the default $_. This routine calls another subroutine to print the URLs.

Printing URLs

The &printURLs() subroutine prints the URLs for each index page. Here it is in its entirety:

```
########################################################################
# Print the URLs contained in the file passed to the subroutine
########################################################################
```

```
sub printURLs {
    local($file) = &setBase($_[0]);
    local($error) = 0;
    open(URL,"$file") || die "unable to open $file\n";
    print "<DL>\n";
    %entry = ();
    while (<URL>) {
        chop;
        if (/\<desc\>/ || /\<end\>/) {
            print "<DT>";
            if ($entry{'gif'} eq '') {
                if ($index{'defgif'} ne '') {
                    print "<IMG SRC=\"$index{'defgif'}\" >";
                }      #if
            } else {
                print "<IMG SRC=\"$entry{'gif'}\" > ";
            }
            print "<A HREF=\"$entry{'url'}\">";
            print "<b>$entry{'name'}</b></A>";
            if ($entry{'desc'} ne '') {
                print ": $entry{'desc'}\n";
            } else {
                print "\n";
            }
            if (/\<desc\>/) {
                print "<DD>";
                while (<URL>) {
                    chop;
                    last if (/\<end\>/);
                    print "$_\n";
                }      #while
            }      #if
            %entry = ();
        } else {
            ($key,@value) = split(/\=/);
            $entry{$key} = join('=',@value);
        }      #else
    }     #while
    print "</DL>";
    close(URL);
    0;
}    #printURLs
```

This subroutine uses many of the statements you've examined before. A couple of interesting things should be pointed out. First, &printURLs defines local variables for use exclusively by this routine. Note that these variables can be declared and set at the same time.

The {*key*}={*value*} pairs are split. But, because a visitor might have entered a statement with an equals sign, you have to put the {value} back together:

```
($key,@value) = split(/\=/);
$entry{$key} = join('=',@value);
```

Notice also that the @value array "sucked up" the remainder of the line ($_ by default) split by the statement. If you place another variable after @value, it will always be empty because @value uses everything from that point to the end of $_.

A bit about style: Notice that there are control statements such as if{} and while{} statements. These are aligned to make reading and debugging them easier.

Comments are also important for understanding a function when you have to maintain it. I like to place a comment block at the start of more complex subroutines and sections of a program. Also, statements such as

```
} #if
} #while
} #printURLs
```

are comments at the end of blocks. They help to document the flow and make following the logic easier. This can be especially helpful when blocks are long and extend more than a screen or page in length. Use whatever style makes sense to you, but do so consistently and use comments to help you understand your script when you come back to it.

The zero (0) on the last line of the subroutine is the return value. By default, Perl returns the result of the last line evaluated by a block.

Handling Forms

So far, you've created Web pages that, although they are dynamically created, aren't really exciting. Now you come to the part of the application that interests most people—the creation and handling of forms.

Printing the form is relatively straightforward and amounts to little more than producing the rest of the page. It is accomplished as part of the GET method code. Here is the code that prints the form:

```
sub showForm {
    print "<A NAME=\"form\"></A>";
    print "<H2>Add your own Links</H2>";
    if  (&Config("$cfgFile",'FormIntro')) {
        foreach (@Cfg) {
            print "$_ ";
        }    #if
    }    #if

    print <<instEOT;
<H3>Entries are in the form</H3>
<B>Category</B><P>
<DL>
<DT>Title: Description
<DD>Notes
</DL><P>
The <B>Title</B> will become the link to your page.  Your link will
<B>NOT</B> become available
immediately.  It will be sent to the Webmaster for evaluation.<p>
If accepted, your suggestion will generally be posted within
hours.  Please be patient.  <B>DO NOT</B> send multiple entries!
instEOT
    ;
```

```
    print "<FORM ACTION=\"$script_http\" METHOD=POST>\n";
    print "<PPE>Category...: <SELECT NAME=\"cat\">\n";
#   sort the category names
    @keys = sort keys %Category;
    foreach (@keys) {
        print "<OPTION>$_\n";
    }
    print "</SELECT>\n";

    $notes = '';

print <<formEOT;

URL........: <INPUT VALUE="http:" SIZE=60 NAME="url">
Title......: <INPUT VALUE="" SIZE=60 NAME="title">
Description: <INPUT VALUE="" SIZE=60 NAME="desc">
Your Name..: <INPUT VALUE="" SIZE=60 NAME="fromname">
E-Mail Addr: <INPUT VALUE="" SIZE=60 NAME="fromaddr">

Notes......:
<TEXTAREA ROWS=5 COLS=60 NAME="notes">$notes</TEXTAREA></Pre>
<INPUT TYPE="hidden" VALUE="$referrer" NAME="home">
<INPUT TYPE="submit" VALUE="Submit Link Suggestion">
<INPUT TYPE="reset" VALUE="Abort Entry">
</FORM>
<HR>
formEOT
    ;
}    #showForm
```

This subroutine is called when the configuration variable is set to allow link creation:

```
if  (&Config("$cfgFile",'PrintForm')) {
    if  ($Cfg[0] eq 'Yes') {
        &showForm();
    }    #if
}    #if
```

`&showForm()` prints the form part of the page using the same techniques you learned for the remainder of the page. Figure 15.8 shows the form from the "Been There..." implementation. I won't get into the HTML that actually produces the form here. This is left for Chapter 25, "Hypertext Markup Language (HTML)." You need to examine a couple of techniques, however.

First, remember the `%Category` associative array that you collected in `&printCategories()`? Here you use it to create a pull-down box containing all the allowable categories:

```
print "<Pre>Category...: <SELECT NAME=\"cat\">\n";
#sort the category names
@keys = sort keys %Category;
foreach (@keys) {
    print "<OPTION>$_\n";
}
print "</SELECT>\n";
```

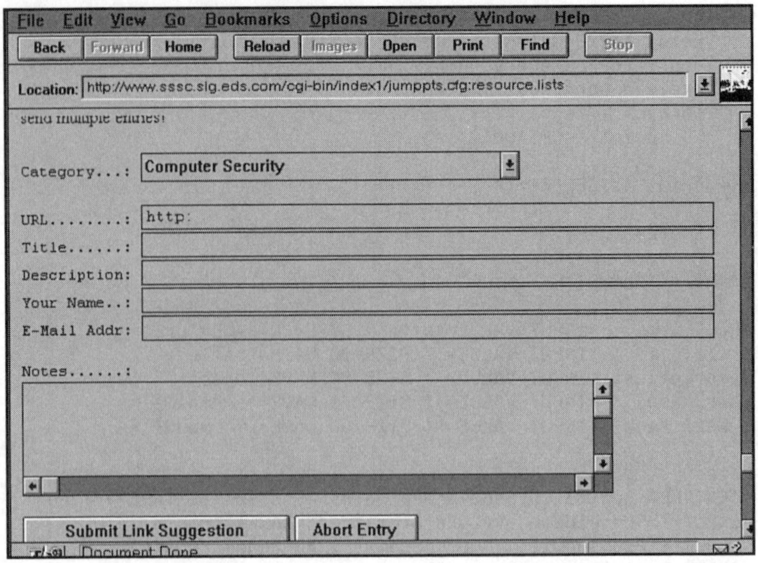

FIGURE 15.8.

The GO application form.

This code displays the categories in alphabetical order because of the sort keys clause in the assignment statement to @keys. It defaults to the first element returned by sort keys. If you want to default to another entry, you might implement code like this:

```
$selected = 'Select Item';
print "<Pre>Category...: <SELECT NAME=\"cat\">\n";
#sort the category names
@keys = sort keys %Category;
foreach (@keys) {
    if $_ = $selected {
        print "<SELECTEDOPTION>$_\n";
    } else {
        print "<OPTION>$_\n";
    }
}
print "</SELECT>\n";
```

Note also that you have included the $referrer variable that you assigned in the initialization code as a hidden variable:

```
<INPUT TYPE="hidden" VALUE="$referrer" NAME="home">
```

Again, I should emphasize that all information that must be retained between page sends must be kept on the page. It can be kept in a cookie or in a file/database from which it can be retrieved based on information returned by the browser.

That's about it for displaying forms. The program writes out the page footer, if any, after the form. Here is the footer code:

```
sub printFooter {
    if (&Config("$cfgFile","Footer")) {
        open(FOOT,&setBase($Cfg[0])) || die "Cannot open $footer";
        while(<FOOT>) {
            print "$_\n";
        }
        close(FOOT);
    }   #if
    if ($referrer ne "") {
    print <<EOR;
<hr>
<A HREF="$referrer"><IMG SRC="/usbbs/button.cgi/Return"></A>
Return to $referrer
EOR
    ;
    }

    print <<footEOT;
<hr>
<IMG SRC="/users/rbreed01/rfbsm.gif" ALIGN="left">
<FONT SIZE=-1>
<b>index</b> version $ScriptEdition by
<A HREF="/users/rbreed01/">Bob Breedlove</A>.<BR>
Last Modified $ScriptDate<BR CLEAR=LEFT>

footEOT
    ;
}   #printFooter
```

This code uses the same routines you have seen before. Note that you include a footer, which can be set from the configuration file. (In fact, the Main Configuration file contains the name of the text file that contains the page contents.) You also include a part fixed in the code. Here, you use the $ScriptEdition and $ScriptDate variables, which were set in the initialization code.

Now that you've displayed the form, you need to see how it is processed. The form information is returned when the visitor fills it out and presses the <SUBMIT> button. The code is contained in the POST method branch of the main if{} statement. Here is that branch:

```
if ($ENV{'REQUEST_METHOD'} eq 'POST') {  # Send them the form
    if (&addLink()) {
        &displayIndex();
    } else {
        print "<H1>ERRORS</H1>$errors";
    }
}   #POST
```

The logic first executes the &addLink() subroutine, which returns either TRUE (nonzero) or FALSE (zero). If all edits are passed and the information has been successfully processed (TRUE), the logic executes &displayIndex(). If there were errors, the logic prints a page with the errors, contained in the scalar $errors.

Let's look at each of the subroutines performed by this logic. The following is the &addLink() subroutine:

```perl
##################################################################
# Send the new link request to the Webmaster
##################################################################
sub addLink {
    &readIndex(0);

    if (&Config("$cfgFile","Webmaster") ) {
            $Webmaster = $Cfg[0];  # Name of the Webmaster
    }

    $errors = '';

    local($cat)    = $in{'cat'};
    local($file)   = &setBase($Category{$cat});
    local($url)    = $in{'url'};
    local($fromname) = $in{'fromname'};

    $Request = "$file: Test Request";

    if ($fromname eq '') {
        $errors .= "You <b>MUST</b> enter your name.<p>";
    }

    local($fromaddr) = $in{'fromaddr'};
    if ($fromaddr eq '') {
        $errors .= "You <b>MUST</b> enter a mailing address.<p>";
    }

    if ($url =~ /[A-Za-z0-9-_.]+\:\/\/[A-Za-z0-9-_.]*/) {
    } else {
        $errors .= "<b>$url</b> appears invalid, please re-enter<p>";
    }

    local($title) = $in{'title'};
    if ($title eq '') {
        $errors .= "You <b>MUST</b> enter a title.<p>";
    }
    local($desc)  = $in{'desc'};
    local($notes) = $in{'notes'};

    if ($errors ne '') {
        0;
    } elsif (-e "$file") {
            open(MAIL,"|$sendmail");
            print MAIL <<EOM;
From: $fromname <$fromaddr>
To: $Webmaster
Subject: $Request

url=$url
name=$title
faddr=$fromaddr
fname=$fromname
desc=$desc
EOM
    ;
```

```
        if (&Config("$cfgFile",'UserLinkGif')) {
            if ($Cfg[0] ne '') {
                print MAIL "gif=$Cfg[0]\n";
            }   #if
        }   #if
        if ($notes ne '') {
            print MAIL "<desc>\n";
            print MAIL "$notes\n";
        }
        print MAIL "<end>\n";
        close(MAIL);
        1;
    } else {
        1;
    }
}   #addLink
```

This is one of the longer routines in the script, but it really doesn't use anything you haven't seen already. It first performs &readIndex() to set the %Category associative array.

The routine edits the information to make sure that it is complete. If errors are found, the error message is added to the variable $errors. On return from &addLink(), $errors is tested and, if it is not null, the contents are displayed on the page and the information is not sent to the Webmaster. You haven't made these edits overly restrictive, but you want to ensure that the visitor has entered enough information to allow you to post a valid and meaningful link. The $errors scalar is first cleared by setting it to the null string:

```
$errors = '';
```

The subroutine then sets a number of local variables, which are used in the link request. Then you examine the values to make sure that they are valid and complete. Here is an example:

```
if ($fromname eq '') {
    $errors .= "You <b>MUST</b> enter your name.<p>";
}
```

The .= assignment operator appends the error message to the $errors scalar. Because these messages are displayed on the Web page, they contain HTML formatting. After checking for errors, the routine checks the $errors scalar:

```
if ($errors ne '') {
    0;
```

The 0; line will be the last statement executed in the subroutine as this leg of the if{} statement. return 0; is an equivalent line because a subroutine returns the value of the last line evaluated. Note that return 0; is safer if you think you might revise your subroutine in the future. This assures that the subroutine returns at that point even if there are other executable statements after this line.

If there are no errors, the subroutine opens a pipe to the mail program defined in $sendmail:

```
} elsif (-e "$file") {
    open(MAIL,"|$sendmail");
```

First, the program checks to make sure that the file for the requested category actually exists. This allows you to temporarily suspend posting to a category by removing the index file. Of course, it also means that you have to have a file for each category, even if it is empty. (Empty files can be created on UNIX systems by using the touch command.)

This version of the open() function creates a pipe to the program contained in the variable. It's the vertical bar (¦) inside the parentheses that performs this magic. You must also be sure that your mailer allows input through STDIN. If it doesn't, you can modify this code to output a text file and then execute your mailer using the system() function.

The routine formats the mail message using a combination of print statements because certain lines vary depending upon the content of the variables returned from the form. The body of the message contains an entry exactly like those formatted for the index file.

The subroutine returns TRUE (1) whether the index file exists or not. This is a judgment call. You could also produce an error message if the posting is temporarily suspended or the index file is missing for some other reason. Again, return 1; could be used in place of the 1; statements.

After a nonzero (TRUE) &addLink() return, the program displays a confirmation message by executing the &ConfirmMail() subroutine. This type of confirmation display is important if you are using forms. It assures your visitors that their entry has been processed correctly. If you don't give visitors complete, positive feedback, they will have a tendency to use their <BACK> buttons to send multiple link requests for the same link.

Here is the &ConfirmMail() subroutine:

```
#######################################################
# Sends page to confirm the mail which was sent
#######################################################
sub ConfirmMail {
    print <<EOP;
<HTML>
<HEAD>
<TITLE>GO Mail Confirmation</TITLE>
</HEAD>
<BODY>
<H1><IMG SRC="$mainGIF">
Index Suggestion</H1>

Thank you for your index suggestion for:<P>

$in{'title'}<br>
$in{'url'}<P>

Your suggestion has been forwarded to the Webmaster.
It will be evaluated and, if accepted, will be posted
within 72 hours.<P>

<A HREF="$script_http">[Table of Contents]</A>
<P>
EOP
    ;
}    # ConfirmMail
```

The subroutine is a simple `print <<to-here` statement—which is nothing new. However, there are a couple of things to point out. First, give visitors enough information to assure them that the process has completed successfully. Here, you display the title and URL that the visitor entered.

You also give visitors information about when to expect that their entry will show up on the index page. Note that if you don't post their link for some reason, you might want to send mail to their `$fromaddr`. Just like when they use the `<BACK>` button on their browser, visitors might have a tendency to send another request if they don't see their link in what they feel is a reasonable length of time.

The last element for a successful confirmation page is to give visitors somewhere to go from this page. If their only alternative is their browser's `<BACK>` button, they might use it and enter another link request for the same link. They might also go elsewhere and miss the other features of your Web site. Here, you direct the user back to the table of contents by using the contents of the `$script_http` scalar as a link:

```
<A HREF="$script_http">[Table of Contents]</A>
```

Finalization Section

There isn't a finalization section in `go.cgi`. But you might want to always display a common footer on your Web pages, write some log records, or perform some other common routines.

That's it for `go.cgi`. As you can see, HTML programming is essentially straightforward. But, the GO application consists of other programs as well. When visitors request the addition of a link, `go.cgi` mails a request to the Webmaster. You still have to get that request into the proper index file. To make this easier, I have designed a system that will allow you to mail an approved link, which will be added by an automated mail module—`postlink.pl`.

`postlink.pl`: The Index Posting Program

The `go.cgi` program displays the link pages and processes the link request form. As you have seen, the request is mailed to the Webmaster. The Webmaster checks the entry and forwards the request to the mailbox for the postlink program.

Of all the services that make up the set of tools commonly referred to as the Internet, mail is perhaps the most ubiquitous. Perl is an excellent language for processing mail messages on UNIX systems. After all, an SMTP mail message is simply a text stream. As you have seen, Perl is in its element when processing text streams.

`postlink.pl` takes advantage of the capability of sendmail and other mailer programs to pipe messages to other processes. Although you'll use it here to append approved links to the GO index files, the same techniques can be used to implement (among other things) an automated mailing list program. (I have implemented similar functionality in a program that maintains my "Diary" page. This page is a "what's new" type of page, which can be maintained by mail from a remote location.)

I have one caution as you examine `postlink.pl`. Sendmail is the most commonly used mailer on UNIX systems. Sendmail and its clones can pipe mail messages to other programs through STDIN. Your mailer might not have that capability or might function differently, especially if your operating system is not UNIX.

Figure 15.9 shows the basic processing of `postlink.pl`. As you'll see, `postlink.pl` can be attached to an existing mailbox and process only those messages matching the required subject line format.

FIGURE 15.9.

The basic flow of the `postlink.pl` *module.*

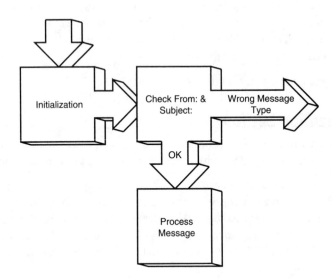

Before examining the code, take a brief look at SMTP messages. These are text streams in a specific format. `postlink.pl` takes advantage of this to determine whether the message is a link-post request coming from an authorized request. Here is a typical message:

```
From - Mon Apr 15 09:09:43 1996
Return-Path: <nobody@apps1.channel1.com>
Received: from apps1.channel1.com by mail5 (8.6.13/Netcom)
     id VAA01910; Fri, 12 Apr 1996 21:43:38 -0700
Received: (from nobody@localhost) by apps1.channel1.com (8.6.12/8.6.9)
   id AAA21390; Sat, 13 Apr 1996 00:42:43 -0400
Date: Sat, 13 Apr 1996 00:42:43 -0400
Message-Id: <199604130442.AAA21390@apps1.channel1.com>
From: breedlov@netcom.com
To: rbreed01@user1.channel1.com
Subject: POSTLINK¦/jumppts.cfg¦Bulletin Board System Homepages
X-Mail-Gateway: USBBS Update Script
X-Mozilla-Status: 0001
```

```
url=http://www.channel1.com/usbbs/
name=The USBBS List Homepage
faddr=breedlov@netcom.com
fname=Bob Breedlove
desc=MS-DOS Based BBS List
gif=/users/rbreed01/images/usbbssm.gif
<desc>
Contains over 4,500 entries for BBS systems throughout
the US and some from other countries.  Add your own
entry to this excellent resource.
<end>
```

The header information starts at the beginning of the message and extends line by line until reaching a blank line (two consecutive line feeds). The message starts after that blank line and continues to the end of the message. Because you will probably forward the approved request, your message can contain the header from the original message.

`postlink.pl` ignores this additional information. When the message has been verified by checking the `Subject:` and `From:` lines, the program searches for the `url=`... line and processes all information until the `<end>` line.

Much of the program processing is straightforward. It uses many of the same techniques that you saw in `go.cgi`. This section examines the parts of the program to point out techniques that will be helpful in this and other mail processing programs. But first, a note about implementing `postlink.pl`.

Implementing PostLink

Ideally, you should set up a special mailbox for the postlink program. But, like me, you might be in a situation where this is impossible or too costly to do. You can implement this program on your existing mailbox. The exact method may vary by system, but on a UNIX system, you can typically create a `.forward` file in your home directory. Place in the file a line that looks like this: `|{path}/postlink.pl`. This executes `postlink.pl` each time a message is received. The message is piped to the program through standard input. If you want to receive other messages, you also have to place your login name in the file on a separate line. Otherwise, all messages are passed to `postlink.pl` exclusively, and you do not receive your mail.

Here is an example. Suppose your logon is `myname`. In order to assure that you received all your other mail, your `.forward` file would have to look like this:

```
myname
| {path}/postlink.pl
```

If you did not include your login name, the mail would be sent to the `postlink.pl` program, and you would never see it.

Initialization

This section starts the postlink.pl program. It performs what little initialization is necessary in this program.

```perl
#!/usr/bin/perl
#########################################################
# PostItem, reads mail and adds to a GO category file
# from selected E-mails.
#
# E-mails must come from an authorized source and the
# subject line must be in the format:
#
#     PostItem¦{Config File}¦{Category}
#
# where {Config file} is one of the GO subject files and
# {Category} is the category title.
#
# The contents starting at the url= line will be
# appended to the subject file and ending with the
# <end> line.
#=======================================================
# Base Directory
#
# Substituted for B+ in configurations
# Do NOT end in trailing slash!
#
# Note, this directory can be reset in the config
# file by the "Base" directive
#########################################################
$baseDir = '/www/etc';
```

PostLink is "lean and mean." Programs that process mail should, as a rule, do the job without a lot of extra processing because they are called each time you receive a piece of mail and do not process the majority of it. PostLink doesn't require extensive initialization. In fact, the only line is the assignment of $baseDir. This will be used to find the configuration file. (Remember that this value was passed to the go.cgi program. PostLink will have to know this information.) Keep the base directory information in synch with the remainder of the GO application programs.

You might want to log the operation of postlink.pl. You could put statements in the initialization section to record the start of the program, including date and time.

Main Processing

The main processing of postlink.pl reads the standard input data stream and processes it one line at a time. The main loop is a while loop:

```perl
#########################################################
# Main loop, assumes standard input.
#########################################################
while(<>) {
    chop;
```

```
    # Get the from line
    &getFrom if (/^From:/);

    # Check subject line to see if it is for us
    &postMessage if (/^Subject:/);

}    # main loop
```

The chop command removes the line feed from the line. Two lines call subroutines when the program finds lines that it recognizes. The program assumes that the From: line will occur before the Subject: line. Both are used to determine whether this is a link-post request from a valid source.

You'll learn about the processing of these lines when you look at the subroutines. Here, note that the loop checks $_ (the default). The ^ indicates the start of the line.

The From: Line

The &getFrom() subroutine gets the information from the From: line. Here it is:

```
######################################################
# Get the from field.  This will be used to verify that
# the message is from a trusted source.
######################################################
sub getFrom {
    ($junk, $from) = split(/\:\s+/);
}    # getFrom
```

At this point, you're probably wondering why you would create a subroutine for a single line that does nothing more than split the input line. Sometimes you might want to design for anticipated future enhancements. For example, at this point, if you were logging the processing, you might want to add code that would record the information from the From: line.

Process the Message

When the program finds the Subject: line in the input stream, it can start processing the message. Here is the postMessage subroutine. It determines whether the message should be processed by parsing the Subject: line to make sure it is valid.

```
######################################################
# Check to see that the message is in the correct
# format.  If it is, post it to the page.
######################################################
sub postMessage {
    ($junk, $subject) = split(/\:\s+/);
    return if ($subject !~ /^POSTLINK/);
    ($junk,$cFile,$Category) = split(/\|/,$subject);

    # name of the configuration file (includes leading slash)
    $cfgFile = &setBase("B+$cFile");
```

```
#####################################################
# Check the Configuration File to see if it resets
# the base directory.
#####################################################
if (&Config("$cfgFile","Base") ) {
    $baseDir = $Cfg[0];  # Name of the index file
}

return if (!&checkFrom());

if (&Config("$cfgFile","Index") ) {
    $indexFile = &setBase($Cfg[0]);  # Name of the index file
}

&readIndex();

while(<>) {
    chop;
        &processPage() if (/^url\=/);
}

}    # postMessage
```

First, the subroutine splits the Subject: line to eliminate the Subject: and then checks to make sure it is a valid line:

```
($junk, $subject) = split(/\:\s+/);
return if ($subject !~ /^POSTLINK/);
```

postMessage processes the default $_ variable. You have seen the use of the split command before. The routine returns immediately if the command line does not match the expected pattern (!~). Note that this implementation uses a relatively simple test. This check can be as complex as needed for your purposes.

If the Subject: line is valid, the program now has enough information to find the configuration file.

```
($junk,$cFile,$Category) = split(/\¦/,$subject);

# name of the configuration file (includes leading slash)
$cfgFile = &setBase("B+$cFile");

#####################################################
# Check the Configuration File to see if it resets
# the base directory.
#####################################################
if (&Config("$cfgFile","Base") ) {
    $baseDir = $Cfg[0];  # Name of the index file
}
```

PostLink uses the same &setBase() routine as go.cgi to expand the path of the configuration file. It then checks the configuration file to make sure that it doesn't alter the base directory.

When the routine has the configuration file, it can check the sender information (From:) to make sure that this request is from an authorized sender. If the sender is not authorized, the routine exits.

```
return if (!&checkFrom());
```

You'll look at the &checkFrom() subroutine later. Note that the return from &checkFrom is negated using the bang (!). The use of the bang is common in C programming; however, it can be confusing when debugging or enhancing programs. You might find that maintenance will be easier if you use an alternative form:

```
return if (&checkFrom() eq 0);
```

Before writing the link information to the file, the program has to get the information about the indexes. It does this by checking the configuration file and reading the index file for this implementation:

```
if (&Config("$cfgFile","Index") ) {
    $indexFile = &setBase($Cfg[0]);  # Name of the index file
}

&readIndex();
```

This is the same logic that you saw in the go.cgi program. The &readIndex() routine has been stripped down to simply produce the %Category associative array.

Now the program can continue to process the input stream. It needs to skip over any other lines in the message and searches for the url=... line using a while loop:

```
while(<>) {
    chop;
        &processPage() if (/^url\=/);
}
```

When the url=... line is found, &processPage() is called to actually write the link file. This is a good place to discuss a style issue—the use of subroutines. This entire program could have been written with all the processing code within a single while{} loop with a set of nested if statements. This would have done the job and not required the overhead of processing subroutines.

Straight-line programming is efficient for small utility programs. After all, subroutines do take some processing cycles to implement. But, if you are programming anything that you hope to maintain or enhance in the future, straight-line programming can be very difficult.

Well-named, organized subroutines can make maintenance and enhancement much easier. Plan subroutines so that they perform only one or two functions. Name subroutines logically, preferably after the function that they perform.

Writing the Index Files

The &processPage() subroutine writes the index file. Here it is:

```
#####################################################
# Process the page and add the message.
#####################################################
sub processPage {
```

```
$file = $Category{"$Category"};

$file = &setBase($file);

open(OUT,">>$file") || die "Unable to open $file.\n";

# Print out the url= line which has already been read
# NOTE: The newline is needed because we have chopped it.
print OUT "$_\n";

# Append the remainder of the entry.
while(<>) {
    print OUT "$_";
    last if (/^\<end\>/);
}

# Print out a trailing blank line to make things easier to
# read.
print OUT "\n";

close(OUT);

}    # processPage
```

First, this routine gets the file corresponding to the category from the Subject: line. It then opens the file to append the link information to the end of the file.

```
$file = $Category{"$Category"};

$file = &setBase($file);

open(OUT,">>$file") || die "Unable to open $file.\n";
```

The >> causes the open() statement to open the file and places the insertion point at the end of the file. Note also that the program will stop processing if the file can't be opened. This is accomplished by the die command and the || operator.

Note, here, that you have used the longer category description. This description is easier for people to read and evaluate. When the Webmaster is determining whether to allow this link, the use of a more detailed category description can be easier to evaluate than a possibly obscure filename associated with the description.

When the file is opened, the program simply reads the standard input text stream into the default $_ variable and uses print statements to write out the output file:

```
# Print out the url= line which has already been read
# NOTE: The newline is needed because we have chopped it.
print OUT "$_\n";

# Append the remainder of the entry.
while(<>) {
    print OUT "$_";
    last if (/^\<end\>/);
}
```

```
# Print out a trailing blank line to make things easier to
# read.
print OUT "\n";

close(OUT);

}    # processPage
```

You have to remember to print out the url=... line that you have already read. You had to add the line feed to the end because you stripped it with the chop command before evaluating the line. Also, you have included a comment to remind a maintenance/enhancement programmer about this unusual situation.

Another while{} loop is used to read and write out the lines from the url=... line and to close with the <end> line. The last statement is used to exit the while{} loop when the <end> line is found. This statement is evaluated after the line has been written.

Before closing the file, the program adds a blank line after the entry. This makes the index file easier to read if you are going to view it with a text editor. Again, you have used a comment to tell why this extra line is added to the program.

Security: Checking the From: Line

The last routine that you'll look at ensures that the message is coming from an authorized source. The security implemented in this routine is minimal. It is not intended as an example of a truly effective security routine. If you are concerned about security at your site, you should modify this routine to also include password checking or other security functions. Here is the routine:

```
#######################################################
# Find the configuration entry for this page and
# check the sender to make sure this is a valid
# id.
#
# ID's are contained in the configuration file one
# per line in the <PostLink> section.
#######################################################
sub checkFrom {
    if (!&Config("$cfgFile","PostLink") ) {
        return 0; # Can't authorize
    }

    foreach $auth (@Cfg) {
        if ($from =~ /$auth/) {
            return 1;
            last;
        }
    }    # foreach

    # If we're here, it's not authorized
    return 0;
}    # checkFrom
```

The <PostLink> section in the configuration file contains the information for each authorized Webmaster. The &Config() subroutine returns an array (@Cfg) containing all these lines. Notice that the routine will fail if the <PostLink> section is not found.

&checkFrom() uses a foreach loop to check the From: line against each line.

```
foreach $auth (@Cfg) {
    if ($from =~ /$auth/) {
        return 1;
    }
}   # foreach
```

The foreach loop returns elements from @Cfg into $auth in a seemingly random order. The loop terminates when all the values have been returned. If the From: line contains $auth exactly, the routine returns 1 (TRUE).

If none of the authorization strings are found, the loop terminates after returning all the values. The subroutine falls through to the next statement:

```
# If we're here, it's not authorized
return 0;
```

Notice, again, the well-placed comment to tell you how you got here and why you're returning a zero (FALSE) value.

Finalization Section

There isn't a finalization section; the program simply terminates after the entire standard input stream has been processed. The finalization section is also a good place to put logging code. For example, you might want to log elements of the link posting to a file.

You might also want to send a message to the originator of the link request, telling that person his or her link has been posted. The faddr=... line contains the mail address of the requester. The same routines used in go.cgi to send the link request message can be modified to send the confirmation.

Utility Programs

go.cgi and postlink.pl form the heart of the GO application. They illustrate Perl's capability to process Web pages and mail messages. These are two of the most common processing jobs on the Internet today.

However, an application might require utility programs, which perform routine maintenance and organization of the application's data. Perl is also excellent for these programs. After all, Perl was originally designed as a general-purpose utility language.

SetIndex: Creating Link Files

go.cgi requires that the link files exist before they can be used. This means that you must have a file for each category, even if there are no entries in that file. In a dynamic system, it can get annoying to have to place the entries in the index file and then create each of the empty link files corresponding to the new entries.

The answer is a routine that will read through the index file and create the empty files—SetIndex. SetIndex is a very straightforward, unremarkable program, but it illustrates a couple of techniques. Here's the entire program:

```perl
#!/usr/local/bin/perl
#
# Automatically set files for CGI indexes by reading the
# 00index file in the current directory.
#
$index = "00index";
if (@ARGV) {
        $baseDir = shift @ARGV;
} else {
        $baseDir = "..";
}


if (-f "$index") {
    open (INDEX, "$index") || die "Can not open $index\n";
} else {
    die "$index does not exist or is not a plain text file\n";
}

while (<INDEX>) {
    chop;
    ($key, $value) = split(/=/);
    if ($key eq "file") {
        $value = &setBase($value);
        if (-f $value) {
            print "$value exists\n";
        } else {
            print "processing $value\n";
            system("touch $value");
            system("chmod 666 $value");
            system("chgrp guest $value");
        }
    }
}

close(INDEX);

sub setBase {
        local($n) = $_[0];
        $n =~ s/\B\+/$baseDir/;
        $n;
}
```

`SetIndex` is written in a straight-line fashion. It contains only a single subroutine that you've seen before: `&setBase()`. The program reads through the Index Directory file, which it assumes to be named `00index`. (As an enhancement to `SetIndex`, you might want to make it read the configuration file to get the name of the index file.)

`SetIndex` also takes some of its configuration information from command-line arguments, if they are entered. This is the first time you've examined the way Perl reads arguments from the command line. In CGI programs, you really can't use the command line to pass in arguments. And, although `postlink.pl` could have used command-line arguments, it didn't.

You decided to pass in some information from the command line because `SetIndex` is a simple, seldom-used utility and should be kept that way. `SetIndex` can be started in one of two ways. The first is by simply using the command name:

`SetIndex`

When started like this, the utility assumes that the `00Index` file is in the current subdirectory, meaning the same directory in which `SetIndex` is started.

`SetIndex` can also be started by placing the base directory on the command line:

`SetIndex {base directory}`

The `check-for` command-line parameters are handled in the following `if` statement:

```
if (@ARGV) {
        $baseDir = shift @ARGV;
} else {
        $baseDir = "..";
}
```

Perl parses the command-line arguments into the array `@ARGV`, where they are available to the program. In general, you will have two types of command-line variables—positional and parameterized. Many programs use both types of arguments.

Positional parameters can use simple `if` statements like those in `SetIndex` to access the array. This `if` statement first checks to see whether there are any parameters. An array used in a scalar context (such as an `if` statement) returns the number of elements it contains. Remember that Perl, like C, assumes nonzero values are TRUE and zero values are FALSE.

If the user has entered command-line arguments, the first one is assumed to be the `$baseDir` argument. The remainder are ignored.

If there are no command-line arguments, the `$baseDir` is assumed to be the parent directory of the current directory. To understand this, you have to know that I place all the index files for GO implementations under a common directory structure like this:

```
base directory
    implementation
        index directory file
        index files
```

```
implementation
    index directory file
    index files
```

Next, the program checks to see whether the index directory file exists. It uses the -f file test:

```
if (-f "$index") {
    open (INDEX, "$index") || die "Can not open $index\n";
} else {
    die "$index does not exist or is not a plain text file\n";
}
```

The -f tests to ensure that the file is a plain text file. This is a bit safer than the -e file test, which simply tests to ensure that the file (of whatever type) exists. The file is opened and assigned to the filehandle INDEX. If the file exists but can't be opened, the program terminates with an error message by using the die command.

Here's a chance to reiterate that there are often many ways to do the same thing in Perl. Many times your choice will be a matter of style or personal choice. In this case, I have chosen a style that is easily readable and familiar to programmers in many languages, including C/C++. Here's code that does the same thing in two lines:

```
die "$index does not exist or is not a plain text file\n" if (!-f "$index");
open (INDEX, "$index") || die "Can not open $index\n";
```

This works because the program exits when the die command is executed. The die command exits with the error value in $! (errno).

SetIndex does its main work in the while statement:

```
while (<INDEX>) {
    chop;
    ($key, $value) = split(/=/);
    if ($key eq "file") {
        $value = &setBase($value);
        if (-f $value) {
            print "$value exists\n";
        } else {
            print "processing $value\n";
            system("touch $value");
            system("chmod 666 $value");
            system("chgrp guest $value");
        }
    }
}
```

The loop reads the INDEX filehandle using the <INDEX> command. The lines are split on the equal sign into a $key/$value pair. If $key is equal to file, the program expands the filename into a full pathname by calling &setBase().

If the file exists and is a text file, the program has nothing to do. It notifies the user and continues processing the index directory file.

If the file doesn't exist or is not a plain text file, the program notifies the user and then uses a series of system() commands to create the empty file. I won't go into the UNIX commands executed because they will vary by operating system.

That's it. Not really much of a program, but it does illustrate that useful utilities can be written quickly in Perl to support the main programs in your application.

SortIndex: Sorting the Index Files

Humans like to see things in some sort of order. This usually means some variation of alphanumeric sequence or time sequence. The Index pages are best sorted in alphanumeric sequence. But because you can't guarantee that visitors will enter link requests in alphanumeric order, you must have a way to sort the links on the page.

If you are using a database or some indexed file system, the entries can be ordered automatically. Because you're using text files, however, you have to manage the files yourself.

I have chosen to provide a maintenance program that can be run periodically against the index files. It is only slightly more complex than the SetIndex program. Here it is in its entirety:

```perl
#!/usr/bin/perl
####################################################
# Utility to sort an index from index.pl
####################################################
# USE: sortindex {full index file name}
####################################################
print "Index File Sort Utility\n\n";

$index = shift @ARGV;
if (@ARGV) {
    $baseDir = shift @ARGV;
} else {
    $baseDir = "../";
}

if (-e "$index") {
    print "  Index: $index\n";
} else {
    print "$index does not exist\n";
    exit(1);
}

open(INDEX,"$index") || die "Unable to open $index\n";

# Search for the "file=" token and process each of
# the files in sequence
while (<INDEX>) {
    chop;
    if (/^file\=/) {
        ($junk, $file) = split(/\=/);
        $file = &setBase($file);
        &sortFile();
    }
}    #while
close(INDEX);
```

```perl
sub sortFile {
    if (-e "$file") {
        print "    Processing: $file\n";
    } else {
        print "    $file does not exist\n";
        return;
    }

    $outfile = $file . ".NEW";

    open(IN, "$file");
    open(OUT, ">$outfile");

    $entry = '';
    @index = ();

    while(<IN>) {
        $entry .= "$_";
        if (/^name\=/) {
            chop;
            ($junk, $name) = split(/\=/);
            $name =~ tr/A-Z/a-z/;
            $entry = "$name¦$entry";
        } elsif (/\<end\>/) {
            push(@index,$entry);
            $entry = '';
        }
    }    #while
    close(IN);

    foreach (sort @index) {
        ($junk, $e) = split(/\¦/);
        print OUT "$e";
    }
    close(OUT);

    system("mv $file $file.OLD");
    system("mv $outfile $file");
    system("chmod 666 $file");
    system("chgrp wheel $file");

}    # sortFile

sub setBase {
        local($n) = $_[0];
        $n =~ s/B\+/$baseDir/;
        $n;
}
```

SortIndex uses the same technique as SetIndex to read the command-line arguments, if any. This time, however, you assume that there are two positional arguments:

```perl
$index = shift @ARGV;
if (@ARGV) {
    $baseDir = shift @ARGV;
} else {
    $baseDir = "../";
}
```

The first line shifts the name of the index file into $index. Then, if there are any remaining command-line arguments, the first one is assumed to be the base directory ($baseDir). Note that after the first variable had been shifted off the array, the remainder of the array can be dealt with as if the first element didn't exist.

Next, the program checks to see whether the requested index file exists:

```
if (-e "$index") {
    print "  Index: $index\n";
} else {
    print "$index does not exist\n";
    exit(1);
}
```

Here, you see a different technique for exiting the program if the file doesn't exist. The program prints a message on the first line of the else leg of the if/else command. The exit command terminates the program with the value (1). This technique might not be as elegant as the die command, but it might be more readable, especially to new Perl programmers who might be familiar with C or Pascal.

The first while loop reads through the Index Directory file and processes each of the files it encounters:

```
# Search for the "file=" token and process each of
# the files in sequence
while (<INDEX>) {
    chop;
    if (/^file\=/) {
        ($junk, $file) = split(/\=/);
        $file = &setBase($file);
        &sortFile();
    }
}     #while
```

The file= line is read, the full pathname of the Index file is constructed, and the &sortFile() function is called to do the work.

The major work of SortIndex is performed in the &sortfile() following function:

```
$outfile = $file . ".NEW";

open(IN, "$file");
open(OUT, ">$outfile");

$entry = '';
@index = ();

while(<IN>) {
    $entry .= "$_ ";
    if (/^name\=/) {
        chop;
        ($junk, $name) = split(/\=/);
        $name =~ tr/A-Z/a-z/;
        $entry = "$name|$entry";
    } elsif (/\<end\>/) {
```

```
        push(@index,$entry);
        $entry = '';
    }
}   #while
close(IN);
```

SortIndex reads from the current Index file and writes to a file with the same filename postfixed with .NEW. It opens the original Index file and assigns it to the filehandle IN. It opens the new file and assigns it to the OUT filehandle. The > parameter causes the program to open the file and clear the contents, if any.

This program also uses a set of while statements to do its work. The first constructs an array, @index, which will be sorted. The index files are typical of configuration files. The set of lines for an entry are in the following format:

```
url={url}
name={title}
faddr={mail address}
fname={from name}
desc={single line description}
gif=$Cfg
[<desc>
{optional multi-line description}]
<end>
```

You can't use a simple text file sort on this type of file. The first chore is to create a structure that can be sorted. SortIndex takes advantage of the fact that strings can be of any length in Perl to create an array of strings that can be sorted.

The while loop appends the lines for each entry to the scalar $entry using the .= operator. If it finds the name= entry, it adds the value of that tag to the front of the line for sorting. You've seen the split operator, which creates the $name value. It then uses the tr/// operator to translate all characters to lowercase.

SortIndex then prepends the resulting string to the $entry scalar. Note also that you have prepended the vertical bar (¦). This will be used later to split this sort string from the remainder of the line.

After the routine recognizes the <end> line, it pushes the $entry scalar onto the @index array and clears the $entry scalar. The push operator places the $entry strings onto the array in a "last in, first out" (lifo) order if the corresponding pop operator is used. However, you will be using the sort operator to extract the entries in alphanumeric order.

After all the entries have been read from the Index file, the @index array is processed in sorted order by the following foreach loop:

```
foreach (sort @index) {
    ($junk, $e) = split(/\¦/);
    print OUT "$e";
}
```

15

Because you have prepended the name entry to the front of the string, the sort will return the strings in alphanumeric order. The name entry is split from the remainder of the entry and the entire entry is written to the output file. Notice that you did not chop the line feeds from the input records. Thus when the entries are rewritten, their original line feeds are present, resulting in the same number of lines as the original file.

After processing the full @index array, the program closes the output file and then performs a set of system() calls to rename the files and set the ownership and permissions. Note that you have chosen to use system() calls. Much of this could have been accomplished with internal Perl commands. This is just another example of the capability of Perl to do things in many different ways.

One note about the way that SetIndex and SortIndex operate: Perl is capable of writing a file in-place, meaning that it overwrites the original file with the new information, but this is *very* dangerous. I recommend that you use techniques similar to those here. That is, write to a new file, rename the original file, and then rename the new file to the required name. This assures that, if something happens, the original file can be restored.

Summary

That's the GO application. The source code for the complete application is included on the CD-ROM. This is a relatively simple application. Perl is quite capable of supporting much more complex applications, including its own socket connections, handling databases, and more. I encourage you to explore options by modifying the GO application to your purposes. Perl is especially suited to exploration because it is interpreted. You can install small, incremental changes and test them in your application with ease. Programming Perl is best learned by programming Perl. Go for it.

Microsoft Implementation Approach

by Rob McGregor

IN THIS CHAPTER

This chapter provides an overview of Microsoft's approach to communications across the Internet. It covers the various levels of communications programming support provided by Win32 APIs and MFC classes. First, you'll get a crash course in computer communications technology, and then you'll look at some of the tools Microsoft provides for Windows programmers to make Windows applications "Internet aware" and to extend client services with ActiveX controls. Finally, you look at security issues relative to Internet application development.

Communications Technology Background

Many communications APIs and Internet programming tools are available for Windows programmers—and all these tools have several things in common: They all provide solutions for communications problems of one sort or another, and they all use standardized protocols to transmit the information they work with from one computer to another using data streams. The remainder of this book provides overviews and details of the most significant of these services and tools. But before you get into the specifics of what's available, the following sections take a quick look at networks and how they relate to the Internet.

Networks

When two or more computers are linked together and can transmit data to each other, you have a network. Admittedly, this is an oversimplification, but the underlying idea is true. Although there are many reasons to connect computers into networks (or, to coin a verb, *to network* the computers), most networks are created for two reasons:

1. To enable people to communicate. Networked computers sending data back and forth over a network are really just another means for people to communicate.

2. To enable people to share resources. Applications and services on a network can be used by anyone who has access to the network. These shared resources free up other valuable resources that can be used for other things.

Although networks are composed of computers and the peripheral hardware that make the magic happen, networks are really just about people communicating more efficiently and saving money by sharing. (And you thought sharing was just kid stuff!)

Communication over a network often involves sending mail and documents or files from one person to another, which is often much more convenient than an audio-only telephone call. If the network has an Internet connection, the mail, documents, and files can be sent to anyone, anywhere in the world, who has Internet access!

Sharing over a network can save money by enabling several users to share the same spreadsheet or word processor applications and by enabling them to print the resulting documents using a shared printer. Emerging technologies promise to enable this type of resource sharing right from a Web browser in the very near future!

Local Area Networks (LANs) and Wide Area Networks (WANs)

A *local area network (LAN)* is a network composed of computer workstations directly connected together, often by a direct cable connection. A *wide area network (WAN)* is a group of LANs connected together, usually with telephone lines. The Internet is composed of uncounted wide area connections that typically use phone lines to transmit data streams. The lack of an advanced or standardized reliable telephone system is the main source of data bottlenecks in LANs, WANs, and the Internet. Data can stream only as fast as the local phone service enables.

Suppose that the computers in your department in the corporate headquarters building are connected with a LAN. Now imagine that other LANs in other buildings also exist. Each LAN can connect to a high-speed link, called a *backbone*, to create a WAN. Special-purpose computers called *routers* are used to connect LANs into WANs and to connect WANs into bigger WANs. These routers also provide connections to the outside world and enable LANs and WANs from one organization to connect to those in another organization. If you can imagine the millions of routers connected to LANs and WANs of computer networks worldwide, you can begin to get a glimpse of the awesome power of the Internet! The sheer volume of information stored on these diverse networks, all connected through the Internet, is absolutely staggering.

Client/Server Systems

The principal way computers communicate with one another is through the use of the *client/server communication model*. Recall that sharing resources is one of the main uses of networks. Most of the time, resource sharing is enabled through the use of two programs working in harmony. A *server* program, also referred to as just "the server," is responsible for providing the resources to a *client* program, also referred to as just "the client." Sounds pretty simple doesn't it? The server provides resources, and the client uses them. Of course, it gets more complex.

Clients and servers typically run on separate machines. For example, you can request stock quotes from a server in New York from your yacht somewhere off the coast of Australia by using a cellular satellite connection. (It's said that common folks like Bill Gates often do this sort of thing.) In this example, the client computer in Australia accesses the server computer in New York, a connection is made, and the client and server programs cooperate to achieve the desired result. This is the client/server relationship.

All Internet services are provided using client/server relationships, and much of the effort expended in learning to use the Internet is really effort expended in learning to use the client software that connects and communicates with the Internet server software. As a developer of Internet-aware applications, you must be aware of both sides of the coin and must have a working knowledge of how both client and server work and communicate.

Modems

Most computer systems communicate with the outside world using a modem and the Internet; Internet servers typically use modems to send and receive data to and from their clients. So what is a modem, anyway? A modem is a hardware device that translates data from digital to analog and vice versa. In fact, the name *modem* itself reflects this functionality.

A modem translates digital data from a computer into an analog signal that can be transmitted over a telephone line. This process is called *modulation*. When the signal from the telephone line reaches another modem, it's converted back to its original digital representation. This process is called *demodulation*. The operations of MODulation and DEModulation gave the *modem* its name.

Modems use various transmission protocols; the modems communicating across the phone line must use the same protocol if they are to understand each other. To put this in perspective, think of the various modem protocols in terms of different spoken languages. If a person who speaks only English has a phone conversation with another person who speaks only Spanish, the result isn't very productive.

Overview of Windows Communications

Windows communications programming isn't just a hot topic—it's almost a necessity these days. Face it: The Internet has been with us in one form or another for nearly 30 years, and it's here to stay. With the advent of the World Wide Web a few years back, and the explosion of Web interest across the globe, it's imperative that today's Windows programmer understand communications programming. In fact, "communications programming" is very nearly synonymous with "Internet programming" these days!

That's not to say that you must become an expert in every facet of communications and Internet programming or commit complex Internet protocols and obscure modem commands to memory. Today's Windows programmer has a great advantage over the programmers of yesteryear. What is this advantage? Experience. Not your own personal experience, perhaps, but you'll definitely benefit from the combined experience of the thousands of programmers who have gone before—those legions of communications gurus who have harnessed the Internet and the Web and made it what it is today.

Tools of the Trade

And those communications gurus aren't really any different from you. Like all good programmers, they don't like to reinvent the wheel—so they've created volumes of code libraries, classes, and components to save themselves (and you!) the time and effort of doing it all over again. Now that's a bargain! Time is money, and many advanced tools are now available for Windows programmers that enable you to just dive in and start hacking out sophisticated communications applications, most with very little time and effort (comparatively speaking).

Microsoft Implementation Approach

CHAPTER 16

455

16

MICROSOFT
IMPLEMENTATION
APPROACH

Microsoft programmers have been busily working over the last several years putting together useful APIs and MFC classes to make the tasks involved in communications programming easier and easier. This part of the book discusses several of these handy, reusable tools and shows several sample programs that can help get you started on the road to creating your own communications masterpieces. The remainder of this chapter introduces some of the technologies integral to Windows communications programming.

Windows Sockets (WinSock)

The Windows Sockets (WinSock) specification enables applications to communicate with each other across networks (including the granddaddy of all networks—the Internet) by means of "socket" communications objects. In general, Windows Sockets are low-level, advanced communications functions that enable a client computer to communicate transparently with a distant host and vice versa. Microsoft has worked with standards committees over the last several years to develop a comprehensive application programming interface for Windows Sockets: the WinSock API.

MFC wraps the complexity of the WinSock API into classes that make it easier to integrate this technology into your applications. Although these low-level classes require some knowledge of socket programming, MFC does a good job of reducing programming tasks. Two classes are provided by MFC for basic socket communications:

- Class CAsyncSocket, which encapsulates the WinSock API. For programmers who know network programming, this class gives low-level access to the WinSock API along with network event callback functions.

- Class CSocket, which provides a high-level interface to WinSock.

The Win32 Internet (WinInet) API

Microsoft has unveiled a new API for creating Internet-enabled applications more quickly and easily than ever before: the Win32 Internet (WinInet) API. This API provides intermediate-to-advanced-level communications functions that enable you to access the main Internet protocols fairly easily. These functions use the familiar Win32 API style and provide a layer of insulation between you and the underlying WinSock implementation that drives it. Here are the four fairly well-defined WinInet API function categories:

1. General-purpose WinInet functions

2. WinInet File Transfer Protocol (FTP) functions

3. WinInet Gopher functions

4. WinInet HyperText Transfer Protocol (HTTP) functions

> **NOTE**
>
> Admittedly, the WinInet API is still evolving. At the time of this writing, it is still in beta versions. To help make WinInet more standardized as the specification is revised, MFC 4.2 encapsulates the WinInet API within a set of classes that use immutable interfaces. Changes to the underlying API specification will affect the MFC classes only internally. The down side to this arrangement is that these classes are available only with MFC 4.2 (and a Visual C++ subscription).

Microsoft's Internet Client/Server Architecture

Microsoft's Internet client architecture has been dubbed *Sweeper*. Sweeper is an API built on Win32 and OLE; it gives you the ability to Internet-enable your applications. Sweeper includes support for extensibility and scripting, asynchronous access, caching, and navigation. Sweeper is composed of a set of redistributable modules that you can use in any Windows-based application. The underlying technology is OLE, and the buzzword is ActiveX.

Most of the functionality provided by Sweeper is present in the *Microsoft Internet Explorer 3.0 (IE3)*, Microsoft's standards-based Internet browser application. IE3 is split into a set of ActiveX components and services that will soon become an integral part of all Windows operating systems. This is good news for developers because, like the Win32 API, the libraries and components needed to use the coolest features of Windows will ship with every copy sold!

The Internet Information Server

The Windows NT Server network operating system (NOS) is Microsoft's top-end system and is quickly becoming the favored operating system for new Web servers. The NT Server networking operating system provides a secure, robust environment with which many types of networks can interact without a hitch—a feature that makes Windows NT Server well-suited for the Internet. The release of Windows NT Server 4.0 has brought the ease of use of the modern Windows 95 interface to what is arguably the best, most robust NOS ever created.

The Microsoft Internet Information Server (IIS) is the only World Wide Web server tightly integrated with the Microsoft Windows NT Server NOS. IIS is designed to deliver a wide range of Internet and *intranet* server capabilities; it delivers high performance, excellent security, and ease of management on the Windows NT Server platform.

The Internet Server API (ISAPI)

The goals of IIS are to be the fastest information server and to enable the server to be extended. How do you extend the server? Through a new open API designed specifically with IIS in mind—the Internet Server API (ISAPI). ISAPI provides you with the tools you need in order to create high-performance, efficient, and secure commercial add-ons for Internet servers that comply to the new IIS standard. In fact, to promote the IIS standard, Microsoft is encouraging other server vendors to adopt ISAPI so that developers can write to a single set of code that will work on several Internet server platforms. In MFC 4.1 and above, the ISAPI is wrapped by MFC classes that, in typical MFC style, make it easier to program ISAPI extensions.

NOTE

ISAPI programming can radically enhance Windows NT Server and IIS by enabling programmers to create custom applications for the Internet and intranet.

ActiveX Controls

ActiveX controls combine the best features of standard OLE controls with the exciting environment of the Web browser. ActiveX technology is changing the Internet, and Microsoft has announced an open ActiveX standard to ensure that industry titans and smaller third-party developers alike can use this new twist on OLE/COM technology. A typical ActiveX control enhances a Web page by providing interactivity, animation, and OLE Automation programmability through scripting languages.

ActiveX controls can be programmed within a Web page by scripting languages such as Microsoft's Visual Basic, Scripting Edition (VBScript), and with the JavaScript language, co-created by Netscape (the founding father of the modern Web browser) and Sun (creator of the Java language).

NOTE

Of course, ActiveX controls also are OLE controls and can be used in programming environments that support OCXs, such as Visual C++ 4.x, Visual Basic 4.0, and Delphi 2.0.

The Messaging API (MAPI)

The Messaging API (MAPI) is based on a powerful object-oriented interface that uses the Component Object Model (COM) as the underlying model for object interaction. MAPI defines a set of objects with many features that enable client applications to give users access to message or recipient properties and customized views of message and address book information.

In addition to full-blown, low-level MAPI, three API sets provide a higher-level interface to support a full range of client application development. These additional APIs are Common

Messaging Calls (CMC), Simple MAPI, and the OLE Messaging Library. These APIs provide messaging capabilities for C, C++, Delphi, and Visual Basic programmers and are easier to use and understand.

All types of client applications can use the powerful and complex MAPI interface, but the less-complex Simple MAPI is usually sufficient to create messaging-aware and messaging-enabled applications.

Internet Security Through Code Signing

As you're probably aware (and if you aren't, you should be!), computer viruses, Trojan horses, and other assorted malicious code-nastiness pose a major security threat to networked systems. On a constantly changing and growing global network the size of the Internet, it's simply impossible to keep viruses and their brethren at bay. The truth is, infected code of one form or another runs rampant in many systems, and code safety is a major concern for developers and for users of Internet applications (including ActiveX controls).

For example, it's possible that a perfectly harmless-looking ActiveX control, executable file, or code from unknown sites or authors could wipe out a user's entire system before he knew what hit him! Worse yet, perfectly harmless code created by one programmer could be tampered with and altered by some other, malicious programmer after its release, possibly wreaking havoc on the systems of users who download and execute the altered code!

Addressing Security Issues

There are two basic ways to address the Internet security issue:

- Sandboxing. This term refers to restricting an application to a certain set of APIs, excluding those that would enable file I/O and other potentially dangerous function groups that could alter or destroy data on a user's system. This security method assumes that you trust the application won't do any harm, and that you trust the source of the application to not act maliciously.

- Shrinkwrapping. This security method uses specially encrypted digital signatures. A *shrinkwrapped* product verifies *signed* code with a private-key/public-key verification scheme. Before any signed code is allowed to execute on a user's machine, its digital signature is verified. This verification process ensures that the code hasn't been tampered with since the code was signed, and it also ensures that the code is from a known, authenticated source.

Digital Code Signing

Digital code signatures are used to verify code authenticity and also to identify and provide details about the publisher of the code. Digital signatures are an industry standard supported by many Web browsers. Such browsers enable a user to choose whether to download and execute code of unknown or suspicious origin.

> **NOTE**
>
> For the most up-to-date information about digital code signing, an industry standard, access the Web site for the World Wide Web Consortium (W3C) at this URL:
>
> ```
> http://www.w3.org/pub/WWW/
> ```

Signed Code and Code Certificates

As an independent software vendor (ISV) who wants to use the benefits of digital code signatures in your applications, you must get something called *certificates* from a *certificate authority* (CA), a third-party company known and trusted by the industry. After a CA verifies that you comply with W3C policies, the CA issues you a digital certificate file for use in code signing. The certificate file contains important information, including the name of the software publisher, your public encryption key, the name of the CA's certificate, and more.

Public and Private Encryption Keys

Public and private keys are created by you for use in encrypting the digital signature block used to verify your code's authenticity. Both keys are created by you, but the private key remains your little secret. The public key must be checked by the CA to ensure that it's unique.

Signing Your Code

You need special tools to sign your code, and these are available in the *ActiveX Development Kit*, available from Microsoft on CD-ROM and online at the following URL:

```
http://microsoft.com/activex
```

Fully debugged, release-ready code is run through a hash function that produces a fixed-length *code digest*. You then encrypt this digest with your private key and combine it with your certificate file. The result is linked back into your executable file. *Presto!* Your digitally signed masterpiece is ready for distribution over the Internet. The tools used for code signing are listed in Table 16.1 and are available in the ActiveX SDK.

Table 16.1. Tools used for digital code signing.

Filename	Description
MAKECERT.EXE	A tool that creates a fake certificate for development purposes.
CERT2SPC.EXE	The tool used to build a signature block from your certificate.
SIGNCODE.EXE	A tool that links the signature block into your executable.
CHKTRUST.EXE	A tool that verifies that code has been successfully signed.

In addition to CHKTRUST.EXE, you can use Internet Explorer 3 (IE3) to verify signed code as well. IE3 provides certificate and code signing options in the Options dialog box (accessed with the View | Options menu command). The Security tab for this dialog box reveals options you can set for verifying signed code, viewing any certificates installed on your system, and setting options for ActiveX components (see Figure 16.1).

FIGURE 16.1.

The Security page in the Internet Explorer 3 Options dialog box.

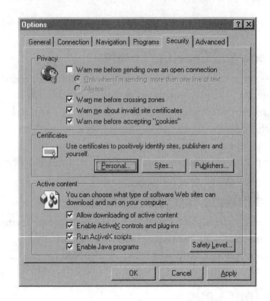

Considering the Cash Factor

As you've seen, code signing is a robust system for creating trustworthy code. Users can rest assured that signed code is safe to download and execute. The nagging question in your mind at this point is probably, "How much does a certificate cost?" Good question!

Microsoft estimates that commercial software publishers will pay around $400 U.S. dollars for the initial certificate and around $300 for an annual renewal. Certificates for individual software publishers will ring in at about $20.

Summary

MFC makes using WinSock, WinInet, ISAPI, ActiveX, and MAPI programming almost easy (especially when compared to standard SDK programming), so you should use these features and experiment with the technologies to better prepare for present needs and future challenges. Windows communications programming is getting more important with each passing day, so don't wait—get connected!

Here are some points to remember:

- Networks enable people to communicate and share resources.

- A local area network (LAN) is a network composed of computer workstations directly connected together, often by a direct cable connection.

- A wide area network (WAN) is a group of LANs connected together, usually with telephone lines.

- The principal way computers communicate with one another is through the use of the client/server communication model; all Internet services are provided using client/server relationships.

- Many communications APIs and Internet programming tools are available for Windows programmers.

- The Windows Sockets (WinSock) specification enables applications to communicate with each other across networks by means of socket communications objects.

- The Win32 Internet (WinInet) API provides intermediate-to-advanced-level communications functions that enable you to access the main Internet protocols (FTP, Gopher, and HTTP) fairly easily.

- ActiveX controls combine the best features of standard OLE controls with the exciting environment of the Web browser.

- The Messaging API (MAPI) is a COM-based set of objects that enable client applications to provide users with messaging, e-mail, and address book information.

Using the Win32 Internet (WinInet) API

by Rob McGregor

IN THIS CHAPTER

CHAPTER 17

This chapter introduces Microsoft's WinInet API functions. It shows how you can use these functions to create your own Internet-enabled applications based on File Transfer Protocol (FTP), gopher, and HyperText Transfer Protocol (HTTP), and how the functions can be used to leverage a program in an internetworked environment.

Overview

You've already been introduced to the Internet, but this chapter introduces some exciting and highly useful new material. The new WinInet API functions provide easy access to common Internet protocols and provide a high-level API that provides a fast and direct path to making Internet-enabled applications.

> **NOTE**
>
> The Win32 Internet API functions described and used in this chapter are based on the beta 1 version of the WININET.DLL, which houses the API. The specifications for the WinInet API are subject to further revision by Microsoft before being moved into the Win32 API at some point in the future, but they are the most current as of this writing.

Introducing the WinInet API

The WinInet API functions are built on the Windows Sockets protocol and fall rather neatly into four categories of functions. Although these are supported by MFC now (currently MFC 4.2), it is important to understand the underlying technology. Microsoft has promised that future versions of MFC will continue to wrap these functions into useful classes in typical MFC fashion and simplify the programming even more.

The four WinInet API function categories are as follows:

- General-purpose WinInet functions
- WinInet File Transfer Protocol (FTP) functions
- WinInet Gopher functions
- WinInet HyperText Transfer Protocol (HTTP) functions

The WinInet API functions are exported from a redistributable dynamic link library called the WININET.DLL. This DLL currently can be redistributed with Win32 applications, and in future releases of Windows this functionality will be incorporated directly into all Microsoft operating systems.

Advantages of Using the WinInet API

The WinInet API functions give applications access to the Internet and provide several advantages to the Win32 application programmer. These advantages stem mainly from the high-level interface provided, which hides many of the gory details and the complexity inherent in programming Internet applications. Let's look at some of these advantages.

TCP/IP and Windows Sockets

Use of the WinInet API all but eliminates the need for a low-level understanding of TCP/IP and Windows Sockets. The API converts these Internet protocols into task-oriented functions that use the familiar Win32 API function style. You don't need to write WinSock code directly. In fact, you don't even need to be familiar with the TCP/IP protocol. The WinInet functions transparently execute WinSock functions for you.

A Friendly Interface

Use of the WinInet API also all but eliminates the need for a low-level knowledge of common Internet protocols such as File Transfer Protocol (FTP) and HyperText Transfer Protocol (HTTP). The concepts behind these protocols are fairly simple, but their actual implementations can be quite complex. The WinInet functions encapsulate the problems inherent in Internet programming and provide a common solution with consistent behavior across applications.

An Up-To-Date API and a Safe Bet

The underlying technology for the Internet is rapidly changing and evolving, and the WinInet API provides a standardized means of programming Internet applications. Because WinInet functions hide the actual implementations of specific protocols within a well structured, well conceived API, you can be assured that your tested WinInet code will work even when specifications change.

The API will remain fairly constant, providing you with a secure code base for your applications that is guaranteed to remain up-to-date. Microsoft programmers will simply update the internal implementation of the WININET.DLL to keep pace with evolving technology.

NOTE

The WinInet API and WININET.DLL are (as of this writing) included in the ActiveX SDK. Download the latest version of the ActiveX SDK from the Web to get the latest version of the WinInet API and WININET.DLL. You'll find this on the Web at the following URL:

```
http://www.microsoft.com/msdownload/activex.htm
```

17

USING THE
WIN32 INTERNET
(WININET) API

A Familiar Programming Interface

The WinInet API functions were designed to feel familiar to experienced Windows programmers. The functions have a familiar look and feel, and most return information in a familiar format. WinInet return values also are easily used in standard Win32 functions. Also, the WinInet API provides its functions in both ANSI and Unicode versions for total compatibility and to facilitate Unicode-only applications.

Multithreaded Application Support

The WinInet API functions are fully multithread safe. You can make simultaneous calls to WinInet functions from multiple threads without worrying about synchronization problems or deadlock. This is possible because the WinInet functions amazingly handle all multithread synchronization internally. (Now that's user-friendly!)

Persistent Data-Caching Support

The WinInet API functions provide persistent caching for all of the Internet protocols. What this means for you is that your application development can focus on the data itself, rather than on managing the data-cache.

Let's take a quick look at the four Win32 Internet API function groups to see what specific services the API offers for Win32 programmers.

Handles and Functions

The WinInet API functions utilize special Internet handles, and there are several different types of these that are used by the various API functions. Although they might all use the HINTERNET moniker on the surface, there are actually 13 different subtypes of Internet handles, and these are shown in Listing 17.1.

Listing 17.1. The 13 HINTERNET types defined in WININET.H.

```
//
// handle types
//

#define INTERNET_HANDLE_TYPE_INTERNET
#define INTERNET_HANDLE_TYPE_CONNECT_FTP
#define INTERNET_HANDLE_TYPE_CONNECT_GOPHER
#define INTERNET_HANDLE_TYPE_CONNECT_HTTP
#define INTERNET_HANDLE_TYPE_FTP_FIND
#define INTERNET_HANDLE_TYPE_FTP_FIND_HTML
#define INTERNET_HANDLE_TYPE_FTP_FILE
#define INTERNET_HANDLE_TYPE_FTP_FILE_HTML
#define INTERNET_HANDLE_TYPE_GOPHER_FIND
#define INTERNET_HANDLE_TYPE_GOPHER_FIND_HTML
#define INTERNET_HANDLE_TYPE_GOPHER_FILE
#define INTERNET_HANDLE_TYPE_GOPHER_FILE_HTML
#define INTERNET_HANDLE_TYPE_HTTP_REQUEST
```

> **CAUTION**
>
> Each of the WinInet functions uses or returns one of these handle types. Although they all appear in code as an HINTERNET, these types are *not* interchangeable. You must be sure to call WinInet functions in the proper order to ensure that the HINTERNET returned from a function is the proper type to use in a subsequent function call.

As I mentioned earlier, there are four main categories of WinInet functions. Let's look at each group of functions to see what services WinInet actually provides.

General-Purpose Internet Functions

The general-purpose WinInet functions apply to all protocols, including HTTP, FTP, and Gopher, and they perform basic Internet file manipulations. The WinInet functions use special Internet handles (HINTERNETs) that aren't compatible with standard Windows system handles but are mandatory for working with the WinInet API functions. The general-purpose WinInet functions are listed in Table 17.1.

Table 17.1. General-purpose WinInet functions.

Function	Description
InternetCanonicalizeUrl()	Converts a URL to a canonical (conventional) form.
InternetCloseHandle()	Closes any Internet handle that an application has opened.
InternetCombineUrl()	Combines a base and relative URL into a single URL. The resultant URL will be canonical.
InternetConfirmZoneCrossing()	Checks for changes between secure and non-secure URLs.
InternetConnect()	Opens an FTP, Gopher, or HTTP session for a given site.
InternetCrackUrl()	Cracks a URL into its component parts.
InternetCreateUrl()	Creates a URL from its component parts.
InternetErrorDlg()	Displays a dialog box that explains why an error occurred.
InternetFindNextFile()	Continues a file search started as a result of a previous call to FtpFindFirstFile() or GopherFindFirstFile().

continues

Table 17.1. continued

Function	Description
InternetGetLastResponseInfo()	Gets error text from the last WinInet function that failed.
InternetOpen()	Initializes an application's use of the Win32 Internet functions.
InternetOpenUrl()	Begins reading an FTP, Gopher, or HTTP URL.
InternetQueryDataAvailable()	Queries the amount of data available.
InternetQueryOption()	Queries an Internet option on the specified handle.
InternetReadFile()	Reads data from a handle opened by the InternetOpenUrl(), FtpOpenFile(), GopherOpenFile(), or HttpOpenRequest() functions.
InternetSetFilePointer()	Sets a file position for InternetReadFile().
InternetSetOption()	Sets an Internet option on the specified handle.
InternetSetOptionEx()	Sets an Internet option on the specified handle.
InternetSetStatusCallback()	Sets up a callback function that WinInet functions can call as progress is made during an operation.
InternetStatusCallback()	This is a placeholder for the application-defined status callback.
InternetTimeFromSystemTime()	Formats a date and time according to the specified Request For Comment (RFC) format.
InternetWriteFile()	Writes data to an open Internet file.

What Is File Transfer Protocol (FTP)?

The File Transfer Protocol (FTP) is the underlying set of specifications that supports Internet file transfer. This is an extremely important service that allows files from one Internet host to copy files to and from any other Internet host.

FTP uses a client/server model that allows the client to send commands to the server (or host), which responds by carrying out the specified command. FTP enables you to upload files to the server and download files to your local machine. If you have the proper access to the server, FTP also enables you to create, browse, and delete files and directories on the server. This is powerful stuff!

Anonymous FTP

Anonymous FTP enables you to log on to a system using the user ID anonymous and use your e-mail address or name as a password. This facility gives you access to any publicly offered files and directories on an incredible number of host machines throughout the world. You can use FTP to browse authorized directories and upload or download files from any number of host machines that are set up to use anonymous FTP.

Using FTP, free of charge, you can download programs that do almost anything, and you can download information about nearly any topic right from the Net. FTP is a powerful facility that acts very much like the glue that holds the Internet together.

WinInet FTP Functions

The FTP functions deal with FTP file and directory manipulation and navigation, and they provide a standard interface to the FTP specification. Table 17.2 lists the WinInet FTP functions.

Table 17.2. WinInet FTP functions.

Function	Description
FtpCreateDirectory()	Creates a new directory on the FTP server.
FtpDeleteFile()	Deletes a file stored on the FTP server.
FtpFindFirstFile()	Begins searching the current directory of the given FTP session.
FtpGetCurrentDirectory()	Retrieves the current directory for the specified FTP session.
FtpGetFile()	Retrieves a file from the FTP server and stores it under the specified filename, creating a new local file in the process.
FtpOpenFile()	Initiates access to a remote file for writing or reading.
FtpPutFile()	Stores a file on the FTP server.
FtpRemoveDirectory()	Removes the specified directory on the FTP server.
FtpRenameFile()	Renames a file stored on the FTP server.
FtpSetCurrentDirectory()	Changes to a different working directory on the FTP server.

The Gopher

The Gopher is a client/server system that enables you to find resources anywhere on the Internet and retrieve the resources without even needing to know where they are coming from. This is an incredibly useful tool! There are thousands of Gopher servers on the Internet, storing all sorts of information. The Gopher provides transparent connection services, using other Internet protocols if necessary, to quickly and easily get the information you need.

> **NOTE**
>
> The original Gopher specification was developed at the University of Minnesota in 1991, and the Gopher got its name for two reasons: first, because it would "go-fer" information on the Net; and second, because Minnesota is nicknamed the Gopher state.

WinInet Gopher Functions

The Gopher functions provide a standard interface to the Gopher specification. Table 17.3 lists the WinInet Gopher functions.

Table 17.3. WinInet Gopher functions.

Function	Description
GopherAttributeEnumerator()	Defines a callback function that processes attribute information from a Gopher server. This callback function is installed by a call to the GopherGetAttribute() function.
GopherCreateLocator()	Creates a Gopher or Gopher+ locator string from its component parts.
GopherFindFirstFile()	Uses a Gopher locator and some search criteria to create a session with the server and locate the requested documents, binary files, index servers, or directory trees.
GopherGetAttribute()	Allows an application to retrieve specific attribute information from the server.
GopherGetLocatorType()	Parses a Gopher locator and determines its attributes.
GopherOpenFile()	Begins reading a Gopher data file from a Gopher server.

HyperText Transfer Protocol (HTTP)

When you access data on the World Wide Web, you'll notice that the address you use to access a Web site looks something like this:

```
http://www.microsoft.com
```

This is the main Web site for Microsoft Corporation, and this address is known as a *Universal Resource Locator* (URL). The first part of the URL describes the type of resource being accessed, and the second part is the actual Internet address for the resource. In the previous example, the first part of the URL is http, which (of course) specifies the HyperText Transfer Protocol. As you might already know, the hypertext format used for HTTP is a scripting format called HyperText Markup Language (HTML). Web documents are created using HTML and are transferred by HTTP.

WinInet HTTP Functions

The WinInet HTTP functions for the Web control the transmission and content of HTTP requests. Table 17.4 describes the WinInet HTTP Web functions.

Table 17.4. WinInet HTTP Web functions.

Function	Description
HttpAddRequestHeaders()	Adds one or more HTTP request headers to the HTTP request handle.
HttpOpenRequest()	Opens an HTTP request handle.
HttpQueryInfo()	Queries for information about an HTTP request.
HttpSendRequest()	Sends the specified request to the HTTP server.

Sample Program: RAWHTML.EXE

Now that you've seen the WinInet functions, turn your attention to a sample program that demonstrates the basic usage of the WININET.DLL for HTTP data transfer. This simple sample shows how you can use this powerful library of functions to create Internet-enabled applications for Win32.

> **NOTE**
>
> RAWHTML.EXE, along with all of its source files, can be found in the SOURCE\CHAP17\RAWHTML folder on this book's companion CD-ROM.

The RAWHTML program simply takes a URL input by a user and requests HTML data from the URL-specified server. The data returned via the WinInet functions then is displayed as raw HTML in a multiple-line edit control. Figure 17.1 shows the RAWHTML program in action.

FIGURE 17.1.

The RAWHTML program displaying a raw HTML source script.

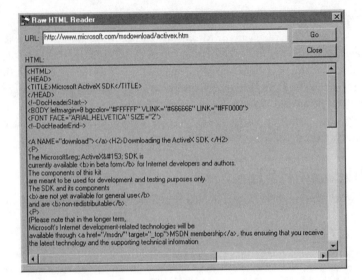

RAWHTML is a dialog-based application that contains three classes: CRawHtmlApp, CRawHtmlDlg, and CAboutDlg. The CRawHtmlDlg class contains the meat of the application's functionality, while the CRawHtmlApp class contains only the minimum necessary code to get the application running. CAboutDlg is simply a trivial About box class.

The CRawHtmlApp Class

The CRawHtmlApp application class interface declares only two methods, and the implementation is basic at best. The application class is declared in the file RAWHTML.H, and it looks like this:

```
///////////////////////////////////////////////////////////////////
// CRawHtmlApp - Application class

class CRawHtmlApp : public CWinApp
{
public:
    CRawHtmlApp();

protected:
    virtual BOOL InitInstance();
};
```

The implementation for this class is found in the file RAWHTML.CPP, and it's only slightly more complex than the declaration, as you can see in Listing 17.2. By now, code such as this should be second nature and self-explanatory to you.

Listing 17.2. The CRawHtmlApp class implementation in the file RAWHTML.CPP.

```
///////////////////////////////////////////////////////////////////
// Module  : RAWHTML.CPP
//
// Purpose : The application class for the RAWHTML program.
///////////////////////////////////////////////////////////////////

#include "stdafx.h"
#include "RawHtml.h"
#include "HtmlDlg.h"

///////////////////////////////////////////////////////////////////
// CRawHtmlApp construction

CRawHtmlApp::CRawHtmlApp()
{
}

///////////////////////////////////////////////////////////////////
// CRawHtmlApp initialization

BOOL CRawHtmlApp::InitInstance()
{
    // Allocate and display main dialog window
    CRawHtmlDlg dlg;
    m_pMainWnd = &dlg;
    dlg.DoModal();

    // Return FALSE so that we exit the application
    return FALSE;
}

///////////////////////////////////////////////////////////////////
// The CRawHtmlApp object

CRawHtmlApp MyApp;

///////////////////////////////////////////////////////////////////
```

The real point of interest for this application is the dialog class that performs the Internet data transfer via HTTP. Let's have a look.

The CRawHtmlDlg Dialog Class Header (HTMLDLG.H)

The CRawHtmlDlg dialog class header declares four controls as data members, along with several methods. The complete class declaration is given in Listing 17.3.

Listing 17.3. The CRawHtmlDlg dialog class header: HTMLDLG.H.

```
///////////////////////////////////////////////////////////////////////
// Module   : HTMLDLG.H
//
// Purpose : The main dialog box interface for the RAWHTML program.

///////////////////////////////////////////////////////////////////////
// CRawHtmlDlg dialog

class CRawHtmlDlg : public CDialog
{
public:
    CRawHtmlDlg(CWnd* pParent = NULL);    // standard constructor

    // Dialog Data
    enum { IDD = IDD_RAWHTML_DIALOG };

    CButton    m_btnClose;
    CButton    m_btnGo;
    CEdit       m_editUrl;
    CEdit      m_editHtml;

protected:
    // DDX/DDV support
    virtual void DoDataExchange(CDataExchange* pDX);

protected:
    HICON      m_hIcon;
    CString   m_strServer;
    CString   m_strPath;

    void ParseURL(CString& strUrl);
    void DisplayRawHtml(char* lpszBuffer);

    // Message map methods
    virtual BOOL OnInitDialog();
    afx_msg void OnSysCommand(UINT nID, LPARAM lParam);
    afx_msg void OnBtnGoClicked();

    DECLARE_MESSAGE_MAP()
};

///////////////////////////////////////////////////////////////////////
```

The CRawHtmlDlg Dialog Class Implementation (HTMLDLG.CPP)

The file HTMLDLG.CPP provides the implementation of the CRawHtmlDlg class, and most of the code should look familiar to you because similar code has been used in several other sample applications elsewhere in this book. The complete HTMLDLG.CPP code is given in Listing 17.4.

Using the Win32 Internet (WinInet) API

CHAPTER 17

475

17

USING THE
WIN32 INTERNET
(WININET) API

Listing 17.4. The CRawHtmlDlg class implementation.

```cpp
/////////////////////////////////////////////////////////////////
// Module  : HTMLDLG.CPP
//
// Purpose : The main dialog class for the RAWHTML program.
/////////////////////////////////////////////////////////////////

#include "stdafx.h"
#include "RawHtml.h"
#include "HtmlDlg.h"

/////////////////////////////////////////////////////////////////
// CAboutDlg dialog used for App About

class CAboutDlg : public CDialog
{
public:
   CAboutDlg();
   enum { IDD = IDD_ABOUTBOX };

protected:
   // DDX/DDV support
   virtual void DoDataExchange(CDataExchange* pDX);
};

CAboutDlg::CAboutDlg() : CDialog(CAboutDlg::IDD)
{
}

void CAboutDlg::DoDataExchange(CDataExchange* pDX)
   { CDialog::DoDataExchange(pDX); }

/////////////////////////////////////////////////////////////////
// CRawHtmlDlg::CRawHtmlDlg() - Constructor

CRawHtmlDlg::CRawHtmlDlg(CWnd* pParent)
   : CDialog(CRawHtmlDlg::IDD, pParent)
{
   m_strServer = "";
   m_strPath   = "";

   m_hIcon = AfxGetApp()->LoadIcon(IDR_MAINFRAME);
}

void CRawHtmlDlg::DoDataExchange(CDataExchange* pDX)
{
   CDialog::DoDataExchange(pDX);

   DDX_Control(pDX, IDCANCEL, m_btnClose);
   DDX_Control(pDX, IDOK, m_btnGo);
   DDX_Control(pDX, IDC_EDIT_URL, m_editUrl);
   DDX_Control(pDX, IDC_EDIT_HTML, m_editHtml);
}

/////////////////////////////////////////////////////////////////
// CRawHtmlDlg Message map
```

continues

Listing 17.4. continued

```cpp
BEGIN_MESSAGE_MAP(CRawHtmlDlg, CDialog)
    ON_WM_SYSCOMMAND()
    ON_BN_CLICKED(IDOK, OnBtnGoClicked)
END_MESSAGE_MAP()

/////////////////////////////////////////////////////////////////
// CRawHtmlDlg::OnInitDialog()

BOOL CRawHtmlDlg::OnInitDialog()
{
    CDialog::OnInitDialog();

    //
    // Add "About..." menu item to system menu. IDM_ABOUTBOX must
    // be in the system command range...
    //

    ASSERT((IDM_ABOUTBOX & 0xFFF0) == IDM_ABOUTBOX);
    ASSERT(IDM_ABOUTBOX < 0xF000);

    CMenu* pSysMenu = GetSystemMenu(FALSE);
    CString strAboutMenu;
    strAboutMenu.LoadString(IDS_ABOUTBOX);
    if (!strAboutMenu.IsEmpty())
    {
        pSysMenu->AppendMenu(MF_SEPARATOR);
        pSysMenu->AppendMenu(MF_STRING, IDM_ABOUTBOX, strAboutMenu);
    }

    // Set the icon for the dialog
    SetIcon(m_hIcon, FALSE);      // Set small icon
    SetIcon(m_hIcon, TRUE);       // Set big icon

// Set the default URL
    m_editUrl.SetWindowText(
        "http://www.microsoft.com/msdownload/activex.htm");
    m_editUrl.SetFocus();

    return FALSE;   // m_editUrl has the focus!
}

/////////////////////////////////////////////////////////////////
// CRawHtmlDlg::OnSysCommand()

void CRawHtmlDlg::OnSysCommand(UINT nID, LPARAM lParam)
{
    if ((nID & 0xFFF0) == IDM_ABOUTBOX)
    {
        CAboutDlg dlgAbout;
        dlgAbout.DoModal();
    }
    else
    {
        CDialog::OnSysCommand(nID, lParam);
    }
}
```

```
/////////////////////////////////////////////////////////////////
// CRawHtmlDlg::OnBtnGoClicked()

void CRawHtmlDlg::OnBtnGoClicked()
{
    // Get the current URL
    CString strUrl;
    m_editUrl.GetWindowText(strUrl);

    // See if the URL looks valid
    if (strUrl.IsEmpty() ¦¦ strUrl.Left(7) != "http://")
    {
        ::MessageBeep(MB_ICONASTERISK);
        AfxMessageBox("Sorry, http address required...",
            MB_OK ¦ MB_ICONINFORMATION);
        return;
    }

    // Parse the URL to get server name and file path (if any)
    ParseURL(strUrl);

    // Initialize the Internet DLL
    HINTERNET hSession = ::InternetOpen("Raw HTML Reader",
        PRE_CONFIG_INTERNET_ACCESS, "",
        INTERNET_INVALID_PORT_NUMBER, 0);

    // See if the session handle is valid
    if (hSession == NULL)
    {
        ::MessageBeep(MB_ICONEXCLAMATION);
        AfxMessageBox("Internet session initialization failed!",
            MB_OK ¦ MB_ICONEXCLAMATION);
        return;
    }

    // Initialize HTTP session
    HINTERNET hConnect = ::InternetConnect(hSession, m_strServer,
        INTERNET_INVALID_PORT_NUMBER, "", "",
        INTERNET_SERVICE_HTTP, 0, 0);

    // See if connection handle is valid
    if (hConnect == NULL)
    {
        ::MessageBeep(MB_ICONEXCLAMATION);
        AfxMessageBox("Internet connection failed!",
            MB_OK ¦ MB_ICONEXCLAMATION);

        // Close session handle
        VERIFY(::InternetCloseHandle(hSession));
        return;
    }

    // Open an HTTP request handle
    HINTERNET hHttpFile = ::HttpOpenRequest(hConnect, "GET",
        m_strPath, HTTP_VERSION, NULL, 0,
        INTERNET_FLAG_DONT_CACHE, 0);
```

continues

17

USING THE
WIN32 INTERNET
(WININET) API

Listing 17.4. continued

```cpp
// See if HTTP request handle is valid
if (hHttpFile == NULL)
{
    ::MessageBeep(MB_ICONEXCLAMATION);
    AfxMessageBox("HTTP request failed!",
        MB_OK | MB_ICONEXCLAMATION);

    // Close session handles
    VERIFY(::InternetCloseHandle(hConnect));
    VERIFY(::InternetCloseHandle(hSession));
    return;
}

// Disable the user interface sending & processing request
m_editUrl.EnableWindow(FALSE);
m_btnGo.EnableWindow(FALSE);
m_btnClose.EnableWindow(FALSE);

// Display wait cursor
CWaitCursor wait;

// Send the request
BOOL bSendRequest = ::HttpSendRequest(hHttpFile, NULL, 0, 0, 0);

if (bSendRequest)
{
    // Get the size of the requested file
    char achQueryBuf[16];
    DWORD dwFileSize;
    DWORD dwQueryBufLen = sizeof(achQueryBuf);

    BOOL bQuery = ::HttpQueryInfo(hHttpFile,
        HTTP_QUERY_CONTENT_LENGTH, achQueryBuf,
        &dwQueryBufLen, NULL);

    if (bQuery)
    {
        // The query succeeded, specify memory needed for file
        dwFileSize = (DWORD)atol(achQueryBuf);
    }
    else
    {
        // The query failed, so guess at a max file size
        dwFileSize = 10 * 1024;
    }

    // Allocate a buffer for the file data
    char* lpszBuf = new char[dwFileSize + 1];

    // Read the file
    DWORD dwBytesRead;
    BOOL bRead = ::InternetReadFile(hHttpFile, lpszBuf,
        dwFileSize + 1, &dwBytesRead);

    // Display the raw HTML
    DisplayRawHtml(lpszBuf);
```

```
        // Clean up buffer
        delete lpszBuf;

        // Close all open Internet handles
        VERIFY(::InternetCloseHandle(hHttpFile));
        VERIFY(::InternetCloseHandle(hConnect));
        VERIFY(::InternetCloseHandle(hSession));
    }

    // Enable the user interface
    m_btnGo.EnableWindow(TRUE);
    m_btnClose.EnableWindow(TRUE);
    m_editUrl.EnableWindow(TRUE);
}

//////////////////////////////////////////////////////////////////
// CRawHtmlDlg::ParseURL()
// Parses the URL to get the server and file names (if any)

void CRawHtmlDlg::ParseURL(CString& strUrl)
{
    if (strUrl.IsEmpty())
        return;

    // Strip off "http://"
    CString strTemp = strUrl.Mid(7) ;

    // Check for a path after the host name
    int nSlash = strTemp.Find("/");

    if (nSlash != -1)  // There's a path specified, so grab it
    {
        m_strServer = strTemp.Left(nSlash);
        m_strPath   = strTemp.Mid(nSlash);
    }
    else
        m_strServer = strTemp;
}

//////////////////////////////////////////////////////////////////
// CRawHtmlDlg::DisplayRawHtml()

void CRawHtmlDlg::DisplayRawHtml(char* lpszBuffer)
{
    m_editHtml.SetWindowText((LPCTSTR)lpszBuffer);
}

//////////////////////////////////////////////////////////////////
```

In the RAWHTML program, the actual Internet-specific code is located in the `CRawHtmlDlg::OnBtnGoClicked()` method, and the first order of business is initializing the Win32 Internet DLL.

Initializing a WinInet Session

To give an application Internet access via the WININET.DLL, for any of the supported protocols, you must first initialize the DLL by calling the InternetOpen() function. This causes the DLL to initialize internal data structures and prepare for future calls from the application. If the function call succeeds, it returns a valid HINTERNET that's used in subsequent function calls. The function has the following prototype:

```
HINTERNET InternetOpen(
    IN LPCTSTR  lpszAgent,
    IN DWORD    dwAccessType,
    IN LPCTSTR  lpszProxyName OPTIONAL,
    IN LPCSTR   lpszProxyBypass OPTIONAL,
    IN DWORD    dwFlags
);
```

The parameters used by this function are as follows:

- lpszAgent is a pointer to a string that contains the name of the application or entity calling the Internet functions (for example, Microsoft Internet Explorer). This name is used as the user agent in the HTTP protocol.

- dwAccessType is the type of access required, which can be any of the values listed later in Table 17.6.

- lpszProxyName is a pointer to a string that contains the name of the proxy server (or servers) to use if proxy access is specified. The InternetOpen() function reads proxy information from the registry if this parameter is NULL.

- lpszProxyBypass is an optional pointer to a list of host names, IP addresses, or both, that are known locally.

- dwFlags is any combination of the flags found in Table 17.5 that specify various options for the function.

Table 17.5. Flags used for the InternetOpen() dwFlags parameter.

Value	Meaning
INTERNET_FLAG_OFFLINE	Satisfy download operations on this handle through the persistent cache only. If the item does not exist in the cache, the function returns an appropriate error code.
INTERNET_FLAG_ASYNC	Future operations on this handle might fail with ERROR_IO_PENDING. A status callback will be made with INTERNET_STATUS_REQUEST_COMPLETE. This callback will be on a thread other than the one for the original request. A status callback routine must be registered or the functions will be completed synchronously.

Table 17.6. Internet access-type values used by `InternetOpen()`.

Value	Meaning
`INTERNET_OPEN_TYPE_DIRECT`	Resolve all host names locally.
`INTERNET_OPEN_TYPE_PROXY`	Pass requests to the proxy unless a proxy bypass list is supplied and the name to be resolved bypasses the proxy. In this case, the function proceeds as for `INTERNET_OPEN_TYPE_DIRECT`.
`INTERNET_OPEN_TYPE_PRECONFIG`	The proxy or direct configuration is retrieved from the registry.

In the RAWHTML program, you initialize the `WININET.DLL` by calling `InternetOpen()` as follows:

```
// Initialize the Internet DLL
HINTERNET hSession = ::InternetOpen("Raw HTML Reader",
   PRE_CONFIG_INTERNET_ACCESS, "",
   INTERNET_INVALID_PORT_NUMBER, 0);
```

> **NOTE**
>
> When your Internet session is over, be sure to call the `InternetCloseHandle()` function with the handle returned from `InternetOpen()` as a parameter. This ensures that any resources allocated by `InternetOpen()` are freed.

Getting a Protocol Handle

When the Internet DLL is initialized and ready for action, you can call other WinInet functions. To get connected to an Internet server, RAWHTML initializes an HTTP session by using the following code:

```
// Initialize HTTP session
HINTERNET hConnect = ::InternetConnect(hSession, m_strServer,
   INTERNET_INVALID_PORT_NUMBER, "", "",
   INTERNET_SERVICE_HTTP, 0, 0);
```

The second parameter, `m_strServer`, is a class data member that represents the name of the server you want to contact to get data. In this case, the server is `www.microsoft.com`, as specified in the `CRawHtmlDlg::OnInitDialog()` method by the following code:

```
// Set the default URL
m_editUrl.SetWindowText(
   "http://www.microsoft.com/msdownload/activex.htm");
```

The default URL is parsed into server and path components with the simple `CRawHtmlDlg::ParseURL()` method (refer to Listing 17.4).

The `InternetConnect()` function takes the HINTERNET returned from the previous call to `InternetOpen()` as its first parameter. The `InternetConnect()` function uses the following prototype:

```
HINTERNET InternetConnect(
    IN HINTERNET hInternetSession,
    IN LPCTSTR   lpszServerName,
    IN INTERNET_ PORT nServerPort,
    IN LPCTSTR   lpszUsername OPTIONAL,
    IN LPCTSTR   lpszPassword OPTIONAL,
    IN DWORD     dwService,
    IN DWORD     dwFlags,
    IN DWORD     dwContext
);
```

The parameters used for this function are as follows: :

■ `hInternetSession` is the handle of the current Internet session (returned by a previous call to `InternetOpen()`).

■ `lpszServerName` is a pointer to a string that contains the host name of an Internet server, or the IP number of the site (in ASCII dotted-decimal format).

■ `nServerPort` is the number of the TCP/IP port on the server to connect to. This can be one of the values in Table 17.7.

■ `lpszUsername` is a pointer to a string that contains the name of the user to log in.

■ `lpszPassword` is a pointer to a string that contains the password to use to log in.

■ `dwService` is the type of service to access, which can be any of the following values: `INTERNET_SERVICE_FTP` for FTP service, `INTERNET_SERVICE_GOPHER` for Gopher service, or `INTERNET_SERVICE_HTTP` for HTTP service.

■ `dwFlags` represents the flags specific to the service used. If `dwService` is `INTERNET_SERVICE_FTP`, then `INTERNET_CONNECT_FLAG_PASSIVE` should be used for this parameter, or you should use NULL.

■ `dwContext` is an application-defined value used to identify the application context for the returned handle in callbacks.

Table 17.7. The values predefined for the nServerPort parameter.

Value	Description
INTERNET_INVALID_PORT_NUMBER	The function uses the default port for the specified service.
INTERNET_DEFAULT_FTP_PORT	Use the default port for FTP servers (port 21).
INTERNET_DEFAULT_GOPHER_PORT	Use the default port for Gopher servers (port 70).
INTERNET_DEFAULT_HTTP_PORT	Use the default port for HTTP servers (port 80).
INTERNET_DEFAULT_HTTPS_PORT	Use the default port for HTTPS servers (port 443).

The `InternetConnect()` function is required before communicating with any Internet service, and RAWHTML calls the function like this in the `OnBtnGoClick()` method:

```
// Initialize HTTP session
HINTERNET hConnect = ::InternetConnect(hSession, m_strServer,
   INTERNET_INVALID_PORT_NUMBER, "", "",
   INTERNET_SERVICE_HTTP, 0, 0);
```

Opening the Desired File

After a connection to the Internet server is established, you can call the `HttpOpenRequest()` and `HttpSendRequest()` functions. These functions work together to open a file—in this case, the file stored in the `m_strPath` class data member.

The `HttpOpenRequest()` Function

The `HttpOpenRequest()` function sends the request parameters to the Internet service and returns a request handle. The prototype for this function is as follows:

```
HINTERNET HttpOpenRequest(
    IN HINTERNET hHttpSession,
    IN LPCTSTR lpszVerb,
    IN LPCTSTR lpszObjectName,
    IN LPCTSTR lpszVersion,
    IN LPCTSTR lpszReferer OPTIONAL,
    IN LPCTSTR FAR * lpszAcceptTypes OPTIONAL,
    IN DWORD dwFlags,
    IN DWORD dwContext
);
```

The parameters for this function are as follows:

- ■ `hHttpSession` is the handle to an HTTP session returned by `InternetConnect()`.

- ■ `lpszVerb` is a pointer to a string that contains the verb to use in the request. Typically GET is the verb, and this is the default.

- ■ `lpszObjectName` is a pointer to a string that contains the name of the target object (a filename, an executable module, or a search specifier) of the verb specified by `lpszVerb`.

- ■ `lpszVersion` is a pointer to a string that contains the HTTP version. If this parameter is NULL, the function uses HTTP/1.0 as the version.

- ■ `lpszReferer` is a pointer to a string that specifies the *referer*. The referer is the URL of the document from which `lpszObjectName` was obtained. Use NULL to specify no referer.

- ■ `lpszAcceptTypes` is a pointer to a null-terminated array of LPCTSTR pointers indicating content types accepted by the client.

- ■ `dwFlags` is a combination of any of the Internet flag values listed in Table 17.8.

- ■ `dwContext` is an application-defined value that associates this operation with any application data.

Table 17.8. The Internet flag values used for the `dwFlags` parameter.

Value	Meaning
INTERNET_FLAG_RELOAD	Get the data from the wire even if it is locally cached.
INTERNET_FLAG_DONT_CACHE	Do not cache the data, either locally or in any gateways.
INTERNET_FLAG_RAW_DATA	Return raw data (`WIN32_FIND_DATA` structures for FTP, and `GOPHER_FIND_DATA` structures for Gopher).
INTERNET_FLAG_SECURE	Request secure transactions on the wire with Secure Sockets Layer or PCT. This flag applies to HTTP requests only.
INTERNET_FLAG_EXISTING_CONNECT	If possible, reuse the existing connections to the server for new requests instead of creating a new session for each request.

The RAWHTML program calls the `HttpOpenRequest()` function as follows:

```
// Open an HTTP request handle
HINTERNET hHttpFile = ::HttpOpenRequest(hConnect, "GET",
   m_strPath, HTTP_VERSION, NULL, 0,
   INTERNET_FLAG_DONT_CACHE, 0);
```

The `HttpSendRequest()` Function

The `HttpSendRequest()` function sends the request parameters to the Internet service and returns a request handle. The prototype for this function is as follows:

```
BOOL HttpSendRequest(
   IN HINTERNET hHttpRequest,
   IN LPCTSTR   lpszHeaders OPTIONAL,
   IN DWORD     dwHeadersLength,
   IN LPVOID    lpOptional OPTIONAL,
   DWORD        dwOptionalLength
);
```

Here are the parameters for this function:

- `hHttpRequest` is an open HTTP request handle returned by `HttpOpenRequest()`.

- `lpszHeaders` is any additional headers to be appended to the request, or NULL if there are no additional headers to append.

- `dwHeadersLength` is the length, in characters, of the additional headers (if any).

- `lpOptional` is the address of any optional data to send immediately after the request headers, or NULL if there is no optional data to send.

- `dwOptionalLength` is the length, in bytes, of the optional data, or zero if there is no optional data to send.

The RAWHTML program calls the `HttpSendRequest()` function using all default values, as follows:

```
BOOL bSendRequest = ::HttpSendRequest(hHttpFile, NULL, 0, 0, 0);
```

Querying for Information

To get the size, in bytes, of the file you want to read, call the `HttpQueryInfo()` function (with a `HTTP_QUERY_CONTENT_LENGTH` flag to specify that you're looking for the file size). The prototype for this function is as follows:

```
BOOL HttpQueryInfo(
    IN HINTERNET hHttpRequest,
    IN DWORD dwInfoLevel,
    IN LPVOID lpvBuffer OPTIONAL,
    IN LPWORD lpvBufferLength,
    IN OUT LPWORD lpdwIndex OPTIONAL,
);
```

Here are the parameters for the function:

- ■ `hHttpRequest` is an open HTTP request handle returned by `HttpOpenRequest()`.

- ■ `dwInfoLevel` is a combination of the attribute to query and any flags that modify the request. Table 17.9 lists the possible query flags.

- ■ `lpvBuffer` is the address of the buffer that receives the information.

- ■ `lpdvBufferLength` is the address of a value that contains the length of the data buffer. When the function returns, this parameter contains the address of a value specifying the length of the information written to the buffer.

- ■ `lpdwIndex` is the address of a zero-based header index used to enumerate multiple headers with the same name.

Table 17.9. Possible query flags for the `dwInfoLevel` parameter.

Flag	Meaning
HTTP_QUERY_CUSTOM	If this query level is specified, `lpvBuffer` contains an ASCIIZ header name. This header name is searched for and its value is returned in `lpvBuffer` on output.
HTTP_QUERY_FLAG_COALESCE	Combine the values from several headers of the same name into the output buffer.
HTTP_QUERY_FLAG_REQUEST_HEADERS	Typically, response headers are queried, but an application can also query request headers by using this flag.

continues

Table 17.9. continued

Flag	Meaning
HTTP_QUERY_FLAG_SYSTEMTIME	For those headers whose value is a date/time string, such as "Last-Modified-Time", specifying this flag returns the header-value as a standard Win32 SYSTEMTIME structure, which does not require the application to parse the data.
HTTP_QUERY_FLAG_NUMBER	For headers whose value is a number, such as the status code, specifying this flag returns the data as a 32-bit number.

The RAWHTML program calls the HttpQueryInfo() function like this:

```
BOOL bQuery = ::HttpQueryInfo(hHttpFile,
    HTTP_QUERY_CONTENT_LENGTH, achQueryBuf,
    &dwQueryBufLen, NULL);
```

Reading the File Data

To actually read the file, now that you've made it this far, you must call the InternetReadFile() function, which has the following prototype:

```
BOOL InternetReadFile(
    IN HINTERNET  hFile,
    IN LPVOID     lpBuffer,
    IN DWORD      dwNumberOfBytesToRead,
    OUT LPDWORD   lpNumberOfBytesRead
);
```

The parameters for this function are as follows: :

■ hFile is a valid handle returned from a previous call to InternetOpenUrl(), FtpOpenFile(), GopherOpenFile(), or HttpOpenRequest().

■ lpBuffer is the address of a buffer that receives the data read from the file.

■ dwNumberOfBytesToRead is the number of bytes to read from the file.

■ lpNumberOfBytesRead is the address of a variable that receives the actual number of bytes read. If dwNumberOfBytesToRead is larger than the actual number of bytes in the file, use this parameter to determine the actual number of bytes read from file.

The RAWHTML program uses the following code to read the file data:

```
// Allocate a buffer for the file data
char* lpszBuf = new char[dwFileSize + 1];

// Read the file
DWORD dwBytesRead;
BOOL bRead = ::InternetReadFile(hHttpFile, lpszBuf,
    dwFileSize + 1, &dwBytesRead);
```

The code is displayed in the `m_editHtml` edit control with a simple call to `SetWindowText()`, as follows:

```
m_editHtml.SetWindowText((LPCTSTR)lpszBuffer);
```

> **NOTE**
>
> To keep the code short and as simple as possible, error checking for this sample program is minimal. In a real-world application, you would certainly want to provide much better error trapping.

Summary

The Win32 Internet functions bring the tools needed to create professional quality Internet access applications well within the reach of most Windows programmers. By providing an insulating layer over the underlying WinSock API, the WinInet API makes Internet programming much easier than ever before!

Here are some points to remember:

- The WinInet API functions are built on the Windows Sockets protocol.
- The WinInet API supports the FTP, Gopher, and HTTP protocols.

17

USING THE
WIN32 INTERNET
(WININET) API

IN THIS PART

III

PART

Internet Scripting Languages

JavaScript and the Internet

by Bill Anderson

IN THIS CHAPTER

CHAPTER 18

Until the proposal of the Multipurpose Internet Mail Extensions (MIME) protocol in 1993, the Internet was a text-oriented environment. The only way to view non-text files was by downloading files via File Transfer Protocol (FTP). Even the Gopher and the first HTML 1.0 protocols require FTP to transfer image files. Although the MIME RFC is an extension to the mail format, the advent of MIME opened the door for a way to introduce non-text documents into Gopher and HTML. The NCSA Web browser provided the first graphical interface for the MIME-enhanced HTML.

Whether it was graphics, sound, movies, word processing documents, or postscript documents, the MIME format gave the information provider a multitude of options for presenting information to the consumer. Using the MIME types, people entered millions of documents to create a virtual worldwide library without the restrictions of traditional information media, but it was not enough. Traditional media lacked a way to interact with the information consumer. Although a lot of files included the `mailto:` scheme in their URL as a method for user feedback, the document was still static. The section on CGI scripts shows the first major step toward creating interactive HTML. With CGI, the server handles all decisions. The client side (the browser) acts only to input data to the CGI script and display any resulting output. The HTML document itself contains no programs or decision logic. The introduction of Java and JavaScript changed the fundamental nature of the HTML document itself.

What Is JavaScript?

Netscape introduced JavaScript as LiveScript in the Netscape Navigator 2.0 beta. When it released version 2.0, the name changed to JavaScript. At the time of its release, many companies hailed the new scripting language as a major step toward enhancing the capabilities of HTML and for the creation and customization of applications for both the Internet and intranets. Both Netscape and Sun Microsystems proposed to introduce JavaScript to the World Wide Web (WWW) consortium and to IETF (Internet Engineering Task Force) as an open Internet scripting language standard. Netscape and Sun hope to encourage the adoption of JavaScript as a widespread Internet standard by making it an open Internet standard, by giving a JavaScript license to Java licensees, and by providing a source code reference implementation of JavaScript.

JavaScript is an easy to learn scripting language designed to create dynamic online applications. These applications link together objects and resources on both the client and the server. Because there are different products for the client side and the server side of the equation, the following discussion reviews JavaScript, as implemented in Netscape Navigator versions 2.0 and 3.0. The focus then changes to the server side and LiveWire.

The Client-Side Features of JavaScript

Netscape created JavaScript as a scripting language for use within the `<SCRIPT>...</SCRIPT>` tags. JavaScript is a completely separate language from Java. Because it is a scripting language, the browser interprets the script after it loads the HTML document. The power of JavaScript derives from the following characteristics:

- It is simple
- It is dynamic
- It is object-based

JavaScript Is Simple

Because JavaScript is a simple scripting language, the Web page developer can create a dynamic Web page without needing to become a programmer. At the same time, programmers can use it to implement Java applets within a Web page.

> **NOTE**
>
> JavaScript is not a programming language; it is a scripting language used within an HTML document. As a scripting language, JavaScript is interpreted and not compiled. Furthermore, its syntax enables a non-programmer to add functionality to his Web pages without first having to acquire a background in programming techniques.

Every language has a role to play. The role of JavaScript is to provide a simple tool that extends the functionality of HTML. The complex tasks are left to plug-ins and Java applets.

JavaScript Is Dynamic

A Web page becomes *dynamic* when it responds to events generated by the user or other objects. With traditional HTML documents, server-side applications had the responsibility of handling events. JavaScript transfers event management to the client side. This makes Web page design more flexible, more dynamic, and more responsive. The trend in programming is to transfer more work to the client, leaving the server to handle the requests of more clients.

JavaScript Is Object-Based

JavaScript is not an object-oriented language like Java or C++, but it interacts with objects. An object-oriented programming language includes classes, inheritance, and strong variable typing, all of which JavaScript lacks. However, it does interact with objects that expose themselves to the scripting environment. JavaScript can, therefore, access objects in the Netscape browser (such as display characteristics or a URL). In Netscape Navigator 2.0, JavaScript can invoke plug-ins or applets. And now, with the release of version 3.0, it can communicate with plug-ins and applets. This capability to interact with different objects gives JavaScript a flexibility beyond that of more complex programs.

Java Versus JavaScript

The similarity of names reflects the commonality of Java and JavaScript. However, even though the JavaScript language resembles Java, it is not a simplified form of Java. JavaScript supports most of Java's expression, syntax, and flow control constructs, but does not support classes or inheritance. JavaScript supports a small number of dynamic data types (numeric, Boolean, and string) that are not typed, whereas Java supports a rich variety of data types that are static and have strong type checking.

JavaScript complements Java by enabling Web page developers to take advantage of the exposed properties of Java applets. JavaScript can get and set exposed properties, which enable it to alter the performance of both applets and plug-ins. Table 18.1 compares the features of JavaScript and Java.

Table 18.1. Comparison of Java and JavaScript.

JavaScript	*Java*
Interpreted by the client	Compiled before execution on client
Object-based	Object-oriented
Integrated with HTML	Applets are distinct applications
Variable types not declared	Strong typing of variables
Dynamic binding of object references	Static binding at compile time

New Features of JavaScript in Netscape Navigator 3.0

With the release of Netscape Navigator 3.0, the people at Netscape added several new features to JavaScript:

- The capability to change GIF and JPEG images automatically, at specified time intervals, or by clicking a button or an icon
- The capability to detect the presence of plug-ins on a Web page and then tailor the user interface according to the plug-ins available

Netscape Navigator 3.0 includes LiveConnect, which enables

- JavaScript to communicate with plug-ins on the same page and vice versa
- Java applets to communicate with JavaScripts running on the same page and vice versa

Web page designers can use LiveConnect to synchronize video and audio files. For example, you can use LiveConnect to make an event trigger an audible alert. With this enhanced communication, JavaScript could collect data from Java applets by accessing its public objects. With all the features of JavaScript, Web pages no longer need to be static documents.

The Server Side of JavaScript

On the server side of the equation, Netscape provides LiveWire for managing Web sites and creating server software. LiveWire consists of the LiveWire Site Manager, LiveWire JavaScript Compiler, and the LiveWire Database Connectivity Library. The JavaScript Compiler and the Database Connectivity Library are the most important features to the programmer.

Netscape servers include the capability to run compiled JavaScript applications. With this addition, the programmer can create platform-independent server applications. When combined with the Database Connectivity Library, server applications can make direct SQL connections to databases from Oracle, Sybase, Informics, and Illustra. The Database Connectivity Library also supports ODBC access to other databases. LiveWire provides an important dimension to applications development. While the server-side features of LiveWire extend the use of JavaScript, these chapters on JavaScript concentrate on the use of JavaScript in HTML documents.

When To Use JavaScript

Whenever you learn about a new language, you probably want to know the best uses for the language. JavaScript is still a young and maturing scripting language, so the following indicate potential uses of this new language:

- It moves much of the action from the server to the client, which lessens the load on the server.
- It enables you to locally validate forms fields before submitting the form to the server.
- It enables HTML documents to respond to local events such as choosing user alternatives and finding out the availability of plug-ins.
- It enables the Web page developer to communicate information to and from applets and plug-ins.
- With server-side JavaScript, each user can have a unique personalized profile that enables them to have a customized Web page.
- Server-side JavaScript also enables users to access popular databases via SQL or ODBC.

With the advent of Java and JavaScript, the days of static HTML documents are over. A new era of interactive user participation, via the Internet and intranets, is now open.

The Limitations of JavaScript

As mentioned previously, JavaScript is a scripting language and not a full-blown, object-oriented programming language. JavaScript was not designed to build complex applications.

At the present, JavaScript exists only in Netscape Navigator, Netscape server products, and Microsoft Internet Explorer 3.0. Anyone designing a Web page for a wider audience must consider this in their Web page design. For example, although JavaScript can eliminate the necessity of using CGI scripts for forms verification, using JavaScript for this purpose would disable users of other Web browsers from forms validation. To design a Web page for a diverse audience, the Web page designer must write CGI scripts that determine whether or not editing is required according to the user's Web browser.

Unfortunately, the rapid growth of JavaScript created a problem with different versions implemented by different products. Netscape Navigator 2.*x* and LiveWire use JavaScript version 1.0. Netscape Navigator 3.0 implements JavaScript version 1.1. Microsoft Internet Explorer 3.0 adds another layer of confusion by using a variation of JavaScript 1.0 called Jscript. All these flavors of JavaScript means that the Web page developer must consider the intended audience when writing his scripts.

When JavaScript was first released, it enabled the sending of mail messages without user knowledge, the reading of the URL history, the reading of directories, and the reading of files. Although these features had valid purposes, hackers used them to gain unauthorized information about the user's system or network. Moreover, because JavaScript is part of an HTML document that flows freely through a firewall, it defeated the protection provided by firewalls that prevented unauthorized users from gaining this information.

In addition, Netscape Navigator 2.0 had a defect termed "stuck onLoad" that enabled a window created in the page to stay open even after the user exited the page. By creating a one-pixel by one-pixel window, hackers could continue to gather information about the user's system, network, or sites visited. Because the window would appear as a very small dot on the screen, the hacker could gather the information without the user knowing it. With the release of Netscape Navigator 3.0, Netscape closed all known security holes. Users of Netscape Navigator 2.0 need to upgrade to version 2.02 or Netscape Navigator 3.0 to close these potential security loopholes. Table 18.2 shows the various problems and the releases that fixed the problems.

Table 18.2. JavaScript security fixes.

Problem	Corrected in release
Capability to read directories	2.01
Capability to track history	2.02
The stuck onload defect	3.0b
Capability to send mail	2.01

With these loopholes closed, users can once again safely use JavaScript. However, they must upgrade to the most current release.

Summary

JavaScript is a new and powerful scripting language that enables Web page developers to write dynamic interactive documents with less reliance on writing server-side scripts. As an object-based language, JavaScript enables the developer to write Web pages that interact with Java applets and plug-ins. The door is now open to a new era of Web page development.

18

JAVASCRIPT AND THE INTERNET

CHAPTER 19

The JavaScript Language

by Bill Anderson

IN THIS CHAPTER

Chapter 18, "JavaScript and the Internet," introduced the purpose and design of the JavaScript language. As mentioned previously, JavaScript is a scripting language used in HTML documents. This chapter shows you how to write JavaScript routines to make dynamic and interactive Web pages. Although LiveWire provides the compiler necessary to create server-side JavaScript applications, this chapter concentrates on using JavaScript in client-side extensions to HTML documents.

> **NOTE**
>
> This chapter assumes that you have a background in creating HTML documents. If you are just getting your feet wet in Internet programming, you should read Chapters 25, "HyperText Markup Language (HTML)" and 27, "Netscape Extensions," before proceeding with this chapter.

This chapter takes you on a fast-paced tour of the JavaScript language. Besides requiring a background in HTML, this chapter also assumes that you have a basic background in programming.

Embedding JavaScript in HTML

There are two ways to incorporate JavaScript in an HTML document:

- By surrounding JavaScript with the `<SCRIPT>...</SCRIPT>` tags
- By using HTML tags to handle events

Using the `<SCRIPT>` Tag

Although Netscape Navigator treats any text bounded by the `<SCRIPT>` tag as JavaScript, the LANGUAGE option declares what scripting language is being used. Because there are other scripting languages for HTML, declaring the name of the scripting language used is good programming practice. Books on programming often start with a simple program that prints `Hello World`. Listing 19.1 shows the JavaScript version of Hello World.

> **NOTE**
>
> I recommend that you enter the JavaScript examples shown in this chapter and see the results.

Listing 19.1. The JavaScript version of Hello World.

```
<HTML>
<HEAD>
<SCRIPT LANGUAGE="JavaScript">
<!-- Hide the script
document.write("Hello world.")
// end hiding -->
</SCRIPT>
</HEAD>
<BODY>
<BR>
This is the first script.
</BODY>
</HTML>
```

Listing 19.1 shows the JavaScript embedded between the <HEAD> and </HEAD> tags. If the JavaScript for Hello World were placed between the <BODY> tags, the script would give the same results as the script in Listing 19.1. Because the heading statements are read before statements in between the <BODY> tags, it is a good programming practice to place all functions and global variable definitions in the heading. By the same token, JavaScript statements related to the document should be placed in the body of the HTML document.

Not every browser processes JavaScript. To keep the HTML document from having errors in these browsers, you need to bracket the body of the script with the comment delimiters:

```
<!-- Hide script form non-JavaScript browser
// End of hidden text -->
```

> **TIP**
>
> Always bracket JavaScript with comment lines so that non-JavaScript browsers ignore any JavaScript statements.

Handling Events

Events turn a static page into a dynamic interactive page. Events result from user actions, such as clicking a mouse button, submitting a form, or exiting a page. Netscape recognizes a certain number of events, such as those involving the use of windows or forms. Instead of discussing events at this point, the events and their related event handlers occur throughout this chapter. In Netscape Navigator 3.0, the source of events expands to include those generated in plug-ins and Java applets.

Variables and Literals

Unlike Java, JavaScript recognizes only a few types of values. They are as follows:

- Numbers, both real and integer (such as 4.156 and 39)
- Strings (such as `"this is JavaScript"`)
- Logical (Boolean) values of true and false
- Null, which is a special keyword denoting a null value

Although the number of data types is small, they are sufficient for the tasks that JavaScript performs. Notice that there is no distinction between integers and real numbers; both data types are just numbers. JavaScript does not provide an explicit data type for a date. However, there are related functions and a built-in date object that enable the Web page designer to manage dates.

Defining Variables

The naming rules for variables require that a variable name begins with a letter or underscore (_) and that the remaining characters are either numbers (0-9), uppercase (A-Z) or lowercase letters (a-z), or the underscore. Following are examples of legal variable names:

```
First_Name
t99
_name
```

> **NOTE**
>
> JavaScript does not check the spelling of variable names. Therefore, the programmer is responsible for the correct spelling of all names. When variables contain unexpected values, check to be sure that the names are spelled correctly.

The only other restriction on variable names is that they must not be the same as a JavaScript reserved word. Table 19.1 lists the JavaScript reserved words.

Table 19.1. JavaScript reserved words.

abstract	extends	int	super
boolean	false	interface	switch
break	final	long	synchronized
byte	finally	native	this
case	float	new	throw

catch	for	null	throws
char	function	package	transient
class	goto	private	true
const	if	protected	try
continue	implements	public	var
default	import	return	val
do	in	short	while
double	instanceof	static	with
else			

Not every word in Table 19.1 is currently used in JavaScript; some are reserved for future use. The reserved words cannot be used for variable names, function names, method names, or object names.

A variable in JavaScript accepts all valid data types. There is no way to automatically force strong typing of data. In the same script, variables can be set to different data types or even mixed data types in a single declaration. The following variable declarations are all valid:

```
temperature =
temperature = "The temperature is"
temperature = "The temperature is " +
```

Because JavaScript is loosely typed, it provides several functions for the manipulation of string and numeric values. The section "Built-In Functions" discusses the `eval`, `parseInt`, and `parseFloat` functions.

Scope of Variables

JavaScript supports two variable scopes:

- Global variables
- Local variables

The local variable applies only within a function and limits the scope of the variable to that function. To declare a local variable, the variable name must be preceded by `var`, as shown following:

```
var MaxValue=0
```

JavaScript considers any variable declaration not preceded by `var` as a global variable. Although JavaScript permits you to use the same variable name for local and global variables, it is not a recommended practice.

> **TIP**
>
> To ensure that functions inherit the correct value for a global variable, declare all global variables at the beginning of the script.

Literally Literals

As opposed to variables, literals represent the fixed values used in JavaScript. JavaScript supports the following literals:

- Integer literals
- Floating point literals
- Boolean literals
- String literals
- Special characters

Integers can be in decimal, hexadecimal, or octal format. A decimal integer is any sequence of digits that is not prefixed by a zero (such as 4, 89, or 157). If the integer is prefixed by a zero, it is an octal value (such as 04, 065, or 0145). An integer expressed in hexadecimal format is prefixed by 0x or 0X (such as 0xff, 0X44, or 0xAE).

A floating-point literal consists of the following components: a decimal integer, a decimal point (.), a decimal fraction, and an exponent. This format allows for both fractional literals (such as 1.23 or 44.6389) or those expressed in scientific notation (3.6E-8, .4E12, or -2.7E12). Every floating-point literal must have at least one digit and a decimal point or an exponent.

Boolean literals are straightforward. Their values are either true or false.

String literals can be enclosed by either single (') or double quotes ("). The beginning and ending quote mark must be the same, as shown in the following examples:

```
"a double quoted literal"
'a single quoted literal'
```

> **TIP**
>
> When you write event handlers, enclose string literals in single quotes because double quotes delimit attribute values.

String literals also might contain special characters to provide a limited degree of line control. Table 19.2 lists the special characters and their functions.

Table 19.2. JavaScript special characters.

Description	Special character
Backspace	\b
Form feed	\f
Newline	\n
Carriage return	\r
Tab	\t

The backslash (\) is the escape character for JavaScript. When used at the end of a line, it acts as a line continuation character. When followed by another character, it escapes that character so that the following character loses its special function. In JavaScript, the programmer uses the backslash to escape another backslash, a single quote, or a double quote.

Expressions and Operators

When literals and variables are linked by operators, the resulting statement is an *expression*. Examples of different types of expressions are the assignment of a literal to a variable or the computation of several literals using mathematical operators. JavaScript provides a rich variety of operators that enable programmers to write expressions ranging from the most simple to the very complex.

The JavaScript operators fall into the following categories:

- Assignment operators
- Arithmetic operators
- Bitwise operators
- Logical operators
- Comparison operators
- String operators

JavaScript includes both binary and unary operators. A binary operator has the format

```
operand1 operator operand2
```

For example, `9 * 7` or `temp = 24` are expressions with binary operators.

The unary operator has two formats:

```
operand operator
```

or

```
operator operand
```

Examples of expressions using unary operators are ++y or y++.

Assignment Operators

The assignment operator (=) is a binary operator that assigns a value to the left operand (usually a variable) based on the value of the right operand (such as FirstName = "John" or x = y * 9). For simple right-hand expressions, JavaScript prefixes the assignment operator with either an arithmetic or bitwise operator. Table 19.3 lists these shorthand assignment operators.

Table 19.3. JavaScript shorthand assignment operators.

Shorthand operator	Meaning	Example
x += y	x = x + Y	x +=
x -= y	x = x - y	x -=
x *= y	x = x * y	x *=
x /= y	x = x / y	x /=
x %= y	x = x % y	x %=
x <<= y	x = x << y	x <<=
x >>= y	x = x >> y	x >>=
x >>>= y	x = x >>> y	x >>>=
x &= y	x = x & y	x &= 0xC0
x ¦= y	x = x ¦ y	x ¦= 0x0F
x ^= y	x = x ^ y	x ^= 0XFF

NOTE

For those who are not familiar with C programming, be careful of the difference between the assignment operator (=) and the comparison operator (==).

Arithmetic Operators

According to the specified arithmetic operators, the purpose of arithmetic operators is to compute a single numerical value from the numerical values of either literals or variables. JavaScript supports the standard arithmetic operators of addition (+), subtraction (-), multiplication (*), and division (/). It also includes operators for modulus (%), increment (++), decrement (--), and unary negation (-).

The modulus operator (%) is a binary operator that returns the remainder of the integral division of *operand1* by *operand2*. For example, the result of 27 % 6 is 4.

The increment unary operators add one to the operand, while the decrement unary operators subtract one from it. However, the value returned depends on the order of the operator and the operand. If the operator is prefix (++x or --x), the value returned is x+1 or x-1, accordingly. When the operator is postfix (x++ or x--), the value returned is x before it is incremented or decremented.

The other special unary arithmetic operator is the unary negation operator. It reverses the sign of the value assigned to a variable. For example, if x = -7, -x changes the value to 7.

Bitwise Operators

For those programmers who need to fiddle with bits, JavaScript provides a set of bitwise operators. For these operators, JavaScript converts the operand into a 32-bit integer before it performs the operation specified by the operator. The bitwise logical operators are

- Bitwise AND (&), which returns the results of the logical AND between each pair of bits. For example, 0x0f & 0x0a returns 0x0a.
- Bitwise OR (¦), which returns the results of the logical OR between each pair of bits. For example, 0x05 ¦ 0x0a returns 0x0f.
- Bitwise XOR (^), which returns the results of the logical exclusive OR between each pair of bits. For example, 0x0f ^ 0x0a returns 0x05.

JavaScript also provides a set of bitwise shift operators that shift the bits of *operand1* by the amount specified in *operand2*. These operands are

- Shift left (<<), which rotates the bits to the left by the amount specified. Excess bits shifted off to the left are discarded, while zero bits are shifted in from the right. For example, 0x0f << 2 returns 0x3c.
- Sign propagating shift right (>>) keeps the value of the sign while shifting bits to the right by the amount specified. Excess bits shifted to the right are discarded, while, excluding the sign bit, zero bits are shifted in from the left. For example, 10 >> 2 returns 2 and -10 >> 2 returns -2.

- Zero-fill right shift (>>>) does not preserve the sign bit while shifting bits to the right by the amount specified. Excess bits shifted to the right are discarded while zero bits are shifted in from the left. For positive numbers, the results are the same as the sign propagating shift right. However, for negative numbers, the sign is lost.

Logical Operators

The logical operators require that the operands are Boolean values (true or false) and they return a logical value. In the case of logical operators, the operands are expressions that evaluate to a logical value. The logical operators are

- Logical AND (&&)
- Logical OR (¦¦)
- Logical NOT (!)

The logical NOT operator is a unary operator that reverses the Boolean value of the expression.

> **NOTE**
>
> JavaScript performs a short-circuit evaluation on logical operations so that `false&&expr` resolves to false and `true¦¦expr` resolves to true. Under these cases, expr is not evaluated.

Comparison Operators

The comparison operators apply to comparisons between numerical and string values and not to Boolean values. Both operands must be of the same type: numbers compared to numbers or strings compared to strings. The result of a comparison, however, is a Boolean value. The comparison operators are

- Equal (==)
- Not equal (!=)
- Greater than (>)
- Greater than or equal to (>=)
- Less than (<)
- Less than or equal to (<=)

JavaScript also supports the conditional expression that takes the form

```
(condition) ? true_value : false_value
```

If the condition is true, the expression has the value of *true_value*. Otherwise, it has the value of *false_value*. Like its cousins in other C-based languages, the conditional expression is like a standard expression and can be used anywhere, as shown in the following:

```
battery_status = (voltage > 1.3) ? "good" : "weak"
```

String Operators

The string operator (+) concatenates two string values and returns a string that is a union of the two values. For example, the expression

```
"Java" + "Script"
```

returns

```
"JavaScript"
```

The shorthand operator += concatenates the string in the left operand with that in the right operand and assigns the new value to the left operand.

Order of Precedence

In complex expressions involving more than one operator, the precedence of the operators determines the order of evaluation. By using parentheses, the programmer overrides these rules. Table 19.4 shows the order of precedence from lowest to highest.

Table 19.4. JavaScript operator precedence from lowest to highest.

Description	Operators
Assignment	= += -= *= /= %= <<= >>= >>>= &= ^= ¦=
Conditional	?:
Logical OR	¦¦
Logical AND	&&
Bitwise OR	¦
Bitwise XOR	^
Bitwise AND	&
Equality	== !=
Relational	< <= > >=
Bitwise shift	<< >> >>>
Addition/subtraction	+ -
Multiply/divide	* / %
Negation/increment	! ~ - ++ —
Call, member	() []

19

Control Statements and Functions

To make a page dynamic and interactive, the Web page developer needs statements that control the flow of information. Depending on computation results or input from the users, the script makes decisions that alter the path of execution. This section covers the conditional and loop statements provided in JavaScript.

Although all of the code could be written in the event handlers, this is not good programming practice. Instead, by using functions, code becomes modularized and reusable. A discussion of the function statement and a more formal discussion of comments round out this section. There are some details of the function statement that apply to objects; the next section covers these details and other control statements related to objects.

Conditional Statements

In addition to the conditional expression discussed in the previous section, JavaScript has one conditional statement—the `if` statement. The syntax of the conditional statement is as follows:

```
if (condition) {
    statements1 }
[else {
    statements2}]
```

The *condition* is any JavaScript expression that evaluates to the Boolean type, either true or false. The conditional *statement* is a JavaScript statement (including another `if`) or JavaScript expression. The following is an example of a valid `if` statement:

```
if (n>3) {
    status = true
    if (j != n) j = 0 }
else j = n
```

> **CAUTION**
>
> C programmers beware of the JavaScript rules for condition evaluation: A numerical condition evaluating to zero is not the equivalent of a Boolean true in JavaScript. Conversely, a non-zero number is not the same as a Boolean false. In JavaScript, the result of the condition must be a Boolean data type.

When there is only a single statement, the braces are not necessary. For example, the following is a legal statement:

```
if (a==b) j=0
else j=1
```

Loop Statements

JavaScript supports two loop structures: the for statement and the while statement. For control within the loop structure, JavaScript provides the break and continue statements.

The for Statement

The JavaScript for statement is the same as the one for Java and C. The for statement repeats a loop until the specified condition evaluates to true or the loop is exited by a break statement. The syntax of the for statement is as follows:

```
for ([initial-expression;] [condition;] [increment-expression]) {
    statements
}
```

The order of processing for the for statement is as follows:

1. The interpreter executes the *initial-expression*. This expression initializes any values needed for loop control.

2. The interpreter then checks the *condition*. If it is true, control passes to the next step. If it is false, control goes to the next statement after the loop.

3. The interpreter then executes the *increment-expression*, which updates the variables used for loop control.

4. The statements then are executed and, unless a break or continue statement is encountered, control returns to step 2.

Listing 19.2 is an example of a for statement.

Listing 19.2. Example of a JavaScript for loop.

```
<HTML>
<HEAD>
<SCRIPT LANGUAGE="JavaScript">
<!-- hide script
for (i=1; i<=10; i++) {
    sq=i*i
    document.write("number: " + i + "square: " + sq + "<BR>")
}
// end script hiding -->
</SCRIPT>
</HEAD>
<BODY>
</BODY>
</HTML>
```

19

THE JAVASCRIPT
LANGUAGE

The while Statement

The while statement continues to repeat the loop as long as the *condition* is true. The syntax for the while statement is as follows:

```
while (condition) {
    statements
}
```

The condition test occurs when the loop in the while statement is first executed and at the end of every loop. When the test returns false, control passes to the next statement after the loop. The for statement turning into a while loop is shown in Listing 19.3.

Listing 19.3. Example of a JavaScript while loop.

```
<HTML>
<HEAD>
<SCRIPT LANGUAGE="JavaScript">
<!-- hide script
i=1
while (i<=10) {
    sq=i*i
    document.write("number: " + i + "square: " + sq + "<BR>")
    i++
}
// end script hiding -->
</SCRIPT>
</HEAD>
<BODY>
</BODY>
</HTML>
```

The break Statement

The break statement terminates the for or while loop and returns control to the next statement following the terminated loop. The following example illustrates how to use the break statement:

```
i=0
while (i<10) {
    if (i==3)
        break
    i++
}
```

The continue Statement

Like the break statement, the continue statement terminates the current iteration of a for or while loop; it does not exit the loop. Where it picks up the next iteration depends on the type of loop.

■ In a while loop, control passes to the *condition*.

■ In a for loop, it passes to the *increment-expression*.

The following shows an example of how to use the continue statement:

```
i=0
while (i<10) {
   if (i==3)
      continue
   i++
}
```

The function Statement

A function is a group of JavaScript statements that performs a specified task. This function can then be called from any point in the document and plays an important role in writing event handlers. The format of the function statement is as follows:

```
function FunctionName(argument list) {
   statements
}
```

The Hello World script example turns into a function like the one shown in Listing 19.4.

Listing 19.4. Hello World as a function.

```
<HTML>
<HEAD>
<SCRIPT LANGUAGE="JavaScript"
<!-- hide the script
function DisplayIt(LineToDisplay) {
   document.write(LineToDisplay + "<BR>")
}
// end hiding -->
</SCRIPT>
</HEAD>
<BODY>
<SCRIPT LANGUAGE="JavaScript"
<!-- hide it
LineToDisplay("Hello World")
// end hiding -->
</SCRIPT>
</BODY>
</HTML>
```

19

THE JAVASCRIPT
LANGUAGE

TIP

Because the browser reads the statements bound by <HEAD>...</HEAD> first, it is good practice to initialize all global variables and define all functions in the HEAD of the document. This prevents errors from non-initialized variables and undefined functions.

The arguments to a function are any JavaScript data types or objects. The array object `functionName.argument[i]`, where `functionName.arguments.length` contains the total number of arguments passed to the function, references arguments by the declared variable names. This feature enables a variable number of arguments to be passed to the function as an argument array. Listing 19.5 illustrates the use of a variable argument list.

Listing 19.5. JavaScript with a variable number of arguments.

```
<HTML>
<HEAD>
<SCRIPT LANGUAGE="JavaScript">
<!-- hide it
UnorderList="UL"
function DisplayList(ListType) {                // Display Variable List
    if (ListType="OL" || ListType="UL") {       // Validate ListType
        document.write("<" + ListType + ">"      // Display type of list
        for (var i=1; i<DisplayList.arguments.length; i++)
            document.write("LI" + DisplayList.arguments[i])
        document.write("</" + ListType + ">")     // End list
        return true
    }
    else return false
}
// end hiding -->
</SCRIPT>
</HEAD>
<BODY>
<SCRIPT LANGUAGE="JavaScript"
<!-- hide it
if (DisplayList(UnorderList, "Bullet 1 text", "Bullet 2 text"))
    document.write("<P>List Display</P>")
else
    document.write("<P>Invalid List Type<p>")
// unhide it -->
</SCRIPT>
</BODY>
</HTML>
```

Listing 19.5 illustrates several important features of functions. A global variable is initialized in the `<HEAD>`. The var statement declared `i` to be a local variable of the function. It also shows how the `return` statement can be used to ensure that a function executed properly. The return statement can also return string and numerical values, as the following illustrates:

```
function RetExam(a, b) {
    var x=0
    x = a+b
    return x
}

TestResult=RetExam(5, 7)
```

Comments

JavaScript supports the two Java style formats:

- The single-line comment preceded by a double slash (//)
- The multiple-line comment preceded by a /* and terminated by a */

The single-line comment, from C++, treats everything from the double slash to the end of the line as a comment. Thus, the following are valid examples of a single-line comment:

```
// this is a comment
if (a=b) c=1 // also a valid comment
```

The multiple-line comment follows the rules of its C equivalent and can be used to bracket any comment. The comment used to bracket the JavaScript statements, as shown in the previous examples, is an HTML comment. However, the last line of the comment needs the double slash to keep JavaScript from interpreting the line.

Fundamentals of Objects

JavaScript is an object-based language and not an object-oriented programming (OOP) language. The designers of JavaScript were not trying to create another OOP; instead, they sought to create a scripting language that provided a tool for integrating objects created with an OOP language into an HTML document. Thus, although JavaScript lacks encapsulation, inheritance, and abstraction features of C++ or Java, it has the means to access their external objects. The ability to access Java applets and plug-ins is limited in version 2.0 of Netscape Navigator, but LiveConnect and the enhanced JavaScript in version 3.0 fully support these features.

Although it lacks the Java class structure, the JavaScript class provides properties and methods for the creation objects. In addition to providing reusable objects, the object provides a means for JavaScript to implement arrays.

Objects and Their Properties

The following shows the notational system used by JavaScript to represent an object and its properties:

```
ObjectName.PropertyName
```

Without calling them objects, this chapter already used several objects and their properties: *ObjectName.arguments* and *ObjectName.arguments.length*. In addition to being referenced by name, JavaScript supports two methods of array referencing: by property name and by an index. For example, the object mydog has the following properties:

```
mydog.breed="small mut"
mydog.age=5
mydog.weight=25
```

The object also could be referenced as an array using the property name as an index:

```
mydog["breed"]="small mut"
mydog["age"]=5
mydog["weight"]=25
```

It also could be referenced as an array using the numerical index:

```
mydog[0]="small mut"
mydog[1]=5
mydog[2]=25
```

Defining Methods

A function associated with an object is referred to as a *method.* After defining a function in the manner described in the "Control Statements and Functions" section of this chapter, the following format associates the function with an object:

```
ObjectName.MethodName = function_name
```

The method then is referenced in the context of working with an object:

```
ObjectName.MethodName(parameters);
```

Before providing an example, I need to cover the JavaScript statements used to work with objects.

Working with Objects

The manipulation of objects requires these additional JavaScript features: for...in statement, with statement, new operator, and this keyword. Only a short description of these features is necessary, because other sections explore them in further detail.

The for...in Statement

The for...in statement provides a loop mechanism for iteration through all of the properties of an object. Its format is as follows:

```
for (variable in Objectname) {
    statements
}
```

The following example uses this statement to list the properties in an object and their associated values:

```
function ListProperties(obj, obj_name) {
    var result = ""
    for (var i in obj) {
        result += obj_name + "." + i " = " + obj[i] + "<BR>"
    }
    return result
PropList = ListProperties(mydog, "mydog")
```

In the preceding example, the variable i is the name of the property. The example then indexes the object using the property name—obj[i].

The **with** Statement

In some situations the same object is referenced several times. The `with` statement establishes a default object for a bracketed set of statements. Its format is as follows:

```
with (ObjectName) {
    statements
i
```

The `Math` object provides an example of how to use the `with` statement:

```
var r =
var x =
with (Math) {
    r = p / (1 - cos(a))
    x = (2 * p * cos(a)) / (sin(a) * sin(a))
}
```

The **new** Operand

For a user-defined object type, the `new` operand provides a means of creating a new instance of that object type. The syntax of this operand is as follows:

```
ObjectName = new ObjectType(param1 [, param2,] … [, paramN])
```

The section "Creating New Objects" contains examples of the use of this operand.

The **this** Keyword

`this` refers to the current object. As the next section shows, it plays an important role in the writing of functions and methods.

Creating New Objects

Although JavaScript contains a large number of predefined objects, the developer can create additional user-defined objects. The creation of objects requires the developer to perform two steps:

1. Define the object type by writing a function.
2. Create instances of the object using the `new` operand.

The function defines the object type, the properties, and the methods. For example, to create an object type for dogs, the following function needs to be written:

```
function dog(breed, age, weight) {
    this.breed = breed;
    this.age = age;
    this.weight = weight;
}
```

In the preceding example, the `this` keyword refers to the instance of the object being created. It is important to note that the assignment of values to a property requires that the statement end with a semicolon.

Using this function, the new operand defines a new instance of the object. For example,

```
mydog = new dog("small mut", 5, 25);
```

In addition to the regular JavaScript data types (string, numeric, and Boolean), another object can be the property of an object. For example, to add a license number to the object type for a dog, the license number also could refer to another object.

```
function doglicense(owner, phone_number) {
   this.owner = owner;
   this.phone_number = phone.number;
}

AZ123 = new doglicense("John Smith", "999-9999");
```

The object type then needs to be modified to include the new information:

```
function dog(breed, age, weight, license) {
   this.breed = breed;
   this.age = age;
   this.weight = weight;
   this.license = license;
}

mydog = new dog("mixed mut", 5, 25, AZ123);
```

To reference the owner of *mydog*, the syntax would be

```
mydog.license.owner
```

> **NOTE**
>
> If a new property is added to an object without changing the object type, the additional property only affects that object and not all other instances of the object type.

> **NOTE**
>
> A string variable or a string literal is a string object. String methods are associated with these objects, as discussed in the section "Built-In Objects and Functions."

Defining Arrays

Unlike other languages, JavaScript lacks an array data type. However, an equivalent function is performed by creating an object that emulates an array. The first step is to define an array object type:

```
function MakeArray(n) {
   this.length = n;
   for (var i = 1; i <= n; i++)
      this[i] = 0;
   return this
}
```

The next step is to define an instance of the MakeArray object type:

```
ExmpArray = new MakeArray(20);
```

When you assign values to array elements, it looks like assigning values to an array data type. The difference is that the array begins with one and not zero, because zero defines the length of the array:

```
ExmpArray[1] = "test1"
ExmpArrya[2] = "another test"
```

Built-In Objects and Functions

The objects and functions described in this section are part of the JavaScript environment and, therefore, they are browser independent. These objects and functions are as follows:

- The string object and its associated methods
- The Math object and its associated methods
- The date object and its associated methods
- The eval, parseInt, and parseFloat functions

Taken as a whole, these objects and their associated methods provide a powerful set of additions to the programmer's toolbox. The string and date objects extend the basic set of data types to cover most development needs. The Math object provides all the standard functions for performing complex mathematical routines.

The String Object

Whether a quoted string is a string variable or a string property of an object, it is a string object; everything placed between quotes is a string object. There are two ways to use a string object:

1. *stringName.propertyName*
2. *stringName.methodName(parameters)*

String Object Properties

The string object has only one property—length. Because it is a property, the following are all valid references:

```
StringLength = stringVariable.length;
StringLength = mydog.name.length;
StringLength = "This is a string".length;
```

String Object Methods

A large number of methods is associated with the `string` object. Besides the normal string manipulation functions, many of these objects wrap the string with HTML tags. The following is a list of the `string` object methods:

- `anchor(nameAttribute)`. With the `nameAttribute` set to the value of the parameter and passed to the method, the anchor method brackets the text with the `<A></A>` tags. Here's an example:

  ```
  document.write("Other Links".anchor("other_links"));
  ```

- `big()`. The string is wrapped with the `<BIG></BIG>` tags.

- `blink()`. The string is wrapped with the `<BLINK></BLINK>` tags.

- `bold()`. The string is wrapped with the `<B></B>` tags.

- `charAt(index)`. This method returns the character to the position specified by `index`, where index ranges from 0 to `stringName.length` - 1. If the `index` is out-of-bounds, a null string is returned.

- `fixed()`. The string is wrapped with the `<TT></TT>` tags.

- `fontcolor(color)`. The string is wrapped with the `<FONT COLOR="color"></FONT>` tags. The `color` parameter is specified in `rrggbb` format.

- `fontsize(size)`. The string is wrapped with the `<FONTSIZE=size></FONTSIZE>` tags. The size can be a value from one to seven, or it can be a relative change (+ or -) to the font size specified in the `<BASEFONT>` tag.

- `indexOf(searchValue, [fromIndex])`. This method returns the index position of the first occurrence of the string specified in `searchValue`. The optional `fromIndex` sets the starting value of the index. If the `searchValue` is not found, JavaScript returns -1.

- `italics()`. The string is wrapped with the `<I></I>` tags.

- `lastOf(searchValue, [fromIndex])`. Starting at the end of the string or the value specified by `fromIndex`, this method searches the string backward for `searchValue`. If the `searchValue` is not found, JavaScript returns -1.

- `link(hrefAttribute)`. The text is wrapped with the `<A HREF=hrefAttribute></A>` tags. The parameter `hrefAttribute` includes all valid URLs.

- `small()`. The string is wrapped with the `<SMALL></SMALL>` tags.

- `strike()`. The string is wrapped with the `<STRIKE></STRIKE>` tags.

- `sub()`. The string is wrapped with the `<SUB></SUB>` tags.

- `substring(indexA, indexB)`. This method returns the subset of `string`, as specified by *indexA* and *indexB*. As with all indexes, the string begins at `0` and ends at `stringName.length -1`. If *indexA* is less than *indexB*, the string returned begins at *indexA* and ends at *indexB-1*. If *indexA* is greater than *indexB*, the string returned begins at *indexB* and ends at *indexA-1*. When *indexA* equals *indexB*, JavaScript returns a null string.

- `sup()`. The string is wrapped with the `<SUP></SUP>` tags.

- `toLowerCase()`. This method converts the string to lowercase and returns it.

- `toUpperCase()`. This method converts the string to uppercase and returns it.

The Math Object

The `Math` object provides a set of standard mathematical values and methods that augment the set of mathematical operators provided with JavaScript. As opposed to other objects, the `Math` object does not require an instance of the object before using the math methods. To simplify the entering of names and to make the script more readable, the `Math` methods often are bounded by the `with` statement. The syntax for the `Math` object is as follows:

1. `Math.propertyName`
2. `Math.methodName(parameters)`

The Math Object Properties

The `Math` object provides eight properties. These properties define various mathematical constants. Table 19.5 describes the properties and gives their approximate values.

Table 19.5. The Math object properties and their values.

Property	Description	Approx. value
E	Euler's constant	2.718
LN2	Natural logarithm of 2	0.693
LN10	Natural logarithm of 10	2.302
LOG2E	Base 2 logarithm of e	1.442
LOG10E	Base 10 logarithm of e	0.434
PI	Ratio of circumference to diameter	3.14159
SQRT1_2	Square root of one-half	0.707
SQRT2	Square root of two	1.414

Math Object Methods

The Math object provides a number of Math methods that augment the set of mathematical operators:

- abs(*number*). This method returns the absolute value of the number.

- acos(*number*). The *number* must be a value between -1 and 1. For a valid *number*, acos returns arc cosine in radians. If the value of *number* is outside of the range of -1 to 1, acos returns 0.

- asin(*number*). The asin method returns the arc sine in radians. The rules for evaluation are the same as those for the acos method.

- atan(*number*). The atan method returns the arc tangent in radians. The rules for evaluation are the same as those for the acos method.

- ceil(*number*). This method returns the next integer greater than or equal to *number*.

- cos(*number*). The *number* is the angle in radians. JavaScript returns the cosine.

- exp(*number*). This method returns e to the power of *number*, where e is Euler's constant.

- floor(*number*). This method returns the next integer that is less than or equal to the *number*.

- log(*number*). The log method returns the natural logarithm (base e) of *number*, where *number* is any positive numeric expression or object. If the number is outside the range, the return value is always 1.797693134862316e+308.

- max(*number1*, *number2*). This method returns the greater of the two numbers.

- min(*number1*, *number2*). Conversely, this method returns the lesser of two numbers.

- pow(*base*, *exponent*). This method raises *base* to the power of *exponent*. If either the *base* or the *exponent* is an imaginary number, JavaScript returns zero.

- random(). This method is available only on UNIX platforms, where it returns a pseudorandom number between zero and one. In Netscape Navigator 3.0, the random() method is available on all platforms.

- round(*number*). JavaScript returns the value of *number* rounded to the nearest integer. For the purpose of rounding, any value of .5 or greater is rounded to the next highest integer.

- sin(*number*). This method returns the sine of the angle, where *number* is expressed in radians.

- sqrt(*number*). The sqrt method returns the square root of any non-negative number. If the *number* is out of range, JavaScript returns zero.

- tan(*number*). This method returns the tangent of the angle, where *number* is expressed in radians.

The Date Object

Although JavaScript does not provide a Date data type, it provides a Date object that allows the handling of date and time information. One caveat is that all dates are in milliseconds from January 1, 1970, 00:00:00. Due to the way JavaScript handles dates, dates before 1970 are invalid dates.

The Date object requires that an instance of the Date object exist prior to the use of its methods. The instance can either be a new object or the property of an existing object. There are four ways to define the new instance:

```
dateObjectName = new Date()
```

```
dateObjectName=new Date("month day, year hours:minutes:seconds")
```

```
dateObjectName=new Date(year, month, day)
```

```
dateObjectName=new Date(year, month, date, hours, minutes, seconds)
```

Format one sets the date and time to the current date and time. Leaving out the time sets the value to zero. Because the Date object does not contain any properties, there is only one format for the Date methods:

```
dateObjectName.methodName(parameters)
```

The exceptions are UTC and parse methods, which are static methods and use

```
Date.UTC(parameters)
Date.parse(parameters)
```

Table 19.6 describes the values returned by the various get commands.

Table 19.6. Extracting information from the Date object.

Date *method*	*Returned value*
getDate()	Day of the month
getDay()	Day of the week
getHours	Hour of the day
getMinutes	Minutes in the hour
getMonth	The month
getSeconds	Seconds in the minute
getTime	Milliseconds since 1/1/1970
getTimezoneOffset	Offset between local time and GMT
getYear	The year

Besides being able to retrieve information on the Date object, the methods in Table 19.7 show how to change date information.

Table 19.7. Setting information into the Date object.

Date method	Valid values
setDate(*dayValue*)	1-31
setHours(*hoursValue*)	0-23
setMinutes(*minutesValue*)	0-59
setMonth(*monthValue*)	0-11
setSeconds(*secondsValue*)	0-59
setTime(*timeValue*)	>=0
setYear(*yearValue*)	>=1970

Two additional methods are used to convert the date to a string value. They are as follows:

- **toGMTString()**. This method converts the date in GMT (Greenwich Mean Time) and returns it as a string. The actual format of the string is dependent on the hardware platform.

- **toLocaleString()**. This method converts the string to the locale format, which varies according to locale.

The Date object also provides two static methods for handling strings; it has the format of *Date.method()*. These methods are as follows:

- **parse(*dateString*)**. This method converts a date string into the number of milliseconds since January 1, 1970, 00:00:00. Local time is the default. However, it also supports a suffix specifying the GMT offset or U.S. standard time zones.

- **UTC(year, month, day [, hrs] [, min] [, sec])**. This method returns the number of milliseconds since January 1, 1970, 00:00:00 Universal Time Coordinate (in other words, GMT).

Built-In Functions

JavaScript supports several built-in functions that are not related to any object. These built-in functions are as follows:

■ eval(*string*). The eval function evaluates the *string*, which contains any JavaScript expression, statement, or sequence of statements, and returns the result. Some examples of the eval function are

```
var x =
var y =
var z = "if (x <= 9) (x*y) else (x/y);"
document.write(eval("x + y / 4"), "<BR>")
document.write(eval(z), "<BR>")
```

■ parseFloat(*string*). This function parses *string* and returns a floating point number. If the first character is not a number or sign, it returns zero on Windows platforms and NaN (not a number) on other platforms. Parsing of the string continues until it reaches the end of the string, or a character that is not a sign, number, decimal point, or exponent.

■ parseInt(*string* [, radix]). The parseInt function parses the string and returns an integer according to the specified radix. The value of radix is 8 for octal, 10 for decimal, and 16 for hexadecimal. If the radix is not specified, a string that begins with 0x is radix 16, 0 is radix 8, and any other value is radix 10. If parseInt encounters a character that is not a numerical value in the specified radix, it stops parsing and returns the value to that point. If *string* begins with a non-numerical value, it follows the same rules as parseFloat.

■ isNaN(*testValue*). This function exists only on UNIX platforms and evaluates *testValue* to determine whether it is a NaN. It returns either true or false.

■ escape("*string*"). This function returns the ASCII encoding of an argument in the ISO Latin-1 character set. The *string* is a non-alphanumeric string or property of existing object. It returns the value as %xx, where xx is the ASCII encoding of a character in the argument. If it encounters an alphanumeric value, it passes the value to the output string without encoding it.

■ unescape("*string*"). This function returns the ASCII character for the %xx, or hexadecimal values specified in the *string* parameter.

Netscape Objects

In addition to the JavaScript objects and methods, the Web page developer has access to the objects and methods in the Netscape browser. This section reviews the Netscape Navigator objects and methods. The next section looks at how to use the objects and methods in the management of windows and frames.

The Navigator Object Hierarchy

Netscape Navigator builds an instance hierarchy that reflects the document being processed. As an instance hierarchy, there are no classes as defined in Java. However, the instance hierarchy works with the JavaScript approach to objects. Figure 19.1 shows the structure of the Navigator object hierarchy.

FIGURE 19.1.

The Netscape Navigator object hierarchy.

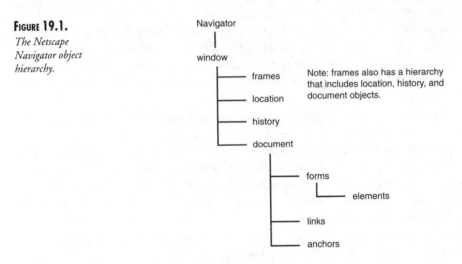

This hierarchy is important for creating references to objects and their properties. The children of an object are properties of the parent object. Because all objects are descendants of the window object, the window object itself is not referenced when referencing any object or property within the current window. For example, the reference to the instance of myform is document.myform. However, referencing a document in another window requires the addition of the window name to the object reference.

The Importance of HTML Layout

The proper use of JavaScript depends on having a basic understanding of how Netscape Navigator processes an HTML document. When an HTML document is loaded, the browser starts processing at the first line of the document. The browser lays out the screen in the order of the HTML statements in the document. After the screen is drawn, it cannot be redrawn without processing a new document. How this affects frames and windows is the topic of the next section.

The corollary to this is that an instance of an object exists only after encountering the HTML that generates the instance. Thus, JavaScript cannot reference an HTML object, such as a form, or execute a function until the browser processes the statement. For example, JavaScript cannot reference a form object until the browser processes the HTML for the form. Similarly, the changing of a property after the browser used the property in the layout of the window does not affect its value or appearance.

Although the constraints seem onerous, understanding the behavior of processing HTML and JavaScript saves a lot of frustration. The key principle to remember is that an HTML document is sequentially processed and JavaScript is part of that sequential process.

The Window Object

The window object is the parent of all objects. It includes the properties that define all windows and frames within a window. When the browser initially loads the HTML document, it starts with a single instance of a window object. If the HTML document creates frames, the frame information is stored in a frame array object. By the same token, opening a new window creates a child window object. The power of JavaScript lies in its capability to utilize the properties and methods of the window object.

The section "Windows and Frames" goes into more detail about the window object itself. This section covers the objects that are properties of the window object. These objects are the

- Location object
- History object
- Document object

Of the three, the document is the most important object in the hierarchy. The document object itself contains properties that refer to other objects. The most important of these are the following:

- form object
- anchor object
- link object

The upcoming sections cover each of these objects. However, they cover only those objects, properties, and methods that are related to JavaScript.

The location Object

The location object contains information about the current URL. The reference to the object is as follows:

```
[windowReference.]location[.propertyName]
```

The properties of the location object refer to the individual parts of the URL:

```
protocol//hostname:port pathname search hash
```

NOTE

The location object and the location property of the document object
(document.location) have different purposes. The location object can be changed, but
the location property cannot be changed.

The properties of the location object are as follows:

- protocol. The protocol specifies the access method of the URL and includes everything up to the first colon.
- hostname. The hostname contains the host and domain name, or IP address, of the destination host.
- port. The port is the TCP/IP port as discussed in Chapter 1, "An Overview of Internet Programming." If the port property is empty, it defaults to the port specified for the protocol as defined in the services file.
- pathname. The pathname specifies the path to the specified resource on the destination host.
- search. The search property is a string that begins with a question mark and is used for CGI scripts.
- hash. The hash property is a string that begins with a hash mark (#) and specifies an anchor name.
- href. This property specifies the entire URL. If reference is made to [windowName.]location, the href property is assumed.
- host. This property is equivalent to hostname:port.

NOTE

Although JavaScript permits the modification of the individual properties, sound programming practice calls for changing the href property. This approach prevents any errors resulting from the browser attempting to access the URL before all changes are made.

The History Object

Access to the History object is a controversial subject because it enables the script to send the history back to the server. To prevent this from being misused, Netscape Navigator versions 2.01 and above no longer enable access to this object.

The document Object

The document object holds the properties, objects, and methods that define the presentation of the document. It refers to that part of the HTML document defined by the `<BODY></BODY>` tags. The following subsections discuss the components of the document object, except for the form object (which is covered in the "The Form Object" section, later in this chapter).

The document Object Properties

The HTML options to the `<BODY>` tag define the document object properties. JavaScript references all of these properties, except for the background image.

> **NOTE**
>
> The string required to change the color properties is in the format of
> `document.colorProperty = "#RRGGBB"` or `document.colorproperty="colorName"`. Any
> color property defined in the `<HEAD></HEAD>` tags takes precedence over the `<BODY>` tag
> option. The outcome of color changes made in the `<BODY>` depends on the color property.

The color document object properties are as follows:

- **bgColor.** This property defines the background color of the document. The bgColor property immediately updates the display.

- **fgColor.** This property defines the text color of the document. After the browser completes the layout of the HTML document, the browser ignores changes to this property. Instead, the `<FONT>` tag or the fontcolor method provide an alternative mechanism for changing the text color.

- **linkColor.** The linkColor represents the color of a link defined by HREF, without prior visits. As with all color involving the links, the colors change after the user selects the link.

- **alinkColor.** This property controls the color of an active link. In other words, it is the color of the link after it is selected and before the destination host replies.

- **vlinkColor.** After the user visits a site, the browser displays this color for the link.

The document object also contains the following non-color related properties:

- **lastModified.** This read-only property reflects the date that the document was last modified.

- **location.** This read-only property usually matches the value of the location object unless redirection alters the URL.

- referrer. This read-only property contains the URL for the document that is linked to the current document.
- title. A read-only property that contains the value specified by the <TITLE></TITLE> tags.

The anchors Object

The anchors object contains an array of all anchors declared by the NAME attribute of the <A> </A> tags. The array begins at 0 and continues through *document.anchors.length* - 1. The value of *document.anchors[index]* is null.

> **TIP**
>
> Before using it to set a value such as location.hash, it is possible to check the validity of the anchor by comparing it to the array length; you use sequential numbers to identify anchors.

The link Object

The link array contains the link objects defined by the <A></A> tags or the link method. The array includes objects for both the HREF and NAME attributes. With the addition of the TARGET attribute, the properties of each link object are identical to those of the location object.

> **NOTE**
>
> The link array is a read-only array. Additional entries are added via the <A></A> tags. The link method modifies existing entries in the link array.

The link object provides two event handlers: onClick and onMouseOver. The section called "The Form Object," later in this chapter, describes how to use these event handlers.

The cookie Property

The cookie property contains a string value of the cookie entry from the cookies.txt file for the document. For a complete description of how to use cookies, see the Netscape cookie specification. The substring, charAt, indexOf, and lastIndexOf string methods can be used to dissect the cookie string. Chapter 18 contains an example of how to read the cookie string.

The document Object Methods

The `document` object contains five methods:

- `document.write()`
- `document.writeln()`
- `document.open()`
- `document.close()`
- `document.clear()`

As shown in previous examples, the `document.write` method, without a window reference, writes text to the current window. The `document.writeln()` method is the same as `document.write`, except that it inserts a newline character at the end of the argument. The format for these methods is as follows:

```
document.write(expression [, expression2] ... [expressionN])
document.writeln(expression [, expression2] ... [expressionN])
```

The default MIME type is `text/html`. However, the `document.open(["mimetype"])` method enables the opening of other MIME types, such as text/plain, image/gif, image/jpeg, image/x-bitmap, and plugIn. The `document.open()` method opens a stream to collect the output of the write and `write.ln` methods. If the MIME type is text or image, the browser opens a stream for layout; for plugIn, the browser opens it to a plug-in. If a document already exists in the target window, the `open` method clears it.

> **NOTE**
>
> Currently, it is not possible to print any text generated by JavaScript via the `write` or the `writeln` methods.

The stream stays open until the browser encounters a `document.close()` method. The `document.close()` forces the content of the stream to display. The `document.clear()` method clears the content of the window.

The Form Object

The HTML `<FORM></FORM>` tags provide the means for user input of data, and output of variable data to the user. The user input might affect choices for client-side use, or it can be sent to the server. On the other hand, variable data such as marquees can be displayed on the form. On the input side, event handlers provide a means to invoke JavaScript routines to perform such tasks as editing data. On the output side, JavaScript plays a bigger role in the managing of data to be displayed in the form.

This section discusses the form object and its properties. Due to the length of forms examples, this section only presents snippets of code. The next chapter gives full-blown scripts illustrating the use of forms and event handlers.

Event Handlers

Event handlers constitute one of the major uses of JavaScript. Events are the result of user actions, such as the clicking of a mouse button, the checking of a box, or the submission of a form. Event handlers are defined in the HTML tags along with the JavaScript related to the event. The following example illustrates the coding of an event handler:

```
<INPUT TYPE="button" VALUE="Submit" onClick="validate(this.form)">
```

In the preceding example, the keyword this refers to the current object, which is the button object. By stating this.form, the reference is made to the form object containing the button. While the preceding example executes a function, JavaScript statements also are valid. When there is more than one statement, each statement must be separated by a semicolon.

TIP

Good programming practice calls for the use of functions because they make code easier to read and can be reused.

NOTE

Until an HTML document is loaded into a window that contains the <BODY></BODY> tags, a window contains no event handlers.

The following is a list of event handlers supported by JavaScript:

- onBlur. The JavaScript for this event handler executes when the user leaves the field causing it to lose focus.
- onChange. The browser executes this JavaScript for the event when the user leaves the field and the value of the object changes.
- onClick. The onClick event occurs when the user clicks on a form or link.
- onFocus. This event occurs when a field receives input focus by tabbing to the field or clicking with the mouse.
- onLoad. This event occurs when the browser finishes loading a document or all frames within the <FRAMESET> tag.

■ onMouseOver. This event occurs when the mouse moves over an object from outside the object. The JavaScript routine for the event handle must return true for the status and defaultStatus properties to be set.

■ onSelect. An onSelect event occurs when a user selects text within a text or textarea field.

■ onSubmit. When the user submits a form, an onSubmit event occurs. If the JavaScript returns false, the form is not submitted. Any other value, including no return statement, enables the form to be submitted.

■ onUnload. This event occurs when a document is exited.

The event handlers are a part of various objects. Some objects support more than one event handler, and some event handlers appear in multiple objects. Table 19.8 shows the relationship between event handlers and objects.

Table 19.8. The relationship between event handlers and objects.

Object	Event handlers
button	onClick
checkbox	onClick
form	onSubmit
link	onClick, onMouseOver
radio	onClick
reset	onClick
select	onBlur, onChange, onFocus
submit	onClick
text	onBlur, onChange, onFocus, onSelect
textarea	onBlur, onChange, onFocus, onSelect
window	onLoad, onUnload

The forms Array

The forms array contains an entry for each form object created by the <FORM></FORM> tags. For JavaScript, it is a read-only array composed of the following properties:

■ action. This property contains the value of the ACTION attribute.

■ element. This is an array of element objects defined for the form.

■ encoding. This property contains the value of the ENCTYPE attribute.

19

THE JAVASCRIPT LANGUAGE

- **length.** This property contains the number of entries in the element array.
- **method.** This property contains the value of the METHOD attribute.
- **target.** This property contains the value of the TARGET attribute.

The following are the valid means of addressing the form objects:

```
formName.propertyName
formName.methodName(parameters)
forms[index].propertyName
forms[index].methodName(parameters)
```

Form Object Methods

The form object has only one method—submit. The submit method performs the same action as the submit button of an HTML form and has the following syntax:

```
document.formName.submit()
```

The element Objects

The element objects reflect the element entries in the `<FORM></FORM>` tags. Table 19.9 lists the element objects and their properties.

Table 19.9. The properties of element objects.

Element object	Properties
button	name, value
checkbox	name, value, checked, defaultChecked
hidden	name, value
password	name, value, defaultValue
radio	name, value, checked, defaultChecked, length
reset	name, value
select	name, length, options array, selectedIndex
submit	name, value
text	name, value, defaultValue
textarea	name, value, defaultValue

The properties are addressed as *document.elementName.property*, or as *document.formName.elements[index].propertyName*, where *elementName* is the value of the name property for the element object.

The element Methods

The `element` methods emulate their cousins, the event handlers. However, there are some caveats, as the following shows:

- ■ `blur()`. This method removes focus from the specified object but does not establish the focus on another object.
- ■ `click()`. This method simulates a mouse click on the specified object. When referencing the radio element, the form is *document.radioName[index].click()*.
- ■ `focus()`. This method gives focus to the specified object.
- ■ `select()`. This method selects the entire input area.

Except for the `radio` object, the methods are addressed as *document.elementName.methodname()*. Table 19.10 lists the element objects and their corresponding methods.

Table 19.10. The methods of element objects.

Element object	Methods
button	click
checkbox	click
hidden	(has no methods)
password	blur, focus, select
radio	click
reset	click
select	blur, focus
submit	click
text	blur, focus, select
textarea	blur, focus, select

Windows and Frames

Windows and frames create more confusion for Web page developers than any other aspect of the browser. When Netscape Navigator starts, it opens a window and, depending on how the options are set, loads a document into the window. If you select the menu option File | New Web Browser, a new window is opened. In this case, closing the original window does not close the new window. .

On the other hand, frames are created according to the <FRAMESET></FRAMESET> tags in the HTML document. It subdivides the screen's real estate into a number of frames. When the document that defined the frames is closed, the frames go away because their existence depends on the document.

Chapter 18 provides examples that illustrate the difference in behavior between windows and frames, even though both are containers for documents. This section concerns itself with the properties and methods of the window and frame objects.

The Window Object Properties

One of the major features of JavaScript is its capability to create and manipulate windows. These windows are not limited to just displaying messages; depending on the parameters set, they can be another instance of the browser. The following properties of the window object reflect the flexibility of the browser window:

- defaultStatus. The defaultStatus is the message that appears in the status bar when no other message is being displayed. If it is set from a onMouseOver event handler, the event handler must return true for the status to change.

- frames. This property is an array that contains the frame objects. The frame inherits all of the properties and methods of the window object.

- length. The value of this property is the number of frames in the frame array.

- parent. From a frame reference, this is the window that the frameset resides in. A frame within the frameset can reference another frame in the frameset by using *parent.frames[index]* without having to reference the window by name.

- self. This is a synonym for the current window or frame.

- status. This is a transient message that is set by the onMouseOver event handler.

- top. This property is used to reference the topmost window. It can be used by child windows or embedded filesets to reference the originating window.

- window. This property is a synonym for the current window.

The forms for referencing window properties are

```
window.propertyName
self.propertyName
top.propertyName
parent.propertyName
windowVar.propertyName
propertyName
```

The Window Object Methods

The following are the window or frame object methods:

- alert("message"). This method creates an alert dialog box with a single OK button. It is used to display a message that does not require a user decision.

- close(). This method closes the referenced window. It must contain a window reference such as *window.close* as *close()* with no reference is the equivalent of *document.close*.

- confirm("message"). The confirm method displays a confirm dialog box with OK and Cancel buttons. OK returns a value of true, and Cancel returns a value of false.

- [windowVar =][window.]open("URL", "windowName" ["windowFeatures"]). This method opens a new Web browser window. The object name *windowVar* is the name of the new window and is used to reference its properties and methods. The URL specifies the URL to open in the new window. If the option is null, a blank window is opened. The variable *windowName* is the name used in the TARGET attribute of the <FORM> and <A> tags. The variable *windowFeatures* is a comma-separated list of the following options:

```
toolbar=yes¦no
location=yes¦no
directories=yes¦no
status=yes¦no
menubar=yes¦no
scrollbars=yes¦no
resizable=yes¦no
width=pixels
height=pixels
```

If no features are set, all features default to true. If any feature is explicitly set, all features default to false. If a feature is set without specifying the value, the value is true. These features refer to the components of the Navigator window. Thus, location refers to the location entry field and directories refers to the standard Navigator buttons.

NOTE

After it is created, the window is independent of the parent window; if the parent window closes, the window created remains open. The onUnLoad event handler closes the windows created.

- prompt("message" [, inputDefault]). The prompt method displays a prompt dialog box with a message, an input field, an OK button, and a Cancel button. The inputDefault is a string, integer, or property of an object that represents the default value for the input field. If the inputDefault is not specified, the input field displays the value <undefined>.

- timeoutID=setTimeout(expression, msec). With this method, the evaluation of the expression is delayed for the number of milliseconds specified. The timeoutID is only used by the clearTimeout method.

- clearTimeout(timeoutID). This method cancels the time-out set by the setTimeout method.

The preceding methods are referenced as follows:

```
window.methodName(parameters)
self.methodName(parameters)
top.methodName(parameters)
parent.methodName(parameters)
windowVar.methodName(parameters)
methodName(parameters)
```

> **CAUTION**
>
> The `open()` and `close()` methods need to be referenced as `window.open()` and `window.close()` to avoid any conflicts of scope with `document.open()` and `document.close()`.

Dividing the Window into Frames

Frames divide a window into multiple, independently scrollable frames on a single screen. Frames are created via the `<FRAMESET></FRAMESET>` tags in an HTML document. Each document creates a frame array for that document. If a document opened in one of the frames contains a `<FRAMESET>` tag, that frame is divided into frames by that document. This hierarchy of framesets is important in referencing the properties and methods of frames.

> **NOTE**
>
> Frames have all the properties of a window. The entire hierarchy for the frame structure is the same as the window structure. (Refer to Figure 19.1.)

The structure under any window or frame can be referenced. Thus, object properties in one window or frame can change object properties in another window or frame using the structure shown in Figure 19.1.

> **NOTE**
>
> The HTML document that uses `<FRAMESET></FRAMESET>` contains only frame statements. After the frames are opened, the original document is no longer visible. The HTML document is one frame that can control the other frames. Thus, the possibilities for screen management give the Web page developer tremendous freedom in the development of interactive Web documents.

Summary

JavaScript is more than a simple scripting language and less than a full-blown, object-oriented programming language. It is the glue that binds many diverse elements into a single dynamic and interactive environment.

This chapter presented the fundamentals of JavaScript and described the objects and their properties that are available to JavaScript. This chapter dealt with the pieces to the puzzle, and Chapter 18 puts the pieces together to illustrate the uses of JavaScript.

19

THE JAVASCRIPT LANGUAGE

JavaScript in Internet Applications

by Bill Anderson

IN THIS CHAPTER

CHAPTER 20

When describing the syntax of a language in the previous chapter, the snippets of JavaScript code kept the focus on the topic. The examples in this chapter illustrate in detail how JavaScript works in HTML documents. Each of the simple examples covered in this chapter focuses on a particular application of JavaScript. The examples in this chapter cover how to verify forms, work with windows, work with frames, and read cookies.

A Forms Example

Without using JavaScript to verify forms, the server side validates a form with little interaction from the user. With the event handlers provided in JavaScript, the client side performs the editing. This gives the user an immediate response to the validity of the data entered. Beyond verification, the event handlers add a means of providing more interactive forms management. Listing 20.1 illustrates the capabilities of event handlers in performing this task.

Listing 20.1. JavaScript and forms.

```
<HTML>
<HEAD>
<TITLE>JavaScript and Forms</TITLE>
<SCRIPT LANGUAGE="JavaScript">
<!--
var lstSex=""
function chkSex(strValue) {
    if (lstSex == "") {
        lstSex = strValue
        return true
    }
    if (lstSex != strValue) {
        if (confirm("Do you wish to change value?")) {
            lstSex = strValue
            return true
        }
        else return false
    }
    return true
}
function getSport(formObj) {
    if (formObj.hobSports.checked == 1) {
        var question = "What is your favorite sport?"
        formObj.favSport.value = prompt(question, formObj.favSport.value)
    }
}
function getPlay(formObj) {
    if (formObj.hobTheater.checked == 1) {
        var question = "What is your favorite Play?"
        formObj.favPlay.value = prompt(question, formObj.favPlay.value)
    }
}
```

```
function getBook(formObj) {
    if (formObj.hobReading.checked == 1) {
        var question = "What is your favorite book?"
        formObj.favBook.value = prompt(question, formObj.favBook.value)
    }
}
function getPlace(formObj) {
    if (formObj.hobCamping.checked == 1) {
        var question = "What is your favorite place to camp?"
        formObj.favPlace.value = prompt(question, formObj.favPlace.value)
    }
}
function chkForm(formObj) {
    if (formObj.exmpName.value == "") {
        alert("\nYour name is required.\nPlease enter and resubmit form.")
        return false
    }
    if (formObj.hobSports.checked == 0 && formObj.favSport.value != "")
        formObj.favSport.value = ""
    if (formObj.hobTheater.checked == 0 && formObj.favPlay.value != "")
        formObj.favPlay.value = ""
    if (formObj.hobReading.checked == 0 && formObj.favBook.value != "")
        formObj.favBook.value = ""
    if (formObj.hobCamping.checked == 0 && formObj.favPlace.value != "")
        formObj.favPlace.value = ""
    formObj.submit()
    return true
}
// -->
</SCRIPT>
</HEAD>
<BODY>
<H1 ALIGN="CENTER">JavaScript and Forms</H1>
<P>Instead of sending the form to the server for editing, the web page
developer has the option to edit the form using JavaScript to validate
the data before it is sent to the server. This example, shows how
JavaScript event handlers execute validation functions.</P>
<HR>
<FORM NAME="example" onSubmit="alert('\nForm submitted')">
<P>Enter your name: <INPUT TYPE="TEXT" NAME="exmpName"
   onFocus='window.status="Please enter your name"'
   onBlur='window.status=""'> (required)</P>
<P>Sex:  Male <INPUT TYPE="RADIO" NAME="exmpSex" VALUE="M"
   onClick='if (!chkSex(this.value)) exmpSex[1].checked=1'>
 Female <INPUT TYPE="RADIO" NAME="exmpSex" VALUE="F"
   onClick='if (!chkSex(this.value)) exmpSex[0].checked=1'></P>
<P>Check the boxes that match your hobbies:<BR>
<INPUT TYPE="CHECKBOX" NAME="hobSports"
   onClick='getSport(this.form)'> Sports<BR>
<INPUT TYPE="CHECKBOX" NAME="hobTheater"
   onClick='getPlay(this.form)'> Theater<BR>
<INPUT TYPE="CHECKBOX" NAME="hobReading"
   onClick='getBook(this.form)'> Reading<BR>
<INPUT TYPE="CHECKBOX" NAME="hobCamping"
   onClick='getPlace(this.form)'> Camping</P>
<INPUT TYPE="HIDDEN" NAME="favSport">
```

20

JAVASCRIPT IN INTERNET APPLICATIONS

continues

Listing 20.1. continued

```
<INPUT TYPE="HIDDEN" NAME="favPlay">
<INPUT TYPE="HIDDEN" NAME="favBook">
<INPUT TYPE="HIDDEN" NAME="favPlace">
<P>Are there any special comments:<BR>
<TEXTAREA NAME="exmpCmnts" ROWS="4" COLS="40" WRAP="VIRTUAL"
    onFocus='window.status="Looking forward to your comments."'
    onBlur='window.status=""'>
</TEXTAREA></P>
<P><INPUT TYPE="SUBMIT" VALUE="Submit Form" onClick='chkForm(this.form)'>
<INPUT TYPE="RESET" VALUE="Clear Form"></P>
</FORM>
</BODY>
</HTML>
```

The onFocus and onBlur event handlers in the input text statement show how to display a message in the status bar. The onFocus event handler displays the message and the onBlur removes it when it is no longer applicable. Although the onBlur event handler looks like a natural candidate for validating the value of the text, it presents a serious problem in that leaving the page causes its execution. Thus, the user, who wanted to exit the page without completing the form, gets an error message. As an exercise, change the event handler to call the chkForm function and see how it behaves.

For the radio buttons, the listing illustrates a simple change test. Both buttons use the same function to determine if a change occurred. If a change occurred, the user is prompted (see Figure 20.1) to verify the change. The false output generated by cancel causes the value of *checked* to change. The variable *checked* modifies both the visual display and the value of the *exmpSex* variable, while the check() method only modifies the variable and not the visual display. Again, the reader can change the script to see the difference between modifying *checked* and using the *check()* method.

The checkbox section of the preceding listing shows how additional information can be gained and stored in a hidden form entry. The function prompts the user for information (see Figure 20.2) when the box is checked and not checked. The script retains the value of the hidden information rather than having the user re-enter the information, then uncheck and recheck the box.

FIGURE 20.1.
Using the Confirm dialog box.

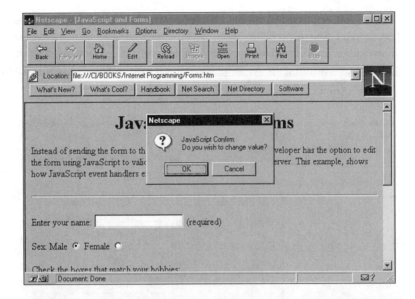

FIGURE 20.1.
Using the Confirm dialog box.

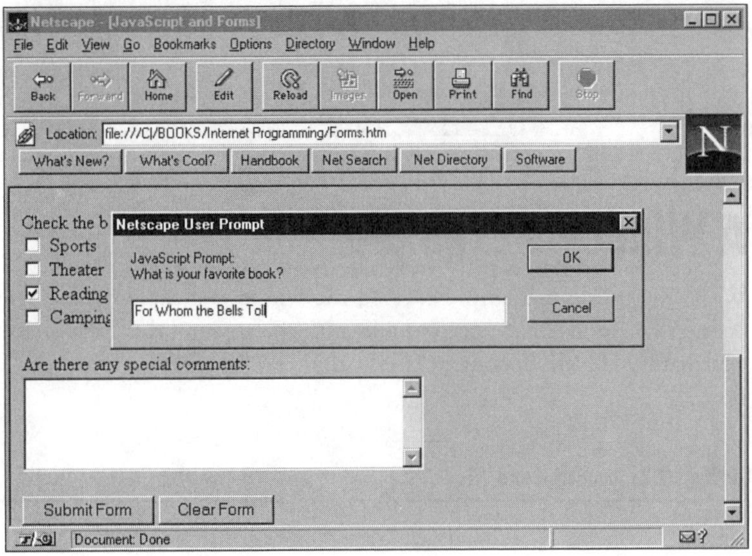

FIGURE 20.2.
Using the Prompt dialog box.

Finally, the script's use of the *onClick()* alert handler for the submit button shows one alternative of validating forms submission. In this approach, the function, after it performs the validation checks, submits the form using the *submit()* method. In addition, the validation function takes care of cleaning up the hidden variables. The *onSubmit()* event handler now displays an alert (see Figure 20.3) that the script submitted the form.

FIGURE 20.3.

Using the Alert dialog box.

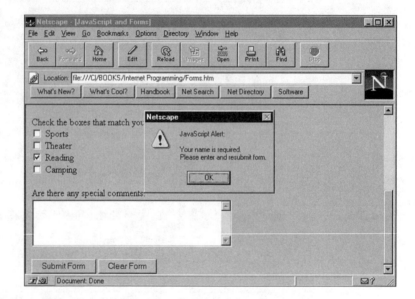

A Windows Example

While the previous example covered the windows created by the alert(), confirm(), and prompt() methods, this example looks at the behavior of the window.open() method. This self-explanatory HTML document (see Listing 20.2) shows windows open under different conditions.

Listing 20.2. JavaScript and Windows.

```
<HTML>
<HEAD>
<TITLE>JavaScript Windows Example</TITLE>
<SCRIPT LANGUAGE="JavaScript">
<!--
var win4Open=false
function winTest4() {
   winTst4=window.open("", "winS", "resizable,width=200,height=100")
   winTst4.document.open()
   winTst4.document.write("<H1>Test 4</H1>")
   winTst4.document.close()
   win4Open=true
}
```

```
function endIt() {
    if (win4Open) winTst4.close()
}
// -->
</SCRIPT>
</HEAD>
<BODY onUnLoad='endIt()'>
<H1 ALIGN="CENTER">A JavaScript Windows Example</H1>
<P>HTML lacks the means to create windows. Frames, yes -- windows ,
no. The best way to learn about the behavior of windows is to play
with this script.</P>
<HR>
<FORM>
<P>This window test generates a new instance of the browser,
with this document as the opening document. Close the first instance
of the browser to see what happens.<BR><BR>
<INPUT TYPE="button" NAME="test1" VALUE="Open Test 1"
    onClick='window.open("window.htm")'></P>
<HR>
<P>By declaring a named windowed object, it is still possible to
create multiple instance of the browser.<BR><BR>
<INPUT TYPE="button" NAME="test2" VALUE="Open Test 2"
    onClick='winTST2 = window.open("window.htm")'></P>
<HR>
<P>When the name argument to window.open is provided, it cannot
another copy with a duplicate name. Instead, it reopens the
same document.<BR><BR>
<INPUT TYPE="button" NAME="test3" VALUE="Open Test 3"
    onClick='winTST3 = window.open("window.htm", "winTest")'></P>
<HR>
<P>This final test shows away to use the onUnLoad option to close
any windows created. You can run test 1 or 2 and run this test
from another instance of the browser.<BR><BR>
<INPUT TYPE="button" NAME="test4" VALUE="Open Test 4"
    onClick='winTest4()'></P>
</FORM>
</BODY>
</HTML>
```

As the various window tests illustrate, windows are independent entities. As long as the window object has a name, it can be explicitly addressed from any other window.

NOTE

The window object name is not the same as the window name argument. The window name argument is related to the TARGET attribute in the <FORM> and <A> tags.

The preceding example shows a simple method for closing windows that are open, as shown in Figure 20.4. Because the window might not be open, the script tests to see if it was opened prior to closing.

FIGURE 20.4.

The Test 4 results.

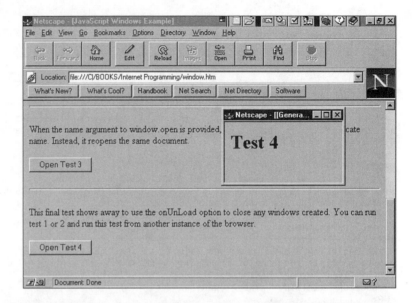

TIP

Unless there is a reason for doing otherwise, a good programming practice calls for the closing of all windows that are opened.

A Frames Example

The HTML equivalent of opening windows is the <FRAMESET> tag, which divides the screen real estate into smaller windows. The <FRAMESET> tag replaces the <BODY> tag so that, except for the <NOFRAMES> tag, the document's sole purpose is to define a set of frames, as shown in Listing 20.3.

Listing 20.3. HTML for parent <FRAMESET>.

```
<HTML>
<HEAD>
<TITLE>JavaScript and Forms</TITLE></HEAD>
<FRAMESET ROWS="20%,*">
<FRAME SRC="fr_top.htm" NAME="topFrame" SCROLLING="NO">
<FRAME SRC="fr_main.htm" NAME="bigFrame">
</FRAMESET>
</HTML>
```

For a frame to actually appear on the screen, a document must be defined, as is done for the *topFrame*. As Listing 20.4 shows, this is a very minimal document.

Listing 20.4. HTML for `topFrame`.

```
<HTML>
<HEAD>
<TITLE>Top Frame Title</TITLE>
</HEAD>
<BODY>
<H1 ALIGN="CENTER">JavaScript and Frames</H1>
</BODY>
</HTML>
```

The document loaded into *bigFrame* is another <FRAMESET> document. (See Listing 20.5.) This approach makes the new <FRAMESET> a child to the first <FRAMESET>.

Listing 20.5. A child <FRAMESET>.

```
<HTML>
<HEAD>
<TITLE>Main Frameset</TITLE>
</HEAD>
<FRAMESET COLS="25%,*">
<FRAME SRC="fr_cntrl.htm" NAME="frameControl">
<FRAME SRC="fr_dsply.htm" NAME="frameDisplay">
</FRAMESET>
</HTML>
```

Other than as an example, there are advantages to this approach over the inclusion of the <FRAMESET> as an embedded <FRAMESET> with the first <FRAMESET>. By creating a child <FRAMESET>, the *bigFrame* is free to receive any kind of document. For example, if the *topFrame* contains a series of buttons describing alternate formats, the <FRAMESET> for *bigFrame* changes, according to the needs of the application.

Like *topFrame*, *frameDisplay* needs an initial document. For this example, the document is a short description of this example as shown in Listing 20.6.

Listing 20.6. Initial document for `frameDisplay`.

```
<HTML>
<HEAD>
<TITLE>Initial Doc for Display Frame</TITLE>
</HEAD>
<BODY>
<H1 ALIGN="CENTER">Initial Document for Test</H1>
<P>For a frame to be define, an initial document must be
opened in the frame. This is different than a window, which
allows a window to be opened with no document. In this
example, the control panel changes the document displayed in
this window.</P>
</BODY>
</HTML>
```

The HTML document (see Listing 20.7) loaded in `frameControl` shows how one document can manipulate other frames.

Listing 20.7. The Control Panel document.

```
<HTML>
<HEAD>
<TITLE>Control Frame</TITLE>
<SCRIPT LANGUAGE="JavaScript">
<!--
function chgHeader() {
var newhdr=prompt("Enter new title for top frame.", "")
if (newhdr.length > 0) {
    top.topFrame.document.open()
    top.topFrame.document.write('<H1 ALIGN="center">'+newhdr+"</H1>")
    top.topFrame.document.close()
  }
}
// -->
</SCRIPT>
</HEAD>
<BODY>
<H2 ALIGN="CENTER">Control</H2>
<FORM>
<INPUT TYPE="button" NAME="test1" VALUE="Load Forms"
   onClick='top.bigFrame.frameDisplay.location="forms.htm"'><BR>
<INPUT TYPE="button" NAME="test2" VALUE="Restore"
   onClick='top.bigFrame.frameDisplay.location="fr_dsply.htm"'><BR>
<INPUT TYPE="button" NAME="test3" VALUE="Change Header"
   onClick='chgHeader()'><BR>
</FORM>
</BODY>
</HTML>
```

Figure 20.5 shows the screen when `frames.htm` is loaded.

The references used in this document illustrate the format required to address the different frames. For the first two buttons, the reference must start from the top window. It includes the references to the parent frame and child frame. The keyword *top* forces the reference to start from the original because the control panel is a document of the child <FRAMESET>. When the Load Forms button is clicked, the forms document described in the first example is loaded into the display frame, as shown in Figure 20.6.

FIGURE 20.5.

Initial window for the Frames example.

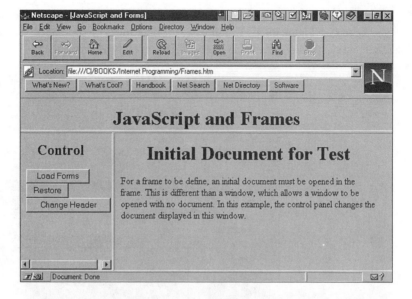

FIGURE 20.6.

Loading the Forms example.

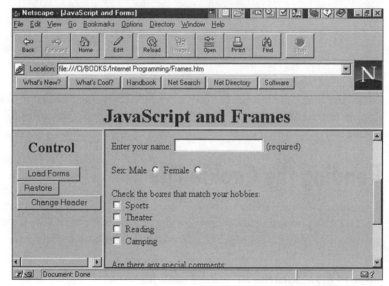

The Change Header button executes a function that prompts the user for a new value for the *topFrame*. (See Figure 20.7.) In this case, the document method opens a new document in the frame, writes the new header to it, and then closes the document.

FIGURE 20.7.

Changing the Header in the Top Frame.

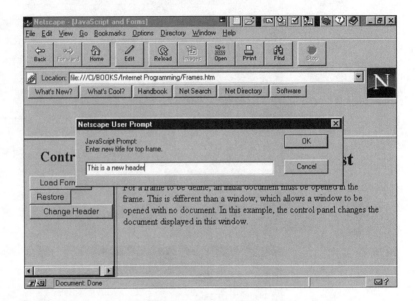

The control frame could change the values for the colors in the other frames. It could also reference the data collected in the form's example. By using JavaScript to enhance the HTML documents, the Web page developer has a much greater degree of flexibility in designing Web documents.

Reading the Cookie File

There are times when trying to improve on the wheel is counterproductive. This is one of them. Bill Dortch's public domain routine for the management of cookies is a straightforward, well-written piece of code. Listing 20.8 is the latest release of his work.

Listing 20.8. JavaScript code for reading a cookie file.

```
<html>
<head>
<title>Cookie Examples</title>
</head>
<body>
<script language="javascript">
<!-- begin script
//
// Cookie Functions - Second Helping  (21-Jan-96)
//  Written by:  Bill Dortch, hIdaho Design <bdortch@netw.com>
```

```
//   Original location:   http://hidaho.com/cookies/
//   The following functions are released to the public domain.
//
//   1.  The expires parameter is now optional - that is, you can omit
//       it instead of passing it null to expire the cookie at the end
//       of the current session.
//
//   2.  An optional path parameter has been added.
//
//   3.  An optional domain parameter has been added.
//
//   4.  An optional secure parameter has been added.
//
//   For information on the significance of these parameters, and
//   and on cookies in general, please refer to the official cookie
//   spec, at:
//
//       http://www.netscape.com/newsref/std/cookie_spec.html
//
//
//   "Internal" function to return the decoded value of a cookie
//
function getCookieVal (offset) {
  var endstr = document.cookie.indexOf (";", offset);
  if (endstr == -1)
    endstr = document.cookie.length;
  return unescape(document.cookie.substring(offset, endstr));
}


//
//   Function to return the value of the cookie specified by "name".
//      name - String object containing the cookie name.
//      returns - String object containing the cookie value, or null if
//        the cookie does not exist.
//
function GetCookie (name) {
  var arg = name + "=";
  var alen = arg.length;
  var clen = document.cookie.length;
  var i = 0;
  while (i < clen) {
    var j = i + alen;
    if (document.cookie.substring(i, j) == arg)
      return getCookieVal (j);
    i = document.cookie.indexOf(" ", i) + 1;
    if (i == 0) break;
  }
  return null;
}


//
//   Function to create or update a cookie.
//      name - String object object containing the cookie name.
//      value - String object containing the cookie value.  May contain
//        any valid string characters.
//      [expires] - Date object containing the expiration data of the cookie.  If
//        omitted or null, expires the cookie at the end of the current session.
//      [path] - String object indicating the path for which the cookie is valid.
```

20

JAVASCRIPT IN
INTERNET
APPLICATIONS

continues

Listing 20.8. continued

```
//      If omitted or null, uses the path of the calling document.
//   [domain] - String object indicating the domain for which the cookie is
//      valid.  If omitted or null, uses the domain of the calling document.
//   [secure] - Boolean (true/false) value indicating whether cookie
//      transmission requires a secure channel (HTTPS).
//
//   The first two parameters are required.  The others, if supplied, must
//   be passed in the order listed above.  To omit an unused optional field,
//   use null as a place holder.  For example, to call SetCookie using name,
//   value and path, you would code:
//
//      SetCookie ("myCookieName", "myCookieValue", null, "/");
//
//   Note that trailing omitted parameters do not require a placeholder.
//
//   To set a secure cookie for path "/myPath", that expires after the
//   current session, you might code:
//
//      SetCookie (myCookieVar, cookieValueVar, null, "/myPath", null, true);
//
function SetCookie (name, value) {
  var argv = SetCookie.arguments;
  var argc = SetCookie.arguments.length;
  var expires = (argc > 2) ? argv[2] : null;
  var path = (argc > 3) ? argv[3] : null;
  var domain = (argc > 4) ? argv[4] : null;
  var secure = (argc > 5) ? argv[5] : false;
  document.cookie = name + "=" + escape (value) +
    ((expires == null) ? "" : ("; expires=" + expires.toGMTString())) +
    ((path == null) ? "" : ("; path=" + path)) +
    ((domain == null) ? "" : ("; domain=" + domain)) +
    ((secure == true) ? "; secure" : "");
}


// Function to delete a cookie. (Sets expiration date to current date/time)
//   name - String object containing the cookie name
//
function DeleteCookie (name) {
  var exp = new Date();
  exp.setTime (exp.getTime() - 1);   // This cookie is history
  var cval = GetCookie (name);
  document.cookie = name + "=" + cval + "; expires=" + exp.toGMTString();
}


//
//   Example
//
var expdate = new Date ()
// 24 hours from now
expdate.setTime (expdate.getTime() + (24 * 60 * 60 * 1000));
SetCookie ("FreqGrafxPath", "http://www.his.com/~smithers/freq/",
expdate,"/~smithers/freq/")
SetCookie ("coName", "Frequency Graphics", expdate)
SetCookie ("tempvar", "This is a temporary cookie.")
SetCookie ("ubiquitous", "This cookie will work anywhere in this domain",
null,"/")
```

```
SetCookie ("inBetaOnly", "This cookie will work in the ./beta/ directory",
expdate,"/~smithers/freq/beta")
SetCookie ("goner", "This cookie must die!")
document.write (document.cookie + "<br>")
DeleteCookie ("goner")
// end script -->
</script>
</body>
</html>
```

Resources on the Web

JavaScript is a new and evolving scripting language. The following resources help one to keep up with the changes:

- Earthweb's Gamelon at `http://www.gamelon.com/` is a great resource and index to what is happening with Java and JavaScript.

- JavaScript 411 at `http://www.freqgrafx.com/411/` is another excellent resource.

- JavaScript-Intro by Voodoo at `http://www.ag.or.at/~fknipp/javascript/jsintro` is a good basic tutorial for JavaScript.

The Netscape site provides other valuable resources, including a JavaScript Guide. You can access the current version of the JavaScript Guide by selecting Help | Handbook from your Netscape Navigator menu bar. There is much more, but all links can be found at the preceding sites.

Summary

This chapter covered examples for forms, windows, frames, and cookies. These are complete examples that the reader can use to explore the world of JavaScript. The sites listed in the resources section provide more examples and tutorials.

VBScript and the Internet

by Keith Brophy and Timothy Koets

IN THIS CHAPTER

The Microsoft Visual Basic Scripting Edition, more commonly referred to as VBScript, is one of several revolutionary new scripting languages at your fingertips today for producing exciting, dynamic Web pages. If you've heard a lot about VBScript and what it can do, but you've been bombarded with so much new information that you can't absorb it all, you're not alone. This chapter was written for you! It will clearly and methodically explain to you the essence of VBScript—that is, what it's all about. Here you will see, in plain English, why VBScript is exciting and what it can do for you. Some of the questions answered in this chapter include

- What is VBScript?
- What can it do?
- What do I have to know to use VBScript?
- What software or tools do I need to use it?
- How secure is VBScript?
- How does it compare to Visual Basic and Visual Basic for Applications?

This chapter presents an overview of VBScript, followed by a condensed guide to the entire VBScript language in Chapter 22, "The VBScript Language." Then, in Chapter 23, "VBScript Application Pages," you will see VBScript in action and examine several Internet applications built using VBScript.

What Is VBScript?

When the World Wide Web first became popular, HTML was the only language programmers could use to create Web pages. They soon learned that HTML had some major limitations. Although HTML presented the user with a "page" of information, the Web page and the user had a limited amount of interaction; the experience was like reading the front page of a newspaper on a computer monitor. Now most computer users, whether they use Windows, Macintosh, UNIX, or a combination of the three, are accustomed to graphical applications that provide interaction. They're used to clicking buttons, entering values into text boxes, and choosing from menus. In fact, the only way to get useful work done with a computer is to interact with it. The first generation of Web pages provided information to the users, but the users could not interact with the Web the way they could with their word processors. If users wanted to interact with their Web pages, they had to send the data to the server, which contained all the "smarts." The server sent its results back to the Web page. This interaction required a great deal of extra time, effort, and overhead, and the user interface was very constrained compared to other popular applications.

Fortunately, the builders of the Internet and the World Wide Web recognized these limitations. They soon realized that if the user was denied the capability to interact with the Web page, the Web itself would become little more than a collection of information, much like a library of books. Although that collection is very useful, users demand more from their computers than a duplication of what they could find elsewhere.

The capabilities of HTML began to grow and become more powerful. Soon, designers began to realize that they needed more than just HTML to make the Internet accessible and useful to the masses. Corporations that wanted to develop enterprise solutions or explore the profit potential of the Internet also began to pressure designers to give them something more.

These demands have resulted in a continued improvement of HTML, the emergence of browsers such as Internet Explorer that tap into the power of HTML, and the advent of scripting languages such as VBScript. To understand what a scripting language is, think of HTML as an airport runway. You can get where you need to go on the ground, but you have an entire sky to travel through above you. Scripting languages are like the airplanes that enable you to lift off the ground. They extend the capabilities of the Web much like an airplane enables you to travel through the sky. A script lets the page become an active, dynamic piece of software, rather than a static piece of content.

> **NOTE**
>
> A *scripting language* is a special type of programming language used to provide control in another host environment. It is interpreted rather than compiled. Therefore, a program built with a scripting language must be run in the environment that contains the scripting language's interpreter and cannot be run as a stand-alone application.

HTML can't interpret a scripting language itself, but it knows enough to call the interpreter of the scripting language to carry out the interpretation. Consequently, you can overcome HTML's limitations by using any browser-supported scripting language to extend the Web page. With scripting languages such as VBScript, the limitations of HTML disappear; the opportunities are now limited only by the power of the scripting language! Although other scripting languages are bound to emerge, two widely used scripting languages in existence today are JavaScript and VBScript. Both of these languages can be embedded in a Web page, and if the browser supports them, they provide the path to smart, active programs that are part of that page.

With HTML you can place controls such as buttons and text boxes on a Web page. Without a scripting language such as VBScript, any actions the user takes on the controls of a Web page must be sent back to the Web page server. That is, the user's computer cannot handle them. Furthermore, the amount of control and flexibility available without a scripting language is very limited. With VBScript you can link to controls on the Web page and also write code to respond to what the user does with those controls. If, for example, a Web page contains a command button, you can write VBScript code that gets executed immediately when the user clicks that button. An example of such a code segment might look like the following:

```
Sub Button_OnClick
    ' The message below will be displayed when the user clicks on the button
    Msgbox "This button was clicked"
End Sub
```

Button is the name of the button, and OnClick is the event that the user causes to occur when he or she clicks the button. You can supply code such as the message statement shown here to be executed every time the user clicks the button. The Msgbox statement, which is discussed in detail in Chapter 22, simply presents a message box to the user. This example is simple, but it shows how VBScript code can enable a page to respond immediately to user actions. VBScript breathes life into otherwise static Web pages, making them dynamic, responsive, intelligent, and interactive.

What Can VBScript Do?

VBScript lets the user interact with a Web page rather than simply view it. Many scenarios are possible for this interaction. For instance, Web pages can ask questions and respond to the user's answers. A VBScript can then take input from the user and check the data to make sure it is valid or meets some criteria. Then it can put an Internet server to work by actually storing the data or causing some action to take place on the server based on the user's input. For example, VBScript could respond to a user's request for an airline reservation by reading in the data, checking to make sure that the request is complete and that the phone number and ZIP code are in a valid format, informing the user of the estimated price, and then notifying the server of the reservation. All these tasks could be performed by the code in the Web page that was downloaded across the Internet as it sits on the user's client PC. The server, in turn, makes sure that the ticket is available, books the flight, and arranges to deliver the tickets to the customer.

Interaction can also be helpful for advertising services or products to a user. A business can use an interactive survey to deliver carefully targeted messages to potential customers. Imagine, for example, a series of Web pages that ask you qualifying questions about your dream car, along with how much you want to spend, and then display information on vehicles that match your criterion. Rather than dealing with a pushy salesperson, you can take your time on the Internet and carefully obtain the facts you need. When you finally go to the dealer's showroom, you can use your knowledge to get the best price.

In this type of interaction, VBScript can play an important role in many ways, including validating data, costing, providing impressive multimedia feedback, and initiating data storage. You can use VBScript to sequence the questions based on responses. For example, if a user wants a van, VBScript can generate an input box that asks him or her to specify the number of seats needed. Throughout the data entry process, VBScript can make sure the user enters a valid order, address, and method of payment, and it can even display a pie chart of how much of the cost goes toward the base price and how much goes toward extras. The sound of a trumpet fanfare can announce the bar graph. The possibilities are endless.

VBScript can also perform calculations on data, such as computing the cost of an item that includes the sales tax. Often, calculations on a Web page enable users to figure out what they want to do or perhaps give them some sort of result. A Web page enables the user to walk away with more than a mere presentation of fixed information. You could, for example, design a Web page that enables customers to choose luxury items for a car and, as the luxury items are selected, adjusts the overall cost. The users could spend as much time as they want and choose as many combinations as they like until they find the perfect combination of features versus price. How often can someone get that level of service from a car dealer?

By utilizing other technologies such as CGI, or *Common Gateway Interface*, which transmits information from the client back to the server, VBScript code can even initiate order placement for that item in the vendor's computer. If the script determines the order meets all criteria for a valid order, it can place the order. Otherwise, it can generate an error message. Using script logic, it could even place the order on a different server, depending on which type of car was requested, and provide an estimated time frame for delivery based on a rule-of-thumb calculation for that type of order. Visual Basic can perform virtually any process that a traditional application can perform. Even in areas in which Visual Basic can't directly cause some action, such as writing to the server database or playing a sound file, it can achieve these results indirectly by using CGI scripts or sound controls, for example. Visual Basic becomes the application behind the Web page that interacts with the user.

Another important aspect of this programming model is that you can also use intrinsic HTML form controls and Microsoft's ActiveX controls with VBScript to give Web pages an attractive look and feel. Intrinsic HTML form controls give the Web page developer a standard set of controls similar to those used in the Windows environment. ActiveX controls include graphs and charts, labels that can be rotated 360 degrees, "new" banners that can remain on a Web page for however many days you want, a timer that enables you to time events on Web pages, a pre-load function that lets you load bitmaps and other time-consuming parts of a Web page before it gets displayed, and so on. These controls give Web pages a professional, polished look. They also provide pages with smarter interactive responses because a Visual Basic program can maintain dynamic control over the control characteristics. For example, your script code can generate a new graph based on user input.

You can also use Microsoft's vast array of OLE controls in VBScript, which opens up a whole world of possibilities for Web pages. Designers can now place ActiveX custom controls directly on Web pages in the Windows environment. OCXs, the forerunner to ActiveX controls, have made languages such as Visual Basic incredibly powerful because programmers can "glue" an OCX that performs some task for them, such as displaying a calendar on the screen, into the application. They don't have to create code to put a calendar on the screen; the OCX does the job for them. Likewise, programmers can now put an ActiveX control on a Web page and access the control through VBScript. The end result is better, more interactive pages for the end user.

In addition to using ActiveX controls, VBScript can also tie other applications into a Web page through OLE automation technology. For example, with the appropriate object declarations, you can tie an Excel spreadsheet into your Web page so that when the user clicks on the spreadsheet, Microsoft Excel runs and loads the spreadsheet for you to edit. Now, you can work within a Web page and also activate other applications within the Web page with the click of a mouse button. The ability to tie external applications to a Web page enables you to show virtually anything on a Web page; the only requirement is that the applications you want to link to a page support the OLE automation standard.

With VBScript and the right controls, you can even create 3-D animation effects, making your Web page come alive with moving objects in response to certain events. You can use animation to make cars careen across the screen, butterflies fly across your Web page, or arrows move and point to where you want the user to interact with the page.

The component incorporation capabilities of VBScript introduce some special considerations and trade-offs in page design. For example, a Web page that includes VBScript code that interacts with Excel and Microsoft Word and uses ActiveX controls (which are currently only supported within Windows), cannot be fully distributed over the Internet with all the support software. The Web page might not run properly on all of the various platforms and operating systems. Still, a page that leverages these technologies would be fully usable for Internet or intranet users who have the necessary hardware and software to successfully support the Web page in question.

At the other end of the spectrum, a page that incorporates VBScript to carry out a series of calculations can be a perfect Internet citizen, fully downloadable over the Internet and running on a variety of platforms and operating systems. In this respect, the flavor and tone of your VBScript Web pages depend largely on how you want to leverage them.

> **NOTE**
>
> Microsoft might support ActiveX controls on other environments such as the PowerMac in the future, but they are currently supported only in the Windows environment.

In order to gain a more complete understanding of how VBScript works with browsers, controls, and objects, consider the simple model shown in Figure 21.1.

FIGURE 21.1.
A simple diagram of the VBScript—host model.

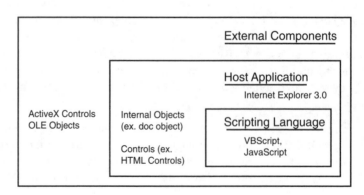

The innermost box contains the core language of the scripting language which, in this model, is VBScript. Other languages, such as JavaScript, could be placed in this box as well. This core language cannot be run alone—it requires the support of a host, which leads to the second, larger box in the figure.

The second, larger box represents the host program that runs the scripting language. At the time of this printing, VBScript could be used with Microsoft Internet Explorer 3.0, which in this case would be the host. Although the host might vary, the core VBScript language stays the same. In other words, the VBScript language is the same regardless of the host. The host might contain a set of internal objects and controls. For example, you can access Internet Explorer's *document object* from VBScript, which is discussed further in Chapter 22. You can also access Internet Explorer's Intrinsic HTML Controls through VBScript, also covered in the next chapter. Any scripting language, such as JavaScript, has the same type and level of access to these browser objects and controls as VBScript has.

The third box represents components external to the browser but available in the Windows environment, such as ActiveX controls, OLE controls, and objects such as OLE automation servers. Figure 21.1 illustrates how VBScript can access these controls and objects through the browser. In order for VBScript to access a control at this level, it must be linked through the host. Each link of the chain must be complete before VBScript can access any objects or controls throughout the chain. Because the browser provides a secure environment, the user will be warned before a script attempts to use a control, provided the default browser options are in place to do so.

Remember that any scripting language operates using this model. JavaScript, another powerful scripting language, would occupy the same position in the figure as VBScript does. Consequently, any scripting language has access to the browser's controls and objects as well as to the system's controls and objects if they are supported by the browser.

The variety of controls and technologies that surround the World Wide Web is likely to increase dramatically over the next several years. Although keeping up with the changes and new controls on the market can be quite dizzying, it's an exciting time to be a part of the Internet revolution. Now that you have had a glimpse at the power of VBScript and the technologies that surround it, the examples in the next section will help you understand further some of VBScript's capabilities!

Learning VBScript

VBScript is much easier to learn than programming languages such as Java, C/C++, and other scripting languages such as JavaScript. Derived from the BASIC language, VBScript should not be difficult for anyone who has any computer programming experience.

To start working with VBScript, you need several things: a browser that supports VBScript, the VBScript runtime interpreter, access to required controls, and an editor or other tool to help you assemble Web pages or edit HTML documents. The first step is to obtain a browser that includes VBScript runtime support if you do not already have one. Microsoft's Internet Explorer 3.0 was the first publicly available browser that supported VBScript. This browser is available free from Microsoft. At the time this was written, you could obtain Internet Explorer 3.0 from the Microsoft Web site at `http://www.microsoft.com/ie`.

Any browser that supports VBScript includes the VBScript runtime interpreter. Therefore, if you install the browser, you have everything you need to run VBScript, including the runtime interpreter. You don't need to obtain any other pieces. However, you might want to refer to the location `http://www.microsoft.com/vbscript` for a general description of runtime capabilities beyond that provided in this book. The runtime interpreter for VBScript is license free, just like Internet Explorer. Even if other browsers incorporate the VBScript runtime interpreter, Microsoft does not charge a licensing fee to the end user or the company that produces the browser. Therefore, you can safely bet that the VBScript interpreter will be widely distributed with most browsers in the future.

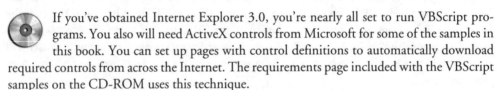 If you've obtained Internet Explorer 3.0, you're nearly all set to run VBScript programs. You also will need ActiveX controls from Microsoft for some of the samples in this book. You can set up pages with control definitions to automatically download required controls from across the Internet. The requirements page included with the VBScript samples on the CD-ROM uses this technique.

If you are a VBScript programmer—in other words, you want to edit VBScript programs or create your own from scratch—then you need one more tool, a Web page editing tool. Such a tool not only enables you to generate Web pages but also enables you to embed VBScript code into those pages. Fortunately, most tools provide this capability. As long as you can enter text insertion mode and type text directly into your page as you create it, you can insert VBScript statements. You can use many different tools to accomplish this task. They range from the Windows Notepad, a simple text editor, to more sophisticated tools such as Internet Assistant, a utility that incorporates itself into Microsoft Word and enables you to quickly and easily build Web pages.

Another available tool for use in Web page design with VBScript is Microsoft's ActiveX Control Pad. This tool is an HTML text editor that enables you to insert HTML and ActiveX controls automatically into your HTML documents with the help of a wizard. Figure 21.2 shows the beta version of the ActiveX Control Pad in action.

FIGURE 21.2.

*Microsoft's ActiveX
Control Pad in beta
form.*

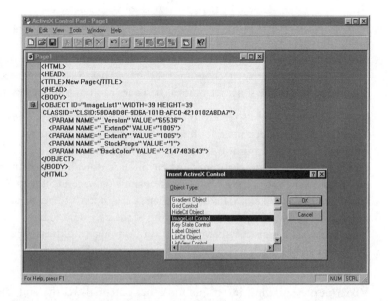

The editor has many additional features that aid in editing Web pages and incorporating VBScript and JavaScript into them. Another useful feature Microsoft has provided in the ActiveX Control Pad is the capability to place controls on a Web page using the Microsoft Layout Control. This placement capability in the Control Pad, together with Internet Explorer's 2-D layout for HTML, enables you to position elements and controls anywhere on a page in a form-like fashion, much like Visual Basic. The layout information is built in a separate file that the layout control interprets and incorporates into your main page when that page is loaded. This approach is discussed in more detail in the next chapter.

Security and VBScript

One of the many questions people ask about VBScript is, "How secure is it?" VBScript was designed as a subset of the Visual Basic language. When you look at the language and compare it to VBScript, you essentially see a stripped-down version of Visual Basic. The designers took any part of Visual Basic that could cause VBScript to be unsafe and insecure and eliminated it. The end result of their work is a language that is safe and "lighter" than its parent, Visual Basic.

When people think about safety and the Internet, their concerns are often valid. The Internet has just recently become popular to the masses, and companies are starting to think of ways to make money on the Internet. This brings to mind images of users entering credit card numbers, making banking and shopping transactions, and paying for other services. Obviously, before such activities can take place, the Internet must be secure. Otherwise, people simply won't want to take the chance of their credit card numbers being intercepted or some secure password being used to access their accounts. The World Wide Web and Internet consortia are working very hard to establish security mechanisms for the Internet. Rest assured; security will be an area of intense interest in the short term until the issues can be firmly resolved.

Users of VBScript are also likely to be concerned about security. They want to make sure that VBScript does not open the door for a devious Web page to damage their computer systems in any way. The most common type of computer damage users fear is the multitude of viruses that are transmitted to computers when files are downloaded from an Internet server and modified on the user's computer. Other possible damage includes a Web page that, for some reason, causes the loss of data on the client's computer system or otherwise causes the computer to crash. Nothing is more frustrating to the user than to have five applications open and lose all the data because of a computer crash. Although multitasking systems such as Windows 95, Windows NT, and UNIX are less susceptible to crashing than the Windows operating system was, system crashes still happen.

VBScript prevents virus infections and other potential security and safety problems by eliminating the cause of such problems entirely. First of all, VBScript does not read and write files or databases in the traditional fashion. This approach might seem like quite a limitation, and it is indeed limiting, but it stops up a very large security leak. Damage could come to a user's computer through a Web page that opens and modifies a file or perhaps deletes a file on the user's computer. Therefore, VBScript itself is not able to open or modify any files on the user's computer.

The second area of safety is making sure a VBScript will not cause the computer to crash. If an important exchange of information is happening in a Web page, the user would certainly not want the computer to crash because of an ill-formed script.

The design of VBScript properly reflects the goal to prevent security leaks and ensure safety with VBScript, but the story does not end yet. Although VBScript works with ActiveX controls, intrinsic HTML controls, OCXs, and OLE objects within a Web page, VBScript has no control over what goes on when the code that composes such controls executes. All VBScript "sees" when working with a control or object is the interface that control provides. A control could, for example, modify a file. VBScript doesn't modify the file—the control does. Although VBScript can't be faulted for causing damage to a user's system, it cannot be responsible for either the security or stability of any controls or OLE objects it works with.

If a control were written with some sort of a glitch or bug inside of it, it could cause a computer to crash or, at the very least, cause the Web page to not function properly. Again, the problem does not lie in VBScript itself but in the control it interfaces with. A Web page is only as stable as its least stable component. If a buggy control is included on a Web page, the potential of that Web page to become unstable is equal to the stability of that control. Therefore, it is essential that the Web page designer choose controls that will work as bug free as possible with any browser or any platform on which the Web page is run.

Microsoft's Internet Explorer 3.0 is a good example of the current state of browser security. Internet Explorer contains a feature called Safe Content that makes sure that no unknown programs or components can be downloaded to the user's computer by a Web page without the user's consent. Refer to Figure 21.3 for the Internet Explorer 3.0 Programs dialog box for setting security options for programs you receive within Web pages from the Internet.

Figure 21.3.

Microsoft Internet Explorer 3.0 Programs dialog box.

As you can see, you have the option of choosing "Expert," which warns you about any security problems before a Web page is displayed, "Normal," which automatically prevents security problems by not displaying content that causes security violations, and "None," which displays all contents without worrying about security violations. The Expert setting will inform you whenever an object is required by the Web page or if a scripting language changes the properties of an existing control on a Web page. These safeguards are an example of part of an evolving process of making the Web browsers more secure in an environment of rapidly growing objects, controls, and scripting languages.

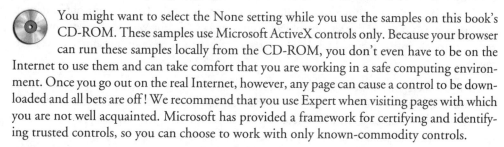

You might want to select the None setting while you use the samples on this book's CD-ROM. These samples use Microsoft ActiveX controls only. Because your browser can run these samples locally from the CD-ROM, you don't even have to be on the Internet to use them and can take comfort that you are working in a safe computing environment. Once you go out on the real Internet, however, any page can cause a control to be downloaded and all bets are off! We recommend that you use Expert when visiting pages with which you are not well acquainted. Microsoft has provided a framework for certifying and identifying trusted controls, so you can choose to work with only known-commodity controls.

The Internet is continuing to develop rapidly in the arena of security, particularly in the area of component distribution and security. It is important to understand that security considerations have shaped the capabilities inherent in the VBScript language.

VBScript Versus Visual Basic and Visual Basic for Applications

Many programmers who are interested in VBScript have used either Visual Basic or Visual Basic for Applications. If you are included in that group, you most likely know that VBScript is a subset of Visual Basic. You've probably also heard Microsoft's claim that if you already know Visual Basic or Visual Basic for Applications, you know VBScript. Yes, well—sort of. You know what you can do, but you might not be so sure about what you cannot do.

One of the first striking differences between VBScript and Visual Basic is that Visual Basic has a design-time environment. When you run Visual Basic, you get an attractive editing environment where you can craft forms and write code using an interactive shell. When you work with VBScript, on the other hand, you have no such environment. VBScript code "lives" within an HTML document, which is a plain text file. At the time of this printing, neither Microsoft nor any other large commercial vendor has a design environment that lets users create VBScript code in the way Visual Basic does. This restriction is due, in part, to the way in which VBScript works. Visual Basic code creates Windows applications that operate in and of themselves. On the other hand, VBScript code works inside of HTML documents and runs along with HTML.

Even though VBScript is an interpreted language, as is its parent, you must create VBScript code manually. Some tools already are emerging to overcome this tedious limitation. Microsoft's ActiveX Control Pad, for example, helps overcome the tedious work of inserting controls and editing HTML code by providing an editing and layout tool that is more sophisticated than Notepad. This tool is currently available for free and can be located on the Microsoft Web site, `www.microsoft.com/workshop`. You can use the tool for automatic insertion of control object definitions and as a layout editor. The layout editor lets you lay out pages interactively, much like Visual Basic 4.0, and stores the results in a separate file for the Layout control to integrate on your page. And the ActiveX Control Pad even provides a Script Wizard that lets you define scripts through an interactive high-level interface, rather than by entering source code statements.

Because the focus in this book is on helping you understand all the details of VBScript, however, we steer clear of the higher level tools that can shield you from some of the underlying details. We want you to learn those details! Therefore, the samples here are presented at the source code level and can be entered with a text editor such as Notepad. After you gain a well-grounded knowledge of VBScript, then you might choose to progress to some of the higher level tools.

The other primary difference between VBScript and Visual Basic, aside from development environments, is the language itself. As mentioned previously, Visual Basic supports many commands, keywords, and data types that VBScript does not support. A summary of the differences between VBScript and Visual Basic for Applications can be found on Microsoft's

VBScript Web site, as well as in *Teach Yourself VBScript in 21 Days* by Brophy and Koets, from Sams.net Publishing. Understanding how to port code from one language to another is very important, and *Teach Yourself VBScript in 21 Days* clearly explains the process.

How VBScript Enhances Browsers and HTML

VBScript enhances Web browsers in a variety of helpful and significant ways. Web browsers are able to read and interpret HTML code, formatting the text and other data in a Web page based on the specifications of the browser. HTML was originally written to address content of a document while enabling the browser itself to worry about how to present the output to the user. As such, it is a relatively simple language that is quite limited in its power. One of its biggest limitations was the inability to support *interaction* with a Web page as fully as users have come to expect from computer-run applications. For instance, people who use sophisticated word processors such as Microsoft Word or MacWrite expect the user-friendly atmosphere of menus, toolbars, and dialog boxes that help them accomplish various tasks. When working with a Web page built with HTML alone, the user is very limited in what he or she can do. Various controls can be placed on a form, but the Web page input must be submitted back to the server in order to perform any processing. This restriction usually makes Web pages fairly rigid in their interactive capabilities.

Web pages built entirely on HTML often require the user to set a series of controls, such as check boxes and text fields. Typically an entire form's worth of data is supplied at a time. After filling in fields on a form, the user can click on a button, usually called Submit, and the contents of the Web page are sent back to the server. The only work that the client's computer performs is to display the Web page to the user. The server performs all the intelligent work and processing. Remote processing not only increases the amount of traffic required on the Internet but also prevents the user from interacting with the Web page. If, for example, the Web page was used to take a survey, HTML would not be able to validate the user's input. In other words, the Web page wouldn't be able to make sure that the user was entering valid information. In fact, the user could spend a long time entering invalid data, only to have the server echo the data back to the user and tell him or her to enter it again. Or, worse yet, the server might discard all of the user's data and force him to start over and enter all the data again!

With VBScript, however, the Web page has its own intelligence. VBScript can, for example, make sure that what a user enters is valid before the user "submits" it to the server. Local validation eliminates a great deal of extra traffic, not to mention the delay the user must experience in waiting for the information to get to the server. One immediate benefit for the user is that faster, more responsive Web pages make the overall Web page experience more enjoyable. Furthermore, many effects, such as multimedia and animation, that are limited, if not nonexistent, in HTML, are relatively easy to implement in VBScript, and they can also enhance the Web page experience.

Another great strength of VBScript is its capability to act as a "glue tool" that can integrate and control all the components on a Web page, such as OLE objects, ActiveX controls, Java applets, Intrinsic HTML form controls, and Virtual Reality Modeling Language (VRML) controls.

> **NOTE**
>
> VRML is a language used to present a three-dimensional, graphical world to the Web user.

This same capability also made Visual Basic the important tool it is today. Therefore, VBScript enhances the power of browsers and HTML because it gives the Web page a higher degree of interaction with the user, allows for processing on the user's computer rather than only on the server, provides the user with more control over the Web page, and glues together various components of a Web page.

Host Environments

VBScript can be supported and used in any browser distributed with VBScript runtime support, as well as with a variety of other tools and components. This section briefly reviews some of the host environments and then turns to the specifics of how to make VBScript work in HTML browsers.

Web Browsers

At the time of this writing, the Internet Explorer browser supported VBScript. Other browsers might add support as well, as VBScript gains enough popularity that market forces and user pressures force the issue. Add-on components already exist to extend VBScript support to Netscape's Navigator browser. Because this is currently the browser with the largest market share, there is hope in many quarters that Netscape might add native support for VBScript. While to date there has been no indication this is planned, if and when that move occurs, VBScript will become virtually a *de facto* standard in the browser arsenal and would likely be a part of all serious browsers.

Microsoft's Internet Explorer is the focus of the discussion in the remainder of the chapters of this book relating to VBScript because it is the most established VBScript platform. If you use VBScript in another environment, recognize and take comfort in the fact that VBScript should work essentially the same everywhere. No matter which browser your script runs in, you can expect consistent behavior from the core language. The runtime interpreter, the engine that interprets and processes the language, will also behave the same because it will be derived from the same Microsoft VBScript source code wherever it is found.

If a browser or tool vendor ports VBScript to a different environment, the vendor can license the source code free of charge from Microsoft and modify it to work in that other environment. But even the modified version must meet Microsoft's criteria for VBScript conformance. However, you might find slight variations in the objects that a host, such as a browser, makes available to VBScript to manipulate. Aside from these differences, though, the language and behavior of VBScript will be consistent from one implementation to another.

Microsoft's Internet Explorer already contains the Visual Basic runtime interpreter. Versions for 16- and 32-bit Windows will become available, as well as versions for the Macintosh and UNIX-based computers. This cross-platform support of VBScript through the Internet Explorer will not restrict VBScript users to the Windows environment, as did Visual Basic and Visual Basic for Applications. Furthermore, Microsoft will provide the Internet Explorer without charge to users across these platforms.

So what do we mean when we say that a browser supports VBScript? When we answer this question later, you will understand the mechanics of running a VBScript within a browser. But first, we need to consider some non-browser environments that also host VBScript.

Other Internet Tools

In addition to Web browsers, a variety of other tools for the Internet will benefit from VBScript support. The first case to consider is custom controls, which can be used as building blocks for standard applications. A variety of companies produce browser controls for Windows applications, for example, that enable developers to build their own Web browsers or incorporate some browser functionality into their applications. If, for example, a designer is building an application for a company, she might want to make the application "Internet aware" and provide a browser interface to the World Wide Web from within the application itself. This type of browser component has the potential to support VBScript code as well, thereby giving application developers who incorporate browsers into their own applications the ability to support Web pages that use VBScript.

Some services not directly related to Web browsers also support VBScript. Microsoft's Internet Information Server product is one example. The Internet Information Server enables computers where Web pages permanently reside to share their pages with the rest of the Internet. The product works in conjunction with Windows NT to deliver Web pages across the Internet in response to a user's request. VBScript is even used to glue server-side solutions together, just as it can be used to glue Web page components and logic together.

VBScript support has also been projected for WebObjects, a dynamic Web page tool from Next Software, Inc. You can use WebObjects for rapid development of sophisticated Web server solutions. Another area where VBScript can be used is Microsoft's Active VRML environment. VRML is quickly becoming very popular on the World Wide Web because it enables designers to create a three-dimensional world, rather than fixed Web pages. The user can then navigate through this world, much like a person would walk through a house, to explore its contents. In the early alpha models of Microsoft's ActiveVRML technology, VBScript can interact with Microsoft's Active VRML standard events and properties of an Active VRML viewer ActiveX control. The ActiveVRML technology is still evolving, but if this level of support remains, VBScript will help enhance the power of VRML and give the Web user even more visually appealing ways to interact with information.

Why is VBScript so prevalent? Precisely because it was intended to be. Microsoft designed VBScript to be a general-purpose scripting language. It was not intended to be constrained just to HTML Web pages. To the contrary, it is specified in such a way that it can easily be incorporated as a smart programming language into any application. Microsoft provides the VBScript runtime license and source code free of charge to any software manufacturer that wants to make its product "VBScript-aware."

Assume, for example, that you are marketing your own spreadsheet software. You want to give your customers a way to write macros that can interact with the contents of a spreadsheet based on instructions provided by the customer. One of the best ways to accomplish this task is to incorporate VBScript runtime support. Then you've extended the capabilities of your product by giving your customers an easy way to control the spreadsheet. It costs you, the manufacturer, virtually nothing, because you were able to leverage Microsoft code. Models of this sort will continue to facilitate the growth of VBScript into arenas beyond the Web page.

Microsoft announced plans to license its more extensive Visual Basic engine, called VBA or Visual Basic for Applications, a few months after announcing the licensing plans for VBScript. Software providers can incorporate VBA into their product in much the same way as they can incorporate VBScript. The difference is that VBA is a high-end product with more function, options, and bulk. VBA 5 has a development environment that can be called from the application that incorporates it, for example. VBScript, on the other hand, is designed to be lightweight, fast, and simple. Because it is derived from VBA, and is in fact a proper subset of VBA, the languages are very similar. Which will most vendors incorporate? Time will tell. Given that VBScript can be licensed for free, which is not the case with VBA, you should expect to see VBScript in more and more applications.

As these examples show, the applications for VBScript are potentially broad. In addition, VBScript can be targeted for networks other than the World Wide Web. It can also be useful in intranet applications, in a sense running over a private mini-Web.

> **NOTE**
>
> An intranet is a scaled version of the Internet that is contained within an organization—an intranet's corporation is equivalent to the Internet's world.

VBScript technology can be used equally well in either an intranet or Internet environment. In fact, VBScript can be especially well suited to the intranet because it can craft very sophisticated solutions on a powerful set of front-end web pages and corresponding customer-made business rules as determined by the organization. Distribution and support of components might be easier to handle when those components are shared just within the organization, rather than with the entire Internet. VBScript could make such a strategy more feasible.

The possibilities for using VBScript are numerous. Still, by far the most common use of VBScript today is as a tool to create great Web pages. In this and the next two chapters, VBScript is demonstrated within the Web browser. Although we have restricted our discussion to preliminary versions of Microsoft's Internet Explorer 3.0 running within Windows 95, you can apply the concepts you learn here in any of the platforms or within any of the tools that support VBScript. Our next task is to show you how a browser supports VBScript. Then you will be ready to create your first VBScript program!

Placing VBScript Code Within an HTML Document

In order to place code from a scripting language into an HTML document, you must use script tags. The script tag looks like this:

```
<SCRIPT>
```

It is closed using this:

```
</SCRIPT>
```

Unlike the other tags you have seen so far, however, the opening script tag requires an argument—namely, the language of the script. The opening script tag embeds VBScript code within an HTML document. For VBScript code, the tags are used as follows:

```
<SCRIPT LANGUAGE="VBScript">
...your VBScript code goes here
</SCRIPT>
```

The language parameter should be specified as `"VBScript"`, including the quotation marks. Early beta versions of Internet Explorer used `VBS` without quotation marks, but later betas and the final release require the parameter as specified above. If you are using another scripting language, such as Java, you need to enter an indicator such as `"JavaScript"` rather than `"VBScript"` in the language argument when you write the opening script tag. When the browser encounters a script tag, it checks to see what language the script has been written in. Then the browser checks whether an interpreter is available that can read the script code. If so, the interpreter takes over. If not, the script tag is ignored and HTML moves on its merry way to the next line of code after the script tag.

You can also use a variety of other tags in an HTML document. Some of these tags are introduced in later chapters because they are important in working with VBScript. Others are not directly applicable to VBScript but are useful to know anyway. Again, you might want to read *Teach Yourself Web Publishing with HTML 3.0 in a Week* or *Teach Yourself More Web Publishing with HTML 3.0 in a Week*, both from Sams Publishing, for more information on how to use HTML in building Web pages.

Now that you have all the pieces of the puzzle, let's put them together so you can see how to place VBScript code in your Web pages. To place a script inside an HTML document, you should use the script and comment tags together. As previously mentioned, the comment tags are important just in case someone reads the Web page with a browser that does not support VBScript. You will see an example of the impact in a moment.

The following is the syntax for placing VBScript code inside an HTML document. You can place the code anywhere within the framework of your HTML document.

```
<SCRIPT LANGUAGE="VBScript">
<!--
    ... your VBScript code goes here
-->
</SCRIPT>
```

Notice that the comment tag appears immediately after the script tag so that if the browser doesn't recognize the script, it will ignore the script tag and treat anything that follows as regular HTML text. The comment tags prevent the browser from displaying the script code just in case it is a browser that doesn't recognize VBScript. The VBScript interpreter will not process the comment tags because when the browser finds an HTML comment, it does not bother to pass the comment on to the VBScript interpreter. As a result, you don't need to worry about VBScript not being able to figure out why the HTML comment tags are present.

Internet Explorer lets you place VBScript code anywhere inside your HTML document. In practice, however, the best place for your VBScript code is at the very end of the body section in your HTML document. This gives you an easy frame of reference to locate all code in the page.

Also, you can place VBScript code within control definitions themselves. If you use this technique within the body of the HTML document, VBScript must also reside in the body of the document. Placing the script code at the end of the body section is, therefore, the safest choice.

Listing 21.1 shows an example of a Web page that contains VBScript code placed at the end of the body section of the document.

Listing 21.1. A Web page using VBScript code.

```
<HTML>
<HEAD>
<TITLE>VBScript Test Page</TITLE>
</HEAD>

<BODY>

<H1>
<A HREF="http://www.mcp.com"><IMG  ALIGN=MIDDLE
SRC="../shared/jpg/samsnet.jpg" BORDER=2 HSPACE=20></A>
<EM>VBScript Test Page</EM></H1>

<HR>

<CENTER><INPUT TYPE=BUTTON LANGUAGE="VBScript"
VALUE="Click Here for a Message!" NAME="TestButton"></CENTER>

<HR>

<center>
Adapted From <em>Teach Yourself VBScript in 21
Days</em><br> by <A HREF="../shared/info/keith.htm">Keith Brophy</A>
and <A HREF="../shared/info/tim.htm">Tim Koets</A><br><br>
Return to <a href="VBSDemo.htm">Content Overview</a><br>
Copyright 1996 by SamsNet<br>
</center>

<SCRIPT LANGUAGE="VBScript">
<!--
     Sub TestButton_OnClick()
          MsgBox "It's easy to create message boxes with VBScript!"
     End Sub
-->
</SCRIPT>

</BODY>

</HTML>
```

This Web page is shown in Figure 21.4.

As you can see, the Web page includes a button that the user clicks to display a message box (which is also shown in Figure 21.4). The code used to create the Web page in Figure 21.4 works fine because the browser recognizes VBScript. If the browser wasn't VBScript-aware, the comments between the script tags would prevent the code from being displayed in the Web page.

FIGURE 21.4.

An example of a Web page using VBScript.

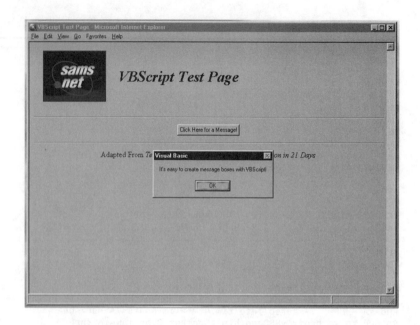

To see what would happen if you didn't use those comment tags and then used a browser that was not VBScript-aware, look at the Web page created in Listing 21.2 and shown in Figure 21.5.

Listing 21.2. A Web page using VBScript code and no comment tags for the script code.

```
<HTML>

<HEAD>
<TITLE>VBScript Test Page</TITLE>
</HEAD>

<BODY>

<H1>
<A HREF="http://www.mcp.com"><IMG  ALIGN=MIDDLE
SRC="../shared/jpg/samsnet.jpg" BORDER=2 HSPACE=20></A>
<EM>VBScript Test Page</EM></H1>

<H2>No comment markers!</H2>

<HR>

<CENTER>
<INPUT TYPE=BUTTON LANGUAGE="VBScript" VALUE="Click Here for a Message!"
➥NAME="TestButton"></CENTER>

<HR>
```

```
<center>
Adapted From <em>Teach Yourself VBScript in 21
Days</em><br> by <A HREF="../shared/info/keith.htm">Keith Brophy</A>
and <A HREF="../shared/info/tim.htm">Tim Koets</A><br><br>
Return to <a href="VBSDemo.htm">Content Overview</A><br>
Copyright 1996 by SamsNet<br>
</center>

<SCRIPT LANGUAGE="VBScript">
      Sub TestButton_OnClick()
          MsgBox "It's easy to create message boxes with VBScript!"
      End Sub
</SCRIPT>

</BODY>

</HTML>
```

Figure 21.5 shows the Web page when viewed with Mosaic, which at the time of this printing did not support VBScript.

FIGURE 21.5.

*An example of
VBScript code with
no comment tags.*

Notice that in this case all the VBScript code is printed in the Web page—a very undesirable result! You can avoid this misfortune by using the comment tags whenever you write VBScript code within a Web page. That's all there is to it!

Summary

This chapter introduced you to the exciting world of VBScript. You learned what VBScript is, what it can do, and how it resembles its parent language, Visual Basic for Applications. You also learned about the tools you need to incorporate VBScript into your Web pages and that VBScript is an easy language to learn. Because security is a big issue on the Internet these days, we also discussed the ways in which VBScript is secure on the Web. Finally, you learned how to place VBScript code within an HTML document. This relatively easy process enables you to work with any browser that supports HTML and VBScript.

The next chapter presents a comprehensive overview of the VBScript language, and you will learn to write VBScript-based Web pages on your own. Then, in Chapter 22, you can examine several useful, working Web pages that take advantage of VBScript and the rich suite of capabilities it offers.

CHAPTER 22

The VBScript Language

by Keith Brophy and Tim Koets

IN THIS CHAPTER

In this chapter, you will learn the fundamentals of programming with VBScript. You will first learn the basics, such as creating variables, using operators, controlling the flow of code, and creating procedures. Then you will see how to use existing HTML and ActiveX controls along with VBScript to enhance your Web pages. You will also learn about Script Object Model Objects and other objects you can use along with VBScript to take advantage of the cutting-edge Internet technology on the Web.

All About Variables

Before you learn the more advanced aspects of VBScript programming, you need to become familiar with the basics. The first thing you need to know about VBScript programming is how to create a variable.

Creating Variables

When you create a variable, you have to give it a name. That way, when you need to find out what's contained inside the variable, you use its name to let the computer know to which variable you are referring. In most cases, the name you assign to the variable helps you recall what the variable is used for. For example, a variable named Age is much easier to remember and understand than a variable named X.

You can be quite creative when you name variables in VBScript, but you can't use just any name you want; you have to follow a few naming rules. The first rule is that the name must begin with a letter. A variable name of 1ToMany, for example, is not allowed. Second, the variable name cannot contain a period or space. A variable named Customer Name is illegal and produces an error. You can't use a period either because VBScript uses periods to reference properties of objects. Third, the length of a variable name cannot exceed 255 characters. You should keep your variables short but meaningful or expect your fingers to get very sore.

After you've decided on a name for your variable, you have two ways to create it. The first way, called the *explicit method,* is where you use the Dim keyword to tell VBScript you are about to create a variable. You then follow this keyword with the name of the variable. For example, if you want to create a variable called Quantity, you would enter

```
Dim Quantity
```

and the variable will then exist. It's that simple! If you want to create more than one variable, you can put several on the same line and separate them by commas, such as

```
Dim X, Y, Z
```

The second way to create a variable is called the *implicit method.* In this case, you don't need to use the Dim statement. You can just start using the variable in your code, and VBScript creates it automatically. If, for example, you want to store the quantity of an item, you can simply enter

```
Quantity = 10
```

using the implicit method. You don't have to create the variable explicitly with a `Dim` statement.

If you take no special steps, you can freely intermix the implicit and explicit methods of declaring variables. When you want to, you can choose to set aside a named storage space before you use it by giving it a name in advance through the `Dim` statement. On the other hand, you can also rely on the fact that when you refer to something by name in a statement and space hasn't yet been reserved for storing that variable, it will be created for you on-the-fly.

This method of intermixing implicit and explicit declarations can produce programs that are confusing to follow, to say the least. Fortunately, VBScript gives you a way to force a consistent explicit declaration approach. To make the explicit method a requirement and prevent the implicit allocation of names, you must place the command

```
Option Explicit
```

in the first line of the first script in your HTML document, as shown in the following segment:

```
<SCRIPT LANGUAGE="VBScript">
<!--
Option Explicit
[the rest of your script code]
-->
</SCRIPT>
```

> **NOTE**
>
> At the time of this writing, VBScript was still in beta form, as was Internet Explorer 3.0. With the beta software, the `Option Explicit` statement was not yet fully implemented and had to be placed in the first line next to the HTML comment tag to be included without errors. The beta implementation of `Option Explicit` did not always explicitly force variable declaration as specified.
>
> I expect that `Option Explicit` will be fully implemented in the final release of Internet Explorer 3.0. You might find further updates on implementation status by visiting Microsoft's Web site at www.microsoft.com/vbscript, the Macmillan Publishing site at www.mcp.com (look for the book title under Sams.net), or the authors' update site at www.doubleblaze.com. In the samples in the book, the `Option Explicit` statement appears next to the comment tag to prevent errors.

The `Option Explicit` statement therefore makes explicit declarations a requirement, and you have to define every variable with a declaration such as `Dim`. With `Option Explicit`, if you have not defined the variable before you use it, you can't use it! Therefore, you need to enter the command

```
Dim Quantity
```

before you enter

```
Quantity = 10
```

In the explicit method, if you assign Quantity with a value of 10 before creating it, you will get an error.

You might be wondering, "Why use the explicit method when I can just start using variables?" The implicit method is certainly more convenient while you are writing the code—that is, until you spell a variable wrong. What will happen? VBScript will go ahead and create another variable based on your misspelling, and you will get the wrong result. Consider, for example, the following code segment:

```
<SCRIPT LANGUAGE="VBScript">
<!--
Quantity = 2
Quantity = Quantity + 3
-->
</SCRIPT>
```

You would expect the result to be 5, right? And it would be. Suppose you misspelled Quantity in the second line of code:

```
<SCRIPT LANGUAGE="VBScript">
<!--
Quantity = 2
Quantity = Quantite + 3
-->
</SCRIPT>
```

The variable Quantite would be created on the fly, and because it was never defined or previously assigned a value, it would be assigned a value of zero. The result variable Quantity, then, would wind up being 3, not 5. If, on the other hand, you were using the explicit method of creating variables, you would enter the code as

```
<SCRIPT LANGUAGE="VBScript">
<!-- Option Explicit
Quantity = 2
Quantity = Quantity + 3
-->
</SCRIPT>
```

which would give you a runtime error if you spelled Quantity wrong because you had not declared it first. The runtime error that results from using Option Explicit typically alerts you to the problem and leads you to correct the error right away. On the other hand, if you didn't use Option Explicit and therefore didn't receive the runtime error, you have a much more subtle problem. You might not even notice the incorrect result, and even if you did, you would probably have a more difficult time targeting the source of the problem.

The Contents of Variables

VBScript is a new product, but it is a language derived from its parent product, Microsoft Visual Basic. VBScript is essentially a subset of Visual Basic. When you create variables in Visual Basic, you have the opportunity to specify what type of data you want to store in a variable. If, for example, you want to store integers in a variable, you can declare the variable as an integer variable using the integer data type. As a result, if you try to store anything other than an integer in the variable, Visual Basic either converts the data automatically into integer format or tells you the assignment cannot be made.

If you can be specific about the type of data you are storing, your code has the potential to be less error-prone because you make fewer mistakes when assigning data to variables. On the other hand, programming is easier if you do not have to worry about restricting a variable to specific types of data. Visual Basic also gives you the choice of creating variables when the kind of data you want to store doesn't matter. This special type of variable is called a *variant*.

> **NOTE**
>
> A *variant* is a special type of variable that can store a wide variety of data types. In many programming languages, variables can contain only a specific predeclared type of information, such as integers or strings. However, you can assign an integer value to a variant in one statement and then replace that integer with a string value in a subsequent statement. Variables in VBScript are based on the variant.

VBScript uses the variant as the basis for variables you create. The variant is used most often to store numbers and strings, but it can store a variety of other types of data. These data types are often called *subtypes* because the variant can represent them all internally. VBScript keeps track of these subtypes on its own; you usually just store whatever you want in the variable. VBScript matches the data to the best subtype and behaves accordingly.

To understand what the variant actually is, you should understand all the other data types that the variant can represent. These data types are taken from VBScript's parent, Visual Basic. By learning about these data types, you will begin to see how the variant works and what you can and cannot store in a VBScript variable. Here is a list of all the subtypes that the variant uses to represent the data you store in a variable:

- Boolean
- Byte
- Integer
- Long
- Single

- Double
- Date (Time)
- String
- Object
- Error
- Empty
- Null

When you are considering how data is stored in a variable, think of a closet full of shoe boxes. Every type of shoe has a certain type of box that can store the shoe. In addition to the boxes that store specific types of shoes, other larger, generic-looking boxes are on hand. These generic boxes can store any of the types of shoes. The shoe boxes that store specific types of shoes represent the subtypes, whereas the boxes that can store any kind of shoe represent the variant. The variant is a "fit-all" data type that can hold any of the subtypes.

The following paragraphs explain what type of data can be stored in VBScript variables.

Boolean

You can set the Boolean data type to either `True` or `False`, which VBScript represents as `-1` and `0`, respectively. This subtype is useful when you want to determine or set a condition for the variable.

Byte

The byte data type can store an integer value between 0 and 255. It is used to preserve binary data and store simple data that doesn't need to exceed this range.

Integer

The integer data type is a number that cannot contain a decimal point. Integers can range from -32,768 to +32,767.

Long

Variables of the long data type are also integers, but they have a much higher range, -2,147,483,648 to 2,147,683,647, to be exact. Because this data type is also an integer, you cannot use decimal points. Long integers are also quite common and are usually used when the range of the number exceeds the smaller range of the integer.

Single

The single subtype represents *floating-point,* or decimal, values, which means that numbers represented by this subtype include decimal points. The range jumps to a whopping $-1.4E^{-45}$ to $-3.4E^{38}$ for negative numbers and $1.4E^{-45}$ to $3.4E^{38}$ for positive numbers. (These numbers are expressed in *scientific notation.*)

> **NOTE**
>
> *Scientific notation* is a way to represent very small or very large numbers. A number is expressed as *x.xxEyyy* where *x.xx* is a number and *yyy* represents how many places to shift the decimal point over in the number. If *yyy* is positive, the decimal moves to the right. If *yyy* is negative, the decimal moves to the left. Thus, the expression 3.45E02 becomes 345 and 2.34E-03 becomes 0.00234.

Double

Double is another floating-point data type, but this data type has an even larger range than the single data type. The range for the double is $-4.9E^{-324}$ to $-1.8E^{308}$ for negative numbers and $4.9E^{-324}$ to $1.8E^{308}$ for positive numbers.

Date (Time)

The date subtype stores dates and times in a special format. This popular subtype places the date in a predefined format that other functions in VBScript can act upon. If, for example, you have a date variable named HireDate and you want to know what year is in the date, you can simply use the function Year(HireDate) to find it. If you use the date subtype to represent HireDate, the function can retrieve the year from the variable.

String

The string is used to store alphanumeric data—that is, numbers, letters, and symbols. The string is another commonly used subtype for VBScript variables.

Object

The object data type is a special subtype used to reference OLE automation objects within a VBScript application or another application. Microsoft created OLE automation to enable one application to share information and control with another.

Error

The error subtype is used for error handling and debugging purposes.

Empty

The empty subtype is used for variables that have been created but not yet assigned any data. Numeric variables are assigned 0, and string variables are assigned " " in this uninitialized condition.

Null

The null subtype refers to variables that have been set to contain no data. Unlike the empty subtype, the programmer must specifically set a variable to null.

How Variables Are Stored

In many languages, you can allocate a variable to accept a specific type of data—say, integer data. As stated earlier, you cannot directly create a variable in VBScript that "knows" ahead of time it will contain only integer data. Instead, you can create a variable that can take on integer values along with any of the other subtypes listed previously. VBScript handles the conversions automatically. Suppose, for example, that you declare a variable in VBScript as

```
Dim Item
```

Then, suppose that you set the variable Item equal to an integer value:

```
Item = 23
```

VBScript stores the value 23 in the Item variable as an integer. If, on the other hand, you were to set Item with a string, as

```
Item = "Tacoma, Washington"
```

the text you place in the variable Item gets stored internally as a string. The great advantage of the variant is that you don't have to worry about placing the wrong type of data in a variable. In Visual Basic 4.0, for example, you can declare an integer value with the statement

```
Dim Distance as Integer
```

You could enter a distance in miles easily by using the statement

```
Distance = 6
```

Suppose, however, that you want to enter a distance of 6.5 miles. If you enter the statement

```
Distance = 6.5
```

Visual Basic 4.0 will store the distance as 7. This happens because you told Visual Basic the variable was based on the integer data type, which cannot store decimal points. As a result, Visual Basic 4.0 obediently stores it as an integer by rounding the value, in this case, up to an even seven miles. This problem is automatically solved for you in VBScript, where you simply enter the declaration

```
Dim Distance
```

and then set the distance using

```
Distance = 6.5
```

or

```
Distance = 6
```

or even

```
Distance = "6 Miles"
```

It doesn't really matter what you set the Distance variable to. Because the variant data type is used, VBScript automatically converts the data into the best possible subtype internally. The first assignment is converted into a single-precision value, the second to an integer, and the third to a string. As you can see, the variant gives you complete flexibility in entering data because you aren't limited by predeclared data types. Furthermore, the variant can automatically convert data from one type to another. If, for example, you have two variables assigned as

```
Distance = 6.75
Units = " feet"
```

you can put the two variables together into a third variable using

```
Result = Distance & Units
```

which makes Result equal to the string 6.75 feet. Now suppose you were using Visual Basic 4.0. If you defined the Distance variable as the single data type and you defined Units as a string, the command

```
Results = Distance & Units
```

would result in a Type Mismatch error. This error simply means that Visual Basic 4.0 isn't able to add a string to a number. It can add strings to strings and numbers to numbers, but not strings to numbers. Visual Basic 4.0 doesn't automatically add a string to a number because the two are incompatible. When using variants, however, VBScript makes some assumptions for you. On its own, it determines that when you're adding a number to a string, you're going to get a string result. Because the variant can take on any of the data types, it simply stores the result in the variable as a string result.

Constants

Sometimes in writing code, you will want to refer to values that never change. The values for True and False, for example, are always -1 and 0, respectively. Values that never change usually have some special meaning, such as defining True and False. These special kinds of values that never change are called *constants*. The constants True and False are sometimes referred to as *implicit* constants because you do not need to do anything to reference their constant names. They are immediately available in any script you write.

You have already seen the `True` and `False` constants in action in the previous code samples. Keep in mind that changing the value of either of these intrinsic constants is illegal. Therefore, the statement

```
False = 10
```

would result in an error because VBScript has already defined `False` to be `0`. VBScript won't let you change a constant, even though you can change a variable.

Unfortunately, you cannot create true constants with VBScript because the language will still enable you to change the value of any constant variable you define. Many languages have special ways to declare a constant so that you cannot alter its value anywhere in the program. VBScript does not offer this level of strict enforcement. However, you can simulate a true constant by following two rules:

- When you create a simulated constant, name the constant with uppercase letters if the constant represents a value unique to your program. If the constant is a special value expected by VBScript, prefix the constant name with the letters `vb`. This naming convention is not required, but it will help you distinguish the constant from other variables.

- After you assign the initial value to a simulated constant, don't change the value of the constant. VBScript will not enforce this for you, so you'll have to make sure you don't change the value of a simulated constant in your code.

As an example, if you want to create a constant that contains your company name so you can use it throughout your code, you can use the following statements to define the constant:

```
Dim COMPANY
COMPANY = "Acme Enterprises"
```

Then use the variable throughout your code, never assigning the variable `COMPANY` to any other value. This convention will help you work with and recognize simulated constants.

The Scope and Lifetime of a Variable

When a variable is created, you can either use it within a specific procedure or share it among all the procedures in the script. A variable's availability within its environment is referred to as the *scope* of a variable. Variables in VBScript can have two kinds of scope. When a variable is declared inside a procedure, it has *local scope* and can be referenced only while that procedure is executed. Local-scope variables are often called *procedure-level* variables because they exist only in procedures. When you declare a variable in a procedure, it automatically has local scope, which means that only the code within that procedure can access or change the value of that variable. However, you might want to share a variable with other procedures. If you declare a variable outside of a procedure, it automatically has *script-level* scope and is available to all the procedures in your script.

> **NOTE**
>
> Scope refers to where within a script a given variable is available based on the declaration, such as locally within a procedure or globally across the script.

Another characteristic of variables is that they exist for different amounts of time, depending on their scope. This property of a variable is often referred to as its *lifetime*. Script-level variables are created outside of any procedures using the Dim keyword, and they exist from the time the variable is declared until the time the script is finished running.

The lifetime of a script-level variable is equal to the entire life of the Web page. On the other hand, when you declare a procedure-level variable using Dim, the variable exists only while the procedure is run. Once the procedure ends, the variable is destroyed.

Arrays

You create arrays using the same keyword you use to create variables—the Dim keyword. An array created with the Dim keyword exists as long as the procedure does and is destroyed once the procedure ends. If you create the array in the main script, outside of the procedure, the values will persist as long as the page is loaded. You can create two types of arrays using VBScript: *fixed* arrays and *dynamic* arrays. Fixed arrays have a specific number of elements in them, whereas dynamic arrays can vary in the number of elements depending on how many are stored in the array. Both types of arrays are useful, and both have advantages and disadvantages.

Fixed-Length Arrays

You can create fixed-length arrays using the following syntax:

```
Dim Array_Name(count - 1)
```

where Array_Name is the name of the array and *count* is an integer value representing the number of containers you want the array to contain. The statement

```
Dim Names(19)
```

creates an array called Names that consists of 20 containers, often called *elements*. You can store 20 different names in this array of data called Names. Consider the shoe box analogy discussed earlier in this chapter. Creating an array is like having 20 shoe boxes, all the same size, in which you can store shoes. Instead of naming each box separately, you can give them all the same name and refer to them using an index, such as ShoeBox(1), ShoeBox(2), Shoebox(3), and so on.

The index of the array always starts at zero and ends at `count -1`. In the case of the `Names` array, the number of containers, or elements, in the array ranges from `Names(0)` to `Names(19)` for a total of 20 elements. To see how this works, look at the following code:

```
Dim Names(19)
Dim i

For i = 0 to 19
    Names(i) = "Unknown"
Next
```

This simple code listing sets every element of the `Names` array equal to the string `"Unknown"`. This process is similar to putting the same type of shoe in every shoe box in your closet. This code listing uses a *loop* to set each element. Essentially, the program treats the variable `i` like a counter and keeps incrementing it by 1 all the way from 0 to 19. The `Names(i) = "Unknown"` code statement is executed 20 times, and each time the `i` value is different. You need to remember that the first container in your array has an index of 0, not 1. In this example, the first element in the array is `Names(0)`, not `Names(1)`. If you forget this rule and start with `Names(1)`, you'll only be able to use 19 of the containers, not 20.

Dynamic Arrays

The second type of array you can create is the dynamic array. The benefit of a dynamic array is that if you don't know how large the array will be when you write the code, you can create code that sets or changes the size while the VBScript code is running. A dynamic array is created in the same way as a fixed array, but you don't put any bounds in the declaration. As a result, your statement becomes

```
Dim Names()
```

Eventually, you need to tell VBScript how many elements the array will contain. You can do this with the `ReDim` function. `ReDim` tells VBScript to redimension the array to however many elements you specify. `ReDim` takes dimensions the same way `Dim` can. The syntax is

```
ReDim Array_Name(Count - 1)
```

So, if you enter

```
ReDim Names(9)
```

you will create an array that has room to store 10 elements. This way, you can set the size of the array while the code is running, rather than when you write the code.

Suppose that you dimension an array in your code, and later on, you need to increase the size of the array. No problem, right? You just use `ReDim` again and increase the number of elements in the array. That method will certainly work, but the entire array will be erased in the process. This situation is like adding more shoe boxes to your closet by taking out all the shoe boxes, emptying them, and putting the total number you want back in empty. Do not despair; VBScript contains a special keyword called `Preserve` that comes to the rescue.

The `Preserve` keyword is very important when using `ReDim`. Suppose, for example, that you create a dynamic array, specify its storage space by using `ReDim`, fill it with data, and then later decide to make it larger so you can fill it with more information without losing your original data.

If you want to erase whatever is in the array when you resize it, leave off the `Preserve` keyword. If you want to keep what you have, make sure to include `Preserve` when you `ReDim` an array.

> **NOTE**
>
> Concepts such as determining the size of an array, creating multidimensional arrays, and erasing the contents of arrays are discussed in *Teach Yourself VBScript in 21 Days* by Brophy and Koets from Sams.net.

Using Operators

Now that you've seen how to create variables, you need to know how to use *operators* to make those variables do useful work for you. Operators are given that name because they *operate* on the variables associated with them. As you begin to write VBScript code, you will use operators so much that their use will become natural to you. In this section, you will learn about each VBScript operator, as well as how to use them.

Arithmetic Operators

The first major class of operators is *arithmetic operators.* Arithmetic operators enable you to perform simple arithmetic on one or more variables.

> **NOTE**
>
> *Arithmetic operators are a special class of operators specifically intended to perform arithmetic on the corresponding data.*

You will be familiar with most of these operators because you have been exposed to them in everyday life. Few people will be surprised to find, for example, that the + operator performs addition. Some operators, however, might be new to you. In any case, you need to understand how to apply these operators to variables and literals in VBScript code.

Addition (+)

The first arithmetic operator is the addition operator. As you surely guessed, the addition operator is used to add values, whether they are stored in variables, constants, or literal numbers. You also use the + operator to concatenate strings, but for now, just focus on its capability to add numbers—I'll discuss string concatenation later in this chapter.

Subtraction (-)

The subtraction operator should also be very familiar to you. This operator works the same way the addition operator does except that it subtracts one or more numbers. Otherwise, the syntax is the same.

Multiplication (*)

Addition and subtraction are important, but you also need a way to multiply values together. Most computer languages use the * symbol to indicate multiplication, not the × symbol. You might be able to use × on paper, but to the computer, × is a variable, not a multiplication symbol. If you enter the command

```
Result = 3 x 2
```

the interpreter will give you a syntax error. To be correct, you should enter the command

```
Result = 3 * 2
```

Division (/ and \)

The division operator is the last of the four commonly used arithmetic operators, and division is the most complicated arithmetic operation a computer performs. This statement shouldn't surprise you if you remember learning long division in grade school math class. VBScript has two types of division operators. The first operator handles numbers with decimal points. Usually referred to as the *floating-point* division operator, it's represented by the / symbol in code listings. If you are relatively new to programming, you might be wondering at this point if you can use a more familiar symbol for the same purpose. The answer is no; you cannot use the familiar ÷ symbol in computer speak—you must instead use the / symbol for floating-point division. The floating-point division operator is designed to divide values with decimal points, but it can also divide numbers without decimals. The syntax for division is the same as for any of the other operators presented so far:

```
c = a / b
```

This code divides the variable b into a and puts the result into the variable c. Similarly, you could use numbers and perform a division such as

```
c = a / 2
```

which, in this case, divides the variable a in half. If the variable a were set to some valid numeric value, say 3, the result stored in c would be 1.5.

From time to time, you might want to divide integer values or perform a division without a decimal point in the result. In that case, you want to use integer division. Integer division is performed the same way floating-point division is, but the operator is different. Rather than use a forward-slash (/), you use a backward slash (\).

Using the same numbers as before, if you were to enter

```
c = a \ 2
```

an integer division would take place. The decimal would be chopped off, and the result would be 2 rather than 1.5. You need to remember that integer division turns your result into an integer by rounding the original values of the operands to integers to calculate the results. For example, consider the result of the following calculation:

```
c = 4 \ 1.9
```

The value of variable c after this statement executes will be 2. VBScript processes this calculation after an internal rounding of the operands. The expression VBScript will act upon in this case is not c = 4 \ 1.9 or c = 4 \ 1. Instead, it rounds the operands to perform the calculation of c = 4 \ 2, which equals 2.

> **NOTE**
>
> Additional operators such as the exponent, the modulo, and negation operators are discussed in *Teach Yourself VBScript in 21 Days* from Sams.net.

Comparison Operators

The first set of operators VBScript provides are arithmetic operators. This section discusses the second type: *comparison operators*. As the name implies, you use comparison operators to compare one or more variables, numbers, constants, or a combination of the three. VBScript has many different types of comparison operators, and each type checks for a different comparison condition.

Equality (=)

You use the equality operator to see if a variable, constant, or number is equal to another. It's common to mistake the equality operator for the assignment operator, which is also represented by an equals sign. You use the *assignment* operator to set a variable equal to another variable, number, string, constant, or other data entity. For example, the statement

```
a = b
```

assigns the value contained in b to the variable a.

The equality operator, on the other hand, is used to test whether one value is equal to another. The syntax for the equality operator looks similar to that for the assignment operator

```
a = b
```

where *a* and *b* can be variables, constants, or numbers. The context in which you use the expression determines whether it is treated as an assignment or an equality check. Equality is always used in the context of checking a condition. For example, a statement such as

```
if a = b then
```

is an example of the equality operator because it is a conditional check. As a rule of thumb, you can assume that if a = b appears in a statement by itself, it is an assignment statement. If you see a = b as part of any other expression, it is used in the equality context.

Inequality (<>)

Another important comparison operator is the inequality operator. You use this operator to test whether a variable is not equal to another variable or some data element. The syntax for the inequality operator is

```
a <> b
```

where *a* and *b* are variables, constants, strings, or numbers. Again, the expression returns True if the condition is indeed true and False if it isn't. For example, you can take the following code

```
If TravelTime = 0 Then
    MsgBox "The speed cannot be calculated because the time is zero.
  Please enter a valid time."
Else
    Speed = Distance / TravelTime
    txtSpeed.Value = Speed
End If
```

and make the following change—that is, use the inequality operator rather than the equality operator—and get the same results:

```
If TravelTime <> 0 Then
    Speed = Distance / TravelTime
    txtSpeed.Value = Speed
Else
    MsgBox "The speed cannot be calculated because the time is zero.
  Please enter a valid time."
End If
```

Using the inequality operator is sometimes more convenient and sensible than using the equality operator.

Greater Than and Less Than (> and <)

You might have a condition where you don't care whether a variable is equal to another, but you do want to know whether it is greater than or less than another variable, number, or constant. In such a case, you need the greater-than and less-than operators. The syntax for these two operators is

a > b

and

a < b

where *a* and *b* are variables, constants, numbers, or strings, and the result is True if the expression is true. Otherwise, the expression returns False. For an example of its use, consider the following code:

```
If TravelTime > 0 Then
    Speed = Distance / TravelTime
    txtSpeed.Value = Speed
Else If TravelTime < 0 Then
    MsgBox "You cannot enter a negative value for the time!"
Else If TravelTime = 0 Then
    MsgBox "The time must be greater than zero!"
End If
```

Here, you see the greater-than, less-than, and equality operators all in use. If the variable TravelTime is greater than zero, a speed can be calculated, but if TravelTime is less than zero or equal to zero, the user must be notified—any such value would not be valid.

You could write the same code in another way if you think carefully about the conditions being satisfied. If a travel time is not greater than zero and not less than zero, you know it must be zero. Even without checking for this value, you can tell that zero is the only possibility left! You could therefore rewrite the code as

```
If TravelTime > 0 Then
    Speed = Distance / TravelTime
    txtSpeed.Value = Speed
Else If TravelTime < 0 Then
    MsgBox "You cannot enter a negative value for the time!"
Else
    MsgBox "The time must be greater than zero!"
End If
```

This code works just as well as the previous code. The first method was used to emphasize the purpose of the equality expression. The first method is also a better approach in some respects; for example, the purpose of each branch of the code is more clearly defined and easier to read and debug when the conditions are explicitly named. Code that is clearer is usually also easier to maintain and less subject to bugs.

> **NOTE**
>
> The less-than-or-equal-to and greater-than-or-equal-to (<= and >=) operators are discussed in *Teach Yourself VBScript in 21 Days* from Sams.net.

Object Equivalence (`Is`)

The last comparison operator is designed for objects, which are discussed in more detail later in the chapter. For now, consider an object such as a command button that you can place on a Web page. The syntax of the `Is` operator is

```
result = object_reference1 Is object_reference2
```

where `object_reference1` and `object_reference2` are references to objects and `result` is either `True` or `False`, depending on whether the statement is true.

This operator does not compare one object to another, nor does it compare values. This special operator simply checks to see if the two object references in the expression are the same object. Suppose, for example, you have a command button in your script that you have defined as `TestButton`. You have another variable, `myObject`, that is set to reference different objects at different points in your program. Assume a statement has been carried out that assigns the variable `myObject` to reference `TestButton`, such as

```
Set myObject = TestButton
```

If the script later carries out the expression

```
result = myObject Is TestButton
```

it will return the `True` in the variable `result` because `TestButton` is indeed the same object as that referred to by `myObject`. If, on the other hand, you were to enter

```
result = myObject Is SomeOtherTestButton
```

`result` would be `False` because the two objects are not the same.

As you can see from this discussion, you must apply some special rules when you deal with objects. For example, you must use the `Set` statement to assign an object's value, as shown previously. You cannot directly compare two objects with an equal statement, such as

```
if myObject = TestButton   ' illegal syntax
```

Logical Operators

The last category of operators in VBScript is *logical operators*. The logical operators are probably the most difficult operators to understand.

Negation (Not)

The first operator is called the *negation* operator. This operator has the following syntax:

```
result = Not expression
```

Table 22.1 shows the `result` variable in relation to `expression`.

Table 22.1. Negation (Not) results.

If expression *is...*	*Then* result *is...*
True	False
False	True
Null	Null

If you enter the expression

```
a = Not 1 > 2
```

where the expression is `1 > 2`, the result is stored in the variable a. The value stored in variable a will be `True`. The expression `1 > 2` is false because 1 is not greater than 2. `Not` simply flips a false over to true or a true over to false. Because the expression is false, the `Not` operator makes the result true. As a result, the VBScript value for true, `True` or `-1`, will be stored in variable a. If the expression is null, the `Not` operator will return a null when applied to the expression.

The `Not` operator is often used when working with if-then conditionals, such as the following example:

```
If Not GetZip(City, State, Zip) Then
    MsgBox "The zip code could not be determined."
Else
    MsgBox "The zip code is " & Zip
End If
```

This simple example calls the function `GetZip`. The arguments for this function are the city, state, and ZIP code. The function returns a Boolean value that indicates whether the function has succeeded. This return variable is often called a *return code*. The function loads the variable `Zip` with the ZIP code and returns `True` if it is successful. If the function fails, it returns `vbFalse`. The function could fail, for example, if an invalid state or city was passed as an argument to the function.

The conditional statement checks the return code. If it is true, the function has succeeded and the code proceeds to show the user the ZIP code. In this case, the `Not` operator is used instead, checking to see whether the result of the function is `True or False`.

Conjunction (And)

The conjunction operator compares two or more variables in some type of test. The syntax for the conjunction operator is

```
result = expression1 And expression2
```

In order to obtain True in the *result* variable, both *expression1* and *expression2* must be true. You often use this operator to make sure two or more conditions are true before performing some action. Suppose you have a Web page for making airline reservations. You have several functions in your code: one to get the customer's name and address, one for the origination point, one for the destination, and one for the day he or she wants to travel. In order to book the reservation, each function must succeed. If any of them fail, the reservation cannot be made. The following statement is an example of what could appear in a VBScript code segment:

```
OkayToReserve =
➥GetCustomer(Name, Address, Phone) And
➥GetDepartureCity(DepartCity) And
➥GetDestinationCity(DestinationCity) And
➥GetTravelDate(TravelDate)
```

If the function that gets the destination city from the customer, for example, does not succeed for whatever reason, your program will not accept the reservation.

This example is simple, but you get the point. Each of these functions must return True. If any one of them fails, the variable OkayToReserve will be false. You can then make a simple check to determine whether to make the reservation:

```
If OkayToReserve = True Then MakeReservation( Name, Address, Phone,
➥DepartCity, DestinationCity, TravelDate )
```

NOTE

VBScript lets you take a shortcut when referencing true in a condition. You don't have to explicitly compare the condition to true. If you have no comparison, VBScript assumes you are checking the true condition. The following statement is functionally equivalent to the previous example without using the True constant:

```
If OkayToReserve Then MakeReservation( Name, Address, Phone,
➥DepartCity, DestinationCity, TravelDate )
```

Disjunction (Or)

Another frequently used logical operator is the *disjunction* operator. This operator has the same syntax as the conjunction operator:

```
result = expression1 Or expression2
```

This operator behaves quite a bit differently from the conjunction operator. In this case, any of the expressions can be true for the result to be true. The result is false only if all the expressions are false. You typically use this operator when you have to make a decision in which any of a number of activities could occur, but only one must occur for the operation to proceed.

Suppose you want to call a function on your Web page that processes an order for flowers. If you have five varieties of flowers, the customer could order one or more types. You simply want to see if any of them are on order. All it takes to process an order is a request for one type. The following code segment handles this request for you:

```
If Order1 Or Order2 Or Order3 Or Order4 Or Order5 Then
    OrderFlowers()
End If
```

In this case, five variables exist that are true or false, depending on whether the user wants to order flowers of that type. If the user wants to order flowers of any type, the script calls the `OrderFlowers` function. That function can then determine the specifics of the flower order.

> **NOTE**
>
> Additional logical operators, such as the exclusion operator (Xor), the logical equivalence operator (Eqv) and the implication operator (Imp) are discussed in detail in *Teach Yourself VBScript in 21 Days* from Sams.net.

String Concatenation

One special operator does not fit in any of the other classes. This operator, called the *string concatenation* operator, is represented by the & symbol.

String Concatenation Using the & Operator

You use the string concatenation operator to merge two strings together. If, for example, one variable holds the string

```
First_Name = "Buddy"
```

and the second holds the string

```
Last_Name = "Bird"
```

to form a complete name, you need to concatenate these two strings. The syntax for the concatenation operator is

```
result = string1 & string2 & ... & stringn
```

String Concatenation Using the + Operator

You should know one more thing about string concatenation. As you begin to see examples of VBScript code on the Internet, you might sometimes see strings concatenated using the + operator, rather than the & operator. For example, you can build a name with this code:

```
Name = First_Name + " " + Last_Name
```

This statement would correctly build the string "Buddy Bird" for you. Although you can indeed use the addition operator to concatenate strings, you're not always guaranteed a correct result because the addition operator is designed for numeric values. It can handle strings, but when strings are mixed with numbers, VBScript can get into an ambiguous state, not knowing exactly how you want to concatenate the values. If, for example, one of the expressions is a number and the other is a string, the + operator gives you an error:

```
Dim a, b, c
a = 10
b = " Apples"
c = a + b
MsgBox c
```

When VBScript encounters the expression c = a + b, a type mismatch error will result. Instead of trying to add a number and a string that cannot be translated into a number, you should use

```
Dim a, b, c
a = 10
b = " Apples"
c = a & b
MsgBox c
```

and you will store "10 Apples" in the variable c.

You must enclose literal numbers in quotes if you want to treat them as strings when you concatenate them to other strings. Because this step is not very convenient and requires extra thought, it's safer and better to use the & operator whenever you're concatenating strings. Any technique that helps reduce potential errors in your code is always a wise decision.

Operator Precedence

Now you have seen all the operators VBScript has to offer. For each type of operator—arithmetic, comparison, and logical—you have seen the order of precedence. What happens when operators from different categories are all combined in the same statement? What is executed first?

VBScript first attends to the arithmetic operators, followed by the string concatenation operator, the comparison operators, and the logical operators, as summarized in Table 22.2.

Table 22.2. Operator precedence summary.

Order	Operation
	Arithmetic
1	Exponents (^)
2	Negation (-)
3	Multiplication (*), division (/ and \)
4	Modulo arithmetic (Mod)
5	Addition (+), subtraction (-)
6	String concatenation (&)
	Comparison
1	Equality (=)
2	Inequality (<>)
3	Less than (<)
4	Greater than (>)
5	Less than or equal to (<=)
6	Greater than or equal to (>=)
7	Object equivalence (Is)
	Logical
1	Negation (Not)
2	Conjunction (And)
3	Disjunction (Or)
4	Exclusion (Xor)
5	Logical equivalence (Eqv)
6	Implication (Imp)

22

THE VBSCRIPT
LANGUAGE

When an expression has more than one operation, each part of that expression is evaluated in this order from left to right across the expression.

Intrinsic Functions

VBScript contains a wide variety of functions you can use to enhance and empower your applications.

Dates and Times

The functions that follow can work with a date, a time, or a time and date. In VBScript, dates and times are often stored together. The date subtype is viewed as representing both a date and time in its own format.

Date, Time, and Now

Some of the easier functions to use are Date, Time, and Now. Date returns a character string with the current date. Time returns a character string with the current time. Now returns a character string with the current date and time.

Date, Time, and Now lead to the same results. The difference is that whereas Date returns an individual date and Time returns an individual time, Now returns both the current date and time, combined into one string. To see the current date and time, for example, you could enter the following statement in a script:

```
Msgbox "Current date / time is " & Now, 0, "Using now"
```

Alternatively, you could use the Date and Time functions to provide the same type of feedback to the user.

```
Msgbox "Current date / time is " & Date & " " & Time,
        ➡0, "Using date and time"
```

Year, Month, Day, Weekday, Hour, Minute, and Second

When you use these functions, working with pieces of a date and time string is easy. If you need to use just the current hour figure to determine what type of data a program runs, you can parse out this information with the Hour function. The same type of helpful function is available if you need to know what day of the week a certain date fell on. Use the Weekday function to get your answer. You don't have to write a detailed procedure to parse this information out of a date because it is already there.

Several similar functions handle dates and extract information. Year returns a number representing the current year, Month returns an integer representing the current month, Day returns an integer representing the current day number, and Weekday returns numbers 1 through 7 to represent Sunday through Saturday, respectively. All the functions take a date specification as an argument and return data about that date supplied as an argument. The date specification argument is typically one of your variant variables, but it could also be the function Now or anything else in date and time format. The following statement shows these functions in use.

```
Dim dtmCurrent

' Start out with current time as value to use
dtmCurrent = now

Msgbox "Current year is " & Year(dtmCurrent) & "; month is " &_
        month(dtmCurrent) & "; day is " & day(dtmCurrent) &_
        ": weekday is " & weekday(dtmCurrent), _
        0, "Using year/month/day/weekday"
```

The time-based functions work much the same. Hour, Minute, and Second can derive this information from the time supplied as an argument. Here is an example of these functions in use.

```
dim dtmCurrent

' Start out with current time as value to use
dtmCurrent = now

MsgBox "Current hour is " & Hour(dtmCurrent) & "; minute is " &_
       minute(dtmCurrent) & "; second is " & second(dtmCurrent) _
       0, "Using hour/minute/second"
```

These code examples are easy to write because the functions are very straightforward to use.

> **NOTE**
>
> VBScript uses additional functions such as DateSerial, TimeSerial, CreateDate, and IsDate. These and other functions are discussed in *Teach Yourself VBScript in 21 Days* from Sams.net.

Advanced Math

Many computer programs written today require some type of math to process user data and provide results. Many require extensive mathematical operations. The ability to carry out precise calculations is an integral part of programming. It comes as no surprise then that an important part of any programming language is the mathematical capabilities it supports.

Rounding and the Integer Functions—Fix and Int

When you deal with numbers and produce results, you need to handle them in different ways. You will want to keep some results, such as the grade point average of a student, in decimal format. Other results, such as the total number of employees you need to hire to staff a factory based on average staffing history, you might round. After all, you would have trouble hiring 20.7 workers if your company doesn't use part-time help. Your best bet is hiring 21 workers. Still other results might need to be truncated. If you are writing a program that provides billing estimates based on the number of days a patient stays at a hospital, but you only charge for full days, you might treat a total of 14.2 days or 14.9 days as simply 14 days.

VBScript provides several easy-to-use functions to carry out all these tasks.. First of all, consider the case of truncating. Truncating a decimal point is essentially the same as returning the corresponding integer. The Int function serves this purpose by returning the integer portion of a number. The statement

```
MsgBox Int(14.9)
```

displays 14, as does the statement

```
MsgBox Int(14.2)
```

These statements work exactly the same way with the `Fix` function. `Fix` also truncates a number to display its integer representation. For example, the following statement displays 15:

```
MsgBox Fix(15.7)
```

One difference between these two functions—and it is a subtle one related to rounding negative numbers—is that `Fix` truncates a negative number so that the value is greater, and `Int` produces the negative integer that is less than the value supplied. The following statement displays -15:

```
MsgBox Fix(-15.7)
```

But the next statement displays -16 instead:

```
MsgBox Int(-15.7)
```

If you need to round a number rather than truncate it, you can always build in the rounding yourself. If you add .5 to a decimal number and then take the integer value using `Int`, the result is to round it to the next higher integer if the number originally contained a decimal portion greater than .5. For example, if `VarA` contains 1.7, then the following statement displays the result 2.0:

```
MsgBox Int(VarA + .5)
```

An easier and slightly different way to round is built into VBScript. The `Cint` function will round a number to the nearest integer. If decimal values are less than .5, `Cint` rounds the number down. If decimal values are greater than .5, `Cint` rounds the number up. If the decimal portion of a number is exactly equal to .5, then it is rounded to the nearest even number. For example, 7.5 would be rounded up to 8. Because 7.5 is between the two even numbers 6 and 8, 8 is the nearest even number and is selected as the rounding result. Likewise, 6.5, sandwiched between 6 and 8, would be rounded down to 6.

A good way to think of these functions is in terms of a number line. If you really want a number to be rounded rather than truncated, you should use `Cint`. This function moves you to the closest integer on the number line and chooses the closest even integer when the choice is a toss-up. If you simply want to truncate the number, and you always want to truncate to a lesser value, then `Int` is the way to go. `Int` always advances you left on the number line to the previous integer. If you do have a special situation where you want to truncate, but you always truncate closer to 0, then use `Fix`. This function will always advance you to the next closest integer to 0, moving you left on the number line when you started with a positive number and right on the number line when you started with a negative number.

> **NOTE**
>
> VBScript has many additional math functions such as `Fix`, `Log`, `Exp`, `Sqr`, `Sin`, `Cos`, `Tan`, `Atn`, `Trig`, `Randomize`, `Rnd`, and `Mod`. These and other mathematical functions are discussed in *Teach Yourself VBScript in 21 Days* from Sams.net.

The MsgBox Function

Sometimes, particularly in a programming language, simple is beautiful. An easy-to-use programming function or element is less likely to cause you bugs, which saves you time, effort, and the pain of banging your head on the monitor in frustration. Simple means good, clear, maintainable code. The message box function is just that—good and simple!

You have seen examples of the message box earlier in this chapter. For example, you can insert a statement in your code that displays a small window with the message Break time! with just 20 characters of typing:

```
MsgBox "Break time!"
```

When this code statement is carried out, a window containing this message pops up in the middle of the screen. Not only does the user see this message in a nice little window, but that window even comes with a handy acknowledgment button. The window hangs around until the user clicks on the button to make it go away.

First, consider the issue of interaction. Users could click OK because it is the only choice! The purpose of forcing users to select OK is to make sure that they read the message. The OK button, in this case, is simply an acknowledgment button.

You can use MsgBox to get much more information from the user than simply an acknowledgment. The second parameter of the function is used to specify message box attributes. One attribute that you can specify is the type of buttons to include in the message box. Consequently, your selection affects the type of information that the user returns to your code.

A specific integer number specifies each type of button choice attribute. The values and purposes are summarized in Table 22.3.

Table 22.3. VBScript button constants.

Value	Purpose
0	Show only OK button
1	Show OK and Cancel buttons
2	Display Abort, Retry, and Ignore buttons
3	Show Yes, No, and Cancel buttons
4	Show Yes and No buttons
5	Show Retry and Cancel buttons

You can use button attribute constants to request different combinations of buttons as well. All the available combinations are documented in Table 22.3. Most of these combinations give the user the opportunity to provide more feedback to the script than just a simple acknowledgment. The vbYesNoCancel constant, for example, provides three choices for the user, as shown in the next example:

```
rc = MsgBox( "rc = MsgBox ""Text"", vbYesNoCancel + vbExclamation, ""Title"" ", _
    vbYesNoCancel + vbExclamation, "vbYesNoCancel")
```

The script can then interpret which button the user selected and perform further processing based on that response. But that's not the whole story of the second parameter. The second parameter has two pieces joined by a plus sign. The button indicator code is on the left side. What's that on the right side? It's a value that indicates the icon to display with the message box.

When the MsgBox function is used, it sends a return value back to the statement that called it. This return code can be assigned to a variable of any name, although the convention of rc for return code is often used. The return code will indicate which button the user selected. This value will be one of the ones shown in Table 22.4.

Table 22.4. VBScript button response values.

Value	Purpose
1	Returned by MsgBox if OK is selected
2	Returned by MsgBox if Cancel is selected
3	Returned by MsgBox if Abort is selected
4	Returned by MsgBox if Retry is selected
5	Returned by MsgBox if Ignore is selected
6	Returned by MsgBox if Yes is selected
7	Returned by MsgBox if No is selected

If you have used programs in a Windows environment, you probably know one very important aspect of the message box window: It is modal. Once a message box is presented, users must respond to it before they can interact further with that Web page. Modality is great news from a script-programming standpoint. When a script puts up a message box, you know that by the time the next code statement is carried out, the user will have already provided a response to that message. Consequently, you have a high degree of control over the interaction. You know the user has to respond to your message, and you know that you will have a record of the user's response in the statement after the message.

Input Boxes

The input box function, InputBox, provides a separate modal window much like the message box. You can use it to present a prompt message to the user and collect an input string that is returned back to the script. The syntax of the function takes the following format:

```
ResultVar = InputBox(prompt_message, optional_title,
optional_default_response, optional_x_position,
optional_y_position, optional_helpfile,
optional_helpfile_context )
```

The first parameter is the prompt message; it prompts the user for a response. The prompt message is required, and the rest of the parameters are optional.

The next parameter is the title of the window, which is displayed in the top caption area. If a title is not supplied, Visual Basic will appear in its place.

The third parameter is the default response, which will appear in the text input area that is supplied for user input when the input box is generated. The default response is a response that the user is likely to provide. To accept the default, he or she can simply select OK without typing in any text. To provide a specific response, the user simply types the response and then selects OK. The new input will automatically replace the highlighted default; no backspacing or deletion is necessary.

The fourth and fifth parameters control the placement of the input box in x and y coordinates from the top of the screen. In the sample, the X and Y were specified to be 0, so the input box appeared at the top-left corner of the screen. If no values are supplied, the input box appears centered horizontally on the screen and one third of the way down.

The sixth and seventh parameters of the InputBox function call are for help file and help file context information. The help file support for the InputBox is the same as that for the message box.

The manner of retrieving the user response for an InputBox call is also similar to that of MsgBox. After the user enters a string into the input area and clicks OK, that user-supplied value is returned.

Controlling the Flow of Code

In this section, you will learn how to control the flow of your programs. This subject is very important when you want your programs to make on-the-spot decisions or execute based on what the user wants to do. You will learn about all the ways you can construct and control the order in which your code is executed. You will learn all the VBScript *control structures* and see several examples of how you can apply them. You will also learn which structures are particularly applicable and useful in various situations.

Using Control Structures To Make Decisions

Fortunately, VBScript gives you a variety of ways to direct the flow of your code with mechanisms called *control structures*. They are called *structures* because you construct your code around them, much like you build and finish a house around its structure. Control structures are like the wood beams and boards in your house that all of your rooms are built upon. You can use each control structure to make your code travel in different ways, depending on how you want a decision to be made. In this section, you will learn about two control structures used in VBScript to choose one path of code versus others. Later, you will see the control structures that choose the same code path over and over based on criteria you specify.

> **NOTE**
>
> A *control structure* is a combination of keywords in code used to make a decision that alters the flow of code the computer executes.

If...Then

The first control structure you should know about is If...Then. The syntax for this control structure is given as

```
If condition = True Then
    ... the code that executes if the condition is satisfied
End If
```

where `condition` is some test you want to apply to the conditional structure. If the condition is true, the code within the `If` and `End If` statements is executed. If the condition is not true, the code within these statements is skipped over and does not get executed.

> **NOTE**
>
> Rather than using the expression
>
> `If condition = True`
>
> you can use the expression
>
> `If condition Then`
>
> instead. VBScript automatically checks to see if the condition is true if you don't explicitly say so. Similarly, if you want to check to see if an expression is false, you can check to see if the condition is equal to false
>
> `If condition = False Then`
>
> or you can have VBScript check the `Not` true condition
>
> `If Not condition Then`
>
> These conventions can be used interchangeably throughout the book.

If...Then...Else

The control structure called If...Then...Else is represented as

```
If condition = True Then
    ...this is the code that executes if the condition is satisfied
Else
    ...this is the code that executes if the condition is not satisfied
End If
```

What if you had a few other cases you wanted to test? You're in luck: You can do as many tests as you want by simply placing more ElseIf statements between the first If statement and the End If statement. The syntax of such a structure looks like this:

```
If condition1 = True Then
    ...the code that executes for condition1
ElseIf condition2 = True Then
    ...the code that executes for condition2
ElseIf condition3 = True Then
    ...the code that executes for condition3
End If
```

where you can have as many ElseIf statements as you want. Notice that the terms Else and If must be concatenated as ElseIf, whereas End and If are separate, as End If. You can use the If...Then and If...Then...Else control structures to control the flow of your code based on decisions made within your code. For more information on these structures, refer to the book *Teach Yourself VBScript in 21 Days* from Sams.net.

The Select Case Structure

In cases in which you have to perform a large number of tests on the same expression, you can use the Select statement. The Select statement often makes your code easier to read and interpret versus a long list of Else and Else If statements. The Select Case structure is defined as follows:

```
Select Case test_expression
    Case expression-1
      ...this is the code that executes if expression-1 matches test_expression
    Case expression-2
      ...this is the code that executes if expression-2 matches test_expression
    Case expression-3
      ...this is the code that executes if expression-3 matches test_expression
    .
    .
    .
    Case Else n
      ...this is the code that executes if expression-n matches test_expression
End Select
```

where *expression-1*, *expression-2* and *expression-3* are one or more expressions that must match the *test_expression* in order for the code below each Case statement to execute. As you can see, the same condition is evaluated throughout the structure. Only one case is executed when VBScript travels through. If more than one case matches, only the first one is executed. If none of the cases match, the code underneath the `Case Else` section is executed. The `Case Else` section is optional. Therefore, if you don't include a `Case Else` section, none of the code within the `case` statement is executed.

Consider the following example that prints a message to the user based on the user's home state:

```
Select Case State
   Case "Michigan"
      Message = "Michigan is a wonderful state to visit if you enjoy " &
                "fresh water lakes."
   Case "Virginia"
      Message = "Visit the Commonwealth for a wide variety of historical " &
                "landmarks and beautiful mountain-scapes."
Case "Arizona"
      Message = "Arizona is a wonderful getaway for those who love heat " &
                "with low humidity"
   Case "Colorado"
      Message = "Colorado is almost unsurpassed for its " &
                "majestic mountains and rivers."
Case Else
      Message = "No specific information is available about this state."
End Select
```

Using Control Structures To Make Code Repeat

On occasion, you will need to write code that repeats some set of statements. For example, you might need to perform some calculation over and over, or you might have to apply the same calculations or processing to more than one variable, such as changing the values in an array. This section explains the VBScript control structures that enable you to write code that repeats.

For...Next

The first structure is often referred to as the `For...Next` *loop*. The syntax for this structure is

```
For counter = start to finish
   ...code that gets repeated
Next
```

where *counter* is a variable used for counting purposes that begins at the number specified by the *start* variable and counts up by one, each time executing the code within the structure, until it reaches *finish*. Usually, *counter* is incremented by one each time through the loop, although you can change the value of the increment. I'll show you how to do this in a moment, but first, check out the `For...Next` loop in action.

Suppose you have an array called `Salaries` that contains 30 elements, and you want to set all these elements to a value of 30,000. You could enter the following code:

```
Salaries(0) = 30000
Salaries(1) = 30000
Salaries(2) = 30000
   .
   .
   .
Salaries(29) = 30000
```

If you did it this way, you would have to enter 30 lines of code. Rather than do all that work, however, you can use a much more efficient *loop*. You're still repeating the same operation 30 times, but each time, you're assigning the value to a different element in the array. Try entering the following code:

```
For i = 0 to 29
   Salaries(i) = 30000
Next
```

The For...Next loop is quite flexible because you can tell VBScript how much you want the counter variable to be incremented each time through the loop. You can also decrement the counter rather than increment it. How do you do this? The counter is incremented by a value of one each time through the loop unless you specify otherwise. You can do so through the use of the `Step` keyword like this:

```
For counter = start to finish Step increment
   ...code that gets repeated
Next
```

where *increment* is a variable or value that tells the loop how much to increment the counter each time through the loop. As before, the moment *counter* falls outside the range of *start* and *finish*, the loop will stop.

Do...Loop

The next conditional structure is the powerful Do...Loop structure, and one variation of this loop structure is the Do While...Loop. The basic syntax for this structure is

```
Do While condition
   ...code within the loop goes here
Loop
```

where the *condition* is either true or false. As long as the condition is true, the code within the loop gets executed. Once the condition becomes false, the loop stops and the code after the loop is executed. The only way for the program to break out of the loop is if the condition becomes false or if an Exit Do statement is encountered somewhere inside the loop. Consider the following example shown in Listing 22.1.

Listing 22.1. Using the Do While...Loop conditional structure.

```
Again = True
DoubleIt = 1

' Keep doubling the number as long as the user desires
Do While Again = True

        '   Show current results and prompt to see if we should continue

        If MsgBox("Current total is " & DoubleIt & ". Double it again ?",
        ➥vbYesNo) = vbYes Then
           DoubleIt = DoubleIt * 2
        Else
           Again = False
        End If

Loop
```

In Listing 22.1, the first line of code sets the variable that gets tested in the loop equal to true. The second line sets the variable that gets doubled in the code equal to one. Setting the loop variable equal to true enables the loop to get off and running because the third line says, "If Again is true, enter the loop." Because the variable has just been set to true, the loop begins. The first statement in the loop displays the result to the user. Because nothing has been doubled yet, the result is one—the initial value of the DoubleIt variable.

When the results are displayed, the user is asked if he or she wants to continue. If the user chooses to go forward, the variable DoubleIt is multiplied by two. When the program hits the Loop instruction, it will return to the top of the loop and once again check to see if the condition is set to true. Because the condition has not changed, the loop executes again. It will continue to execute until the user chooses not to continue. Once that happens, the variable Again is set to False. Now, when Loop is reached, the code swings back up to the top of the loop and evaluates the condition once more. This time, the condition is false, so the loop does not execute again. The code moves on beyond the loop.

> **NOTE**
>
> VBScript has many additional conditional structures, such as Do...Loop While, Do Until...Loop, and Do...Loop Until. For a comprehensive discussion of all the conditional structures available in VBScript, refer to *Teach Yourself VBScript in 21 Days* from Sams.net.

Building a Home for Your Code

In this section, you will learn how VBScript code is organized. VBScript, like most other languages, stores code in *procedures*. Procedures come in two varieties: *subroutines* and *functions,* each of which is explored in this section.

Subroutines

The first type of procedure is the *subroutine.* You declare subroutines using the `Sub` keyword and end them using the `End Sub` statement. The structure of a subroutine is

```
Sub Subroutine_Name(argument1, argument2, ..., argumentn)
    ...code within the subroutine
End Sub
```

where `Subroutine_Name` is the name of the subroutine and `argument1` through `argumentn` are optional *arguments,* often called parameters, that you can pass to the subroutine. If you choose not to pass any arguments to the subroutine, the parentheses are optional, as you will see in a moment.

You can design a subroutine to require that the code statement that calls that subroutine provide one or more *arguments,* or variables that the subroutine can work with. Any time you need preexisting data to perform the task within the subroutine, arguments are very helpful. For example, the argument that the following subroutine accepts is actually a message that the subroutine displays to the user.

```
Sub ShowMessage(CurrentMessage)
    MsgBox CurrentMessage, vbOkOnly, "Important Message"
End Sub
```

In this case, `CurrentMessage` is the argument, and it is treated like any other variable in the subroutine. It is treated exactly as if it had been declared with a `Dim` statement with one very important difference. The `CurrentMessage` argument variable starts out pre-initialized with a value that was supplied by the code that called this subroutine.

Frequently, a subroutine might not require any arguments, and you can drop the parentheses. For example, if you have a subroutine that simply displays information to the user, it doesn't need any arguments, as in the following code:

```
Sub ShowAboutMessage
    MsgBox "This Web page was designed by the WebWizard."
End Sub
```

Because the code lists no arguments, it does not require the parentheses. On the other hand, if you declared a procedure using one or more arguments, you'd use the parentheses as shown in the following example:

```
Sub ShowAboutMessage(Message)
    MsgBox Message
End Sub
```

Now that you've learned how to create a subroutine, how do you call one? You can call a subroutine throughout the rest of the application once you've declared and created it by using the `Call` keyword or by entering the name of the subroutine on a line of code. For example, to call a subroutine called `ShowMessage`, you could enter

```
ShowMessage "This is the message."
```

22

THE VBSCRIPT
LANGUAGE

You could also use the `Call` keyword and enter

```
Call ShowMessage("This is the message.")
```

Although the choice is up to you, I generally recommend that you always use the `Call` statement when calling subroutines for the sake of readability.

The code within your subroutine will execute until one of two things happens. First, the subroutine might get down to the last line, the `End Sub` line, which terminates the subroutine and passes the baton back to the caller. This statement can appear only once at the end of the subroutine declaration. The second possibility is that VBScript could execute

```
Exit Sub
```

when placed inside the subroutine. You might use `Exit Sub` if you need to provide more than one exit point for the subroutine. However, you shouldn't need to use this statement very often if your subroutine is constructed properly.

Functions

The second type of procedure is called a *function*. Like a subroutine, a function also holds a series of VBScript statements. The only difference is that a function actually returns a value to the code statement that called it. You've already seen earlier in this chapter how you can fill a variable with a value supplied on the right side of an assignment statement:

```
ZipCode = 49428
```

In the same manner, you can fill a variable with a value supplied by a function you define:

```
ZipCode = GetZipCode("Jenison")
```

As with the subroutine, the flow of code is redirected to the function while the code within the function executes. Once the function has finished executing, control returns to the code that called the function, the value from the function is assigned to the calling code, and execution resumes.

To declare a function, use the `Function` keyword instead of the `Sub` keyword. You end functions using the `End Function` statement. The structure of a function is

```
Function Function_Name(argument1, argument2, …, argumentn)
     ...code within the function
End Sub
```

where `Function_Name` is the name of the function and `argument1` through `argumentn` are optional arguments you can pass to the function. As with the subroutine, the parentheses are not required if no arguments are passed to the function.

Now that you've seen how to declare a function, you need to know how to call it. The benefit of using a function is that you can pass back a piece of data to the caller. The subroutine does not enable you to do this because it does not return anything. You will see a way to change variables in the calling code with a subroutine later in the chapter, but the function is a better way to transfer data back and forth. To call a function, you simply use the following syntax:

```
return_variable = function_name(argument1, argument2, …, argumentn)
```

Notice that the syntax for a function is quite a bit different from the syntax for a subroutine. Here, you can assign the function to a variable (or another expression that can be updated with a value, such as a property), or you needn't assign it to anything. Also, the parentheses are optional. Even if you pass arguments to the function, the parentheses are not required. This syntax is quite a change from the familiar parentheses Visual Basic requires for functions.

Suppose you have a function called GetAge. To use the GetAge function, you could enter the statement

```
UserAge = GetAge()
```

or

```
UserAge = GetAge
```

Notice that this function doesn't need any arguments and that the result is assigned to a variable named UserAge. The following function requires three arguments—hours, minutes, and seconds—and returns the number of seconds:

```
Function GetSeconds(Hrs, Min, Sec)
   GetSeconds = Hrs * 3600 + Min * 60 + Sec
End Function
```

You could then call this function using a statement like

```
NumSeconds = GetSeconds(2, 34, 25)
```

or

```
NumSeconds = GetSeconds 2, 34, 25
```

where the total number of seconds is returned to the variable NumSeconds.

To exit a function, you use the same method as when you exit a subroutine, namely, the End Function statement. This statement can appear only once at the end of the function declaration. You have seen this statement used in the functions discussed so far. You can also use the statement Exit Function to break out of a function in the same way as you used the Exit Sub statement to exit a subroutine. As before, exiting a function naturally when your code reaches the final End Function statement is a better technique than using an Exit Function line of code to terminate the function in the middle of the statements. The code is simply easier to follow when you avoid such forced exit statements.

Passing Arguments into Procedures

When you call a procedure, you either provide a copy of a variable to a procedure so that it has a local copy to modify if necessary or refer the procedure to the original variable itself. Either way, the procedure cannot modify the variable owned by the caller. If you refer the procedure to the original variable, you are, in effect, supplying the memory address of that variable to the procedure. However, VBScript hides the memory address details from you. From the programmer's perspective, you are simply providing the variable name to the procedure. But VBScript does not enable you to change the variable—the interpreter will trigger an error when the Web page loads, if you try to do so.

> **NOTE**
>
> The current VBScript in beta Internet Explorer does not support the "ByRef" parameter familiar to many Visual Basic programmers. In Visual Basic 4.0, for example, if you use a ByRef parameter, you can make changes to that variable within the subroutine that defined the parameter and the changes are reflected back to the variable supplied in that parameter position by the calling code. This capability might be introduced in subsequent releases. You might want to check the current documentation to ascertain the implementation level if you are interested in this feature.

> **NOTE**
>
> Passing *by value* means that a copy of the original value is given to the procedure. The procedure can change its own copy, but it won't affect the original owned by the caller.

To refer the procedure to the original without giving it a copy of the variable, you omit the ByVal keyword. This case is the default and is called passing a variable "by reference." If you try to modify a variable passed to a procedure by reference, VBScript displays an error message when the Web page loads into the browser. The procedure can read the contents of a variable passed in by reference, but it cannot change its contents because the procedure doesn't own the variable.

> **NOTE**
>
> Passing *by reference* means that the procedure is allowed to read the variable owned by the caller. The procedure is not allowed to change the value of the variable because it does not own that variable.

If you wish to pass variables into a procedure by value, you simply declare the procedure using the format

```
Sub Subroutine_Name(ByVal argument1, ByVal argument2, ... ByVal argumentn)
```

when creating a subroutine and

```
Function Function_Name(ByVal argument1, ByVal argument2, ... ByVal argumentn)
```

when creating a function. To pass variables by reference, you simply omit the ByVal keyword as shown here for a subroutine:

```
Sub Subroutine_Name(argument1, argument2, ... argumentn)
```

and here for a function:

```
Function Function_Name(argument1, argument2, ... argumentn)
```

Event Procedures

When you work with controls and other components, you frequently interface with them using *event procedures*. Event procedures are subroutines that are called automatically by the browser. They are different from regular subroutines in that regular subroutines must be called within the program by statements you write or else they are never used. An event procedure is called as a result of some action taken by the user, such as clicking a command button or checking a box on a Web page, or by the system, such as detecting that a predefined timer has expired.

> **NOTE**
>
> An *event* is a subroutine called automatically by VBScript as a result of a user or system action. Although the programmer must manually specify subroutines and functions calls through normal calls in code, event subroutines are called automatically as a result of what they represent. For example, you can define a subroutine to be carried out when the user clicks on a particular button by means of a special name. Then, when the user clicks the button, the button control object itself generates an "OnClick" event. VBScript responds to this *event* by calling the named subroutine associated with the event.

You don't have to worry about calling event procedures in your code because they are called automatically by the system and the browser, but you do need to create them if you want to write code that responds to these events. For example, if you place a button on your Web page, you probably want your program to respond in some way when the user clicks it. If you construct an event procedure, you can write the code to do just that. If you fail to place the event subroutine in your code, however, your users can click the button all day long, and nothing will happen because no event procedure is available to process the click events.

The rules for creating and naming event procedures are more rigid and structured than regular procedure naming rules. First of all, the naming conventions for an event procedure are very specific. Except with some special cases discussed later in the chapter, you can't just name an event procedure anything you want. To name an event procedure, you must know two things: the name of the control, or component, and the name of the event you want to respond to. Suppose, for example, you have a command button on your Web page labeled `TestButton`. Buttons have an event called `OnClick` that you can write code for. This event occurs when the user clicks the button. To create an event procedure for this action, you must name your procedure

```
TestButton_OnClick
```

Notice that the name of the control comes first, followed by an underscore character, followed by the name of the event. You must spell everything correctly, or else VBScript will be unable to connect the event procedure to the button. The rule for assigning a name to a control or component is

```
Sub ControlName_EventName()
```

where `ControlName` is the name of the control and `EventName` is the name of the event corresponding to the control. You'll learn more about event procedures later in the chapter when intrinsic HTML controls and ActiveX controls are introduced.

Method Procedures

You might have also heard of *method procedures*. Method procedures are similar to predefined procedures you can call, but they are provided by an object. You can't actually see the code for them, nor can you create them. Objects can have a set of methods that were created when the programmer designed the object.

> **NOTE**
>
> A *method* is an object-associated procedure you can call. Methods accomplish some specific task or service that the object provides. Methods might or might not return values, depending on what they do.

To invoke the method of an object, you can simply call the method using the following convention:

```
object.method
```

where `object` is the name of the object and `method` is the name of the method. You'll learn more about objects later in the chapter.

Where To Put Procedures

Finally, you need to understand where you can place procedures in your HTML document. You can place procedures within one script tag:

```
<SCRIPT LANGUAGE="VBScript">
<!--
    Sub GetMiles()
        ...code for subroutine
    End Sub

    Function CalculateTime(RunnerTime)
        ...code for function
    End Function
-->
</SCRIPT>
```

You can also place procedures in separate scripts:

```
<SCRIPT LANGUAGE="VBScript">
<!--
    Sub GetMiles()
        ...code for subroutine
    End Sub
-->
</SCRIPT>

<SCRIPT LANGUAGE="VBScript">
<!--
    Function CalculateTime(RunnerTime)
        ...code for function
    End Function
-->
</SCRIPT>
```

Also, notice that you do not have to store all VBScript code within a procedure. However, if you have code outside a procedure, as shown in the following example, keep in mind that this code is automatically executed in order from top to bottom when the browser first loads the Web page.

```
<SCRIPT LANGUAGE="VBScript">
<!-- Option Explicit

   Dim Miles_Ran
   Dim Total_Miles
   Dim Start_Time
   Call InitializeVariables

   Sub InitializeVariables
      Miles_Ran = 0
      Total_Miles = 0
      Start_Time = 0
   End Sub
-->
```

22

THE VBSCRIPT LANGUAGE

Intrinsic HTML Form Controls

Now that you've learned some of the important fundamentals of VBScript programming, you are ready to put these skills and techniques to practical use. Controls and objects are entities you can place on a Web page to provide an interactive user interface. You can also use controls and objects as the front ends to perform behind-the-scenes operations, such as submitting information to a program on a server.

> **NOTE**
>
> *Controls* and *objects* are elements you can include in a Web page that enable the user to interface with the page or perform some specific task from within the HTML document.

An Introduction To HTML Forms

As you can see by the title of this section, intrinsic HTML controls apply to HTML forms. You need to understand what an HTML form is and what its capabilities are in order to appreciate the roles and capabilities of the intrinsic controls. Forms serve as containers whose information can be sent across the Internet to the server that supplied the Web page to the client.

> **NOTE**
>
> A *form* is a container into which you can place controls and objects. The form can transmit the values of intrinsic controls to the server for processing in response to selection of a Submit button. Even if the controls in a form are not intended to gather data for a server, a form can still provide a convenient grouping of the controls it contains.

The form is particularly useful when you want to collect data on a page and then submit it to a server. An example of such a page is one that collects survey data and then submits that data for storage in a central database. You typically submit such data to a server using the HTML form submittal and CGI capabilities to launch a script on the server.

Often, you will create Web pages that simply "do their own thing" and have no need to send information back to a server. If your Web page doesn't need to use CGI to submit information to a server, then you don't need to place your controls in a form.

Now that you understand forms and the relationship that controls have to them, you are ready to examine the controls themselves. You can use HTML form controls independently of CGI. Before the development of scripting languages such as VBScript, programmers had to submit data to servers through CGI in order to give Web pages even the simplest intelligence. Now that we have a sophisticated scripting language, however, this restriction is less burdensome.

Still, CGI is often vital and necessary to send data to a server, such as when ordering products or inquiring about information.

The Button Control

Buttons give the user the capability to execute VBScript code that performs some action indicated on the caption of the button. You have seen buttons in use throughout this chapter because they are such an important part of a Web page.

To create a button on a Web page, you need to use a special tag called an INPUT tag. The INPUT tag tells the browser you are about to create a control used to get input from the user. The button is just one type of control you can create using the INPUT tag. The actual input could come in the form of text, an indication of whether the user has checked the control, or a recognition of the control by clicking it. In any case, information is being exchanged with the user. The input tag takes at least two attributes: TYPE and NAME.

TIP

The <INPUT> tag is used to place intrinsic HTML controls on a Web page.

The TYPE attribute is very important because it tells the browser what type of control you want to create. You use the input tag to create text controls, radio button controls, and check boxes, just to name a few. The TYPE attribute will be set equal to the keyword BUTTON. As you will see, other keywords are used for the other control types.

The second attribute that you must supply is the NAME attribute, which gives the control a name. Why would you want to name a control? To work with a control, you have to refer to it, and to do that, you must give it a unique name. The name can be any string as long as it starts with a letter.

NOTE

You can use many more standards to help make your code clear, readable, and easy to maintain. You won't really understand all the recommended standards until you've been exposed to the full VBScript language. Refer to the book *Teach Yourself VBScript in 21 Days* for detailed coverage of all the important standards.

When you work with button controls, you want to set one more attribute—the VALUE attribute. The VALUE attribute sets the caption of the button. The caption tells the user what the button does. Make sure the caption of your button is descriptive enough to let the user know what happens if he or she clicks it.

Here's a simple example of a line of HTML code that creates a button:

```
<INPUT TYPE="Button" NAME="cmdGetCost" VALUE="Get the Cost">
```

The name of the control is `cmdGetCost`, and the caption that will appear on the Web page is `Get the Cost`.

How do you connect the button with your VBScript code? Quite easily, in fact. Earlier in the chapter, you learned about a special procedure called an *event procedure.* You saw that event procedures are designed to respond to events initiated by the user, usually on controls. To get your VBScript code to respond to a button click, you have two options. First, you can use the *implicit* event procedure, which has the following format:

```
Sub ButtonName_OnClick()
    ...place your code here
End Sub
```

where *ButtonName* is the name of the button. You gave the button this name using the `NAME` property of the input tag when you created it. Consider Listing 22.2, which shows VBScript code that responds to the click of the button by showing the user a message box.

> **NOTE**
>
> In HTML terms, the `NAME` property of the input tag is an attribute. Because you will use it as a property of the control, I use the term *property* here.

Listing 22.2. A simple Web page with an HTML button control and VBScript code that responds to the user's click.

```
<HTML>

<HEAD>
<TITLE>The Button Control</TITLE>
</HEAD>

<BODY>

<CENTER><INPUT TYPE="BUTTON" NAME="cmdBegin" VALUE="Click to Begin"

<SCRIPT LANGUAGE="VBScript">
<!-- Option Explicit

    Sub cmdBegin_OnClick()
        MsgBox "You have clicked on the command button.
            ➥I knew you couldn't resist!"

End Sub

-->
```

```
</SCRIPT>

</BODY>

</HTML>
```

As you can see, the implicit event procedure is named according to conventions. If you do not name the subroutine properly, it will not connect to the button and will never be called.

The other way of connecting a command button to code is through the *explicit* event procedure. Rather than create a procedure that uses the naming convention required by the implicit event procedure, in this case Sub *buttonname*.OnClick(), you can specify the subroutine you want to call and give it any name you like. To implement an explicit event procedure, you use a special attribute called ONCLICK when you create the button. Set the ONCLICK attribute equal to the procedure you want to call when the user clicks the button and then create the subroutine in your code. Consider the following declaration of a button:

```
<INPUT TYPE="Button" NAME="cmdGetCost" VALUE="Get the Cost"
LANGUAGE="VBScript" ONCLICK="GetCost">
```

In this example, the attribute ONCLICK executes VBScript code that calls the GetCost subroutine. Obviously, this subroutine must exist within the Web page. The benefit of this approach is that you do not need a unique event procedure for each event of a control. You can share a procedure among several controls, if you like. Also note that you should set the LANGUAGE attribute to VBScript. If you don't, the browser might not be able to identify what scripting language you are using. It might, for example, assume that you are using JavaScript instead. Therefore, you should always set this attribute to tell the browser what scripting language you are using.

The ONCLICK attribute not only lets you indicate procedures to be activated when the event occurs but also lets you create script code on the fly in the button definition. To do so, enclose your code in single quotes immediately after the ONCLICK attribute. For example, if you want to display a pop-up message box when the user clicks a button without triggering a separate event procedure, you can simply use the following definition for the button:

```
<INPUT TYPE="BUTTON" NAME="cmdButton1" LANGUAGE="VBScript"
VALUE="Button One" ONCLICK='MsgBox "You just clicked on Button #1"' >
```

This approach is a very convenient way to throw a bit of code here and there in response to controls, but beware! The more you scatter your code around in attributes of controls, the more difficult it will be to find and debug your code later. A better idea is keeping your code within procedures and calling those procedures using the ONCLICK attribute or using the implicit event procedure approach for your controls.

NOTE

You can also specify code in the ONCLICK event by enclosing it in double quotes, but you need to specify two double quotes in a row in the inner statement. They will be interpreted as one, as shown here:

```
<P><INPUT TYPE="BUTTON" NAME="cmdButton1"
VALUE="Button One" LANGUAGE="VBScript"
ONCLICK="MsgBox ""You just clicked on Button #1"" " >
```

This rule applies to all VBScript code inside or outside script procedures.

Another interesting feature of VBScript is its support of a special block of script code that responds to a control event without placing it within a procedure at all! You can implement this feature by using the EVENT and FOR attributes in an opening script tag. Assign the EVENT attribute to a string indicating the name of the event, and assign the FOR attribute to the control to which the script applies. To write a script that presents a message box for the button cmdButton1, you could create the following script:

```
<SCRIPT LANGUAGE="VBScript" EVENT="ONCLICK" FOR="cmdButton1">
<!--
    MsgBox "You just clicked on button #1"
-->
</SCRIPT>
```

In this case, the entire script applies to one specific event. You don't need to create a procedure because the entire script is devoted to the control and event you specify. Usually, any script statements between the <SCRIPT> and </SCRIPT> tags that are not enclosed in procedures execute as soon as the page loads into the browser. However, if you use the EVENT attribute, these statements of code execute only when the event occurs. You can use this technique to declare several different scripts within the same page and enable other scripts to access data declared in each script. You could build a good event-handling approach by dedicating a separate script (enclosed in <SCRIPT> and </SCRIPT> tags) for each event instead of creating a separate procedure for each event. For purposes of clarity, using procedures within the same script might be easier because all your information is in one place.

The Text Control

Another versatile and useful control in your HTML control toolkit is the text control. This control displays a simple region on the Web page into which the user can enter alphanumeric data such as numbers, strings, and so on. Using the text control is as easy as using the button control. The text control is another of the suite of HTML input controls and is commonly defined as follows:

```
<INPUT TYPE="TEXT" NAME="txtCost" SIZE="10">
```

Notice that the TYPE attribute is set to "TEXT" rather than "BUTTON". By the way, "TEXT" is the default value of the attribute, so if you do not specify any TYPE with an input definition, you'll get a text control. Notice that you must also set the familiar NAME attribute. The typical convention when creating a text control is to prefix the name with txt. The rules for naming controls are the same for all types.

The SIZE attribute is an optional attribute that enables you to specify the width of the text control in approximate characters. Because of differences in font representation, the size of your text box will probably not be exactly that many characters wide on the page. If you omit the size, the browser determines a default size. Typically, you set the size equal to the maximum number of characters that you want the user to enter into the control. In a moment, you will learn how to restrict the number of characters that a user can enter.

The VALUE attribute is not included in the preceding example, but you can use it to assign initial text to the text box. If you want to fill the text box with data when the Web page is loaded, you can specify it in the definition. Whatever you set for the VALUE attribute will appear in the text control when the page is loaded into the browser. Listing 22.3 shows an easy way to include a text control on a Web page.

Listing 22.3. Getting a user's age from a text control and reporting it through a button using an explicit event procedure.

```
<HTML>

<BODY>

<INPUT TYPE="TEXT" NAME="txtData">
<INPUT TYPE="BUTTON" NAME="cmdBegin" VALUE="Get Text Control Data">

<SCRIPT LANGUAGE="VBScript">
<!--

   Sub cmdBegin_OnClick()

       MsgBox "You are " & txtData.Value & " years old."

   End Sub

-->
</SCRIPT>
</BODY>
</HTML>
```

This code prompts the user to enter his or her age. The Web page loads the text control with a default value of 25. If the user clicks the button labeled Get Age, he or she will see a message box that echoes the age. Notice how the subroutine that responds to the button click retrieves the text control's text. The data of the text control is read by accessing the VALUE property of the control. If you wanted to place the control within a form, you would first need to refer to the form. You could refer to the form and text box on it with the name `document.MyForm.txtData.Value`. This name is obviously fairly long and somewhat intimidating! Fortunately, VBScript provides a shorthand method to reference the same control. You simply declare a variable, in this case called `form`, and set that variable using the `Set` keyword so that the variable refers to the form defined in the body of your HTML document. That form is referenced using the statement

```
Set form = document.FormName
```

where *FormName* is the name of the form you created in your HTML document using the FORM tag and NAME attribute for that form. Notice the use of the object named `document`. The document object represents the entire HTML document. Because a form is a specific part of the entire HTML document, the form is referred to as one of the properties of the `document` object. To refer to the form, you must first refer to the document and then to the document's form as shown. Once you've entered this command, you can then reference any control on the form using the following syntax:

```
form.control.property
```

With the `cmdResult_OnClick` subroutine, you must use

```
form.txtData.Value
```

to refer to the text of the text control you want if you place the controls within a form. You access a control through a form, and you access a form through a document. If you use the structure outlined previously, you will make the necessary connections in your code.

Both the text control and the button control have various events and methods that you can use. Two equally useful events are the `OnFocus` and `OnBlur` events. The `OnFocus` event occurs whenever a control, in this case the text control, receives focus. A control can receive focus in one of two ways—the user can press the Tab key to place focus on the control, or the developer can use the `Focus` method to put the control into focus using code (as was the case with the `Click` event using the `Click` method). When a control receives focus, a gray box typically silhouettes the control.

NOTE

Focus is a term used to indicate a control that is recognized as being the control the user is interested in. When a control on a Web page has *focus*, certain keys cause the control to react in some way. For example, pressing the Enter key when a button has focus simulates clicking the button.

The button control discussed in the previous section supports many more methods and events, such as the `OnClick` and `OnFocus` events and the `Focus` method. The text control, in addition to supporting the `OnFocus` and `OnBlur` events, also supports events such as `OnChange` and `OnSel`, as well as methods such as `Focus`, `Blur`, and `Select`.

> **NOTE**
>
> For a description of additional intrinsic HTML controls such as the text area control, the check box control, and the radio button control, refer to *Teach Yourself VBScript Programming in 21 Days* from Sams.net. You will find a comprehensive survey of many of the most commonly used intrinsic HTML controls.

Using Objects and ActiveX Controls

You've just looked at some of the intrinsic controls you can manipulate from your scripts. If you've been a Web page author for a while, you probably recognized the intrinsic control types; HTML has always supported the check box, text box, radio button, and other controls. Traditionally, the intrinsic controls collected input to pass to the server, but with the advent of VBScript, you can control the controls directly.

What if you want to offer some level of interaction not supported by those intrinsic controls? Some very powerful alternatives exist. One of the easiest, most powerful ways to extend those bounds is through a type of object introduced by Microsoft as part of its Internet strategy called ActiveX controls. These controls are packaged in separate files and defined to the operating system through system-wide classes. Some means is necessary to tell the browser and script the location, calling conventions, and characteristics for these components.

Defining an Object

The tag to indicate an object is one that makes perfect intuitive sense: <OBJECT>. You might need to insert objects for a wide range of purposes other than those that ActiveX controls fulfill. A Web page can consist of many types of elements, including images, controls, Java applets, video, audio, and embedded compound documents, as well as other new forms of media that might yet spring into existence. As the World Wide Web Consortium (W3C) assessed these needs, it realized that a hodgepodge of different approaches for incorporating different media, each with its own tag, was not ideal. Instead, a well-defined <OBJECT> methodology provides a general solution for all objects that you want to incorporate into a page.

> **NOTE**
>
> The World Wide Web Consortium defines Web standards. You can find more information on the W3C working draft for "Inserting Objects into HTML" at http://www/w3.org/pub/WWW/TR/WD-object.html. You can find a list of W3C working drafts at http://www.w3.org/pub/WWW/TR.

Use of the <OBJECT> tag is best understood by looking at some simple examples, starting with the label control. You use the label control to define, through appropriate statements in an object declaration, a string of text characters that can appear anywhere on a page. So far it sounds like a heading, but you will notice a few differences. One difference is that the label text can be positioned at an angle, so it can appear diagonally across a page. Another is that the label, like most objects, can be modified by a VBScript program even after a page has been initially generated. Listing 22.4 shows the format for this object definition used to include a label control on a Web page.

Listing 22.4. The object definition declaration for an ActiveX label control.

```
<OBJECT
classid="clsid:99B42120-6EC7-11CF-A6C7-00AA00A47DD2"

    id=lblAd
    width=240
    height=240
    align=left
    hspace=5
    vspace=5
>
<param name="angle" value="45" >
<param name="alignment" value="2" >
<param name="BackStyle" value="0" >
<param name="caption" value="50% off studded trail running shoes!">
<param name="FontName" value="Arial">
<param name="FontSize" value="20">
<param name="FontBold" value="1">
<param name="FontItalic" value="1">
<param name="ForeColor" value="255">
</OBJECT>
```

Object Attributes

The object tag is similar to the standard HTML <BODY> tag format in many respects. It has both a start tag <OBJECT> and an end tag </OBJECT>. Within the start tag, you can define additional attributes that describe characteristics common to all objects.

The CLASSID is an essential part of any ActiveX object declaration. It identifies the implementation of an object to the browser. In other words, it provides the browser with a path to the code behind an object. It describes what kind of class an object belongs to and thereby identifies the code that defines its behavior.

In the early beta versions of Internet Explorer, this class registration information consists of a cryptic-looking string of digits that corresponds to information in the registration database. The registration database, in turn, knows the location of the library file (with an OCX extension in Windows) that provides the code for this class. In later versions of the Internet

Explorer, this string will probably evolve to a more easily understood program ID (such as `="PROGID:Internet.Label.1"`), rather than the corresponding number reference in the previous example `"clsid:{99B42120-6EC7-11CF-A6C7-00AA00A47DD2"`.

According to the object attribute specification, you can also identify the base location of an object in terms of a URL through the CODEBASE attribute, which means that an object can be specified as a file available on the Web. Using a URL opens the door to some of the most exciting possibilities for object components.

You can access and download controls across the Web with pages that use them. If a control doesn't exist on your system (which the browser verifies using the CLASSID), the CODEBASE URL is used, if present, to retrieve the component from wherever it resides.

> **NOTE**
>
> Many programming environments for software that runs under graphical operating systems now provide sophisticated visual tools to incorporate components into programs. Often, you can just drag and drop a component icon onto a program interface to add the component to your program.
>
> Fortunately, at the time of this writing, such tools are starting to appear in some forms. Microsoft's ActiveX Control Pad editor inserts object tags for ActiveX controls and represents controls visually in the left margin of the editor. This tool is currently free on the Microsoft Web site (www.microsoft.com/workshop). Short of having such a snazzy tool, however, the only way to add objects to forms is to insert the lines of code of the object declaration right into your source file.
>
> Tools will evolve with time as the state of the art seems to change from month to month. You would be wise to check online resources and industry periodicals for the most recent information when you read this book.

Object Parameters

If you've used HTML to build Web pages, the attributes of the object tag are probably somewhat familiar to you. The attributes are common to other tags such as <BODY> and <IMG> as well as <OBJECT>. Another aspect of the object tag—the <PARAM> tag—is unique to it. <PARAM> specifies object parameters within an object definition. An object parameter is a characteristic of an object that is defined by the object itself, rather than by the HTML standards. If you have experience with Visual Basic or an object-oriented programming language, you can picture a parameter as a property of the object.

<PARAM> is a tag that is embedded between the <OBJECT> and </OBJECT> tags. <PARAM> requires no ending tag and carries with it just two main attributes: NAME and VALUE. NAME is used to

designate the name of a property, and VALUE determines its initial value. If you refer to Listing 22.5, you can see that the label ActiveX control object definition defines a font name property:

```
<param name="FontName" value="Arial">
```

You first assign object properties when authoring a page to create the initial state of an object. You also will probably reference many properties in your scripts to control the behavior and characteristics of an object. You can reference a specific property in your code by designating the ID of the object, a period to indicate that what follows is a property, and then the specific property. When you reference the name of the object and property in a statement, the corresponding value is returned. When the object and property indicator appear on the left side of an assignment statement, such as

```
"lblAd.Caption = "Sales Off"
```

the object's property value changes to the new value indicated in the assignment. Being able to set and retrieve the value of object properties provides a powerful means to interact with controls within your scripts. You can write code to inspect and control any aspect of the controls you incorporate in your programs.

ActiveX Controls

ActiveX is a technology standard that was introduced by Microsoft in March 1996. It defines a standard approach for implementing controls that can be easily integrated into applications, including Web pages. You can obtain ActiveX controls from Microsoft or from third-party vendors, or you can write them yourself.

Microsoft has provided many free-of-charge ActiveX controls already, and you can expect more to be available to help foster growth of their Internet and operating system environments. In addition, many companies sell ActiveX controls that perform specific tasks. Purchasing a control is usually less costly than expending the labor to write the same code yourself, so a steady market for controls exists. Suppose, however, that you want to integrate some type of functionality into your program but cannot locate a control on the market that serves the purpose. The prospect of writing it yourself and using it in many VBScript programs might start to sound appealing.

Using Label Control Properties

The following sample line of code shows a VBScript statement that changes the value of the label control caption property. The name of the control, lblAd, was designated when the object was declared earlier in the HTML source through the <OBJECT id="lblAd"> attribute. Caption was designated as a property within this object declaration by the <PARAM NAME="Caption"> parameter. This example assigns a new string to the caption property of the label object. This statement could appear within any block of script code; for example, it could execute in response to a button click. As soon as the script code containing this statement finishes, the new caption is displayed for the label:

```
lblAd.caption = "This is a new caption!"
```

In addition to manipulating object properties, you can also use object methods in your code. When you use an object's method, you are essentially calling prepackaged function or subroutine calls from the object. In the following example, the lblAd control's AboutBox method is called to display an About box associated with that control. The AboutBox method is an intrinsically defined method or function built into the control. You do not have to explicitly define such methods in your Web page <OBJECT> declaration. You get access to all the methods of an object simply by including the <OBJECT> tag.

```
' Show the about box for this control
lblAd.AboutBox
```

As you can see, you can weave a lot of programming around controls. You can set properties of ActiveX controls and call methods that trigger code performed in the control. You've covered all the bases except one. What if the user interacts with the control on the Web page, or the control reaches a certain state you want your code to react to? How can you write code that reacts to these events? (Recall that events are predefined conditions of the control with which you can associate code. When the condition occurs in the control, your code is triggered.) ActiveX controls provide the same solution for handling events as you read about in the section on intrinsic controls.

Consider again the label control. A predefined event for the label control is the Click event. If the user clicks a label, the control's Click event handler subroutine is performed (if one is defined in the script). The block of code in Listing 22.5 is the event-handling code for the Click event of the label.

Listing 22.5. The Click event for the label control.

```
<SCRIPT LANGUAGE="VBSCRIPT">
<!--
   Sub lblAd_Click
       MsgBox "Our studded trail shoes are especially well-suited " & _
              " for running over glaciers or through muck-covered " & _
              " streams with nary a slip!",0,"A Steal at $49.00!"
   End Sub
-->
</SCRIPT>
```

22

THE VBSCRIPT LANGUAGE

The name of the lblAd_Click subroutine associates this code with the label's Click event. The first part of the subroutine name, lblAd, associates it with the ID of the ActiveX control object. The underscore (_) is the notation that indicates an event definition might follow. Then, because the Click that follows is the name of a predefined label event, the code in subroutine lblAd_Click will be performed whenever that specific label is clicked. Whenever the user clicks the label, the message box pops up to provide more details.

> **NOTE**
>
> In addition to the label and timer controls, ActiveX has the New Item, Chart, Preload, and Layout controls. Microsoft might have introduced more controls since this book was printed. Refer to *Teach Yourself VBScript in 21 Days* for much more information about these ActiveX controls.

Summary

This chapter presented an overview of the VBScript language. You learned how to create variables, apply operators to those variables, work with strings, use math functions and other specialized functions, control the flow of code with conditional structures, and present and query information from the user. Then, you learned how to include intrinsic HTML controls, objects, and ActiveX controls in an HTML document with VBScript. These concepts are all fundamental to your understanding of VBScript. In the next chapter, you will see some actual Web pages that use the concepts discussed in this chapter.

VBScript Application Pages

by Keith Brophy and Tim Koets

IN THIS CHAPTER

In Chapter 22, "The VBScript Language," you learned the language mechanics of VBScript. This chapter shows VBScript in action and puts those techniques to use. The samples that follow encompass a spectrum of uses ranging from pages that calculate running pace per mile on the user's local PC to pages that perform front-end validation before submitting orders to a server. Keep in mind, however, that even though these samples cover a lot of ground, they just touch the surface of VBScript's potential. Because VBScript is a full-fledged language that lets you build programs around any object you want to incorporate, the only real limit to the type of solutions you can implement is your own creativity. As you study the samples in this chapter, you will see how to assemble the capabilities of this language into a comprehensive program and perhaps develop a sense of VBScript's range of possibilities.

> **NOTE**
>
> For more details on many facets of VBScript, see the Sams.net book *Teach Yourself VBScript in 21 Days*; it includes more sample programs with comprehensive discussions of each technique.

Metric Conversion Application

The Metric Converter application page is a good example of relatively simple code that still accomplishes a very useful function for the user. This application converts a distance specified on the page in feet and inches into the corresponding metric equivalent. Figure 23.1 shows the implementation of this code on the corresponding page.

> **NOTE**
>
> This sample page is contained in the file `meters.htm` on this book's CD-ROM. I recommend that you access this page by starting with the main index page to VBScript samples, `VBSDemo.htm`.

This page is built around a primary conversion function. User input supplied on the page through text input boxes is passed as parameter data to the function call in the VBScript call. This core function is shown in the following code:

```
Function ConvertToMeters(ByVal Inches, Feet)
     Inches = Feet * 12 + Inches
     ConvertToMeters = Inches * 0.0254
End Function
```

Figure 23.1.

The Metric Converter Web page.

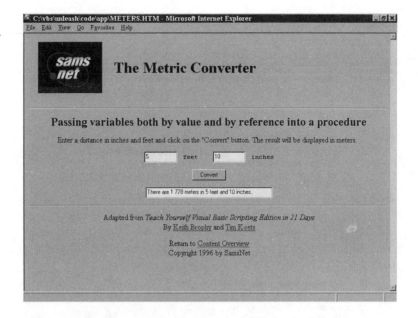

Standard VBScript mathematical operators carry out the conversion. Then, the function returns the conversion result to the calling code by setting the result equal to the name of the function itself, `ConvertToMeters`. The calling code displays the result to the user by updating a text box on the Web page.

The code listing for the entire Web page is shown in Listing 23.1.

Listing 23.1. The Metric Converter Web page code.

```
<HTML>

<HEAD>
<TITLE>The Metric Converter</TITLE>
</HEAD>

<BODY>

<H1><A HREF="http://www.mcp.com"><IMG  ALIGN=BOTTOM
SRC="../shared/jpg/samsnet.jpg" BORDER=2></A>
The Metric Converter</H1>

<HR>

<CENTER><H2>Passing variables both by value and by
reference into a procedure</H2>

<P>Enter a distance in inches and feet and click on the "Convert" button.
The result will be displayed in meters.
```

continues

Listing 23.1. continued

```
<PRE><INPUT NAME="txtFeet" SIZE=10 > feet
<INPUT NAME="txtInches" SIZE=10 > inches</PRE>
<P><INPUT TYPE="BUTTON" NAME="cmdConvert" VALUE="Convert">
<P><INPUT NAME="txtResult" SIZE=50 ></CENTER>

<HR>

<center>
from <em>Teach Yourself VBScript in 21 Days</em> by
<A HREF="../shared/keith.htm">Keith Brophy</A> and
<A HREF="../shared/tim.htm">Tim Koets</A><br>
Return to <a href="..\default.htm">Content Overview</A><br>
Copyright 1996 by SamsNet<br>
</center>

<SCRIPT LANGUAGE="VBScript">
<!-- Option Explicit

    Sub cmdConvert_OnClick()

       Dim Inches, Feet, Meters

       Inches = txtInches.Value
       Feet = txtFeet.Value

       Meters = ConvertToMeters(Inches, Feet)

       txtResult.Value = "There are " & Meters & " meters in " & Feet &
                          ➥" feet and " & Inches & " inches."

    End Sub

    Function ConvertToMeters(ByVal Inches, Feet)

       Inches = Feet * 12 + Inches
       ConvertToMeters = Inches * 0.0254

    End Function

-->
</SCRIPT>

</BODY>

</HTML>
```

As you can see from Figure 23.1, the user simply enters the number of inches and feet in the appropriate text boxes and clicks the Convert button. That action calls the function ConvertToMeters, which converts the values into meters and returns the value. The value is then displayed in the result text box on the Web page. The entire conversion process is carried out without requiring any server-side interaction.

Interactive Tutorial Application

A tutorial program called the VBScript ActiveX Tutorial demonstrates how you can use the label control to give your users a high degree of feedback during their interaction with your scripts.

This tutorial uses standard HTML code to display a series of questions on the screen. Next to each question is a standard input text control to collect the answer. To the right of the text control is a column of hints, displayed with the label control. All question-related information is presented within an HTML table to help align the columns of information.

> **NOTE**
>
> The tutorial is available on the CD-ROM in the file `interact.htm`.

The user interacts with this program by entering his or her responses in the appropriate text boxes and then pressing the Provide Feedback command button. This button triggers script code that evaluates each answer. If an answer is correct, a green label displays "Correct!" If an answer is incorrect, a red label provides the correct answer. To provide a high degree of visual cue feedback, a correct answer changes the angle of the feedback label to point slightly upward with a jaunty air. If an answer is incorrect, the feedback label angle changes to droop slightly downward. A label at the bottom of the feedback area shows the total number of correct answers. Figure 23.2 shows the feedback label's response to both correct and incorrect answers.

23

VBScript
Application
Pages

FIGURE 23.2.

Interactive tutorial feedback for user responses.

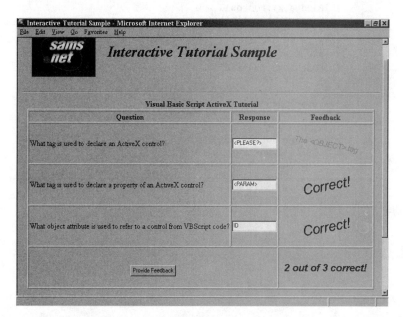

The degree to which the feedback of this program impresses you probably depends on your background. If you're coming to VBScript from a traditional programming background, you might think, "This interactivity is very much like what I can already do with a Windows program." If you're approaching VBScript from a heavy Web page development background, you might be thinking, "This really lets me do a lot more than I ever could before in my Web pages." Both of these perspectives are accurate. VBScript integrates controls and provides programmability much like its parent product, Visual Basic, has for some time in the Windows environment. VBScript now extends this power to the Web page.

Listing 23.2 shows the code that assesses the answers to the tutorial questions and provides the feedback. A comparison is performed on each text box answer. For the sake of the example, the comparison is very simple. In an actual tutorial, you would probably perform much more extensive comparisons, converting the response to uppercase, checking for close variations on the correct answer, and so on. With this sample program, if an exact match occurs on the answer, it is considered a correct response.

Listing 23.2. Providing feedback based on responses.

```
<SCRIPT LANGUAGE="VBSCRIPT">
<!--

    Sub cmdFeedback_OnClick
    'This routine is called when the user clicks the feedback button.

        dim Correct

        Correct = 0

        ' Change all feedback labels to italic rather than bold
        lblFeedback1.fontbold = 0
        lblFeedback1.fontitalic = 1
        lblFeedback2.fontbold = 0
        lblFeedback2.fontitalic = 1
        lblFeedback3.fontbold = 0
        lblFeedback3.fontitalic = 1


        ' Assess Question 1
        if txtQuestion1.Value = "<OBJECT>" then
            ' Correct response
            Correct = Correct + 1
            lblFeedback1.angle = "10"
            lblFeedback1.fontsize = "24"
            lblFeedback1.caption = "Correct!"
            lblFeedback1.ForeColor = "65280"
        else
```

```
        ' Incorrect response
        lblFeedback1.angle = "350"
        lblFeedback1.caption = "The <OBJECT> tag"
        lblFeedback1.ForeColor = "255"
    end if

    ' Assess Question 2
    if txtQuestion2.Value = "<PARAM>" then
        ' Correct response
        Correct = Correct + 1
        lblFeedback2.angle = "10"
        lblFeedback2.fontsize = "24"
        lblFeedback2.caption = "Correct!"
        lblFeedback2.ForeColor = "65280"
    else
        ' Incorrect response
        lblFeedback2.angle = "350"
        lblFeedback2.caption = "The <PARAM> tag"
        lblFeedback2.ForeColor = "255"
    end if

    ' Assess Question 3
    if txtQuestion3.Value = "ID" then
        ' Correct response
        Correct = Correct + 1
        lblFeedback3.angle = "10"
        lblFeedback3.fontsize = "24"
        lblFeedback3.caption = "Correct!"
        lblFeedback3.ForeColor = "65280"
    else
        ' Incorrect response
        lblFeedback3.angle = "350"
        lblFeedback3.caption = "The ID attribute"
        lblFeedback3.ForeColor = "255"
    end if

    ' Show the results
    lblResults.caption = cstr(Correct) & " out of 3 correct!"

  end sub
-->
</SCRIPT>
```

When the user gives a correct response, the label angle, caption, font size, and ForeColor are all adjusted accordingly. Likewise, if an answer is incorrect, the angle, caption, and ForeColor are adjusted for incorrect response feedback. The lblResults label that is updated in the last line of the script illustrates a particularly useful technique. You can make a response appear at just the right moment. The lblResults label does not initially appear to the user because the following parameter is used to declare the starting object caption:

```
<param name="caption" value="">
```

When you want a caption to appear, you simply assign one in your code, and presto! The user sees text where there was none before. This program uses many labels—four to be exact—to provide a dynamic page that updates with user feedback. In the old Web programming model, you probably would have needed at least two Web pages, one of them custom-generated by a CGI script on the server, to produce the equivalent function. The simple addition of the label control and VBScript enable you to integrate all this feedback into one relatively simple page.

> **NOTE**
>
> A rather interesting behavior occurs with early beta versions of the label control if you don't include any parameter tag for the caption in your object declaration. When the label is drawn on screen, it appears with the caption "Default"! You can still assign values to properties even if they are not declared with the parameter tag in an object declaration. You can change the caption at some point in your program if you start with this default caption. However, if you don't want to generate a caption until some interaction with your program occurs, you would prefer that your user see nothing for the label, rather than the confusing "Default" on screen. Setting the parameter equal to the empty string, as defined previously, solves this problem.

Pace-Pal Application

Pace-Pal is the running-pace calculation program shown in Figure 23.3. This program resembles other VBScript page applications in that it consists of a standard HTML Web page with embedded VBScript. Pace-Pal allows the user to specify a distance in either miles or kilometers, and a time in minutes/seconds format. (Hours can also optionally be entered if the user has run a distance that takes them that long to cover!) With this information, a runner can calculate his pace per mile. For example, if someone ran a 6.2 mile race (10k) in 37 minutes and 12 seconds and supplied that information to Pace-Pal, Pace-Pal would calculate that the runner averaged a 6-minute mile.

> **NOTE**
>
> The Pace-Pal program is available on the CD-ROM in the file `PacePal.htm`.

FIGURE 23.3.

The Pace-Pal program.

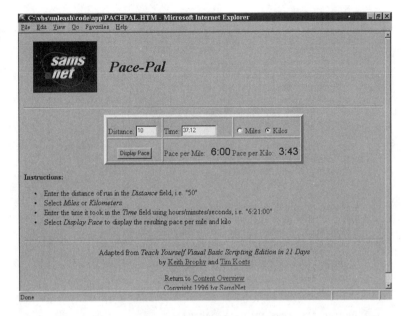

The Pace-Pal application performs a rather lengthy series of conversions and calculations to derive the pace per mile from the user-supplied input. The Calculation button click event handler, `Calc_OnClick`, uses underlying functions to carry out these computations. The code for this event appears in Listing 23.3.

Listing 23.3. `Calc_OnClick` event handler.

```
Sub Calc_OnClick
    ' Processes request to calculate pace
    '------------------------------------------------------------------------
    Dim sngDistanceMiles    ' How far was the distance in miles
    Dim sngDistanceKilos    ' How far was the distance in kilos
    Dim iDuration           ' How long did it take

    Dim iHoursPos  ' What position is ":" for hours located at
    Dim iMinPos    ' What position is ":" for minutes located at
    Dim iSecPos    ' What position is ":" for seconds located at

    Dim sTemp      ' Temp holder for user input

    if (len(document.frmPace.txtDistance.Value) = 0) or _
       (len(document.frmPace.txtTime.Value) = 0) then
       msgbox "A valid time and distance is required!",0,"More Data Required"
       exit sub
    end if

    ' Convert user string to time in seconds
    sTemp = document.frmPace.txtTime.Value
    ' iDuration = ConvertStringtoTotalSeconds(sTemp)
```

continues

Listing 23.3. continued

```vbscript
iDuration = ConvertStringToTotalSeconds(sTemp)

' Divide time by distance
' Convert units if needed
If sCurrentUnits = "Kilos" Then
    sngDistanceKilos = CSng(document.frmPace.txtDistance.Value)
    ' Convert kilos to miles
    sngDistanceMiles = sngDistanceKilos * 0.62
Else
    sngDistanceMiles = CSng(document.frmPace.txtDistance.Value)
    ' Convert miles to kilos
    sngDistanceKilos = sngDistanceMiles * 1.613
End If

' Determine pace per unit
' Derive the average pace per mile
iSecPerUnit = Int(iDuration / sngDistanceMiles)

' Convert pace in total seconds to formatted pace string
➥showing minutes/seconds
document.frmPace.lblPaceMiles.Caption =
➥ ConvertSecondsToString(iSecPerUnit)

' Derive the average pace per kilo
iSecPerUnit = Int(iDuration / sngDistanceKilos)
' Convert pace in total seconds to formatted pace string
'    showing minutes/seconds
document.frmpace.lblPaceKilos.Caption =
➥ ConvertSecondsToString(iSecPerUnit)

End Sub ' Calc_OnClick
```

The function `ConvertStringToTotalSeconds` is called to put the original user input string into a calculation-ready numeric format of total seconds. Calculations are then performed using the data in this format. Once a final pace in seconds has been derived from the calculations, the result must be returned to the user. The function `ConvertSecondsToString` is called to transform the seconds-only data into a more readable minutes-seconds form before it is updated on the page for the user to see. Both of these functions are user-defined functions that are also defined in the VBScript code of the Web page. Listing 23.4 shows the logic for `ConvertStringToTotalSeconds`.

Listing 23.4. ConvertStringToTotalSeconds function.

```vbscript
Function ConvertStringToTotalSeconds (ByVal sDuration)
    '-------------------------------------------------------------------
    ' Takes HH:MM:SS format string and converts to total seconds

    ' When error occurs, continue with next statement rather than halting program
        on error resume next
```

```
    Dim iPosition        'Position of ":" seperator
    Dim vHours           ' Number of hours required
    Dim vMinutes         ' Number of minutes required
    Dim vSeconds         ' Number of seconds required

    'Start working from right of string, parsing seconds
    sMode = "Seconds"

    ' Get leftmost time component
    iPosition = InStr(sDuration, ":")
    if iPosition = 0 then
        ' no more time info, assume time info just in ss format
        vSeconds = sDuration
    else ' more time info is on string
        ' store first portion in hours for now, assume hh:mm:ss format
        vhours = left(sDuration,iPosition - 1)
        ' Parse string for further processing
        sDuration = right(sDuration, len(sDuration) - iPosition)

        ' Get middle time component
        iPosition = InStr(sDuration, ":")
        if iPosition = 0 then
            ' no more time info, must just be mm:ss format
            vMinutes = vHours
            vSeconds = sDuration
            vHours = 0

        else ' time info must be in hh:mm:ss format

            vminutes = left(sDuration,iPosition - 1)
            seconds = right(sDuration, len(sDuration) - iPosition)
        end if
    end if

    ' Represent all components in terms of seconds
    vHours = vHours * 3600
    vMinutes = vMinutes * 60

    ' Return total seconds value
    ConvertStringtoTotalSeconds = CInt(vHours) +
  ➥ CInt(vMinutes) + CInt(vSeconds)

    if err.number <> 0 then
        msgbox "Error #:" & err.number & " Description:" & err.description _
        & " Source:" & err.source, 0, "Error in ConvertStringtoTotalSeconds!"
    end if

End Function ' ConvertStringtoTotalSeconds
```

This sample program illustrates that you can build a rather sophisticated program directly into a Web page's script code. The modular use of functions and good comments helps to keep your code manageable. Some rules of thumb that have been published about scripting suggest that a page should never contain "a lot" of script code. This line of reasoning maintains that if a program has more than a few lines, it should be bundled in a separate Java applet or ActiveX control that's included with the page, rather than as a script that is part of the page itself.

A program such as Pace-Pal refutes this argument. It is very easy to implement in VBScript and was developed in a much shorter time frame than the alternative approaches. If you have a substantial programming task that could be implemented in script or as a control, consider factors such as time, maintenance, and development effort; then base your decision on the circumstances.

Information Submittal Application

So far, the applications presented have focused solely on the scripts that relate to the page running on the client computer without much regard for the Web server. The server has another role that goes beyond just downloading pages or components. In many cases, VBScript code in a page can affect what happens on the server.

At first glance, VBScript might appear to be a periphery player in the server-side communication. After all, many of the pages that a server downloads to a client computer serve simply as front ends for collecting data. However, VBScript can serve as the basis of the front end for data validation and final submittal of the data to the server to ensure clean data and thereby enhance server performance.

The Advantage of Validating Server-Bound Data

For some time, HTML has had a model for collecting data on a page and submitting it to a server. Although that model is evolving with the help of technologies such as VBScript, the concepts are still much the same. Input control fields collect data from the user. Two specific HTML definitions are required for the page to submit that data to a program on the server. The input controls must be defined within a form so that the data from them can be submitted as one data set. Some specific action must trigger the submittal, which is accomplished through an input control that resembles a regular command button but has a type of submit.

Consider the form definition further. When the data is provided to the server, the server must be able to tell which program to submit that data to. After all, the server can't just assume the data should be added to a database or saved in a file or ignored. Therefore, the form tag has an ACTION attribute, which specifies the program on the server that processes the input from the client. (These server-side programs that process page data are sometimes called server *scripts*.) In addition, the form tag definition sets a method attribute to indicate how the information should be passed from the client back to the server.

The full details of this interaction are beyond the scope of this section, but you should understand some of the technologies involved. In the past, the primary protocol for supplying data back to the server and launching a script was CGI, or Common Gateway Interface. CGI is still in broad use today. In addition, other technologies such as Internet Server Application Program Interface (ISAPI) and Internet Database Connectivity (IDC) have emerged. An ISAPI-launched program on a Windows NT server works in the same address space as server software, which means that it can be significantly faster than a traditional CGI server script. The related technology of IDC can even result in direct database interaction through the use of a template file.

> **NOTE**
>
> You can also use VBScript directly on NT Server with the Internet Information Server Web server software. The focus of this section is illustrating the use of VBScript at the browser level, so I do not consider this topic in detail. However, the same VBScript core syntax rules and language fundamentals covered here apply in the server environment as well.

Although technical differences exist in the way these approaches are implemented, the concept is the same from the standpoint of your page and your script code. When the user clicks a Submit button on the form, the browser submits all the input fields on the form as well as the action parameter to the server. The server activates the specified application and provides the field names from the form and their associated data as well.

The application is responsible for responding to the request. Typically, the CGI or ISAPI application on the server might store the information from the page into a database. It might also generate another page to download to the client. These tasks are accomplished with assistance from the Web server. Typically, the CGI or ISAPI application generates one long string for a page. This string contains all the tags that make up the Web page to be sent to the client. The server takes care of passing that data through the HTTP protocol back to the client. All this interaction is fairly transparent to the user. From the perspective of the end user, she supplies some data, submits it, and suddenly another page appears.

An example can help illustrate the process and also show the specific way that VBScript comes into play as a front-end validator. Listing 23.5 shows a simple form definition on a page.

23

VBScript Application Pages

Listing 23.5. Form definition.

```
<form name="frmOrder"
    action="/scripts/oleisapi.dll/Order.clsOrder.ProcessOrder" method="POST">
Your Name: <input name="txtName">
Street Address: <input name="txtAddress" >
City: <input name="txtCity">
State: <input name="txtState">
Zip: <input name="txtZip">

<input type="submit" name="cmdOrder" value="Submit Order">
</form>
```

> **NOTE**
>
> Usually, the data in the form would be presented in a more visually attractive format, such as with each element placed in the cell of an HTML table. For the sake of simplicity, the example is shown without any frills.

Note that a Submit button is defined at the bottom of the form. When the user selects the Submit button, the browser automatically submits the form to the server. No VBScript code or any kind of code is required to make this happen! This process is part of the HTML form and submit element definition. The server receives data that includes the following string:

```
/scripts/oleisapi.dll/Order.clsOrder.ProcessOrder
```

Also appended to this string is other information about the contents of `txtName`, `txtAddress`, `txtCity`, `txtState`, `txtZip`, and the form method attribute. The string

```
/scripts/oleisapi.dll/Order.clsOrder.ProcessOrder
```

tells the server to pass this request to the ISAPI OLE automation director, `/scripts/oleisapi`. (OLE automation is a special method of communicating that some applications, including those generated by Visual Basic 4.0, can respond to.)

`Oleisapi` is actually a dynamic link library (DLL) on the server system. `Oleisapi` starts the requested program. It can locate the requested program because it is registered in the system registration database as an OLE automation server. `Order.clsOrder` specifies the DLL name and class of the program intended to handle this request. `ProcessOrder` specifies the method of this program that is initiated. `Oleisapi` initiates the `Order.clsOrder.ProcessOrder` method, passing it two important parameters. The first is the data from the Web page in one long string. The second parameter is used by `Order.clsOrder` to supply a return page that `oleisapi` directs back to the server and subsequently back to the client.

> **NOTE**
>
> This discussion of server-side software focuses on an NT Server Web server solution and the OLEISAPI technology, but the general concepts largely apply to other server environments as well.

Listing 23.6 shows the code for the Order.clsOrder.ProcessOrder method. This sample is Visual Basic 4.0 code, not VBScript. It is shown here because it gives you a good, representative idea of what a server-side application might do with data from a Web page.

Listing 23.6. Server application called in response to page form submittal.

```
Public Sub ProcessOrder(strRequest as String, strResponse as String)
    Dim strName as String
    ' Extract the name from the data that came from the page
    strName = GetNameField (strRequest)

    ' See if a valid name was supplied
    if len(strName) = 0 then
        ' Name is missing, can't process the order.
        '    Generate a page scolding the user
        strResponse = <html><head><h1>The name is missing!</h1>" & _
            </head><body><p>Please supply a valid name with the order!" & _
            </body></html>"
    else
        ' Store order info from page in database
        StoreInDB (strRequest)
        '    Generate a page confirming to the user
        strResponse = <html><head><h1>Order Confirmation</h1>" & _
            </head><body><p>Thanks for placing the order with us!" & _
            </body></html>"
    end if

    'Add the standard header that is needed when sending new page from
    '   the server to the browser to the front of the response string
    strResponse = "Content-Type: text/html" & vbCrLf & vbCrLf & strResponse
End Sub
```

The comments in this code segment provide a pretty good overview of what the code is doing. The code calls a user-defined procedure to return only the name field from all the string information that originated from the page. It makes a check to see if a name was supplied. If the name is missing, the code assigns to a string a series of HTML tags that make up the new pages. If the name is present, the order is stored in the database by calling a user-defined procedure. The page is built in a string with HTML tags thanking the user. Then the code adds a required header to the response string to indicate that HTML text format data is returned. The ProcessOrder method procedure then terminates, and the server returns the response string to the client. The client receives the new page, which came from an application-generated string rather than from a file. Of course, the end users don't realize the difference; they just see that a result page has arrived from their original query.

Consider the flow of this interaction when the user forgets to supply a name while specifying an order on the original Web page, as illustrated in Figure 23.4.

The request went all the way to the server, which then detected the missing name, so no data was saved. The response page went back to the user. That's too much overhead for what was accomplished considering that nothing was saved in the database. The interaction involved the user's time, network communication, and server processing time, all for the end result of no change to the server database.

FIGURE 23.4.

Server validation of bad input.

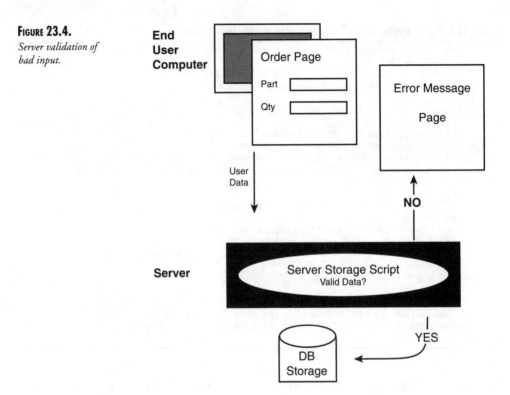

Now, you can finally see an alternative implementation where VBScript comes to the rescue! Suppose that you define exactly the same form, but you add a block of script code to the page, as shown in Listing 23.7.

Listing 23.7. VBScript page-resident validation.

```
<script language="VBScript">
<!--
    function frmOrder_OnSubmit
    ' Submit order if the request is valid

    ' Make sure user has supplied name before submitting order to server
    if len(document.frmOrder.txtName) = 0 then
        ' No name was supplied, order won't be submitted
        MsgBox "You must supply a name.",vbOKOnly, "Can't submit order"
        ' Cancel the submittal
        frmOrder_OnSubmit = False

    else
        ' Order OK, submit it to server
        MsgBox "Order was submitted. Thanks.",vbOKOnly, "Confirmation"
```

```
        ' Submit the order
        frmOrder_OnSubmit = True
    end if
  end sub
-->
</script>
```

NOTE

The Submit program is available on the CD-ROM in the file `Submit.htm`. Note that the Submit program is provided only as a client-side sample. The full submittal process does not work unless you provide your own server-side application to receive the input from the client VBScript page.

The comments in this code once again provide pretty full details about what transpires. If the text box string has a length of 0, no submittal takes place. How is that accomplished? You simply return a false for the form's `OnSubmit` event handler. If you had no VBScript event handler, the browser would submit all data automatically. If you supply code for the `OnSubmit` event of a form, the data is not submitted if the VBScript code returns a false for the event. It will be submitted if the script returns a true for the event. You can see the use of this method in the `Else` branch of the conditional statement. If the name is present, the data is submitted. Once the form is submitted, the server application that was described earlier will be launched on the server to carry out further processing.

On the form for this example the `cmdOrder` button was declared to be a special HTML Submit button, by setting its type to `TYPE=SUBMIT` in the `<INPUT>` tag. If no event handler was defined, then the form would be automatically submitted when the user clicked on the button. When a form submit event handler is defined, that will be called first.

The event handler is declared by creating the function named `"yourform_OnSubmit"`. This function name is made up of the form name followed by an underscore and then the predefined `"OnSubmit"` syntax. There is another way to name the event handler, however. You could also plug your own routine into the form tag and associate it with the `OnSubmit` event:

```
<FORM ID="YourForm" LANGUAGE="VBScript" OnSubmit="YourVBFunction"
➥ ACTION="serversidescript">
```

Both approaches accomplish the same end result. Your function would do the validation and return a true if the submit was to proceed or false if it wasn't.

However you implement the solution, validation provides great advantages. The code has done something very significant: It has eliminated the need for any server-side validation. The Visual Basic code that stores data in the database no longer needs to check whether a name exists. It is only called if valid data was first verified by the VBScript code that resides at the client computer. This approach saves processing time on the server when the data is saved. You use fewer lines for error-checking code. Better yet, consider what happens when an error does occur. Before, you had communication between the client to the server, processing on the server, and communication from the server to the client just to generate an error message to the user. Now, the client-side processing by VBScript generates the error message directly. VBScript completely eliminates all the network traffic, not to mention the user wait for the network and the server-side processing!

Figure 23.5 shows the flow for this interaction. Compare Figures 23.5 and 23.4, and observe the difference in approaches. This very simple, scaled-down example shows the advantages of placing the validation load on VBScript rather than on the server. Even this simple example shows significant savings.

FIGURE 23.5.

*VBScript form
validation flow.*

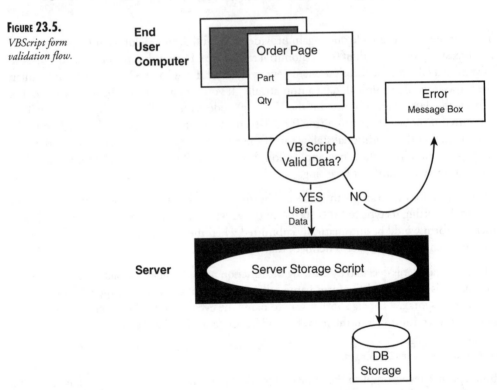

As you can see, even though VBScript performs the processing on the client, it can have a close association with any programs on the server that might process data from the page. VBScript can execute front-end validation processing before form data is submitted to the server. It can screen out bad data or modify questionable data before submitting it to the server. The front-end processing reduces server load, network load, and even user wait time in the event that the data is bad and an error response must be generated for the user. VBScript can provide feedback right away without the server program generating a response and sending it back.

Of course, when you develop software in this manner, you must plan the scripts in conjunction with the server-side software. You don't gain much by having a script validate data if it's not validating the data according to the right rules. Generally, this kind of in-sync planning of server application and script works out well because the server application must be planned in concert with the form anyway. VBScript can generate smoother performance from the entire server when you use it to perform the type of validation described here.

Browser Objects

Most examples presented so far have focused on core capabilities of the VBScript language. For example, the VBScript interpreter directly supports language keywords such as `if` and `dim`. This language is consistent whether you use VBScript hosted in the Internet Explorer browser, in some other browser, in the Internet server, or even in some application that supports VBScript not related to the Web at all.

Other examples looked at objects defined externally to the browser, including ActiveX controls. The host environment enables VBScript to control objects. Support in the Internet Explorer browser and its interface with the VBScript interpreter lays the framework for your VBScript to access such objects. If you use VBScript in another host environment, such as a different browser or a non-Web-related application, it may very well provide the same support. On the other hand, it may not. The VBScript language definition does not require every host to provide this capability. Clearly, the host environment makes a difference in what you can do with VBScript.

You still need to consider one more area: objects the host itself exposes. The Internet Explorer, which is the host I focus on, provides VBScript with access to information about itself and with interfaces to control its own behavior through objects such as the document object.

The Internet Explorer provides access to this browser information by making available several intrinsic browser objects. This concept is not unique. Other browsers such as Netscape Navigator expose a range of objects to JavaScript. For the most part the objects exposed by Microsoft Internet Explorer to JavaScript and VBScript are the same as those exposed to JavaScript by other browsers. Consequently, intrinsic objects in scripting are likely to be very consistent from browser to browser. However, the intrinsic objects exposed by the browser are not an inherent part of the VBScript language. If you work with VBScript in other environments, these objects might not be available to you, but if you're in another browser host, odds are they will be.

Objects exposed by the Internet Explore browser include the window object, the document object, the element object, the frame object, the history object, the script object, the anchor object, the element object, the form object, and the navigator object. With these objects you can do many things. From your code, you can link to other pages. You can detect the version of the browser that is used. You can respond to mouse movements and clicks on link areas. You can work with the browser history list. You can even find out the name of the referring page for the current page. In other words, you can tell the page that your user visited before he or she linked to the page that contains your VBScript. You can also use these objects to provide control over multiple frames from your code. This script statement, for example, could reside in a script in a currently displayed frame page and update the contents of another visible frame:

```
parent.frames(1).document.writeln
  "<HTML><BODY><h2> You can " & "generate HTML to a
  ➥ page!</h2></BODY></HTML>"
parent.frames(1).document.close
```

> **NOTE**
>
> A *frame* is an independent HTML window created through the <FRAMESET> and <FRAME> tags. You can find more details on frames from any HTML reference. Frames can be referenced in VBScript through the objects and properties exposed by the browser. The parent keyword references the parent window of the current frame. That window contains a collection of all existing frames created underneath it. The first is referenced as parent.frames(0) and the second as parent.frames(1). The document keyword indicates the document object belonging to that frame. Writeln is a method of the document object that you can use to generate HTML content to a page, and close is a method used to conclude the document changes.

The possibilities are limitless. A good representative summary of these intrinsic browser objects appears in the sample program Browser.htm on the CD-ROM. This page includes samples of script control between frames, various ways to advance from one page to another, and methods to determine information ranging from the browser version to the last date that a page changed. You can inspect the source code to observe the various techniques used. A table of some of the key properties and methods of the browser objects appears on this page. Browser.htm serves as a good initial reference point to the browser objects for you. A detailed discussion of all the objects would be very lengthy given the range of capabilities. Refer to Microsoft's documentation for the comprehensive documentation. However, the samples you can inspect in Browser.htm should be enough to get your script-creation efforts off to a good start.

Summary

As the samples in this chapter demonstrate, VBScript has very few limitations. You saw several examples of the types of page-resident application solutions that VBScript can provide. For example, one application carried out a simple metric conversion, using very little code. Another sample demonstrated an interactive tutorial that provides user question-and-answer feedback through an ActiveX label control with no server-side intervention. You saw a script that uses a more complex series of calculations in the Pace-Pal running-calculator program, as well as a sample of how to use front-end techniques for validating data before submitting it to a server. Finally, you examined an application that addressed a broad range of capabilities for interacting with browser objects. Separating hype from reality in the rapidly evolving Internet technology arena is not easy, but the examples here underscore the fact that VBScript is the real thing. With some creativity, persistence, and a good knowledge of the capabilities of VBScript, you can deliver quick-to-develop, impressive solutions.

CGI Scripting with the UNIX Shell

by Dave Taylor

IN THIS CHAPTER

CHAPTER 24

So far you've spent a lot of your time learning about complex and sophisticated languages for working with the Internet. All of them are powerful approaches to developing Common Gateway Interface (CGI) solutions for the World Wide Web. If you've been around the UNIX system for a while, though, you already know the majority of what it takes to make a powerful programming environment from your day-to-day command-line usage: the UNIX shell. This chapter explores the capabilities of the shell and looks at how it can be the ideal solution for a variety of simple to sophisticated Web back-end processes.

How CGI Scripts Work, a Redux

First, you can admit it: The Web, and all that it has spawned, is ugly and pretty much a huge hack. It's somewhat miraculous that it all works as well as it does and that it appears so seamless, when underneath, it is weird and remarkably inconsistent. Not just the markup language itself, mind you, but the actual protocol and even the way that the server identifies the type of information being sent to the client is the result of this combination of software and luck.

It all works similar to the depiction in Figure 24.1.

FIGURE 24.1.

The basic client/server communication.

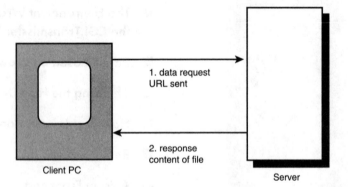

The simplest case is when the client program (the Web browser) asks for a specific file using the file's address, or Uniform Resource Locator (URL). The server looks for the file, and if it finds it, sends back the contents of the specified file. If not, an error occurs and you get an ugly one-liner such as `404 File not found`.

However, instead of the server sending back the contents of a file, the request can instead be "run this program on the server and send the output." Better yet, what if the program itself could output information in HTML so that the results are attractive and consistent? That's what interactivity is all about on the Web.

To have a program, rather than a file, be the target of a URL, you need to have that program live on the server and output HTML code. At its simplest, a shell script like the following does the trick:

```
#!/bin/sh -f
echo "Content-type: text/html"
echo ""
echo "<HTML><BODY>"
echo "<H1>Hello World</H1>"
echo "</BODY></HTML>"
exit 0
```

> **NOTE**
>
> Web servers typically execute programs only in certain directories on the server, most commonly cgi-bin (Common Gateway Interface Binaries). Drop your programs into that directory on your server if that's how your server is configured, or you have another possibility. All scripts must have the .cgi suffix, even if they're shell scripts, but they can live anywhere in the file system. Check with the person who built the server—or, for your own system, look in the config files—to find out how the system is installed.

After you've figured out the necessary naming scheme for your server, you're ready to roll with simple programs; change the ownership of the script using the UNIX chmod command to ensure that the script is executable, and figure out the full URL including your host name (such as http://www.intuitive.com/script.cgi). Any output that your program emits is sent to the browser (the client program) on the other end of the wire.

Local Time and Who's Logged In

You can write a simple output-only CGI script that shows what time it is and who is logged on to the server itself by using the UNIX date and who commands, all wrapped up with standard HTML commands (see Listing 24.1).

Listing 24.1. Providing the time and a list of users to the client.

```
#!/bin/sh -f
echo "Content-type: text/html"
echo ""
echo -n "<h1>Welcome to "
hostname
echo -n " It's "
date
echo "</h1>"
echo "Here's Who is Logged In Right Now:"
echo "<BLOCKQUOTE><PRE>"
who
echo "</PRE></BLOCKQUOTE>"
echo "</BODY></HTML>"
exit 0
```

The output looks like the following:

```
Welcome to www.intuitive.com It's Fri Jul 26 14:06:41 CUT 1996

Here's Who is Logged In Right Now:

        sol          pts/2      Jul 06 00:48              (server.iadfw.net)
        taylor       pts/5      Jul 26 13:56          (ws3.hostname.com)
```

This script isn't too gorgeous, but it's quite utilitarian and serves as a basis for some interesting status scripts and such.

> **NOTE**
>
> In addition to the standard HTML formatting instructions output from your script, the first two lines of output are critical to the Web browser's understanding of what to do with the information in the output: the two lines must be "Content-type: text/html" followed by a blank line. If you omit this, you'll see "document has no data" error messages when you try to access the scripts from a browser.

The Environment Wrapped Up in the CGI Transmission

The request for a URL from the Web browser comes wrapped in a package that contains various snippets of useful information. When that information gets to the CGI program, it becomes part of the calling environment. Listing 24.2 shows a simple script that lets you see what you've got.

Listing 24.2. Obtaining browser information.

```
#!/bin/sh -f
echo "Content-type: text/html"
echo ""
echo "<PRE>"
env ¦¦ printenv          # SVR4 or BSD - skip errors
echo "</PRE>"
exit 0
```

The output from the server when I connect via the Web shows what kind of client I'm using, from what system I'm connected, and lots of other interesting information, if you look closely.

```
DOCUMENT_ROOT=/home/httpd/htdocs
GATEWAY_INTERFACE=CGI/1.1
HTTP_ACCEPT=*/*, image/gif, image/x-xbitmap, image/jpeg
HTTP_USER_AGENT=Mozilla/2.1N (Macintosh; I; PPC)
PATH=/bin:/usr/bin:/usr/ucb:/usr/bsd:/usr/local/bin
QUERY_STRING=
REMOTE_ADDR=205.149.165.109
REMOTE_HOST=ws3.hostname.com
REQUEST_METHOD=GET
SCRIPT_NAME= /test.cgi
SERVER_NAME=www.intuitive.com
SERVER_PORT=80
SERVER_PROTOCOL=HTTP/1.0
SERVER_SOFTWARE=NCSA/1.4.2
```

Notice that there's no remote login name or e-mail address in this collection of information. The best you can get automatically from a connection (today) is the user's remote host name (variable REMOTE_HOST) and the type of browser that the client is running (variable HTTP_USER_AGENT). You can extract the specific browser with a couple of simple UNIX tools:

```
x="`echo $HTTP_USER_AGENT ¦ sed 's:/: :g'`"
browser="`echo $x ¦ cut -d\  -f1`"
```

The sed invocation replaces the slash that separates the browser from its version ID, so it has arguments separated by spaces. Then, cut gives you the first field (-f1) in the argument as variable browser.

There are a variety of different browsers on the Net today, but a small number represent a large percentage of the user population. Here are some of the most common user agent identification strings:

```
HTTP_USER_AGENT=Lynx/2-4-2  libwww/2.14
HTTP_USER_AGENT=Microsoft Internet Explorer/4.40.308 (Windows 95)
HTTP_USER_AGENT=Mozilla/0.96 Beta (Windows)
HTTP_USER_AGENT=Mozilla/1.1N (Macintosh; I; PPC)
HTTP_USER_AGENT=Mozilla/1.22 (Windows; I; 32bit)
HTTP_USER_AGENT=NCSA Mosaic for the X Window System/2.4 libwww/2.12 modified
HTTP_USER_AGENT=NetCruiser/V2.00
HTTP_USER_AGENT=PRODIGY-WB/1.3e
HTTP_USER_AGENT=Spyglass Mosaic/1.0  libwww/2.15_Spyglass
```

TIP

Mozilla is the internal name for Netscape's Navigator and has crept out in various releases of the browser.

Being able to automatically identify the browser software within your script offers a terrific capability: browser-sensitive pages.

Pages Based on Browser Software

Suppose you want to have two versions of the same Web page, one for people with graphic capabilities and another for those using the utilitarian Lynx text-only Web browser. Listing 24.3 shows how you can do it.

Listing 24.3. Producing browser-dependent Web pages.

```
#!/bin/sh -f
echo "Content-type: text/html"
echo ""

x="`echo $HTTP_USER_AGENT | sed 's:/: :g'`"
browser="`echo $x | cut -d\  -f1`"

if [ $browser = "Lynx" ] ; then
  cat $text_only_home_page
else
  echo $graphical_home_page
fi
exit 0
```

One drawback to this approach is that you must maintain two parallel HTML pages with the same basic information. Web page development tools that can help with this problem are just starting to show up on the market; you could also use m4 or a similar UNIX macro processor to allow #ifdef-style conditionals within a single version of the file that would automatically split into separate browser-specific documents.

Checking the Host Domain

One common use for the Web is to provide information that's available for the public and simultaneously provide other information only for people in the same institution or type of business. There's a very straightforward way to accomplish this by using the REMOTE_HOST environment variable. Its value is computer.domain.top-level-domain—for example, www4.intuitive.com. To extract the relevant information, use a pair of UNIX commands:

```
TOPMOST="`echo $REMOTE_HOST | rev | cut -d. -f1 | rev`"
DOMAIN="`echo $REMOTE_HOST | rev | cut -d. -f1,2 | rev`"
```

Note the double use of the obscure UNIX rev command, which reverses characters in the line. By reversing the remote domain name (to moc.evitiutni.4www), you can get the first field only (-f1 to cut) as the topmost domain and the first two fields as the regional domain. Then, flip it back with another call to rev, and you're ready to use the domain name.

How could you use this? The following shows an example:

```
echo "<h2>Our Favorite Links</h2>"
if [ $TOPMOST = "com" ] ; then
  cat commercial_links
elif [ $TOPMOST = "edu" ] ; then
  cat educational_links
else
  cat other_links
fi
```

The rage in Web site promotion is advertising, and this tool gives you the capability to tailor a portion of your page—perhaps to your advertisers—based on their domain. For example, you can list different sets of advertisements or sponsors for students and commercial users (which includes subscribers America Online, the Microsoft Network, and all the dial-up services, too).

How Fast Is Your Connection?

When a browser connects to a server, its host name is sent as the environment variable REMOTE_HOST. Knowing that, you can write a shell script to run on a server and indicate the speed of the connection between the visitor and the server system. Listing 24.4 shows how that would look.

Listing 24.4. Checking the client/server connection.

```
#!/bin/sh -f
echo "Content-type: text/html"
echo ""
echo "<HTML>"
echo "<H1>Ping info to host $REMOTE_HOST:</h1>"
echo "<BLOCKQUOTE><PRE>"
ping -c 10 $REMOTE_HOST
echo "</HTML>"
exit 0
```

If you connect to this script via the Web, you might see the following output:

```
Ping info to host test.intuitive.com:

     PING test.intuitive.com (205.149.165.109): 56 data bytes
     64 bytes from 205.149.165.109: icmp_seq=0 ttl=47 time=351 ms
     64 bytes from 205.149.165.109: icmp_seq=1 ttl=47 time=286 ms
     64 bytes from 205.149.165.109: icmp_seq=2 ttl=47 time=310 ms
     64 bytes from 205.149.165.109: icmp_seq=3 ttl=47 time=293 ms
     64 bytes from 205.149.165.109: icmp_seq=4 ttl=47 time=291 ms
     64 bytes from 205.149.165.109: icmp_seq=5 ttl=47 time=293 ms
     64 bytes from 205.149.165.109: icmp_seq=6 ttl=47 time=302 ms
     64 bytes from 205.149.165.109: icmp_seq=7 ttl=47 time=284 ms
     64 bytes from 205.149.165.109: icmp_seq=8 ttl=47 time=289 ms
     64 bytes from 205.149.165.109: icmp_seq=9 ttl=47 time=297 ms

     --- test.intuitive.com ping statistics ---
     10 packets transmitted, 10 packets received, 0% packet loss
     round-trip min/avg/max = 284/299/351 ms
```

Because `ping` computes an average round-trip time (see the last line of the preceding output), you could even add some smarts to your script that would let you take different actions based on the speed of the connection between the server and the browser system.

The first step is to extract the average round-trip packet speed:

```
ping -c 10 $REMOTE_HOST > /tmp/pingme.$$
average="`tail -1 /tmp/pingme.$$ ¦ awk -F/ '{ print $4 }'`"
```

Now `average` has the average `ping` speed, in milliseconds, which you can then use as a gauge to deliver different information based on connection speed. The following is a very simple example of different graphics that you might include on your page based on whether the client has a fast or slow connection (fast connections get larger images in this case). Listing 24.5 shows how you could write a script to exploit this idea.

Listing 24.5. Delivering graphics based on connection speed.

```
if [ $average -lt 100 ] ; then
  echo "<img src=hi-rez.jpg>"
elif [ $average -lt 200 ] ; then
  echo "<img src=low-rez.jpg>"
else
  echo "<img src=black+white.gif>"
fi
```

Users who connect over a slow line see the black-and-white GIF format, but users with a reasonable speed connection see a color graphic. However, if your users connect to the same site over a really fast line, they are surprised to see a beautiful, high-resolution JPEG image.

Remote `ping`

What if you want to specify what machine you want to ping? It turns out that there's another environment variable that can be sent from the browser to the server called `QUERY_STRING`. If you simply specify the URL of a particular CGI program or script and add a `?`, anything following that question mark—up to the first space—is sent as the value of the `QUERY_STRING` variable.

Listing 24.6 shows how you could easily modify the `ping` script to check the connection between the server and any arbitrary system on the Internet.

Listing 24.6. Using `ping` for a specific machine.

```
#!/bin/sh -f
echo "Content-type: text/html"
echo ""
echo "<HTML>"
if [ "$QUERY_STRING" = "" ] ; then
```

```
  echo "<h1>no query string? No host to check</h1>"
else
  echo "<H1>Ping info to host $QUERY_STRING:</h1>"
  echo "<blockquote><pre>"
  ping -c 10 $QUERY_STRING
  echo "</pre></blockquote>"
fi
echo "</HTML>"
exit 0
```

Suppose the script in Listing 24.6 is called `query.cgi` and that it lives on `test.intuitive.com`. The URL for that particular script is then `http://test.intuitive.com/query.cgi`. Now you can actually send it some arguments—in this case, the host name of a machine to check—by appending the desired system name to the URL itself. For example, within Netscape Navigator, you can click the Open URL button within your browser and type

```
http://test.intuitive.com/cgi-bin/query.sh?pipeline.com
```

The following output is shown as the contents of that page:

```
Ping info to host pipeline.com:

        PING pipeline.com (198.80.32.3): 56 data bytes
        64 bytes from 198.80.32.3: icmp_seq=0 ttl=244 time=39 ms
        64 bytes from 198.80.32.3: icmp_seq=1 ttl=244 time=36 ms
        64 bytes from 198.80.32.3: icmp_seq=2 ttl=244 time=41 ms
        64 bytes from 198.80.32.3: icmp_seq=3 ttl=244 time=42 ms
        64 bytes from 198.80.32.3: icmp_seq=4 ttl=244 time=29 ms
        64 bytes from 198.80.32.3: icmp_seq=5 ttl=244 time=32 ms
        64 bytes from 198.80.32.3: icmp_seq=6 ttl=244 time=31 ms
        64 bytes from 198.80.32.3: icmp_seq=7 ttl=244 time=30 ms
        64 bytes from 198.80.32.3: icmp_seq=8 ttl=244 time=32 ms
        64 bytes from 198.80.32.3: icmp_seq=9 ttl=244 time=31 ms

        --- pipeline.com ping statistics ---
        10 packets transmitted, 10 packets received, 0% packet loss
        round-trip min/avg/max = 29/34/42 ms
```

As you can see, Pipeline in New York has a much, much faster TCP packet turn-around speed with the server than the test workstation used in the previous example (34 milliseconds compared to 299 milliseconds); that's almost 10 times faster!

A Form Front End

Being able to add arguments to a URL as a way to pass information is useful, but it's somewhat limited. After all, what you really want to have on your Web pages are boxes and checklists—places where users can specify information and then press a Do It or Submit button and have that information quickly relayed to the waiting CGI script.

You include such elements with the `<FORM>` HTML tag set within your documents, as shown in Listing 24.7.

Listing 24.7. Creating a form to reach your script.

```
<HTML>
<h1>How fast is your connection?</h1>
<hr>
<FORM METHOD=get
ACTION="http://test.intuitive.com/query.cgi">
Look for?
<input type=string name=ping>
<P>
<input type=submit value="ping this host">
</form>
</HTML>
```

Most of this script is typically straightforward Web markup until you get to the `<FORM>` section. The `FORM` tag has two attributes: the mechanism by which the information should be transmitted to the server and the URL of the CGI program that should receive the information. In this case, you can see that the `ACTION` specifies that the remote script is referenced as

```
http://test.intuitive.com/query.cgi
```

and that the `METHOD` is `Get`.

The two basic `METHOD`s for sending information from a browser to a CGI script are `Get` and `Post`. `Get` is the easiest to work with because the information is all tucked neatly into the `QUERY_STRING` environment variable, but it has some serious size limitations. Instead, complex Web forms invariably use `Post`, which sends all the information as standard input to the CGI script, allowing an arbitrary amount of data to flow from the browser to the CGI script.

Every input field from an HTML form is sent as a *name=value* pair with multiple pairs separated by an ampersand. In the case of this particular form, the `<input type=string>` HTML tag produces a small box within which the user can type the name of a system to `ping`. That information is actually sent to the CGI script as `ping=`*whatever-they-typed* (that's what the `name=ping` does in that `<INPUT>` tag). There's a variety of different `input type` fields, including those shown in Table 24.1.

Table 24.1. Form input types.

Input type	Meaning
string	One line of text requested from the browser
password	One line of text—not echoed as typed

Input type	Meaning
radio	One of a set of radio buttons
checkbox	A yes/no checkbox
submit	The submit or do it button
reset	The reset or restore default values button

Many good references are available both online and in books at your local bookstore, so I won't belabor the point here.

Now you have a simple Web page that prompts for a host to ping and presents an action button right below the prompt that users can click to have their information sent to the script and acted upon. This is shown in Figure 24.2.

FIGURE 24.2.

A simple form-based Web page inviting input.

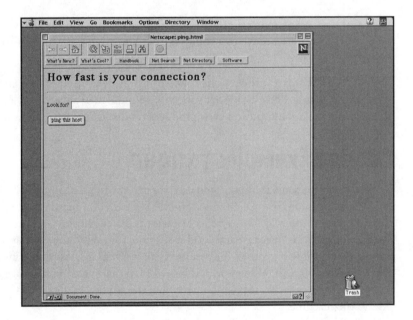

How does this variation of the CGI script look? It's surprisingly similar to the last version you saw; indeed, all you need to add is the capability to extract the host name from its name=value form, as shown in Listing 24.8.

24

Listing 24.8. ping script that accepts input.

```
#!/bin/sh -f
# modified to accept name=value pairs...
echo "Content-type: text/html"
echo ""
echo "<HTML>"
if [ "$QUERY_STRING" = "" ] ; then
  echo "<h1><I>no query string? No host to check</i></h1>"
else
  host="`echo $QUERY_STRING | awk -F= '{print $2}'`"
  echo "<H1>Ping Info to Host $host:</h1>"
  echo "<blockquote><PRE>"
  ping -c 10 $host
  echo "</pre></blockquote>"
fi
echo "</HTML>"
exit 0
```

You use the awk program to split the information received at the =, which works fine for a single value. However, if you move to a multiple-variable script, a more sophisticated technique is required.

With this HTML page and the script shown in Listing 24.8, users can now pop over to the Web site and ping any host on the network with wild and merry abandon. Entering pipeline.com and pressing the Submit button even produces results identical to those shown earlier.

Another Example: finger

You can apply the same technique you used for ping to another simple UNIX command—one that would be useful to access from within the Web environment: the finger command. This is an interesting command because its behavior is dependent on the type of information that you give it; use it to finger a name, and it searches for everyone with that information in the password file, showing you all the results. Give it a remote host name instead—in the form @hostname.com—and it tells you who is logged in to that machine. Use a fully qualified e-mail address—user@hostname.com—and it tells you, the requestor, about that person if it can connect to the machine.

Listing 24.9 shows an HTML file that's a quick and simple finger front end. You'll see that it's remarkably similar to the ping page.

Listing 24.9. Form front end for finger queries.

```
<HTML>
<h1>Finger:</h1><h2>find out about users or computers</h2>
<hr>
<form method=get action="http://test.intuitive.com/cgi-
bin/finger.sh">
```

```
Look for?
<input type=string name=finger>
<P>
<blockquote><font size=+1>
<I>Try an email address for a specific user, or just the '@hostname'
format to see who is using a particular computer on the net</i>
</font></blockquote><P>
<CENTER><input type=submit value="look up this user or host">
</CENTER>
</form>
</html>
```

This time, you've also included some helpful information for the user in the form of a brief italicized comment below the input box, as you can see in Figure 24.3.

FIGURE 24.3.

Simple Web front end for the finger *command.*

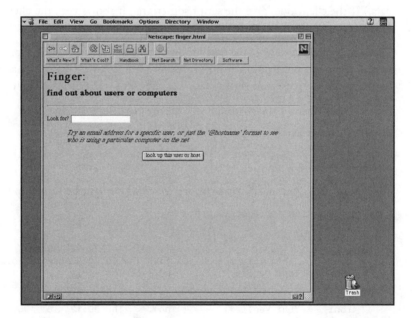

The script at the other end looks like Listing 24.10.

Listing 24.10. The finger **CGI script.**

```
#!/bin/sh -f
# Finger user or user@host or @host
echo "Content-type: text/html"
echo ""
echo "<HTML>"
if [ "$QUERY_STRING" = "" ] ; then
  echo "<h1><I>no user or host to check?</i></h1>"
else
```

continues

Listing 24.10. continued

```
value="`echo $QUERY_STRING | awk -F= '{print $2}'`"
echo "<H1>Finger information for $value:</h1>"
echo "<blockquote><PRE>"
finger $value
echo "</pre></blockquote>"
fi
echo "</HTML>"
exit 0
```

In the spirit of good coding, you again include some error checking—this time, the CGI script can produce an error message (as proper HTML, of course) if you hit the script without going through the HTML page. (If you leave the box blank, it sends finger=, so there's still some data.) If the client does give the script something, it shows you, the client, the results of the finger command run on the server with the information you've specified.

Take a quick look at some of the possible output formats. Note in these examples that the $value sent also appears as part of the output. As an interface rule, this is a great bit of positive user feedback, allowing users to verify that what they sent was processed accurately.

First, what happens if the client doesn't specify anything?

```
Finger information for :

    Login      Name            TTY    Idle    When      Site Info
    taylor    Dave Taylor      p0       2  Thu 12:57
```

What happens if you specify @usenix.org to see who might be logged in there?

```
Finger information for @usenix.org:

        [usenix.org]
        Login       Name            TTY Idle    When      Where
        zanna     Zanna Knight      KA 1:46 Thu 09:00  Zanna's Mac:8.23
        toni      Toni Veglia       co   13: Tue 14:59
        diane     Diane DeMartini   p6    8 Thu 08:44  131.106.3.16:0.0
        ellie     Ellie Young       p7 1:22 Thu 09:04  boss:0.0
        toni      Toni Veglia       pb      Thu 09:12  131.106.3.17:0.0
        carolyn   Carolyn Carr      pe 1:26 Thu 09:20  bigx:0.0
        ah        Alain Henon       q0   12 Thu 09:29  131.106.3.29
        zanna     Zanna Knight      q3   59 Thu 09:48  131.106.3.20:0.0
        eileen    Eileen Curtis     q5   36 Thu 10:04  131.106.3.19:0.0
```

The Usenix Assocation has a lot of people and a lot of things going on. You can also pick someone and submit that person's name @usenix.org to find out more about him or her:

```
Finger information for zanna@usenix.org:

        [usenix.org]
        Login name: zanna                    In real life: Zanna Knight
        Directory: /staff/zanna              Shell: /bin/csh
        On since Dec  7 09:00:41 on KA0.0 from Zanna's Mac:8.23
```

```
1 hour 45 minutes Idle Time
No unread mail
No Plan.

Login name: zanna                    In real life: Zanna Knight
Directory: /staff/zanna              Shell: /bin/csh
On since Dec  7 09:48:06 on ttyq3 from 131.106.3.20:0.0
58 minutes Idle Time
```

Here, Zanna is actually logged in on two different lines, which is why you see two entries for her in this output. Notice that the top entry indicates that she's actually connected from a Macintosh, too. Ah, the things you can glean when you poke around on the network...

Another Script Trick: Redirection

One nuance of CGI response that's quite cool is if your program emits a line `"Location: url"` with some valid URL for a page anywhere on the network, the connection to your server is instantly replaced with a connection to the specified other server. Suppose you're at `www.intuitive.com` and you have a CGI script `elsewhere.sh` in the `cgi-bin` directory. The script `elsewhere.sh` proves to be a tiny script that looks like this:

```
#!/bin/sh -f
echo "Content-type: text/html"
echo "Location: http://www.tntMedia.com/"
echo ""
exit 0
```

You connect to the URL `http://www.intuitive.com/elsewhere.cgi` and what's returned is actually `http://www.tntMedia.com/`. The net result of invoking this CGI script is that you'll be looking at the home page of TNT Media at `www.tntMedia.com`.

> **NOTE**
>
> The `Location:` line is output in addition to the `Content-Type:` header. Notice that the blank line still must appear after these lines.

What can you do with this? The most obvious answer is a random forwarding service, a so-called URL roulette, where you connect to this URL, and it randomly picks another URL from a file and sends you there instead—somewhat like the following pseudo code:

```
randomurl = `pick-random-line-from  urllist`
print "Location: " $randomurl
```

More interestingly, you can combine what I've been discussing to make a page that takes people to the home page of their browsers, as shown in Listing 24.11.

Listing 24.11. Jumping to the right home page.

```
#!/bin/sh -f
echo "Content-type: text/html"

x="`echo $HTTP_USER_AGENT ¦ sed 's:/: :g'`"
browser="`echo $x ¦ cut -d\   -f1`"

case $browser in
  Cello )         loc=http://www.law.cornell.edu/cello/cellotop.html;    ;;
  Spyglass )      loc=http://www.spyglass.com/three/index.html;          ;;
  Lynx )          loc=http://www.cc.ukans.edu/about_lynx/about_lynx.html; ;;
  NCSA )        loc=http://www.ncsa.uiuc.edu/SDG/Software/;            ;;
  Mozilla )       loc=http://www.netscape.com/;                        ;;
  NetCruiser )    loc=http://www.netcom.com/faq/;                      ;;
  Microsoft )
           loc=http://www.windows.microsoft.com/windows/ie/ie.htm;   ;;
      * )       loc=http://www.yahoo.com/;                            ;;
esac
echo Location: $loc
echo ""
exit 0
```

If you don't know what to do with their browsers, you send 'em to Yahoo!

Summary

This chapter shows only the tip of the proverbial iceberg for shell-based CGI scripting. In particular, any time you either display pages based on processing, without user input, or process only a single variable of information, a shell script is probably the fastest and easiest solution available within UNIX.

Other scripting languages are available on UNIX—notably TK, TCL, and Python—and they have very specific capabilities that make them useful for UNIX programming but not for CGI work.

IV
PART

Internet Markup Languages

HyperText Markup Language (HTML)

by Rick Tracewell

IN THIS CHAPTER

So, you think that HTML is easy? Do you think that it's a waste of time to learn HTML when you've got more exciting things such as Shockwave, Java, and VRML to develop for? If so, it's time for a reality check. Granted, HTML is pretty simple as far as programming languages go. Some people go so far as to claim that it isn't programming at all. The fact is that HTML is the virtual glue that holds together all of these exciting new multimedia and interactive technologies on the Web. Without HTML, there wouldn't be any global way to present the "fancy" stuff.

HTML keeps everything on the World Wide Web anchored to a common ground. So, keeping up with the latest upgrades and features supported (or not supported) by the major Web browser players, such as Netscape and Microsoft, is not only a good idea, but it is a necessity if you are planning to stay competitive in this medium. Multimedia (audio, video, interactive applications) is being integrated into HTML for Web use at a very rapid rate, so making sure that you are in tune with the latest tags supported in HTML could save you a considerable amount of time in the long run.

In this chapter, you will learn some of the new features supported in HTML 2.0 (and proposed for HTML 3.0), and you will be introduced to some of the built-in HTML/multimedia functionality supported by the major Web browsers that virtually eliminates some of the harder-to-learn languages such as JavaScript. Providing all HTML tags would be a little overkill, so I opted to include the most up-to-date tags and the proposed tags that will probably be in use by the time this book is published. I highly recommended that you look through and test each of these tags, because they can be very useful in creating effective Web pages for you and your clients.

I wrote this chapter assuming that you have at least a working knowledge of the basics of HTML. Therefore, I used easily understandable and accessible resource information rather than tons of walk-through examples. The chapter covers the most basic of HTML commands (see the sections "The Basics: What Every HTML Document Needs" through "Text Styles" later in this chapter), as well as the newest tags supported by proposed HTML 3.0 and the two top Web browsers: Netscape Navigator 2.*x*/3.*x* and Microsoft Internet Explorer 2.*x*/3.*x*.

Simple gray backgrounds were all that were available for Web page designers "way back" in 1993 and early 1994, but today there are many commands and specifications that enable color to be placed almost anywhere and in almost every shade (see the section "Color Values" later in this chapter). Choose any graphic as a background and add unique flair to your Web page, or simply choose a color from your computer's palette to keep the background graphic in the background and the text and graphics on your page as the main focus of a visitor's attention. With newer browsers (at the time of this writing, only Internet Explorer), you can now colorize tables within individual cells to really enhance your documents.

Hyperlinks are what make the Web dynamic. The ability to create a *tag* that enables users to jump to anywhere in the world by simply clicking their mouse cursor is one of the powerful features of HTML (see the section "Hyperlinks"). Since the early incarnations of HTML, hyperlinks have evolved along with everything else to include graphics—"clickable images" that enable the designer to specify coordinates and send people to multiple locations from one graphic—and much more (see the "Images" section).

Images are an important part of any Web page layout. But, how do you get the image to place correctly with the text on the page? Why won't the graphic enable text to flow around it? Can I force the graphic to one or the other side of the page? What if someone is using a text-only browser or is on a slow connection and has graphics turned off? Will that person know what the text on a hyperlinked button graphic says? These are common questions that are addressed in the following pages.

It's great to have lots of useful information available on your Web pages for clients, friends, and relatives or fans, but what if you want to get some information from *them*? With HTML, a simple form will do the trick. Forms can be used for applications, to request more information, as order forms, as guest books, and much more (see "Forms" in "HTML Interactions and Enhancements"). Your HTML document takes the information provided in the <FORM> fields and sends it to a CGI (Common Gateway Interface) application that (depending on how it is written) processes the data and returns it to you either on a Web page or through e-mail. This feature of HTML is a very valuable tool in gathering information from your Web site visitors—and a great way to collect marketing data!

Tables are another powerful feature of HTML that enable Web designers to actually have control over text and graphics by placing them in rows and cells (see "Tables" under "HTML Interactions and Enhancements"). This HTML tag is perfect for displaying in an easy-to-read format information such as price sheets, inventory reports, profit/loss statements, company projections, schedules, and anything else you can think of. Tables can also be used for restraining graphics and text so that they are positioned exactly how you want them. (Table borders can be turned off so that they are invisible.)

Integrating audio clips, animated graphics, video clips, and more is currently the craze (see the section "Multimedia: Audio, Video, Applications"). HTML and the leading Web browsers have had to come up to speed quickly in order to handle these new commands: background audio, scrolling text, Shockwave, JavaScript, and more. As you can imagine, with these new features being introduced at a rapid pace, only a few browsers support them. Each feature will note a few of the more popular browsers that support it or don't support it.

The latest creation for Web browsers (thanks to the team at Netscape Communications) is the <FRAMESET> tag (see the "Frames" section). The <FRAMESET> tag enables multiple documents to be simultaneously active on a page, giving the visitor several independent windows (or frames) in which to view information. Instead of forcing a Web designer to create huge HTML documents, one Frame document enables the designer to use hyperlinks within the frames of the Frame document to link with other HTML documents. One nice thing about using <FRAMES> is that you can have a logo and/or a table of contents on-screen at all times while the main frame is where the visitor sees the information he wants—which is a handy navigation tool!

This feature can only be viewed by a few browsers, so the <NOFRAMES> tag enables the designer to provide access to the information in another manner for visitors with non-frame compatible browsers (see the section "Frames" for more details).

NOTE

HTML tags are not case-sensitive. I happen to prefer using uppercase in my programming, so that is what I use in this chapter.

Body and Text Commands

These are the most common HTML commands. Each HTML document is filled with them. What you might *not* know is how much some of them have been enhanced in the latest incarnations of HTML.

The Basics: What Every HTML Document Needs

Increasingly, the basic tags in HTML that used to just get copied from one document to another without ever changing are becoming important to the overall layout of a Web page. From changing the color of the text (hyperlinks, visited hyperlinks, and so on) to changing the color of the background (or using an image) to specifying fonts or style sheets to adjusting margins, these tags need to be looked at and mastered.

<HTML> : </HTML>

This tag is placed at the beginning and end of the entire HTML page and lets the server know that it is an HTML document.

<HEAD> : </HEAD>

This tag is placed at the top of the document, encompassing the <TITLE> tag.

<TITLE> : </TITLE>

This tag encompasses the title of the document (usually displayed in the top frame of the browser window).

<BODY> : </BODY>

This tag surrounds all HTML tags within the body of the document. Any changes to the background, colors of text, and the margins of the document are applied within the <BODY> tags. The following attributes are applicable to this tag.

<BODY BACKGROUND=>

This attribute selects a graphic file and tiles it as the background for the HTML document. Here is an example:

```
<BODY BACKGROUND="/images/graphicname.gif">
```

<BODY BGCOLOR=>

This attribute solidly colorizes the background of the HTML document with the specified color. The default background color (if none is specified in the BODY tag) is gray. For example, this code changes the background color to white:

```
<BODY BGCOLOR="#FFFFFF">
```

For newer browsers, see Table 25.1.

```
<BODY BGCOLOR="WHITE">
```

<BODY TEXT=>

This attribute colorizes the text in the HTML document. The default text color (if none is specified in the BODY tag) is black.

<BODY LINK= VLINK=>

The LINK attribute changes the color of the text hyperlinks, and the VLINK attribute changes the color of the text hyperlink *after* it has been visited. In most browsers, the default link color (if none is specified in the BODY tag) is blue, and the visited link is usually red (Microsoft Internet Explorer) or purple (Netscape Navigator).

<BODY BACKGROUND= BGPROPERTIES=>

The BGPROPERTIES attribute can only be used in conjunction with the BACKGROUND tag, and it has only one value: FIXED. Basically, this attribute holds the background graphic so that it does not "scroll" down with the rest of the content (Internet Explorer-only).

<BODY BGSOUND SRC=>

The BGSOUND tag enables a Web designer to play a sound file (music, voice, sound effect, and so on) without the visitor having to actually click on anything. The sound file loads last (after graphics and text) and immediately starts playing. At the time of this writing, only Internet Explorer supports this tag. This tag has the following attributes:

<BODY BGSOUND= LOOP=>

The LOOP attribute defines the number of times the sound file is to play—for example, LOOP="2". To make the sound file play continuously, use this command:

```
LOOP="infinite"
```

Combinations

Any combination of the preceding BODY attributes can be used within the BODY tag, with the exception of the BGCOLOR and BACKGROUND attributes because they essentially serve the same purpose, and the BGPROPERTIES attributes, which can only be used in conjunction with the BACKGROUND attribute. Here are two examples:

```
<BODY BGCOLOR="#FFFFFF" TEXT="#000000" LINK="#FFFFFF" VLINK="#FFFFFF">

<BODY BACKGROUND="/images/graphicname.gif" TEXT="#FFFFFF">
```

Basic Paragraph Text Tags

As with the basic HTML body tags mentioned previously, the paragraph tags are becoming more dynamic. Whereas a simple centered paragraph used to have a <P> tag and a <CENTER> tag before with a </CENTER> tag after, you can now encompass all three of them in one tag (beginning and ending); <P ALIGN=CENTER> : </P>. Such new HTML extensions are fast becoming the norm, so become very familiar with them; they just might save you a lot of time.

<P>

The paragraph break can be placed at the beginning or end of a paragraph. It can also be used before or after a graphic to move it "down" from the above text or graphic. The paragraph break has the following attribute:

<P ALIGN=>

This is an HTML extension. Therefore, only the newest browsers support it. The following are examples of its use in justifying text to the right and left:

```
<P ALIGN=RIGHT>

<P ALIGN=LEFT>
```

Here is how to center the text:

```
<P ALIGN=CENTER>
```

The default justification for anything on a page is left.

<DIV>

This is a proposed addition to HTML 3.0. Although this tag is similar to <P>, it will be able to handle several types of paragraph breaks within this command. At the time of this writing, Netscape Navigator is the only browser supporting it and is only supporting the ALIGN attribute (covered next).

`<DIV ALIGN=>`

Until the other features mentioned earlier are implemented, this is the only attribute recognized by Netscape Navigator, and it is identical to the `<P ALIGN=>` attribute (see above). The following are examples of aligning left and right:

`<DIV ALIGN=RIGHT>`

`<DIV ALIGN=LEFT>`

The following line centers the text:

`<DIV ALIGN=CENTER>`

Again, the default justification for anything on a page is left.

`<BR>`

The line break inserts a line break smaller than the paragraph break. It can be placed at the beginning or end of a line. As with the `<P>` tag, it can also be used in front of or after a graphic to manipulate how close the item is to the text or graphic above. An available attribute is

`<BR CLEAR=>`

Instead of stopping all text flow as with the `<BR>` tag alone, this attribute stops text from flowing to either side of a graphic that is aligned to the left or right and resumes the text below the graphic. Here is an example:

`<BR CLEAR=LEFT>`

This is used when a graphic is aligned to the left, which forces the text below the graphic instead of enabling it to run alongside the graphic in the right margin. Also, `<BR CLEAR=RIGHT>` and `<BR CLEAR=ALL>` are each related to the margin.

`<PRE>` : `</PRE>`

This signifies preformatted text. The `<PRE>` tag renders text exactly as it is typed between the `<PRE>` and the end tag: `</PRE>`. Normal line breaking is disabled, creating text that flows off to the right of the browser window. This tag is shown on-screen as monospaced in order to enable a designer to retain specific spacing needs (such as source code).

> **TIP**
>
> Any literal markup tags (style markup tags are allowed) must be given entity equivalents such as < for <, and > for >.

<CENTER> : </CENTER>

When placed inside the beginning and ending tags, this tag centers text, graphics, and/or applets in the body of the document.

<HR>

The horizontal rule creates a visible line that enables you to easily separate sections of your page. The default line looks like it is embedded into the page with a 3-D look.

> **NOTE**
>
> The <HR> tag automatically creates a line break causing text to begin underneath the line.

The following are the available attributes for the <HR> tag:

<HR SIZE=>

This attribute enables you to thicken the line by pixels. <HR SIZE=5> would be a line that is 5 pixels high.

<HR NOSHADE>

This creates a 2-D flat black line that can be used in combination with the SIZE, WIDTH, and ALIGN attributes.

<HR WIDTH=>

This attribute enables you to select the width of the line that is centered by default (other justifications are covered next). This attribute's value can be in pixels or a percentage of the document width. Just as with the other attributes for the <HR> tag, this can be used in combination with the others. For example, this is how to select the width by pixel:

```
<HR WIDTH="340">
```

Here is how to select by percentage:

```
<HR WIDTH="66%">
```

<HR ALIGN=>

Internet Explorer and Navigator enable three values for this attribute: LEFT, CENTER, and RIGHT. The default is CENTER. Again, this can be used in combination with all other <HR> attributes.

Comments

The comment tag (<!-- -->)is not displayed by the browser, so it is useful for explaining commands or reminders for others designing the same pages or to place a copyright notice. Here is an example:

```
<!-- Web design by TNT Media www.tntmedia.com -->
```

> **CAUTION**
>
> Be careful what you write in your comments, because anyone can download your HTML source and read it.

<UL> : </UL>

The Unordered List tag is for lists of items with no particular order or sequence. This tag creates an indent of the text, which continues until the end tag is given. It is commonly used with the <LI> command (covered later) to create an unordered list of bullet items.

> **TIP**
>
> To indent further, use several <UL> tags at once because they compound and indent more with each tag:
>
> <UL><UL><UL>
>
> The body of the text you want to indent.
>
> </UL></UL></UL>
>
> Remember that you must match the number of end </UL> tags at the bottom with the number of <UL> tags at the top.

The following are the available attributes:

<UL> Nesting

Technically, there isn't a tag for this, but it is a feature of the <UL> tag. This enables you to *nest* several indentations, similar to a tree structure. You'll notice in the following family tree example that to create this effect, you simply continue indenting instead of adding the end (</UL>) tag. This technique is cumulative, so your information continues off the right side of the view window if you aren't careful. Notice that in Figure 25.1, the bullet styles change as the items are indented. The bullet style can be changed with the TYPE attribute.

```
<FONT SIZE=5>The O'Brien Family Tree:</FONT>
<UL>
    <LI>James C. O'Brien and Mary McMillen
    <UL>
        <LI>Lindsey R. O'Brien
        <LI>Thomas J. O'Brien
        <UL>
            <LI>Stephanie A. O'Brien
        </UL>
        <LI>James C. O'Brien, Jr.
    </UL>
</UL>
```

25

FIGURE 25.1.

Bullet style samples.

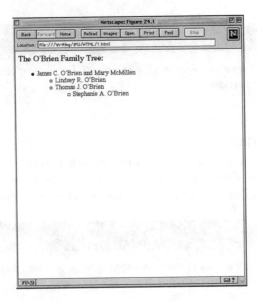

```
<UL TYPE=>
```

This is a Netscape-only attribute that enables the change of a bullet (the `<LI>` tag) within the `<UL>` tag. Values are DISC, CIRCLE, or SQUARE.

> **TIP**
>
> I've found that if the `<UL>` tag is left without the TYPE attribute and there are bullets within the tags, Navigator for Windows machines default to square bullets. I recommend using `<UL TYPE=DISC>` when using bulleted lists.

`<BLOCKQUOTE>` : `</BLOCKQUOTE>`

This is similar to the `<UL>` tag, but it is commonly used for indenting text from the rest of a lengthy document. It is also used to make quotes stand out from the rest of a body of text.

`<OL>` : `</OL>`

The Ordered List tag provides a way to create numbered or alphanumeric lists rather than simple bullets. Internet Explorer and Navigator also enable two handy extensions that enhance this feature even further (covered later). Here are the available attributes:

`<OL START=>`

Without this attribute, your ordered list starts with number 1 and works its way up by default. The START attribute enables you to choose where the numbering starts, as in `<OL START=4>`. This attribute can be used in combination with the TYPE attribute (covered next).

`<OL TYPE=>`

Browsers use Arabic numerals by default, so this attribute gives you more options, such as `<OL TYPE="A">` for capital letter numbering, `<OL TYPE="a">` for lowercase numbering, `<OL TYPE="I">` for capital Roman numerals, or `<OL TYPE="i">` for lowercase Roman numerals.

`<LI> & <OL TYPE=>`

The `<LI>` tag can also be used with the TYPE attribute when inside an `<OL>` tag. The cool thing is that you can change the type on any of the `<LI>` tags that you have inside an `<OL>` tag, and it won't alter the order of the list!

`<LI>`

The List Items tag creates bullets in front of lines of text. It can be used inside the `<UL>`, `<OL>`, and `<BLOCKQUOTE>` tags.

> **NOTE**
>
> For attributes specific to Ordered Lists (`<OL>`), see the `<OL>` section earlier in this chapter.

Here are the available attributes for list items:

`<LI TYPE=>`

This is used in the first `<LI>` tag of a multiple list of bullets. The values are DISC (solid black bullet), CIRCLE (hollow bullet), and SQUARE.

> **CAUTION**
>
> When the TYPE attribute has been set, there is no way to revert back to the default TYPE. (All subsequent bullets in the list are changed with the first TYPE attribute.) You must change the item where you want to start a different TYPE attribute and change the next one after it.
>
> For example:
>
> `<LI TYPE=DISC>`
>
> is text with a black circle as a bullet.
>
> *continues*

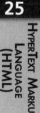

continued

```
<LI TYPE=SQUARE>
```

is a bulleted item with a square bullet.

```
<LI>
```

The bullet is still square because it hasn't been changed since giving the `"TYPE=SQUARE"` command.

```
<LI TYPE=DISC>
```

Back to the black circle bullet.

Text Styles

As with any printed material, you will undoubtedly want to use stylized text to get your point across clearly. The standard bold and italics are covered here as well as tags that make text look like computer code and tags that enable you to adjust the font size of selected text for use in headings or subtitles.

`<B>` : `</B>`

The Bold tag boldfaces the text within the beginning and end tags.

`<I>` : `</I>`

The Italics tag italicizes the text within the beginning and end tags.

`<TT>` : `</TT>`

As with the `<CODE>` tag, the text contained between the beginning and end tags is monospaced and is usually represented by the browser with a Courier font.

`<H>` : `</H>`

The Headline font size is used to change the size of text. Attributes are numerical and are limited to 1-7, with 1 being very small and 7 being very large. The default text size in HTML is 4. It is used as `<H5>Headline Five</H5>`

NOTE

The differences between the `<H>` and the `<FONT>` tag are twofold. First, browsers usually use a different font for each tag. (I prefer the look of the `<FONT>` tag, myself.) Second, the `<H>` tag does not wrap text, meaning that text automatically breaks to the next line. If you want more control of your text, I suggest using the `<FONT>` tag.

`<FONT>` : `</FONT>`

This tag enables you to change the appearance of the text displayed in a document. The available attributes are as follows:

`<FONT SIZE=>`

The SIZE attribute (recognized by most current browsers) must use the numeral values 1-7 to change the size of the text with 1 being the smallest and 7 being the largest size. You can also place a + or - symbol in front of the value, such as `<FONT SIZE=+3>`, which then increases or decreases the base font size by that amount.

> **NOTE**
>
> When you change the font size, you are changing the basefont size (see `<BASEFONT>` tag) of the document, not the size of the current paragraph of text. The default `<FONT>` size of an HTML document is 4, and the default `<H>` size is `<H3>`.

`<FONT COLOR=>`

This attribute (recognized by most current browsers) changes the default color, which is usually set in your browser's preferences (default is black). This attribute uses Pantone (RGB) color values or Navigator extension color names (see Table 25.1).

`<FONT FACE=>`

The FACE attribute enables you to actually specify a font from the machine on which the browser is installed. The author can actually select several fonts separated by commas. This is an Internet Explorer-only tag. Here is an example:

```
<FONT FACE="Times, Futura, Friz Quadrata>TNT Media</FONT>
```

If the user's machine does not have any of the fonts installed, the browser simply displays TNT Media in the default font as set in the user's browser preferences.

`<BASEFONT>`

This tag defines the normal document text size. Recognized by Navigator and Internet Explorer, the `<BASEFONT>` tag is typically used at the beginning of a document (above the `<BODY>` tag). The tag only has one attribute, SIZE, which is required. The available attribute is as follows:

`<BASEFONT SIZE=>`

As with the `<FONT>` tag, this attribute uses the numerical values of 1-7 to constitute the size of the body text.

_:

The Subscript tag is not a part of the current HTML 2.0, but it is supported by the latest versions of Navigator, Internet Explorer, and NCSA's Mosaic. Text contained between the beginning and end tags is displayed half of a character lower than the rest of the text in the line but in the same font. This tag is usually used in mathematical equations.

[:]

The Superscript tag is similar to the <SUB> tag. Any text contained within the tags is displayed half of a character above the rest of the text in the line but in the same font. This tag is usually used for trademark symbols.

Color Values

Before the last six months, to specify a color value you either had to have a chart of the RGB values or you had to keep running to Netscape's Web site to find the correct value. All of that has now changed because Navigator and Explorer use color names instead of the code values. (See Tables 25.2 and 25.3.)

> **NOTE**
>
> Because the RGB values are no longer the value of choice, I will only list a handful of the most popular colors.

Table 25.1. Pantone (RGB) color names.

Pantone (RGB) Values	
Black	"#000000"
White	"#FFFFFF"
Yellow	"#FFFF00"
Red	"#FF0000"
Green	"#00FF00"

Table 25.2. Microsoft Internet Explorer-supported color values.

aqua	black
blue	fuchsia
gray	green
lime	maroon

navy	olive
purple	red
silver	teal
yellow	white

NOTE

Navigator supports many more color values than Internet Explorer, so instead of listing them all, I listed some of the most popular. For the complete list, see Netscape's support Web site.

Table 25.3. Netscape Navigator-supported color values.

antiquewhite*	aquamarine*
azure*	beige
black	blue*
brown*	coral*
cyan*	deeppink*
deepskyblue*	dodgerblue*
firebrick	forestgreen
gold*	gray (can also be spelled "grey")
green*	hotpink*
khaki*	lavender
lawngreen	limegreen
magenta*	maroon
midnightblue	mistyrose*
navyblue	orange*
orchid*	peachpuff* (no, I didn't make this one up)
pink*	plum*
purple*	red*
salmon*	seagreen*
skyblue*	snow*
steelblue*	tan*
turquoise*	white
yellow*	yellowgreen

25

HYPERTEXT MARKUP
LANGUAGE
(HTML)

Hyperlinks

What good would the Web be if you couldn't get anywhere? Designing Web pages that don't go anywhere would be pretty frustrating, don't you think? Thankfully, there are now many ways to enable a visitor to freely navigate through your site while at the same time keeping a visually appealing site. Standard hypertext (a word or words linked to a URL) is still generally the same (with the exception of "anchors"—see the `<A NAME>` tag), but now designers can link graphics (without the ugly blue border!) and even link parts of graphics (see the `<MAP>` tag).

`<A> : </A>`

This tag creates links to other documents, URLs, e-mail addresses, or anchors within a document. It is most commonly used with the HREF attribute.

`<A HREF=> : </A>`

This attribute is used to link a portion of text or an image to a URL (Universal Resource Locator or Uniform Resource Locator) or e-mail address (see HREF=MAILTO:). Here is an example:

```
<A HREF="http://www.tntmedia.com">TNT Media</A>
```

If a visitor clicks on the TNT Media text, the browser retrieves the document at the URL `http://www.tntmedia.com`.

`<A HREF=MAILTO:> : </A>`

This attribute enables linking to an e-mail address using the e-mail functions of the browser. Most current browsers now support this function. Here is an example:

```
<A HREF=MAILTO:rick@tntmedia.com>Email me!</A>
```

The visitor clicks on the `Email me!` text, which brings up a pre-addressed e-mail message from within his or her browser.

TIP

When you are placing the HREF attribute around a graphic that is to be linked to another URL, use the BORDER=0 attribute in the `<IMG>` tag to remove the link border (see the section on "Images"):

```
<A HREF="http://www.tntmedia.com"><IMG SRC="/images/logo.gif" BORDER=0></A>
```
Without this attribute, there would be a blue (or whatever the link color is) border around the graphic, which is considered very amateurish in HTML design.

<A NAME=> : </A>

This attribute creates an *anchor* anywhere within a document, so that an HREF somewhere else (either on the same HTML document or elsewhere) can link to it. It is commonly used in FAQs (Frequently Asked Questions) and long documents. The NAME attribute is invisible because the text inside of the beginning and end tags does not appear as a hyperlink.

For example, within a FAQ page titled faq.html you would have

```
<A NAME="tech">Technical Support Questions</A>
```

Now, here's how to link to it from another HTML document or from the same faq.html document:

```
<A HREF="faq.html#tech">Tech Support</A>
```

> **TIP**
>
> Technically, you do not have to have any text between the <A NAME=> and the </A>, so you can place this attribute above a headline, before a graphic, and so on.

<A TARGET=>

This attribute is used within a frame document (see the "Frames" section). It enables the author to point the hyperlink to a specific frame. This is a Netscape-only tag.

<IMG SRC= ALT=>

This is an attribute of the <IMG> tag (see the section on "Images"), but it has an attribute that relates to the <A HREF=> tag. If you are placing a link around a graphic, be aware of visitors using text browsers or visitors with slow modem connections. The ALT attribute gives a text link for the image so that visitors with text browsers can see what is written or displayed on the image. For slow connections, most browsers will display the ALT text while the image is loading, which gives the visitor a chance to see what the link is. Here is an example:

```
<A HREF="funstuff.html"><IMG SRC="/image/funbutton.gif"
➥BORDER=0 ALT="Fun Stuff!">
```

<MAP> : </MAP>

The client-side image map tag enables the author to create multiple links within a single graphic using coordinates. It encompasses the <AREA> tag (discussed next). The available attribute is as follows:

<MAP NAME=> : </MAP>

The NAME attribute simply tells the browser the name of the image map:

```
<MAP NAME="imagemap1">
```

<AREA>

This tag defines the area coordinates of the image map. In simpler terms, it says, "If a visitor clicks in this area, take him here." The <AREA> tag requires the COORDS, SHAPE, and HREF attributes (covered next). The available attributes are as follows:

<AREA COORDS=>

This attribute provides the coordinates of the image map and is required in order for the <AREA> tag and SHAPE attribute to work. The SHAPE attribute defines how the coordinates are interpreted. See "<AREA SHAPE=>."

> **TIP**
>
> An easy way to find out coordinates is to use an image map application. Many are free for downloading on the Web. These applications enable you to select the area of an image map with your cursor, and then they calculate the coordinates. Simply look at the text file when you have selected all of your "link spots," copy the coordinates into your HTML document, and add the appropriate URL.

<AREA SHAPE=>

This attribute defines the shape of the area selected in the image map. At the time of this writing, Netscape Navigator only supports the RECTANGLE attribute, while Microsoft Internet Explorer supports RECTANGLE, CIRCLE, and POLYGONS. You can have different SHAPE attributes within an image map. Simply define each one within the <AREA> tag.

<AREA HREF=>

Like the <A HREF=> tag, this attribute points the browser to a URL.

<AREA NOHREF>

This attribute enables you to define a region in an image map where there is no HREF link. Here is an example:

```
<MAP NAME="imagemap1">
<AREA SHAPE="RECTANGLE" COORDS="50,50,75,75" HREF="page2.html">
<AREA SHAPE="RECTANGLE" COORDS="0,0,45,45">
</MAP>
```

Images

Whether or not you like a lot of graphics on your Web pages, you really can't avoid them entirely. With the mass market glomming onto the World Wide Web, you are now dealing with visitors who have the attention span of a common gnat. That said, as a Web designer, you need to keep their attention long enough to get your point across. The most effective way to do that is with clean, to-the-point graphics.

<IMG>

The Image tag enables you to insert a graphical image into an HTML document. Most popular browsers only support .gif or .jpg graphics files. The available attributes are as follows:

<IMG SRC=>

The Image source attribute is required in order for the browser to locate the graphic file:

```
<IMG SRC="/images/graphicname.gif">
```

<IMG ALT=>

This is the Alternative text attribute. As explained earlier in the section "Hyperlinks," the ALT attribute gives visitors a text description of the image in case they are using a text-only browser or they stop the image from loading. It is especially useful when the image has the <A HREF> tag around it. It is used like this:

```
<IMG SRC="/images/store.jpg" ALT="Our Grocery Store!">
```

<IMG BORDER=>

The border attribute defines a border around the graphic with the value in pixel width: <IMG SRC="/images/graphicname.jpg" BORDER=3>. This tag displays a three-pixel border around the graphic. The graphic does not have a border in default tags (no BORDER attribute). As mentioned in the "Hyperlinks" section, to remove a border when it is placed within the <A HREF>, simply define the BORDER attribute as BORDER=0.

<IMG ALIGN=>

Just as it says, this attribute aligns the image with these values: RIGHT, LEFT, TOP, MIDDLE, and BOTTOM. Navigator also supports ABSMIDDLE, ABSBOTTOM, BASELINE, and TEXTTOP.

<IMG LOWSRC=>

The low speed source attribute, which is currently a Netscape-only feature, helps speed up the loading of a graphic on a page. It precedes the SRC attribute in the <IMG> tag with the URL of

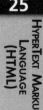

a lower resolution image. When implemented, the LOWSRC attribute causes a low-resolution version of the graphic to load first, giving the visitor a quick glimpse of what the actual graphic looks like until the entire graphic is loaded. It makes an interesting effect, so some designers use it with a "special effects" angle in mind. Browsers that don't support this attribute will simply ignore it and load the graphic normally. Here is an example:

```
<IMG LOWSRC="/images/apple-low.gif" SRC="/images/apple.gif">
```

<IMG HEIGHT= WIDTH=>

By default, browsers display the image in its original size. But, behind the scenes, the browser is examining the image size and making room for the image on the page before rendering it. The HEIGHT and WIDTH attributes, currently supported by both Navigator and Internet Explorer, enable the author to tell the browser up front what the size is, so that the image rendering time is considerably less because the browser reserves space for the image and continues to load the rest of the page. Both attributes require the value in pixels, like this:

```
<IMG HEIGHT="50" WIDTH="100">
```

> **TIP**
>
> Use the HEIGHT and WIDTH attributes to create a quick thumbnail of an image. Simply give the values for the image in the size that you want the thumbnail to be. The browser still has to load the entire image before it resizes it, but it is still cool. Be careful! Non-supporting browsers still show the full-sized image.

<IMG HSPACE= VSPACE=>

Typically, the space surrounding an image is two pixels, which can place the image a little too close to text or another image. With these attributes, you can supply another pixel separation:

```
<IMG HSPACE="5" VSPACE="5">
```

HTML Interactions and Enhancements

With the massive numbers of businesses now utilizing the Web for corporate uses, it was inevitable that there would be the need for more interaction from HTML. These are a few of the enhancements that enable businesses of all sizes to gather information and process orders online.

Forms

What good would the Web be to businesses if they couldn't process orders or request for orders online? The answer is, not a lot, which is why HTML forms were invented. Coinciding with CGI scripting, forms serve two purposes; they can send information in a cohesive manner so that the information can easily be viewed and processed (orders, requests for information, and so on) and they can send requests to the server for information (database searches).

<FORM> : </FORM>

The <FORM> tag can be placed anywhere inside an HTML document with the sub-tags within the beginning and end <FORM> tags. You must have a form-processing application in CGI (Common Gateway Interface) somewhere on your server in order to process the data retrieved in your form (ask your service provider).

> **TIP**
>
> Because there are no layout restrictions on any sub-tags within a <FORM> tag, use the <BR>, <P>, and other attributes just as you would within normal text situations to create a clean document layout.

The available attributes are as follows:

<FORM ACTION=>

This attribute is required in the <FORM> tag. ACTION provides the URL of the form application (usually located in the `cgi-bin` directory on a server, so I'll use it here) that will process the data:

```
<FORM ACTION="/cgi-bin/forms.cgi">
```

<FORM METHOD=>

This is another required attribute in the <FORM> tag. This attribute defines the way that the information is sent to the server for processing. There are two values: POST and GET. The POST value sends the data to the server in two steps: It contacts the form application and then sends the data to the server in a separate transmission. The GET value contacts the application and the server in one transmission separated by a ?. The method that you use depends on what your forms application requires.

Form Tags

<INPUT>

This tag can include many different form elements, from text fields and multiple-choice fields to submission buttons. The only required attributes are TYPE and NAME, although there are many others (covered next). The available attributes are as follows:

`<INPUT TYPE="TEXT">`

This attribute is used for single-line text fields (for Text Areas where people would write a comment, see the following Tip) that hold name, address, company name, and so on. (See Figure 25.2.)

FIGURE 25.2.

Here are some visual examples of the most common <FORM> tags in action.

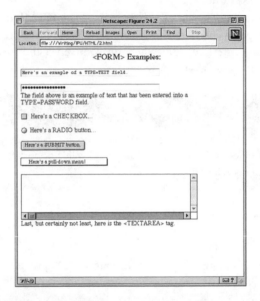

`<INPUT SIZE=>`

The SIZE attribute sets the character width of a TEXT field. Although it is not required, it is recommended to not only keep visual style on a page, but to coincide with the information that is to be typed in. For example, if you had a TEXT field for State, the SIZE value would be 2:

`<INPUT TYPE="TEXT" NAME="State" SIZE="2">`

`<INPUT MAXLENGTH=>`

This attribute defines the maximum number of characters allowed in a given text field such as the following:

```
<INPUT TYPE="TEXT" NAME="Company Name" SIZE="30" MAXLENGTH="80">
```

`<INPUT TYPE="PASSWORD">`

This TYPE value is used when you want to have someone enter a password or any other type of text that you want hidden. The data entered is displayed exactly the same as the TEXT value; it just displays dots or something similar instead of revealing the entered text. (Refer to Figure 25.2.)

`<INPUT TYPE="CHECKBOX">`

This attribute creates an easy way for visitors to select items in your Web form. CHECKBOX creates an empty box that, when clicked on (selected) by a visitor, becomes checked. A required attribute is VALUE, which tells the form application what it is that the visitor has selected. It is used like this:

```
<INPUT TYPE="CHECKBOX" NAME="Item" VALUE="Watch"> Watch
```

When you place several CHECKBOX tags with the same NAME value, you create a group of checkboxes. (Refer to Figure 25.2.)

`<INPUT TYPE="RADIO">`

Radio buttons are similar to the CHECKBOX value, with the exception that the visitor can only choose one selection in each group of RADIO buttons. Each RADIO button should be given a different VALUE. (Refer to Figure 25.2.)

`<INPUT CHECKED>`

This attribute does not require a value; it is a stand-alone feature. When you have a list of checkboxes or radio buttons, using the CHECKED attribute on one of the selections makes it checked. The visitor can simply choose another item if he or she chooses.

`<INPUT TYPE="SUBMIT">`

This value does just what it says: It submits the form data to the form application as specified in the <FORM ACTION=> tag described earlier. The VALUE= attribute enables you to define the text that shows on the button:

```
<INPUT TYPE="SUBMIT" VALUE="Click here!">
```

The default VALUE (if none is given) is Submit. It is commonly placed next to a RESET button that enables the visitor to clear the form and start over again. (Refer to Figure 25.2.)

`<INPUT TYPE="RESET">`

Again, this is basically self-explanatory. The RESET value clears the form data that has been entered thus far. As with the SUBMIT value, the VALUE= attribute can be used to change the text on the button to be Clear Data or something similar. The default value (if none is given) is Reset.

`<INPUT TYPE="HIDDEN">`

This value is hidden from the visitor. The HIDDEN value can be used in many different ways, one of which is to send data along with the form for internal use, such as to supply a form version.

`<TEXTAREA>` : `</TEXTAREA>`

This is the field in which you enable a visitor to enter more information than a single-line text field can handle, such as comments. However, you might restrict the amount of text area and text the visitor is given. Also, any text outside of the tags but between the beginning and end tags is displayed in the TEXTAREA. This must be plain text with no HTML tags, so that the user can modify or delete the given text. Refer to Figure 25.2. The attributes are as follows:

`<TEXTAREA NAME=>`

As with the NAME attribute in the previous tags, this defines the name of the TEXTAREA for the form application.

`<TEXTAREA COLS= ROWS=>`

This is where you are able to restrict the size of the TEXTAREA. Although text will flow above and below the TEXTAREA, it will not flow around it. As with the previous values, COLS and ROWS values are given in character spacing. The browser automatically supplies the scrollbars (both horizontally and vertically, if needed) if the user provides more text than there is room for with the COLS and ROWS set.

`<TEXTAREA WRAP=>`

This attribute has three values: OFF, VIRTUAL, and PHYSICAL. The OFF value functions the same as not including the WRAP attribute at all, so it is not commonly used. In default mode, if TEXTAREA has a line of text that is longer than the width of the TEXTAREA, the text will continue to the right and the visitor has to scroll right to see the rest of the text. The text is sent to the form application as one line of text.

With the value set to VIRTUAL, the long line of text automatically breaks to the next line in the TEXTAREA and is sent to the form application as one line of text (this is the most popular value).

With the value set to PHYSICAL, the long line of text breaks to the next line, as with the VIRTUAL value, but the text is sent to the form application as two lines.

<SELECT> : </SELECT>

With a list of items that have the `<OPTION>` tag in front of them placed between the beginning and end tags, this attribute displays multiple choice pull-down menus as shown here:

```
Please tell us where you heard about our site:
<SELECT>
<OPTION> Search Utility
<OPTION> Newspaper Ad
<OPTION> Flyer
<OPTION> A Friend
</SELECT>
```

The available attributes are as follows:

<SELECT MULTIPLE>

If `MULTIPLE` is not used, only one item can be selected from the list. With this attribute in place, the visitor can select multiple items from the list.

<SELECT NAME=>

As with other `NAME` attributes, this enables you to provide the `<SELECT>` data field with a name for easy sorting when the data is retrieved in any format.

<SELECT SIZE=>

This attribute determines how many `<OPTION>` items are shown in the pull-down menu window. The default is one. This is best used with the `MULTIPLE` attribute for selecting more than one item.

<OPTION>

The `<OPTION>` tag is used at the beginning of an item within the `<SELECT>` beginning and end tags.

Tables

Previously, there was no good way to control text flow. There was no way to constrain text or graphics on a Web page. The team at Netscape Communications conceived the `<TABLE>` tag and its many features. Tables (with or without borders) can display information, whether it is a corporate spreadsheet or a graphic with a subtitle, in a clean, easy-to-read format.

<TABLE> : </TABLE>

This tag and its end tag encapsulate the tags and data that define the table. Tables are aligned left by default, but as with images, they can be centered by placing the `<CENTER>` tag above the `<TABLE>` tag and the `</CENTER>` tag after the `</TABLE>` tag.

`<TABLE ALIGN=>`

Just as with the `<TABLE>` tag, the text within the table cells is justified left by default. With the `ALIGN` attribute and its values (`LEFT` and `RIGHT`), you can place the text flush against the left or right margin of the text flow. This attribute is used differently than the `ALIGN` attribute in `<TR>`, `<TD>`, and `<TH>`. This attribute is supported only by Internet Explorer and Navigator.

`<TABLE BGCOLOR=>`

This Internet Explorer-only attribute enables you to make the table background color different from the background of the rest of the HTML document. As with other color attributes, the value is either RGB codes or color names (refer to Table 25.1). Individual table cells can be changed even from the table background color by adding the `BGCOLOR` attribute to the individual cell.

`<TABLE BORDERCOLOR= BORDERCOLORLIGHT= BORDERDARK=>`

This is another Internet Explorer-only set of attributes. These attributes enable you to change the color of the border surrounding the table. Again, the values are in RGB code or color names (refer to Table 25.1). `BORDERCOLOR` shades the middle part of the border, and `BORDERCOLORLIGHT` and `BORDERCOLORDARK` give the border a 3-D effect.

`<TABLE BORDER=>`

Without this attribute, the table would simply have a default border given by the browser. Internet Explorer and Navigator enable an integer value (pixels) with the `BORDER` attribute, which gives you the power to create borders of a certain pixel width. (See Figure 25.3.)

Figure 25.3.

A few of the most common `<TABLE>` attributes.

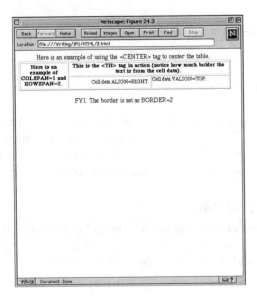

> **TIP**
>
> If you want to simply restrain text so that it lines up properly in columns, but you don't want to show that the text is set in a table, simply give the value of 0 for the BORDER attribute:
>
> `<TABLE BORDER="0">`
>
> The BORDER="0" is also handy when restraining a graphic along with a textual subtitle.

`<TABLE CELLSPACING=>`

This Navigator only attribute controls the amount of pixel space between individual cells and the sides along the edges of the table. To make a thinner border between cells, give the value as follows:

`<TABLE CELLSPACING=0>`

`<TABLE CELLPADDING=>`

Like the CELLSPACING attribute, this is a Navigator-only attribute. CELLPADDING enables you to define the amount of pixel space between the cell border and the text inside of the cell.

`<TABLE HSPACE= VSPACE=>`

Just as with images (see the "Images" section) these attributes—supported only by Internet Explorer and Navigator—provide you with a way of allowing space (HSPACE for horizontal and VSPACE for vertical) around the table so that text and images surrounding the table aren't too close to it.

`<TABLE VALIGN=>`

This Internet Explorer-only attribute sets the vertical alignment of text within its cell for the whole table. To achieve this effect in Navigator, you must use the VALIGN attribute in the <TR>, <TD>, and <TH> tags for each individual cell (see the next section).

`<TABLE WIDTH=>`

Almost all current browsers simply make the table the size of the data inside that makes up the table. With Internet Explorer and Navigator, you can set the table width with the WIDTH attribute, which supports a pixel integer. Alternatively, you can set the width of the table by the percentage of the display window:

`<TABLE WIDTH=75%>`

This makes the table 75 percent of the size of the display window in the browser.

`<TR> : </TR>`

The Table Row tag creates each individual row within a <TABLE>. The <TH> and <TD> tags go between the beginning and ending <TR> tags. The attributes are as follows:

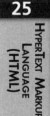

`<TR ALIGN= VALIGN=>`

These attributes enable you to change the alignment of the text within all cells in the row. `ALIGN` has a default of `LEFT`; `VALIGN` has a default of `CENTER`. `ALIGN` values are `LEFT`, `RIGHT`, and `CENTER`. `VALIGN` values are `TOP`, `BOTTOM`, and `BASELINE`.

`<TR BGCOLOR=>`

As described previously, this Internet Explorer-only attribute sets the color of the cells within the current row. Values are RGB code and color names.

`<TR BORDERCOLOR= BORDERCOLORLIGHT= BORDERCOLORDARK=>`

This is another Internet Explorer-only set of attributes. These attributes enable you to change the color of the border of the cells in the current row. Again, the values are in RGB code or color names (refer to Table 25.1).

`BORDERCOLOR` shades the middle part of the border, and `BORDERCOLORLIGHT` and `BORDERCOLORDARK` give the border a 3-D effect.

`<TD> : </TD>` and `<TH> : </TH>`

These tags go between the beginning and end `<TR>` tags, and they define the table data and cells. `<TD>` is Table Data that is plain text, and the `<TH>` tag is Table Header with a bolder font used for headers above or next to table data.

> **NOTE**
>
> Because the attributes for the `<TD>` and `<TH>` tags are identical, I've shown the examples using `<TD>` to avoid confusion. Again, all of the examples can be used with the `<TH>` tag as well.

`<TD ALIGN=>`

Just as with the `<TR>` tag, the text within the table cells is justified left by default. With the `ALIGN` attribute and its values (`LEFT` and `RIGHT`), you can place the text flush against the left or right of the cell border. This attribute is supported only by Internet Explorer and Navigator. Refer to Figure 25.3.

`<TD VALIGN=>`

This enables you to change the alignment of the text within the cell. Values are `LEFT`, `RIGHT`, and `CENTER`. `VALIGN` values are `TOP`, `BOTTOM`, and `BASELINE`. (Refer to Figure 25.3.)

<TD WIDTH=>

With Internet Explorer and Navigator, you can set the cell width with the WIDTH attribute, which supports pixel integers (WIDTH=300). Alternatively, you can set the width of the cell by the percentage of the display window:

<TABLE WIDTH=75%>

This makes the table 75 percent of the size of the display window in the browser.

<TD COLSPAN=>

When you would like to have data occupy more than one cell across in a table row, use this attribute:

<TD COLSPAN=2>

This makes the data in that <TD> cell occupy the space of two horizontal cells. (Refer to Figure 25.3.)

<TD ROWSPAN=>

As with COLSPAN, this attribute tells the cell to occupy a certain number of cells going down:

<TD ROWSPAN=2>

This makes the data in a cell occupy the space of two cells in a vertical direction (down). (Refer to Figure 25.3.)

<TD NOWRAP>

The NOWRAP attribute is used to force data in a cell to continue on one line (unless there are <BR> and/or <P> tags in place), instead of enabling the data to wrap to the next line when it gets to the end of the cell border.

<TD BGCOLOR=>

As described previously, this Internet Explorer-only attribute sets the color of the cell. Values are RGB code and color names.

<TD BORDERCOLOR= BORDERCOLORLIGHT= BORDERCOLORDARK=>

This is another Internet Explorer-only set of attributes. These attributes enable you to change the color of the border of the cell. BORDERCOLOR shades the middle part of the border, and BORDERCOLORLIGHT and BORDERCOLORDARK give the border a 3-D effect.

Multimedia: Audio, Video, Applications

Lights, camera, action! Multimedia has arrived on the Web in full force, and HTML has been furiously trying to keep up with the tags necessary to encompass it all. Although Netscape

Navigator has done a nice job lately with proposed HTML extensions, Microsoft Internet Explorer has jumped ahead in this area by creating easy-to-understand tags.

<BGSOUND>

The <BGSOUND> tag enables visitors using Internet Explorer to hear audio clips in the background while viewing a Web document. No file needs to be downloaded and separately played; all of this is done behind the scenes within Internet Explorer. All other browser applications simply ignore this tag, so it is safe to use on universal pages.

> **TIP**
>
> It is easy to go overboard with this tag. Be aware that the audio file loads last, and at the time of this writing, Internet Explorer loads the graphics along with the audio. In other words, if you have a very large audio file (which is extremely easy to do), the page won't fully load until the audio clip is completely downloaded. Find a good audio editing application and edit the sound file if it's too large.

The attributes are as follows:

<BGSOUND SRC=>

This is a required attribute for the <BGSOUND> tag. As with other SRC attributes, this specifies the URL of the sound file. Only three different types of sound files are supported: .wav, .au, and MIDI files.

<BGSOUND LOOP=>

This attribute specifies the amount of times that the sound file is played. The two optional values are

```
<BGSOUND SRC="/audio/soundfile.wav" LOOP="8">
```

which is a numeric value, or

```
<BGSOUND SRC="/audio/soundfile.wav" LOOP="INFINITE">
```

This value naturally makes the sound file loop continuously as long as the page is loaded on the screen.

<MARQUEE> : </MARQUEE>

This is another Internet Explorer-only tag. It creates text that scrolls across the screen. <MARQUEE> is very similar to the Java Script effect in which the text scrolls at the bottom of the browser frame, except that you have control over where on the page the action takes place. The attributes are as follows:

`<MARQUEE ALIGN=>`

The `<MARQUEE>` tag is treated as an image, so this attribute enables text to flow around it. It accepts the values TOP, MIDDLE, and BOTTOM.

`<MARQUEE BEHAVIOR=>`

In order to control the direction, style, and duration of the text, you need the BEHAVIOR attribute. It accepts several values: SCROLL causes the text to come in from one side or the other (specified with the DIRECTION attribute). SLIDE causes the marquee to start with an empty box. When the text comes out, it stops so that it is visible in the box. ALTERNATE causes the text to start as fully visible in the box, and when the text reaches the end of the box, it reverses itself.

`<MARQUEE DIRECTION=>`

This sets the direction in which the text flows onto the screen. The values are LEFT (default) and RIGHT.

`<MARQUEE LOOP=>`

Like the LOOP attribute in `<BGSOUND>`, this attribute defines how many times the marquee is shown. Again, the values are either numerical (1, 2, 3, and so on) or INFINITE for never-ending repetition.

`<MARQUEE BGCOLOR=>`

As with all other BGCOLOR attributes, this enables the specification of the background color in the marquee box. Accepted values are RGB code (#FFFFFF) or color names.

`<MARQUEE HEIGHT= WIDTH=>`

These attributes determine the size of the marquee box. If these attributes are not used, the marquee box extends the entire width of the browser display window and is just tall enough to enclose the height of the text. Values are either in pixels (200) or a percentage of the browser display window (50 percent).

`<MARQUEE HSPACE= VSPACE=>`

These attributes enable space around the marquee to separate it from surrounding text. Values are given in pixels, like this:

`<MARQUEE HSPACE="5" VSPACE="5">`

This creates a five-pixel space around the marquee.

`<MARQUEE SCROLLAMOUNT= SROLLDELAY=>`

Use these attributes for controlling the smoothness or quickness of the marquee text. SCROLLAMOUNT values are given in pixels, with lower numbers creating slow but smooth movement and larger numbers creating fast and jerky motion.

25

HYPERTEXT MARKUP
LANGUAGE
(HTML)

SCROLLDELAY is the number of milliseconds that the text waits between successive scrolling. Larger numbers create slower delays, and lower numbers make quicker movements.

\<APPLET\> : \</APPLET\>

This tag is supported only by Hot Java (Sun Microsystems) and Netscape Navigator. \<APPLET\> defines the application to be used in the current document. The following attributes define the placement and behavior of the application to be loaded.

The attributes are as follows:

\<APPLET ALIGN=\>

As with the \<IMG ALIGN=\> attribute, this attribute defines the alignment of the \<APPLET\> with regards to the surrounding text on the page. Values include ABSMIDDLE, ABSBOTTOM, BASELINE, BOTTOM, MIDDLE, TOP, and TEXTTOP, along with LEFT and RIGHT.

\<APPLET ALT=\>

Using this attribute is a very good idea. Similar to images, the text placed as the value here is displayed if there is a problem in loading the application.

\<APPLET CODE=\>

The CODE attribute defines the type of \<APPLET\> code that is to be used. The value should be the name of the class or the package.

\<APPLET CODEBASE=\>

This defines the URL in which the CODE is located.

\<APPLET NAME=\>

As with forms, this enables you to provide a unique name for the \<APPLET\>.

\<APPLET HEIGHT= WIDTH=\>

These determine the size of the \<APPLET\> display area. Values are either in pixels (200) or percentage of the browser display window (50 percent).

\<APPLET HSPACE= VSPACE=\>

Similar to the \<MARQUEE\> tag covered earlier, these attributes enable space around the marquee to separate it from surrounding text. Values are given in pixels, like this:

\<APPLET HSPACE="5" VSPACE="5"\>

This would create a five-pixel space around the \<APPLET\>.

<PARAM>

Although this tag does not have content or an end tag, it is used within the beginning and end <APPLET> tags to specify parameters.

The attributes are as follows:

```
<PARAM NAME= VALUE=>
```

Some <APPLETS> enable you to supply information in which to define a certain part of an application. In that case, you could use these attributes. Suppose that you have a calendar application, and you want to specify what year to display. It might look like this:

```
<APPLET CODE="Calendar">
 <PARAM NAME="Year" VALUE="1997">
</APPLET>
```

Frames

Frames are the latest and greatest feature of HTML. They give a lot of power back to the Web designers that keeps the visitor within the Web site they are perusing while still enabling them to link to other sites.

<FRAMESET> : </FRAMESET>

This is another Navigator-only tag, and it is the main tag that defines the size and location of all frames in the document. The <FRAMESET> replaces the <BODY> tag in frame documents. You must exclude all other HTML tags other than the <HEAD> and <TITLE> tags or Netscape will ignore the frame tags altogether.

> **CAUTION**
>
> If you include the <BODY> tag out of habit, your <FRAMESET> tags will be completely ignored by Navigator. Make sure this is a frame document only!

Frame documents do not contain data themselves; instead, they contain <FRAME> tags that point to URLs that will fill in the frames specified in the <FRAMESET> tags.

> **NOTE**
>
> You can place several <FRAMESET> tags within a frame document for precise placement of frames. The only limit is the visible area within the browser window. The other <FRAMESET> tags must be placed within the beginning and end of the first <FRAMESET> tag. Placing more than one <FRAMESET> tag is often called *nesting*.

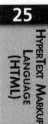

The attributes are as follows:

`<FRAMESET ROWS= COLS =>`

These attributes define the number of columns as well as the size of the columns and rows of frames and framesets. Both attributes can accept values in pixels or a percentage of window view to occupy (separate row values with a comma such as `200,350,100`). Like tables, Navigator will not extend the frames outside of the viewing window. Instead, it creates scrollbars within the framesets. Frameset documents do not have scrollbars surrounding the entire document, as regular HTML documents do. When using percentages, the numbers do not have to necessarily have to add up to 100 percent. Navigator adjusts and resizes each frame to fit the window.

A nice feature value with these attributes is the * value, which is the equivalent of a wild card. If you know exactly what pixel size or percentage of space you want the first frame to be and the other row (as in the following example) you want to fill the empty space (you never know how big a visitor's browser window is), use this value:

`<FRAMESET ROWS="200,*">`

In this case, one frame will be 200 pixels wide and the second frame will fill whatever space is left over. (See Figure 25.4.)

TIP

If the values are set in pixels to a smaller size than the Navigator window, the browser will compensate and stretch the frames to fit. In light of this, I recommend using percentages so that you have more control of where the frames are placed. (See Figure 25.4.)

`<FRAME>`

This tag is placed between the beginning and ending `<FRAMESET>` tags; together with the SRC attribute (covered next), it specifies the URL of an HTML document to be placed in a specific frame.

The attributes are as follows:

`<FRAME SRC=>`

The required source attribute specifies the URL of the HTML document that is to be placed into the frame. There are no limitations on what these HTML documents can contain—applets, Java, animations, and so on. (Refer to Figure 25.4.)

`<FRAME NAME=>`

The NAME attribute is optionally used in conjunction with Navigator's TARGET attribute for anchoring (the `<A>` tag). See `<A TARGET=>` for more information on this technique.

FIGURE 25.4.

A simple <FRAMESET>
document.

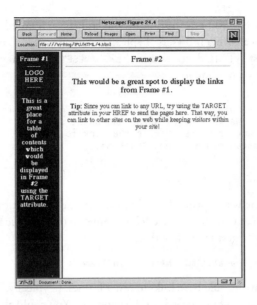

<FRAME NORESIZE>

With Navigator version 2.0, visitors could resize the frames as they chose, which would ruin the layout that you created. (Version 3.0, which is in beta at the time of this writing, is supposed to change this.) The NORESIZE attribute locks the proportions of a frame so that it cannot be manipulated. Here is an example:

```
<HTML>
<HEAD><TITLE>Figure 25.4</TITLE></HEAD>
<FRAMESET COLS="20%,*" NORESIZE>
<FRAME SRC="frame1.html">
<FRAME SRC="frame2.html">
</FRAMESET>
</HTML>
```

<FRAME SCROLLING=>

Normally, if the content of a frame fits in the allotted space, no scrollbars appear. If the SCROLLING value is set to YES, scrollbars appear whether they are needed or not. When the value is NO, scrollbars will not be added to the frame.

<FRAME MARGINHEIGHT= MARGINWIDTH=>

These attributes are similar to the HSPACE and VSPACE attributes in tables. Use these to create space around a frame. Values are in pixels.

<NOFRAMES> : </NOFRAMES>

Considering that there are very few browsers capable of viewing frames, this tag is a very good idea (and pretty courteous to those with non-frame compliant browsers). Use this tag only within the "main" <FRAMESET> tag (if you are nesting <FRAMESET> tags).

25

HYPERTEXT MARKUP LANGUAGE (HTML)

Any text placed within the beginning and end tags is ignored by frame-compliant browsers but comes up for all other browsers. Typically, this tag is used to point visitors to a non-frame URL or to the first HTML document in the <FRAMESET>, assuming that it is linked to the rest of the pages. Here is an example:

```
<NOFRAMES>
If you are viewing this, your browser does not support frame documents.
Don't worry! We've thought ahead and built our site to be navigational
with non-frame browsers. Here's the link to our
<A HREF="noframes.html">Home Page</A>.
</NOFRAMES>
```

<A TARGET=>

This attribute was explained briefly earlier in the NAME attribute section. This attribute to the <A> tag enables you to direct a URL to come up in a specific frame window. Suppose that you named your largest frame like this:

```
<FRAME SRC="frame1.html" NAME="main-frame">
```

In this case, you could have links in other frames. (Typically, designers place a narrow "table of contents" frame along one side of the window.) You could also have the document come up in the large frame. Here's what the tag would look like:

```
<A HREF="page1.html" TARGET="main-frame">Page One</A>
```

What if you have a bunch of HREFs? Do you have to type the TARGET attribute on every one? Not when you use the <BASE TARGET=> tag.

<BASE TARGET=>

This tag, placed within the <HEAD> and </HEAD> tags in the HTML document, enables you to specify a target for all HREFs included in the current document. For example, with the code written as it is here, all three HREFs will go to the "main-frame" target frame.

```
<HTML>
<HEAD>
<TITLE>Links!</TITLE>
<BASE TARGET="main-frame">
</HEAD>
<BODY BGCOLOR="White">
<FONT SIZE=6>Here are some links!</FONT>
<P><A HREF="page1.html">Page One</A>
<P><A HREF="page2.html">Page Two</A>
<P><A HREF="page3.html">Page Three</A>
</BODY>
</HTML>
```

Summary

If you are an old HTML hacker, you can probably see that HTML has come a long way since its "college days," so to speak. If you are new to HTML programming, we "old HTML hackers" think that you've got it made. Thanks to the latest extensions explained in this chapter, you don't have to spend hours upon hours trying to come up with a clever way to display information in a visually pleasing manner.

The best advice I can give to anyone venturing into the HTML world (or to someone just trying to keep up with the new extensions) is to visit as many Web sites as you can stand. If you see some layouts that you like, use the "View Source" feature of your Web browser application to see how it was done. There's no better way to learn HTML "tricks" than by seeing it in action and implementing it on your own Web pages.

SGML

by Edward Hooban

IN THIS CHAPTER

The Problem

One of the great things about technology over the last couple of decades is its increasing functionality and role in our everyday lives. Technology now plays a key role in one of the most fundamental office activities: writing text. Word processors are among the most prevalent applications in the microcomputer's existence. A major problem with computers and text over the last several decades, however, is that numerous proprietary storage means for text have been invented. All storage ideas have certain features that merit consideration, but most limit portability because they are a particular vendor's embodiment of the perfect text storage format, which does not necessarily correspond with another vendor's storage format.

Recently, we have witnessed an explosion in information dissemination with the advent of the World Wide Web, creating an acute need for a standard document interchange format. This explosion of information dissemination is directly attributable to the widespread use and adoption of the HyperText Markup Language (HTML) to mark up text. Microsoft Word, WordPerfect, and other word processors never achieved this level of ubiquity because they stored their text in proprietary formats. They did not conform to a standard, therefore documents created with a particular word processor were of little use to someone not equipped with that particular word processor. Because the rules of HTML markup are created according to an international standard (Standard Generalized Markup Language, or SGML), anyone can publish a document that can be viewed by the world as long as they mark up their document according to the standard. HTML is as close as we come to a universal interchange standard for text, but it really only taps a small portion of the expressive power of SGML.

Without an agreed-upon standard for storing textual information, vendors devise their own means for storage and management of text. Each vendor may feel that its system affords the user numerous advantages that they cannot get anywhere else. Users are bound to a particular vendor's application and its feature set. In the short term, they get great features, but the long term portability of their data suffers because it is stored according to a particular vendor's closed and proprietary scheme. When that vendor's product is obsolete and those original features are outdated, there is a huge issue with migrating that text to another vendor's product or platform. To solve the issue of information being stranded in a particular environment with a particular vendor, the International Standards Organization (ISO) defined a standard, Standard Generalized Markup Language (SGML), for representing and storing textual information to meet the portability and reuse requirements of an increasingly digitized world.

The Solution

Standard Generalized Markup Language (SGML) defines a standard for creating a markup language to describe the structure of a document. It provides a method for generically marking up an infinite variety of documents based strictly on that document's unique structure. For example, a sales report on fourth-quarter earnings might be structurally different from an engineering report on the specifications for maintaining an aircraft part. Each of these particular document types would have unique structural rules. Table structures might be more rigidly defined in a quarterly report, and explanation of parts might be more richly structured in a parts document for engineers. In an SGML authoring environment, the structure of the documents is more important than stylistic formatting issues such as font sizes (where structural meaning may have to be inferred). This enables documents to be produced in a variety of formats that require different markup codes.

Stylistic formatting is one of the biggest problems that plagues the interchange of electronic information. After you have authored a document for a particular vendor's application environment, you are tied to that vendor's proprietary method for defining the structure and style of documents. This is typically not compatible with another vendor's implementation of the same structural and stylistic markup. Within the same editing package, authors might attempt to convey widely varying structural meaning for the exact same stylistic element. Each vendor and author has developed what they consider to be an efficient and effective means for marking up documents.

For example, suppose you and a co-worker want to share a document. If you use Microsoft Word and your co-worker uses WordStar, you might have difficulty exchanging documents between the two formats. You and your co-worker might have different ideas of what 12-point bold means. If you want to exchange document drafts with a co-worker, you must find some neutral method for saving and interchanging work. Given the proprietary nature of storage for each word processing product, this can be a difficult issue. Another scenario is if you want to send out an electronic document company wide via e-mail but you are not sure if everyone has the word processor you used to create the document (actually, the World Wide Web solves this problem for simple documents with the prevalence of the intranet for broadcasting information).

SGML attempts to solve the problem of information becoming stranded in a particular application or on a particular platform. It is a generic, international standard. Markup rules are not controlled by any particular vendor, only by an international standards committee. The standard is vendor neutral, so adherence to it facilitates the long-term use and re-use of information. In addition, documents are validated against a particular structural rule set so that processing programs know the exact structure of what they are getting with the assurance that it has been validated against a specific rule set.

Listing 26.1 shows an example of marking up text. Instead of indicating that Section One is 12-point, bold Helvetica and embedding the style commands that are only understood by a particular application, we are indicating that Section One is Heading Level 2 and surround the text with the appropriate tags, thus conveying its structural meaning and not its stylistic presentation.

Listing 26.1. An example of marking up text.

```
.point 12 .attribute bold .font Helvetica Section One  [Word Processor 1]
!pointsize=12!attribute=bold!font=Helvetica! Section One [Word Processor 2]
<H2>Section One</H2>
```

This increases the document's flexibility when you want to move it to another editing application or process it for a new medium of distribution. Stylistic details are left to a particular processing program for a specific output medium. The output processing engine uses whatever stylistic elements are at its disposal for output on its unique medium.

You need to send along with your document a set of rule descriptions (known as a document type definition or DTD) and an instance (markup and data) so that the document can be easily processed for various outputs. For example, one processor for CD-ROM might make Section One 18-point italic, another processor such as a browser for the World Wide Web might make it 14-point bold, and yet another processor for a book might make it Arial, 16-point bold. The point is that it doesn't matter how each application renders the information. What matters is that they all know the exact structure of a document and can make their own formatting judgments. Additionally, they should verify that the document conforms to the agreed upon structure as defined in the DTD.

One of the most commonly held misconceptions is that HTML is a subset of SGML. HTML is a particular implementation of SGML. SGML just sets the ground rules by which you may create a markup language. The World Wide Web consortium is responsible for creating and maintaining the HTML document type definition, or rules files for Web-distributed documents. Browsers are free to render documents marked up according to the HTML DTD in any way they see fit. For example, one browser might interpret emphasis tags as bold and another might interpret them as italic. Both browsers know that, within the structure of this particular document, this text should be emphasized. The style of emphasis is completely up to the browser.

The key components of an SGML document include a declaration, a document type definition (DTD), and an instance. The declaration defines what character set is used and what the delimiters are. Unless you are a serious SGML professional, you are generally not concerned with the declaration. The DTD defines the rules by which you author documents, including markup tags and the order and relationship among them (these are pretty inscrutable, too). The instance contains the marked-up text according to the rules as defined by the DTD and the constraints and character sets as defined by the declaration.

Standards

Standard Generalized Markup Language (SGML) is an official international standard (ISO/IEC 8879:1986 "Information Processing—Text and Office Systems—Standard Generalized Markup Language (SGML)" is the title of the official standard available from the International

Standards committee) for exchange of digital information. It is a meta-language (language for creating languages) or grammar for defining specific implementations of markup schemes. It is a flexible system for defining a rich set of markup languages to precisely define the structure of an unlimited set of documents. The standard was primarily driven by Dr. Charles Goldfarb, who worked extensively with markup languages for many years at IBM on GML (Generalized Markup Language), which eventually became SGML.

Portability

An illustration will help to clarify some of the benefits of SGML. In Figure 26.1, you can see that a document is authored according to a particular set of markup rules. From this source document, which is explicitly defined and rigidly structured, your processing programs have a known textual quantity. This isolates any filtering issues to a particular program and not to the data itself. Conformance to international standards ensures that documents created according to SGML are truly portable across hardware systems and application software vendor systems.

FIGURE 26.1.

Document with a particular set of markup rules.

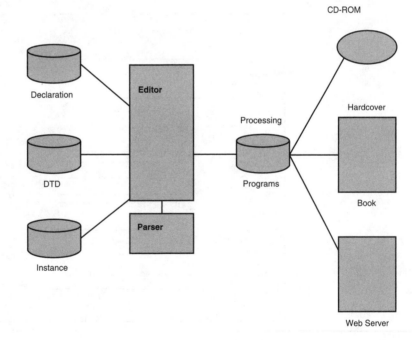

Form and Structure

One of the key tenets of SGML is that the format of a document is separated from the structure of a document. A traditional word processor, such as Microsoft Word, allows you to intermingle your formatting codes with your structural codes. Each word processor or desktop publishing application has its own proprietary markup schemes. This makes the interchange of documents very cumbersome. It also limits their capabilities for being rendered by different word processing, desktop publishing, and electronic publishing engines.

These are issues that SGML attempts to address. An author can generically mark up a document according to a document type definition (DTD). The author is not concerned with exactly how the document looks but with how the document is structured. SGML markup works with the logical structure of the document, not the document's appearance. There are no stylistic concerns at this stage, so documents are more flexible for porting to various platforms and publishing environments. One set of source, SGML-marked-up files can be used to generate numerous output on various media such as the World Wide Web, CD-ROM (any number of electronic publishing engines), desktop publishing, and even hard copy (see Figure 26.2).

FIGURE 26.2.

A generic document.

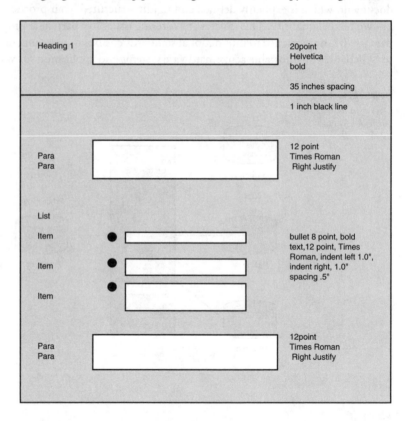

A widely held misconception is that authoring and using SGML is overly complex and unforgiving. Although it is true that some SGML applications have been known as user-unfriendly, SGML authoring systems have become richer and more robust, including WYSIWYG (What

You See Is What You Get) graphical authoring environments with on-the-fly validation and graphical tree representations of document models. In the long run, the increased effort required to use an SGML authoring system makes document management issues easier.

Authoring Systems

SGML authoring systems have varying levels of integration. There are several essential components to any SGML system. The following list describes these components in detail.

- The *editing application* consists of a text editor (usually graphical) and a validating parser for managing the creation and editing of SGML documents. If you have used any editor for marking up HTML, then you used an SGML editor. Some of these HTML editors are more rigid than others. Some do not interactively parse your document; they do not check while you are authoring whether you are conforming to the DTD. HTML editors usually enforce one particular version of an HTML DTD and probably do not accommodate another DTD. This behavior is very limiting because such editors can validate and verify the integrity of only one document type. For a truly powerful SGML authoring environment, you need an editor with the capability to parse any DTD that is fed into the system.

- The *document type definition* (DTD) is a file containing the valid markup language for a particular document type. For example, documents from the engineering department might have their own DTD that is different from documents from the accounting department. They both conform to the SGML standards and may even be authored with the same package. A DTD expert creates and modifies the library of document types. A number of specialized tools for editing DTDs are available, and some tools include tree-like graphical representations of the information.

- The *instance* is the document that you create, which includes content and markup. Instances consist of individual textual elements and entities, the individual components of a document. This end-user document is validated against the DTD that is associated with it. The instance is the end product of an authoring session. After the content is entered and marked up, a parser processes the content and tags to validate its structural integrity against the DTD.

- *Processing software*: After you create an SGML document, you want conversion programs to take it to various streams of output. These output media might include hard-cover books, CD-ROM, or the World Wide Web. The processing software can be written in any particular language. One particular software processing language with numerous features is Omnimark. Omnimark includes a validating parser in its processing environment and an English-like, event-driven programming language optimally designed to process SGML documents. Other languages for processing output include Perl and C (with freeware parsers available for both environments).

Instance Components

The instance must contain a reference to a particular DTD. This must come at the beginning of the document with the `<!DOCTYPE>` tag, indicating the type and location of the DTD. This is a critical piece of information to the parser because it needs to know what context it is in. The other components of an instance are the actual text and the markup that surrounds the text (tags as defined by the DTD referenced).

Elements

With SGML, consider your document a collection of objects. The object name, behavior, and characteristics are defined in the DTD. The objects are instantiated when you write the content and surround it with the appropriate markup. For example, a tag can have certain attributes that enable you to define information about that piece of text, such as a unique ID, object author, object topic, and object creation date, as shown in the following line:

```
<H1 ID="145981" TOPIC="MATH" AUTHOR="JOHN SMITH"> Functions and Graphs </H1>
```

The preceding line is a self-contained unit of a document called an *element*; it is a standard SGML textual unit. Think of it as an object with certain characteristics (known in SGML parlance as *attributes*). Elements can also contain other elements but not particular text content. An element set that encloses other elements (with no text of its own) is called a *content model*. Listing 26.2 shows a very simple example of a book to illustrate markup and elements.

Listing 26.2. Illustration of markup and elements.

```
<!-- SGML Example -->
<BOOK>
<PART><TITLE>Databases</TITLE>
<CHAPTER><TITLE>Object-Oriented Databases</TITLE>
<HEADING>Free OODBMS's</HEADING>
<PARA>There are a number of free Object Oriented Databases:</PARA>
<LIST>
<ITEM>Ingres</ITEM>
<ITEM>Hyper-G</ITEM>
</LIST>
<PARA> And there are also a variety of commercial databases:</PARA>
<LIST>
<ITEM>Gemstone</ITEM>
<ITEM>O2</ITEM>
</LIST>
</CHAPTER>
</PART>
</BOOK>
<!-- End SGML Sample -->
```

From this example, you can see a number of characteristics for an SGML document. First of all, notice that all the content is surrounded by tags. These tags are very important for conveying the structure of the document. A begin tag is created by using a <TAGNAME> and denotes the beginning of some structural element in the document. An end tag is similar, with the exception of a slash inserted, </TAGNAME>.

The first and last tags are comments and do not have a begin and end tag set; they are delimited with <!-- COMMENT -->. The next tag is the <BOOK> tag and indicates that everything that follows until the closing </BOOK> tag is part of the book element construct. The BOOK tags are known as a content model. (<HTML> </HTML> are very similar tags structurally.) They do not directly contain text; they are merely containers for other tags and their text. The next tag, <PART>, is also a content model. It merely contains other tags and their content. These two tags represent an important concept in SGML, rich structural markup for flexible processing.

The next tag, <TITLE>, actually contains some text. It is delimited by an opening tag, <TITLE>, and a closing tag, </TITLE>. In between is the actual text. Next in the example, you see another content model, a <CHAPTER> tag. It doesn't contain content but merely delimits the structural boundary for a book chapter (a content model). Within the <CHAPTER> tag is a set of <TITLE> </TITLE> tags to indicate the actual name of the chapter.

Chapters have <HEADING> tags to delimit subsections. The <HEADING> is designed to have content. The rest of the chapter is structured in a similar manner.

The structure of the preceding book must be formally defined in a document type definition. Look at the table of contents for this book. You will notice how the book is broken down into sections and chapters. If you look at the individual chapters you will notice that they are further broken down into section headings within chapters and paragraphs within headings. Going back to the preceding simple example, you can infer some rules about the content markup:

- A BOOK element always contains one or more PART elements.
- A PART can have only one TITLE and must precede a HEADING. Optionally, you can leave out a TITLE element.
- A CHAPTER can have zero or more of HEADING or PARA or LIST elements that must follow the TITLE.
- A TITLE must contain non-parsable character data (ASCII text).
- A HEADING must contain non-parsable character data (ASCII text).
- A LIST must contain one or more ITEMs.
- An ITEM must contain non-parsable character data (ASCII text).

Note that I have not made any figure references. Figures are usually handled with an external entity reference, indicating where on the file system they are located. Figure contents are not parsed, just the reference to them.

Minimization

Noting the rules that were set forth for authoring a book, you can see that this markup is a bit verbose. That is, every begin tag has an end tag that explicitly ends the textual unit. Many times, you can determine from the context whether or not an end tag is explicitly required. For example, in the following code, an `<ITEM>` tag is implicitly ended by the beginning of a new `<ITEM>` tag; therefore, you do not need to explicitly end it, as shown in the following:

```
<LIST>
<ITEM>Ingres
<ITEM>Hyper-G
</LIST>
```

The capability to omit tags, known as *minimization*, is dictated by the document type definition (rules file). The DTD indicates what tags can and cannot be minimized.

Attributes

Every SGML element can have one or more attributes (or none). *Attributes* are information about that particular element—you can think of them as adjectives to the element's noun. In an object-oriented class, attributes would be the instantiated object's instance variables. For example, every `<PARA>` tag might have an ID attribute as a unique identification code for that textual element that looks something like the following:

```
<PARA ID="1111-2222-3333-4444">This is a sample paragraph with
➥an attribute</PARA>
```

This PARA container has a unique label, so you can distinguish and catalog each of your elements in a fine-grained manner. This identification could be useful if you have a distributed electronic authoring system with constant additions and deletions from a document. If the document is sufficiently large, you wouldn't want to lock the whole thing and check it out to one author. Instead, you'd like to control editing in a more sophisticated manner. The capability to lock certain discrete sections of a document facilitates the multiple author edit process. Authors could work simultaneously on different sections of document with no conflict. Within the attributes for each of the elements, an AUTHOR attribute could track who was responsible for each textual unit in a document.

Additionally, you can define access control to certain parts of a document. When an author checks out elements from the payroll section of a budget with the attribute GROUP="ACCOUNTING", you can verify that person as someone with access to this information. In contrast, a group of elements comprising the mission statement might have an attribute of GROUP="ALL", thus allowing everyone access to this information. The element, with its attributes, is a self-contained unit of information that can be processed in any number of ways. Attributes can be very powerful features. Hypertext systems (such as the World Wide Web) are highly dependent on the use of attributes. Tags such as `<IMG>` and `<A>` indicate particular object types, but attributes indicate the specific resources for those object types.

Advantages of Structured Markup

SGML provides facilities for defining the rules that govern the authoring process and provide for rigidly structured document creation. What are the benefits of marking up data in such a manner? In the case of a technical book, processing programs could automatically generate the table of contents as part of their conversion to an output format. This means that the author or editors do not have to worry about generating a table of contents; they let the processing program take care of that. The document is validly structured, making this a trivial task. Additionally, the author or editor can make major structural changes until the last minute without affecting the table of contents. The table of contents is generated by a processing program after you have completed a valid document.

> **NOTE**
>
> Another interesting thing that you can do with a well-structured document is contextual analysis. A processing program familiar with the document type could automatically generate weighted indexes for search engines based on the placement of words. (For example, words within the <HEADING> </HEADING> tags would have a higher weight than words within the PARA tags.) This technique is used by some World Wide Web crawlers in examining HTML documents. Words within the <H1> </H1> tags have a higher weight than words within the <H5> </H5> tags. With a highly structured and rigidly defined document, you can utilize some powerful processing capabilities for manipulating the data.

Document Type Declaration

A document type definition is written according to the rules as set forth in the SGML standard. SGML lays the ground rules for how to define markup, and a DTD is a particular implementation of markup rules. Specifically, a DTD defines the names of elements, how often such elements may appear, the order in which the elements must appear (in the document and relative to one another), and whether elements may be safely omitted.

Usually, a DTD is created for a particular class of documents. An example might be a corporate division business plan DTD with a unique structure different than an engineering document. What is common to both DTDs is that they define the valid range of tags allowed to mark up a particular type of document. A DTD can be as loosely defined or as rigidly defined as a particular document type requires. This is where the real power (and danger) of SGML is manifested. A DTD can be written as the most complex and rigidly defined of documents, or it can be used to give loose and informal structure to a document. Good design is imperative.

722

Additionally, the DTD defines where tags could go in relation to other tags for a particular document type. Both the structure and syntax of the DTD and any documents created in accordance with it are verified as syntactically correct by a validating parser.

Listing 26.3 is written according to the following DTD, which lays out all the available tag names and how they relate to each other. Don't worry about the syntax. (I have already explained the rules for this particular document type.) Just realize that Listing 26.3 is part of what a DTD looks like (without the attributes).

Listing 26.3. Sample document type definition (DTD).

```
<!ELEMENT BOOK      - -  (PART+)>
<!ELEMENT PART      - -  (TITLE?, CHAPTER+)>
<!ELEMENT TITLE     - 0  (#PCDATA)>
<!ELEMENT CHAPTER   - -  (TITLE?,(HEADING ¦ LIST ¦ PARA)+)>
<!ELEMENT HEADING   - -  (#PCDATA)>
<!ELEMENT PARA      - 0  (#PCDATA)>
<!ELEMENT LIST      - -  (ITEM+)>
<!ELEMENT ITEM      - 0  (#PCDATA)>
```

Do not worry if the markup makes no sense to you. Typically, a DTD is written and maintained by a skilled SGML analyst. These rule sets are too vital and complex to be left to an author who cares only about creating content. If you have a poorly written DTD, the repercussions can be disastrous. Processing systems will break and output will be unreliable (especially across various media).

Many of the authoring and processing environments provide access to a validating parser. The parser's job is to make sure that the DTD and the rules it sets forth are rigidly enforced against every document that claims to abide by that particular DTD. For example, in Listing 26.3, the <BOOK> tag cannot contain a <PARA> tag. A <PARA> tag is only allowed within a <CHAPTER> tag. If you tried to put the <PARA> tag before the <PART> tag in Listing 26.3, the parser would complain.

```
<BOOK><PARA>I am going to talk about databases</PARA>
<PART><TITLE>Databases</TITLE>
```

This is certainly possible to do, if the rules permit it. (If you need such flexibility, you must change your DTD accordingly.) In this particular DTD, placing the <PARA> tag as in the preceding example is an invalid construct.

Without these assurances of the integrity of the authoring process, programs would have an unreliable input stream. The obvious consequence is an unreliable output stream. A parser's job to validate documents is vital to the success of an SGML system.

Coming Together—The SGML Authoring System

The varieties of systems for authoring SGML documents range from GUI-based, on-the-fly validation environments to a crude UNIX-based vi text editor with a freeware validating parser. The choice depends on the publishing environment. Paradoxically, SGML's vendor independence and implementation flexibility can make it a tremendously complex environment to set up.

Depending on the type of publishing operation you intend to run, the training and software costs can be high. Each of the authors will likely need a WYSIWYG SGML authoring system with a fully compliant validating parser. Authors need training for such a system. It often takes a bit of adjustment, psychologically, to get attuned to a structured authoring environment. It can be frustrating for the authors because they prefer to concentrate on writing rather than conforming to a particular DTD (or even worrying about a DTD).

A document analyst must do a significant amount of work to assess your various document structures. After assessing your structural requirements, you must author and debug the DTDs. Then, the DTDs must be constantly maintained. Once you have a body of data that you'd like converted to other formats, you need to write programs to perform the conversion. These conversion programs must also change to reflect the changing structure of your DTD.

In short, developing and maintaining an SGML authoring system is no small task. It requires significant up-front investment of both time and money, but the long-term rewards can be invaluable.

The Future of SGML

Richer SGML systems will have increasing prominence in information technology shops of the future. The advent of the World Wide Web is a proven SGML application. HTML is a very simple DTD. HTML 3.0 proposes numerous features, including enhanced table markup, mathematical symbols, and greater attribute control. The groundwork and protocols for interchange of information has been established (TCP/IP). HTML has effectively addressed a short-term need to structurally define bits of information distributed throughout the world. As the demand for distribution of information via the Internet increases, the need for a more sophisticated and robust method of marking up a wider variety of information will become paramount.

Already, certain browser manufacturers are adding additional parsing functionality to their products to support extensions to the HTML DTD. This is because the market needs a product that allows it to represent a richer set of information. Demand is present. As a greater body of increasingly complex information requires a platform- and vendor-independent form of distribution, SGML will become a greater utilized standard. Presently, the most successful implementation of SGML, HTML, has bumped up against severe limitations in the range of data that it can represent. Browsers such as Arena and Panorama parse a wider variety of DTDs on-the-fly and render them in a hypertext environment.

The dream of a uniform and complete hypertext-linked environment is getting closer to realization with the advent of SGML standards.

Netscape Extensions

by Stig Erik Sandø

IN THIS CHAPTER

Netscape is. By most standards, there is nothing more to say. Netscape is probably the hippest, coolest, dandiest, most loved, and most hated Web browser of them all. Every self-respecting Net surfer has noticed imposing Ns and Netscape logos everywhere, and three out of four surfers may have noticed the renowned N in the corner of their very own browsers.

Trouble in Paradise

Why does the Netscape Navigator (hereafter just called Netscape) generate such strong feelings and cause such a big furor? It is, after all, just another Web browser, right? Basically, Netscape is "just another browser," or at least it started out that way in October 1994 when Mosaic Communications released the first beta version. Netscape was then (and still is) a very good browser that did its job with style and seldom crashed. It was faster and easier to use than NCSA Mosaic, which was the hot browser at the time. There was no trouble in paradise, and everyone was happy until March 1995, when some new and useful HTML enhancements were added to Netscape; for example, a tag to center text and pictures. All in all, a centered header or a picture is really quite nice. The fact that the accepted standards lacked a general center tag was the problem. Netscape Communications Corporation (which was its new name) had not proposed the additions to the Web committees and subcommittees and gone through a lengthy process until the additions became part of the accepted standard, which is about as close you can come to committing deadly sins on the Net. All other browser vendors had more or less grudgingly agreed to wait for HTML 3.

> **NOTE**
>
> Hypertext Markup Language (HTML), an easy-to-use layout language, is the foundation of nearly every Web page. With millions of Web pages and dozens of computer architectures and operating systems, it is of vital importance that HTML is standardized so your computer and your software can display all Web pages properly, and that the rest of the world is also able to enjoy your Web pages fully.
>
> HTML currently has two accepted standards: HTML 1.0 and HTML 2.0. As of September 1996, the current discussed standard is HTML 3.2 and all references to HTML 3 in this chapter are to the HTML 3.2 Working Draft (September 9, 1996). The discussion is not moving very fast and might not be very interesting to the average Web user. However, a big part of the Web, and the Net itself, has evolved from discussions in various committees and subcommittees, and this dialog is generally considered to be the best way of reaching good standards on the Net. The latest HTML standards and documents connected to Web standards can be found at the WWW Consortium's Web pages at http://www.w3.org/.

Netscape has implemented a variety of new HTML extensions in its latest versions, which have more or less revolutionized Web design, providing sites all over the Net with new and intriguing possibilities not available in HTML 2. As of September 1996 the newest version of Netscape, 3, includes among other things a news- and mail-reader, an HTML editor, and support for

Java applets, JavaScript, and many other plug-ins. Other browsers, such as Microsoft Internet Explorer (MIE) and Spyglass Mosaic, to name a few, have adopted many of Netscape's extensions, and many of these extensions one can be fairly certain that most browsers will accept.

However, extension users must be careful to allow people with older versions of Netscape and other not-so-dandy browsers to access the information created with the extensions. The cheeky chaps at Netscape have more or less created their own standard, and HTML 3 is, as of September 1996, not yet completed.

Sound advice and good technical information will enable you to create trendy Web pages and ensure everyone of a satisfactory result, regardless of the browser being used.

Structuring Netscape HTML

The basis of all HTML is the structure of the document, something it has inherited from its "foundation," the Standard Generalized Markup Language (SGML). HTML is defined by an <HTML> element, which again is divided into a <HEAD> and a <BODY> element. The <HEAD> element is generally used for the document title, special commands for the browser, and simple input fields. The <BODY> element is quite simply your document with all the text and pictures.

The <HEAD> Element

Netscape extends a few of the typical <HEAD> elements in HTML. Netscape 1.0 adds a PROMPT attribute to the <ISINDEX> element, which enables you to get rid of the dreadful standard message:

```
This is a searchable index. Enter keyword(s)
```

<ISINDEX> is mainly used with CGI scripts that accept the GET method and is not of much use in forms. MIE supports the PROMPT attribute, and it is part of HTML 3. Listing 27.1, searchable.html, shows an example of basic HTML structure and how to use the PROMPT attribute.

Listing 27.1. searchable.html.

```
<HTML>

<head>
  <title>This is THE gourmet-database</title>
  <isindex prompt="Please enter the name of the
  delicious food you wish our cook to serve:">
</head>

<body>
 <P>Welcome to the Restaurant at the End of the Universe. </P>

</body>
</HTML>
```

Netscape 1.1 introduced the <META> elements, which give commands directly to the browser. Including the following line in the <HEAD> causes the document to refresh itself in 10 seconds:

```
<META HTTP-EQUIV="Refresh" CONTENT=10>
```

You have just given the browser an order, which it has to obey. If you like the idea of ordering other people's browsers around, you can order other browsers to do even more. Let's say that you want all browsers peeking into your newly created virtual bathroom on the Web to peek into your neighbor's bathroom. Just include a rather complex tag such as this in your bathroom .html file:

```
<META HTTP-EQUIV="Refresh"
CONTENT="42; URL=http://www.neighbour.se/bathroom.html">
```

You're actually telling the browser that after 42 seconds it should tiptoe along and look in bathroom.html at www.neighbour.se.

CAUTION

You must place all <META> tags in your <HEAD> element and before any text or images. If you want to order the browser to load another URL, give the full address to the URL, not a relative URL.

The HTTP-EQUIV and CONTENT tags translate their contents into an HTTP response header, which you might use directly from your CGI scripts. The format is given as the values of

```
HTTP-EQUIV: CONTENT
```

The previously mentioned bathroom redirecter produces an HTTP response header, which would look like this:

```
Refresh: 42; URL=http://www.neighbour.se/bathroom.html
```

The <BODY> Element

The <BODY> element is the main element of HTML and contains all the text and graphics. Netscape 1.1 added attributes to the BODY tag, which enable you to choose background color, background images, and the color of the text. The different <BODY> attributes are part of the proposed HTML 3, and both Spyglass and MIE support the attributes. A peek at the HTML reveals this format:

```
<BODY BACKGROUND="image_url" BGCOLOR="#rrggbb"
TEXT="#rrggbb" LINK="#rrggbb" ALINK="#rrggbb" VLINK="#rrggbb">
```

You thought the META stuff was difficult? This code seems even more confusing, but you're in luck; the format is simpler than it looks. The attributes in the preceding <BODY> element can be summarized as follows:

- ■ BACKGROUND: Uses the named GIF or JPEG as background. This picture does not load if you have turned off images.
- ■ BGCOLOR: Background color.
- ■ TEXT: The normal text color in the document.
- ■ LINK: The color of unvisited links.
- ■ ALINK: The color of a link that is currently clicked.
- ■ VLINK: The color of a visited link.

27

NETSCAPE EXTENSIONS

To specify the colors accurately for the preceding attributes you need the tricky "#rrggbb"s, which really are hexadecimal red-green-blue codes for the color. An example of a valid value is #f0a543 where f0 is the amount of red, a5 is the amount of green, and 43 is the amount of blue; the result is a shiny, happy orange color. Don't worry; a sane system supposedly lurks behind the scheme. Play around with the numbers, and you might get lucky. (The maximum number of combinations is only 16.8 million.) You might even understand the system.

A good way to find colors, for example, is to search the Net for a color table that has the color in a more readable language, as well as the matching hex number. You can also check if your favorite drawing program supports this system and has a color picker (most do), or just grab the color of a Web page you like with a peek at the HTML source. If you are certain that all your visitors will be using Netscape 2.0 or higher, you can write the color directly, as shown in the following example:

```
<BODY BGCOLOR="orange">
```

Voilà, a bright orange color. Naming colors may work for Netscape 1.1, MIE, and Spyglass, but even then you can name only the most basic colors. I recommend the use of hex numbers to maintain portability. Listing 27.2, bodysnatcher.html, is an example of a full document with BODY attributes and a META tag.

Listing 27.2. bodysnatcher.html.

```
<HTML>
<head>
<title>A body more or less..</title>
<META HTTP-EQUIV="Refresh" CONTENT="42; URL=http://localhost/nextbody.html">
</head>

<body bgcolor="#808000" text="#000000" link="#ff0000"
 alink="#ffff00" vlink="#0000ff">
<h1>The snatching of a body</h1>
```

continues

Listing 27.2. continued

```
<P>Once upon a time someone took a closer look at
   a body with olive background, black
   text, and an anchor to
   the <a href="index.html">index</a> which is red
   when the document it links to has not been visited,
   is yellow when you click it and finally becomes blue
   when you have visited the document it links to. When you've looked at
   the page for 42 seconds it goes off to
   find  <b>http://localhost/nextbody.html</b>
</P>.
</body>
</HTML>
```

Formatting, Paragraphing, and Other Wonders

The core and value of Web sites are the information they provide, but the presentation has become almost as important. The new Netscape extensions to HTML give users much more control of the appearance of text and other information.

Earlier in the chapter, I mentioned that HTML 2.0 lacks decent tags to align pictures and text. Netscape's controversial <CENTER> tag enables everyone to center text, pictures, and other elements. The problem with Netscape's <CENTER> tag was that it did not fit 100 percent into HTML's structure.

HTML 3 defines the alignment of elements as an attribute and not as an element. Here is an example of an HTML 3-compatible tag:

```
<p align=center>
```

Netscape allows the following ALIGNs: LEFT, RIGHT, and CENTER. Netscape supports this form of aligning in paragraphs <P>, divisions <div>, horizontal rulers <HR>, and headers <Hx>.

I recommend that instead of using the <CENTER> tag, you use the more powerful division tag <DIV> with an appropriate ALIGN attribute. The tag

```
<DIV ALIGN=center>
```

is in practice equal to Netscape's <CENTER> tag. As of April 1996 only Netscape 2 and later supports the <DIV> tag, but most browsers will probably support it soon. To get the expected result from most browsers, you can use both tags, as shown in the following example:

```
<DIV ALIGN=center><CENTER>Text, Pictures and other
centered elements</CENTER></DIV>
```

The implementation in other browsers varies widely. Some stay close to the philosophy in HTML 3, others copy Netscape's extensions directly, and others wait patiently for HTML 3 to be an accepted standard.

Text Gone Haywire

The regular text is pretty daft, and one sometimes wishes to spice it up. Luckily, Netscape gives you the opportunity to manipulate the size of your fonts directly, and the latest version lets you color the text, too. The <FONT> tag in Netscape 2 and later and the proposed HTML 3 currently has two attributes: SIZE and COLOR. The format is

```
<FONT SIZE=value COLOR="#rrggbb">
```

The COLOR value accepts the same values as the various color attributes used in the <BODY> tag. The default SIZE value is 3, and the SIZE attribute accepts values between 1 and 7. You can also use positive and negative values, such as +1 and –2, as size values, which adjusts the font size relative to the size of the base font.

```
Normal font here and
<FONT SIZE="+3" COLOR="#ffffa3"> very large colored font here</FONT>
```

You probably noticed that you can make every letter in different sizes and colors, but take my advice...don't!

You can also specify how you want the general font in the document to be with the <BASEFONT> tag:

```
<BASEFONT SIZE=value COLOR="#rrggbb">
```

Netscape extends text formatting beyond the capability to merely format font sizes and colors. The browser accepts several fast and easy tags for formatting text where the actual size is relative to your settings and your browser.

- <BIG>: Uses a big font.
- <SMALL>: Uses a small font.
- <SUB>: Text appears as subscript and in a smaller font.
- <SUP>: Text appears as superscript and in a smaller font.

These tags are supported by Netscape 1.1 and later and HTML 3, but not yet by many other browsers. The subscript and superscript tags may be very useful and are apparently the crude beginnings of a <MATH> element, which is sorely needed. Listing 27.3, texted.html, makes all these new extensions a bit clearer.

Listing 27.3. texted.html.

```
<html>
<head> <title>Catching the bus</title> </head>

<body bgcolor="#ffffff">
<basefont size=3 color="#000000">
<div align=right>
```

continues

27

NETSCAPE
EXTENSIONS

Listing 27.3. continued

```
<h2 align=center>Centered Hitchhiking</h2>
<p align=left>This text is aligned to the left</p>
<p>This text is aligned right in Netscape 2.0 because
    of the &lt;DIV&gt;-tag, but is on the
left side in Netscape v1.22</P>
<p align=center>These <big>BIG</big> letters and these
<small>small</small> letters are centered.</p>
<p>The formula of water in blue <small>(only Netscape 2.0)</small>
is <font size="+2" color="#0000ff">H<sub>2</sub>O</font></p>
</body>
</html>
```

You've Been Enlisted

With Netscape's extensions you get even more control of your lists than HTML 2. The basic unnumbered list <UL> has a different bullet for every indented level. Now you can choose the type of bullet with the TYPE attribute, which accepts disc, circle, and square. To produce an unordered list with circled bullets, you use

```
<UL TYPE=circle>
```

The numbered list <OL> also has a TYPE attribute. The allowed TYPEs include

- TYPE=A: Counts with capital letters (A, B, C, ...).
- TYPE=a: Counts with small letters (a, b, c, ...).
- TYPE=I: Counts with large Roman numerals (I, II, III, ...).
- TYPE=i: Counts with small Roman numerals (i, ii, iii, ...).
- TYPE=1: Uses the default numbers.

If this variety is not enough for you, you can start your list with values other than 1 by using the START attribute in the <OL>:

```
<OL START=4>
```

starts counting on 4, and based on the TYPE, you get D, d, IV, iv, or 4.

You may also change the TYPE in the list element <LI>. The list tag <LI> accepts the same TYPEs as the list it is part of (for example, you may specify discs and other markers for an unnumbered list <UL>). An <LI> in a numbered list can also specify a specific value, but this changes the counting for all subsequent items. To specify a list element <LI> with the value 3, type the following:

```
<LI VALUE=3>
```

HTML 3 supports all of these extensions and some browsers have adopted some of the attributes; for example, MIE supports the VALUE in <LI> elements. These extensions are nice and dandy, but avoid making your information dependent on them due to the different representation in the various browsers. If you need different bullet shapes and want your HTML to be portable, try using the image element <IMG> with appropriate images. Listing 27.4, enlisted.html, contains a more extensive example of the list tags.

Listing 27.4. enlisted.html.

```
<html>
<head> <title>A few small lists</title> </head>

<body bgcolor="#ffffff">
<basefont size=3 color="#000000">
<h2 align=center>Available Jobs</h2>
<big>Pentagon:</big>
 <ul type=square>
  <li> HTML-designer </li>
  <li type=circle> OO-Wizard </li>
  <li type=disc> CGI-programmer </li>
 </ul>
<hr>
<h2 align=center>Where to go?</h2>
<big>Nice places (in order):</big>
 <ol type=I>
  <li> Norwegian Fjords </li>
  <li> Stonehenge</li>
  <li value=2> Bermuda </li>
  <li> Taj-Mahal </li>
 </ol>
</body>
</html>
```

Rulers of the Web

The <HR> element defines a horizontal ruler, which most browsers draw as a shaded line. Netscape has added these extra attributes to the <HR> tag:

- ■ SIZE=number: Lets you specify the height of the ruler in pixels.
- ■ WIDTH=number¦percent: The default ruler has a width of 100%. You can decide the length in pixels or as a percentage of the browser window.
- ■ ALIGN=alignment: Defines the alignment of the ruler and accepts LEFT, RIGHT, and CENTER as arguments.
- ■ NOSHADE: Gives you a solid ruler with no shadow.

HTML 3 supports all of these attributes and major browsers such as MIE and Spyglass Mosaic also accept them.

Listing 27.5, `rulersofWeb.html`, sums up the rulers quite nicely.

Listing 27.5. `rulersofWeb.html`.

```
<html>
<head> <title>To rule or not to rule</title> </head>

<body bgcolor="#ffffff">
<basefont size=3 color="#000000">
  <h2 align=center>Rule the world, please</h2>
<P>Basic ruler:</p>
<hr>
  <P>A halfscreen centered ruler:</p>
<hr width="50%" align=center>
  <P>A noshaded 10 pixels thick ruler,
     aligned right and with a width of 125 pixels:</p>
<hr size=10 width=125 align=right noshade>
</body>
</html>
```

Images and Imagination

The Web's capability to combine text and images has probably made it the most popular application of the Net. For example, pretty ladies, flashy logos, and small, colorful buttons seem to be just about everywhere. Netscape has several new tags and new attributes for already existing tags that facilitate the use of images in documents. Unfortunately, the Net is still painfully slow, and image loading takes most of the time. The following section suggests a few tricks that you can try to help your users access your images more quickly.

The core of images in HTML is the `<IMG>` element, and Netscape has made this element one of the most extensive. Here is the format of the `<IMG>` element:

```
<IMG SRC="image_url" ALIGN=alignment WIDTH=value HEIGHT=value BORDER=value
VSPACE=value HSPACE=value ALT="text" LOWSRC="image_url" USEMAP=#map ISMAP>
```

The SRC attribute names the URL of the image and is the main part of the `<IMG>` element. The ALIGN attribute extends the TOP, MIDDLE, and BOTTOM values in HTML 2 to quite a few new values:

- **LEFT**: A left-aligned image is placed as close to the left margin as possible. Any subsequent text or pictures wrap around the right part of the image.

- **RIGHT**: Works the same as LEFT aligning but positions itself near the right margin. The text and pictures wrap around the left part of the image.

- **TEXTTOP**: The top of the picture aligns with the top of the tallest text. TEXTTOP is not supported by HTML 3.

- **ABSMIDDLE**: The middle of the picture aligns with the middle of the current line. ABSMIDDLE is not supported by HTML 3.

- BASELINE: The bottom of the picture aligns with the baseline of the current line (equal to ALIGN=BOTTOM). BASELINE is not supported by HTML 3.

- ABSBOTTOM: The bottom of the picture aligns with the bottom of the current line. ABSBOTTOM is not supported by HTML 3.

The floating alignment in LEFT and RIGHT are so useful that you'll soon want to jump to the end of the picture with a simple tag. Netscape allows you to do so by extending the <BR> tag with a CLEAR attribute. The <BR> tag usually inserts a regular line break, but the CLEAR attribute can add a vertical jump that you specify and is very useful when you are working with images.

The CLEAR attribute currently accepts three values:

- LEFT: Breaks the line and moves vertically down until you have a clear left margin.

- RIGHT: Breaks the line and moves vertically down until you have a clear right margin.

- ALL: Breaks the line and moves vertically down until both margins are clear.

This system is not very difficult to use, as Listing 27.6 clearly shows. It loads myWebPictures/sheep.gif, aligns it to the left, and prints some text.

Listing 27.6. sheepy.html.

```
<html>
<head> <title>Sheepish look</title> </head>

<body bgcolor="#ffffff">
<basefont size=3 color="#000000">
  <h2 align=center>Sheep</h2>
  <p align=center>As defined by: Oxford Advanced Learner's Dictionary</p>
  <img src="myWebPictures/sheep.gif" align=left>

<b>sheep</b>:
  <ol type=i>
   <li>grass-eating animal with thick fleecy coat, kept in
       flocks for its flesh as food and for its wool.</li>
<li>(idm) <b>like 'sheep</b> too easily influenced or led by others</li>
  </ol>
</body>
</HTML>
```

Image Sizing

The image sizing is built into Netscape with the <IMG> attributes HEIGHT and WIDTH. These attributes allow you to resize your picture and give the size either in pixels or as a percentage of the browser window. Whatever size you give it, Netscape and other good browsers stretch and squeeze the picture until it has the proportions you want.

Another benefit of this feature is that Netscape does not have to query the server for the size of every image when it creates the layout. Because the browser does not need to connect to the server to check the size of the images, the page can load more quickly.

> **NOTE**
>
> Remember that the image sizing feature is no excuse for putting larger images on your pages. Keep your images as small as possible!

Most browsers and HTML 3 have adopted these sizing attributes, and you should use them whenever possible.

Border Patrol and *Lebensraum*

Somewhere along the line you might want to let your images link to bigger, better, and meaner places. If you try

```
<a href="searchable.html"><img src="myWebPictures/sheep.gif"></a>
```

you get a colored border around your image. Everyone knows that a color border is clickable and always leads to some fun, but if you already have a well-designed page where "looks are everything," you might want to make the border unique. Netscape and most other browsers enable you to change the size of your border in pixels with the BORDER attribute. If you want a border but want it invisible, just set the BORDER attribute to zero. To make an invisible link to searchable.html on the sheep picture write the following line:

```
<a href="searchable.html"><img src="myWebPictures/sheep.gif" border=0></a>
```

When you let your text flow around your images, which creates a very nice effect, you may notice that the text is clinging to the image. A little extra space, or *Lebensraum,* for your images can improve the look and make the text more readable. Most browsers support the horizontal HSPACE and vertical VSPACE space attributes.

```
<a href="searchable.html">
<img src="myWebPictures/sheep.gif" border=0 hspace=8 vspace=4>
</a>
<P>Lots and lots of text that has been moved
8 pixels away from both sides of the image,
and 4 pixels away from the bottom and the top of the image.</P>
```

> **NOTE**
>
> HTML 3 supports the border attribute and the two SPACE attributes.

If you're worried about the slow Net and that people will never see the giant-size pictures you have on your page, one more trick might help you. This trick is not used very much, which is a pity, and unfortunately, it works only with Netscape and has yet to be included in HTML 3.

Suppose you have a huge picture that takes eons to download even if you have set the WIDTH and HEIGHT attributes correctly, like this picture of a big sheep:

```
<img src="myWebPictures/bigsheep.jpg" height=410 width=282 ALT="My giant sheep">
```

Consider adding a smaller picture for people to watch while the huge one downloads. When all other text and pictures are loaded, Netscape downloads the big picture and puts it in its rightful position. To implement this magic, include the LOWSRC attribute in your <IMG> tag, pointing to the image you want to load first:

```
<img src="myWebPictures/bigsheep.jpg" height=410 width=282
lowsrc="myWebPictures/sheep.gif" ALT="My giant sheep">
```

> **NOTE**
>
> Remember that both pictures use the same image size. If you don't specify the size, Netscape uses the LOWSRC's image size. Specify the large picture's size and the LOWSRC picture will be stretched and squeezed to fit the area. The LOWSRC attribute can point to any image of any size.

Netscape also supports interlaced GIFs, animated GIFs (GIF89a), JPEGs, and other image formats.

Image Mapping Made Easy

Image mapping is one of the impressive features that gives the Web a true feeling of a point-and-click interface. The problem until now is that all image maps had to depend on CGI scripts on the server. Netscape 2.0 has made image mapping easier with its implementation of client-side image maps, which the browser, instead of a remote server, parses and interprets. The best part of this feature is the simplicity, and it allows everyone to create outstanding image maps. All you have to do is to define a "map," and include the USEMAP attribute in your <IMG> tag.

The syntax of the USEMAP attribute is

```
<IMG SRC="image_url" USEMAP="map_url#mapname">
```

where #mapname specifies the name of the map in the map file. The <MAP> element describes the different regions and parts of the image. The default syntax of a <MAP> element is

```
<MAP NAME="name">
<AREA [SHAPE="rect"] COORDS="x,y,.." [HREF="reference"] [NOHREF]>
</MAP>
```

So far, Netscape has implemented only one SHAPE—RECT—which is a rectangle whose coordinates are specified as "left, top, right, bottom." The HREF attribute points to a URL relative to the file that contains the map. To use another URL as base, include a `<BASE HREF="url">` in the document. The NOHREF tells the browser that clicking in the specified NOHREF region does not lead to any action, which enables you to make a "hole" in an otherwise hot-linked area. If a region is not specified at all it will not lead to an action.

> **TIP**
>
> If you define regions that overlap other regions (like a hole in an otherwise hot-linked area) declare the smaller region (like the hole) first. The general rule is that if two or more areas overlap, the first region defined in the map takes precedence over subsequent regions.

Listing 27.7, buttons.html, shows how to use buttons in a real-life, client-side image map for Netscape 2 and later.

Listing 27.7. buttons.html.

```html
<html>
<head> <title>Buttons which was used in Real Life</title> </head>

<body bgcolor="#000000" text="#fffff0"
 link="#ffff00" vlink="#00ff00" alink="#00ff00">
<P align=center>
<img border=0 alt="Main Buttons"
 usemap="buttonmap.html#mainlinks"
 src="myWebPictures/mainbut.gif">
</P>
<base href="http://www.ii.uib.no/~stig/NetscapeChapter/">

<map name="mainlinks">
  <area shape="rect" coords="1,1,90,28" href="index.html">
  <area shape="rect" coords="1,28,90,56" href="information.html">
  <area shape="rect" coords="1,56,90,84" href="tome.html">
  <area shape="rect" coords="1,84,90,112" href="trivia.html">
  <area shape="rect" coords="1,112,90,140" href="newspaper.html">
  <area shape="rect" coords="1,140,90,168" href="world.html">
  <area shape="rect" coords="0,0,91,169" nohref>
</map>

</body>
</HTML>
```

Notice how the `<BASE>` tag specifies the base URL, which all the following relative URLs use. When the `<BASE>` tag has not been used, the browser will use the document's URL.

Tables and Their Possibilities

A *table* is a collection of cells divided into rows and columns. An HTML table consists of several containers for your data. Netscape 1.1 implemented the tables in the proposed HTML 3 specification. Simply stated, tables are probably the most powerful Web design tools you can use on your Web pages.

> **CAUTION**
>
> When you use tables, you have the opportunity to make a lot of mistakes. The best advice is to stick rigorously to the syntax. Tables are constantly under development, both by Netscape, other browsers, and in HTML 3, so new tags and attributes might show up. Unfortunately many browsers don't support tables fully, and your pages might in some cases be totally unreadable.

The basic table tag is `<TABLE>`, which contains the whole table. The table tag has several attributes:

- `ALIGN=alignment`: This attribute works exactly like the one in the `<IMG>` tag and enables you to create floating tables or wrap text around the table, for example. This attribute exists only in Netscape 2.0.

- `BORDER=value`: The `BORDER` attribute enables you to specify the width of the border. Setting `BORDER` to zero gives no lines around cells and the outside.

- `CELLSPACING=value`: `CELLSPACING` is the number of pixels between the cells in a table. The default value is two.

- `CELLPADDING=value`: `CELLPADDING` is the number of pixels between the `cellborder` and the content of the cell. The default is one.

- `WIDTH =value¦percent`: Works as the `WIDTH` attribute in the `<IMG>` tag. You should let Netscape do table sizing due to its complex nature.

The table row tag `<TR>` defines all rows and may define specific attributes for all cells in that row. All table cells are either left-aligned, normal data cells `<TD>` or centered, bold table headers `<TH>`. You can also give the table a caption in a `<CAPTION>` tag. All table tags share the following attributes:

- `ALIGN`: If `ALIGN` is an attribute for a `<CAPTION>`, you can decide whether the caption should appear at the `TOP` or the `BOTTOM` of the table. The default for `<CAPTION>` is `TOP`. If `ALIGN` is an attribute for `<TR>`, `<TD>`, or `<TH>`, it controls the horizontal alignment of the contents. `LEFT`, `RIGHT`, and `CENTER` are valid alignments.

- `VALIGN`: May be used with `<TR>`, `<TD>`, or `<TH>` and controls the vertical alignment of the contents. `TOP`, `MIDDLE`, `BOTTOM`, and `BASELINE` are valid alignments.

- NOWRAP: May be used with \<TD> and \<TH> and enables you to decide that the cell should not wrap its contents.

- COLSPAN/ROWSPAN: You can use these attributes in \<TD> and \<TH> tags. They tell the browser how many columns and rows the table should span, which is very useful for table headers and special cells. Take care when using these tags because columns and rows may be truncated. The default for both values is one.

Listing 27.8, aNiceTable.html, shows how to create a table that contains basic information. You must understand how to create a table because Listing 27.9, newspaper.html, combines all I've shown so far and makes heavy use of tables.

Listing 27.8. aNiceTable.html.

```html
<html>
<head> <title>A nice table</title> </head>

<body bgcolor="#ffffff">

<table border=10 align=right>
  <caption align=top><font size="+3"
  color="#005500">Fiscal Budget</font></caption>

  <tr>  <th> </th>  <th>March</th>  <th>April</th>
        <th>May</th>  <th>Total</th>  </tr>
  <tr valign=top>
        <td><b>Money In:</b></td>  <td>15.8</td>
        <td>16.8</td>  <td>16.6</td>  <td> </td>
  </tr>
  <tr valign=top>
        <td><b>Money Out:</b></td>  <td>5.7</td>
        <td>1.2</td>  <td>10.3</td>  <td> </td>
  </tr>
  <tr valign=top>
        <td><b>Difference:</b></td>  <td>10.1</td>
        <td>15.6</td>  <td>6.3</td>  <td nowrap>32.0</td>
  </tr>

</table>

<h2 align=center>An easy table</h2>
<P>
  In Netscape 2.0, this table is right-aligned, but
  in Netscape 1.1 it is left-aligned.
Apart from that they're equal. As you can see, it
  is now possible to create spreadsheets and other tables with relative ease.
  Several other good examples of
  tables are available at
  <a href="http://www.netscape.com/">Netscape's</a> Homepages.
</P>
</body>
</HTML>
```

Listing 27.9, `newspaper.html`, uses most of what has been described in this chapter to create the newspaper *Sheep Times*. An intriguing part of `newspaper.html` is the small subtable with a border that is placed within a data cell. Creating a newspaper is just one of the many things you can do with tables.

Listing 27.9. `newspaper.html`.

```
<html>
<head> <title>A REAL Newspaper</title> </head>

<body bgcolor="#ffffff">
<div align=center> <center>
<img src="myWebPictures/stimes.gif">

<table bordeR=0 width="100%" cellpadding=4>
  <tr>
    <td><a href="index.html"><img src="myWebPictures/arrowxmb.gif" border=0
    ➥alt="Back"></a></td>
    <td><b>Issue 12</b></td>
    <td><b>Woolmonth</b></td>
    <td><b>$0.00</b></td>
    <td><b>Netscape-Enhanced</b></td>
    <td align=right><a href="aNiceTable.html">
        <img src="myWebPictures/arrowxma.gif" border=0 alt="Forward"></a></td>
  </tr>
  <tr>
    <td colspan=6> </td>
  </tr>
  <tr valign=top>
    <td rowspan=5 colspan=4>
        <img src="myWebPictures/sheep2.gif" align=left
            alt="His Royal Sheepiness" border=2 hspace=10
            vspace=5>
<P><big>His Royal Sheepiness proposes to the Web</big></P>
        <font size="-1">
        <P>This morning His Sheepiness proposed to his
            beloved Net. The romance has
been known for several months, but His Sheepiness has been to shy to
        propose to his beloved. We hope that they both will live long, prosper
        and grow fine wool.</P>
        <P align="right"><b>Read more on Page 12</b></P></font>
    </td>
    <td colspan=2>

        <table border=1>
            <tr><td><b>In this issue:</b></td></tr>
            <tr><td colspan=2><img src="myWebPictures/ballxgre.gif"
                            hspace=8>Lamb-Psychology</td></tr>
            <tr><td colspan=2><img src="myWebPictures/ballxpin.gif"
                            hspace=8>Sheep-cults</td></tr>
            <tr><td colspan=2><img src="myWebPictures/ballxgre.gif"
                            hspace=8>Where the wool go</td></tr>
            <tr><td colspan=2><img src="myWebPictures/ballxpin.gif"
                            hspace=8>News and Rumours</td></tr>
```

continues

Listing 27.9. continued

```
        </table>
      </td>
    </tr>
</table>

</center> </div>
</body>
</HTML>
```

You've Been Framed

Netscape 2.0 introduced frames to Web users. Frames allow you to split your browser window into several separate, independent regions. The possibilities of frames are nearly endless. You may now, for example, have a constant set of quick links in one part of the window, normal browsing in another part of the window, and a totally different set of tools in some other region of the window. Frames enable you to, among other things, target links to other regions, create new windows, and retrieve multiple documents. When you use frames with JavaScript functions, they can become very powerful.

> **CAUTION**
>
> Frames are not part of the proposed HTML 3 standard and the whole concept of frames is under development in one of the many Web specifications at the WWW-Consortium.

The code for implementing frames is fairly easy and resembles the table syntax. Frames are generated by <FRAMESET> tags, <FRAME> tags, and FRAME documents. You need a main page that sets up the frames and loads the framedocuments into the different parts of the window.

The main container is the <FRAMESET>, which defines the <FRAME> information area. The tag has two attributes COLS and ROWS; each defines a list of comma-separated values that may be in pixels, percentages, or the special, relative-sized * sign that depends on the other values for its size. All values are scaled to a total of 100 percent. For example, the following line divides the screen in three parts:

```
<FRAMESET COLS="100,*,30%">
```

The first column has a width of 100 pixels, the last column has a width of 30 percent of the width of the browser window, and the column in the middle uses the rest of the space.

You put <FRAME> tags, which define names of the different frames and their content, into the <FRAMESET> area. The <FRAME> tag has the following attributes:

- **SRC="url"**: The URL of the document to put in the frame.
- **NAME="window_name"**: Assigns a name to a specific frame, which allows other documents to address it.
- **MARGINWIDTH="value"**: Defines the width of the left and right margins in pixels. This value must be greater than or equal to one.
- **MARGINHEIGHT="value"**: Defines the height of the top and bottom margins in pixels. This value must be greater than or equal to one.
- **SCROLLING="yes¦no¦auto"**: Lets you control whether a scrollbar should be visible. The default is auto, which lets the browser decide.
- **NORESIZE**: This attribute says that the frame is not resizable by the user. By default, all frames are resizable.

Another special tag is the <NOFRAMES> tag that contains information that browsers with frames ignore. Listing 27.10, framed.html, is a frame document that calls Listing 27.11, framedata.html, into its three frames. To allow other browsers to read the content, framed.html gives an anchor to the framedata.html file.

Listing 27.10. framed.html.

```
<FRAMESET COLS="150,*">
<NOFRAMES>
<html>
<head> <title>A framed document</title> </head>
<body bgcolor="#ffffff">

<h1 align=center>You've been framed</h1>
  <P>This document should be read by a
     frame-capable browser. The document which is
     framed may be <a href="framedata.html">found</A>
     even if you don't have the latest
     version of Netscape.</P>
</body>
</html>

</noframes>
  <frameset rows="100%">
    <frame src="framedata.html" name="frame1">
    <frame src="framedata.html" name="frame2">
  </frameset>
</frameset>
```

Listing 27.11. framedata.html.

```
<html>
<head> <title>A framed document</title> </head>

<body bgcolor="#ffffff">
  <h1 align="center">Frames may be useful</h1>
  <P>You've now created a frame and put a document in it.
     You should now have two frames,
     with this document in both. Congratulations</P>
</body>
</HTML>
```

Aiming for a Window

Now when you have the power to create windows or frames within the browser, you soon might want to specify into which frame a document should be loaded or *targeted*. You can add the following attribute to elements that load other documents:

```
TARGET="window_name"
```

You may add TARGETs to anchors, the <BASE> tag, the <AREA> tag (Imagemaps), and <FORM> tags. Any window_name that begins with an alphanumeric character is valid.

Some TARGET names are special and have a special effect; all the special TARGET names begin with an underscore.

- TARGET="_blank": The link is loaded in a new blank window.
- TARGET="_self": The link is loaded in the same window you clicked in. Overrides any <BASE> tags.
- TARGET="_parent": The link is loaded into the window that created the frame.
- TARGET="_top": The link loads in a full window and wipes out any frames.

If you use frames, always remember to have a <NOFRAMES> area where people with other browsers can read the information.

JavaScript and Java

Java is the trendiest stuff on the Web nowadays, and Netscape has included Java in its browsers for most UNIX flavors, the Macintosh, Windows 95, and Windows NT. Java is a full programming language with special libraries for the Web that was developed by Sun Microsystems. On the Web, you can find several compiled byte codes (Java classes), which are often referred to as Java applets. You can use on your home page applets you find on the Web.

Netscape and other Java-capable browsers have their own <APPLET> tag, which has the following syntax:

```
<APPLET CODEBASE=codebaseURL CODE=appletFile
 ALT=alternateText NAME=appletInstanceName
WIDTH=pixels HEIGHT=pixels ALIGN=alignment
 VSPACE=pixels HSPACE=pixels>
   <PARAM NAME=appletAttribute1 VALUE=value>
   <PARAM NAME=appletAttribute2 VALUE=value>
   . . .
</APPLET>
```

The attributes you must include are CODE, HEIGHT, and WIDTH. The others are optional. Refer to a Java manual for more information on the parameters and other attributes not explained earlier in this chapter. To create your own Java applets, you need a Java compiler, which is now available on most computers with 32-bit architecture (most UNIX flavors, Windows 95/NT, and some Macs). You can learn more about Java at Sun's Java pages at http://java.sun.com/ or in the newsgroup hierarchy comp.lang.java.

Another great invention is JavaScript, which is a programming language in your browser. JavaScript is easier to use than Java and has some nifty features that may be of use to anyone who makes Web pages. You can get more information about JavaScript either at Netscape's home page at http://www.netscape.com/ or in the newsgroup comp.lang.javascript.

Miscellaneous

Netscape has created even more additions to HTML. Among them is the dreaded and much hated <BLINK> tag. Don't even think of using it.

Netscape has also added an ENCTYPE attribute to the <FORM> tag that allows you to write forms that take a file as input. This feature is quite useful for larger systems with the Web as their interface.

```
<FORM ENCTYPE="multipart/form-data" ACTION="url_to_fileParser" METHOD=POST>
Send: <INPUT NAME="inputfile" TYPE="file">
<INPUT TYPE="submit" VALUE="Send File Flying">
</FORM>
```

> **NOTE**
>
> With the ENCTYPE attribute you can specify with which MIME format the form's content should be encoded. The attribute is mainly for CGI programmers who want to use other encoding methods than the standard encoding. Don't mess with it if you're not sure what you're doing.

To print characters in HTML documents that are not part of the main ASCII character set, HTML uses what is called *entities*. HTML 2 defined a list of entities that enabled me, among other things, to put the character ø at the end of my name with the entity ø. Netscape has introduced two new entities, which also have been adopted by HTML 3:

■ `&reg;`—Registered trademark ® symbol.

■ `&copy;`—Copyright © symbol.

Netscape's browser is in constant development, and updated information is available at Netscape's home page at `http://www.netscape.com/`. You should check this site frequently.

Summary

Netscape has so far been by virtually all standards the best and most powerful Web browser around, and the cheeky chaps at Netscape have introduced many new and eminent concepts to the Web. Unlike other notable browsers, Netscape is made for virtually all computer platforms, which again makes it available to everyone and not just people running Windows 95. This makes Web pages written with the help of Netscape's HTML extensions available to just about every Web surfer, ranging from top-notch scientists with beefy UNIX workstations to tea-drinking landladies with Macintoshes.

The extensions to HTML and the Web that have come from Netscape are rapidly becoming tomorrow's standards, and taking advantage of the many extensions to make a tremendous page should not be considered a sin. Be careful when you use the newest and hippest extensions, because not everyone is using the funkiest browser, and letting the browser-challenged get an unreadable Web page will not serve much of a purpose. The best advice if you want to use some effort on your Web design and have a fairly beefy machine is probably to grab a couple of browsers and install them on your computer and check what your pages look like with other browsers before you put your pages on the Web. Due to the vast difference between Netscape 1.*x* and Netscape 2.*x*/3.*x*, getting both versions is a good solution if you want to make sure everyone gets a satisfactory result.

Filling your hard disk with 20 different browsers to check just a couple of HTML files is, however, not a very good solution. Using the hints and guidelines in this chapter will probably let your pages be understood by most (if not all) browsers in existence and provide the best possible end result for everyone. Make an option for other browsers whenever you use the coolest and most fancy stuff—frames, tables, Java, and JavaScript to name a few—because there is nothing people hate more than the message

```
"Sorry, you cannot access this page because you don't
have a browser that supports all the fancy extensions
I have filled my incredible and gigacool pages with"
```

Most of the Netscape extensions have been adopted by proposed HTML 3 standard and the different HTML specifications, which means that eventually other browsers will try to catch up with the standard Netscape has set. This makes your immensely good and Netscape-extended Web pages available to an even larger audience and lets everyone enjoy them. So don't be afraid to use the many good extensions in your Web pages, but give the people that have not downloaded Netscape yet a chance to enjoy your Web pages, too.

CHAPTER 28

Microsoft Internet Explorer-Only HTML Tags

by Rick Tracewell

IN THIS CHAPTER

Less than a year ago, if anyone asked who the king of the Web browser universe was, there was no hesitation in the response: Netscape Communications's Navigator. You can imagine that the engineering team at Microsoft Corporation, the company that dominates almost every portion of the software industry worldwide, probably viewed this as a little bit of a challenge. Or, perhaps, they realized that they almost missed the Internet boat altogether by taking a *laissez faire* attitude toward this "new" medium. (Actually, they didn't have to realize it. Industry pundits and analyzers were printing it in periodicals all over the place.)

Fortunately for Microsoft, the company has deep pockets and good programmers who work very quickly. Consider this: There wasn't a devoted Internet division at Microsoft in December 1995, whereas in July 1996, the new Internet Platform & Tools Division boasted 2,500 employees (which is more than Netscape and six more new Internet companies combined).

Suddenly, Microsoft's Internet Explorer Web browser application has become a strong rival to Netscape's Navigator Web browser. Taking the path of vying for ease-of-use multimedia dominance over Navigator, Explorer implemented several HTML extensions that Netscape Navigator and other browsers do not support. Among them, the <BGSOUND> tag allows background sound to play behind the scenes on a Web page. The nice thing about this feature is that the user is not required to have any special sound playing applications, Internet Explorer plays the sound files right inside the browser.

Another Explorer-unique tag is <MARQUEE> (see "Multimedia: Audio, Video, Applications"). This upscale take on the old (and, to most people, extremely annoying) <BLINK> tag enables authors to create customized scrolling text anywhere on a Web page. Attributes give the options to change the marquee and text colors as well as change the direction and speed of the scrolling text. As with most moving objects on a Web page, using this tag sparingly is good advice in order to not scare visitors away.

For those gazillions of Windows users out there, Internet Explorer now recognizes bitmap graphic files (.bmp), the Windows graphic format of choice, as opposed to all other browsers that only support .gif and .jpg files. Also added to Internet Explorer 3.0 is the recognition of animated .gif files, which are built-in layers using an animated .gif utility. (Check the Web for the several very good freeware apps for both Windows and Macintosh.) The animated .gif files are displayed as the browser recognizes the layers and loads them in succession, which creates the animated effect.

Internet Explorer has also enhanced a few of Netscape's own inventions along the way, namely the <TABLE> and <FRAME> tags. With tables, Internet Explorer added some of its own attributes that allow designers to add color to individual table cells (see the "Tables" section), as well as allowing them to control the look and color of the borders in and around a table. Now, with Internet Explorer version 3.0, Microsoft is reaching even further to widen the gap between Internet Explorer and Navigator, starting with frames. Explorer didn't just stop at the standard frame tags and attributes that were already in place. Instead, Microsoft created "floating" frames (see the "Frames and Floating Frames" section of this chapter).

Internet Explorer's new style sheets (an HTML 3.2 proposal) are a powerful way of adding text and paragraph formatting to HTML pages. Using style sheets, authors can specify font sizes in points, set margins and indents, and change link colors, which are then propagated throughout one Web page, sections of a Web page, or an entire Web site (see Figure 28.1).

The good news resulting from Microsoft and Netscape battling each other is that those of us who design and author Web pages end up winning in the end. I, for one, am very happy that there are two quality Web browsers on the market. The only tough part is keeping up on which browser supports which extension and creating work-arounds for the browser that doesn't support the other's tag. That is why this chapter helps you—maybe for the first time—to have a good list of Microsoft's Internet Explorer-only HTML extensions and proposed HTML extensions for the latest version 3.0.

This chapter describes Microsoft Internet Explorer-only tags and attributes—not *all* of the tags it supports. Therefore, in order to fully design sites using these tags and the rest of the common HTML tags, you should also see Chapter 25, "HyperText Markup Language (HTML)."

> **NOTE**
>
> HTML tags are not case-sensitive. I prefer to use uppercase in my programming, so that is what I used in this chapter.

The \<BODY\> of the Page

`<BODY> : </BODY>`

The `<BODY>` tag surrounds all HTML tags within the body of the document. You place the `<BODY>` tag just beneath the `<HTML>` tag, and you place the `</BODY>` tag just above `</HTML>` at the end of a document. Any changes to the background, text colors, and the margins of the document (for Internet Explorer attributes) are specified within the `<BODY>` tag.

\<BODY BACKGROUND= BGPROPERTIES=\>

The `BGPROPERTIES` attribute can only be used in conjunction with the `BACKGROUND` tag, and it has only one value: `FIXED`. Basically, this attribute holds the background graphic so that it does not scroll down with the rest of the content.

\<BODY BGSOUND SRC=\>

The `BGSOUND` tag enables a Web designer to play a sound file (music, voice, sound effect, and so on) without the visitor having to actually click on anything. The sound file loads last (after graphics and text) and immediately starts playing. The available attributes are as follows:

```
<BODY BGSOUND= LOOP=>
```

The LOOP attribute defines the number of times the sound file is to play, as in the following example:

```
LOOP="2"
```

To make the sound file play continuously, use this command:

```
LOOP="infinite"
```

Paragraph and Text Style Tags

One of the drawbacks to early HTML is the limitation on font usage and control of text (that is, margin settings and so on). Although there have been many advances in this area in recent times, Internet Explorer 3.0 has taken the first major step to provide solutions for Web designers. The <STYLE> tag and its attributes enable the author to specify fonts (more than one so that the browser scans the user's system and finds one that is loaded), margin sizes, indents, and more.

<STYLE> : </STYLE>

The Style Sheets tag is a proposed HTML 3.2 tag that enables the author to change font sizes in points, set margins, change link colors, and more—all within a section of a document, on the whole Web page, or throughout an entire document by linking to an external style sheet (see the section, "Using an External <STYLE> Sheet").

NOTE

Unlike most HTML tags, the <STYLE> tag places its attributes within the beginning and ending tags rather than <STYLE=attribute>, like this:

```
<STYLE>
H1 {font: 14pt Arial bold}
P {font: 10pt Arial}
</STYLE>
```

The preceding code specifies that the <H1> : </H1> tag should be displayed in Arial bold 14 point, and the <P> tag should display paragraph text as Arial 10 point.

Here is the attribute format to be used within the <STYLE> tags:

```
P {font: 14pt Helvetica; text-indent: 1in}
```

First is the tag. (Notice that there are no brackets < around the tag.) The tag is followed by the attributes in brackets ({). To apply more than one attribute, you simply use a semicolon.

The available attributes for the STYLE tag are as follows:

font:

This attribute specifies font attributes such as bold, italic, font size/font leading, and list of font names.

This attribute sets many font properties within the same attribute tag. You can specify more than one font, separated by commas. If the first font is not available, the next one will be tried, and so on until a font is found on the visitor's machine. Here are examples:

```
font: 12pt Arial
```

```
font: italic 12pt "Arial,Helvetica"
```

font-family:

This attribute chooses which font family should be used to display paragraph text. As for the previous attribute, you can specify a list of font names separated by commas. Here is an example:

```
font-family: Times New Roman
```

font-size:

This attribute enables you to select font sizes in four different integers: inches (`in`), centimeters (`cm`), pixels (`px`), or the most popular, points (`pt`). Here are examples:

```
font-size: 14pt
```

or

```
font-size: 5px
```

font-weight:

This attribute is not for weight in pounds. The only two values at this time are bold and normal.

font-style:

For this attribute, italic is the only value currently supported.

text-decoration:

This attribute sets text decoration. Values include none, underline, italic, or line-through. Here is an example:

```
text-decoration: underline
```

28

> **TIP**
>
> This attribute can be useful if you want to turn off link underlining: Simply set text-decoration to none.

background:

This attribute sets a color or image behind text to highlight it. Values are RGB codes (#FFFFFF), color names (WHITE), or a URL (/images/background.gif). Here are examples:

```
background: GRAY
```

or

```
background: "/images/background.gif"
```

margin-left: and **margin-right:**

These attributes set the left and right margins. As with the previous attributes, values can be in inches (in), centimeters (cm), or pixels (px). Here are examples:

```
margin-left: 1in
```

```
margin-right: 25px
```

text-align:

This attribute is pretty straightforward. It uses the values left, right, and center.

text-indent:

This attribute enables the author to indent a block of text using the common integers used by previous attributes (inches, centimeters, and pixels). Here is an example:

```
text-indent: .025in
```

<SPAN> : </SPAN>

Another way to change text within an area of a document is to use this attribute. Span doesn't really do anything itself; it simply specifies a select area of text, like this:

```
<SPAN STYLE="text-indent: .5in">
```

> **NOTE**
>
> The STYLE tag can also be used within paragraph tags, like this:
> ```
> <P STYLE="font-size:32pt>
> ➥The paragraph within these beginning and ending tags will be
> ➥displayed in 32 point type.</P>
> ```

Using <STYLE> Attributes for an Entire Document

To use attributes within the <STYLE> tags for an entire HTML page, the <STYLE> tags and attributes must be placed after the <HTML> tag but before the <BODY> tag, like this:

```
<HTML>
<HEAD><TITLE>My web page!</TITLE></HEAD>
<STYLE>
BODY {background: white; color: blue}
H1 {font: 16pt Futura bold}
A {text-decoration: none; color: red}
</STYLE>
<BODY>
```

Using an External <STYLE> Sheet

If you want to have a specific <STYLE> sheet for an entire Web site and you don't want to have to place the attributes on every page, here's the answer.

You need to create a text file with the extension .css and have it include only the attributes that normally go between the <STYLE> tags, such as these:

```
BODY {background: white; color: blue}
H1 {font: 16pt Futura bold}
A {text-decoration: none; color: red}
```

Then, within the <HEAD> tags of all of the documents that you want to have the style sheet attributes, place the link to your new style sheet, like this:

```
<HTML>
<HEAD>
<TITLE>My web page!</TITLE>
<LINK REL=STYLE TYPE="text/css" SRC="/styles/style1.css">
</HEAD>
<BODY>
```

<FONT FACE=>

The FACE attribute enables you to actually specify a font from the machine on which the browser is installed. The author can actually select several fonts separated by commas. This is an Internet Explorer-only tag. Here is an example:

```
<FONT FACE="Times, Futura, Friz Quadrata>TNT Media</FONT>
```

If the user's machine does not have any of the fonts installed, the browser simply displays TNT Media in the default font as set in the user's browser preferences.

NOTE

One of the good things about using the <FONT> tag or the font-family: and font: attributes is that they are safe to use. This is true because they enable you to choose several fonts. Therefore, if the first font isn't available on the visitor's machine, the machine chooses the next one, and so on. If none of the fonts are available, the machine ignores the tag or attribute altogether and uses the visitor's browser's default font. So, you can only win by utilizing these features. Your design will succeed either way without showing an error or broken page.

The simple example in the following HTML code shows the different font (Arial) and the indentation of text (.05 inches) for the display shown in Figure 28.1:

```
<HTML>
<HEAD><TITLE>Figure 28.1</TITLE></HEAD>
<STYLE>
BODY {background: white; color: black}
H1 {font: 24pt Arial bold}
P {font: 14pt Arial; text-indent: .05in}
A {text-decoration: none; color: red}
</STYLE>
<BODY>
<P>The body text is indented .05 inch and is displayed in 14pt Arial.
<CENTER>
<H1>Here's a headline in 18-point Arial bold!</H1>
<P><A HREF="http://www.tntmedia.com">Check out our web site!</A>
</CENTER>
<P>Notice that the above link is not underlined because text-decoration was set
➥to "none" (unless you have your browser's preference set to
➥"no underlined links").</P>
</BODY>
</HTML>
```

FIGURE 28.1.

A display of different fonts and indentations of text.

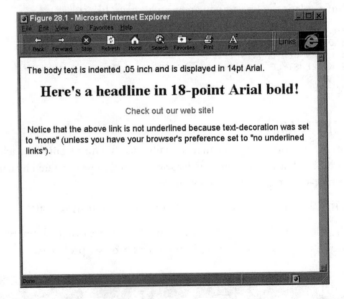

Color Values

Previously, to specify a color value, you either had to have a chart of HTML-supported color tags (Pantone's RGB values) or you had to keep running to an HTML resource Web site to find the correct values. All of that has now changed because Explorer uses color names instead of the code values. Although Netscape Navigator currently supports the color names in Table 28.1 (and close to three dozen more), the list reflects Internet Explorer-only supported names as specified at the time of this writing so that if you are authoring Web sites specifically for Internet Explorer users, your colors will be correctly displayed.

Table 28.1. Pantone (RGB) color names.

Microsoft Internet Explorer supported color values	
aqua	black
blue	fuchsia
gray	green
lime	maroon
navy	olive
purple	red
silver	teal
yellow	white

Tables

When tables were introduced to HTML in 1995, it revolutionized the way text and graphics are displayed on Web pages. Before tables, there was very little anyone could do to constrain blocks of text in a readable format. Microsoft Internet Explorer 3.0 has taken over the table feature where Netscape Navigator left off. Changing the look of a table by manipulating the borders and colorizing individual cells or rows of cells has really enhanced this HTML tag.

<TABLE>

These Internet Explorer-only attributes give the Web author more control over how a user views the information within a table. With these attributes, an author can decide to highlight a certain cell to make a point by adding a color background behind that individual cell. Or an author can decide to make the tables on a page stand out from the rest by adding a background graphic behind the entire table. With these new attributes, you'll certainly find some new ideas to enhance your Web site.

<TABLE BGCOLOR=>

This attribute enables you to make the table background color different from the background of the rest of the HTML document. As with other color attributes, the value is either RGB codes or color names (refer to Table 28.1). Individual table cells can be changed even from the table background color by adding the BGCOLOR attribute to the individual cell.

`<TABLE BACKGROUND=>`

With Internet Explorer 3.0, authors can now place a graphic behind an entire table for a very unique effect. Just as with the BACKGROUND attribute in the `<BODY>` tag, you simply point to the URL of the graphic, like this:

```
<TABLE BACKGROUND="images/bg-graphic.jpg">
```

`<TABLE RULES=ROWS>`

Use this attribute if you want borders only between the table rows. For borders only between the columns, use RULES=COLS. To create a table with no borders inside the rows and columns (the BORDER= attribute still defines the outside border), use RULES=NONE.

`<TABLE BORDERCOLOR= BORDERCOLORLIGHT= BORDERDARK=>`

These attributes enable you to change the color of the border surrounding the table. Again, the values are in RGB code or color names (refer to Table 28.1). BORDERCOLOR shades the middle part of the border, and BORDERCOLORLIGHT and BORDERCOLORDARK give the border a 3-D effect.

`<TABLE VALIGN=>`

This attribute sets the vertical alignment of text within its cell for the whole table. Values are TOP, BOTTOM, and MIDDLE.

> **NOTE**
>
> Because the `<TR>` and `<TD>` tags use the same attributes, I decided to avoid confusion by showing examples using only the `<TD>` tags. Again, all of these attributes can be used with the `<TR>` tag as well.

`<TD>`

Table Data (`<TD>`) and Table Rows (`<TR>`) are simple tags, yet they can be used to really enhance information that is displayed in tables. The following attributes for Internet Explorer show that Microsoft has taken tables to another level so that you, the author, can design a table much as you would design a Web site (you can decide how you want it to look). Until these attributes were introduced in 1996, authors were stuck with simple, boring tables. Now, you can add color and boldness to your information.

`<TD BGCOLOR=>`

As described previously, this attribute sets the color of the cells within the current row. Values are RGB code and color names.

`<TD VALIGN=BASELINE>`

This attribute is used to align the baselines of different font sizes of text in a table.

`<TD BACKGROUND=>`

As with the `<TABLE>` attribute, you can use this attribute to place a graphic behind an individual cell.

`<TD BORDERCOLOR= BORDERCOLORLIGHT= BORDERCOLORDARK=>`

These attributes enable you to change the color of the border of the cells in the current row. Again, the values are in RGB code or color names (refer to Table 28.1). BORDERCOLOR shades the middle part of the border, and BORDERCOLORLIGHT and BORDERCOLORDARK give the border a 3-D effect.

Multimedia: Audio, Video, Applications

Microsoft's Internet Explorer used to play catch-up to Netscape's Navigator. With the release of Internet Explorer 3.0, however, it has taken a leap ahead of Navigator in the area of multimedia. Some of the features that these tags represent can be used when you are authoring for Navigator, but the tags for them are cryptic and often require plug-ins and knowledge of Java or other programming languages. Internet Explorer has given authors easy-to-use tags that simply make adding multimedia to their Web pages much easier.

`<BGSOUND>`

The `<BGSOUND>` tag allows browsers using Internet Explorer to hear audio clips in the background while viewing a Web document. Because no file needs to be downloaded and separately played (all of this is done behind the scenes within Internet Explorer), this command makes it quick and easy to add a voice greeting or a pleasant musical intro to your site. All other browsers simply ignore this tag, so it will not cause any problems when someone using another browser visits it.

> **TIP**
>
> It is easy to go overboard with this tag. Many times, depending on the speed of the visitor's modem, the Web page will not fully load until the audio file is completely downloaded. So, naturally, if someone is using a slow Internet connection, the wait can be extremely frustrating. Find a good audio editing application and edit the sound file (both in length and in frequency) until it is a more reasonable file size.

The <BGSOUND> tag has the following attributes:

<BGSOUND SRC=>

This is a required attribute for the <BGSOUND> tag. As with other SRC attributes, this specifies the URL of the sound file. Only three different types of sound files are supported: .wav, .au, and MIDI files.

<BGSOUND LOOP=>

This attribute specifies the amount of times that the sound file is played. The two optional values are a numerical value

```
<BGSOUND SRC="/audio/soundfile.wav" LOOP="8">
```

or

```
<BGSOUND SRC="/audio/soundfile.wav" LOOP="INFINITE">
```

The "INFINITE" value makes the sound file loop continuously as long as the page is loaded on the screen.

<MARQUEE> : </MARQUEE>

This tag creates text that scrolls across the screen. <MARQUEE> is very similar to the JavaScript effect in which the text scrolls at the bottom of the browser frame, but with <MARQUEE> you have much more control over where on the page the action takes place, as well as other advantages discussed under the following attributes. The available attributes are as follows:

<MARQUEE ALIGN=>

The <MARQUEE> tag is treated as an image, so this attribute allows text to flow around it. It accepts the values TOP, MIDDLE, and BOTTOM.

<MARQUEE BEHAVIOR=>

In order to control the direction, style, and duration of the text, you need the BEHAVIOR attribute. It accepts the following values: SCROLL, which makes the text come in from one side or the other and is specified with the DIRECTION attribute; SLIDE, which causes the marquee to start with an empty box in which the text stops so that it is visible; and ALTERNATE, which causes the text to start fully visible in the box and reverse when it reaches the end of the box.

<MARQUEE DIRECTION=>

This sets the direction in which the text flows onto the screen. The values are LEFT (default) and RIGHT.

`<MARQUEE LOOP=>`

As with the LOOP attribute in `<BGSOUND>`, this attribute defines how many times the marquee is shown. Again, the values are either numerical (1, 2, 3, and so on) or INFINITE for never-ending repetition.

`<MARQUEE BGCOLOR=>`

As with all other BGCOLOR attributes, this allows the specification of the background color in the marquee box. Accepted values are RGB code (#FFFFFF) or color names.

`<MARQUEE HEIGHT= WIDTH=>`

These attributes determine the size of the marquee box. If these attributes are not used, the marquee box will extend the entire width of the browser display window and be just tall enough to enclose the height of the text. Values are either in pixels (200) or percentage of the browser display window (50%).

`<MARQUEE HSPACE= VSPACE=>`

These attributes allow space between the marquee and the surrounding text. Values are given in pixels, like this:

```
<MARQUEE HSPACE="5" VSPACE="5">
```

This would create a 5-pixel space around the marquee.

`<MARQUEE SCROLLAMOUNT= SROLLDELAY=>`

Use these attributes for controlling the smoothness or quickness of the marquee text. SCROLLAMOUNT values are given in pixels, with lower numbers creating slow but smooth movement and larger numbers creating fast and jerky motion.

SCROLLDELAY specifies the number of milliseconds in which the text waits between successive scrolling. Larger numbers create slower delays, and lower numbers make quicker movements.

Because it's difficult to show scrolling text in a figure, I opted to at least show you what a colored (BGCOLOR=) marquee box would look like with this sample code:

```
<HTML>
<HEAD><TITLE>Figure 28.2</TITLE></HEAD>
<BODY BGCOLOR="BLUE">
<CENTER>
<PRE>
</PRE>
<MARQUEE BEHAVIOR=SLIDE LOOP=1 WIDTH=60% BGCOLOR=WHITE>This is a MARQUEE
➥with the background color white.</MARQUEE>
</CENTER>
</BODY>
</HTML>
```

28

EXPLORER-ONLY HTML TAGS

Notice in the preceding HTML code that I specified the width as 60 percent of the browser window, but I did not specify the height. This caused the marquee box to simply be as tall as the text. (See Figure 28.2.)

FIGURE 28.2.

A sample marquee box.

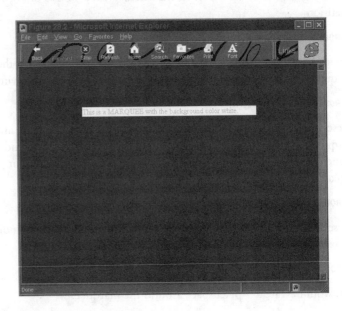

Frames and Floating Frames

Again, as with the Table feature, Internet Explorer has enhanced this Netscape invention to give the author more control over the way his Web design is viewed. Frames enable the visitor to link to other sites and or other pages while the "framework" of the current site (usually in the form of navigation buttons or logos) remains around the viewing area. This is a very powerful tool for authors who want to give the visitor freedom to link elsewhere, yet don't want to lose the visitor to "Web surfing."

<FRAMESET>

This tag specifies the area of an individual frame (which displays an individual HTML page inside it). Creative authoring can provide a site with some interesting combinations of frames that give the visitor freedom to navigate throughout the site while keeping the navigating tools at hand at all times.

<FRAMESET FRAMESPACING=>

This attribute enables you to create spacing borders (in pixels) between frames.

> **TIP**
>
> Use the value 0 to delete the 3-D looking borders between frames, creating a seamless look to your frame document, like this:
>
> ```
> <FRAMESET FRAMEBORDER="0" FRAMESPACING="0">
> ```

Floating Frames

`<IFRAME>`

This new Explorer 3.0 tag creates a "floating" window (frame) into which you place a URL (Web page address). Although this looks like a separate Web browser-like window, the tag actually launches a separate small (depending on the size attributes) browser window that allows the visitor to link to other sites within this window just like the full-size browser window that is open beneath it.

Don't let the name fool you, though. The name, *floating frames*, makes it sound like you can move the box around—but you can't. Rather, the *floating* pertains to the fact that you can place this mini-browser window anywhere in your document (similar to placing a graphic) in order to show an example, link to another site, and so on.

This tag must be placed within the `<BODY>` and `</BODY>` tags. Most of the common frame attributes apply to this tag as well (such as VALIGN, VSPACE, SCROLLING, and so on), although many features and rules will be in place when the final version of Internet Explorer 3.0 is released. (At the time of this writing, it is still in beta testing.)

For example, the following tag and attributes create a 250×250 pixel floating frame:

```
<IFRAME WIDTH=250 HEIGHT=250 SRC="float.html">
```

You can also use percentage values to create a floating frame that is in relation to the current Explorer window, as follows:

```
<IFRAME WIDTH=60% HEIGHT=60% SRC="float.html">
```

> **TIP**
>
> If you want the Web page that appears in the floating frame to be aligned with the top and left side of the floating frame, use this attribute in the `<BODY>` tag of the Web page inside the floating frame:
>
> ```
> <BODY TOPMARGIN=0 LEFTMARGIN=0>
> ```
>
> If you want a 5-pixel space between the top and left sides of the floating frame, do this:
>
> ```
> <BODY TOPMARGIN=5 LEFTMARGIN=5>
> ```

The following HTML code places a simple 500×300 pixel floating frame on a page. You'll notice that there is an extra frame tag within the `<IFRAME>` and `</IFRAME>` tags. Microsoft recommends this when used within a `<FRAME>` document so that Internet Explorer 2.0 users will be able to view the frame.

```
<HTML>
<HEAD><TITLE>Figure 28.3</TITLE></HEAD>
<BODY BGCOLOR="WHITE">
<CENTER>
<P><FONT SIZE=5>Here's a floating frame!
<IFRAME WIDTH=500 HEIGHT=300 SRC="http://www.tntmedia.com/">
   <FRAME WIDTH=500 HEIGHT=300 SRC="http://www.tntmedia.com/">
</IFRAME>
</CENTER>
</BODY>
</HTML>
```

In this example, you can see that there is actually another little browser window embedded into the Web page (see Figure 28.3). Notice the scrollbar on the left side. When writing the HTML code, keep in mind the pixel width and height. If the page you are pointing to is larger than the area you have specified, you will have scrollbars on the right and bottom of the floating frame, showing only the upper-left portion of the page within the frame.

FIGURE 28.3.

An example of a floating frame.

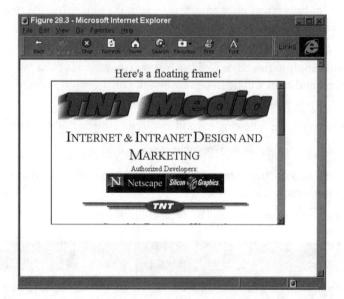

Summary

Overall, these new Internet Explorer features and enhancements are very encouraging. Instead of trying to outdo Netscape's Navigator, Microsoft obviously listened to Web authors and added to what was already there rather than reinventing the wheel.

The easy-to-use multimedia tags are sure to catch on with Web authors of all skill levels because they are easier to implement than programming Java or other cryptic languages.

As the browser wars continue, it seems that Web authors will certainly have to keep on their toes and watch for the latest features. From the information you learned in this chapter, you can probably see that multimedia, whether it be audio, video, or floating frames, is dominating the Web at a fast clip. Make sure that you aren't left behind by learning which browser recognizes the new tags and more important, what happens when someone visits using another browser that doesn't support the new tags. The one thing you don't want to do is alienate someone from your site just because he isn't using your favorite browser.

Keep that in mind, make sure you accommodate everyone you can, and you should have no trouble designing world-class Web sites.

28

EXPLORER-ONLY
HTML TAGS

Shockwave and Lingo

by Richard Wainess

IN THIS CHAPTER

What Is Shockwave?

If you've ever heard of Shockwave, you probably think it's a powerful tool for creating interactive multimedia for the Internet or intranets (*intranets* are private networks that use Internet and WWW standards). Well, you're wrong. First of all, Shockwave is not a development tool; it's a runtime routine. Second, there are three different Shockwaves. Two are runtime routines for multimedia applications. (Actually, one is for a multimedia application, and one is for a computer-based training, or CBT, application.) The third version is for a graphics package. Confusing? Don't worry; the situation is not as complicated as it sounds.

> **NOTE**
>
> At the time of this writing, Shockwave Audio Streaming and Shockwave for Xres were released.

When you hear the word *Shockwave*, think Shockwave and Afterburner. They go hand in hand. Afterburner is the application that works with the authoring and design applications to turn them into Internet-ready pieces. Shockwave is a browser plug-in that enables these applications to play on an Internet Web site or on an intranet. When I say "these applications," I'm referring specifically to three programs from Macromedia, Inc.: Macromedia Director, Macromedia Authorware, and Macromedia Freehand. Although Shockwave is not a development tool, it does enable the applications that have been shocked to include Web-related commands, such as the loading of HTML pages, and to become interactive tools for the World Wide Web.

What exactly are the three packages that can be shocked? Director is a multimedia authoring package, Authorware is a CBT authoring package, and Freehand is a vector-based draw package. Even though Freehand is, in its standard form, a static application, Afterburner for Freehand enables Freehand's vectored objects to contain hypertext links, turning them into hotspots capable of providing jumps to HTML documents.

Throughout this chapter, you will see the word *currently* quite often. Shockwave is a new technology and is rapidly improving and expanding. Each week Macromedia posts news on updates and changes to its Shockwave technology, including new Macromedia products capable of being shocked and new browsers capable of playing shocked applications. Visit Macromedia, Inc., regularly, at `http://www.macromedia.com` to stay current with Shockwave developments.

System Requirements

As with all applications, Shockwave and Afterburner have system requirements. Because Afterburner is an extension of the authoring package, if you own Director, Authorware, or Freehand, you have met Afterburner's system requirements. Of more concern are the system requirements for Shockwave (the browser plug-in).

Shockwave

Shockwave is an Internet browser plug-in that was developed by Macromedia to enable users to view and interact with Web-based multimedia files. Shockwave currently supports the following platforms:

For Director:	Mac PPC and 68K; Windows 3.1 and 95
For Authorware:	Mac PPC and 68K; Windows 3.1 and 95, NT 3.5.1
For Freehand:	Mac PPC and 68K; Windows 3.1 and 95, NT 3.5.1

At the time this book was written, Shockwave plug-ins were available for Netscape 2.0 and 2.01, and for browsers compatible with Netscape plug-ins, and Microsoft's Internet Explorer 3.0 and Internet Starter Kit (Shockwave for ActiveX is also included in Microsoft's Windows 95 OEM Kit). However, plug-ins are currently in development for CompuServe's NetLauncher, America Online's Navisoft, and for Silicon Graphic's UNIX-based computers. Additionally, Netscape has chosen Shockwave as its *de facto* multimedia standard and will include the Shockwave code in all future Netscape browsers, alleviating the need for the plug-in.

> **NOTE**
>
> Macromedia, Inc., at `http://www.macromedia.com` updates its compatibility list weekly.

Shockwave for Director (4.0*x* and 5)

Up until now, I have talked about Shockwave as a Netscape plug-in and Explorer ActiveX component for various Macromedia applications. Now, you'll examine each application and the power they bring to the Internet. I'll begin with Director.

Director is a powerful multimedia authoring tool. It has two components: a design package capable of creating sophisticated animations and an extremely powerful programming language, called Lingo. Lingo contains the core of Director's power and adds complex interactive and decision-making components to an already robust design tool.

Afterburner

After you create a Director movie, you must turn it into a shocked movie before it can play on the Internet. Afterburner is the Macromedia application that accomplishes this task. During the conversion process, Afterburner also compresses the Director movie (by an average of 60 percent, and often much more), which assists in keeping the file small. Afterburner is available on all current Macromedia platforms—Windows 3.1, Windows 95, Windows NT, Mac, and PowerPC.

Adding a Shocked Movie to an HTML Document

To add a shocked movie to an HTML document, you use an HTML EMBED tag. In its simplest form, the EMBED tag for a Director Shockwave movie looks something like the following:

```
<EMBED SRC="myMovie.dcr" WIDTH=320 HEIGHT=240 palette=background>
```

The EMBED tag comprises several components.

<EMBED SRC>

The tag begins with <EMBED SRC="??????".

The phrase SRC= refers to the source, or filename, of the shocked file to appear (that is, to be embedded) on the Web page. The filename (in quotes) follows the equal sign (for example, <EMBED SRC="MyDirectorFile.dcr").

WIDTH and HEIGHT

Next come the WIDTH and HEIGHT tags, which refer to the actual pixel size of the files. ALL shocked files must include these two tags.

PALETTE

Director uses the PALETTE= tag, followed by either foreground or background (for example, PALETTE=foreground).

Foreground causes Director to load the movie's palette. The palette is then used for the whole Web page. This palette, of course, affects the colors of all elements on the page and must be planned carefully in order to achieve the expected result.

Background causes Director to ignore its internal palette(s) and to use the computer's system palette.

If you do not include the EMBED tag, Director uses PALETTE=foreground as the default.

If you do include the EMBED tag, PALETTE=background is the default.

NOTE

As with all HTML tags, the EMBED tag ends with >.

Broken Icons

Unfortunately, the world is not a simple place, and neither is HTML programming. If everyone had a Shockwave-compatible browser and the Shockwave plug-in, the EMBED tag would be all that was needed in the HTML document. But many browsers, many versions of browsers, many platforms, and many operating systems are in use. If your browser does not support shocked files, you will see a broken icon on your Web page.

JavaScript

Fortunately, you can avoid broken icons simply by using JavaScript. Don't worry: You don't have to become a Java programmer to avoid broken icons. You will be given a simple template to follow. But before you look at the template, look a little more closely at the problem the template addresses.

HTML is a perceptive, or forgiving, language. Typically, languages either see something they understand, they display an error message, or they crash. Browsers, however, just ignore any HTML code they do not understand, and that behavior is the key to the EMBED tag.

When most browsers come across the EMBED tag, they have no idea what to do with it. Consequently, they ignore the tag, or at least they try. Unfortunately, some of the items within the EMBED tag can't be ignored—particularly the SRC tag. When a browser sees the SRC tag, it tries to display the object referenced. In the case of a Shockwave file, the browser tries to display the file. However, a browser that isn't familiar with the object type will display a broken icon in its place.

Netscape Navigator 1.1*x* has a different reaction to the EMBED tag. That browser recognizes the EMBED tag as an OLE link under Windows 3.1. However, the object does not conform to the expected model, so Navigator will display a broken icon.

Currently, the only browser that knows what to do with a shocked file is Netscape Navigator version 2.0. To that browser, the EMBED tag signifies that a plug-in (in this case, the Shockwave plug-in) will process the content within the tag. If you have the plug-in installed, you will see the shocked file. If not, you will see a broken icon.

Now comes JavaScript. JavaScript is a programming language that is built into Netscape Navigator 2.0. The key to JavaScript is HTML comment tags, `<!-->` and `<-->`. When all other browsers see the comment tags, they ignore anything within those tags. When Netscape 2.0

sees a comment tag that is prefaced by `<SCRIPT LANGUAGE="JavaScript">`, it will read the information inside the comment tags. The format for Shockwave files is

```
<SCRIPT LANGUAGE="JavaScript">
<!-- Information inside this comment area is only recognized by Navigator 2.0.
document.write( '<EMBED SRC="shockedfile" WIDTH=x HEIGHT=y>' );
<!-- This ends the hidden JavaScript from non-Navigator 2.0 Browsers -->
</SCRIPT>
```

Replace the (`'<EMBED SRC="shockedfile" WIDTH=x HEIGHT=y>'`); as described earlier in this section.

You've almost taken care of the broken icon problem. Yes, you've eliminated the broken icons. For browsers that don't recognize JavaScript and don't have the Shockwave plug-in, what does the Web page display in place of the shocked file? With the preceding command, nothing, because you have not given HTML any display alternatives. Usually, when a graphic is to be displayed on a Web page, the `SRC="graphic"` command is followed by an `ALT="text string"` command. Because not all browsers are capable of displaying graphics or a particular graphic format, the `ALT` command enables you to display alternative text in place of the graphic, for browsers that don't understand the particular graphic format. Because JavaScript is hidden with a comment section, only browsers capable of reading JavaScript will see and display the shocked image. Fortunately, there is a solution to this problem.

The NOEMBED Tag

Netscape Navigator ignores anything it encounters between the `<NOEMBED>` and `</NOEMBED>` tags. Other browsers, however, will read any tags within this area, which is where the solution to a missing alternate graphic exists.

By placing an alternative to the Shockwave file between the `<NOEMBED>` and `</NOEMBED>` tags, non-Navigator 2.0 browsers will display the alternative on the HTML document. The format is as follows:

```
<SCRIPT LANGUAGE="JavaScript">
<!-- Information inside this comment area is only recognized by Navigator 2.0.
document.write( '<EMBED SRC="shockedFile" WIDTH=x HEIGHT=y>' );
<!-- This ends the hidden JavaScript from non-Navigator 2.0 Browsers -->
</SCRIPT>
<NOEMBED>
<IMG SRC="alternativeFile" WIDTH=a HEIGHT=b>
</NOEMBED>
```

Replace the (`'<EMBED SRC="shockedfile" WIDTH=x HEIGHT=y>'`); as described earlier.

Replace it with `<IMG SRC="alternativeFileName" WIDTH=a HEIGHT=b>`, using the width, height, and name of an alternative JPEG, GIF, or PNG image file.

Multiple Movies

Netscape enables you to include as many shocked movies as you wish on an HTML page. However, the way Director works with shocked movies is to place the entire movie into RAM before it can play. As you add more movies to a page, you need more RAM. Because pages might be accessed by computers with limited RAM, Macromedia recommends placing no more than three movies per page.

After the browser loads a new page, the Shockwave plug-in removes the previous movies from RAM. If you want to have numerous movies on your Web site, try to limit yourself to three movies per page and use as many pages as you need.

Multiple Movies Utilizing Sound

Sometimes Netscape has problems playing sound tracks (called *sound channels*) from two or more shocked movies at the same time. To avoid these problems, either include sound on just one movie on a page or require the user to trigger a sound from the movies with mouse clicks.

Looping

Although you can easily program a Director movie to loop constantly, this process can tie up the user's computer processor. I recommend that you include either an active Stop button or a counter in the shocked movie to limit the number of times the movie can loop.

Asynchronous Operations

Developers can create multimedia applications entirely, or almost entirely, using just the design and animation portion of the Director package. Typically, such an application supports little or no user interaction—for example, a simple animated fish tank. If you were developing a Web site for an aquarium company, you could use Director in this way to spice up a simple non-interactive site with a dynamic design element. Just create the animation and use Afterburner to turn it into a shocked movie. Fish will leisurely swim about the fish tank on the Web site.

Most developers, however, use Lingo to add control and interactivity to Director movies. Lingo, as Director's programming language, adds the capability of clicking buttons, branching choices, controlling animations, and much more. For example, you could use Lingo to enable viewers to select various fish (tropical, saltwater) or to view photos of various fish tanks. Lingo enables you to turn your Web sites into interactive experiences.

You can also use Lingo to incorporate Web-related commands into shocked movies. For example, viewers could click an Order button that would take them to a new HTML page where they could fill out an order form.

Although Lingo has over 200 commands, numerous additional Web-related commands—*extensions*—have been added to the Lingo language for creating shocked Web sites.

You can divide these extensions into asynchronous operations and functions.

> **NOTE**
>
> Shockwave for Director versions 4.0x and 5 have a great deal in common. However, the Director 5 version offers additional commands and control. In the following section, I note Director 5-only commands and functions.

getNetText uri

`getNetText uri` is the Lingo command that retrieves an HTTP text item for Lingo to read.

> **NOTE**
>
> Although Lingo is not case-sensitive, protocol dictates starting all Lingo commands in lowercase and beginning all other words within a group command phrase in uppercase (for example, `startMovie` or `mouseDown`).

The URI portion of the command refers to the universal resource identifier. Universal resource locators (URLs) are a subcategory of URIs, as are file extensions.

An example of the `getNetText uri` command is

```
getNetText "http://mywebsite.com/newsletter.text"
```

> **NOTE**
>
> The `NetDone` command determines if the `getNetText` command has finished.

gotoNetMovie uri

The `gotoNetMovie uri` command enables one Director movie to call, and be replaced by, another Director movie. The new shocked movie appears in the same place on the page as the first movie. When the command is called, the first movie continues to play until the second movie is fully loaded into RAM. Then, the first movie stops and is instantly replaced by the new movie.

The uri defines the location and name of the new movie.

An example of the gotoNetMovie command is

```
gotoNetMovie "http://mywebsite.com/movies/mynextmovie.dcr"
```

> **NOTE**
>
> If you issue a second gotoNetMovie command before the first new movie has finished loading, the second command cancels the first command and the second gotoNetMovie command will be accomplished. In other words, you can change your mind after selecting a new movie and select a different new movie instead.

gotoNetPage uri, target

gotoNetPage uri is a Net-related Lingo extension that opens a new URI. The URI target does not have to be a Director movie. It can be another MIME type, such as an HTML page.

The target parameter is optional. It references a target frame if you have designed a page using the Netscape frame feature.

> **NOTE**
>
> Only Director 5 shocked movies support the target parameter.

preloadNetThing uri

The preloadNetThing uri Lingo command preloads an HTTP item into Netscape's disk cache so that you can access, or download, the item without any delays.

You need to keep a few things in mind when you use the preloadNetThing command. First, you have no way of knowing if the item has been removed from the disk cache. Also, you can load only one item at a time. If, for example, you want to load an HTML page containing a logo, two photos, and a shocked movie, you must load each item separately with its own preloadNetThing command.

An example of a preloadNetThing command is

```
preloadNetThing "http://mywebsite.com/graphics/logo.gif"
```

29

**SHOCKWAVE
AND LINGO**

Functions

Functions return a result based upon the preceding asynchronous commands. Macromedia added to Lingo a small group of functions that are specific to the Internet. They are referred to as *net functions*, and are identified by the inclusion of the letters net in their name.

netDone()

If the asynchronous operation is complete, netDone() returns a result of TRUE. netDone() returns a result of FALSE if the operation has been started, but has not finished. The netDone() command defaults to TRUE.

An example of the netDone() function is

```
If netDone() then puppetSound "Trumpet"
```

> **NOTE**
>
> The preceding example is the same as writing
>
> ```
> If netDone() = TRUE then puppetSound "Trumpet"
> ```
>
> netDone() and Netdone()=TRUE are equivalent.

netError()

netError() returns one of three results:

- If an operation has not finished, netError() returns an empty (netError()=EMPTY) string.
- If an operation has completed successfully, netError() returns OK (netError() = "OK").
- If an operation has not completed successfully, netError() returns a string that describes the error.

netTextResult()

netTextResult() returns the result of the getNetText command. An example of this command is

```
If netDone() then
        put netTextResult() into field "Headline"
end if
```

netMime()

netMime() returns the MIME type of an HTTP item. Only Director 5 shocked files support this function.

netLastModDate()

`netLastModDate()` returns the last modified date string located in the HTTP header for the item referenced. An example of this function is

```
put netLastModDate() into field "Page Updated On"
```

Only Director 5 shocked files support this command.

getLatestNetID()

`getLatestNetID()` returns a unique identifier describing the last asynchronous operation started. This function is handy when using the `netAbort` command or the `netDone()` function.

Other Lingo Extensions

In addition to `net`-related asynchronous commands and functions, one other `net`-related command has been added to Lingo.

netAbort

`netAbort` stops a Net operation that is in progress. Only Director 5 shocked movies support this command.

Director Commands Disabled for Shockwave

Although the good news is that additional Net-related commands were added for shocked movies, the bad news is that other Director commands have been disabled.

Although a variety of commands have been disabled, most of them relate to data transmission. The primary reasons for disabling commands are to prevent the transfer of viruses and to block the capability to read information off of a user's hard drive and transfer that information back through the shocked movie to a Web site. Lingo, like virtually all other programming languages, can read, write, and delete files. Therefore, if certain capabilities were not disabled, the shocked movies, via Lingo, would have access to users' hard drives, where they could extract information (upload local files, including both data and programs), delete information (delete local files and programs or entire drives), or introduce information (alter files, add files, add viruses).

The following commands have been disabled in Director 4.0*x* and Director 5 shocked movies.

Table 29.1 shows Director-related commands that open, close, paste, print, and save files.

Table 29.1. Disabled Director-related commands.

Command	Description
openResFile	This Mac-only command opens a specific resource file. Because shocked movies might be played in Windows or another operating system, this command has been disabled to prevent errors.
closeResFile	The counter command to the openResFile command closes a resource file that has been opened on a Mac. It has been disabled for the same reasons as the openResfile command.
open window	Director has the capability of playing a second movie inside of an opened Director movie. You can size this "windowed" movie from very small to large enough to occupy the entire screen size of the current movie.
	Because the Windows version of Shockwave currently has problems with Director windows, and because Netscape supports only Director windows if the EMBED command is used, this feature has been disabled. Macromedia is working to resolve this problem.
close window	This command closes an open Director window, but because opening Director windows has been disabled, this command is also disabled.
importFileInto	Castmembers (the objects—graphics, scripts, videos, and so on) that are used in a Director movie are all referred to as castmembers. Most often, all castmembers are saved inside of the Director movie. The importFileInto command enables an external file to be loaded into a castmember position of a Director movie, either replacing one of the movie's castmembers or adding a new castmember to the movie. As already mentioned, to maintain system integrity, all I/O or data transfer functions have been disabled; importFileInto falls into this category and has been disabled.
saveMovie	Because the content of the movie might change while it is being played (from importfileInto commands, data entry, and so on), Director enables you to save movies that are playing—that is, to retain the changes. Again, this function is an I/O or data transmission function, so this command has been disabled.

Command	Description
printFrom	The printFrom command enables the user to print a hard copy of the content of the stage, or what is being viewed by the user. This command has been disabled for two reasons. First, the user might not have a printer, or the printer might not be capable of printing graphical information. Second, some printer setups are designed to print to file, so the issue of I/O or data transmission occurs.
pasteFromClipboard member x	This command pastes the contents of the user's Clipboard into the castmember location specified by x. Director 5 adds castlib y to the end of the command, which enables the viewer to specify a castlibrary. As with all data transfer functions, this command has been disabled.

Table 29.2 shows system-related commands that are used to open and close programs.

Table 29.2. Disabled system-related commands.

Command	Description
open	This command is used to start, or launch, another application while the Director movie is playing. Because users might not have that particular application on their system or because they might not have enough RAM to run both applications, this feature has been disabled.
openDA	This Mac-only command opens a Mac desk accessory. (Windows ignores this command.)
	Not all Macs have the same accessories, so this function has been disabled.
closeDA	As the counterpart to the openDA command, closeDA has also been disabled.
quit	This command exits Director. In Windows, quit returns you to Program Manager; in Windows 95, it returns you to the main interface. On the Mac, quit returns you to Finder. Because quit will also close your browser, it has been disabled for shocked movies.
restart	On Macs, this command restarts the computer. This action is even more drastic than the quit command, so the reasons for disabling this command should also be obvious.

continues

Table 29.2. continued

Command	Description
shutDown	As with the quit and restart commands, this command has dramatic effects on the computer. On Macs, shutDown closes any applications that are open and then turns the computer off. In Windows, the shutDown command exits the Director movie (or Director, if in an authoring mode) and then exits Windows.

NOTE

As already stated, all I/O or data transmission commands have been disabled. This includes all commands relating to filenames and file paths.

Table 29.3 shows filename commands that return or alter filenames. Path commands return or locate file paths or define what local folder paths are to be searched.

Table 29.3. Disabled path and filename commands.

Command	Description
fileName of cast	This command changes the name of the externally linked file associated with a castmember.
fileName of Window	Because Director does not currently support windows, this command, which defines the name of the Director movie to be placed into the window, is also disabled.
getNthFileNameInFolder	This command returns the name of a file with a directory (Windows 3.*x*) or folder (Mac or Windows 95). The parameters of the command include a number that refers to the Nth file within that folder. This function has been disabled because it could enable a shocked movie to read filenames from a user's computer.
moviePath	This disabled command returns the pathname of the folder or directory in which the current movie is located.
pathName	This command is the same as the moviePath command.
searchCurrentFolder	This flag command can be set either to TRUE or to FALSE. If TRUE, Director searches the movie's current folder first, before searching any other folders (see searchPaths).
searchPaths	The searchPaths command defines the various paths that the Director movie may search in order to locate files.

Table 29.4 shows the MCI, a Windows-only feature that accesses Windows' media controller. Via the controller, media devices can be accessed and controlled by shocked movies. Although MCI is a single command, it has dozens of parameters for controlling the functions of various devices.

Table 29.4. Disabled MCI command.

Command	Description
mci	In a Windows environment, this command gives Director access to the Windows media controller and various media control functions, including recording sounds, triggering a video disk player, and playing music tracks on a CD-ROM. Because not all Windows systems are alike (for example, not everyone has a CD-ROM), this command has been disabled.

XObjects, XCMDs, XFCNs

XObjects, XCMDs, and XFCNs refer to external objects, commands, and functions. Although both Windows and Macs can use XObjects, only the Mac can use XCMDs and XFCNs.

XObjects enable third-party developers to create new features and enhancements for Director 4.0x. For example, Director 4.0x does not include database functions, but outside developers have used XObjects to add this feature.

Macromedia added an entirely new function, called Xtras, to Director 5. Xtras technology enables third-party developers to create and distribute sophisticated add-ons to Director, including new transitions, database management, sophisticated printing capabilities, and new commands.

XObjects, XCMDs, and XFCNs can be either internal (included within a Director movie) or external (referenced or pointed to by a Director movie). Shocked movies support only external XObjects, XCMDs, and XFCNs.

In order for a movie to use external XObjects, XCMDs, or XFCNs, these files must be located in the user's Plug-In directory. Users need to download the external files prior to using them in a shocked movie.

29
SHOCKWAVE
AND LINGO

NOTE

The purpose of this chapter is to introduce and explain Shockwave and programming as it applies to the Internet and intranets. Programming for XObjects, XCMDs and XFCNs is beyond the scope or intention of this chapter. Please refer to the Director manuals for instructions on how to use these features.

Disabled Director 5 Commands

Director 5 added a new feature called multiple casts. Although Director 4.0*x* used only one internal cast, Director 5 can open and use multiple external casts. This function enables you to have different casts for different languages or to divide casts by object type (for example, a digital movie cast, a script cast, a text cast, a graphics cast).

In some cases, Shockwave has entirely disabled these multiple cast functions. In other cases, Shockwave has limited the function. More specifically, shocked movies cannot specify paths for locating cast libraries. Shocked movies can use only cast libraries located in the Plug-In directory. To use multiple casts, allow users to download the additional casts and place them in their Plug-In directory.

Previously, commands that were disabled for both Director 4.*x* and 5 were described. Table 29.5 shows commands disabled only for Director 5 Shockwave. In most cases, these commands are disabled by Director 5 but not by Director 4.*x*, because they are commands new to Director 5.

Table 29.5. Disabled Director 5 commands.

Command	Description
OpenXLib	This command can access cast libraries in any path by specifying the complete path and filename. Because shocked movies can use the Plug-In directory only for locating cast libraries, just specify the filename, not a complete path.
CloseXLib	As the counterpart to the OpenXLib command, follow the same restrictions as for the OpenXLib command.
opencastlib x importFileInto member x of castlib y	This command is similar to the importFileInto command described earlier. The difference is that this command takes advantage of Director 5's multiple cast by enabling you to import a file type into both the movie's main, internal cast, and an external cast library. Because this is a data transmission function, this command has been disabled.
save castlib	This command enables Director to save cast libraries. Depending upon the parameters, Director either updates the original cast library or creates a new cast library.

Work Arounds for Other Director-Disabled Features

Director shocked movies do not support the score's tempo channel. The elements that appear on the screen (the stage) of a Director movie are placed onto Director's score. The score has spots (channels) for 48 items at any given moment. In addition to the 48 channels, known as *sprite channels,* Director has five other special channels: a script channel, two sound channels, a transition channel, a palette channel, and a tempo channel.

The tempo channel includes four features:

■ The capability to change the tempo, or speed, of the movie from 1 frame per second (fps) to 120 fps in 1fps increments

■ The capability to pause the movie for intervals of 1 to 60 seconds before proceeding

■ A toggle to turn on Director's internal function that makes the movie pause in a particular frame and not continue until someone either clicks a mouse button or touches a key

■ The capability to make the movie remain with one frame until either a sound in one of the two sound channels finishes or a digital movie (an AVI or MOV file) finishes playing in one of the sprite channels

Although this situation might seem to be somewhat limiting, it is not. You can use Lingo to re-create all the functions of the tempo channel. As a matter of fact, using Lingo affords even greater control of the functions. For example, the tempo channel enables the movie to pause in increments of one second only, but you can define Lingo pauses in 1/60 of a second increments. Another example of additional control through Lingo is the wait for mouse click or key press feature. Through Lingo, you can specify the mouse, a key, or both; you can specify either the left or right mouse button or both; or you can specify a key combination (such as Shift+Alt+A) that the user must press to continue with the movie.

The following are examples of Lingo work arounds for the tempo channel functions.

Wait (Seconds)

In this example, the movie will wait three seconds.

```
on exitframe
    startTimer -- this resets the timer to zero
    repeat while the timer < 3 * 60  -- the 60 represents 60 ticks per second
        nothing
    end repeat
    go to the frame
end
```

Mouse or Key Clicks

In the first example, the movie will wait for a mouse click, at which time it will advance to the next frame containing a marker.

29

```
on exitFrame
    go to the frame
end


on mouseDown
    go to next
end
```

A variation to the preceding scenario follows. Note that it uses only one handler instead of two.

```
on exitFrame
    if the mouseDown then
        go next
    else
        go to the frame
    end if
end
```

In the next example, the movie waits for a mouse click or any key to be pressed. (Note the third variation of the mouseDown line in the exitFrame handler.)

```
on exitFrame
    if the mouseDown then go next
    go to the frame
end

on keyDown
    go to next
end
```

In the final example, the movie waits for the F key to be pressed or for the right mouse button to be pressed on a PC or the Control Key/Mouse button combination on a Mac. (This command works only in Director 5.)

```
on exitFrame
    if the rightMouseDown or (the key = "f") then next
    go to the frame
end
```

> **NOTE**
>
> In order for the right mouse button feature to work, you must add the following phrase to the Director movie before you use the rightMouseDown command.
>
> ```
> set the emulateMultiButtonMouse to TRUE
> ```
>
> In a typical movie script, this phrase appears in the startMovie handler.

Tempo

You can use the `puppetTempo` command to change the tempo of a movie. The following example sets the movie's tempo to 30 fps when the movie begins playing.

```
on startMovie
    puppetTempo
end
```

Waiting for Sounds To Finish

Lingo uses the `soundbusy(x)` command to determine if a sound is still playing. Although the tempo channel can test only the two sound channels located in the score, the `soundbusy(x)` command can check all eight sound channels available to Director. The additional six channels can be activated only through the sound `playfile` command, but all eight are tested by the `soundbusy(x)` command. The following example tests the fourth sound channel and branches to a marker called `"Menu"` if the sound in sound channel 4 has finished.

```
on exitFrame
    if not soundbusy(4) then go to "Menu"
    go to the frame
end
```

Waiting for Digital Videos To Finish

The current version of Director does not support Quicktime or Video for Windows files because shocked files cannot use linked files (and in Director, digital video is always linked). Because Macromedia might remove this restriction in the future, take a look at how to test if a digital video has finished playing. This test requires two Lingo commands: the `movieTime of sprite` command and the `duration of cast x` command. Director measures the length of digital videos in ticks. Each tick represents 1/60 of a second. The `duration of cast x` command returns the length, in ticks, of a digital video. The `movieTime of sprite` command points to the current tick being played in a digital movie.

When the `movietime of sprite` command returns the same value as the `duration of cast x` command, the movie has finished playing. Here is an example of the command sequence:

```
if the movieTime of sprite 6 = the duration of cast "MyMovie" then
    go to the frame +
end if
```

> **NOTE**
>
> Until Director can support digital video , you can use PICT sequences to achieve the illusion of digital video.

Director Bandwidth Issues

Director can create highly complex and very large movies, but you must be aware of the band-width restrictions of the Internet when you are developing shocked movies.

Although some people have the luxury of accessing the Internet through T1 or T3 lines, and many people have access to ISDN lines, most people are using 14.4 and 28.8 modems. And because these slower modems slow down the Internet in general, many T1 lines have the effec-tive throughput of a 28.8 modem.

A 14.4 modem transfers information at about 1K (one kilobyte, or 1024 bytes) per second. At this speed a user would have to wait at least two minutes to download a 120K shocked movie. Remember, the movie will not begin playing until the entire movie downloads.

Table 29.6 shows some relative download times, based upon file size.

Table 29.6. Relative download times (in seconds).

Movie Size	14.4Kbps	28.8Kbps	64Kbps	1.5Mbps
50K	50	17	10	1.7
100K	100	34	20	3.4
500K	500	170	100	17
1MB	1,000	340	200	34
10MB	10,000	3,400	2,000	340

Considering that most people have 14.4 and 28.8Kbps modems, you can see that 100K is about the largest file size you should create for a shocked movie—at least until technology catches up and bandwidth issues no longer exist.

You can use various techniques to keep files small, including tiling backgrounds; using 1- and 2-bit graphics whenever possible; limiting the number of cast members; using short 11KHz, 8-bit, mono sounds; and resizing images to make them as small as possible.

Another way of keeping file sizes small is to take advantage of the two ways in which Director 5 creates text: the text tool and the field tool (or the text window and the field window). The text you create with the text tool turns into bitmapped text when you create the shocked movie. Field text, on the other hand, remains as font descriptions (that is, TrueType fonts) even after the movie has been shocked. Because bitmapped fonts must describe every pixel that makes up the text, and field text uses only text descriptions, field text takes up much less room than bitmapped text. The advantage of using field text is smaller movie sizes, but this method also has a disadvantage.

If the computer that the movie is playing on does not have the particular font used to create the field text, the computer will provide a substitute font. The results can be very unpredictable. Also, in cross-platforming, font sizes vary for equivalent fonts. The PC Arial font is smaller than the Mac Helvetica font. The same is true for their equivalent Times fonts. If you decide to use field text, stick to basic fonts, such as Arial, Courier, Symbol, Times New Roman, and Wingdings on the Windows platform and Chicago, Courier, Helvetica, Symbol, and Times on the Mac platform. Also, be sure to allow for varying font sizes within your stage design and the width of field castmembers.

Shockwave for Authorware

Authorware is Macromedia's icon-based authoring package. Because of its inherent features, it is primarily used to develop CBT. Like Director, Authorware supports very sophisticated interactivity, including the use of clickable buttons or graphics (hotspots).

Currently, Shockwave works only with Authorware 3.5 and on Netscape 2.0 or 2.01.

Although Authorware shocked applications can be used either on the Internet or on intranets, Authorware is currently targeted primarily for use with intranets. (*Intranets* are private networks that use Internet and WWW standards.)

> **NOTE**
>
> The Shockwave plug-in is available for Windows 3.1x, Windows 95, Windows NT, 68K Macs, and PowerPCs.

Afterburner

Like Director, Authorware uses the Afterburner tool to convert Authorware applications into shocked applications. Afterburner is available both for Windows and Mac.

Afterburner performs three functions:

1. It compresses Authorware files and libraries.

2. It divides the files into several segments.

3. It creates one map file for locating each segment when needed. Map files are explained later.

The Mac version of Afterburner performs one additional function. It flattens external files so they can be downloaded properly from intranets to Mac computers.

The file segments, the map, and the flattened external files are assigned MIME types.

`application/x-authorware-map`	MIME type for the Authorware map.
`application/x-authorware-seg`	MIME type for a file segment.
`application/x-authorware-bin`	MIME type for a flattened external file.

Using Afterburner for Authorware

Afterburner for Authorware is more complex than Afterburner for Director, which only requires that you run Afterburner and select the Director file to be shocked.

1. Package the Authorware application. This is accomplished by performing the following steps:

   ■ Choose `Package` from Authorware's File menu and select `Without Runtime` from its dialog box. (The Netscape Shockwave plug-in for Authorware will act as the Runtime application.)

   ■ Select any option you want.

   ■ Choose Save File(s) and Package.

2. Compress the application by performing the following steps:

   ■ Run Afterburner for Authorware.

   ■ Select the file you want to turn into a shocked application (most likely, the file you just packaged) from the Select Package Source File dialog box.

   ■ Open the File menu and select Afterburn. (The Windows shortcut is Control+B. The Mac shortcut is Command+B.)

   ■ Choose the location of the map file from the Select Destination Map File dialog box. This location will also become the location of the segment files.

   ■ Access the Segment Settings dialog box and enter from one to four characters to be used as a prefix for the segment files. Segment files are numbered sequentially and start with the characters you select here. The first segment will be appended with 0000. The four digits are incremented by one for each subsequent segment. The digits are in hexadecimal format. For example, if you choose `abcd` as the four-character prefix, the first segment file would be `abcd0000.aas`, the second would be `abcd0001.aas`, the tenth would be `abcd0009.aas`, and the eleventh would be `abcd000a.aas`.

NOTE

Authorware segment files have the extension `.aas`.

   ■ Decide on a size for the segments and enter that number. This value tells Afterburner the average size to make each segment. The default value is 16,000 bytes. Depending on the size of the entire project and depending upon the speed of the intranet or Internet (that is, bandwidth), this number can vary. You might want a lower or higher number.

3. Wait for Authorware's Afterburner to compress and segment the Authorware application. It will create just one map file, along with one or more segments, depending on segment size and file size. In addition, Authorware's Afterburner automatically adds entries for external files (for external content and for external libraries) to the map file.

> **NOTE**
>
> Authorware's Afterburner creates all files with lowercase names. Some systems (for example, UNIX) are case-sensitive. Be aware of any case changes when using case-sensitive HTTP servers.

Editing Map Files

If you need to change filenames in your map file or if your Authorware application uses Xtras or Xobjects, you will need to edit your map file. Currently, the Windows version of Afterburner for Authorware has a built-in map edit facility. Mac users will need to read the following explanation of how to edit Mac map files.

The Elements of a Map File

The map file consists of up to seven line types. The primary line types are

- ver
- get
- put
- set
- lib
- bin
- #

ver

The first line of a map file, ver, provides the version of the map file.

get

The second line, get, provides the path to the map file's location on the server. If the map file is located in the same directory as the HTML document, the get line contains a period. You will need to change this entry if your map file is not in the same location as your HTML page or if you change its location.

If the map file is not located in the same directory as the HTML document, you can provide either an absolute path (the full path) or a relative path (a subdirectory or subdirectory path off the HTML document). For example, if the HTML document is `c:\mysite\HTML` and the Authorware application files are in `c:\mysite\HTML\myapps`, the absolute path is `c:\mysite\HTML\myapps`, while the relative path is `myapps`. The relative path starts at the location of the HTML document and adds only the subdirectories that point to the correct folder or directory.

put

The `put` line describes where on the user's computer external files will be downloaded. The default location is the `Download` directory or folder. The Authorware plug-in automatically creates this folder when the plug-in sees the line `put DOWNLOAD` in a map file. If you want to download files into other folders or directories, you must specify those locations. If they do not exit on the user's computer, the plug-in will create them.

set, lib, bin

The line types `set`, `lib`, and `bin` refer to the internal and external files that make up the Authorware application.

#

The seventh line type is a comment line, which begins with the number sign.

As mentioned at the beginning of the Authorware portion of this chapter, map files provide the name(s) and location(s) of file segments, libraries, and external files. The map tells the Shockwave for Authorware plug-in where to find the elements required to play the Authorware application and provides pointers to various files.

> **NOTE**
>
> Note that Map files have the `.aam` extension.

Of the seven line types in map files, the line type you will most likely be editing is the `bin` line referencing external files. You might also need to edit the segment and library lines and add `Xtras` and drivers to the map file. Another very important reason for editing map files is cross-platforming. If you are developing an application to run on both Mac and Windows, by editing the map file, you can combine both the Mac and Windows maps into a single file.

Editing Map Files in Windows

When you are editing map files, three types of lines typically might be edited. They are external lines, library lines, and segment lines.

Editing Segment Lines

The segment line has five columns. Moving left to right, they are

- The type (in this case, `seg` for segment).
- The platform the application is designed to run on. Currently, this column can have five possible entries:

  `all`—Mac and Windows

  `mac`—Mac only

  `win`—Windows only (both 16-bit and 32-bit Windows)

  `win16`—16-bit Windows (Windows 3.1*x*)

  `win32`—32-bit Windows (Windows 95/NT)

- The segment's filename. As described in item 2 of the section "Using Afterburner for Authorware," a segment filename consists of from one to four characters, followed by four digits and the extension `.aas`.
- The starting byte of the segment, in relation to the beginning of the application. For example, if the segments that come before this particular segment had comprised 8,015 bytes of the application, the number listed in this column for this particular segment would be 8016, because 8016 is the starting byte of this segment in relationship to the entire application.
- The size, in bytes, of the segment.

If you are changing any of the line entries in the segment, you are most likely changing its filename.

To edit a segment line, just double-click on the line to open an edit window. The edit window contains three editable windows: a pull-down window for changing the line type, a pull-down window for changing the platform designation, and a window containing the filename. The starting byte and file size are listed in the edit panel, but are not changeable.

Make whatever changes you wish and close the window; that is, click OK to keep the changes or Cancel to abort the changes.

Editing Library Lines

Library lines have the following four columns:

- The type (in this case, `seg` for segment).
- The platform the application is designed to run on (for example, `win` for Windows).

■ The library's map file.

■ The library's original name—that is, the name of the library at the time the application was packaged. Although Shockwave for Authorware is not case-sensitive, you should use all uppercase in this column to indicate that this name is the file's original name.

As when you edit segment lines, the column you will most likely edit for library lines is the filename column (column 3).

And, as with the segment lines, to make changes to a map line, just double-click on the line to open an editing dialog box. This box consists of five editable fields. The top field equates to the first column and is a pull-down window for editing the line type. Moving down, the second field, which equates to the second column, is a pull-down window for specifying the platform for which this library has been created.

The third field is the filename as located on the server, and the fourth field is the filename as it will appear when downloaded to the local (or client) device.

The final field is a `Preempt` flag (either checked or unchecked). If checked, this flag forces the user's browser to download the file located on the HTTP server. If, for example, the user had previously downloaded the file, this flag would force the user to download the file again, instead of using the version located on his or her computer. This step would be useful if, for example, the file had been updated or changed entirely.

Make your changes and click OK.

Editing External Lines

The lines of a map file that refer to external content consist of four or five columns—the fifth column is optional.

■ The first column is the file type. All external files are binary files, so the external line always begins with `bin` in the first column.

■ As with the other lines, the second column of an external line refers to the platform on which this file will play.

■ The third column defines the filename of the external file as it appears on the server. Because a large number of HTTP servers are case-sensitive, you must adhere to the server's naming conventions and match cases precisely.

■ The fourth column holds the filename that will be given to the file when it is downloaded to the client computer (the user's computer). Macromedia convention recommends using all uppercase letters for this column.

■ The final column is optional and can affect how a file is downloaded. These download options are defined in Table 29.7.

To edit an external file line, double-click on the line to open an editing dialog box. This box consists of five editable sections. The first four refer to columns 1 through 4 and consist of one field each. The top field equates to the first column and is a pull-down window for editing the line type. Moving down, the second field, which equates to the second column, is a pull-down window for specifying the platform for which this library has been created.

The third field is the filename as located on the server, and the fourth field is the filename as it will be downloaded to the local (or client) device.

The next section is the flags section and consists of four check boxes that determine when or how a file is downloaded. The download options are described in Table 29.7.

Table 29.7. Download options.

Option	Purpose
Preempt	If checked, the map file will override any files that exist on the user's computer or CD-ROM and force the file to be downloaded from the HTTP server. This option is useful for updating external files on a client computer.
OnDemand	Because Authorware is an interactive application, a user might not want to access all elements within the application. Instead of downloading all external files, the user can save time and space by downloading only certain files. The OnDemand flag specifies that the user wants to download an external file only if it is needed to run a particular portion of the Authorware application.
Recycle	By default, external files are deleted when an Authorware application ends. To prevent a file from being deleted, check the Recycle box. This option is particularly useful for intranet applications in which a user might be regularly accessing an Authorware application (for example, an interactive employee manual). Once the user downloads the external file, it will remain on his or her computer for further use.
MacBinary	This flag creates a flattened file with the extension .aab, which combines the data fork and resource fork of the file into a single MacBinary file, thereby preserving the Mac file creator and file type information required to ensure proper downloading of movies, Xtras, and XCMDs. Normally, HTTP does not transfer this information.
Empty	Empty is the default state. By not checking any of the preceding four options, the column will remain empty. Empty downloads external files at the beginning of an Authorware application and deletes them from the user's computer when the user closes the application. For Internet applications, Empty is the desired condition. For intranets, this condition will cause unnecessary delays for regularly accessed applications.

NOTE

Multiple flags are separated by commas, for example, `macbinary, recycle`.

The final section of the dialog box for editing external lines is the Creator/Type section and consists of two fields: File Type and File Creator. This section is applicable only if the `MacBinary` check box has been checked (see earlier).

Make whatever changes are necessary and click OK to save.

Adding New Lines to a Map File

Adding a new line is simple. Click on the line that you want the new line to follow. From the map editor's Edit menu, select `Insert Line`. Afterburner will display a dialog box for constructing the elements of the new line.

The following external file types are not automatically added to a map file; you must add them by inserting new lines:

```
MOA Asset Xtras (.x16, .x32, etc.)
Authorware Video Player DLLs (.VDR)
Authorware Movie Player DLLs (.XMO)
Director M5 executables and support files
```

To add a new line, include the following five column entries:

```
File Type: bin
Platform: win, mac, all, etc.
Server filename:
Local filename:
Flags: Preempt, OnDemand, etc.
```

After you add a line, you can double-click and edit it like any other map file line.

Using Custom Windows Fonts

You cannot include Windows fonts (FNT files) in a map file. If they are present, Afterburner for Authorware will ignore them. If you want to use custom Windows fonts, you must download them separately and install them into Windows in the normal fashion for installing fonts.

Editing a Map File on a Mac

Until Macromedia adds an internal map editor to Afterburner for Authorware for Macintosh computers, like the one it has for Windows, you must adhere to the following procedures to edit map files on the Mac.

An Authorware map file is a text file. Therefore, you can use any text editor to edit it. As an alternative, you can edit Mac map files in Windows by using the map editor in the Windows version of Afterburner for Authorware.

The format of the lines that appear in a Mac map file is identical to the format of the lines in a Windows map file. Refer to the previous Windows section for a complete description of the line types and their content.

Downloading External Mac Files

Before you download a Mac file, you need to perform two tasks: flatten the file and add the `MacBinary` flag to the map file. The `MacBinary` flag tells Shockwave for Authorware that the file has been flattened. (See "Editing External Lines," earlier in this chapter, for an explanation of flattening and the `MacBinary` flag.)

The Afterburner software automatically flattens external files for use by Shockwave for Authorware on a Mac. Next, using a text editor, add the word `macbinary` to the fifth column of the `bin` line containing the flattened file reference. Multiple flags can appear in the fifth column if they are separated by commas (for example, `macbinary, recycle`).

Text and Quicktime Files on a Mac

Two types of external files do not need to be flattened before Shockwave for Authorware can use them on a Mac—text files and Quicktime movies that have been cross-platformed and saved with a `.mov` extension. Text files do not contain a resource fork, so you won't have to combine resource and data forks (which is the function of flattening). The flattening process (or cross-platforming) moves critical information to the data fork. The `.mov` extension tells the Shockwave plug-in the file creator and file type for the Quicktime movie.

Using Custom Mac Fonts

Unlike custom Windows fonts, you can package custom Mac fonts with an Authorware application. Authorware will recognize these fonts and include them when the application is run by Afterburner for Authorware on a Mac.

Allowing Windows and Macs to Share External Files

Windows doesn't recognize flattened files. Mac requires flattened files. Mac recognizes a flattened Quicktime movie as flattened, but Windows just sees it as a file that it understands. In order for both Mac and Windows to recognize a Quicktime movie, the map line must appear in a format that both platforms can recognize.

Depending on the intended platform(s), one of three lines must appear. Following are descriptions of those three lines.

The following is an external line referencing a Windows Quicktime file:

```
bin    win    mymovie.mov    MYMOVIE.mov
```

The following is an external line referencing a Mac Quicktime file that has been flattened:

```
bin    mac    mymovie.mov    MYMOVIE.mov    macbinary
```

The following is an external line referencing a Quicktime file for cross-platform use:

```
bin    all    mymovie.mov    MYMOVIE.mov    type='MV93',creator='MD93'
```

The Windows-only line contains the file type, the platform, and the server and client filenames.

The Mac-only line contains the file type, the platform, the server and client filenames, and the `macbinary` flag indicating that the file has been flattened.

The third entry, the cross-platform line, contains the file type, the platform, and the server and client filenames. In addition, it contains explicit file type and file creator references.

Speeding Up Mac and Cross-Platform Files

Rather than using Afterburner to flatten files, you can improve the performance of external files by manually entering the file type and file creator information, as shown a few paragraphs earlier.

By providing the file type and file creator information, you do not need to flatten files. This information improves performance because flattened files must be unflattened before playing. However, some files, such as Quicktime files, must be flattened to play in a Windows environment.

Using Transition Xtras

You won't need to download the Director transition Xtra as an external file, because it is included with the Shockwave for Authorware plug-in. However, if you plan to use transition Xtras (transitions created by third-party developers, not as part of the basic Director package), you will need to download those Xtras into an Xtra folder at the start of the application.

For the Windows environment, you can accomplish this task by adding the line put XTRAS immediately preceding the Xtras entry(s) in the map file, such as the following example:

```
put    XTRAS
bin    win32         xtraTrans.x32    XTRATRANS.X32
```

For the Mac, follow the same format as the Windows version, but add `macbinary` in the options column (the fifth column):

```
put    XTRAS
bin    mac           xtraTrans.ab     XTRATRANS.aab         macbinary
```

Combining Windows and Mac Map Files

After creating both Shockwave versions of an Authorware Application, you will end up with two map files. You need to create links for both versions to your HTML page—one link for the Mac map file and one for the Windows map file. However, if you combine map files into one file, you will need to reference only one map file on your HTML page. This file can contain Mac-only references, Windows-only references, and cross-platform references.

The following is an example of a combined map file. Note the use of comment lines (lines preceded with a number sign—#).

```
# Combined windows/Mac map file
ver 0
get .
put .
# Windows segments
seg    win    funw0000.aas    0         16840
seg    win    funw0001.aas    32931        16905
seg    win    funw0002.aas    49836        15602
# Mac segments
seg    mac    funm0000.aas    0         17002
seg    mac    funm0001.aas    17002        15603
seg    mac    funm0002.aas    32605        18010
# Windows library lines
lib    win    winlib1.aam       WINLIB1.APR
lib    win    winlib2.aam       WINLIB2.APR
# Mac library lines
lib    mac    maclib1.aam       "LIBRARY1"
lib    mac    maclib2.aam       "LIBRARY2"
# Shared external files
bin    all    mymovie.mov    MOVIE1.MOV    onDemand
bin    all    mymovi2.mov    MOVIE2.MOV    onDemand
```

Referencing Files in Multiple Locations

Like `seg` and `bin` entries, you can include multiple `get` and `put` lines in a single map file. This technique is useful for grouping files by location.

A `get` or a `put` entry applies to subsequent line entries. With the `put` line, if you refer to a folder or directory that doesn't exist on the user's computer, the Shockwave for Authorware plug-in will create it.

With a `get` line, you can refer either to an absolute or a relative path. For example, if the HTML document is `c:\mysite\HTML` and the Authorware application files are in `c:\mysite\HTML\myapps`, the absolute path is `c:\mysite\HTML\myapps`, while the relative path is `myapps`. The relative path assumes the location of the HTML document and adds only the subdirectories needed to point to the correct folder or directory.

If you plan to use `Xtras` (other than the Director transitions `Xtra` that comes with Shockwave), use a `put XTRAS` line before the lines that refer to the `Xtras`. Remember, you must download transition `Xtras` to the `XTRAS` folder before the application begins.

With a put line, use relative paths only. The Shockwave for Authorware plug-in does not recognize absolute paths.

The following map file includes multiple put lines. Transitions are put into the XTRAS folder (a relative path off the HTML document folder). Text files are put into a TEXT folder that is located in another folder, MEDIA, off the directory containing the HTML document. The movie file is put into a MOVIE folder that is also a subdirectory (or subfolder) of the MEDIA folder.

```
ver 0
get .
# this is a Windows-only map file
seg    win    news0000.aas    0        24404
seg    win    news0001.aas    24404    28003
seg    win    news0002.aas    52407    22915
# this line directs the next files to be placed into the XTRAS folder
put    XTRAS
bin    win16    transit.x16    MYTRANS.X16
bin    win32    transit.x32    MYTRANS.X32
# this line directs the next files to be placed into the MEDIA/TEXT folder
put    MEDIA\TEXT
bin    win    readme.txt    README.TXT
bin    win    ordering.txt    ORDER-ME.TXT
# the above text file platform entries could have been all, instead of win
# because text files are cross-platform files. However, because this  is
# a Windows-only
map file, it seemed appropriate to make reference only to Windows.
#
# The next line directs the files that follow to be placed
# into the MEDIA/MOVIE folder
put MEDIA\MOVIE
bin  win  movie1.mov  MYMOVIE.MOV  onDemand
```

You can make an external file accessible to more than one Authorware application by using the same put line and external filename in different map files. Be sure to include the recycle option, to prevent the file from being deleted when the application is closed.

Authorware Bandwidth Issues

As with Director, Authorware must contend with bandwidth issues—at least if it is on the Internet rather than on an intranet. If the application is on an intranet, the bandwidth is typically 1.5Mbps (a T1 line) or greater. However, applications are quite often on the Internet, or are on intranets but connected off-site via ISDN lines (or 28.8 or 14.4Kbps modems).

Even if you are accessing an Internet application with a T1 or ISDN, slower modems tend to slow down the Internet, giving these faster lines the throughput of a 28.8Kbps modem.

A 14.4Kbps modem transfers information at about 1KB (one kilobyte, or 1024 bytes) per second. At this speed, a user would have to wait at least two minutes for a 120KB application to download.

For a chart showing some relative download times, based upon application size, refer to Table 29.6 earlier in this chapter.

Because most people use 14.4 and 28.8Kbps modems, 100KB is about the largest file size you should create for a shocked application. To reduce delays, use the onDemand flag to prevent files from downloading, unless needed. You can also use segment sizes to alter access times. With small sizes, the delays are shorter but there are more delays. With larger segments, the delays are longer, but less frequent.

On intranets with T1 lines, file size is much less of an issue. A 1MB file will take only a little more than 30 seconds to load.

Until technology catches up and bandwidth issues no longer exist, you will have to be aware of file size and continue to use onDemand to reduce download delays.

New Shockwave-Specific Functions and Variables

Several new functions and variables

 make Authorware easier to use for Internet and intranet applications. These functions and variables address needs specific to Internet and intranet environments. The needs focus primarily on references to HTML documents (Net pages) and URLs.

GoToNetPage(URL), window

Attaching the GoToNetPage(URL) function to a button or hotspot causes Netscape to load the Web page listed in (URL).

You can also add a second optional argument to this function. This argument is a target to HTML windows. Windows are a part of Netscape's Frame technology, and you should study Netscape Frame Scripting to understand the use of frames and HTML windows. Table 29.8 lists possible target options for the second (the window) argument.

Table 29.8. Options for the GoToNetPage window argument.

Option	Meaning
_blank	Causes the Authorware application to remain in a window while a second window displays the new Web page. You can use this method to return to the Authorware application after viewing the Web page.
_self	Causes the new Web page to open in the same window as the current page.
_parent	Causes the new Web page to open in the same frameset parent window as the current page. When you are using target windows, this option overrides a globally assigned base target (the default window). If there is no parent, this argument functions the same as the _self argument.

continues

29

SHOCKWAVE
AND LINGO

Table 29.8. continued

Option	Meaning
_top	Causes the new Web page to open in the body of the current window. This option is equivalent to the _self argument. It is also used to return from frame nesting.
	If you do not include a second argument, the Authorware application closes as soon as it locates the new Web page.

> **NOTE**
>
> Use a comma to separate arguments; for example, URL, "_blank".

An example of the GoToNetPage(URL) function is

```
GoToNetPage("http://www.mysite.com", "_blank")
```

NetDownload(URL)

The NetDownload(URL) function

downloads the file listed in (URL) to the user's computer. The full pathname is returned if the operation was successful. This function, in combination with the onDemand flag in the map file, enables files to be downloaded only when requested.

NetDownload(URL) looks at the map file and downloads to the location listed by the put line of the map file that precedes the line entry for the file being downloaded. If the map file does not have an entry for the file being downloaded, it will be downloaded to the DOWNLOAD subfolder of the folder containing the Authorware plug-in.

In the following example, an Adobe Acrobat file is downloaded and, when the process is complete, returns the pathname to a string called WherePut:

```
WherePut:= NetDownload("http://www.mysite.com/files/newletter.pdr)
```

The file was located on the HTTP server in the folder FILES. After downloading, the WherePut: variable will contain the location of the file on the client computer (the user's computer). If the map file does not have a line for newsletter.pdr, then WherePut: might contain "C: \NETSCAPE \PLUGINS\AP32ASW\DOWNLOAD".

However, if the map file includes an entry for newsletter.pdr, and a put line precedes the entry, the file will be placed into the folder specified by the put line. The folder location will be a subfolder off the Authorware plug-in folder. If, for example, the put line was put PDRS, the WherePut: variable would contain "C:\ \NETSCAPE\ \PLUGINS\AP32ASW\PDRS".

NetPreload(IcondID@"IconTitle")

NetPreload(IcondID@"IconTitle") is an

asynchronous command that downloads whatever segment files the icon specified by IconTitle requires to execute. If the IconTitle is a map, interaction, decision, or framework icon, "all" icons that are either attached to (external) or within (internal) the IconTitle are preloaded.

The primary function of the NetPreload function is to initiate background preloading of segments required for sounds, movies, or graphics, so that the segments are on the user's system when needed.

NetPreload does cause the system to slow down or halt during the load process, so you should time the function to operate during the most optimum moments. For example, a good time to initiate a NetPreload function might be when a user is looking at a newly downloaded map, since the system is halted for the moment.

> **NOTE**
>
> Preload cannot asynchronously preload external files, such as digital video files. It downloads segments (seg), not executables (bin). Use the NetDownload(URL) function to download executables.

The difference between the NetPreload function and the preload option is that the preload option stores the data in Authorware's memory, while NetPreload stores the information on the user's computer drive.

The function returns information, but the information serves no purpose and Authorware ignores it.

NetConnected

NetConnected is a flag variable (1=TRUE, 0=FALSE). It tells the Authorware application if it is running via Shockwave. The value is 1 if the application is running under Shockwave and 0 if it is running either under Authorware's runtime routine or in the authoring environment.

This variable is useful with calculation icons or decision icons to branch according to the environment on which the Authorware application is playing, for example:

```
if NetConnected then
    Platform := "Running on an HTTP server"
else
    Platform := "Running stand-alone"
end if
```

The NetConnected variable is a handy way of building a single piece of code that can run in multiple environments. The appropriate media will be accessed according to the results of the NetConnected variable. For example, you might want to use 8-bit, 11KHz, mono sound on an intranet, but 16-bit, 44.1KHz, stereo sound on a stand-alone application.

NetLocation

The NetLocation flag returns the URL of the current Shockwave application. A useful routine is to use the NetConnected flag to determine if the Authorware application is running on the Internet or as a stand-alone application. Then, either retrieve a file off the HTTP server in a file relative to the NetLocation if the application is running on the Internet or retrieve the file off the hard drive or a CD-ROM using a local address if the application is running in stand-alone mode.

Existing Authorware Functions

The following are functions that already exist in Authorware but have been adapted for use on the Internet or on an intranet:

- Jumpfile
- JumpFileReturn
- ReadExtfile

Jumpfile and JumpFileReturn

The Jumpfile and JumpFileReturn functions enable Authorware to jump from one Authorware application to another and return to the calling Authorware application. The function has been altered to accept a URL as its first argument. The following is an example:

```
JumpFile("http://www.mysite.com/pgms/sale-cbt.aam")
```

> **NOTE**
>
> Jumpfile and JumpFileReturn might be affected by user-selected security settings—they might be disabled. (See "System Security," later in the chapter.)

ReadExtFile

ReadExtFile now accepts an absolute URL as an argument. The URL must begin with either http://servername/ or file:///.

The following code reads an external file and returns its entire contents to the string MyText:

```
MyText := ReadExFile("http://hostserver/mysite/mytextfile.txt")
```

As with the JumpFile and JumpFileReturn functions, the ReadExtFile function might be affected by user-security settings.

System Security

With the Shockwave for Authorware plug-in, users have the opportunity to set one of two security modes: trusting and nontrusting. Simply put, *trusting* mode says that you trust the integrity of external files and are willing to download them. *Nontrusting* mode says that you are afraid that your system might become corrupted, that plug-ins might read confidential files off your system and transfer them back to an HTTP server, or that a virus might be introduced and that you would rather not download any files that could compromise your computer.

Both of these modes apply to Authorware running on the Internet. On intranets, the assumption is that the MIS staff has taken the responsibility of assuring system and file integrity and that all downloads are safe.

Nontrusting mode disables the following functions and variables:

Functions:

```
AppendExtfile

Catalog

CreateFolder

DeleteFile

JumpFileReturn

JumpOut

JumpOutReturn

JumpPrintReturn

PrintScreen

ReadExtFile*

RenameFile

SaveRecords

WriteExtFile
```

Variables:

```
DiskBytes

FileLocation

FileType

OrigWorkingDirectory

RecordsLocation

SearchPath
```

29

SHOCKWAVE
AND LINGO

The `ReadExtFile` is disabled only for reading files off the user's hard drive, not for reading files off the HTTP server (files whose path begins with `http://`).

Because nontrusting mode prevents the automatic downloading of UCDs, DLLs, XCMDs, and Xtras, you must place these files on the user's system manually.

In nontrusting mode, Xtras are not looked for by Authorware in the following locations, depending upon the client system:

System	Location
Windows 3.1*x* and NT	`windows/system/macromedia/xtras`
Windows 95	`Program Files/Macromedia/Xtras`
Mac	`System Folder:Macromedia:Xtras`

Invoking Security

Whenever you launch an Authorware application via an HTTP server (an Internet or intranet), the first thing you see is a security dialog box. You also see the security dialog box whenever you use either the `JumpFile` or `GoToNetPage` function.

The Security Dialog Box

The Security dialog box opens with the full HTTP pathname of the Authorware file, followed by two check boxes—one to select trust mode and one to select nontrust mode.

You can also select the Security Options button to access another dialog box, which has two more boxes: `Trust All Sites` and `Trust Only Listed Sites`. If you check the second option, the bottom half has a screen for entering the names of the sites you trust.

Just below the top of the Security Options box is a section titled `Show Security Dialog When:` followed by two check boxes, one for when `Opening Trusted Sites`, and one for when `Opening Non-Trusted Sites`. By checking one of the boxes, you can select when you want to display the Security dialog box.

The Security Options dialog box also has buttons for adding, deleting, and renaming sites, as well as for saving current settings.

Remember, even though you can open an Authorware application in nontrusting mode, it might not function properly because you might have inhibited some of its functions or features.

Integrating Authorware into Browsers

To access Authorware using a browser, you must have the Shockwave for Authorware plug-in, and you must be using a browser compatible with the plug-in. Currently, the only browser compatible with the Authorware plug-in is Netscape (versions 2.0 and 2.01).

You add Authorware shocked applications to an HTML document the same way that you add Director Shockwave files to an HTML document—via the EMBED tag, as follows:

```
<EMBED SRC="myapp.aam" WIDTH=640 HEIGHT=480 WINDOW=onTop>
```

<EMBED

<EMBED begins the HTML tag sequence.

SRC="?????.aam"

SRC="?????.aam" defines the filename of the Authorware shocked file.

WIDTH=

WIDTH= ### describes the width, in pixels, of the Authorware application.

HEIGHT=###

HEIGHT=### describes the height, in pixels, of the Authorware application.

WINDOW

The WINDOW setting defines how the Authorware application will appear on the Netscape browser. This command has three possible options: inPlace, onTop, and onTopMinimized.

inPlace

The inPlace option embeds the application within the HTML page in the browser. The option is only applicable when viewing in the Windows environment.

This option does not enable you to include a title bar in the application. If you try to include a title bar, it will not display, but the application's height will be reduced by the size of the title bar (even though it is not displayed).

Because Netscape's active window is smaller than the screen's full window size, be sure to create applications with height/width settings smaller than 640×480. Otherwise, users with screens set to 640×480 (the current LCD—lowest common denominator) will have to scroll vertically and horizontally to see the entire application.

Also, the ResizeWindow and MoveWindow functions can produce unpredictable results.

onTop

onTop displays the application in a separate window on top of the Netscape browser windows. This window makes the Authorware application appear to be a separate application, that is, not part of the HTML document.

onTopMinimized

This final option, `onTopMinimized`, like the `onTop` option, places the Authorware application in a separate window. However, `onTopMinimized` also minimizes the browser, which makes the Authorware application appear to be a stand-alone application.

Displaying an Alternate Image on Noncompatible Browsers

Because the only browsers that can read the Authorware application (as of this writing) are Netscape 2.0 and 2.01, all other browsers need something else to view. The `<NOEMBED>` command accomplishes this task.

<NOEMBED>

When Netscape sees the `<NOEMBED>` command, it ignores anything that follows until it sees the `</NOEMBED>` tag, which designates the end of the `<NOEMBED>` sequence.

All other browsers do not understand the `<NOEMBED>` tag. Instead of ignoring everything that follows the `<NOEMBED>` tag, they read everything that follows.

To provide an alternate image for non-Netscape browsers to view while Netscape browsers access the Authorware application, place the alternate image information within the `<NOEMBED>` and `</NOEMBED>` tags. In the following code, Netscape will play the Authorware application `myapp.aam` while all other browsers will display the image `alt-img.gif`, which is located in the IMAGES folder on the server.

```
<EMBED SRC=myapp.aam" WIDTH=320 HEIGHT=240 WINDOW=inPlace>
<NOEMBED> <IMG SRC="images/alt-img.gif"> </NOEMBED>
```

Shockwave for Freehand

The final Macromedia application that a Shockwave plug-in has ported to the Internet is Freehand.

Freehand is a cross-platform, vector-based, draw package that incorporates sophisticated special effects via `Xtras` plug-ins, such as Smudge, Fisheye Lens, and 3D Rotation, along with powerful page layout capabilities to rival programs such as PageMaker and QuarkXPress.

You can use Freehand to create exciting page-based documents. With the inclusion of Shockwave, these pages can appear on the Web.

Obtaining Shockwave and URL Managers

In order to turn a Freehand graphic into a shocked graphic, you need to download Afterburner for Freehand and URL Manager Xtras for Freehand. These files are available, free of charge, from the Macromedia's Web site at `http://www.macromedia.com`.

Embedding a Freehand Graphic on an HTML Page

When a graphic is created in Freehand, you can use Freehand's Page inspector to determine the page size. First, use the Page inspector to set the unit of measure to points. There are 72 points to the inch. This measurement is equivalent to the number of pixels per inch. For example, a 3-inch wide graphic is 216 points (72×3) wide, which means that it is approximately 216 pixels wide.

Macromedia recommends following these steps:

1. Select all the objects on the Freehand page.

2. Group them together.

3. Move the group to the lower-left corner of the page.

4. Make a note of the measurements (height and width, in points) that Freehand's Object inspector displays.

5. Enter the measurements you just wrote down as custom page dimension in Freehand's Page inspector.

6. Notice that the page size matches the size of the grouped items.

Now that you have a page designed to match the size of the graphic element it contains, you can add the document to the HTML document.

The EMBED Tag

As with Director and Authorware shocked files, Freehand shocked files are placed into an HTML page via the `<EMBED>` tag, using the following format:

```
<a> <embed SRC="fh-file.ext" WIDTH=480 HEIGHT=360 toolbar=top></a>
```

<a> </a>

The `<a>` tag and closing `</a>` tag denote that the information between them is a hypertext link.

SRC

The `SRC` element defines the name of the freehand file to be embedded.

WIDTH and HEIGHT

WIDTH and HEIGHT define the size, in width and height, of the Freehand graphic image. Use the width and height dimensions that you copied down during the preceding step 4 for the WIDTH and HEIGHT dimensions.

You can also display the Freehand graphic in a size that is smaller than its original size. If, for example, the original graphic is 480×360 and you want to display it at 50 percent of its original size, just enter 240 for the WIDTH and 180 for the HEIGHT.

TOOLBAR

You can display a toolbar on a Freehand graphic by using the TOOLBAR element of the EMBED tag. The TOOLBAR element has two possible values: top and bottom. With top, the toolbar will appear at the top of the Freehand graphic. With bottom, the toolbar appears at the bottom of the Freehand graphic.

The toolbar gives users access to the panning, zooming, and linking features of Shockwave for Freehand.

If you are using a toolbar, be sure to add the height of the toolbar (20 pixels) to the HEIGHT listing of the EMBED tag. For example, if you want to use a toolbar in the example with the 480×360 graphic, the HEIGHT becomes 380 (360 + 20 pixels).

To use a toolbar, the graphic must be at least 85 pixels wide. The toolbar automatically resizes itself to fit the width of the Freehand graphic. However, unless the toolbar is 150 pixels wide, it does not have enough room to display the Shockwave logo. Although not displaying a logo might not seem important, it is, because the logo is a hotspot. Clicking on the logo returns the graphic to its original view. If you cannot see the logo, either you will have to guess at the original view and use the zoom and hand tools to re-create that view as best you can, or you will have to use a keyboard command for the return-to-original-view function normally accomplished by clicking the logo. On the Mac, the keyboard combination is Command+Shift-click. On the PC, it's Ctrl+Shift-click. See Table 29.9 for the keyboard alternatives to the toolbar.

Table 29.9. Keyboard alternatives to the toolbar.

Operation	Computer	Method
Zoom in	Mac	Command-click.
Zoom out	Mac	Command-Option-click.
Home view	Mac	Command-Shift-click.
Zoom in	PC	Right-click or Ctrl+Left-click.
Zoom out	PC	Alt+Right-click or Ctrl+Alt+Left-click.
Home view	PC	Shift+Right-click.

Operation	Computer	Method
Zooming a selection	Either	Click and drag a selection box.
Panning	Mac	Hold down the control key and click and drag.
Panning	PC	Hold down the spacebar and click and drag.

Activating a Link in Netscape

When you move the cursor around the Freehand graphic in Netscape, the cursor turns into a pointing finger when it rolls on top of a hyperlink. Click to activate the link.

The URL Xtra

Although being able to place vectored graphics onto a Web page is certainly nice, Shockwave for Freehand also enables you to attach hyperlinks to vectored objects, turning them into hotspots.

In the Freehand program, you can use the URL Xtra to add hyperlinks to the graphics.

Freehand accesses the URL Xtra via Other in the Windows menu.

Creating a hypertext link is a two-step process. First, you add the URL information to the URL palette, and then you attach the URL to an object.

Adding a URL

To add a URL to Freehand, access the URL Xtra from the Windows menu and select New from the Options menu. Enter the URL into the New URL dialog box. URLs can either be absolute or relative paths (full or partial paths). Relative paths are relative to the folder containing the Freehand graphic.

> **NOTE**
>
> You cannot add URLs to groups, but you can add them to individual objects within a group.

Attaching the URL to an Object

From the URL palette, drag the URL to an object. To attach the URL to multiple objects, select the multiple objects and click the URL in the URL palette.

> **NOTE**
>
> URLs that have not been attached to at least one object before the Freehand graphic is saved will be deleted and not saved. This rule also applies to closing or zooming the URL's window or sending the graphic to the background.

Editing, Copying, and Deleting URLs

To edit a URL, just double-click it (or click it and select Edit from the Options menu on the URL palette). Press Enter when you are finished editing.

To copy a URL, click the URL to select it. Then select Duplicate from the Options menu on the URL palette.

To delete a URL, click on the URL to select it. Then select Remove from the Options menu on the URL Links Manager.

> **NOTE**
>
> Note that this step will also remove any hotspots (the link, not the objects) associated with the URL.

Finding URL Associations

After URLs have been attached to Freehand objects, you can find them by using the Find button located in the URL palette. By clicking on a URL, selection handles will appear around any and all objects associated with that URL.

Afterburner for Freehand

Now that you've created your graphic and added hotspots with URL links, you need to turn the graphic into shocked graphics so it can be played on the Internet.

As soon as you save a Freehand graphic (in its normal fashion), it is ready for use in an HTML document. All you need to do is add either a .fh5 or .fh4 extension, depending upon which version of Freehand you used to create the graphic. Although this method is simple, the more appropriate procedure for creating a shocked Freehand document is to use Freehand's Afterburner Xtra, located in the Freehand Xtras menu.

The reason the Afterburner Xtra is used is because it compresses the file, reducing its size. As with all other shocked file formats mentioned in this chapter, size is important because of Internet and intranet bandwidth considerations.

To compress Freehand graphics, select `Compress Document` from the Afterburner menu. (Be sure to save your document before compressing.)

Afterburner saves compressed graphics with the `.fhc` extension, which signals the Netscape Shockwave for Freehand plug-in to decompress the document.

While compressing, you can lock the compressed graphic by clicking the Locked option. However, Freehand cannot reopen locked files; you will need a browser to view them. If you plan to lock your graphic, be sure to save an original version first so you have a version of the graphic that Freehand can reopen and alter.

Opening Compressed Graphics in Freehand

After Afterburner compresses a file, Freehand can reopen it, as long as you did not select the `Locked` option.

From Freehand's Afterburner menu (under Freehand Xtras), choose `Decompress Document`. Locate and select the file you wish to decompress.

When the file opens, its name will be untitled. You will need to name the file before saving and before compressing again.

Using Fonts

As with Director and Authorware, fonts are always an issue when creating cross-platform applications or when using custom or specialized fonts, even within a single platform.

To reduce problems, use the most common fonts (Courier and Times). However, even these fonts are not the same across platforms and might produce results that you do not expect.

To ensure that what you want is what you get, turn all fonts into vectored polygons (freeform objects).

Features Disabled for Shockwave for Freehand

Certain Freehand features have been disabled in the shocked version of Freehand. Primarily, they are effects or features available on the development platform but not necessarily available on the delivery platforms.

- Encapsulated Postscript (EPS) file format. Because file size is a paramount concern in the Internet, and because EPS files are not space-efficient, this format is not supported for shocked files.
- Multiple pages. The page that was active (selected) when the document was saved will be the one displayed on the HTML document. Other pages can be viewed by panning.
- PostScript lines and fills (for example, custom fills).

- Linked TIFF files (embedded TIFFs are supported).
- Text effects.
- Tab leaders.
- Range kerning.

Configuring Servers

In order for HTTP servers to display Shockwave files properly, you must configure the servers to accept the appropriate MIME type for each type of Shockwave file. Depending upon the host server, the code will vary. The following are the formats for configuring various server types for the different Shockwave formats.

Three server types are covered.

- UNIX
- Mac
- Webstar

UNIX

The UNIX system was the first system used on the Internet. Until recently, all Internet servers were UNIX-based.

Shockwave for Director 4.0*x*–The Do-It Yourself Method

In order to have a server display the various Shockwave MIME types (file extensions), references for the MIME types must be added to the appropriate server file(s). Each server type locates the MIME information in a different file or group of files and in a different format. Also, some files can be edited simply by opening them with a text editor, while others require access through specialized programs. The UNIX file containing MIME information is edited via any text editor.

1. Create or open a file called `htaccess` (or a variation, depending upon your system).
2. Set the file access permission by adding the following lines to the file:
   ```
   user = read and write
   group = read
   world = read
   ```
3. Set file privileges to world readable by adding
   ```
   chmod 644 .htaccess
   ```
4. Add the following lines:
   ```
   AddType application/x-director dcr
   AddType application/x-director dir
   AddType application/x-director dxr
   ```
5. Save the file to the root level of your Web pages.

Shockwave for Director 4.0*x*—The System Administrator Method

The system administrator must add the following lines to the system file that registers MIME types for the server:

```
MIME type: application
Sub Type: x-director
Extensions: dcr,dir,dxr
```

Shockwave for Director

Follow the same procedure as for Director 4.0*x*.

Shockwave for Authorware—The Do-It-Yourself Method

Follow the same procedure as for Director 4.0*x*. However, for the AddType entries, type the following:

```
AddType application/x-authorware-map aam
AddType application/x-authorware-seg aas
AddType application/x-authorware-bin aab
```

Shockwave for Authorware—The System Administrator Method

The system administrator must add the following lines to the system file that registers MIME types for the server:

```
MIME type: application
Sub Type: x-authorware-map
Extension: aam

MIME type: application
Sub Type: x-authorware-seg
Extension: aas

MIME type: application
Sub Type: x-authorware-bin
Extension: aab
```

Shockwave for Freehand

The system administrator must add the following lines to the system file that registers MIME types for the server:

```
MIME type: image
Sub Type: x-Freehand
Extensions: fh4,fh5,fhc
```

Mac

As with the UNIX system, the Mac file containing MIME type information can be edited using any text editor.

29

SHOCKWAVE
AND LINGO

Shockwave for Director 4.0*x*

Add the following lines to the file MacHTTP.config:

```
BINARY .DIR TEXT * application/x-director
BINARY .DXR TEXT * application/x-director
BINARY .DCR TEXT * application/x-director
```

Shockwave for Director

Follow the same procedure as for Director 4.0*x*.

Shockwave for Authorware

Add the following lines to the file MacHTTP.config:

```
BINARY .AAM TEXT * application/x-authorware-map
BINARY .AAS TEXT * application/x- authorware-seg
BINARY .AAB TEXT * application/x- authorware-bin
```

Shockwave for Freehand

Add the following lines to the file MacHTTP.config:

```
BINARY .FH4 TEXT * image/x-Freehand
BINARY .FH5 TEXT * image/x-Freehand
BINARY .FHC TEXT * image/x-Freehand
```

Webstar

Unlike the UNIX- and Mac-based servers, MIME information for Webstar servers can be changed only with the WebSTAR Admin application. For each Shockwave format, the steps required to add the MIME information are described next.

Shockwave for Director 4.0

1. Start the application called WebSTAR Admin.

2. Select your server (it must be running) from the Pick A Server window.

3. Select Suffix Mapping from the Configure menu.

4. Choose the following settings:

   Action: BINARY

   File Suffix: .DCR

   File Type: TEXT

   Creator: *

   MIME Type: application/x-director

5. Repeat the last four steps to add MIME information for DIR and DXR suffixes.

6. Close the application.

Shockwave for Director

Follow the same procedure as for Director 4.0*x*.

Shockwave for Authorware

The process for adding Authorware MIME type information is the same as the procedure for adding Director MIME information. Only the entry information varies.

1. Start the application called WebSTAR Admin.
2. Select your server (it must be running) from the Pick A Server window.
3. Select `Suffix Mapping` from the Configure menu.
4. Choose the following settings:

   Action: `BINARY`

   File Suffix: `.AAM`

   File Type: `TEXT`

   Creator: `*`

   MIME Type: `application/x-authorware-map`

5. Repeat the last process for `AAS` and `AAB` suffixes with MIME types as `application/x-authorware-seg` and `application/x-authorware-bin`, respectively.
6. Close the application.

Shockwave for Freehand

Just like adding Authorware and Director MIME types to a WebSTAR server, the WebSTAR Admin program must be used in the following manner.

1. Start the application called WebSTAR Admin.
2. Select your server (it must be running) from the Pick A Server window.
3. Select `Suffix Mapping` from the Configure menu.
4. Choose the following settings:

   Action: `BINARY`

   File Suffix: `.FH4`

   File Type: `TEXT`

   Creator: `*`

   MIME Type: `image/x-Freehand`

5. Repeat the last process for `FH5` and `FHC` suffixes.
6. Close the application.

Summary

Shockwave is a powerful plug-in for experiencing interactivity on the Internet and intranets. Afterburner is the developer's tool that turns a Shockwave-compatible application into a shocked file, ready for use in the HTTP environment.

In some cases (such as for Director files), Afterburner is virtually a one-click operation. In other instances (as with Authorware), Afterburner is a more complex process, requiring dialog box entries and even text editing. But, in all cases, Afterburner and Shockwave are only afterproducts of sophisticated programs.

Authorware and Director in particular are extremely powerful applications capable of creating limitless interactivity and animation, incorporating sound, pictures, and digital video. Afterburner and Shockwave are just a small portion of a very long learning curve. For both programs, Afterburner and Shockwave provide additional language interpreters, enabling the programs to utilize HTTP-specific commands and functions.

With all three programs—Authorware, Director, and Freehand—Afterburner turns a desktop or LAN-based product into an Internet- and intranet-capable program, adding features important for an interactive experience, including point-and-click hypertext linking to URLs and to Internet-compatible media.

To assist you in finding more information on the subjects covered in this chapter, and the products and vendors mentioned, the following list of Internet resources has been compiled:

CompuServe: `http://www.compuserve.com`

Macromedia: `http://www.macromedia.com`

Microsoft: `http://www.microsoft.com`

Navisoft: `http://www.aol.com`

Netscape: `http://www.netscape.com`

Silicon Graphics: `http://www.sgi.com`

V

PART

Special Topics

Creating an ActiveX Control To Activate a Web Page

by Rob McGregor

IN THIS CHAPTER

ActiveX controls are the new standard for OLE Control Extensions (OCXs) that use the OLE Control 96 specification. Because ActiveX controls are changing the face of the World Wide Web, they are having an enormous impact on the world of Windows communications programming. This chapter shows you how to create a new ActiveX control and add it to a Web page to help activate the Internet.

Overview of ActiveX Controls

An ActiveX control is an OLE control with some special features. The control must be a COM object and must export the functions DLLRegisterServer() and DLLUnRegisterServer(). The control must also implement the IUnknown interface. MFC makes this all very easy by providing convenient wrapper classes; the Visual C++ OLE Control Wizard makes it easy to create a skeleton control. The Visual C++ 4.2 Control Wizard has been updated to support advanced features of ActiveX controls. The most important new feature is support for asynchronous code and property downloading. This feature allows control code and properties to load in the background, preventing application blocking.

OLE controls are programmable software components that can be used in a variety of OLE-enabled containers, including COM-aware (ActiveX-enabled) Web browsers on the Internet. The most exciting thing about an ActiveX control is that it is inherently an Internet control. This means that an ActiveX control can be used within an ActiveX document or it can be a direct part of a Web page!

> **NOTE**
>
> ActiveX controls aren't limited to use on the Web. They can also be used in any ActiveX-enabled container (if the control supports the COM interfaces required by that container).

The OLE Controls 96 Specification

ActiveX controls are special because they use the OLE Controls 96 specification. Like standard OLE controls, ActiveX controls are self-contained, plug-in software components. The OLE Controls 96 specification provides some advanced features for OLE controls not available previously, including these:

- Mouse interaction and drag-and-drop services for inactive controls
- Special drawing optimizations
- Flicker-free activation and deactivation
- Flicker-free drawing (note that this feature isn't yet implemented in any container objects)

- Support for windowless controls
- Support for transparent objects
- Support for nonrectangular objects

> **NOTE**
>
> Because the primary purpose of ActiveX technology at this time is to provide useful components over the Internet, it's desirable to keep the code size small for an ActiveX control. To help ensure this, Microsoft Visual C++ 4.x doesn't allow static linkage for ActiveX controls. The controls must use the shared MFC DLLs at runtime, which means that these DLLs must be present on the user's system.

A Sample ActiveX Control: `JIGGLER.OCX`

Let's now implement a basic—but useful and fun—ActiveX control. This control was inspired by the Java applet "Nervous Text," which was written by Daniel Wyszynski from the Center for Applied Large-Scale Computing (CALC).

> **NOTE**
>
> The source code for the `JIGGLER` ActiveX control has no relation whatsoever to the original "Nervous Text" Java applet source code; I started from scratch. (Thanks for the idea though, Dan!)

The basic idea for the control is that a text string, supplied by the user of the control, becomes visually hyperactive in the container, whether it be an ActiveX-enabled Web page or an OLE container window. Each character in the text string must be offset from the next by a random amount on both the x and y axes. This random offset is controlled by a window timer internal to the control; the randomly offset characters are redrawn with each `WM_TIMER` message received by the control. This causes the text string to appear to dance, or jiggle, on the display (thus the name `JIGGLER`).

> **NOTE**
>
> `JIGGLER.OCX`, along with all its source files, can be found in the `SOURCE\CHAP30\JIGGLER` folder on this book's companion CD-ROM.

To test the completed `JIGGLER.OCX` control, you use the Test Container application that ships with Visual C++ and create a simple Web page for Microsoft's ActiveX-enabled Web browser, Internet Explorer 3 (IE3), to test the control in a typical active Web setting.

Creating an OLE Control Skeleton

The first step in creating the `JIGGLER` ActiveX control is to create an ActiveX-compliant control skeleton. The easiest and most effective way to do this is to use the Visual C++ 4.2 OLE Control Wizard, which provides new ActiveX features in step 2 of the Wizard (see Figure 30.1).

FIGURE 30.1.

Creating a new ActiveX control project with the Visual C++ 4.2 OLE Control Wizard.

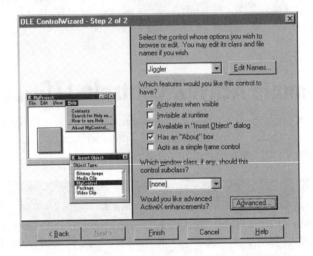

The OLE Control Wizard walks you through the two simple steps needed to create a robust ActiveX control skeleton. Then it's just a matter of adding the methods needed to implement the control's desired functionality (in this case, the jiggling of some text).

> **NOTE**
>
> The Visual C++ OLE Control Wizard enables you to select advanced ActiveX options for your control. The most important of these is *asynchronous download*. For this skeleton control, it's the only option you need to check.

Testing the Skeleton Control

After you select the Finish button in the Control Wizard dialog box, the Control Wizard generates a set of header, source, and support files for the new control. The resulting classes for the `JIGGLER` control from a run of the Control Wizard are shown in Figure 30.2, as displayed in the Visual C++ ClassView pane.

FIGURE 30.2.

The classes and methods generated automatically by the OLE Control Wizard.

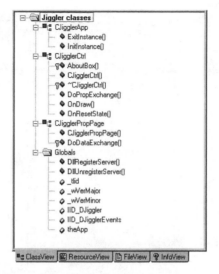

The skeleton control can be compiled at this point. Visual C++ automatically creates a type library and registers the new control with the system registry at this time. If you insert the control into the Test Container application (included with Visual C++), the default visual representation of the control simply draws an ellipse. You can modify the visual aspects of the control by adding the desired code.

Adding Functionality to the Skeleton

Now that you have an ActiveX skeleton to build on, let's add the functionality needed to create an OCX that has some useful purpose—in this case, jiggling text. Your `JIGGLER.OCX` control will have the following features:

- A programmable text string (you know, the one that jiggles) up to 50 characters long. (This can be easily changed to allow for longer strings.) The control automatically resizes to the size of this text.

- Many possible text and background colors.

- Many possible fonts and font styles. The default font is 24-point Arial.

- Variable jiggling speed, determined by the timing interval for the internal window timer used by the control.

Customizing the Project Resources

The default resources for the skeleton control are a good starting point, but they need to be customized for the professional look users have come to expect. For this control, you change the default bitmap used to identify the OCX in client programming system tool palettes (such as the Visual Basic tool palette) to that shown in Figure 30.3.

Figure 30.3.

The new customized bitmap for the JIGGLER *control under construction in the Developer Studio resource editor.*

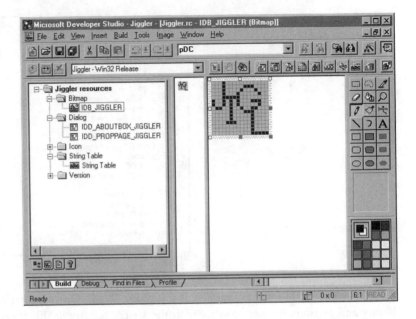

After recompiling, the OCX uses the new bitmap to help users differentiate a JIGGLER control from other controls in a tool palette.

The Property Page Dialog Resource

To enable users to control the JIGGLER.OCX properties at design time, you add controls to the control's property page dialog box resource (IDD_PROPAGE_JIGGLER) to represent the state or value of each property exposed by the control. After adding the appropriate controls for every property (as discussed next), the dialog resource looks like the one shown in Figure 30.4.

The dialog box resource has only four controls: two static text boxes and two edit controls. The edit controls allow the user to specify a text string (for the jiggling text), and the interval (in milliseconds) at which the jiggling occurs. The entire dialog resource script should look something like that shown in Listing 30.1.

Listing 30.1. The IDD_PROPPAGE_JIGGLER dialog resource.

```
IDD_PROPPAGE_JIGGLER DIALOG DISCARDABLE  0, 0, 250, 62
STYLE WS_CHILD
FONT 8, "MS Sans Serif"
BEGIN
    LTEXT           "Jiggle Text:",IDC_STATIC,5,7,45,10
    EDITTEXT        IDC_EDIT_CAPTION,55,5,180,12,ES_AUTOHSCROLL
    LTEXT           "Interval:",IDC_STATIC,5,22,45,10
    EDITTEXT        IDC_EDIT_INTERVAL,55,20,40,12,ES_AUTOHSCROLL
END
```

FIGURE 30.4.

The customized property page dialog resource in the Developer Studio resource editor.

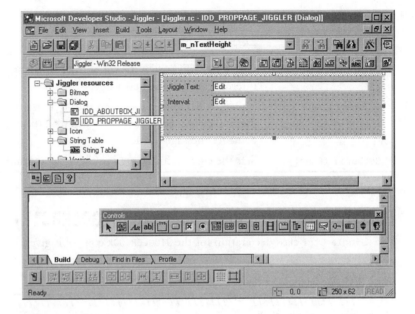

The CJigglerCtrl Class

To fill out the new JIGGLER.OCX CJigglerCtrl class and make it fully functional, perform the following steps:

1. Use the Class Wizard to add OLE Automation properties to the class; alternatively, add the dispatch map code manually.

2. Implement the code to provide the jiggling functionality you need.

Here are the properties you'll add:

- ■ Caption: The text used for jiggling.
- ■ Interval: The interval (in milliseconds) used for the control's internal timer.
- ■ DefaultFont: The font used to display the jiggling text.

The methods you'll add are listed in Table 30.1.

Table 30.1. The additional methods used by the JIGGLE.OCX control.

Method	Description
GetDefaultFont()	Gets the custom font stored in the m_fontDefault data member.
JiggleText()	The method that implements the text-jiggling functionality.
OnCreate()	Starts the internal timer when the control window is created.
OnDestroy()	Kills the internal timer when the control window is destroyed.

30

CREATING AN ACTIVEX CONTROL

continues

Table 30.1. continued

Method	Description
OnIntervalChanged()	Called by MFC when the timer interval changes and resets the internal timer to the new value.
OnTimer()	Called by MFC in response to the WM_TIMER message. This method calls JiggleText() for each WM_TIMER message in the control's message queue.
SetDefaultFont()	Sets the custom font stored in the m_fontDefault data member.

The CJigglerCtrl Class Interface (JIGGLERC.H)

The CJigglerCtrl class declaration for the JIGGLER.OCX control is given in Listing 30.2.

Listing 30.2. The interface for the CJigglerCtrl class (JIGGLERC.H).

```
///////////////////////////////////////////////////////////////////
//   Module  : JIGGLERC.H
//
//   Purpose : Interface for the CJigglerCtrl OLE control class.

#define IDC_TIMER1   100

///////////////////////////////////////////////////////////////////
// The CJigglerCtrl class

class CJigglerCtrl : public COleControl
{
    DECLARE_DYNCREATE(CJigglerCtrl)

// Constructor
public:
    CJigglerCtrl();
    virtual void DoPropExchange(CPropExchange* pPX);

protected:
    CRect          m_rcBounds;     // Control bounding rect
    CFontHolder    m_fontDefault;  // Custom OLE font

    void JiggleText();

    DECLARE_OLECREATE_EX(CJigglerCtrl)    // Class factory and guid
    DECLARE_OLETYPELIB(CJigglerCtrl)      // GetTypeInfo
    DECLARE_PROPPAGEIDS(CJigglerCtrl)     // Property page IDs
    DECLARE_OLECTLTYPE(CJigglerCtrl)      // Type name and misc status

    // Message map entries
    afx_msg int OnCreate(LPCREATESTRUCT lpCreateStruct);
    afx_msg void OnDestroy();
    afx_msg void OnTimer(UINT nIDEvent);
    afx_msg void AboutBox();
```

```
    DECLARE_MESSAGE_MAP()

    // Event maps
    DECLARE_EVENT_MAP()

    // Dispatch maps
    short m_nInterval;
    afx_msg void OnIntervalChanged();
    afx_msg LPFONTDISP GetDefaultFont();
    afx_msg void SetDefaultFont(LPFONTDISP newValue);

    DECLARE_DISPATCH_MAP()
public:
    // Dispatch and event IDs
    enum {
        dispidInterval    = 1L,
        dispidDefaultFont = 2L,
    };
};
```

//

Implementing the `CJigglerCtrl` Class

The `CJigglerCtrl` class is the heart of your ActiveX control, providing all the functionality the control needs. The helper methods and dispatch map methods listed in the class declaration in Listing 30.2 must, of course, be implemented. The default font is described by the FONTDESC type, which is used by OLE to create the font (in this case, 24-point Arial). This is shown in the following code:

```
// Default OLE font for the control
static const FONTDESC _fontdescDefault =
{
    sizeof(FONTDESC), OLESTR("Arial"), FONTSIZE(24),
    FW_NORMAL, ANSI_CHARSET, FALSE, FALSE, FALSE
};
```

The class data member `m_fontDefault` is used to hold the resulting `CFontHolder` object. The `CFontHolder` class encapsulates the functionality of a Windows font object and the OLE `IFont` interface. You use this in the Jiggler control to implement the custom `DefaultFont` property.

The `IFontDispatch` Interface

The `CFontHolder` class implements an OLE font object that uses the `IFontDispatch` OLE interface. This interface exposes a font object's properties through OLE automation. Table 30.2 describes the dispatch IDs for the various font properties.

30

CREATING AN
ACTIVEX CONTROL

Table 30.2. The dispIDs for various OLE font properties.

Symbol	Value
DISPID_FONT_NAME	0
DISPID_FONT_SIZE	2
DISPID_FONT_BOLD	3
DISPID_FONT_ITALIC	4
DISPID_FONT_UNDER	5
DISPID_FONT_STRIKE	6
DISPID_FONT_WEIGHT	7
DISPID_FONT_CHARSET	8

The properties in the IFontDisp interface support both read and write access, and they are listed in Table 30.3. These properties will become very useful later in this chapter when you want to manipulate font characteristics for your JIGGLER control with a scripting language in your sample Web page.

Table 30.3. The properties for the IFontDisp interface.

Property	Type	Description
Name	BSTR	The face name of the font (for example, Arial)
Size	CY	The point size of the font
Bold	BOOL	Indicates if the font is bold
Italic	BOOL	Indicates if the font is italic
Underline	BOOL	Indicates if the font is underlined
Strikethrough	BOOL	Indicates if the font is strikethrough
Weight	short	The boldness of the font
Charset	short	The character set used for the font

The CJigglerCtrl Constructor

The CJigglerCtrl constructor simply calls the COleControl method InitializeIIDs() with the appropriate parameters, as you can see here:

```
CJigglerCtrl::CJigglerCtrl() : m_fontDefault(&m_xFontNotification)
{
    InitializeIIDs(&IID_DJiggler, &IID_DJigglerEvents);
m_lReadyState = READYSTATE_LOADING;
}
```

The COleControl member m_1ReadyState is set to the value READYSTATE_LOADING to indicate that the control is currently loading its properties.

The Jiggler Control Properties

The dispatch map for the CJigglerCtrl class is used to set up the connection between class data members and property values. Listing 30.3 shows the dispatch map for the CJigglerCtrl class.

Listing 30.3. The dispatch map for the CJigglerCtrl class.

```
/////////////////////////////////////////////////////////////////
// Dispatch map

BEGIN_DISPATCH_MAP(CJigglerCtrl, COleControl)
    DISP_PROPERTY_NOTIFY(CJigglerCtrl, "Interval", m_nInterval,
        OnIntervalChanged, VT_I2)

    DISP_PROPERTY_EX(CJigglerCtrl, "DefaultFont", GetDefaultFont,
        SetDefaultFont, VT_FONT)

    DISP_DEFVALUE(CJigglerCtrl, "Caption")
    DISP_STOCKPROP_CAPTION()
    DISP_STOCKFUNC_REFRESH()
    DISP_STOCKPROP_READYSTATE()
    DISP_STOCKPROP_BACKCOLOR()
    DISP_STOCKPROP_FORECOLOR()
    DISP_FUNCTION_ID(CJigglerCtrl, "AboutBox", DISPID_ABOUTBOX,
        AboutBox, VT_EMPTY, VTS_NONE)
END_DISPATCH_MAP()
```

> **NOTE**
>
> The JIGGLER control uses the stock property Caption, which is the default property for the control. This is evident from the use of the DISP_STOCKPROP_CAPTION and DISP_DEFVALUE macros.

There are three property pages for this control: one custom page (the General page) and two predefined pages (Colors and Font), as specified with this code:

```
/////////////////////////////////////////////////////////////////
// Property pages

BEGIN_PROPPAGEIDS(CJigglerCtrl, 3)
    PROPPAGEID(CJigglerPropPage::guid)
    PROPPAGEID(CLSID_CColorPropPage)
    PROPPAGEID(CLSID_CFontPropPage)
END_PROPPAGEIDS(CJigglerCtrl)
```

At runtime, The General property page (defined by your customized dialog template resource) looks like the one in Figure 30.5.

FIGURE 30.5.
The customized General property page
(CJigglerPropPage::guid).

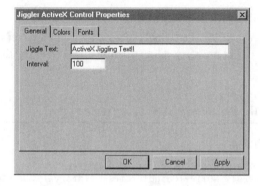

The identifiers CLSID_CColorPropPage and CLSID_CFontPropPage are predefined values that MFC uses to add the Colors and Font property pages to the control's property sheet. Figure 30.6 shows the predefined Colors property page with the two stock properties BackColor and ForeColor present.

FIGURE 30.6.
The predefined Colors property page
(CLSID_CColorPropPage).

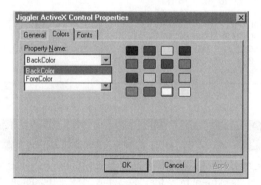

Figure 30.7 shows the predefined Font property page with the default Arial font selected.

FIGURE 30.7.
The predefined Font property page
(CLSID_CFontPropPage).

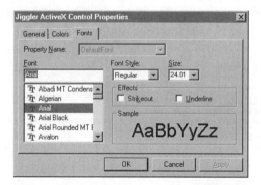

Object Persistence with DoPropExchange()

To make sure that your OLE control "remembers" settings applied to properties at design time when it executes at runtime, you must implement object persistence for the control. By doing this, you can ensure that property settings made with a property editor will remain valid at runtime without writing additional code on the client side. This is achieved by using the PX_* group of persistence support functions provided by MFC.

The CJigglerCtrl::DoPropExchange() method makes calls to MFC's predefined persistence methods to provide property persistence for the JIGGLER control. The method is given in Listing 30.4.

Listing 30.4. The DoPropExchange() method.

```
///////////////////////////////////////////////////////////////////////
// CJigglerCtrl::DoPropExchange - Persistence support

void CJigglerCtrl::DoPropExchange(CPropExchange* pPX)
{
    ExchangeVersion(pPX, MAKELONG(_wVerMinor, _wVerMajor));

    // Set a default caption
    if (InternalGetText() == "")
        SetText(_T("ActiveX Jiggler!!"));

    COleControl::DoPropExchange(pPX);

//
// Call PX_* functions for each persistent custom property
//
    // Property exchange for default font
    PX_Font(pPX, _T("DefaultFont"), m_fontDefault,
        &_fontdescDefault);

    PX_Short(pPX, _T("Interval"), m_nInterval, 100);
}
```

Miscellaneous OLE Control Housekeeping

When the CJigglerCtrl class was generated by the OLE Control Wizard, it generated some very important OLE housekeeping functions in the JIGGLERC.CPP source file. These functions perform the following tasks:

- Initialize the class factory and GUID
- Implement code to specify the type library ID and control version information
- Define the control's interface IDs (IIDs): IID_DJiggler and IID_DJigglerEvents
- Specify control type information
- Add or remove system registry entries for CJigglerCtrl

30

CREATING AN
ACTIVEX CONTROL

Listing 30.5 shows the code for these tasks.

Listing 30.5. OLE housekeeping functions for the CJigglerCtrl class.

```
///////////////////////////////////////////////////////////////////
// Initialize class factory and guid

IMPLEMENT_OLECREATE_EX(CJigglerCtrl, "JIGGLER.JigglerCtrl.1",
    0x5cd2fc83, 0xe7bd, 0x11cf, 0xa3, 0xbc, 0x44, 0x45, 0x53,
    0x54, 0, 0)

///////////////////////////////////////////////////////////////////
// Type library ID and version

IMPLEMENT_OLETYPELIB(CJigglerCtrl, _tlid, _wVerMajor, _wVerMinor)

///////////////////////////////////////////////////////////////////
// Interface IDs

const IID BASED_CODE IID_DJiggler =
{
    0x5cd2fc81, 0xe7bd, 0x11cf,
    {
        0xa3, 0xbc, 0x44, 0x45, 0x53, 0x54, 0, 0
    }
};

const IID BASED_CODE IID_DJigglerEvents =
{
    0x5cd2fc82, 0xe7bd, 0x11cf,
    {
        0xa3, 0xbc, 0x44, 0x45, 0x53, 0x54, 0, 0
    }
};

///////////////////////////////////////////////////////////////////
// Control type information

static const DWORD BASED_CODE _dwJigglerOleMisc =
    OLEMISC_ACTIVATEWHENVISIBLE |
    OLEMISC_SETCLIENTSITEFIRST |
    OLEMISC_INSIDEOUT |
    OLEMISC_CANTLINKINSIDE |
    OLEMISC_RECOMPOSEONRESIZE;

IMPLEMENT_OLECTLTYPE(CJigglerCtrl, IDS_JIGGLER, _dwJigglerOleMisc)

///////////////////////////////////////////////////////////////////
// CJigglerCtrl::CJigglerCtrlFactory::UpdateRegistry -
// Adds or removes system registry entries for CJigglerCtrl

BOOL CJigglerCtrl::CJigglerCtrlFactory::UpdateRegistry(
    BOOL bRegister)
{
```

```
        if (bRegister)
            return AfxOleRegisterControlClass(
                AfxGetInstanceHandle(),
                m_clsid,
                m_lpszProgID,
                IDS_JIGGLER,
                IDB_JIGGLER,
                afxRegInsertable | afxRegApartmentThreading,
                _dwJigglerOleMisc,
                _tlid,
                _wVerMajor,
                _wVerMinor);
        else
            return AfxOleUnregisterClass(m_clsid, m_lpszProgID);
}
```

The JiggleText() Method

Typically, MFC calls the OnDraw() method whenever a control needs to be redrawn. In this case, OnDraw() simply isn't needed because the control is continually redrawn in response to the internal timer firing WM_TIMER messages. Instead, the drawing code all takes place within the JiggleText() method, shown in Listing 30.6.

Listing 30.6. The JiggleText() method.

```
//////////////////////////////////////////////////////////////////
// CJigglerCtrl::JiggleText() - The meat of the control!

void CJigglerCtrl::JiggleText()
{
    // Get the client DC
    CClientDC dc(this);

    // Prepare a memory DC for holding a memory bitmap
    CDC dcMem;
    dcMem.CreateCompatibleDC(&dc);

    // Get the current caption text and text length
    const CString& strText = InternalGetText();
    int nMsgLen = strText.GetLength();

    // Select font and set transparent text mode, forecolor
    CFont* pFontOld = SelectFontObject(&dcMem, m_fontDefault);
    int nModeOld = dcMem.SetBkMode(TRANSPARENT);
    int crTextColorOldMem = dcMem.SetTextColor(
        TranslateColor(GetForeColor()));

    // Get the text char size for current font
    TEXTMETRIC tm;
    dcMem.GetTextMetrics(&tm);

    int nTextHeight = tm.tmHeight + tm.tmExternalLeading * 2;
    int nAveCharWidth = (int)(tm.tmAveCharWidth * 1.5);
```

continues

Listing 30.6. continued

```cpp
// Get the bounding rect for the entire string (current font)
int nCtrlWidth = nAveCharWidth * nMsgLen + (nAveCharWidth / 2);
int nCtrlHeight = nTextHeight + (nTextHeight / 4);

// Autosize the control to the text (if needed)
int nWidth, nHeight;
GetControlSize(&nWidth, &nHeight);
CRect rcOld(0, 0, nCtrlWidth, nCtrlHeight);
CRect rcCurrent(0, 0, nWidth, nHeight);

if (rcCurrent != rcOld)
    SetControlSize(nCtrlWidth, nCtrlHeight);

// Prepare a memory bitmap
CBitmap bmp;
bmp.CreateCompatibleBitmap(&dc, nCtrlWidth, nCtrlHeight);

// Select the bitmap
CBitmap* pbmpOld = dcMem.SelectObject(&bmp);

// Fill with current background color
CRect rc(0, 0, nCtrlWidth, nCtrlHeight);
CBrush brBack(TranslateColor(GetBackColor()));
dcMem.FillRect(&rc, &brBack);

// Create a random number generating object
CRand rand;

// Jiggle the chars
for (int i = 0; i < nMsgLen; i++)
{
    CRect rc;
    UINT cx = rand.MapRand(nAveCharWidth) / 2;
    UINT cy = rand.MapRand(nTextHeight) / 4;

    rc.left   = (nAveCharWidth * i) + cx;
    rc.right  = rc.left + nAveCharWidth + cx;
    rc.top    = cy;
    rc.bottom = rc.top + nTextHeight + cy;

    // Draw next character on the bitmap
    dcMem.DrawText((CString)strText[i], rc, DT_CENTER);
}

// Blast bitmapped text to the window
dc.BitBlt(0, 0, nCtrlWidth, nCtrlHeight, &dcMem, 0, 0, SRCCOPY);

// Clean up
dcMem.SelectObject(pbmpOld);
dcMem.SelectObject(pFontOld);
dcMem.SetTextColor(crTextColorOldMem);
dcMem.SetBkMode(TranslateColor(nModeOld));
bmp.DeleteObject();
}
```

This code might look somewhat tricky at first glance, but the idea is really quite simple. To make the text jiggle, you get the bounding rectangle of the text using the text metrics of the current font. Then you subdivide this rectangle into smaller rectangles, one for each character in the string. You then draw the text, one character at a time (within a loop) on a memory bitmap, with each character offset by a random amount in the x and y axes.

The memory bitmap is then blasted to the control's client area using the `CDC::BitBlt()` method. Using `BitBlt()` instead of drawing directly in the control prevents flashing and makes the jiggling look much smoother. The control's client area is resized automatically to the maximum size of the jiggled text string. This provides the smallest area needed for the `BitBlt()` and optimizes the speed of the bit block transfer operation.

> **CAUTION**
>
> It's very important to clean up by calling the `DeleteObject()` method for the GDI bitmap object. If this isn't done, the control will allocate a new bitmap every time the timer fires a `WM_TIMER` message, and the GDI heap will be quickly exhausted. This will cause unpredictable results, always resulting in the text no longer jiggling, but it could also easily cause a system crash under Windows 95!

The `CJigglerPropPage` Class

The `CJigglerPropPage` class provides the user interface needed to control `JIGGLER.OCX` properties at design time from development environments such as the Visual C++ Developer Studio. The interface for the `CJigglerPropPage` class is given in Listing 30.7.

Listing 30.7. The interface for the `CJigglerPropPage` class.

```
/////////////////////////////////////////////////////////////////
//   Module  : JIGGLERC.CPP
//
//   Purpose : Interface for the CJigglerPropPage property page
//             class.

/////////////////////////////////////////////////////////////////
// The CJigglerPropPage class

class CJigglerPropPage : public COlePropertyPage
{
    DECLARE_DYNCREATE(CJigglerPropPage)
    DECLARE_OLECREATE_EX(CJigglerPropPage)

public:
    CJigglerPropPage();    // Constructor

    // Dialog Data
    enum { IDD = IDD_PROPPAGE_JIGGLER };
```

continues

Listing 30.7. continued

```
   CString   m_Caption;
   int       m_nInterval;

protected:
   // DDX/DDV support
   virtual void DoDataExchange(CDataExchange* pDX);

// Message map
DECLARE_MESSAGE_MAP()
};

///////////////////////////////////////////////////////////////////
```

This class uses two data members, m_Caption and m_nInterval, to handle the data exchange to the Caption and Interval properties. The complete implementation source code for this class is given in Listing 30.8.

Listing 30.8. The implementation of the CJigglerPropPage class.

```
///////////////////////////////////////////////////////////////////
//   Module  : JIGGLERP.CPP
//
//   Purpose : Implementation of the CJigglerPropPage property
//             page class.

#include "stdafx.h"
#include "Jiggler.h"
#include "JigglerP.h"

IMPLEMENT_DYNCREATE(CJigglerPropPage, COlePropertyPage)

///////////////////////////////////////////////////////////////////
// Initialize class factory and guid

IMPLEMENT_OLECREATE_EX(CJigglerPropPage,
    "JIGGLER.JigglerPropPage.1",
    0x5cd2fc84, 0xe7bd, 0x11cf, 0xa3, 0xbc, 0x44, 0x45, 0x53,
    0x54, 0, 0)

///////////////////////////////////////////////////////////////////
// CJigglerPropPage::CJigglerPropPageFactory::UpdateRegistry -
// Adds or removes system registry entries for CJigglerPropPage

BOOL CJigglerPropPage::CJigglerPropPageFactory::UpdateRegistry(
    BOOL bRegister)
{
    if (bRegister)
       return AfxOleRegisterPropertyPageClass(
          AfxGetInstanceHandle(), m_clsid, IDS_JIGGLER_PPG);
    else
       return AfxOleUnregisterClass(m_clsid, NULL);
}
```

```
////////////////////////////////////////////////////////////////////
// CJigglerPropPage::CJigglerPropPage - Constructor

CJigglerPropPage::CJigglerPropPage() :
    COlePropertyPage(IDD, IDS_JIGGLER_PPG_CAPTION)
{
    m_Caption   = _T("");
    m_nInterval = 100;
}


////////////////////////////////////////////////////////////////////
// CJigglerPropPage::DoDataExchange - Moves data between page
//   and properties

void CJigglerPropPage::DoDataExchange(CDataExchange* pDX)
{
    DDP_Text(pDX, IDC_EDIT_CAPTION, m_Caption, _T("Caption"));
    DDX_Text(pDX, IDC_EDIT_CAPTION, m_Caption);
    DDV_MaxChars(pDX, m_Caption, 50);

    DDP_Text(pDX, IDC_EDIT_INTERVAL, m_nInterval, _T("Interval"));
    DDX_Text(pDX, IDC_EDIT_INTERVAL, m_nInterval);
    DDV_MinMaxInt(pDX, m_nInterval, 10, 1000);

    DDP_PostProcessing(pDX);
}

////////////////////////////////////////////////////////////////////
```

Testing the Control in the OLE Control Test Container

To test the new functionality of the JIGGLER control, you first drop it into the Test Container application to verify that all the properties are functioning properly and that the behavior of the control is what you expect. The result of this test is shown in Figure 30.8.

Just to verify that everything works properly at design time in an actual Windows development environment, you dropped JIGGLER.OCX into a new Visual Basic 4 form. The result of this small test can be seen in Figure 30.9.

FIGURE 30.8.

The fully implemented JIGGLER *OLE control in the Test Container application.*

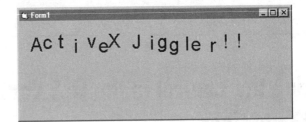

FIGURE 30.9.

The JIGGLER *ActiveX control in a generic Visual Basic 4 form.*

Using the New Control on a Sample Web Page

ActiveX controls are the hot new way to activate the World Wide Web, bringing previously static Web pages to life. Now that the control has been successfully tested in both the Test Container application and a generic VB form, it's time to write a Web page of your own to fully test the control in a Web browser. To "activate" this sample Web page, you'll use three instances of the JIGGLER control and programmatically control them with OLE Automation by using VBScript, Microsoft's trimmed-down version of Visual Basic for the Internet.

NOTE

The source for the sample Web page can be found in the SOURCE\CHAP30\JIGGLER folder on this book's companion CD-ROM as the file JIGGLER3.HTM.

Creating a Simple HTML Web Page

Before you can add a control to a Web page, you must first create an HTML document that defines the page. There are several HTML generating utilities and applications available, but you'll start your sample page by using one that comes free with every version of Windows: Notepad. Yes, with the venerable Notepad and a little knowledge of HTML syntax, you can create a simple Web page in no time. The source code for a basic Web page contains just a few simple HTML tags, as shown in Listing 30.9.

Listing 30.9. The HTML source for a minimal Web page.

```
<HTML>
<HEAD>
<TITLE>Some Title</TITLE>
</HEAD>
<BODY>

</BODY>
</HTML>
```

Of course, this code is pretty useless, because nothing appears in the browser! You must customize the page by adding some text that describes the new JIGGLER ActiveX control, as shown in Listing 30.10.

Listing 30.10. The modified HTML source for describing the JIGGLER ActiveX control.

```
<HTML>
<HEAD>
<TITLE>Rob's Jiggler ActiveX Control</TITLE>
</HEAD>
<BODY BGCOLOR="#FFFFFF">

<H2><I>Rob's ActiveX Jiggler Control</I></H2>
<HR>
This is my new JIGGLER ActiveX control!! Pretty cool, eh?
 It was inspired by the "Nervous Text" Java applet, but this was totally
 redesigned from scratch and written in C++ for ActiveX! It supports many
 background and text colors, and it's easily extensible, so go for it!<p>

</BODY>
</HTML>
```

Note that you've set the BODY tag to include a background color set to white:

```
<BODY BGCOLOR="#FFFFFF">
```

When opened in Microsoft's ActiveX-enabled Web browser Internet Explorer 3 (IE3), this code results in a Web page that resembles the one in Figure 30.10.

30

CREATING AN
ACTIVEX CONTROL

FIGURE 30.10.
*The basic Web page in
Internet Explorer 3.0.*

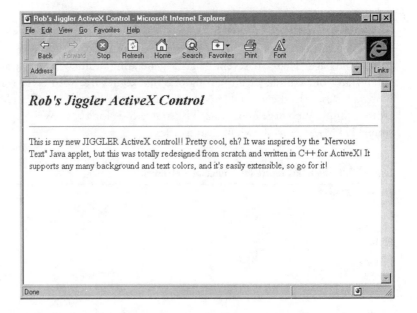

Adding the JIGGLER Control to the Web Page

Now that the basic HTML file is ready, how do you add the ActiveX control to the page to activate it with some exciting jiggling text? The easiest way to add the JIGGLER.OCX to the Web page is with a very useful tool: Microsoft's ActiveX Control Pad. The Control Pad is a free utility designed to insert ActiveX controls into Web pages. This utility also generates basic VBScript and JavaScript source code for the controls on your pages.

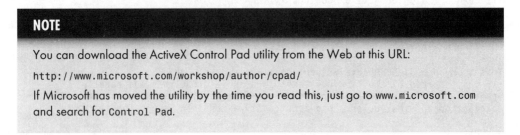

NOTE

You can download the ActiveX Control Pad utility from the Web at this URL:

`http://www.microsoft.com/workshop/author/cpad/`

If Microsoft has moved the utility by the time you read this, just go to `www.microsoft.com` and search for `Control Pad`.

To add the JIGGLER control to the Web page, just open the JIGGLER3.HTM file in Control Pad and then select the Edit | Insert ActiveX Control menu command. This action activates the Insert ActiveX Controls dialog box (see Figure 30.11).

FIGURE 30.11.

Inserting the
JIGGLER.OCX *into*
an HTML document
using the ActiveX
Control Pad.

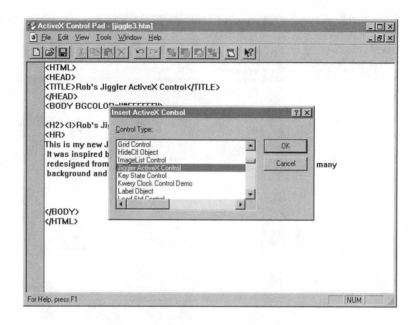

Select JIGGLER ActiveX Control from the list; the Control Pad opens an editing window similar to the one found in Visual Basic (see Figure 30.12). By setting the Caption, ForeColor, and BackColor properties in the Properties dialog box, you can visually set these stock OLE control properties.

NOTE

If the JIGGLER control isn't on the Insert Control list, you'll need to manually register the control. You can do so in the Test Container application by choosing the File | Register Controls menu command.

Set the Caption property to ActiveX using the property editor. Next, visually set the BackColor property to the color white by double-clicking the BackColor property in the Properties window and choosing the white square from the resulting color-selection dialog box (see Figure 30.13). Set the ForeColor property to the color red using the same technique. The changes are immediately reflected in the Edit ActiveX Control window.

When you're finished, close the Properties and Edit ActiveX Control windows. At this point, the Control Pad generates and inserts the code for the JIGGLER control into the HTML document. The code added by Control Pad is shown in Listing 30.11.

30

CREATING AN
ACTIVEX CONTROL

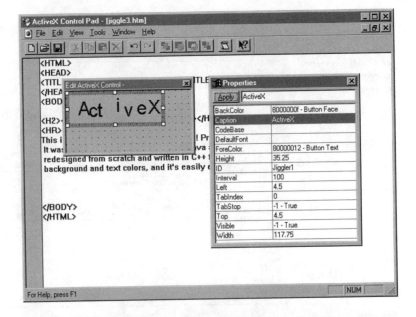

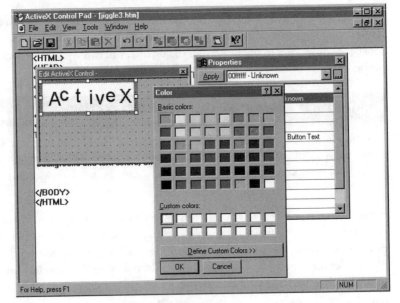

Listing 30.11. The basic JIGGLER control source code generated by the Control Pad.

```
<OBJECT ID="Jiggler1" WIDTH=157 HEIGHT=47
  CLASSID="CLSID:5CD2FC83-E7BD-11CF-A3BC-444553540000">
    <PARAM NAME="_Version" VALUE="65536">
    <PARAM NAME="_ExtentX" VALUE="4154">
    <PARAM NAME="_ExtentY" VALUE="1244">
```

```
    <PARAM NAME="_StockProps" VALUE="11">
    <PARAM NAME="Caption" VALUE="ActiveX">
    <PARAM NAME="ForeColor" VALUE="255">
    <PARAM NAME="BackColor" VALUE="50331647">
</OBJECT>
```

This code uses the World Wide Web Consortium (W3C) <OBJECT> HTML tag to describe the ActiveX control. The CLASSID on line 2 gives the JIGGLER control's CLSID, which Control Pad automatically looked up in the registry for you. This is a very convenient feature! Notice that the second line ends the <OBJECT> tag with a closing bracket (>) after the CLSID number. You'll add a new line *inside* the <OBJECT> tag that specifies the actual URL of the JIGGLER ActiveX control on your Web server.

The CODEBASE keyword lets IE3 find and download the control to a user's machine if the control doesn't exist on that machine already. For your purposes, assume that the control exists in a subdirectory of the directory in which your JIGGLER3.HTM file lives. Let's call this directory ocx. This gives you the following relative CODEBASE:

```
CODEBASE = "./ocx/Jiggler.ocx">
```

The preceding CODEBASE line now ends the <OBJECT> tag, which gives IE3 everything it needs to know about where to find the control. The <OBJECT> tag is followed by several PARAM NAME lines that define the values for control properties. This change yields the following code, which fully describes the JIGGLER ActiveX object, named Jiggler1, in HTML:

```
<OBJECT ID="Jiggler1" WIDTH=157 HEIGHT=47
 CLASSID="CLSID:5CD2FC83-E7BD-11CF-A3BC-444553540000"
 CODEBASE="./ocx/Jiggler.ocx">
    <PARAM NAME="_Version" VALUE="65536">
    <PARAM NAME="_ExtentX" VALUE="4154">
    <PARAM NAME="_ExtentY" VALUE="1244">
    <PARAM NAME="_StockProps" VALUE="11">
    <PARAM NAME="Caption" VALUE="ActiveX">
    <PARAM NAME="ForeColor" VALUE="255">
    <PARAM NAME="BackColor" VALUE="50331647">
</OBJECT>
```

By simply copying this object definition and pasting two more copies into the document, you create a total of three JIGGLER controls on the page. Each control must have a unique name, so you must change the names of the pasted controls. Change the name of the second control from Jiggler1 to Jiggler2, and change the name of the third control from Jiggler1 to Jiggler3.

The Control Pad editor window displays buttons in the left margin that you can click to bring up the edit and property windows for each control (see Figure 30.14). Use these buttons to change the Caption and ForeColor properties of the second and third instances of the JIGGLER control. Set the Caption property for Jiggler2 to Text and the ForeColor to the color green (value 65280). Set the Caption property for Jiggler3 to Jiggling and the ForeColor to the color blue (value 16711680). There! A nice red, green, and blue trio of JIGGLER objects.

FIGURE 30.14.

The Control Pad editor provides edit buttons for each ActiveX control in an HTML document.

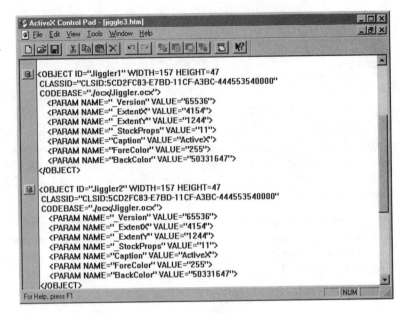

```
<OBJECT ID="Jiggler1" WIDTH=157 HEIGHT=47
CLASSID="CLSID:5CD2FC83-E7BD-11CF-A3BC-444553540000"
CODEBASE="./ocx/Jiggler.ocx">
   <PARAM NAME="_Version" VALUE="65536">
   <PARAM NAME="_ExtentX" VALUE="4154">
   <PARAM NAME="_ExtentY" VALUE="1244">
   <PARAM NAME="_StockProps" VALUE="11">
   <PARAM NAME="Caption" VALUE="ActiveX">
   <PARAM NAME="ForeColor" VALUE="255">
   <PARAM NAME="BackColor" VALUE="50331647">
</OBJECT>

<OBJECT ID="Jiggler2" WIDTH=157 HEIGHT=47
CLASSID="CLSID:5CD2FC83-E7BD-11CF-A3BC-444553540000"
CODEBASE="./ocx/Jiggler.ocx">
   <PARAM NAME="_Version" VALUE="65536">
   <PARAM NAME="_ExtentX" VALUE="4154">
   <PARAM NAME="_ExtentY" VALUE="1244">
   <PARAM NAME="_StockProps" VALUE="11">
   <PARAM NAME="Caption" VALUE="ActiveX">
   <PARAM NAME="ForeColor" VALUE="255">
   <PARAM NAME="BackColor" VALUE="50331647">
</OBJECT>
```

The Control Pad makes creating these definitions of your JIGGLER objects easy and convenient, but the objects aren't very flexible on their own. After all, an ActiveX control is, at its core, an OLE Automation server. To take programmatic control of the object in a Web page, you must use a scripting language. The next section uses VBScript for this example.

Programming the JIGGLER Control with VBScript

Now that the HTML code is in place for the control, you can write some simple VBScript code to set JIGGLER property values when the document is loaded into the IE3 browser window. Much more can be done with VBScript, but let's keep it simple.

> **NOTE**
>
> For the full documentation on VBScript, visit the Microsoft Web site. While you're there, check out the cool VBScript code samples. You can find this stuff at the following URL:
>
> http://www.microsoft.com/vbscript

To begin, you want to change the Interval property for each control, and you also want to change the DefaultFont properties for each control. This should be done when the page is first loaded into a browser. By selecting the Tools | ScriptWizard menu command in the Control Pad, you can generate a default script with the proper syntax already in place. To get an idea of how this tool works, follow these steps:

1. Select the `onLoad` event for the `window` object in the left pane, highlighting it in the tree control.
2. Select the `Interval` property for the `Jiggler1` control in the right pane, highlighting it in the tree control.
3. Click the Insert Action button and enter the number `50` in the resulting input dialog box.

These steps result in the Script Wizard associating the value of `50` with the `Interval` property of the `Jiggler1` object when the page is loaded, as you can see in Figure 30.15.

FIGURE 30.15.

Defining a basic script in the Control Pad Script Wizard.

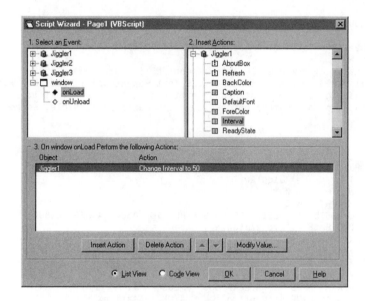

Click OK at this point to generate the following VBScript code:

```
<SCRIPT LANGUAGE="VBScript">
<!--
Sub window_onLoad()
   Jiggler1.Interval = 50
end sub
-->
</SCRIPT>
```

Because the `DefaultFont` property uses the `IFontDispatch` interface, you can use the OLE Automation properties presented earlier in Table 30.3 to programmatically set font properties. The font properties you'll set are all `IFontDispatch` interface subproperties of the `DefaultFont` property, including `Name`, `Size`, `Italic`, and `Bold`. The following is an example using these properties in VBScript code:

```
Jiggler1.DefaultFont.Name   = "Times New Roman"
Jiggler1.DefaultFont.Size   = 20
Jiggler1.DefaultFont.Italic = True
Jiggler1.DefaultFont.Bold   = True
```

30

**CREATING AN
ACTIVEX CONTROL**

As the final step, duplicate the VBScript code for the other two JIGGLER object instances, changing the names to Jiggler2 and Jiggler3 (of course). This gives you the final HTML source code found in Listing 30.12. You're finished! The JIGGLER3.HTM Web page is ready to be loaded into IE3, and the three JIGGLER objects will jiggle away until the cows come home.

Listing 30.12. The complete source code for the final version of JIGGLER3.HTM.

```
<HTML>
<HEAD>
<TITLE>Rob's Jiggler ActiveX Control</TITLE>
</HEAD>

<BODY BGCOLOR="#FFFFFF">

<H2><I>Rob's Jiggler ActiveX Control</I></H2>
<HR>
This is my new JIGGLER ActiveX control!! Pretty cool, eh?
 It was inspired by the "Nervous Text" Java applet, but this was totally
 redesigned from scratch and written in C++ for ActiveX! It supports many
 background and text colors, and it's easily extensible, so go for it!
<P>

<!-- Create 3 Jiggler ActiveX controls -->

<OBJECT
    ID       = "Jiggler1"
    WIDTH    = 0
    HEIGHT   = 0
    CLASSID  = "CLSID:5CD2FC83-E7BD-11CF-A3BC-444553540000"
    CODEBASE = "./ocx/Jiggler.ocx">

    <PARAM NAME = "_Version"    VALUE = "65536">
    <PARAM NAME = "_ExtentX"    VALUE = "11933">
    <PARAM NAME = "_ExtentY"    VALUE = "1244">
    <PARAM NAME = "_StockProps" VALUE = "11">
    <PARAM NAME = "Caption"     VALUE = "ActiveX">
    <PARAM NAME = "ForeColor"   VALUE = "255">
    <PARAM NAME = "BackColor"   VALUE = "16777215">
</OBJECT>

<OBJECT
    ID       = "Jiggler2"
    WIDTH    = 0
    HEIGHT   = 0
    CLASSID  = "CLSID:5CD2FC83-E7BD-11CF-A3BC-444553540000"
    CODEBASE = "./ocx/Jiggler.ocx">

    <PARAM NAME = "_Version"    VALUE = "65536">
    <PARAM NAME = "_ExtentX"    VALUE = "11933">
    <PARAM NAME = "_ExtentY"    VALUE = "1244">
    <PARAM NAME = "_StockProps" VALUE = "11">
    <PARAM NAME = "Caption"     VALUE = "Jiggling">
    <PARAM NAME = "ForeColor"   VALUE = "65280">
    <PARAM NAME = "BackColor"   VALUE = "16777215">
</OBJECT>
```

```
<OBJECT
    ID       = "Jiggler3"
    WIDTH    = 0
    HEIGHT   = 0
    CLASSID  = "CLSID:5CD2FC83-E7BD-11CF-A3BC-444553540000"
    CODEBASE = "./ocx/Jiggler.ocx">

    <PARAM NAME = "_Version"    VALUE = "65536">
    <PARAM NAME = "_ExtentX"    VALUE = "11933">
    <PARAM NAME = "_ExtentY"    VALUE = "1244">
    <PARAM NAME = "_StockProps" VALUE = "11">
    <PARAM NAME = "Caption"     VALUE = "Text">
    <PARAM NAME = "ForeColor"   VALUE = "16711680">
    <PARAM NAME = "BackColor"   VALUE = "16777215">
</OBJECT>

<P>

<!-- Program the controls with OLE Automation via VBScript -->

<SCRIPT LANGUAGE="VBScript">
<!--
Sub window_onLoad()

    rem Set the properties for Jiggler1

    Jiggler1.Interval          = 100
    Jiggler1.DefaultFont.Name  = "Times New Roman"
    Jiggler1.DefaultFont.Size  = 20
    Jiggler1.DefaultFont.Italic = True
    Jiggler1.DefaultFont.Bold  = True

    rem Set the properties for Jiggler2

    Jiggler2.Interval          = 75
    Jiggler2.DefaultFont.Name  = "Arial"
    Jiggler2.DefaultFont.Size  = 24
    Jiggler2.DefaultFont.Italic = True
    Jiggler2.DefaultFont.Bold  = True

    rem Set the properties for Jiggler3

    Jiggler3.Interval          = 50
    Jiggler3.DefaultFont.Name  = "Courier New"
    Jiggler3.DefaultFont.Size  = 30
    Jiggler3.DefaultFont.Italic = True
    Jiggler3.DefaultFont.Bold  = True

end sub
-->
</SCRIPT>

</BODY>
</HTML>
```

30

CREATING AN ACTIVEX CONTROL

Figure 30.16 shows the end result of all your hard work, with the JIGGLER3.HTM file loaded in the IE3 browser window. (Take my word for it; the control text is red, green, and blue.)

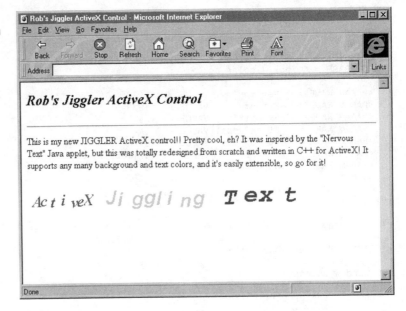

FIGURE 30.16.

The final JIGGLER3.HTM *Web page, complete with three JIGGLE ActiveX controls using different fonts, colors, and jiggle intervals.*

Summary

ActiveX controls are at the forefront of new technology that's activating the Internet. These new controls are fun and exciting and, they bring the Web to life. Visual C++ 4.2 fully supports ActiveX controls and makes creating them fairly easy, thanks to the updated OLE Control Wizard.

Here are some points to remember:

- ActiveX controls support OLE Automation by implementing and exposing a set of methods and properties.

- ActiveX controls can be placed into any OLE control container and can be used with any OCX-compliant programming language, as well as ActiveX-enabled Web browsers on the Internet.

- Property pages provide the self-contained user interface ActiveX controls need to provide true component software ease of use to the developer.

- ActiveX controls are OLE controls that comply with the updated OLE Controls 96 specification.

- Because ActiveX controls are generally for use over the Internet, their file sizes should be kept small. Therefore, static linking isn't supported.

- The ActiveX Control Pad makes inserting ActiveX controls into Web pages easy; the Control Pad Script Wizard makes short work of writing basic scripts.

- ActiveX controls can be controlled on a Web page with a scripting language. A scripting language can also allow ActiveX controls on the same Web page to communicate with each other.

VDOlive Technology

by Antonio Miguel Ferreira

VDOlive is a relatively new technology that supports both video and audio broadcasting on the Internet or on other TCP/IP networks such as intranets. VDOlive broadcasts resemble RealAudio audio broadcasts; the main difference is that VDOlive adds a video signal to the stream.

Traditionally, when a Web page contains a video, the user must download the whole file (MPEG, AVI, or any other format) and display it by using an external program running on his or her PC. Browser plug-ins and helper applications (built-in or external programs) enable downloading and automatic viewing. Unfortunately, downloading big video files (1MB to 10MB or more) can be a discouraging operation when you don't have a 56Kbps link (at least) to the Internet.

VDOlive technology is based on a scaleable video and audio compression algorithm and a protocol for transmissions of resulting files through the Internet. This technology enables you to view and download videos simultaneously; and the quality of the picture is proportional to the available Internet link bandwidth! The video file downloads and at the same time the player displays the part of the video that resides in the memory buffers. You do not have to download the entire video in order to watch it; you can see it while it is downloading. (The process is similar to listening to a radio station while it broadcasts its signal.) At the time of this writing, a VDOlive server could transmit only pre-prepared video files, but VDOnet Corp., the creator of VDOlive technology, is working to improve the technology to suit real-time compression and, consequently, real-time video broadcasting.

Finding Out How VDOlive Works

VDOlive is based on a client/server architecture, the client being the VDOlive player and the server being a VDOlive server (either the limited Personal Server version or the complete Video Server version). The client enables users to receive and view video clips, whereas the server transmits video over the Internet to users. Figure 31.1 summarizes the function of the VDOlive system.

FIGURE 31.1.
A VDOlive player connected to a VDOlive server.

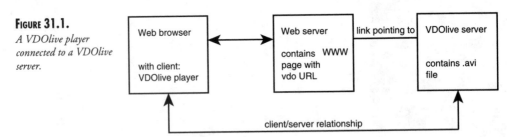

Standard browsers cannot display real-time video and audio, so you must install a helper or plug-in application. This special-purpose program, which runs on the user's PC, interprets the video stream and displays it on a TV-like screen window. The plug-in to view VDOlive video clips is called VDOlive player. It is available for Windows and Macintosh platforms and works with most Web browsers.

On the server side, everything you need in addition to your Web server is a VDOlive server. This program runs in the background, listening to the default TCP port 7000, reads a file in VDO format from the local file system and transmits it over the Internet to a given client, using the UDP protocol. Two VDOlive servers are currently available: Personal Server and Video Server. The first is a limited test version, and the second is the complete program that can serve many video streams at the same time and scale up to different bandwidth connections.

You will have to capture video and audio sources (from VHS or Beta magnetic tapes) and then edit and compress them to the VDO format file, which is compatible with the AVI format. (In fact, the only good reason to have your own on a Web site is to broadcast original video clips over the Internet.) You can use VDOlive Personal Tools, along with specialized video and audio capture hardware, to create your own video files. Other third-party tools, in particular tools for converting existing video formats (such as MPEG and QuickTime) to VDOlive format, are also available.

As for hardware, the VDOlive Web site (`www.vdo.net`) presents a list of video acquisition devices that can be used with VDOlive tools for content (video) creation.

You can find both VDOlive players and servers, as well as complete installation documentation and FAQs, on the VDOlive Web site at `http://www.vdo.net/`. Read on for an overview of the installation process for VDOlive products.

Installing a VDOlive Player

Installing a VDOlive player is easy. First, make sure you have the latest version of the software for your operating system. At the time of this writing, the current version is 2.0, either as a plug-in for the Netscape browser on Windows or Macintosh platforms or as a helper application for many other browsers. Video for Windows (a standard feature in Windows 95) optimizes the overall performance of VDOlive player, but isn't required.

After you download VDOlive player, run the executable file to start the installation process. If you are installing VDOlive player as a plug-in, you will be asked to name the folder in which Netscape 2.0 resides and to read the license agreement (please do). If you proceed, you must enter some personal information (name, e-mail address, and company) in order to customize your copy of the player. This information is logged in the VDOlive server's log files when you watch video clips over the Internet (be aware that companies that provide video clips may use the information concerning you for marketing or other business purposes).

Next, you must choose a folder in which to install the VDOlive player. A good choice is the plug-ins folder within the Netscape folder; if you plan to use VDOlive player as a helper application, choose any other folder. The setup program finishes by asking if you want to add icons to the Program Manager. Answer Yes, choose the program group for the icons, and the installation process will finish.

You are now able to connect to a VDOlive site and watch video clips over the Internet. A good starting point is, naturally, VDOlive's Web site. You can find lots of pointers to many other sites that deliver video content in VDOlive format.

If you experience problems, contact your Web site's administrators. They may have to open a UDP port on their Internet server so that the VDOlive server can send its video stream. You should configure your VDOlive player (Setup | Settings) to this specific UDP port.

Installing a VDOlive Server

VDOlive server can be installed in different hardware and software platforms: UNIX (all popular flavors) or Windows NT/95. Once again, make sure you have the latest version (as of this writing, it is version 2.0) of either the VDOlive Personal Server, which you can obtain from VDOlive's Web site, `http://www.vdo.net/`, or the VDOlive Video Server.

This section explains the installation process on a Linux server. (Installation on other UNIX systems is similar.) The VDOlive Personal Server is as easy to install as the VDOlive player is to install. After downloading the trial version of the server (about 1.4MB), you must run the executable (for example, `vdoaout.exe`) as root. You should read the license agreement carefully when it appears. The installation program creates a directory (`/usr/local/vdosrv` by default) for the `vdosrv` file (the server) and the VDOlive Personal Tools. By default, this directory also contains the server log files.

Finally, you can add a line to the file—`/etc/rc.d/rc.local`—(for other UNIX systems you should locate a similar file, the one that executes commands at system boot process) pointing to the vdosrv server, which will run in the background, listening to default TCP port 7000. (You can override this setting with the `-d` parameter.) If you do not want the server to run all the time, you can start it manually by running the binary file in the background. It is the best option if you just want to try the server for a while.

The VDOlive Personal Server version available at `www.vdo.net` has some limitations:

- The maximum number of streams it can serve at any time is two. Therefore, the maximum number of players you can connect to your server at any time is two.

- The maximum stream transmission rate scales up to 256Kbps, even if a greater link is available. This rate is adequate for normal dial-up connections to the Internet.

■ The maximum video length that the Personal Server version can make available to users is 60 seconds.

■ The server has an expiration date. After that you should upgrade to either a new Personal Server or, preferably, to the VDOlive Video Server, the complete version.

The license agreement of the VDOlive programs should give you any relevant information on using the server.

The VDOlive Personal Server is intended for testing purposes on home or small systems. If you plan to serve many clients over the Internet or to serve big video files, you should obtain the VDOlive Video Server, which can be adapted to as many video streams as you want.

Creating Video Clips

Both versions of the server include software tools (VDOlive Personal Tools) that enable you to produce your own video clips in VDO format. The latest version is available only for Windows 95 or NT.

You can use one of the tools to capture analog video and audio from an analog source (VHS or Beta) and convert it to digital format. (For this conversion, you must also use a dedicated video capture card and Video for Windows.) Another "tool" enables users to compress previously prepared uncompressed videos to the VDOlive format, saving them as AVI files, which a VDOlive server can then transmit. There are also tools available to help you handle videos on MPEG or Quicktime formats.

A typical 160×120 video, with 15 frames per second and 24 bits per pixel, requires from 200KB to 1000KB per minute, depending on its compression rate.

Linking Video on WWW Pages

A video link on a Web page is the URL of a VDO file; for example, `http://www.foo.com/film.vdo`. This VDO file is in fact a container of another URL (written in ASCII in the file), and the actual video file; for example, `vdo://www.foo.com:7000/usr/src/videos/film.avi`. The MIME type for the VDO files is `video/vdo` (the file `mime.types`—or similar file, containing all the MIME types supported by the Web server—on the Web server should include a line for this MIME type).

The actual video can be displayed on the browser's window, inside the Web page, or in an external VDOlive player window.

You can see the appearance of a Web page with the TV-like screen in Figure 31.2.

FIGURE 31.2.
The VDOlive video screen inside a Web page.

Watching Video Clips Over the Internet

While you are surfing the Internet for videos, you may notice that most of the time you will find only demonstration videos, not real-life applications with a special purpose. The VDOlive technology is quite new, and its use is still evolving. In the future, we might be able to watch real-time videos (broadcasting) such as news programs over the Internet. Also, companies might consider video distribution over the Internet as an alternative to TV commercials or other presentations.

Although VDOlive works reasonably well over a 28.8Kbps link, at a maximum rate of 10 frames per second under ideal conditions, overall transmission quality (audio and video synchronization) is superior over an ISDN or T1 line—naturally—from which you can view 20 (or even more) frames per second. If you use a near site (to which your Internet provider has fast links), you will probably enjoy better video quality, because many times packets—and consequently frames—are lost over distant or saturated Internet links.

The transmission quality adapts to the quality of the receiving Internet connection. Although you can watch videos over a 28.8Kbps modem link (maximum rate of 10 frames per second), a 56Kbps, ISDN, or T1 link produces better quality.

The ideal transmission conditions depend not only on the available bandwidth, but also on the volume of Internet traffic over the various links traversed by the video stream and on the load on VDOlive servers. For example, viewing videos over a 14.4Kbps modem may be impossible unless conditions are ideal (that is, low traffic and low overload).

Also, video screens (the windows in which the video is displayed on your personal computer) are still limited to 160×120, 24 bits per pixel, which is big enough for viewing and enjoying the video clips but too small for viewing real applications (real-time broadcasting or film presentation clips, for example). This screen size limits the videos to only simple ones. Improvements on Internet links and in VDOlive technology should yield bigger and better video screens in the future.

Resources

The VDOlive site on the Internet is `http://www.vdo.net/`. You can find information concerning the VDOlive servers and player, as well as many links to other Internet sites delivering video content. VDOlive is a trademark of VDOnet Corporation, California (USA).

Creating Netscape Navigator Plug-Ins

by Zan Oliphant

IN THIS CHAPTER

With the release of Netscape Navigator 2.*x* in the first quarter of 1996 came support for Netscape Navigator plug-in code modules—otherwise known as plug-ins. Plug-ins are similar in functionality to Java, an interpreted language developed by Sun Microsystems. In contrast to Java, Navigator plug-ins are binary code modules written and compiled for each host operating system or hardware platform. Why write a plug-in instead of a Java applet? The answer is speed. Navigator plug-ins are especially well suited for handling high bandwidth data transfers needed for demanding data types such as audio and video over the Internet.

Most of the material in this chapter first appeared in *Programming Netscape Plug-ins*, also published by Sams.net, and I refer to it throughout this chapter. If you do decide to write a plug-in for Netscape's Navigator or Microsoft's Internet Explorer, you should consider getting a copy of *Programming Netscape Plug-ins*; it is an authoritative, Netscape-reviewed, plug-in API reference and contains numerous code examples.

Plug-In Design and Architecture

Netscape Navigator's plug-in architecture is based on dynamically loaded code modules. These modules reside in a subfolder or directory called PLUGINS that Navigator reads during its initialization. Each module has a resource that determines which MIME type it can handle. When Navigator finds this MIME type embedded in a Web page through HTML or as a single file, it loads the appropriate code module.

For embedded plug-ins, the HTML EMBED tag tells Navigator the size of the plug-in's window in a given Web page so that Navigator can create the window for the plug-in. The plug-in is given a handle to this newly created window for drawing graphics and processing events.

When a plug-in is loaded, an instance of the plug-in is created with a call to the NPP_New API. The plug-in can be loaded multiple times, creating multiple instances. Web pages frequently have more than one instance of a plug-in. Therefore, if your plug-in uses a restricted resource such as an audio card, you must share this resource across multiple plug-in instances.

Data streams are a big part of Netscape's plug-in architecture. Most plug-ins have data pushed from the server for processing, but others might choose to pull it down, perhaps in a random-access fashion. Just as a plug-in can have multiple instances, it can also have multiple streams per instance. The plug-in API also provides for stream-instance data.

With the introduction of Netscape Navigator 3.0 comes LiveConnect. LiveConnect extends the plug-in architecture by adding communication between plug-ins, Java applets, and JavaScript. The Java Runtime Interface (JRI) plays an important part in this architecture.

How It All Fits Together

As you can see in Figure 32.1, the Navigator 3.*x* plug-in architecture consists of a plug-in code module, Navigator, Java Applet and JRI, JavaScript, and HTML. A bare minimum plug-in could go without Java, JavaScript, and HTML.

FIGURE 32.1.

Netscape's Navigator
3.x plug-in architecture.

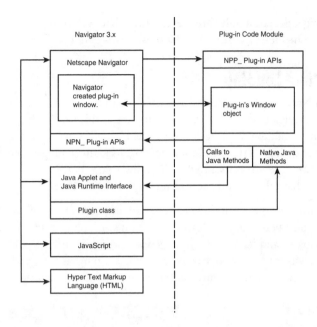

32

The core of the plug-in interface is the plug-in API. These APIs are prefixed by NPN for methods located within Navigator and by NPP for methods in the plug-in. By using the APIs, the plug-in becomes part of Navigator's code.

LiveConnect

Netscape's LiveConnect enables you to integrate Java, JavaScript, and plug-ins. New plug-in methods for LiveConnect are NPP_GetJavaClass, NPN_GetJavaEnv, and NPN_GetJavaPeer. Chapter 14 of *Programming Netscape Plug-ins,* "LiveConnect," documents these Java-specific APIs for plug-ins and gives more details on the LiveConnect interface. Also, Chapter 23 of that volume includes a LiveConnect example written by Netscape.

For the purposes of this chapter, you should understand what LiveConnect does. With LiveConnect you can perform the following tasks:

- Call a Java method from a plug-in
- Call a native method located in a plug-in from Java
- Call Java methods from JavaScript
- Call JavaScript methods from Java

As you can see, LiveConnect extends not only JavaScript and Java but also plug-ins. Notice the absence of a 33a direct connection between plug-ins and JavaScript in Figure 32.1. Any plug-in to JavaScript communication must go through Java. To learn more about LiveConnect, make sure to get the latest Software Development Kit (SDK) from Netscape and read the documentation. The Netscape SDK has the most up-to-date LiveConnect information.

Runtime Loading

When Navigator initializes itself, it checks for installed plug-ins in the PLUGINS subdirectory or folder. Navigator does not load any plug-ins at this time; it just parses out the resource information containing the plug-ins' supported MIME types, file extensions, and the name for the file-open dialog. At the time of this writing, Macintosh plug-ins enable a user to configure plug-in/MIME type association, while Windows does not. Navigator release 4.0 for Windows is slated to have this feature, according to Netscape sources.

Navigator beta 4 for Windows contains an updated version of the Help | About Plug-ins menu item. The About Plug-ins feature tells you what plug-in you have installed, the full path of each plug-in and its MIME type, its description, its suffixes, and whether it is enabled. Only after Navigator finds a MIME type to which a plug-in is registered is the plug-in loaded into memory and executed. Figure 32.2 shows the Windows Navigator beta 4 About Plug-ins screen.

FIGURE 32.2.

Windows Navigator beta 4 About Plug-ins screen.

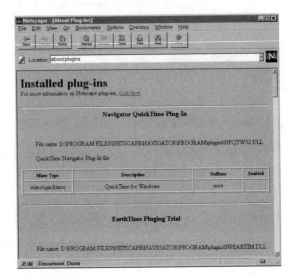

Plug-In Instances and Instance Data

An important feature of a plug-in is that it can be loaded multiple times, depending on a given Web page. For example, a Web page might contain three audio files of the same type. Navigator then creates three instances of the audio plug-in using the NPP_New API. Each of these instances has its own instance data that is allocated by the plug-in and attached to a Navigator-maintained instance data pointer. Each time Navigator calls one of your plug-in methods, you must dereference the Navigator-provided instance pointer and get access to your instance data.

All of the examples found on the CD-ROM included with *Programming Netscape Plug-ins* show how to do this.

In many cases, your plug-in code can be oblivious to other instances. However, in some cases, a plug-in needs to communicate among its instances. The RealAudio plug-in does so by enabling a Web author to load a console instance to control other instances associated with audio files. You can read more about the RealAudio plug-in in Chapter 5 of *Programming Netscape Plug-ins*, "Using a Plug-In."

Windows and Events

Navigator creates a window for your plug-in and gives you a handle to this window during a call to the NPP_SetWindow method. The HTML EMBED tag attributes WIDTH and HEIGHT determine the size of this window. The HTML code also determines the relative window position. Each operating system (UNIX, Windows, and Macintosh) handles window and event processing a little differently.

In Windows and UNIX, a child window is created in the window hierarchy. This child window automatically sees all window events. In the Windows programming environment, you can subclass the Navigator-created window to process any given window event.

In the Macintosh environment, the plug-in and the Navigator share a Macintosh window. Therefore, the plug-in must draw only in the specified area of this shared window. You must save, set up, and restore the shared drawing environment around any drawing operations. Events are sent to the Macintosh plug-in with the plug-in provided with the NPP_HandleEvent API.

Seamless Web Page Embedding

The big advantage of a Navigator plug-in over a Navigator helper application is that a plug-in can embed itself directly in the Navigator-displayed Web page. This feature is similar to the way that a Java applet provides seamless Web page integration. A plug-in differs from Java in that the plug-in's code is native to the local machine and is installed. A Java applet is downloaded before each use and is platform independent.

A plug-in can run in either embedded, full page, or hidden modes. Of these modes, embedded is used most often because it provides seamless Web page integration. Full page mode enables a plug-in to run by itself, taking the whole Navigator display area. Hidden mode, as the name implies, is for plug-ins that have no visible attributes. An example of a hidden plug-in is the Background Musical Instrument Device Interface (MIDI) Player sample code found in *Programming Netscape Plug-ins*, Chapter 21.

Data Streams

Netscape Navigator plug-ins are built around the concept of client/server data streaming. A stream is a constant flow of data. One of the first implementations of streams was for the UNIX

I/O subsystem, which provided a full-duplex, modular connection to a given device driver. As multimedia becomes more prevalent on the home computer, streaming becomes very important to handle data flow for audio and video.

A simple stream can be implemented with a pool of fixed-length buffers. The producer of data continuously fills empty buffers, buffer order is maintained, and data is delivered to the consumer. Such problems as overruns (no more empty buffers) or underruns (no more full buffers) make the life of the stream more complicated.

The Navigator plug-in API provides many methods for managing data streams both to and from a plug-in. A stream that sends data from Navigator to a plug-in (the most common type of stream) uses NPP_NewStream to create it, NPP_Write to write the data, and NPP_DestroyStream to destroy it. A stream that sends data from a plug-in to Navigator (new with the Navigator 3.0 plug-in API) uses NPN_NewStream for creation, NPN_Write to write data to the stream, and NPN_DestroyStream to destroy it. Additionally, your plug-in can have multiple incoming and outgoing streams running concurrently.

> **NOTE**
>
> For further reading, see Chapter 10, "Stream Creation and Destruction," and Chapter 11, "Reading From and Writing to Streams," in *Programming Netscape Plug-ins*. Be sure to look at the code samples in Chapter 17, "A Streaming Audio Sample," and Chapter 18, "The Buffer Classes," to see how your plug-in can handle a real-time data stream from Navigator.

Sequential and Seekable Streams

After a plug-in is loaded, for all intents and purposes it's part of the Navigator client. A plug-in is compiled machine code and requires no interpretation, in contrast to platform-independent languages such as Java that do require interpretation. Tight coupling enables a plug-in to maintain a very high-speed bond to the Navigator client and, in turn, to the Web server. Data flows between the plug-in and Navigator in either sequential or seekable streams.

A plug-in can change the stream type to seekable by setting *stype to NP_SEEK. Setting this mode enables a plug-in to pull data from a server with calls to the NPN_RequestRead method. This technique puts the onus on a plug-in to continuously call Navigator for data buffers and is not considered a true continuously flowing stream. A seekable stream is generally slower than a sequential stream, which is driven by Navigator with calls to the plug-in implemented method NPP_Write. Your plug-in should use only seekable streams when the random access benefits outweigh the performance penalty.

When Navigator creates a stream for your plug-in, it is in sequential mode. In most cases, Navigator creates a sequential type stream for each plug-in instance. The NPP_Write API automatically notifies your plug-in as chunks of data come across the net. This data flow can come from the Internet via TCP/IP, a local area network (LAN), a local client file, or Navigator's file cache. A sequential stream, as the name implies, is a continuous sequential stream of data true to the streaming definition. In most cases, a sequential stream is the preferred stream type for a plug-in to use.

> **NOTE**
>
> Navigator's cache plays an important role in your plug-in's performance. Netscape Navigator 2.0 has both a memory-based and a disk-based caching system. The caching scheme is based on whole files. If you abort a file download, it is not saved to cache. Both cache sizes are user configurable.
>
> Navigator 3.0 introduced LiveCache. LiveCache provides progressive caching, which enables you to continue where you left off if a file download is aborted. LiveCache also enables you to preload content from slow devices such as CD-ROMs for fast access and viewing.

Assisted Installation

A common problem with plug-ins is that users don't know where to find them. To view a Web page that needs a specific plug-in, the user must have that plug-in installed on his or her local machine. Navigator's assisted installation feature helps users install new plug-ins. This feature is automatically activated when a user displays an HTML page that requires a plug-in that is not currently installed.

When a user hits a Web page that requires a plug-in not found in that user's current plug-in installation, a dialog box opens and enables the user to select either `Plug-in Info` or `Cancel`. If the user clicks the Plug-in Info button, Navigator loads a new URL to get the given plug-in. This URL can be specified in the `PLUGINSPACE` attribute of the `EMBED` tag. If the tag does not contain the `PLUGINSPACE` attribute, Navigator goes to a current plug-in list.

Netscape's SDK

You should download Netscape's Plug-in SDK to use in conjunction with this book. The SDK contains the authoritative and most up-to-date plug-in documentation. This SDK is currently located at the following FTP site:

```
ftp://ftpXX.netscape.com/pub/navigator/sdk
```

In this address `ftpXX` is any one of Netscape's 20 or so FTP servers.

The Plug-in SDK provides the following benefits:

■ Documentation in HTML format
■ Header and source files

- Source code examples
- Special tools for LiveConnect

Navigator Plug-In Design Considerations

Before you jump into the wonderful world of Netscape Navigator plug-in development, you need to do some planning. The tools you use, cross-platform compatibility, and the performance will affect your plug-in's success in the quickly growing plug-in market. As you design your Netscape Navigator plug-in, consider the following factors:

- What development language should you use? Most Navigator plug-ins today are written in C++. You can use C or even assembler. Any language that is capable of generating machine language for your given platform will work.

- Will your plug-in be compatible with all versions of Netscape? Will your plug-in work with Navigator 2.*x*? How about 3.*x*? Make sure you have a good reason for not supporting these older Navigator versions.

- Can your plug-in handle a 28.8Kbps Internet connection? How about 14.4Kbps? Bandwidth requirements for your plug-in should be well-planned.

- Do you want a Java or JavaScript interface to your plug-in?

- What about MIME types? How many should you support? Is MIME contention an issue?

- Can you write your plug-in so that it processes data in a real-time streaming fashion? Or, must a user wait for a complete file to download?

- Does your plug-in require a CGI program?

The following discussion will help you plan your plug-ins.

Choosing a Development Language

Unlike a Java applet, a plug-in is native machine code and is not interpreted, which means that you can write a plug-in in any language that compiles to native machine code. However, some issues make certain languages easier to use than others.

For example, in Windows a plug-in must be a dynamic link library (DLL). The development language you use must be capable of generating a DLL code module to build a stand-alone plug-in. Many languages such as Microsoft's Visual Basic and Borland's Delphi are quite capable of generating Windows DLLs, but these languages might not be able to generate the special resources required for plug-ins. You might be better off using one of these high-level languages to generate an OLE library for use with a third-party plug-in, such as ActiveX from NCompass or OpenScape from BusinessWeb.

The best documented language for Navigator plug-in development is C++. *Programming Netscape Plug-ins*, along with Netscape's Plug-in SDK, uses C++ exclusively. In addition, you can use assembler inline or in separate routines. In some cases, such as software decompression, an assembler routine might provide the performance you need. And don't hesitate to consider other possibilities, such as a hybrid solution using C++ to call routines implemented in other languages.

Navigator Version Compatibility

Which versions of Netscape's Navigator should your plug-in support? Navigator 2.*x* introduced plug-in support, and Navigator 3.*x* added many new and cool features such as LiveConnect and streaming data from a plug-in to the Navigator. Can you design your plug-in so that it works with both Navigator 2.*x* and Navigator 3.*x*? What about Navigator 4.*x*? Your plug-in can also "turn on" more features such as streaming data from the plug-in to the Navigator, depending on the Navigator version under which it is running.

Be sure to check out the NPN_Version API for determining the current Navigator version. Also keep in mind that the version number returned by NPN_Version corresponds to the plug-in API it supports, not to the Navigator version (such as 2.0, 3.0, and so on). You can read more about version support in Chapter 9 of *Programming Netscape Plug-ins*.

Planning for Bandwidth Limitations

What about network bandwidth? Is your plug-in geared toward Internet usage for cases in which a typical Internet Service Provider (ISP) is connecting users at 14.4Kbps or 28.8Kbps? Or, perhaps you are developing a plug-in for your company's local intranet. Intranet plug-ins, used mostly on local area networks, need not worry about slow modem connections. Multimedia audio and video formats have huge bandwidth requirements. Most of today's multimedia data throughput minimums were defined by CD-ROM speeds, not by comparatively slow Internet connections. Data compression for audio and video media types has never been more important.

Streaming Audio

Now look at audio and how you can stream it in real time. A common modem speed today is 14,400 bits per second. Low-quality audio is generally sampled at 11,025 samples per second, using 1 byte per sample. A speed of 11,025 samples per second is 11,025 bytes per second, which means 88,200 bits per second (bps):

```
11,025 bytes/second * 8 bits/byte = 88,200 bits/second
```

How are you going to fit 88,200bps through a 14,400bps Internet connection? The answer, of course, is data compression.

Using the preceding numbers, a 7 to 1 compression ratio would squeak you by.

```
88,200bps / 14,400bps ~
```

Some of today's plug-in vendors are claiming compression ratios as high as 50 to 1! This more than ample compression is obtained by using *lossy compression*, or removing some data, such as dead space between words. In fact, much of what you see on the Web today uses lossy compression, such as JPEG, AVI video, and audio compression.

Remember that the preceding numbers were taken from a perfect world. You won't get 14,400bps from a 14.4Kbps modem. Other factors such as TCP/IP error correction, the speed of your computer, and server load also play an important part in actual throughput.

Multiplatform Compatibility

Multiplatform compatibility is a big design consideration that determines your plug-in's marketability. Although this chapter is geared toward Windows plug-ins, Netscape's plug-in API was designed for platform independence. You will see how Netscape's design is portable later in this chapter. The Netscape development staff worked hard to keep the API set consistent across the Macintosh, UNIX, and Windows platforms. Rumors that Navigator will support even more platforms (such as OS/2) are now coming across the Internet.

If you are a Windows developer, don't be too quick to rule out a version of your plug-in for the Macintosh and UNIX platforms. Try to develop your plug-in with an eye toward other platforms. Consider using Java in conjunction with your plug-in for a user interface. Tight integration between Java and the plug-in comes with LiveConnect. You can read more about LiveConnect in Chapter 14 of *Programming Netscape Plug-ins*. You should use native operating system level APIs only when you have no other recourse.

Expanding To Java with LiveConnect

Netscape introduced LiveConnect with the release of Navigator 3.0. LiveConnect enables Navigator plug-ins, Java, and JavaScript to communicate with each other. How can this technology benefit your development efforts? Does it make sense to add a Java extension to your plug-in, or are you doing it strictly for the hype value?

Using Java in conjunction with a plug-in can certainly reduce your development efforts. The most dramatic reduction occurs with a Java/plug-in applet that uses a plug-in for platform-specific duties and Java for an interactive user interface. In that case, your only job is to port the hardware-dependent plug-in; you don't have to touch the user interface written in Java.

Netscape's LiveConnect AVI video player is a simple example of using Java and JavaScript for the user interface and leaving the video implementation to a plug-in. The LiveConnect video player is documented in Chapter 23 of *Programming Netscape Plug-ins*.

HTML EMBED Tag Attributes

The EMBED tag in the Web page's HTML code starts an embedded plug-in. When the plug-in is loaded, it is displayed as part of the HTML document, rather than within another window.

This technique is very similar to how graphics are embedded in a Web page. As you design your plug-in, you should think about which EMBED tag attributes your plug-in will support. Additionally, define new attributes that are specific to your plug-in.

Current Attributes

The next few sections document Netscape's current EMBED tag attributes. The EMBED tag has the following syntax:

```
<EMBED attributes> ... </EMBED>
```

HEIGHT="value"

Example:

```
HEIGHT=50
```

The HEIGHT attribute defines the vertical size of the plug-in window in units defined by the UNITS attribute. Default UNITS are pixels.

HIDDEN=true or HIDDEN=false

Example:

```
HIDDEN=true
```

The HIDDEN attribute determines whether the plug-in is visible. A value of true indicates that the plug-in is hidden and not visible. This value overrides any HEIGHT or WIDTH parameters and makes the plug-in zero in size. An example of a hidden plug-in is a Web page background MIDI player (a sample in *Programming Netscape Plug-ins*). Be sure to use the HIDDEN attribute to define an invisible plug-in rather than defining HEIGHT and WIDTH to zero. If you use the HIDDEN attribute with no parameters, it defaults to true.

PALETTE=foreground or PALETTE=background

Example:

```
PALETTE=background
```

The PALETTE attribute is for the Windows platform. This attribute instructs the plug-in to realize its palette as either a foreground or background palette. The attribute is useful for embedding multiple palette-aware plug-ins in a single page. The default value is background.

PLUGINSPAGE="URL"

Example:

```
PLUGINSPAGE=http://www.yourcompany.com
```

The PLUGINSPAGE attribute is used by the assisted installation feature if the plug-in registered for the MIME type of a given EMBED tag is not found. Its argument is a standard URL that usually contains the location of the needed plug-in.

> **NOTE**
>
> The PLUGINSPACE attribute is not implemented in Navigator 2.x.

SRC="URL"
Example:

SRC=sound.wav

The HTML argument of the SRC attribute indicates the location of a plug-in's data file. The MIME type of this data file determines which plug-in is loaded to handle the file, and the file's extension usually determines the MIME type. The EMBED tag must use either the SRC or TYPE attribute.

TYPE="type"
Example:

TYPE=audio/x-wav

The TYPE attribute is used instead of SRC to load a plug-in that does not require a data file for startup. The argument for this attribute is a MIME type that maps to a plug-in. The EMBED tag must use either the SRC or TYPE attribute.

WIDTH="value"
Example:

WIDTH=200

The WIDTH attribute defines the horizontal size of the plug-in window in units defined by the UNITS attribute. Default UNITS are pixels.

UNITS="value"
Example:

UNITS=en

The UNITS attribute defines which measurement units the HEIGHT and WIDTH attributes use. The value can be either pixels or en. Pixels are the default. (An en is half the point size.)

Adding Your Own Attributes

Adding attributes for your plug-in's private use is easy. Just put them in the EMBED command line. Navigator ignores all nonstandard attributes while parsing the HTML EMBED tag. You can retrieve any additional name=value pairs during your plug-in's NPP_New API.

For example, many plug-ins use the AUTOSTART and LOOP attributes, which you can add to the EMBED tag such as the following:

```
<EMBED SRC="video.avi" WIDTH=320 HEIGHT=200 LOOP=true AUTOSTART=true>
```

Notice how you can put additional private attributes in the EMBED tag command line just like standard attributes. For an example of extensive use of private attributes, check Chapter 5 in *Programming Netscape Plug-ins,* "Using a Plug-in," which shows how the RealAudio plug-in uses this technique.

Multiple MIME Types

Your plug-in can support more than one MIME type. This feature can be really handy for plug-ins that support more than one file format. Consider Netscape's LiveAudio plug-in, which is included with Navigator 3.x. This plug-in currently supports seven different MIME types! It covers the most popular audio formats for UNIX, Macintosh, and Windows. Table 32.1 shows the MIME types, descriptions, and suffixes that the LiveAudio plug-in supports.

Table 32.1. LiveAudio MIME types.

Mime type	Description	Suffixes
audio/basicl	AU	au
audio/x-aiff	AIFF	aiff, aif
audio/aiff	AIFF	aiff, aif
audio/x-wav	WAV	wav
audio/wav	WAV	wav
audio/x-midi	MIDI	midi, mid
audio/midi	MIDI	midi, mid

MIME Contention

MIME contention occurs when more than one installed plug-in supports the same MIME type. The Macintosh Navigator has solved this problem by letting the user configure appropriate plug-ins for each MIME type. At the time of this writing, Windows and UNIX do not yet have this plug-in user configuration.

When designing your plug-in, you should be aware of these MIME contention issues. The best defense, until Netscape resolves this problem, is a good installation program and user documentation.

File Base Versus Streaming Plug-Ins

Try to design for a streaming plug-in rather than a file-based plug-in whenever possible. A streaming plug-in processes data on a buffer-by-buffer basis as it is downloaded from the network. The advantages of using this design are twofold. First, your plug-in can operate in real time, such as the RealAudio plug-in. And second, your plug-in can take advantage of extra processing time while the data file is being downloaded.

Despite the popularity of the streaming plug-in design, in many cases using this design does not make sense. Consider a plug-in that plays AVI video files. Because the AVI format was designed for CD-ROM streaming at 150KB per second (not your everyday Internet connection speed), you cannot possibly play this file format in real time over the Internet. As you will see with Netscape's AVI player plug-in example, this type of plug-in has to be file-based.

Streaming to the Navigator

Navigator 3.*x* enables you to stream data from your plug-in to Navigator by creating a new stream with NPN_NewStream, writing to it with NPN_Write, and destroying it with NPN_DestroyStream. These APIs are fully documented in *Programming Netscape Plug-ins*, Chapter 10.

Why would you ever want to stream data from your plug-in to Navigator? Maybe you could create a plug-in that reads raw data from a Web server, converts it to HTML, and streams that HTML data to the Navigator for display. For example, you could write a plug-in that displays UNIX manual pages in a nice HTML format.

Your plug-in can make Web pages on-the-fly using this technique.

Client Server Design

With the addition of a common gateway interface (CGI) program residing on the Web server, your plug-in implementation can have a true client/server design. Your CGI server back end can do things such as database searches while the browser client handles the display.

You can send data to your CGI program with NPN_GetURL or NPN_PostURL. Navigator 3.*x* adds NPN_GetURLNotify, NPN_PostURLNotify, and NPP_URLNotify to the mix for better error checking. Be sure to check out the Server CPU Monitor sample in *Programming Netscape Plug-ins* for an example of using these APIs with a CGI program.

The Plug-In API

In order to maintain similarity across multiple platforms, the Windows plug-in API is not built in the usual Windows fashion. A Netscape Navigator plug-in is implemented in a dynamically linked code module. In Windows, this module is the standard DLL. Microsoft designed the DLL with an eye toward implementations, such as a Netscape plug-in, but Netscape has taken a slightly different approach.

This section explains the difference between a Netscape API and a plug-in API. It includes implementations for both types of APIs and how code is called. Additionally, the section briefly explains all APIs (including platform-specific APIs). A complete reference of these APIs, reviewed by Netscape, is available in *Programming Netscape Plug-ins*.

Who Is Calling Whom?

If you scan through the plug-in documentation, you might notice two types of APIs. The first type begins with the convention NPP. These routines are implemented by your plug-in and are called from the Navigator. The letters *NPP* stand for Netscape Plug-in: Plug-in Defined. The second type begins with the convention NPN. These routines are implemented by the Navigator and are called from your plug-in. The letters *NPN* stand for Netscape Plug-in: Navigator Defined. Figure 32.3 shows the calling direction for NPN and NPP plug-in APIs.

FIGURE 32.3.
API calling techniques.

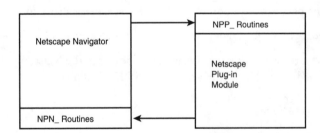

Dynamically Loaded

All plug-in types—UNIX, Macintosh, or Windows 3.1/95/NT—are dynamically loaded code modules. This architecture calls code on demand and over the years has proved to be an effective technique to save system resources. As a Windows developer, you are probably familiar with Windows DLLs, and you might have used them in your projects.

Entry points defined during compile time call routines within a DLL. An application might implicitly load a DLL by linking to a stub library during compile time or explicitly load a DLL by using a Windows API, such as LoadLibrary, followed with calls to GetProcAddress to retrieve function addresses.

How Netscape Calls Your DLL

Unfortunately, these linking methods are very specific to Windows and do not fit Netscape's criteria for cross-platform equivalence. If you look at the header of a typical plug-in DLL, you'll notice only three entry points:

```
NP_GETENTRYPOINTS
NP_SHUTDOWN
NP_INITIALIZE
```

That design certainly doesn't give Netscape much to work with—or does it?

NPWIN.CPP

Netscape provides a file called NPWIN.CPP for Windows developers in its plug-in developer's kit. This file contains code for Windows DLL entry points. You might want to review this file before proceeding with this chapter.

Because NPWIN.CPP is intended as a layer to hide Windows platform-specific entry points from your plug-in, Netscape asks developers not to touch this file. To ensure that no one changes this code, Netscape has mentioned that it might convert NPWIN.CPP to a binary library in the future.

NP_Initialize

Immediately after the plug-in is loaded, the DLL routine NP_Initialize is called. This routine has one parameter—a pointer to the NPNetscapeFuncs structure:

```
NPError WINAPI NP_EXPORT NP_Initialize (NPNetscapeFuncs* pFuncs)
```

The NPNetscapeFuncs structure, which is located in the Netscape-provided header file npupp.h, is defined in the Navigator 3.0 Plug-in SDK as follows:

```
typedef struct _NPNetscapeFuncs {
    uint16 size;
    uint16 version;
    NPN_GetURLUPP geturl;
    NPN_PostURLUPP posturl;
    NPN_RequestReadUPP requestread;
    NPN_NewStreamUPP newstream;
    NPN_WriteUPP write;
    NPN_DestroyStreamUPP destroystream;
    NPN_StatusUPP status;
    NPN_UserAgentUPP uagent;
    NPN_MemAllocUPP memalloc;
    NPN_MemFreeUPP memfree;
    NPN_MemFlushUPP memflush;
    NPN_ReloadPluginsUPP reloadplugins;
    NPN_GetJavaEnvUPP getJavaEnv;
    NPN_GetJavaPeerUPP getJavaPeer;
    NPN_GetURLNotifyUPP geturlnotify;
    NPN_PostURLNotifyUPP posturlnotify;
#ifdef XP_UNIX
    NPN_GetValueUPP getvalue;
#endif /* XP_UNIX */
} NPNetscapeFuncs;
```

The first things to notice are the structure members size and version. The size is simply a sizeof NPNetscapeFuncs. During NP_Initialize, the size is checked against your plug-in's internal NPNetscapeFuncs structure to assure compatibility:

```
if(pFuncs->size < sizeof NPNetscapeFuncs)
    return NPERR_INVALID_FUNCTABLE_ERROR;
```

The version is checked in a similar fashion:

```
if(HIBYTE(pFuncs->version) > NP_VERSION_MAJOR)
    return NPERR_INCOMPATIBLE_VERSION_ERROR;
```

> **NOTE**
>
> The version numbers indicated by NP_VERSION_MAJOR and NP_VERSION_MINOR can't be directly correlated to the version of the Navigator. These values refer to the version of the API. When the major version number of the API increases, it is a breaking change. Plug-ins written for version 0 of the API (the current major version number) won't work if the API in the Navigator progresses to major version 1. Minor version changes indicate nonbreaking changes in the API. Thus, the major version number returned by Atlas (Navigator 3.*x*) continues to be 0, while the minor version is incremented with each change to the API. NP_VERSION_MAJOR and NP_VERSION_MINOR are predefined in the header file, so those numbers indicate the version of the API against which the plug-in was compiled.

Further down in the structure, notice the 12 function pointer prototypes beginning with NPN. You remember that NPN stands for a routine within the Navigator. This structure holds function pointers to all Navigator entry points that your plug-in calls. In addition, your plug-in maintains a global pointer to this structure for future calls to the Navigator.

```
g_pNavigatorFuncs = pFuncs; // save it for future reference
```

The NP_Initialize routine ends with a call to your internal NPP_Initialize method, which is documented in Chapter 9 of *Programming Netscape Plug-ins.*

Mapping Your API Calls to Netscape

As your plug-in is running, it makes calls to Navigator. For instance, a call to allocate memory from Navigator is NPN_MemAlloc. (See *Programming Netscape Plug-ins,* Chapter 12, "Memory Management.") NPN_MemAlloc is really a routine within your plug-in. Look again in the file NPWIN.CPP and find the following routine:

```
void* NPN_MemAlloc(uint32 size)
{
    return g_pNavigatorFuncs->memalloc(size);
}
```

Notice that this routine simply maps your call to NPN_MemAlloc to the previously mentioned structure of function pointers NPNetscapeFuncs and uses calls the saved pointer g_pNavigatorFuncs to call the routine memalloc.

NP_GetEntryPoints

After NP_Initialize is called and returns successfully, the DLL entry point routine NP_GetEntryPoints is called. Just as NP_Initialize gives you the means to call Navigator routines, NP_GetEntryPoints enables Netscape to call your plug-in's routines without using standard DLL calling conventions. Look at the prototype for this routine:

```
NPError WINAPI NP_EXPORT NP_GetEntryPoints (NPPluginFuncs* pFuncs)
```

As with NP_Initialize, this routine passes a pointer to a structure. In this case, the pointer is to the structure NPPluginFuncs, which is currently defined as follows:

```
typedef struct _NPPluginFuncs {
    uint16 size;
    uint16 version;
    NPP_NewUPP newp;
    NPP_DestroyUPP destroy;
    NPP_SetWindowUPP setwindow;
    NPP_NewStreamUPP newstream;
    NPP_DestroyStreamUPP destroystream;
    NPP_StreamAsFileUPP asfile;
    NPP_WriteReadyUPP writeready;
    NPP_WriteUPP write;
    NPP_PrintUPP print;
    NPP_HandleEventUPP event;
    NPP_URLNotifyUPP urlnotify;
    JRIGlobalRef javaClass;
} NPPluginFuncs;
```

Again, the first two members size and version are provided for compatibility checking. In this case, your plug-in only checks the structure size because the version refers to the plug-in:

```
if (pFuncs->size < sizeof NPPluginFuncs)
    return NPERR_INVALID_FUNCTABLE_ERROR;
```

Later in the structure, notice the function pointers and prototypes to routines such as NPP_NewUPP newp. The prototype for these routines begins with NPP, which identifies them as calls from the Navigator to your plug-in's methods.

The plug-in fills the function pointers in this structure with the appropriate internal routines during NP_GetEntryPoints:

```
pFuncs->version       = (NP_VERSION_MAJOR << 8) | NP_VERSION_MINOR;
pFuncs->newp          = NPP_New;
pFuncs->destroy       = NPP_Destroy;
pFuncs->setwindow     = NPP_SetWindow;
pFuncs->newstream     = NPP_NewStream;
pFuncs->destroystream = NPP_DestroyStream;
pFuncs->asfile        = NPP_StreamAsFile;
pFuncs->writeready    = NPP_WriteReady;
pFuncs->write         = NPP_Write;
```

```
pFuncs->print        = NPP_Print;
pFuncs->event        = NULL;        /* reserved */
```

Versions `NP_VERSION_MAJOR` and `NP_VERSION_MINOR` are defined in `NPAPI.H` and indicate the plug-in API release and point version, respectively.

Netscape Calls Your Code

After `NP_GetEntryPoints` returns, the Navigator structure `NPPluginFuncs` is filled with valid function pointers that will be directly called as needed. If you are using a compiler other than Microsoft's, you should make sure that your plug-in APIs are prototyped correctly for your compiler. See Part IV of *Programming Netscape Plug-ins*, "Plug-in Programming Resources for Windows," for more information.

Because the plug-in is running, you no longer need to use the standard Windows DLL interface. The Navigator doesn't use any other DLL entry points until it unloads your plug-in from memory. At this point, `NP_Shutdown` is called.

NP_Shutdown

The last of the Windows DLL entry points, `NP_Shutdown`, is called immediately before the plug-in is unloaded. It simply calls your internal `NPP_Shutdown` routine (see Chapter 9 in *Programming Netscape Plug-ins*), in addition to zeroing out the global functions pointer.

```
NPError WINAPI NP_EXPORT NP_Shutdown()
{
    NPP_Shutdown();

    g_pNavigatorFuncs = NULL;

    return NPERR_NO_ERROR;
}
```

A Quick Look at the Plug-In API Methods

For a complete reference of Navigator's plug-in API methods, consult either Netscape's Plug-in SDK or *Programming Netscape Plug-ins*. Table 32.2 shows plug-in-implemented APIs, and Table 32.3 shows Netscape-implemented APIs.

Table 32.2. The plug-in APIs, which are called from Netscape.

API Name	Description
NPP_Destroy	Deletes an instance of a plug-in
NPP_DestroyStream	Called when a data stream is complete
NPP_GetJavaClass	Returns the plug-in associated Java class
NPP_HandleEvent	Macintosh-only event handler

continues

Table 32.2. continued

API Name	Description
NPP_Initialize	Global initialization
NPP_New	Creates a new instance of a plug-in
NPP_NewStream	Called when a new stream has been created
NPP_Print	Print handler
NPP_SetWindow	Called during plug-in's window activity
NPP_Shutdown	Global termination
NPP_StreamAsFile	Gives the filename for the stream
NPP_URLNotify	Notifies the completion of a URL request
NPP_Write	Called to write data to a plug-in
NPP_WriteReady	Determines whether a plug-in is ready for data

Table 32.3. The Netscape APIs, which are called from the plug-in.

API Name	Description
NPN_DestroyStream	Terminates a data stream
NPN_GetJavaEnv	Returns the Java execution environment
NPN_GetJavaPeer	Returns the plug-in associated Java object
NPN_GetURL	Requests that a new stream be created
NPN_GetURLNotify	Requests that a new stream be created with notification
NPN_MemAlloc	Allocates memory
NPN_MemFlush	Macintosh-only flush memory
NPN_MemFree	Frees memory
NPN_NewStream	Creates a new stream of data
NPN_PostURL	Posts data to a URL
NPN_PostURLNotify	Posts data to a URL and notifies of result
NPN_RequestRead	Requests bytes from a stream
NPN_Status	Displays a status message
NPN_UserAgent	Gets Navigator's user agent field
NPN_Version	Gets Navigator's plug-in version
NPN_Write	Writes to a stream

Summary

Throughout this chapter you learned about Netscape Navigator's plug-in architecture, plug-in design, and plug-in APIs. Plug-ins are dynamically loaded code modules. A plug-in that is loaded more than once is considered to have multiple instances. Navigator creates a child window in UNIX and Windows, but it shares the main window with a Macintosh plug-in.

A Windows DLL is not called in the traditional DLL entry point fashion, but rather through direct function pointers retrieved by Navigator. The Netscape SDK file NPUPP.H contains structures to accomplish this calling mechanism. Calls from your plug-in to Navigator, although more straightforward, use the same technique with function pointers.

This chapter also suggested ways to design plug-ins. Among the many factors to consider when you design and develop plug-ins are Navigator compatibility, development languages, bandwidth requirements, LiveConnect, EMBED attributes, and MIME types. Remember, streaming plug-ins are generally considered much cooler than file-based plug-ins. Also, you can use a CGI program to provide server software as needed. For further reading, *Programming Netscape Plug-ins*, also published by Sams.net, is an excellent resource for more in-depth information on topics covered in this chapter.

Pulling Web Information

by Mark Bishop

IN THIS CHAPTER

CHAPTER 33

Inundated with information, the Internet is like a hungry monster kept alive by thousands of connections and fed each day millions of bytes of data from a number of information sources. One becomes lost even with the best search engines and Web browsers. However, a new era of services and programs makes finding information from the Web easy, painless, personal, and sometimes fun! Pulling Web information using the new programs and services truly enriches your personal Web life.

What Do You Call "It?"

Many buzzwords are flying around for the intelligent agents or Personal Information Gathering Services (PIGS) that essentially fetch information from the Internet and bring it back to your desktop in one form or another. The *Los Angeles Times* (`www.latimes.com`) news retrieving program is titled Hunter, depicted as a puppy dog acting like your canine personal agent; the program fetches a personalized newspaper based on your own profile. Like many such services, Hunter is free!

Accordingly, you can have the latest headlines, stock reports, sports, finances, weather, world news, politics, and even your local TV guide listings and horoscope delivered to you. Leave behind those days of opening your front door and looking for your delivered newspaper. (Mine was stolen most of the time anyway.) Now you can display the news automatically right on your own desktop computer. Some services deliver all the information you've requested right to your e-mail box every morning.

Imagine reading the latest news about Yahoo!, Netscape, and Microsoft in just one click. Picture yourself searching a dozen major newspaper and wire service stories, all at the same time and all in a flash. Would you like a personalized Web page that contains everything you need in a single place and opens when you start your favorite browser? We have those too! Maybe you want a program that silently retrieves the selected news of your choice and caches the HTML news pages for viewing offline. Yes—got those too!

Indeed, the Web is the medium that's growing information services such as Yahoo!'s My Yahoo!, Infoseek Personal, and a host of others. If you don't use your browser to gather information, other programs such as PointCast and Freeloader take care of you. These programs reside on your computer and silently traverse the Internet to retrieve your selected information automatically. Amazing.

It seems that every day a new PIGS-type program comes into being. First, the various Internet search engines such as `www.search.com`, `www.yahoo.com`, and `www.infoseek.com` started using the expression "personalized" Web pages. Personalized Web page services let you click the types of information you want, and presto-magic—they deliver a page that is updated with current information. Accordingly, these search engines reach out to other, larger search engines and draw upon their news sources. In short, the type of information you get back depends on the raw news sources being tapped.

Evolving Capabilities

Following the search engines, the news sources themselves jumped into the personalized information services game and offered even more personalized information. Noted online news companies such as clnet (www.cnet.com), ZD Net (www.zdnet.com), Iworld (www.iworld.com), and others give you a personalized Web screen that bypasses the Internet search engines and goes right to the heartbeat of their news and search engines. Other PIGS-type programs have custom software that sits on your hard drive and, like a faithful dog, fetches whatever information you want. News, news, and more news.

Basically, all the personal search programs perform the following tasks:

- Track information on specific subjects, issues, companies, and people.

- Get relevant and timely news releases from literally hundreds of sources worldwide, from major newspapers online to wire services, Usenet newsgroups, mailing lists, and more.

- Find additional links to other sources on your favorite topics.

- Search archives of collected data. This is especially true for larger content providers and newspaper and magazine companies.

- Open 24 hours a day with news often refreshed hourly or daily. Those PIGS that deliver the news to your e-mail account usually work Monday through Friday. You can customize PIGS such as Freeloader to work when you want them—hourly, daily (you indicate which days), or weekly.

- Change your personalized information page whenever you want, such as adding new categories to search and designing how your page displays. Make them a part of your own home page!

- Act as a screen saver for your system. PointCast and Freeloader do this already. In Freeloader, you just point and click, and it uses your dialer to connect to your provider and get the latest news.

- Entertain you with plenty of advertisements. Well, nothing is truly free. Although you incur no cost using these PIGS programs and services, you can expect advertisements. Some services have so many ads that it might make you want to use another PIGS program. Some services are tasteful enough with their advertisements that they don't slow you down in getting your information. Most of these PIGS work through your Web browser.

- Creates a real contender in replacing your own newspaper in that it will change the way you get your news. Many of these PIGS enable you to tell your computer when to dial out and connect to your ISP and then connect to your news sources.

The many information-gathering programs available are not all the same. They do overlap in the features they provide, but they each have nuances that I discuss to help you decide whether the program or service is for you. The following sections help you decide which PIG program or service to use.

The PointCast Network (PCN)

You can find PointCast at

`http://www.pointcast.com/`

PointCast Incorporated was founded in 1992 to provide current news and other information to the Internet community (see Figure 33.1). The service is free but makes heavy use of advertisements, which are creatively done and shown while you use the program. PointCast also includes a very nice screen saver option. The program itself works fine with Windows, and a Mac version is beta testing in the fall of 1996 (to be notified via e-mail when a Mac PointCast is available, visit `http://www.pointcast.com/mac/mac_signup.html`). PointCast for the Mac will run on PowerMacs only. PointCast does work on NT but will not be fully supported until the arrival of a 32-bit PointCast coming out late 1996. And although PointCast version 1.0 is not supported at all, it seems to work well in a Win OS/2 environment. And due out in late summer 1996 is the PointCast I-Server which will enable businesses to broadcast their own internal news over their intranets. A PointCast I-Server software can support around 500 clients using a Pentium 75MHz system. Indeed, you'll see more of these news server programs for intranet and Internet environments.

Figure 33.1.

PointCast, a resident PIGS program.

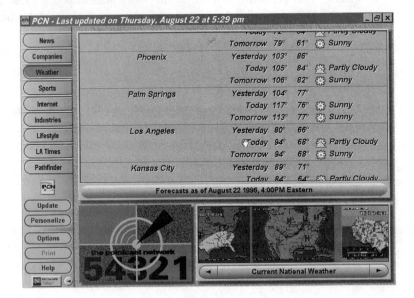

PCN was the first PIGS-type program I used. The program looks and feels nice with many customizable features and different categories of information that include Companies, Weather, Sports, Internet, Industries, Lifestyle, the *Los Angeles Times*, and Pathfinder. In each of these areas, you can click to select which sources of information you want. For example, under Sports, you can select any or all of the following:

- General Sports News
- Major League Baseball
- National Basketball Association
- Men's College Basketball
- Women's College Basketball
- National Football League
- College Football
- National Hockey League
- Golf and Tennis

This list gives you an idea of how most of these information-gathering programs operate—providing a wide selection of choices.

"It's like CNN on your desktop...It's the most compelling app I've ever seen for a personal computer," said Dave Winer of *Wired* magazine. Over a million users use PointCast with largely favorable reviews. PCN software is a resident program that occupies about 3.5MB of your hard-drive space. At specific times you select, PCN ventures out into the Internet and connects with various information sources. On a 486DX2/66MHz, PCN took about ten minutes with a 28.8 modem to get all the information I requested. Currently, PCN is a 16-bit application, which makes it a bit on the slow side for performance, but a 32-bit version is due out late Fall of 1996.

The PCN graphical user interface is well designed and is both efficient and easy to use. Each category that has multiple news feeds quickly displays a summary report that lists all the various stories being offered. Just double-click to get the full story. Even if the annoying advertising box bothers you like it did me, just click the story again, and it maximizes for easier reading.

Features and More Features

PCN is rich in options such as its Smart Screen, which enables you to use PCN as a screen saver. Smart Screen brings to your idle computer news it has retrieved earlier. It activates automatically after a certain amount of idle time elapses, which you indicate in minutes, or you can simply select an active corner of your monitor's screen. Another feature is PCN's Update option. You can update your information from PCN all day long, which I recommend only for live Internet connections. In addition, you can update by scheduling or clicking the Update button. The Proxy option is for network users. If your PCN software is behind a firewall, it must be configured in order to successfully update files. See your network administrator for this information.

Pros of PCN

The direct news feed to Knight-Ridder information sources, a cool GUI interface, and the fact that it's free of charge make PCN a hot and appealing item. Its Smart Screen technology actually makes it a decent screen-saver application, too. PCN now sells a retail version of its search program bundled with AT&T Corporation's WorldNet Internet Access software and Netscape Communications Corporation's Navigator browser software.

Cons of PCN

The downside of PCN is that the current version is still 16 bit and relatively slow. Although PointCast enables you to personalize certain topics, the content is little more than a dressed-up news feed. PCN is loaded with advertisements, but you can expect that from all personal information programs and services.

Freeloader, Inc.

You can find Freeloader at

`http://www.freeloader.com/`

The name alone somewhat exemplifies what Freeloader does—it brings content to you and displays it attractively within your Web browser (see Figure 33.2). Supporting Netscape Navigator and Microsoft Internet Explorer, Freeloader is a small engine that sits on your hard drive. After it surfs the Net to collect the information you subscribe to, Freeloader places the information on your hard drive for viewing at your leisure. With a toolbar that sits nicely under your Web browser and is automatically placed there, Freeloader can easily be adjusted and customized on the fly.

Don't be alarmed: The word *subscribe* here doesn't mean that you are charged because both the program and many sources of information are free. Think of it like programming your VCR to record your favorite upcoming movie. You do virtually the same thing with Freeloader. You subscribe to the types of information you want, and each day it taps into Net sources of information to bring it back to you. Although you don't need a browser for Freeloader to work, you do need one to see the collected information (HTML pages).

FIGURE 33.2.

Freeloader, a resident PIGS program that works with your Web browser.

Freeloader is actually an offline browser that enables users to download any Web content they want, including information from *U.S.A. Today* and *The Wall Street Journal*, any e-zine, sports sites, entertainment of all sorts, and business and headline news. The Freeloader search engine can find things quicker than if I searched the Web myself. I can set the time I want Freeloader to dial out and pick up my requested information. Moreover, Freeloader doesn't lock me in to what news I get, as do other PIGS-type programs.

After Freeloader starts its work, you'll notice that the HTML pages of information are cached to your Freeloader directory. I use this program almost every day and have not yet filled the 10MB I allotted for Freeloader. Reading the news and other selected information is easy and quick because I'm not gathering it online and reading it offline. Freeloader provides users with a powerful Internet tool that enables them to control the Web rather than feel overwhelmed by it.

How fast is it? On my 486DX2/66MHz with a 28.8 modem, I can run the Freeloader program and keep other applications open with no decrease in performance. However, if I open more than one browser and goof off, I notice a minor slowdown. Version 2.0 of Freeloader is significantly faster, and on anything higher than a 486, you don't even notice Freeloader working in the background. You can also configure Freeloader to search up to 12 sites at the same time;

the default is four sites. As with PCN, you can configure Freeloader to update your information hourly, daily, or weekly. Users who pay hourly connect charges to the Internet can save money by reading the information from Freeloader offline. In addition, Freeloader's interactive screen saver alerts you when new content is available either online or locally. Indeed, you can actually click items from the screen saver to instantly load the selected story. In short, you enjoy high bandwidth content at hard-drive speeds rather than modem speeds. The following sections outline some of the features that make Freeloader a unique personal information gathering program.

The Toolbar

Freeloader's toolbar is a horizontal bar that appears at the bottom of your browser's screen. It was designed so that you can easily customize and edit your Freeloader content subscriptions. Earlier versions of the Freeloader toolbar bothered me because it resized my browser screen without my permission, but the newer versions seem to have fixed this. From the toolbar, you can quickly adjust your settings, add new content to search and collect, turn on the search engine, and much more.

Channels and Subscriptions

With Freeloader, the service and content are free of charge. Resembling a television in its terminology, Freeloader offers channels of information categories such as Politics, Sports, the Net, Travel, Computers, Entertainment, Marketplace, Music, News and Weather, Personal Finance, and more. Under each of these headings are scores of information providers and content that you can easily click to receive and indicate how often you want it. Beyond these channels is a personal channel (for example, "Mark's page") that delivers TV programming, local movie listings, local weather, and much more. Users can also create their own channels for hard-to-organize content.

Smarter Screen Saver

Version 2.0 of Freeloader calls its screen-saver feature FL TV. Alerting you when new content is available, this smart screen saver enables you to quickly access new content information via a graphical interactive screen saver. With its polished and animated look, this screen saver appears to be a cut above the rest.

A Time Saver

After you set up Freeloader and select the sites you want it to visit, Freeloader takes only about 10 minutes to get your information. Freeloader also presents suggestions of new content that its staff finds. Because my Freeloader dials out in the morning hours, I rarely get a busy server because there's less Internet traffic at that time.

Content

Freeloader has a good business reputation with many popular and entertaining sites of information. Operating on a quid-pro-quo basis, the folks at Freeloader promote other Web sites in exchange for mentions of Freeloader. They collaborate with giants such as ZD Net, HotWired, Excite, Yahoo!, GeoCities, MovieLink, TV1, Match.Com, SportsLine, Travelocity, iWorld, and *U.S.A. Today.* According to Freeloader's Ricardo Perez, Distribution Manager, Freeloader has evolved from a content provider to a "content facilitator." With the many sites and types of Web information that Freeloader taps, it's turning out to be just that—the facilitator for our Web browsers!

Pros of Freeloader

I can say many good things about Freeloader. It works for you when you want it to. It collects everything and places it on your hard drive for faster viewing. Version 2.0 offers great flexibility in making Freeloader a truly personal type of PIGS program. The screen saver is more than decent—it's great.

Cons of Freeloader

I don't have many disadvantages to report. On my 486, Freeloader was a bit sluggish at times, but that was largely because I ran about a dozen TCP/IP applications along with my active Freeloader engine.

Zippo

You can find Zippo at

```
http://www.zippo.com/
```

When you think in terms of Usenet news and newsgroups, you often think of the popular news programs such as Fagent and News Xpress and so many other fine readers (see `www.stroud.com` or `www.tucows.com` for the latest news readers). Zippo offers a news service without the need for a traditional newsreader application and NNTP protocol (see Figure 33.3). According to Joe Zip, Editor of Zippo News Services, "With our interface, first-time users can read, decode, and post Usenet news with our easy-to-use, icon-driven or point-and-click Web sites."

33

PULLING WEB
INFORMATION

All it takes is your Web browser to use the Zippo services because you don't need the old re-quirements for accessing Usenet newsgroups, such as tricky configurations or separate utilities for decoding newsgroup images. Those days are gone; Zippo does everything for you through your Web browser. In short, Zippo took all the functionality of a typical news server and the traditional NNTP access and made it accessible through a Web interface. Just visit Zippo's site, and you can start doing it all!

Is Zippo the Same as Excite or PointCast?

Zippo is a Usenet news server. Excite, for example, can pull up Web and Usenet-related infor-mation, but there are limitations in what is actually received, especially if that search engine is not tied into Usenet news servers. When you submit your inquiry to other search engines such as Excite, they draw their information from other various databases. Some databases are their own, and some they plug into and use. Because these are only databases, your response is lim-ited to what the database contains and how often the information is updated. Generally, the Usenet information returned to you from other non-Usenet news servers is not as varied and informative as what you get accessing a straight news server such as Zippo. Services such as Zippo plug directly into many information news servers and other worldwide information feeds and news resources. From this propagation of news sources, Zippo can offer the best in timely and thorough Usenet information.

Because Zippo lets you use your own Web browser, you can do everything in one location from searching and replying to interacting and decoding a message. The folks at Zippo claim that their service is the only one that permits Usenet access through the Web, whereas other Usenet services must access with a newsreader or non-graphical NNTP protocol. Zippo offers

5,000 to 6,000 of the core Usenet newsgroups, and they have a Super Zippo that extends the total to 18,000 newsgroups through its subscription service that costs $9.95 a month or $69.00 a year. Receiving over 200,000 new incoming articles or messages a day, Zippo maintains a large depository of fresh news, and it enables you to interact with its servers and its information in real time.

How To Use Zippo's Direct Read News

To check out Zippo for yourself, use your Web browser and follow these easy steps:

1. Point your browser to Zippo's home page at `http://www.zippo.com`.
2. Find a newsgroup category that interests you and click any newsgroup listed.
3. To decode a multi-part file, click any segment, and the Zippo server finds the other parts and puts together the whole article or file automatically.
4. If it's a graphic file, simply click the icon to the left of the header, and Zippo decodes it for you automatically.
5. To read an article, click the header of the message.
6. To save an article, use your browser's Save feature under the File menu.
7. To reply to an article from the open article, click Post at the top of the page.
8. To post a new article, click Post at the top of the header list.

Pros of Zippo

Zippo is an excellent service for those who want quality Usenet news and newsgroups—and lots of them! Unlike other fine Usenet services such as DejaNews (`http://www.dejanews.com`), Zippo does it all for you within your browser. From over 18,000 newsgroups and binary files to an easy-to-use system, you get it all. I highly recommend it!

Cons of Zippo

It was hard to convince myself that Zippo does everything through my Web browser after I got used to my Free Agent NNTP program. The basic free 500 Usenet newsgroups were not enough for me, but then, that's why they offer a Super Zippo service. I hope more Internet services providers (ISPs) find Zippo useful and offer it to their subscribers.

My Yahoo!

`http://www.my.yahoo.com/`

My Yahoo! is one of the many personalized services that's customizable, and it's tied into the powerful Yahoo! search engine. Like many other personal news pages, it offers the latest news, stocks, weather, classifieds, sports, technology, and much more—free! Figure 33.4 shows a sample.

FIGURE 33.4.

My Yahoo! screen.

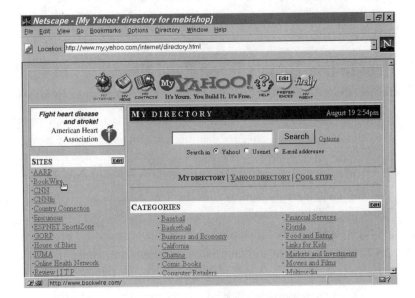

The Personals

The personals are everywhere these days. You name the Internet company—from Yahoo! to Excite, Netcom, Intel, MSNBC, and many others—and it probably has them. What is a personal page? Generally, it's a page that you can customize online so it displays all your favorite topics instantly if you make it your default page with your Web browser. For example, with My Yahoo!, you can select or edit a list of your favorite Web sites for quick access. You can pick Categories and Keyword Searches and add or remove sites at your leisure.

I enjoyed using My Yahoo! because it enabled me to select from a huge arrangement of information. Even the layout of the page itself and the loading speed as my default page was impressive. The title bar indicates your exact location among your personal Yahoo! pages. For example, you can customize the way you want to display main categories such as Internet, News, Contacts, Help, References, and Firefly (an intelligent agent that deals largely with the entertainment industry).

When you visit www.my.yahoo.com for the first time, you are introduced to a guided tour that is decent and informative. It was on the tour that I learned about one of the subcategories of Contacts. This feature ties in all the databases and search engines, such as White Pages, Yellow Pages, and E-Mail Addresses, that help you find information about people. Under each of the subcategories are other choices. I am surprised how often I use this section to look up someone and see whether he or she has a home page. For business people, this feature will come in handy. Overall, My Yahoo! is a great service.

Pros of My Yahoo!

For providing a default home page with my favorite browsers, Navigator and Explorer, My Yahoo! is among the best services available. The page is easy to configure and edit (add or remove) for all the various categories and their respected content. The nice layout means you can quickly click and read what you want. In addition, My Yahoo! also supports multiple users on the same machine.

Cons of My Yahoo!

Sometimes, the Yahoo! servers get quite busy, and I see delays, even on my T1 connection. These delays are rare and exceptional. The Instant Online News ticker-tape program (see the next section) is adequate but has no outstanding qualities, and I prefer my browser's display of My Yahoo!

Instant Online News (ION) for 95

New from Net Controls (`www.netcontrols.com`) in conjunction with the folks at Yahoo!, Instant Online News is a small ticker-tape program that synchronizes with your personal My Yahoo!. All your news in the ticker program appears in your Windows 95 tray bin or the Windows NT 4.0 task bar (see Figure 33.5). The ticker tape scrolls with the latest news that you've customized with My Yahoo!, and you click whatever interests you to display that story within your browser.

FIGURE 33.5.

The Instant Online News ticker-tape program at work.

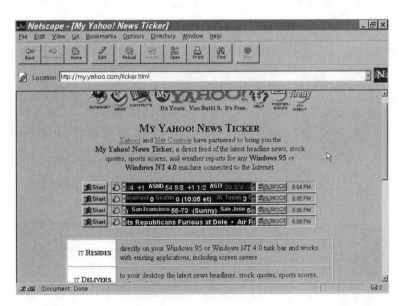

ION works with both Netscape Navigator and Internet Explorer. This program doesn't display advertising, but it lacks configuration options and its interface is plain boring. A more intuitive interface would be nice. I prefer using the My Yahoo! service rather than ION, but it might find a niche of popularity. You can download this program through your My Yahoo! page.

Another Ticker Tape?

Among the other ticker-tape programs available is IBM's infoMarket NewsTicker, which is a part of IBM's infoMarket service of information. Although the program and the information service are free, expect IBM to begin charging for the news feeds at some upcoming date. I personally thought the design and layout of this program was excessively large (including their advertisements and font sizes) for residing on the toolbar. I do expect to see this program grow and improve in the months ahead. For more information, visit `http://www.infomkt.ibm.com/ht3/ticker.htm`.

Personal Excite

`http://www.excite.com/`

If you haven't yet used Excite (see Figure 33.6) as one of the powerful Internet search engines, then you don't get around much, do you? Excite boasts over 50 million full-text URLs and claims it has more indexed pages than Alta Vista, Lycos, Infoseek, or Inktomi. Excite offers some impressive features such as a confidence rating of relevant hits along with click URLs, and it seems to work very fast. Taking the service a step further, it also offers a personalized Excite.

FIGURE 33.6.

A personalized version of the major search engine Excite.

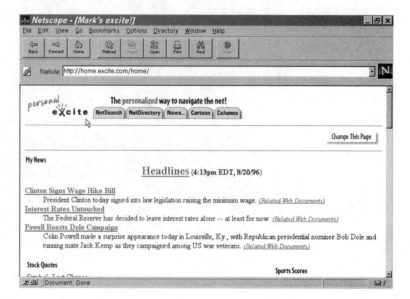

Many of these present and future PIGS-type programs and services basically offer you the same type of information. Personal Excite (PE) takes you a few steps ahead and provides a broad selection of configuration options. The following sections outline some of Personal Excite's features.

Event Reminders

Do you forget birthdays or anniversaries? You will no longer end up in the dog house because Personal Excite starts reminding you a week before the dates you schedule. Other neat features include an extensive hot list of your favorite URLs and Saved Searches, which saves your most frequent searches and keywords for new searches. In addition, Personal Excite can extract your query from its Web, Usenet, Classifieds, and Reviews categories. I entered a search on Earthquakes and Information and was surprised at how many sites had an Excite review.

Has More Than One Person Used Your Computer?

Personal Excite enables multiple people to maintain their own Personal Excite pages on the same machine. This is great if your computer is shared. With Personal Excite tied into one of the leading news agencies, Reuters News, you can be sure that your information is timely and complete. If the headlines, business, sports, international, politics, and entertainment topics are not enough, include also local ski reports, TV listings, cartoons, and more with your Personal Excite.

The following list outlines some of Personal Excite's features:

- Works from your Web browser with no requirements for special software.
- Defines the colors for the background, text, links, active links, and visited links.
- Provides back links from the Excite search page on your personal page.
- Enables you to choose the order of the sections on your personal page.
- Displays up to seven stock quotes along with Reuters News, Dow Jones, and NASDAQ prices under the Business Headlines section.
- Adds a `mailto:` option to your favorite links.
- Supports viewing your personal page from multiple locations and maintaining separate pages for multiple users.
- Displays on your personal page when the news was last updated.
- Provides powerful search functions that are tied into the regular Excite database and search engine.

Pros of Personal Excite

Personal Excite's service provides excellent performance and information tied into one of the Internet's largest search engines. Your page is easy to configure and change when needed. It's a handy page to attach to your home page or make your default search page.

Cons of Personal Excite

The information from Personal Excite is somewhat dry if you prefer heavy graphics and colors.

Personal NewsPage Direct from Netcom

http://www.netcom.com/newspage/direct.html

With over 500,000 paid subscribers to Netcom's credit, you can't easily overlook this nation-wide ISP and what it provides in news and information with a news program called Personal NewsPage Direct. In collaboration with Individual Inc., Netcom brings to the forefront of electronic delivery news customized to your personal news interests that's delivered right to your e-mail address rather than your Web browser.

Every morning (Monday through Friday), you receive an e-mail that includes the top 20 head-lines and other news summaries for you to peruse. There are no fancy graphics (actually none at all) and no links—you see just the facts in abbreviated form with just enough information so you know what's happening in the world. You do have access to full-text stories at NewsPage with this Netcom service, and you save money compared to if you didn't belong to Netcom and paid for the service directly.

Netcom offers three different versions of its service. The Basic service is free and represents about 40 percent of the news stories on NewsPage. The Premium news service and Pay Per View service represent the remainder of the news, providing additional features. Of course, if you want more, expect to pay more. The Premium news service costs an additional $3.95 per month with your Netcom account, but if you use another ISP such as America Online, for example, you pay $6.95 a month for the same service.

Who is Individual Inc.? They are the folks who produce NewsPage, a single-user, online infor-mation service designed to provide WWW users with current and presorted news. Formed back in 1989, Individual Inc. collects over 25,000 pages a day from over 600 news sources. NewsPage also incorporates a smart technology that sorts through the thousands of pages of news and puts them into over 2,300 news topics. Do not panic; all these topics are organized in an intui-tive, hierarchical structure, making it fast and easy to find what you want!

Pros of Netcom's NewsPage Direct

NewsPage Direct is a unique service because it's free if you are a paid Netcom subscriber and because it's delivered to your e-mail address every morning. Although you get only summary information, you do have access to full-text versions after you link to NewsPage's site.

Cons of Netcom's NewsPage Direct

With NewsPage Direct, news arrives only during the week, minus weekends and holidays. Because news doesn't wait for weekends and holidays, a major story can happen at any time, so the limitation makes this service weak. Also, if you click a URL from a given news summary, the program connects you to the NewsPage site, but then many stories display an obtrusive Upgrade page if you want the full-text story. I guess they have to make money somehow.

The Rest of Them

With so many fine PIGS programs and services available, this section could be labeled "The Never-Ending PIGS Story." You've probably noticed a pattern by now—you can get a lot of news with a customized way to search and display—but you'll like some programs and services better than others. Just take a test drive and try them all out; they're free and they cause no pain to your computer or browser. The following sections outline some other services I enjoy.

MSNBC Personal News Page

`http://www.msnbc.com/news/samplepfp.htm/`

MSNBC provides a hot site with professional staffing to make it a great place for you to visit. What do you expect when you put together Microsoft and NBC News? Both the news and pictures are stimulating and timely. Indeed, when the pipe bomb exploded during the Olympics, this site provided a sound recording in what seemed like minutes. MSNBC has just about everything you want in way of news, and you can customize what you want displayed on your personal page, including local news and traffic reports. You can also get other items of information about concert listings, child care, and pregnancy.

c | net: The Community Network

`http://www.cnet.com/`

c|net is among the leading-edge media companies that provide integrated television programming with the World Wide Web. Its television programming alone is broadcast by the Sci-Fi Channel and USA Network to over 50 million households. c|net also recently joined forces with E! Entertainment Television and developed E! Online (`http://www.eonline.com/`), which combines information and entertainment news.

c|net offers a lot of information with its leading Web magazine for news, product reviews, and other resources. In addition to the information, you can find its `Shareware.com` site (`http://www.shareware.com/`), which houses one of the Internet's largest collection of shareware and freeware software. Its famous `Search.com` (`http://www.search.com/`) offers a categorized assortment of every Internet search engine you can imagine. At c|net, you can customize your own personal search page (look under the "Search.Com" category for setting up your own Personal Page). This site is truly amazing to behold and use.

Infoseek Personal

http://www.infoseek.com/

Another famous name in Internet search engines and information is Infoseek Personal. Infoseek Personal offers a personalized news page that is well laid out and easy on the eyes for getting your news on a daily basis. Like other search engines, this service also provides a search field. This is a great site to get personal with the Internet; check it out.

Intel

http://www-pwn.intel.com/

The Intel site is slanted toward its own products. Although this might limit the quantity of information Intel can offer to its users, this site is geared toward the "brains" of computers and the components that make them what they are. If you want technical information regarding the Intel platform, you need to be at the Intel site. For example, the following list outlines some of the content preferences that you can select:

- Cool Uses of Pentium Processor Technology
- Pentium Pro Processors
- Universal Serial Bus Components
- Intel Souvenirs and Screen Savers
- Latest Web Technologies
- Embedded Intel Architecture
- Motherboards

Intel also offers an electronic newsletter about new Web content in selected areas.

ZD Net Personal View

http://www.zdnet.com/

ZD Net provides another fine example of using your Web browser to access information. Much of what you see in the other PIGS services is available in ZD Net Personal View. Your content is nicely laid out within your browser's window, and configuration is easy, too. Furthermore, ZD Net is probably one of the better places to find an extensive amount of computer industry news. With its Personal View, you have your own clipping service to such publications as *Computer Life*, *Inter@ctive Week*, *Computer Shopper*, *Computer Gaming World*, *MacUser*, *PC Computing*, *PC Week*, and many others. ZD Net offers some of the best shareware programs available, which are often highlighted so you know what's free and hot to use. For example, I downloaded a ZD Net utility called Password Pro for Windows. The ZD Net Member newsletter is a very informative biweekly news source sent to you via e-mail.

Timecast and RealAudio Player Plus

`http://www.realaudio.com/`

The word *personal* takes on new meaning when it comes to computers and the Internet. First, it was personal screen savers that identified us in some personal way (from Star Trek to Flying Toasters to scrolling text). Now, our own information-gathering programs plaster our names on the pages, making even our information choices personal. To take the personal visual perception of Web information even further, we can now listen to the news—yes—with a service that provides sound.

Introducing Timecast: The RealAudio Guide

Timecast enables users to customize their own personal daily news with audio content that is timely and informative. It truly is amazing to listen to your news and even music over your Internet connection. Timecast makes it easy to find and immediately hear the news you want (see Figure 33.7).

FIGURE 33.7.

Timecast and RealAudio Player Plus give you the option to listen to the news rather than see it in Web pages.

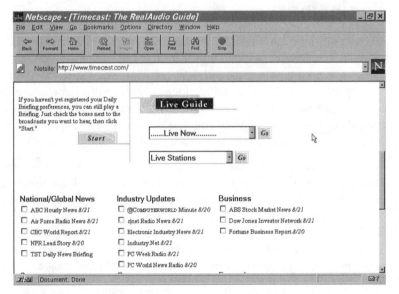

The foundation of Timecast is its Daily Briefing feature that enables users to build their own custom newscast with stories and features from many noted news and entertainment organizations such as ABC, clnet, Entertainment Tonight, CBC, Fortune, ComputerWorld, Web Review, and many others. Timecast also provides a list of more than 600 Web sites that deliver audio content, including a search facility.

RealAudio Plus

A new era of RealAudio performance essentially makes you your own program director for listening to what you want, when you want. Player Plus makes it easier to organize the large amount of audio on the Net by providing Preset buttons of your favorite audio content. These buttons are similar to the presets on your stereo system.

Another advantage of Player Plus is the Scan feature, which cycles through 20 or more Internet radio stations for your listening pleasure. One of my favorite options with this program is the capability to selectively record other RealAudio files. You can save .RA files to your hard disk and listen to them later.

With RealAudio Player Plus and the Internet, you can listen to the news around you and choose what you want to hear. The RealAudio Player Plus, which retails for $29.95, is available through online order. Visit `http://www.realaudio.com/` for more information.

Our Friends from Yesterday—Usenet's Beginnings

It wasn't that long ago before the Internet explosion that BBSs and FidoNet systems delivered what we thought was a world of information to our computers, consisting of hundreds of different newsgroups, echo mail, and ARPA mailing lists. I can still remember configuring my SeaDog software to link with other modems to share this information. But news grows fast. Imagine back in late 1979 when two Duke University grad students, Tom Truscott and Jim Ellis, thought of hooking two computers together to exchange information with the UNIX community. We have jumped miles ahead of those important days.

From those experiments came new releases of other newsreader programs and the jump from UUCP to Network News Transfer Protocol (NNTP), which enabled hosts to exchange information via the TCP/IP connections. Newsreader programs developed for just about every operating system, including Vnews (written by Kenneth Almquist), rn (developed by Larry Wall, author of Perl), tin, pine, and other popular Usenet newsgroup readers such as Agent for Windows and Microsoft Internet News for Windows 95. Although online newsgroups add up to the thousands, yet another new round of news-collecting programs, PIGS, come into play.

With the continuing popularity of Usenet newsgroups and the Web, a blending of the two sources enables us to use our favorite Internet tool, the browser, for accessing information and files and interacting with that information in the manner we choose.

Where Are We Headed Next?

Expect to see very smart agents and programs that not only go out onto the Internet and gather your selected information, but find and organize all your information both on your computer's hard drive, your network, or intranet, as well as everything you got from the Internet and more. Future agent type programs will be capable of going from service to service and information source to information source, both on and off networks. Soon you will find PIGS that will leave a message to your friend, check back at a given time to see whether your friend read his message, and if he hasn't read it, turn around and fax that message to him.

A couple programs to watch include Alta Vista's Private Extensions (www.altavista.com) and the Grasp Information Corporation's Knowit All (www.grasp.com), which stores, organizes, and delivers all your information at the click of a button. It basically replaces your bookmark program for something better! Other programs to keep your eye on include Symantec's Internet FastFind, which automatically uses many Internet search engines and brings back your results pre-sorted and prioritized on one Web page minus any duplicated information. FastFind is available in retail software stores now. Also visit the noted Verity site, www.verity.com, and check out its Search'97 program, which helps you search multiple corporate sites of information plus the Internet.

The list of PIG services and programs goes on and on. You should experiment and try them out for yourself. As mentioned before, some you will like; others you will hate. Don't be surprised to see more of them. What is now available for free might turn into a cost someday—so enjoy and use them now while you have them. Obviously, the competition is heating up, and major search engine sites and news agencies want your Web traffic.

The Internet offers so much for us to see, hear, and use. A plethora of data fed by other sources eventually trickles its way down to our monitors and hard drives. Sooner or later, we'll be inundated with tons of information, not knowing what to do with it all. I guess by that time, we'll have another new program to help us sift through that mess, and on we go again!

33

**PULLING WEB
INFORMATION**

International Considerations

by Mark Bishop

IN THIS CHAPTER

CHAPTER

34

The news today is filled with mind-boggling statistics about the Internet. Visit any Usenet newsgroup and you'll read that 30 million people or more use the Internet regularly, and 2.5 million people have made a purchase over the Internet! In its October 1, 1996, edition, *PC Week Online* says that advertising revenues alone, estimated at $12 million for 1995, could jump up to $300 million for 1996 and reach as high as $3.8 billion by the year 2000. Almost everyone who surfs the Net already knows that the Internet is blowing up exponentially in size. Although the actual number of people using the Internet might be unknown, the fact remains that business-related Web sites are dominating the growth of the Internet and that the Internet is doubling in size each year. Suddenly this big world we live in becomes small and connected. So where does that leave you?

If you already have a Web site or your own Web pages, being on the Internet can be busy work—especially if you are trying to make a business out of your cyberspace presence. Doing business on the Internet means confronting all types of Internet issues, ranging from making cool Web pages and maintaining them, to learning the myriad of ongoing tricks and tags, to making your pages hot. And, if you're selling or promoting a corporate image through your Web pages, the job is even harder because you have to stay on top of much more. Now imagine adding an international presence, having Web pages and information in a language other than English.

Taking into consideration the growth of the Internet, how could any sensible business person not have an international Web site? For example, how can anyone with something to sell ignore the Chinese market, with 800 million people and computer sales that are doubling every year?

Don't forget the 70 million people who speak Cantonese. With the takeover of Hong Kong by mainland China imminent, almost half a million Chinese alone have already immigrated to Canada. The market is there! There are also 78 million in this world who speak French, as well as 98 million people who speak German (in Germany, Switzerland, and Austria). In addition, 300 million people in Spain, Central and South America, and the Philippines speak Spanish. Internet experts tell us that by the year 2010 everyone between the ages of 25 and 55 will have an Internet connection.

Marketing Today

True, you might already know how to market and promote your Web pages via the various search engines. You also know that if you don't register your URLs, no one will know your pages exist. But, what if you wanted to promote or sell products and services to customers beyond the United States and Canada? What if you want to reach billions of people in China, Europe, or Mexico? What if you want to sell a product or service to a specific group of people—how would you market your site? These are tough questions, indeed.

Marketing Changes

Since the explosion of the Internet, many businesses are coming to grips with the fact that many of the traditional marketing approaches used outside the Internet don't necessarily always work on the Internet or one's Web site. Today, the audiences and marketing are different. People are online in more than 100 countries, and they speak many different languages. What was once a tradition-driven market is now an information-driven market.

Not long ago, businesses used demographics and psychological profiles to help identify their customers. Now on the Internet, almost anything goes! In fact, innovation is sometimes the factor that distinguishes a heavily trafficked site from one that is dead. However, to compete in an international market, you need to know more than how to write HTML pages.

A competent Web site needs at least someone who understands the basics of Internet technology, communication, advertising, and marketing. And for a truly global Internet presence, you need to think about other issues, too.

International Concerns

What do you need to develop an international Web site that will be visited by people who speak a variety of languages? Assuming that your Web site is already functional, you need to ask yourself the following questions:

■ Is your product, service, or information content exportable to your target market on the Internet?

Although one of the marketing bonuses of the Internet is that you don't have to buy a local business license for each country, state, or city that you're doing business in (unlike regular merchants who maintain a physical presence), you still need to figure out if you can deliver to that marketplace. The logistics range from translating your content into another language and placing it into your HTML page to shipping your product out of the country. The job is more complex than building a Web page or calling UPS for a pickup.

■ Is your foreign market even on the Internet?

You could waste a lot of time and energy creating an international Web site if no one is online to view it. For example, if I'm trying to sell T-shirts to Tibetan monks and my Web site is in Los Angeles, I could have some problems, such as finding Tibetan monks on the Internet and writing Cool Monk Shirts in their language on my Web page. Do your homework before you start. Professional Internet marketing groups can make a difference if you're unsure.

■ Can you speak the language of your intended market?

Even if you can create your Web page in a foreign language, you still have to consider how you will respond to customer inquiries. Obviously, having someone on staff who can translate and respond effectively in the language of the people you are marketing to is important. Larger companies need to employ full-time translators and cross-train them in HTML and other Internet skills.

■ What about the nuts and bolts?

So, you know how to use a graphic editor such as Paint Shop Pro and can slap together an HTML page, but what if you need to make an image with Japanese or Spanish text characters in it? Fortunately, the tools to make such a graphic are pretty much the same as you use to make any type of graphic for the Internet. After you have your original source of text in the appropriate language, you cut and paste and manipulate. For example, if you were using the Spanish keyboard option in Windows, you could type out the text and manipulate it with bold or change the font, and then cut and paste that text into a graphic program for other special effects.

■ Is what you see what you get?

Will visitors to your Web site need special software to see your non-English text? Do any converter programs work with major Web browsers such as Navigator and Explorer? Do the major browsers display or accept input from languages other than English? These mechanics and behind-the-scenes work become paramount when you are developing a multilingual Internet site. Microsoft's Internet Explorer 3.0 will eventually support 23 languages. Netscape's Navigator 2.0 International version already supports French, German, and Japanese versions. At this time neither supports Chinese dialects. When you are downloading either of these two browsers, look for the "International" versions. Other companies, such as Twinbridge (`www.twinbridge.com`), offer a free program called AsianViewer. This program enables users to display Chinese, Japanese, and Korean language Web pages, e-mail, newsgroups, and other Internet applications.

■ Have you considered how you will ship the product? What about tariffs? Will you accept returns?

If you are largely promoting information and not products for sale, this point is moot. However, if you want to sell to a given foreign market, you must consider these essential issues. Selling over the Internet begins to sound like an import/export business and might very well become such a thing. Be ready for this eventuality!

Defining an International Web Site

An international Web site is largely about displaying your HTML page in more than one language. An international Web site is, at least, bilingual and allows for some type of non-English response or input. The nature of the global audience that you are targeting will also dictate how you should think about and create your page. For example, if you are aiming for an Hispanic market, you surely want to be aware of Hispanic customs, culture, and business practices.

Who's Speaking What?

The Internet is surely a worldwide network, and English (the prevailing language on the Internet) is not the native language of many people who access the Internet! English is actually a second language for many Internet users. And, according to the 1996 edition of *Almanac and World Facts*, of the almost 6 billion people in the world, only about 326 million learn English as their native language. Consequently, millions of people cannot read the millions of English-only Web pages.

True, not everyone in this world has access to a computer, let alone the Internet. However, many industrialized nations do have access and will continue to grow in their number of connections. Along those lines, universities will always connect students and others to the Internet.

Your Competitive Advantages

If you look at the foundation of successful Web sites, you'll notice that they all have what I call GIGSGD. Don't even try to pronounce it! GIGSGD stands for Good Information, Good Shift, and Good Delivery, and in dealing with a truly global Web community, these points take on an important meaning. Following these principles will put you in the same league as other successful Web site owners.

Good Information

Having a successful Web presence is like baking a cake, and your content is the most important ingredient. If you don't have quality information, you cannot expect return visitors. A charismatic site, on the other hand, builds enthusiasm and brings people back for more. A good site covers everything from what a user clicks to navigate through your site to your content, and even your advertisements—if you have any. And it can be as simple as changing the poem you have on your home page to keeping the company Web site up-to-date with the latest products and services you offer. And for an international site with multiple languages, this means translating any changes in your English Web pages to the foreign language pages you're displaying. You need to keep your Web site fresh and exciting!

Good Shift

If you work in a large company, you know that paper is information: tons and tons of pages and information. The world is made up of information from the entertainment community, businesses, government, and individuals. What does one do with all the data? You'll have to shift the information from a non-digital paper format to a digital one as displayed through a given Web page. But, how do you do that?

Your first job is to know about the programs and technology that can take you from a world of hard copy to a world of digital information, such as converting printed items to HTML; learning how to convert standard audio sources such as tapes to digital audio formats using programs such as RealAudio and TrueSpeech; or learning how to convert large-scale word-processing documents into HTML pages, using HTML Transit from InfoAccess. To create multilingual Web pages for your international site, you will need more specialized programs and utilities, such as word-processing software for other languages, translation programs that convert one language into another, and Web browsers that support different languages and their respective fonts. These products are just a few of the tools you can use to get your data ready for the Internet.

Good Delivery

Good delivery is having the required working parts of your Web site to present your information in a pleasant and efficient manner to your viewing audience. For an international site, good delivery could mean informing your users ahead of time that they need, for example, an international Web browser or special viewing software.

If you have good digital information, people from all parts of the world, speaking all types of languages, will come to it. Your content can be compelling information, games, or connections to powerful relational databases, using products such as WebDBC, R:WEB, or CGI Perform. You will have to work hard to make your online information suitable for an international market.

To help put into perspective which applications work nicely in creating an international Web site (defined as using a language other then English), I visited Sprint's Asian division Web site, www.aan.net, and learned how its Webmasters create a Chinese Web page. This scenario helps you to see the steps and tools used to make a multilingual page.

First, according to Wendy Hsu, Webmaster, she first develops her graphic, using professional graphic software such as Paint Shop Pro 4.0 and Photoshop. Second, if text is involved in either the HTML document or the graphic, she uses a Chinese word processing software called Chinese Pro that enables her to use almost any text editor and type directly as Chinese characters. She prefers not to use Microsoft Word to cut and paste because each Chinese word actually takes two spaces, and Word distorts the spacing. She is concerned that those viewing her Chinese Web page have a browser that supports these Chinese characters she has created. Although any browser can display a graphic, the text portion of the HTML document must be displayed correctly via a Web browser that supports multiple languages.

Multilingual Web Browsers and Other Tools

The big names in the universe of Web browsers—Microsoft's Internet Explorer 3.0 and Netscape's Navigator 2.0 International version—support multiple languages. Microsoft promises that its browser will soon be available in 23 languages, enabling users to select the character set of the language they want and thereby enabling the browser to display the page correctly. Netscape's Navigator International version enables customers to use e-mail and join threaded discussion groups.

The Power Players of Multilingual Helper Software

A growing market of software companies is scuttling to write helper programs for non-native English speakers so that they too can surf the Net and see pages in multiple languages. Some of these new programs not only support foreign languages on the Web but also work with many other software programs. Essentially, a mouse click enables a user to switch between English and other languages. Remember that Asian languages generally require helper programs; on the other hand, many of the European languages are built into the popular Web browsers. Many of the following programs support Chinese, Japanese, and Korean (CJK), and offer fonts for these languages too. Here's a list of some of the more popular helper programs:

- **UNIONWAY:** `http://www.unionway.com/`

  A popular suite of programs supporting Chinese, Japanese, and Korean languages under Windows, and also a 32-bit version for NT 3.51 and 4.0. This program provides multilanguage support for Windows-based applications (word processing, desktop publishing, presentation graphics, spreadsheets, and more), by displaying the selected language so that all text you enter from any Windows-based application is displayed in that given language. Also includes an extensive font list for each language.

- **TWINBRIDGE:** `http://www.twinbridge.com/`

  Another very popular suite of applications designed for Asian languages. Offering much of the same as Unionway, Twinbridge provides extensive technical support to its clients. After you click the Twinbridge icon, a new toolbar appears on your Windows desktop, enabling various features. In addition, Twinbridge offers a free utility program called AsianViewer. This very handy utility has a click-down map of Asia that requires users only to click in what Asian country they want to view their Web pages. The program supports the popular Chinese internal codes of BIG5, GB, HZ, and ISO2022-CN, Korean, and Japanese dialects. This intuitive map makes it easy for Web surfers to select in what language or dialect of that language to view multilingual pages.

- **CHINESE PRO:** `http://www.chinapro.com/`

  China Pro is a very flexible and popular Asian utility used by many who do extensive word processing in an Asian language such as Chinese. Its Web site is only in Chinese, so if you want to contact it, have a translator close by.

- **ALIS:** `http://www.alis.com/` European language support

  Known for its popular Tango multilingual browser that not only enables you to display any of over 90 languages, it will automatically retrieve your Web pages in the same languages, too. The big plus here is that most multilingual browsers will display the page in a foreign language, but you can't input a URL in the same language. Tango enables you to input text into its browser. Visit its site to get all the details.

34

INTERNATIONAL
CONSIDERATIONS

- **NJWIN:** `http://www.njstar.com.au/` Shareware version

  Hongbo Data Systems, makers of the NJSTAR and NJWIN suite of applications, produces a wide range of Chinese and Japanese language programs that work with MS-DOS or MS Windows. Its site also has some good links to other online Chinese resources.

- **PROVANTAGE:** `http://www.provantage.com/`

  Provantage is unique in that it comes on a CD-ROM and enables anyone using Netscape 2.0 to translate German, Spanish, and French Web sites into English just by clicking a button. You can buy the product from the Provantage Web site for only $43.00. Not bad!

- **ACCENT:** `http://www.accentsoft.com/`

  The people at Accent Software claim that only 9 percent of the world's population speaks English, and they see the Internet as the network to reach the other 91 percent of the world's global village. Their Internet with an Accent software program is rich in features such as Multilingual Mosaic browser; Multilingual Publisher, which is an HTML editor that enables you to make quick and easy foreign language Web pages; Multilingual MailPad, which lets you correspond in the language that both you and the recipient prefer; and much more. Out in software retail stores now is Navigate with an Accent, which is a plug-in for Netscape's Navigator. This application displays up to 35 different languages and their respective fonts correctly. It also enables multiple character sets on the screen at the same time and provides multilingual help screens and documentation.

To get an idea of how these programs work, you might want to try out the shareware version of NJWIN. The company has a Web site with clear instructions for installing the program (and in English, too), and this program was highly rated by students on the various Chinese IRC talk channels. Figure 34.1 shows a Netscape browser using the NJWIN helper program. Notice the pull-down box that allows for the various Asian languages and their dialects.

For additional information on multilingual Web browsers, visit any English search engine and type `Multilingual Browsers`.

FIGURE 34.1.
*NJWIN multilingual
Web support.*

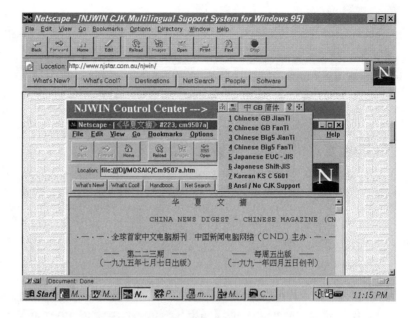

Preparing a Multilingual Document

Although all Web browsers can display a GIF or JPG graphic having foreign characters in the graphic, to view the foreign text within the HTML page your browser must support that language. You can start to prepare a multilingual document by using the international language support that is probably built into your computer. Windows users can change or add keyboard properties for languages and dialects, such as Central European (Danish, Finnish, French, German, Italian, and so on), Cyrillic, Baltic, Greek, Spanish, and others. The Windows keyboard selection supports almost all European languages. However, Asian languages require special software, as described earlier, because the type of characters, such as Chinese, Japanese, and Korean, are double-byte characters. This means that whereas a Spanish character occupies one space, a Chinese character will take up two spaces. This might not seem important until you begin to cut and paste from one application to another and your sentences look distorted.

To add a little confusion with an explanation, HTML publications written in Chinese don't have a unique Chinese code that all Chinese can read or understand. In fact, the Chinese language has a few popular dialects, which is one reason why even the large browsers such as Navigator and Explorer still have not supported it yet, but the two styles of Chinese code that dominate on the Internet are the BIG5 format (traditionally used in Taiwan and Hong Kong) and the GB format (used in mainland China, Singapore, and other places).

Obviously, one can almost see a fatal limitation in having a software program with so many character sets and also having to support them. This enormous diversity is one reason why there

34

INTERNATIONAL
CONSIDERATIONS

is not a universal Web browser that supports all foreign languages. However, the major Web browsers such as Netscape and Microsoft are slowly making support for all languages into reality.

However, don't blame the Asian languages for this technical glitch. After all, HTML and the Web were developed at CERN in Europe, which explains why they have provisions for European languages that use standard escape sequences and existing 8-bit character sets.

Making a Multilingual Web Page

Webmasters who maintain international Web sites tend to use the same tools that any Web person would use to create a hot HTML page, for example, Adobe's Photoshop, CorelDRAW!, and Paint Shop Pro. The difference is in how you turn your multilingual characters into a real Web document for everyone to be able to view.

Cut and Paste! You thought there was an easier way? Actually, cut and paste is a popular and relatively simple method for taking a word or sentence from your multilingual word processor and capturing the text from its original source. An example might be inserting a Chinese Word file into your Adobe Photoshop file, resizing it, and adding your special effects. This method works fine when you are making a GIF file and inserting it into your Web page. In fact, because most browsers can support the GIF and JPG file formats, most of your users won't need any special software to read your non-English text.

Making the multilingual text can be as easy as using a multilingual editor and typing directly into the text or HTML editor. This area is not so difficult as making a multilingual graphic file, because several programs enable your keyboard input to display the foreign letters you've selected. For example, to produce a Microsoft Word document in Chinese, you need the Chinese version of Word for Windows 95, which sells for about $240.

One company that has done an amazing job of converting Chinese text files into regular GIF files is SINANET. In fact, it can convert an entire page of Chinese characters from a major Taiwanese newspaper into an 8-bit GIF file smaller than 15KB. This size means that any Web browser at even a modest connection speed could view multiple pages easily. The idea of having your multilingual text saved as a graphic itself is not a bad idea. It solves for now the difficulty in worrying who can see your page or who can't. And although the folks at SINANET won't say exactly what their process is, one can achieve the same effect scanning a document and saving it as a GIF or JPG file. The trick is to minimize the colors used (black and white), making the scanned page small in size. Visit the SINANET site and see how a nicely laid out multilingual Web page looks. When you're there, click the News Center.

http://sinanet.com/

Probably the same graphics programs you use for your Web pages were the ones used at this site. Programs such as Paint Shop Pro with Kai Power Tools, Photoshop, and CorelDRAW! were all used to make this multilingual Chinese site (English version, too). Visit the site at http://www.aan.net/.

> **NOTE**
>
> Visit `http://www.chasecom.com/price-ms.htm/` for more information on obtaining Chinese-oriented computer products. This site is extremely popular in the Chinese community.

In addition, Windows 3.*x* and Windows 95 already offer character sets in many other languages that you can access with a click. Check Keyboard properties in the Control Panel for more information.

However, be careful not to confuse the making of a foreign language document with building an HTML page. You can use the `<PRE>` `</PRE>` tag to insert your text, but the browser still needs to be in the language you're writing in to view your page correctly. Keep in mind that word wrapping often doesn't recognize foreign characters, so use the `PRE` command often.

Key Components: Translation and Promotion

Delivering your international Web pages to an international audience takes the following:

1. Writing your Web pages in, or having your original page translated to, the language of your choice.
2. Promoting your translated Web page(s) to the world. This type of marketing means thinking globally, because much of the world speaks a language other than English.

Web Translation Services

If your business is too strapped for funds (or time) to take on an international Web venture of designing, making, and delivering multilingual Web pages, or if you want to ease into this project gradually, a Web translation service might be in order. These companies specialize in transforming your English-version Web page(s) into any language(s) you choose.

Fees for Web translation services start around $75 per hour. (You can figure on about an hour per page.) If you use search words such as multilingual and Web or International Web Sites, a search engine will return a decent listing of businesses that can assist you with an international Web look. Here are a few Web translation services. (Most of these companies offer free quotations.)

■ `http://netpromo.com/translation/translation.html`

This company translates Web pages into Chinese, English, and Spanish. It also translates lengthier documents, and charges per word.

■ `http://www.loop.com/`

This is another good company that can handle almost any European or Asian language; translations start at about $100 per page.

■ http://www.globalstrategies.com/

This site designs Japanese-language Web pages. Fees start at about $200 per page, in addition to a charge for each word on the page.

■ http://www.gen.com/euromktg/eurobus.html

This international Web-promotion business understands the European market very well and has an outstanding awareness on how to successfully market your site.

NOTE

For an excellent example of how to handle multiple languages, multilingual sites, launching from a single site, and branching off to other foreign sites, check out

http://www.gen.com/euromktg/index.html

Web translation services are also doing a good business in translating foreign-language HTML into English, which tells me that Europeans, and soon Asians, are also tuned into the possibilities of doing international business on the Internet. I hope this chapter is a wake-up call to readers who want to reach the millions around the world in their own languages.

Apple and IBM sites offer a language-selection drop-down box that takes you to their page in the language of your choice. A good international landing page should have languages in some type of graphic that all browsers can read, followed by a selection of other languages that the user can shoot to quickly. Figure 34.2 shows how a simple point-and-click feature can help navigate to a site with international pages.

FIGURE 34.2.

The www.apple.com *international site.*

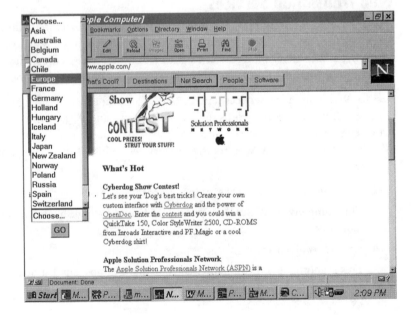

Beyond Web Translating: Promoting Your Site

The other key component in a successful international site is promotion. The minimum effort required is that you register your multilingual Web pages with the major search engines on the Internet; you should also register with various foreign search engines and indexes.

The following are some suggestions that will assist you in promoting your site worldwide:

- Consider hiring a professional marketing company that specializes in international exposure of Web pages. Many of the Web translation businesses can help you; other marketing professionals, such as a public relations firm, can also help.

- Learn about foreign search engines and indexes. Of course, you won't be able to do much unless you speak that language. For example, a new Japanese version of the Open Text Index can access tens of thousands of Japanese Web pages. You'll need a Japanese Web browser (such as Netscape Navigator or Explorer) to see these particular pages, but you can visit the site in English and then select a search language. This powerful and leading-edge search tool is the type of thing you want to be placed in, as it supports languages other than English.

> **NOTE**
>
> The Open Text search engine will also be the basis of other non-English search engines. In your travels to other multilingual sites, you'll find other smaller search engines and Yellow Pages. Expect to see many non-English search engines and indexes soon. Figure 34.3 shows the landing page for Open Text.

- Establish mutual links with a foreign business. This partnership is a great way to bring foreign traffic to your pages and at the same time establish a working relationship with another country. It puts your business on a personal level. Do a keyword search of EuroBusiness Centre in `http://www.altavista.digital.com/`, and you'll be astonished at all the different sites that come up in different languages. You will find a lot of important Internet information that you can use to promote your own international Web pages.

- Send out e-mail, newsletters, and autoresponders. Try to capture your foreign visitors by having a form that asks for their personal information, such as name, phone, e-mail address, and mailing address. Ask if they'd like to receive a newsletter or other information in their own language. Autoresponders enable you to automatically send a prepared document to the visitor's e-mail address. Ask your ISP for more information on autoresponders.

34

INTERNATIONAL
CONSIDERATIONS

- Learn about the business practices of the foreign market you are tapping into with your Web information. For example, Europeans would appreciate a voice call to establish a business relationship rather than just an e-mail message sent to them. The same holds true for Spanish speakers worldwide. Search the Internet for `Business Practices in foreign countries` to get an idea what to expect from various countries.

- Keep your international Web page simple. Graphics are time-consuming and expensive to download.

- Understand the culture and customs of the host country. Believe it or not, some colors are considered offensive in certain countries, and some colors are considered lucky. So do your homework!

- Add sound clips to your pages to enhance the theme of your international pages.

- Make your pages clickable, and easy to navigate. If your page starts out in English, for example, make it clickable so a foreign visitor can spot his or her language and reach the corresponding pages quickly and without confusion. Test run your international pages with people who speak the language your pages are written in.

FIGURE 34.3.

The Open Text multilingual search engine on the Internet.

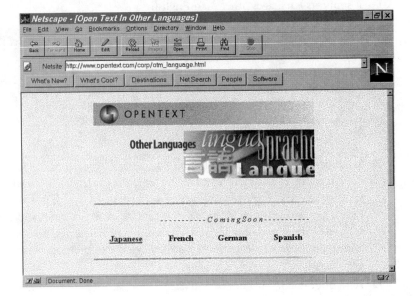

Summary

All the signs point to a lot of people cascading onto the Internet. People everywhere, speaking many different languages, want to visit you on the Internet. Think of these international considerations as a business opportunity that you can't afford to miss. Remember that not all of your business will come from obvious sources; some will show up from places you don't expect. Be prepared to meet these new opportunities and challenges and become a truly international Web person.

Creating a Custom, Integrated Application with Multiple Protocols

by Antonio Miguel Ferreira

CHAPTER 35

IN THIS CHAPTER

This chapter describes the creation of a Web application that deals with multiple Internet protocols. It covers the basics of building such an application and gives you some ideas for enhancements that could be used on your own multi-protocol based applications.

The application described here is called WebPOP, a Web-based mail reader.

A Multi-Protocol Application

Careful planning of a multi-protocol application should be finished before you start to write the program code. If you take some time to think about the application you want to write, you could save many hours of work. Here is a checklist you can follow to write your own multi-protocol applications:

- Think about the functions your application will provide and the protocols it needs to use.

- Take some time to search for something similar on the Internet that might suit your needs.

- Get the specifications (usually an RFC, or Request For Comments, document) of the protocols you will use.

- Take a look at the sockets (communication) interface of the programming language of your choice.

- Make a draft of the overall design (such as subroutines and modules) of the application.

- Code the application in the language of your choice.

- Test your application, taking special care with the subroutines that implement the different protocols.

A Multi-Protocol Application on the Web

Web servers and Web browsers exchange information using the *HyperText Transfer Protocol* (HTTP), but several Internet services are based on other well-known protocols such as SMTP (mail), NNTP (news), FTP (file transfer), and so on. Fortunately, there are ways to exchange information between different servers and to present it all under the same Web-based interface. The integration of several protocols in one application requires a careful design process from the programmer and, most important of all, a good knowledge of the protocols and languages used. A common characteristic of multi-protocol Web-based applications is the use of the CGI (*Common Gateway Interface*) specifications. Unless an application uses a proprietary Application Programming Interface (API), it probably uses the CGI because it is the standard way of communication between a Web server and a custom application.

CGI applications can be written in virtually any computer language, such as Perl and C; it is just a matter of using their communication possibilities (using the sockets library, for example, available for all major platforms) in order to write an application that talks with different servers and outputs the results in HTML format. This is the idea behind multi-protocol applications based on the Web: Talk with other applications; treat the information they provide; and present the results in HTML.

One of the advantages of using CGI applications is that you don't have to worry about making a version for every known platform. Because the program is executed in the server-side, and because the output is in standard format (HTML, plain text, and so on), CGI is a good choice for creating multi-platform applications.

WebPOP

To illustrate the use of an integrated application with multiple protocols, presented here is a CGI program called WebPOP (POP stands for Post Office Protocol, the most common Internet protocol for mailbox contents retrieval). It is a very simple and practical mail-reading program that gets user input and presents results formatted in HTML so that the user's browser can display it correctly.

WebPOP was created to fill the need to offer Internet users an easy-to-use mail program. Internet and the World Wide Web are attracting a lot of new users, most of whom are not computer experts—some aren't even computer literate. These users need a very simple mail program that they can use to process a few messages per day. The use of a standard Web browser, along with WebPOP on the server-side, eliminates the need for a special purpose (platform-dependent) mail reader. These are generally good mail readers, but they frequently offer more possibilities than many newcomers need or want.

On the client side (the user side), the only piece of software needed to use such an application is a common Web browser. On the server side, the Web server must comply with the CGI specification, as do all well-known Web servers today.

WebPOP is a CGI application written in Perl (version 4.036), a very useful scripting language commonly used for CGI development. The complete source code of this application is listed at the end of the chapter. If Perl does not come with your operating system, you should consider installing it. To try it out, take a look at the Web site whose address is

`http://www.perl.com`

> **NOTE**
>
> You might need the help of the Webmaster of your site if you do not have direct access to the `cgi-bin` directory (in which you put programs and scripts that will be executed in the Web). Also, it is important to know the exact locations (paths) of the finger, grep, and smail applications as well as the name of your mail server. See Listing 35.1 for more details.

35

CREATING A
CUSTOM
APPLICATION

Entities

An *entity* is a program executing a particular function; it is independent from other software components on the system. There are five entities that participate in the functioning of the application presented in this chapter: the CGI application itself (WebPOP), the user's Web browser, the Web server, the POP3 server, and the SMTP server. See Figure 35.1 for an illustration of the participating entities.

FIGURE 35.1.

The entities and protocols of the integrated application.

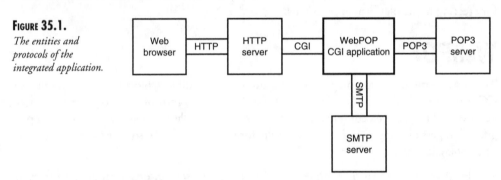

Protocols Used

In order to provide the functionality expected from a mail reader, your application must be able to use multiple protocols:

- POP3 protocol, in order to talk to the mailbox server
- SMTP protocol, in order to send messages via a mail server

At the same time, the Web browser and server communicate with each other using the standard HTTP protocol. The integration of all these protocols is done via CGI, the standard specification that permits the dialog between the Web server and the application. Finally, WebPOP formats the results in HTML and sends them to the Web server that is responsible for forwarding it to the user's Web browser. The protocols are also illustrated in Figure 35.1.

Mail Functions

A mail program must offer some core functions—it must be able to

- Check user authenticity
- Check mailbox contents

■ Read a mail message

■ Send a mail message

The following list shows the functions in detail:

user authentication	A mailbox contains messages that are private to a given user. The mail program must confirm the identity of a user before retrieving that user's messages. The authentication function is the process of asking the user her username and password, and then verifying the information provided against a list of authorized users.
check mailbox contents	When the user wants to read incoming mail, the mail program checks the electronic mailbox and presents a list of the messages sent to that user.
read a mail message	When the user wants to read a particular message, the mail program displays it on the screen.
send a mail message	When the user wants to send a message to someone, either a reply or a new message, the mail program forwards it to its destination.

WebPOP Functioning

Having defined the entities, protocols, and core functions that the integrated application must offer, take a look at the overall functioning. The CGI application must receive orders from the Web server (transmitted by the Web browser, because it is the only entity taking initiatives) and must communicate with the SMTP and POP3 servers. The results obtained are sent back to the Web server and finally to the Web browser in HTML format.

In addition to operating under normal circumstances (consulting a mailbox or sending messages), the application must also operate in abnormal situations, such as facing an unknown user, receiving a bad password or, more critically, dealing with a communications error. In fact, you must try to make the application as robust as possible because it will probably be used by many people at the same time, day and night. Special care should be taken to predict every possible execution sequence of a Web application, under both normal and abnormal circumstances. If possible, test the application using different browsers, too, and check to see that everything runs as expected.

See Figure 35.2 for an illustration of the functioning of the application.

35

CREATING A
CUSTOM
APPLICATION

Figure 35.2.

The functioning of the application.

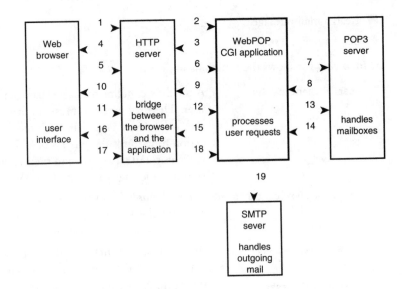

Here is a description of the steps described in Figure 35.2:

1. Original HTTP request is received from Web browser.
2. Server runs CGI script with GET method.
3. CGI script sends back initial form to Web server.
4. Server forwards initial form to browser.
5. User authenticates himself and requests list of messages in mailbox.
6. Server runs CGI script with POST method.
7. CGI script talks to POP3 server for client authentication and retrieval of messages (if authentication is successful).
8. POP3 server returns list of messages.
9. CGI script creates a list box and sends the new form to the Web server.
10. Web server forwards message list form to the browser.
11. User asks to read a message from the list.
12. Server runs CGI script with POST method.
13. CGI script talks to POP3 server for message body retrieval.
14. POP3 server returns message body.
15. CGI script creates a page with the message and sends it back to the server.
16. Web server forwards the message page to the browser.
17. User asks to send a message.
18. Web server runs CGI script with POST method.
19. CGI script talks to SMTP server in order to send the message.

Getting Data from the User

The user of the CGI application must provide information concerning himself or his mailbox. This is entered in the data fields of HTML forms; and when completed, the form is sent (submitted) to the application. The form is then decoded by a function of the cgi-lib.pl library, called ReadParse. It takes a reference to a hash table (you can think of a hash table as an array in which elements are related two by two, the key and the key's corresponding value) as an argument and retrieves the hash table in which each form field name is a key. The value of a field is the value associated with the hash key.

 In the application, the hash table that stores the form fields data is called input. Every form is sent to the Web server with the POST method, which means the function ReadParse must read data from standard input (instead of reading the environment variable QUERY_STRING, if the method GET were used). This function is one of the general CGI application functions found in the useful cgi-lib.pl, which is included in this book's CD-ROM.

The following is an example of a form using the SendNewMessage function:

```
    $fromaddr = $input{'login'}.'@'.$mailserver;
    print <<EOM;
<HTML>
<HEAD>
<TITLE>New message</TITLE>
<BODY BACKGROUND="$pathBackground">
</HEAD>
<BODY>
<FORM ACTION="$url" METHOD=POST>
<P>
<CENTER>
<B>De:</B> $fromaddr<P>
<B>Para (email):</B> <INPUT VALUE="$oldTo" NAME=to SIZE=50><P>
<B>Assunto:</B> <INPUT VALUE="$oldSubject" NAME=subject SIZE=50><P>
<INPUT TYPE=image SRC="$pathButtonSend" NAME=send BORDER=0
➥WIDTH=$bwidth HEIGHT=$bheight>
<INPUT TYPE=image SRC="$pathButtonReturnMailbox" NAME=return BORDER=0
➥WIDTH=$bwidth HEIGHT=$bheight>
<P>
<TEXTAREA ROWS=18 COLS=70 NAME=body>$body</TEXTAREA>
</CENTER>
<INPUT TYPE="hidden" VALUE="$input{'login'}" NAME=login>
<INPUT TYPE="hidden" VALUE="$input{'password'}" NAME=password>
</FORM>
</BODY>
</HTML>
```

Using Hidden Form Fields To Pass Arguments

When a Web browser requests a document from a Web server, a connection (using the HTTP—over TCP—protocol) must be established between the two parties. After the required page is sent to the browser, the connection and any information concerning this connection are lost.

But, each time the user asks the CGI script to perform an action (such as deleting a message from the electronic mailbox), there is data that the CGI script must know, such as the user's login name or password; otherwise, it cannot identify the correct mailbox.

Due to the design of HTTP protocol described earlier (which is transaction-oriented), a Web server is stateless. WebPOP is also stateless, which means that no user information is kept by the application (on a separate file or database) during the interval between connections. If you want to store information between two consecutive requests from the same user, some sort of keep-alive mechanism needs to be provided between the browser and the server in order to keep a connection as long as needed. You can also use the functionality provided by *cookies*, which are special bits of data constructed by the server that the browser keeps and sends to the server at each request).

It is up to the browser, or to the documents transferred between client and server, to keep any relevant user information. To save data, I have chosen to use hidden form fields (invisible to the user) on an HTML page. The form itself is sent to the CGI script with the POST method, read from stdin (stdin stands for standard input, and represents the "place" from which input data is obtained), and then decoded in order for all relevant data to be obtained. This way, you can transparently keep every important data field on the user's side; it will be sent to WebPOP each time there is a request on behalf of the user.

Sending Results Back to the Browser

Output from the CGI script is always in HTML format so that the browser can display it correctly. WebPOP is capable of producing a limited number of HTML pages. In normal functioning, one of the following pages is displayed on the browser:

- Initial form (for user identification) (See Figure 35.3.)
- List of mailbox contents (eventually empty)
- Message
- Reply form
- Help form

Additionally, the following are some status pages that report successful operation or errors:

- Sent message (success)
- Deleted message (success)
- Unknown username or password (error)
- Bad username or password (error)
- getHostByName function error
- Socket error
- Connect error
- Uncompleted form (error)

FIGURE 35.3.

WebPOP's initial page.

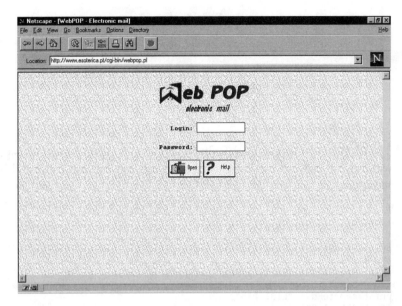

Before receiving and displaying a page, the browser must identify its contents. The page contents are identified by the CGI application, which sends the MIME-type header Content-Type: text/html, followed by two newline characters \n before any HTML tags.

Dealing with the Protocols

Having seen how the browser, server, and CGI application communicate, now look at the use of the protocols POP3 and SMTP. The finger protocol is also used by the application in order to find the user's name to include it in the From field of outgoing messages.

Talking with the POP3 Mail Server

The Post Office Protocol version 3 (RFC1725) was created to permit mail clients (who are not permanently connected to the Internet) to access remote mailboxes in an easy and useful fashion. The application uses some of the most important commands that a POP3 server understands:

- ▪ USER username

  The client sends user identification.
- ▪ PASS user_password

  The client sends the user password.
- ▪ TOP message_number

  Request for the headers of a message.

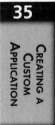

- ◼ `RETR message_number`

    Request for the complete message text.

- ◼ `DELE message_number`

    Request to delete a message.

- ◼ `QUIT`

    End of connection.

The POP3 server listens, by default, to port 110. A client must establish a TCP connection with it in order to start a dialog using these commands. Each command issued to the POP3 server must be followed by a CRLF (Carriage Return and Line Feed) pair (\r\n).

Look at an example of a connection (message request) between WebPOP and the POP3 server (`POPGetMessage` function):

```
print remoteHost "USER $input{'login'}\r\n";
&POPReplyOK;
print remoteHost "PASS $input{'password'}\r\n";
&POPReplyOK;
print remoteHost "LIST\r\n";
if (&POPReplyOK) {
    $nbMessages = &POPCountMessages();
    if ($messageN <= $nbMessages) {
        print remoteHost "RETR $messageN\r\n";
        &POPGetMessageHeader;
        &POPGetMessageBody;
    } else {
        &ShowSimpleForm($errorOutMessageTitle, $errorOutMessageBody);
    }
} # else there's something wrong because there are no messages
print remoteHost "QUIT\r\n";
&POPReplyOK;
```

The function that retrieves and presents the message list is `POPListMessageBox`, similar to the preceding function, but using the LIST command. Besides talking with the POP3 server, this function has to deal with the formatting of the messages list box. There were several choices in the presentation of the list of mail messages:

- ◼ One link (URL) per message. A page would use no forms; so instead of hidden fields, you would have to have another mechanism for passing the username and password. This could be done with a dynamically created database in which each entry would contain user information, and the user would send his entry number as a parameter in the URL.

- ◼ One subform per message. A page would have as many forms as the number of messages, each one with its different buttons and user information in hidden fields.

- ◼ One list box line per message. There would be only one form (with the hidden fields) on the message list page.

For your application, this final choice was taken in order to limit the message list to a pre-defined size. Otherwise, lots of messages in a mailbox would produce an HTML page too big to fit on a computer screen.

See Figure 35.4 for an example of the resulting page.

FIGURE 35.4.

The contents of a mailbox.

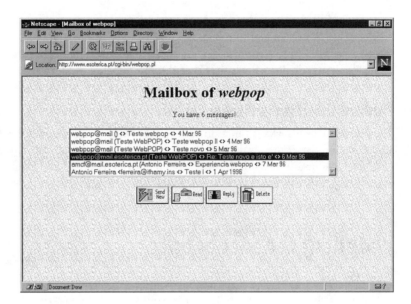

Sending Mail

Mail is sent using the Simple Mail Transfer Protocol—SMTP (RFC821) server, which will forward any mail to the destination specified in the mail header. An SMTP server is somewhat more complicated than a POP3 server because it offers a lot more functionality; but, in your application, you use it indirectly in order to simplify functioning. In fact, mail is sent by invocation of either `sendmail` or `smail`, two well-known UNIX mail-handling systems. The function `SendMessage` in your application is responsible for the mailer invocation:

```perl
$destaddr = $input{'to'};
$fromaddr = $input{'login'}.'@'.$mailserver;
$subject = $input{'subject'};
$body = $input{'body'};
if ($destaddr eq '' || $fromaddr eq '' || $subject eq '' || $body eq '') {
    &ShowSimpleForm($noFieldsTitle, $noFieldsBody);
}
else {
    $userName=&GetUserName($input{'login'});
    open(MAIL,"| $sendmail \"$destaddr\"");
    print MAIL <<EOM;
```

```
From: $fromaddr ($userName)
To: $destaddr
Reply-To: $fromaddr
Subject: $subject
X-Mail-Program: WebPOP - Web/Mail interface
$body
EOM
    close(MAIL);
```

As you might have noticed, the message sent to the SMTP server is composed of To, From, Subject, Reply-To, and custom X-Mail-Program fields and a message body. The mail-handling system understands those fields (in particular the To field) and forwards the message.

Finding the User's Name

The preceding GetUserName function executes the finger program with the From address as the argument and parses the results in order to search the complete user's name. It would also be possible to communicate with the SMTP server through port 25 and issue the VRFY command, but I found the use of finger simpler (although it might not work on systems that refuse finger connections).

Installing the CGI Script

Installing WebPOP is a relatively simple task.

1. Copy webpop.pl (see Listing 35.1) to your cgi-bin directory.

2. Copy the GIF files, representing the buttons, to a directory within your document root hierarchy. Place them in a directory called Images/webpop, for example.

3. Change the paths in every variable $path... in the ##### HTML Text and Buttons ##### section of webpop.pl. You can also customize the messages the user sees by changing all the text variables in the same section. Change the information concerning the URL of the CGI application and paths to system binaries, in the section ##### Paths, binaries and system specific information ##### (adapt $url, $sendmail, $mailserver, $grep, and $finger to reflect your system's settings).

4. Run your browser and launch the URL you have chosen for WebPOP. In the example, it is

    http://www.esoterica.pt/cgi-bin/webpop.pl

 The file install.txt on the CD-ROM explains the installation process. There is one part of the listing that contains hard-coded values, generally found in socket.ph or socket.h.

```
$AF_INET = 2;                  # Internet protocols,
                               ➥specified in "socket.h"
$SOCK_STREAM = 1;              # Semantic (sequenced,
                               ➥two-way, reliable)
$PROTOCOL = 0;                 # Protocol used to support
                               ➥the semantic chosen (TCP)
```

If you have problems or just want to improve portability of the application, you should consider including `socket.ph` in you Perl script (using the `require` directive).

Performance

WebPOP is an interpreted application that depends on the Perl interpreter of your system (either version 4 or version 5). As with every interpreted application, it is somewhat slower than it could be if it were executed using a binary format (precompiled). If you have a fast and resource-full system or do not plan to have many people using your application, this kind of functioning is just fine. But if you have either a surcharged server or plan to have many people using your application, you should probably consider porting the program to a language that can be compiled, such as C. That would limit the performance hit of the application on your system.

Ideas for Improvements

The CGI application presented in this chapter is a simple one and is intended to be a practical example. Several improvements could be made to it—in fact, most of the possible improvements listed here will probably appear in a future version of WebPOP. Anyway, feel free to change the code to suit your own needs or expectations. Here are some ideas:

- Support of MIME types in mail
- Support of URLs in the mail body for embedded links to other web resources
- Support of signatures appended to outgoing messages (that would involve keeping user's information in a database or reading user's `.signature` file in their home directories, if they reside on the same server as the CGI script)
- User customizable mail server (extra input field in initial form)

The Complete Listing

 You can also find Listing 35.1 on the CD-ROM included with this book.

Listing 35.1. WEBPOP.pl—A simple HTML to POP3-mail interface.

```
#!/usr/bin/perl

############################################################################
# webpop.pl 1.3sp - A simple HTML to POP3-mail interface                   #
#                                                                          #
# How does it work?                                                        #
# This program acts as a WWW to POP3 interface. It gets user login and     #
# password from a HTML form (form A) and then returns the user mail list,  #
```

continues

35

Listing 35.1. continued

```
# from the POP3 server. This list is another HTML form (form B), so that   #
# the user can pick a message to read, reply to, or delete. If the user    #
# asks to read a message, another request is sent to the POP3 server,      #
# now returning a HTML form (form C) with the message body. When in        #
# form B, the user can request to delete or reply to a message, too.       #
# That's it, no more bells or whistles.                                    #
#                                                                          #
# Todo list:                                                               #
# - Support MIME / Attachments mail                                        #
# - Save message options                                                   #
# - Support for URLs on messages                                           #
#                                                                          #
# Antonio Ferreira                                                         #
# amcf@esoterica.pt                                                         #
#                                                                          #
# January 1996                                                             #
############################################################################

require '/usr/lib/cgi-lib.pl';                       # The useful cgi-lib

####################### Variables #######################

##### HTML Text and Buttons #####
$formATitle = 'WebPOP - Electronic mail';
➥ # Title of form A (input form)
$formBTitle = 'Mailbox of';
➥ # Title of form B (list of messages)
$formBHeading = 'Mailbox of';
➥ # Heading of form B preceding user's login
$formCTitle = 'Message';
➥ # Title of form C (message)
$formErrorTitle = 'Error';
➥ # Title of error forms
$error1 = 'Error 1: gethostbyname';
➥ # Body of form reporting error on gethostbyname function
$error2 = 'Error 2: socket';
➥ # Body of form reporting error on socket function
$error3 = 'Error 3: connect';
➥ # Body of form reporting error on connect function
$userInfoTitle = 'Unknown user info';
➥ # Title of form reporting missing user info (login, password)
$userInfoBody = 'You must enter your login and password!';
➥ # Body of form reporting missing user info (login, password)
$wrongLoginPassword = 'Wrong login or password!';
➥ # Body of form reporting bad login or password
$noMailBody = 'Sorry, you have no mail...';
➥ # Body of form reporting no mail
$errorOutMessageTitle = 'Invalid message number';
➥ # Title of form reporting invalid message number
$errorOutMessageBody = 'The requested message does not exist!';
➥ # Body of form reporting invalid message number
$noFieldsTitle = 'Uncompleted form';
➥ # Title of form reporting 'missing fields on message'
$noFieldsBody = 'You must fill in the form!';
➥ # Body of form reporting incomplete form
$deletedMessageTitle = 'Deleted message';
➥ # Title of form reporting deleted message
```

```
$deletedMessageBody = 'The message was deleted!';
➥ # Body of form reporting deleted message
$sentMessageTitle = 'Message sent';
➥ # Title of form reporting sent message
$sentMessageBody = 'Your message was sent!';
➥ # Body of form reporting sent message
$fromLine = 'From';
➥ # String introducing "From" field on a form
$toLine = 'To';
➥ # String introducing "To" field on a form
$subjectLine = 'Subject';
➥ # String introducing "Subject" field on a form
$dateLine = 'Date';
➥ # String introducing "Date" field on a form
$pathBackground = '/bg/esot_bg.gif';
➥ # Path to background GIF
$pathLogo = '/Imagens/webpop/webpop.gif';
➥ # Path to webpop logo GIF
$pathButtonHelp ='/Imagens/webpop/help.gif';
➥ # Path to button Help GIF
$pathButtonOpenMailbox ='/Imagens/webpop/open.gif';
➥ # Path to button OpenMailbox GIF
$pathButtonReturnMailbox = '/Imagens/webpop/return.gif';
➥ # Path to button ReturnToMailBox GIF
$pathButtonSendNewMessage = '/Imagens/webpop/sendn.gif';
➥ # Path to SendNewMessage button GIF
$pathButtonSend = '/Imagens/webpop/send.gif';
➥ # Path to Send button GIF
$pathButtonReadMessage = '/Imagens/webpop/read.gif';
➥ # Path to ReadMessage button GIF
$pathButtonReplyMessage = '/Imagens/webpop/reply.gif';
➥ # Path to ReplyMessage button GIF
$pathButtonDeleteMessage = '/Imagens/webpop/delete.gif';
➥ # Path to DeleteMessage button GIF
$lwidth = 197;                                             # Width of logo
$lheight = 68;
➥ # Height of logo
$bwidth = 70;
➥ # Width of buttons
$bheight = 37;
➥ # Height of buttons

##### Paths, binaries and system specific information #####
$url = 'http://www.esoterica.pt/cgi-bin/webpop.pl';        # webpop URL
$sendmail = '/usr/bin/smail';
➥ # Path and parameters for the mailer
#$sendmail = '/usr/bin/sendmail -t -n';
➥ # Path and parameters for the mailer
$mailserver = 'mail.esoterica.pt';
➥ # Complete default POP3 mail server hostname
$POP3_Port = 110;
➥ # Port which the POP3 server is listening to
$grep = '/usr/bin/grep';
➥ # Path for the grep program
$finger = '/usr/bin/finger';
➥ # Path for the finger client program
```

35

CREATING A
CUSTOM
APPLICATION

continues

Listing 35.1. continued

```perl
$AF_INET = 2;
    # Internet protocols, specified in "socket.h"
$SOCK_STREAM = 1;
    # Semantic (sequenced, two-way, reliable)
$PROTOCOL = 0;
    # Protocol used to support the semantic chosen (TCP)

$template = 'S n a4 x8';
    # Template used to pack lists of values

######################### Start of Main Program #########################

&ReadParse(*input);
    # cgi-lib, constructs list of key=value form data
print &PrintHeader();
    # cgi-lib, prints header "Content-type: text/html\n\n"

if (&MethGet()) {                   # GET was used, so...
    &InitialForm();              # ... retrieve the initial form
} else {                          # POST was used, so process POP3 query
    $messageN = $input{'messageN'};
    if ((!$input{'login'} || !$input{'password'}) && (!$input{'help.x'})) {
    # No info given
        &ShowSimpleForm($userInfoTitle, $userInfoBody);
    } else {
        if ((defined $input{'open.x'}) || (defined $input{'return.x'})) {
    # User asked to list messages (needs: login, password)
            &ShowMessageList();
        } elsif (defined $input{'read.x'}) {
    # User asked to read a message (needs: login, password, msgnumber)
            &ShowMessage();
        } elsif (defined $input{'sendn.x'}) {
    # User asked to send a new message (needs: login, password)
            &SendNewMessage();
        } elsif (defined $input{'reply.x'}) {
    # User asked to reply to a message (needs: login, password, msgnumber)
            &ReplyMessage();
        } elsif (defined $input{'send.x'}) {
    # User asked to send to a message (needs: login, password)
            &SendMessage();
        } elsif (defined $input{'delete.x'}) {
    # User asked to delete a message (needs: login, password, msgnumber)
            &DeleteMessage();
        } elsif (defined $input{'help.x'}) {          # User asked for help
            &HelpUser();
        }
    }
}

exit(0);

######################### End of Main Program #########################

#################### Start of subroutines definitions ####################

##### Shows the initial form asking for user's login and password #####
```

```
sub InitialForm {
    print <<EOM;
<HTML>
<HEAD>
<TITLE>$formATitle</TITLE>
<BODY BACKGROUND="$pathBackground">
</HEAD>
<BODY>
<P ALIGN=center><IMG SRC="$pathLogo" BORDER=0 WIDTH=$lwidth
➥ HEIGHT=$lheight></P>
<P>
<FORM ACTION="$url" METHOD=POST>
<CENTER>
<PRE>
<B>   Login</B>: <INPUT VALUE="$input{'login'}" NAME=login SIZE=12><BR>
<B>Password</B>: <INPUT VALUE="$input{'password'}" TYPE="password"
➥ NAME=password SIZE=12>
</PRE>
</CENTER>
<P>
<CENTER>
<INPUT TYPE=image SRC="$pathButtonOpenMailbox" NAME=open BORDER=0
➥ WIDTH=$bwidth HEIGHT=$bheight>
<INPUT TYPE=image SRC="$pathButtonHelp" NAME=help BORDER=0 WIDTH=$bwidth
➥ HEIGHT=$bheight>
</CENTER>
</FORM>
</BODY>
</HTML>
EOM
}


##########################################################################
# Subroutines for option "open", that is, ShowMessageList               #
##########################################################################

##### Gets and displays the list of mail messages #####
sub ShowMessageList {
    if (($name, $aliases, $addrtype, $len, $remote_addr) =
➥ gethostbyname($mailserver)) {
        if (socket(remoteHost, $AF_INET, $SOCK_STREAM, $PROTOCOL)) {
            $remoteStruct = pack ($template, $AF_INET, $POP3_Port,
➥ $remote_addr);
            if (connect(remoteHost, $remoteStruct)) {
                &POPListMessageBox();
            } else {
                &ShowSimpleForm($formErrorTitle, $error3);
            }
            close(remoteHost);
        } else {
            &ShowSimpleForm($formErrorTitle, $error2);
        }
    } else {
        &ShowSimpleForm($formErrorTitle, $error1);
    }
}
```

35

CREATING A
CUSTOM
APPLICATION

continues

Listing 35.1. continued

```perl
##### Talks with POP server, gets and prints the list of messages #####
sub POPListMessageBox {
    local($nbMessages);
    select(remoteHost); $¦ = 1;
    select(STDOUT); $¦ = 1;

    print <<EOM;
<HTML>
<HEAD>
<TITLE>$formBTitle $input{'login'}</TITLE>
<BODY BACKGROUND="$pathBackground">
</HEAD>
<BODY>
<H1 ALIGN=center>$formBHeading <I>$input{'login'}</I></H1>
<FORM ACTION="$url" METHOD=POST>
<P>
EOM
    $nbMessages = 0;
    $_ = <remoteHost>;
    print remoteHost "USER $input{'login'}\r\n";
    if (&POPReplyOK) {
        print remoteHost "PASS $input{'password'}\r\n";
        if (&POPReplyOK) {
            print remoteHost "LIST\r\n";
            if (&POPReplyOK) {
# If 0 messages POP returns -ERR, so it skips this if
                $nbMessages=&POPCountMessages();
                if ($nbMessages > 0) {
# If POP replied +OK after LIST, but there are no messages
                    print "<CENTER>You have $nbMessages message";
# User can have one or more messages
                    ($nbMessages>1) ? print "s" : print "";
                    print "!<P>";
                    if ($nbMessages>10) {
                        print "<SELECT NAME=\"messageN\" SIZE=10>";
                    } else {
                        print "<SELECT NAME=\"messageN\" SIZE=$nbMessages>";
                    }
                    $messageN = 0;
                    while ($messageN < $nbMessages) {
                        $messageN = $messageN +1;
                        print remoteHost "TOP $messageN 50\r\n";
# 50 lines should be enough to get the headers
                        &POPGetMessageHeaders();
                    }
                } else {
                    print "$noMailBody";
                }
            } else {
                print "$noMailBody";
            }
        } else {
            print "$wrongLoginPassword";
            $nbMessages = -1;
        }
```

```
    } else {
        print "$wrongLoginPassword";
        $nbMessages = -1;
    }
    print remoteHost "QUIT\r\n";
    &POPReplyOK;
    if ($nbMessages > 0) {
        print "</SELECT>";
    }
    if ($nbMessages > -1 ) {
    print <<EOM;
<P>
<INPUT TYPE=image SRC="$pathButtonSendNewMessage" NAME=sendn BORDER=0
➥ WIDTH=$bwidth HEIGHT=$bheight>
EOM
    }
    if ($nbMessages > 0) {                    # Only if there are messages
        print <<EOM;
<INPUT TYPE=image ALIGN=top SRC="$pathButtonReadMessage" NAME=read BORDER=0
➥ WIDTH=$bwidth HEIGHT=$bheight>
<INPUT TYPE=image ALIGN=top SRC="$pathButtonReplyMessage" NAME=reply BORDER=0
➥ WIDTH=$bwidth HEIGHT=$bheight>
<INPUT TYPE=image ALIGN=top SRC="$pathButtonDeleteMessage" NAME=delete BORDER=0
➥ WIDTH=$bwidth HEIGHT=$bheight><BR>
EOM
    }
    print <<EOM;
<INPUT TYPE="hidden" NAME=login VALUE=$input{'login'}>
<INPUT TYPE="hidden" NAME=password VALUE=$input{'password'}>
</CENTER>
</FORM></BODY></HTML>
EOM
}

##### Gets headers (From, Date, ...) from message sent by POP server #####
sub POPGetMessageHeaders {
    local($from, $date, $subject, $replyto);
    $_ = <remoteHost>;
    while ($_ !~ /^\.\r\n/) {
    ➥ # Seeks . in one line to end
        if ($_ =~ /^From: (.+)$/) {             # Seeks "From: ..."
            ($from) = /^From: (.+)$/;
            ($from) =~ s/</&lt;/g;              # Replace <'s
            ($from) =~ s/>/&gt;/g;              # Replace >'s
            ($from) =~ s/\r//;                  # Replace carriage return's
            ($from) =~ s/\n//;                  # Replace newline's
            $_ = $from;
            ($replyto) = /&lt;(.+)&gt;/;
            if ($replyto eq '') {
                $replyto=$from;
            }
        } elsif ($_ =~ /^Subject: (.+)$/) {
            ($subject) = /^Subject: (.+)$/;
            ($subject) =~ s/</&lt;/g;           # Replace <'s
            ($subject) =~ s/>/&gt;/g;           # Replace >'s
            ($subject) =~ s/\r//;               # Replace carriage return's
            ($subject) =~ s/\n//;               # Replace newline's
```

35

CREATING A
CUSTOM
APPLICATION

continues

Listing 35.1. continued

```
            } elsif ($_ =~ /^Date: (.+) .+$/) {
                ($date) = /^Date: (.+) .+$/;
            }
            $_ = <remoteHost>;
        }
        # Fixed size list items
        $from = substr($from,0,40);
        $_ = $date;
        ($date) = /.* ([0-9]+ [a-zA-Z]+ [0-9]+) .*$/;
        $date = substr($date,0,11);
        $subject = substr($subject,0,24);
        $selected = ($messageN==1 ? "SELECTED" : "");
        print "<OPTION VALUE=$messageN $selected>$from <> $subject <> $date\n";
}


##### Counts the number of messages available from the POP3 server #####
sub POPCountMessages {
    local($nbMessages);
    $nbMessages = 0;

    while (<remoteHost> !~ /^\.\r\n/) {
        $nbMessages = $nbMessages + 1;
    }
    return $nbMessages;
}



#########################################################################
# Subroutines for option "read", that is, ShowMessage                   #
#########################################################################

##### Gets and displays the a given message #####
sub ShowMessage {
    if (($name, $aliases, $addrtype, $len, $remote_addr) =
➡ gethostbyname($mailserver)) {
        if (socket(remoteHost, $AF_INET, $SOCK_STREAM, $PROTOCOL)) {
            $remoteStruct = pack ($template, $AF_INET, $POP3_Port,
➡ $remote_addr);
            if (connect(remoteHost, $remoteStruct)) {
                &POPGetMessage();
                $messageBody = $body;
                $body =~ s/</&lt;/g;
                $body =~ s/>/&gt;/g;
                $body =~ s/"/&quot;/g;
                print "<HTML>";
                print $messageHeader.$body;
                print <<EOM;
</PRE>
<HR>
<FORM ACTION="$url" METHOD=POST>
<CENTER>
<INPUT TYPE=image SRC="$pathButtonReturnMailbox" NAME=return BORDER=0
➡ WIDTH=$bwidth HEIGHT=$bheight>
<INPUT TYPE=image SRC="$pathButtonReplyMessage" NAME=reply BORDER=0
➡ WIDTH=$bwidth HEIGHT=$bheight>
<INPUT TYPE=image SRC="$pathButtonDeleteMessage" NAME=delete BORDER=0
➡ WIDTH=$bwidth HEIGHT=$bheight>
```

```
</CENTER>
<INPUT TYPE="hidden" VALUE="$input{'login'}" NAME=login>
<INPUT TYPE="hidden" VALUE="$input{'password'}" NAME=password>
<INPUT TYPE="hidden" VALUE=$messageN NAME=messageN>
</FORM>
</BODY>
</HTML>
EOM
            } else {
                &ShowSimpleForm($formErrorTitle, $error3);
            }
            close(remoteHost);
        } else {
            &ShowSimpleForm($formErrorTitle, $error2);
        }
    } else {
        &ShowSimpleForm($formErrorTitle, $error1);
    }
}

##### Asks POP server to retrieve a message #####
sub POPGetMessage {
    select(remoteHost); $¦ = 1;
    select(STDOUT); $¦ = 1;
    $_ = <remoteHost>;
    print remoteHost "USER $input{'login'}\r\n";
    &POPReplyOK;
➥   # This time, no need to check login or password...
    print remoteHost "PASS $input{'password'}\r\n";
    &POPReplyOK;
➥   # ... because it was WEBPOP that sent it!
    print remoteHost "LIST\r\n";
    if (&POPReplyOK) {
        $nbMessages = &POPCountMessages();
        if ($messageN <= $nbMessages) {
            print remoteHost "RETR $messageN\r\n";
            &POPGetMessageHeader;
            &POPGetMessageBody;
        } else {
            &ShowSimpleForm($errorOutMessageTitle, $errorOutMessageBody);
        }
    } # else there's something wrong because there are no messages
    print remoteHost "QUIT\r\n";
    &POPReplyOK;
}

##### Gets the Header of the message sent by the POP server #####
sub POPGetMessageHeader {
    local($from, $subject, $date, $replyto);
    do {
        $_ = <remoteHost>;
        if ($_ =~ /^From: (.+)$/) {
            ($from) = /^From: (.+)$/;
            ($from) =~ s/</&lt;/g;
            ($from) =~ s/>/&gt;/g;
            ($from) =~ s/\r//;
            ($from) =~ s/\n//;
```

continues

Listing 35.1. continued

```
        } elsif ($_ =~ /^Subject: (.+)$/) {
            ($subject) = /^Subject: (.+)$/;
            ($subject) =~ s/</&lt;/g;
            ($subject) =~ s/>/&gt;/g;
            ($subject) =~ s/\r//;
            ($subject) =~ s/\n//;
        } elsif ($_ =~ /^Date: (.+)$/) {
            ($date) = /^Date: (.+) .+$/;
            ($date) =~ s/</&lt;/g;
            ($date) =~ s/>/&gt;/g;
            ($date) =~ s/\r//;
            ($date) =~ s/\n//;

        }
    } until ($_ =~ /^\r\n/);
    $_ = $from;
    ($replyto) = /.*&lt;(.+)&gt;.*/;
    if ($replyto eq '') {
        $replyto = $from;
    }
    $messageHeader = "<HEAD><TITLE>$subject</TITLE>
➡ <BODY BACKGROUND=\"$pathBackground\"></HEAD>
<BODY>
<H2>$fromLine: $from</H2>
<H3>$subjectLine: $subject<BR>
$dateLine: $date</H3><HR><PRE>";
    $oldTo = $from;
    $oldSubject = "Re: ".$subject;
}


##### Gets the Body of the message sent by the POP server #####
sub POPGetMessageBody {
    do {
        $_ = <remoteHost>;
        $body = $body.$_;
    } until ($_ =~ /^\.\r\n/);
}



#########################################################################
# Subroutines for option "sendnew", that is, SendNewMessage             #
#########################################################################

##### Asks for data (header+body) and then sends the message #####
sub SendNewMessage {
    $fromaddr = $input{'login'}.'@'.$mailserver;
    print <<EOM;
<HTML>
<HEAD>
<TITLE>New message</TITLE>
<BODY BACKGROUND="$pathBackground">
</HEAD>
<BODY>
<FORM ACTION="$url" METHOD=POST>
<P>
<CENTER>
<B>De:</B> $fromaddr<P>
```

```
<B>Para (email):</B> <INPUT VALUE="$oldTo" NAME=to SIZE=50><P>
<B>Assunto:</B> <INPUT VALUE="$oldSubject" NAME=subject SIZE=50><P>
<INPUT TYPE=image SRC="$pathButtonSend" NAME=send BORDER=0
➥ WIDTH=$bwidth HEIGHT=$bheight>
<INPUT TYPE=image SRC="$pathButtonReturnMailbox" NAME=return BORDER=0
➥ WIDTH=$bwidth HEIGHT=$bheight>
<P>
<TEXTAREA ROWS=18 COLS=70 NAME=body>$body</TEXTAREA>
</CENTER>
<INPUT TYPE="hidden" VALUE="$input{'login'}" NAME=login>
<INPUT TYPE="hidden" VALUE="$input{'password'}" NAME=password>
</FORM>
</BODY>
</HTML>
EOM
}


##### Uses the mailer defined to send a message #####
sub SendMessage {
    $destaddr = $input{'to'};
    $fromaddr = $input{'login'}.'@'.$mailserver;
    $subject = $input{'subject'};
    $body = $input{'body'};

    if ($destaddr eq '' ¦¦ $fromaddr eq '' ¦¦ $subject eq '' ¦¦ $body eq '') {
        &ShowSimpleForm($noFieldsTitle, $noFieldsBody);
    }
    else {
        $userName=&GetUserName($input{'login'});
        open(MAIL,"¦ $sendmail \"$destaddr\"");
        print MAIL <<EOM;
From: $fromaddr ($userName)
To: $destaddr
Reply-To: $fromaddr
Subject: $subject
X-Mail-Program: WebPOP - Web/Mail interface

$body
EOM
        close(MAIL);
        print <<EOM;
<HTML>
<HEAD>
<TITLE>$sentMessageTitle</TITLE>
<BODY BACKGROUND="$pathBackground">
</HEAD>
<BODY>
<H1 ALIGN=center>$sentMessageBody</H1>
<P>
<B>$fromLine: </B> $fromaddr<BR>
<B>$toLine: </B> $destaddr<BR>
<B>$subjectLine: </B> $subject
<P>
<FORM ACTION="$url" METHOD=POST>
<CENTER>
<INPUT TYPE=image SRC="$pathButtonReturnMailbox" NAME=return BORDER=0
➥ WIDTH=$bwidth HEIGHT=$bheight><BR>
```

35

CREATING A
CUSTOM
APPLICATION

continues

Listing 35.1. continued

```
</CENTER>
<INPUT TYPE="hidden" VALUE="$input{'login'}" NAME=login>
<INPUT TYPE="hidden" VALUE="$input{'password'}" NAME=password>
</FORM>
</BODY>
</HTML>
EOM
    }
}


##########################################################################
# Subroutines for option "reply", that is, ReplyMessage                  #
##########################################################################

##### Reads from POP server, presents reply-form and sends the message #####
sub ReplyMessage {
    if (($name, $aliases, $addrtype, $len, $remote_addr) =
➡ gethostbyname($mailserver)) {
        if (socket(remoteHost, $AF_INET, $SOCK_STREAM, $PROTOCOL)) {
            $remoteStruct = pack ($template, $AF_INET, $POP3_Port, $remote_addr);
            if (connect(remoteHost, $remoteStruct)) {
                &POPGetMessage();
                $body = "> ".$body;
                ($body) =~ s/\n/\n> /g;
            } else {
                &ShowSimpleForm($formErrorTitle, $error3);
            }
            close(remoteHost);
        } else {
            &ShowSimpleForm($formErrorTitle, $error2);
        }
    } else {
        &ShowSimpleForm($formErrorTitle, $error1);
    }
    &SendNewMessage();
}


##########################################################################
# Subroutines for option "delete", that is, DeleteMessage                #
##########################################################################

##### Deletes a message #####
sub DeleteMessage {
    if (($name, $aliases, $addrtype, $len, $remote_addr) =
➡ gethostbyname($mailserver)) {
        if (socket(remoteHost, $AF_INET, $SOCK_STREAM, $PROTOCOL)) {
            $remoteStruct = pack ($template, $AF_INET, $POP3_Port,
➡ $remote_addr);
            if (connect(remoteHost, $remoteStruct)) {
                &POPDeleteMessage();
            } else {
                &ShowSimpleForm($formErrorTitle, $error3);
            }
```

```
                close(remoteHost);
            } else {
                &ShowSimpleForm($formErrorTitle, $error2);
            }
        } else {
            &ShowSimpleForm($formErrorTitle, $error1);
        }
    }

    ##### Deletes a message using the POP server #####
    sub POPDeleteMessage {
        select(remoteHost); $¦ = 1;
        select(STDOUT); $¦ = 1;
        $_ = <remoteHost>;
        print remoteHost "USER $input{'login'}\r\n";
        &POPReplyOK;
        print remoteHost "PASS $input{'password'}\r\n";
        &POPReplyOK;
        print remoteHost "LIST\r\n";
        if (&POPReplyOK) {
            $nbMessages = &POPCountMessages();
            if ($messageN <= $nbMessages) {
                print remoteHost "DELE $messageN\r\n";
                print <<EOM;
<HTML>
<HEAD>
<TITLE>$deletedMessageTitle</TITLE>
<BODY BACKGROUND="$pathBackground">
</HEAD>
<BODY>
<H2 ALIGN=center>$deletedMessageBody</H2>
<P>
<FORM ACTION="$url" METHOD=POST>
<CENTER>
<INPUT TYPE=image SRC="$pathButtonReturnMailbox" NAME=return BORDER=0
➥ WIDTH=$bwidth HEIGHT=$bheight><BR>
</CENTER>
<INPUT TYPE="hidden" VALUE="$input{'login'}" NAME=login>
<INPUT TYPE="hidden" VALUE="$input{'password'}" NAME=password>
</FORM>
</BODY>
</HTML>
EOM
            } else {
                &ShowSimpleForm($errorOutMessageTitle, $errorOutMessageBody);
            }
        } # else there's something wrong because there are no messages
        print remoteHost "QUIT\r\n";
        &POPReplyOK;
    }


#############################################################################
# General subroutines                                                       #
#############################################################################
```

continues

Listing 35.1. continued

```perl
##### True if POP reply's '+OK', false otherwise #####
sub POPReplyOK {
    $_ = <remoteHost>;
    if ($_ =~ /^\+OK/) {
        return 1;
    } else {
        return 0;
    }
}

##### Shows a simple form with a title a short message #####
sub ShowSimpleForm {
        print <<EOM;
<HTML>
<HEAD>
<TITLE>$_[0]</TITLE>
<BODY BACKGROUND="$pathBackground">
</HEAD>
<BODY>
<H2>$_[1]</H2>
</BODY>
</HTML>
EOM
}

##### Gets user's name from finger information, using login as the key #####
sub GetUserName {
    local($tmp);
    $login = $_[0];
    $_ = '$finger $login@$mailserver | $grep \"Name:\"';
    ($tmp) = /.*Name: (.+).*$/;
    return $tmp;
}

##### Adds or removes charaters from a string in order to
➥ have a fixed length #####
sub fixedLength {
    if (length($_[0])<$_[1]) {
        foreach $num (1 .. ($_[1]-length($_[0]))) {
            $_[0] = $_[0]." ";
        }
    } elsif (length($_[0])>$_[1]) {
        $_[0] = substr($_[0],0,$_[1]);
    }
        return $_[0];
}

##### Shows help page #####
sub HelpUser {
    print <<EOM;
<HTML>
<HEAD>
<TITLE>WebPOP - Help</TITLE>
<BODY BACKGROUND="$pathBackground">
</HEAD>
<BODY>
```

```
<H1 ALIGN=center>WebPOP<BR><I>Help </I></H1>
<P>
```
Welcome to WebPOP, the web application that helps you manage your
electronic mail, in a pratical and simple manner! The author of this
application, `<A HREF="http://www.esoterica.pt/amcf/">António Ferreira</A>`,
would like to know `<A HREF="mailto:amcf@esoterica.pt">your opinion and
suggestions</A>` on WebPOP.
```
<P>
```
About WebPOP:
```
<UL>
<LI><B>What is WebPOP?</B>
<BR>
```
It is an application that helps you manage your electronic mailbox
from a World-Wide Web page, which is an interface certainly familiar
to you. Besides reading your mail, you can also send messages to other
people on the Internet and/or delete old messages from your mailbox.
```
<P>
<LI><B>How does it work?</B>
<BR>
```
The initial screen asks for your identification (login and password).
Only that way you can have access to your mailbox!
```
<BR>
```
After entering the identification, you are given the list of messages
from your electronic mailbox. 3 of the 4 buttons at the bottom of the
list permit you to `<B>Read</B>`, `<B>Reply</B>`, or `<B>Delete</B>` the selected
message. If you wish to send a new message, you must click on the first
button, titled `<B>Send new</B>`.
```
<BR>
```
Finally, when you are reading a message, 2 additional buttons permit you
to `<B>Reply</B>` to that message (send a message with the same subject
to the person who wrote to you before) or `<B>Delete</B>` the message
(permanently erase it from your mailbox). If you wish to save a copy
of a particular message, you must use the option `<B>Save as...</B>` (or
an equivalent one) from your browser's File menu. The browser is the
program you are using to access the World-Wide Web.
```
<P>
<LI><B>Can I save my messages on my personal computer and organize my mail?</B>
<BR>
```
Yes. You can create, in your personal computer's hard disk, some
directories (folders), each one dedicated to a person or subject. You
should have your own mail organization strategy. Those folders can all be put
inside a main folder called `<B>MAIL</B>` or `<B>WEBPOP</B>`, for example.
Then, when you are reading a message from your browser's window, you can
choose the option `<B>Save as...</B>` and save the message in your hard disk,
inside the desired folder and with a suggestive name. After saving the
message, you can delete it from your mailbox... it is very important to do
so every once in a while (or every time you save a message) otherwise your
mailbox will grow forever, and accessing it will become progressively slower.
```
<P>
<LI><B>Is there any way to attach a file to a message?</B>
<BR>
```
Not really. The only way is to use the options `<B>Cut</B>` and `<B>Paste</B>`
from your operating system's Edit menu. This only works if your file is
not too big and is composed only of simple (ASCII) text.
```
<P>
<LI><B>If I send a message with WWW links (URL's) in the text, will it be
possible to click on them so that the browser executes the action indicated?</B>
```

continues

35

CREATING A
CUSTOM
APPLICATION

Listing 35.1. continued

```
<BR>
Not yet. This is a feature that will probably appear with the next version
of WebPOP. It will offer you the possibility to click on a URL inside a given
message, just as you would on a link inside an ordinary HTML page. Support for
MIME types (so that messages can be composed with different file formats) is
also a future feature.
</UL>
<P>
<A HREF="$url">Return to the initial form</A>
</BODY>
</HTML>
EOM
}
```

Summary

In this chapter you created an application that enables users to read their mail through Web pages. This application has served as an example of the principles and characteristics of multi-protocol applications. Not only have you created what can be a very useful application, but you have also gone through all the steps in the creation process of such applications and have acquired the know-how needed to proceed with the development of other applications.

RealAudio

by Mark Bishop

IN THIS CHAPTER

It's hard for me to imagine that anyone who uses the Internet doesn't already know about RealAudio—or any other audio or sound program. (More than 4 million Internet users have downloaded and installed RealAudio Players.) Yet for most Internet users, audio and sound issues are seemingly nonexistent. Everyone wants to have cool Web pages and neat Java scripts, but no one seems to care much about sound.

The time has come to add sound to your Web pages! Sound adds life and excitement and complements the carefully crafted visual elements of your Web site. RealAudio is the product that enables you to become an active participant in the exciting new world of real-time audio on demand.

Traditional uses of audio over the Internet were just like the old days of BBSing. You saw a sound file, downloaded it, and then played it using one of the many existing sound players. Indeed, the way we transfer files today via FTP, Gopher, or e-mail makes excellent use of this conventional method. Many Web page designers wanted to do more than store sound files for users to download—they wanted to create real-time performances with neat things that make a Web page come alive!

The process of delivering sound over the Internet involves many factors. Delivering a sound file in real time through your Web page, or maybe even coordinating your Web pages into some type of presentation, means coping with a multitude of time-lapse variables, such as the speed of your Internet connection (bandwidth), a program to deliver the sound file from the server (audio server) to the end user (client), and the modem/connection (TCP/IP) speed of which the audio file travels to and from.

Time-lapse considerations make the difference between what you hear when you listen to a recording of a single person talking into a microphone (AM quality sound) and what you hear when you listen to a high-quality recording of a symphony orchestra playing Beethoven (FM quality sound). It either sounds decent (sounds are clear and strong) or it sounds lousy (sounds break up and are scratchy). All the non-computer audio devices that we take for granted (our telephones and stereos, for example) have specialized equipment that make them work as separate machines. That is, they sound and operate fine. The difficulty occurs when you put these devices into a single computer (now sound and fax cards) and connect them to the Internet and then try to make them work and sound as they did as separate devices. RealAudio works with your computer's sound devices and makes listening to sound over the Internet enjoyable. RealAudio makes sound happen!

Progressive Networks, Inc., based in Seattle, develops and markets software products (such as RealAudio) that enable users of personal computers and other digital devices to send and receive audio files using their existing sound cards. Figure 36.1 shows the Progressive Networks home page at http://www.realaudio.com/.

FIGURE 36.1.

Where sound on the Internet began: The Progressive Networks home page.

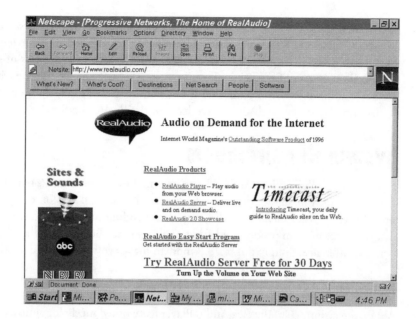

The RealAudio client/server software enables Internet and online users who have a PC, sound card, and telephone line to browse, select, and play back audio or audio-based multimedia content in real time and on demand over a TCP/IP network. The key term here is real time. Being able to play an audio file while it's being delivered (you can say downloaded) in real time to your computer is a real breakthrough in technology, especially if you compare it with typical audio-download experience. Audio files using conventional online methods can take five times longer to download than to play!

How Do They Do That?

How does RealAudio work its magic? The short answer is that the RealAudio Player works as a plug-in with your Web browser, such as Netscape or Explorer. The client side (the RealAudio Player) plays the downloaded sound file as it's being transferred to your computer, and the server side (the RealAudio Server) delivers the audio file with only a modest CPU impact to your server. The original sound performance was only AM broadcast quality (8-bit, 11KHz sample), but RealAudio 2.0 has better performance: The 14.4 algorithm has very good speech transmission and the 28.8 algorithm delivers monophonic FM quality audio.

The RealAudio Server delivers the audio in streams, using advanced compression algorithms and other specifications. Think of a stream as each user listening to an audio file while it's being transferred—no delays. If you want more users to listen to more audio files on your server at the same time, you obviously need a RealAudio Server version with multiple streams. Each stream requires about 10Kbps of network bandwidth and more money.

Accordingly, for this technology to come together and work, you must first create, or "encode," RealAudio files into a RealAudio format (for example, `welcome.RA`). This job requires a RealAudio Encoder. The Encoder encodes your sound input in real time with lots of hot features. The RealAudio Player and Encoder are free. By now, you might be wondering why you need three programs to have RealAudio, and what else you need. Let's talk shop on the following: the RealAudio Player, the RealAudio Encoder, and the RealAudio Server.

System Requirements

Before you launch your RealAudio Player, you might want to know its requirements. Although the player works in all Windows environments, the new 2.0 version can play and create versions for either 14.4 or 28.8 modem speeds depending on your hardware. The difference is that the faster modem produces a higher quality sound. Believe me when I tell you that there is a vast difference. Simply put, a 28.8 modem makes your files sound good!

Using Windows

Although version 1.0 of the RealAudio Player has worked nicely for almost a year now, the 2.0 has many significant new features that make this latest version of RealAudio Player the one to use. Among those features are 14.4 (monophonic AM quality sound) and 28.8 (FM mono quality sound) RealAudio (RA) type files. These files are hardware specific, meaning if your Internet connection and modem speed are fast enough (28.8Kbps for example), the server will send the 28.8 RA sound file, so get used to seeing two speeds for RA formats, 14.4 and 28.8. This will be a standard feature as RealAudio servers upgrade because it benefits the server.

If you want to play the 14.4 RealAudio files, you'll need at least a 486/33 DX or faster computer with a 14.4Kbps modem, 4MB of memory, 2MB of free disk space, an 8-bit sound card (a 16-bit card is recommended), TCP/IP (WinSock or equivalent), and an SLIP/PPP Internet or LAN connection. To play the 28.8 high-quality RealAudio sound files, you'll need at least a 486/66 DX or faster computer with a 28.8Kbps modem, 8MB of memory, 2MB of free disk space, your sound card, and a TCP/IP stack and Internet connection. Accordingly, most of you probably already have the necessary components.

If you're a Windows NT user, you must use the 32-bit RealAudio Player because the 16-bit player does not support Windows NT. The RealAudio Player supports over a dozen popular Web browsers, including Netscape Navigator, the Microsoft Internet Explorer, Netcruiser 2.0 or later, and Internet MCI Navigator.

> **NOTE**
>
> If you use Windows 95 and a later 16-bit `winsock.dll` driver, such as those found in America Online or CompuServe Internet software, you must use the Windows 3.1 (16-bit) RealAudio Player.

Macintosh Users

Macintosh users who want to play a 14.4 algorithm file need a 25MHz 68030 or faster computer. For 28.8 high-quality sound, Mac users need a 25MHz 68040 with floating-point processor or a PowerPC. Modem speed, memory, hard drive space, and Internet connection are equivalent for Windows and Mac. Web browsers for the Macintosh that support the RealAudio Player include Netscape Navigator, Internet Explorer, NCSA Mosaic, Netcruiser 2.0 or later, and MacWEB. New browsers are continually added, so keep updated by visiting Progressive Networks's Web site at `http://www.realaudio.com/`.

The RealAudio Player is the crux of the family of audio software products developed by Progressive Networks. It's free to download and widely used, as is the Encoder program. When you visit a Web page that has a RealAudio file, you usually see the icon shown in Figure 36.2, which means that a RealAudio file is present. Icons with a 28.8 designation mean you need a 28.8Kbps modem to handle the file.

FIGURE 36.2.

The RealAudio icon.

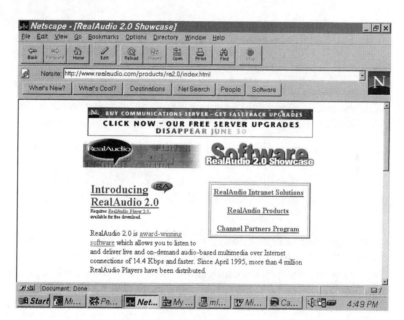

Clicking the icon launches your RealAudio Player and plays the audio file associated with that page. Version 2.0 of the player enables Web authors to play background music automatically or even embed real player controls in Web pages for user interaction.

The RealAudio Player is about 61KB in size, yet it provides a good punch for playing RA sound files. Figure 36.3 shows how the RealAudio Player looks after it is launched.

FIGURE 36.3.

A RealAudio Player.

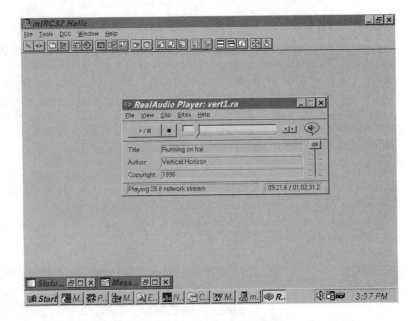

The player offers all the regular functions found in a typical tape player: start, pause, fast forward, rewind, stop, and volume control. You can also play an RA file directly from your hard drive or, of course, in a live real-time performance.

Other neat features include a file opening feature for a given URL address (for example, pnm: //audio.realaudio.com/welcome.ra) under the File section and also a statistics feature under the View section that shows you the number of lost packets sent over your TCP/IP connection. You can use this information to diagnose poor quality sound coming through your sound card.

On the right side of Figure 36.3, you'll see a small speaker. I always wondered why it went in circles. When you see it revolving, the RealAudio Player is looking for the RealAudio Server. Once it's connected, you'll see little sound waves come forth. When you see yellow or red lightning bolts displayed from the speaker, you know that data loss is occurring. Data loss can occur for a number of reasons: a bad connection, too much Internet traffic, or trouble from your own computer and sound card. Just be patient and see if it clears up. I found that running two Web browsers simultaneously made my RealAudio Player choke and the sound quality poor on more than one occasion.

RealAudio Player's Advanced New Features

For those of you with an earlier RealAudio Player, here's a list of the best new features in version 2.0:

■ Live broadcasts: These broadcasts are live audio events over the Internet, and this feature is becoming quite popular. Imagine the possibilities here—from news broadcasts to real-time entertainment. Progressive Networks offers a Live Events directory. I had the pleasure of listening to Classic KING FM 98.1 in Seattle, Washington, while in my office in southern California. This feature is amazing, and many radio stations across America are offering this type of event.

■ Cybercasting in real time: What do you need to start your own real-time broadcasting via the Web? You'll need the RealAudio 2.0 server and the Encoder program, which includes a small utility program called Life Transfer Agent (LTA.EXE) to link RealAudio Server with the Encoder program. The free LTA is used to broadcast a live event from the RealAudio Server. The RealAudio encoder connects to the LTA via TCP, and then it creates a RealAudio file for the Server to serve.

Does it work? While surfing the Web, I first clicked to a classical radio station in Seattle, Washington, called KING FM 98.1. Take note that I live in southern California, a bit out of Seattle's radio range. I wasn't hearing the music through my radio at all. I was listening to a real-time orchestrated performance on my RealAudio Player.

The quality of the music was decent considering that it was coming right over the Internet in real-time form. I would describe the quality as almost FM and a big improvement over the previous version of RealAudio.

To see this, or rather to see and hear, and other live presentations via your Web browser and a RealAudio Player, point your browser to

```
http://www.realaudio.com/products/ra2.0/features/live.html
```

■ Synchronized multimedia: Now you can make your own presentation synchronize visual and sound effects on your Web pages and add a real bang to your Web efforts! This feature is a neat way to do demos, slide shows, and tours of your Web site. By creating an ASCII input file with the start and stop times and the URL for this sound event, you can run CEVENTS.EXE, a utility program that comes with the RealAudio Server software and converts your ASCII file into a RealAudio binary event file with the extension .rae that the server reads. Here's a sample of the syntax you use in your HTML page to make a synchronized slide show with RealAudio sound. The u always goes at the beginning of a time event.

```
u <space> start time <space> end time <space> URL for event
u 00:00:10.0 00:00:59.9 http://www.somewhere.com/page1.htm
u 00:00:10.0 00:03:00.0 http://www.somewhere.com/page2.htm
```

This feature doesn't work with "live" broadcast feeds at this time, but anything from the RealAudio Server or even a local file work nicely. You can find a nice collection and sampling of synchronized presentations using RealAudio at

```
http://www.realaudio.com/products/ra2.0/features/synchmm.html
```

■ Great firewall support: We hear the word *intranet* often these days—and for good reason. Take an average Fortune 500 company with hundreds of divisions and thousands of employees. What you have is a mini-Internet of people, departments, documents, and much more. The capability to have an integrated and secure RealAudio-compatible firewall enables the corporation, large or small, to use RealAudio. Imagine being able to train new employees via a Web presentation using RealAudio files or displaying the corporate annual report using sound! You can download (FTP) a new Firewall Administrator's Proxy Kit free of charge. With Progressive Network's TCP Data Option, you can hear RealAudio from the Internet without any modification to your existing firewall. Many firewall vendors support RealAudio.

■ Server bandwidth performance: A new "bandwidth negotiation" feature enables the RealAudio Player to ask the RealAudio Server for either one of the new (14.4 and 28.8) file types. For example, if your RealAudio Server has little bandwidth or is often busy, you can use this negotiation feature to tell the server to send the correct RA file for that selected speed. If my `welcome.ra` file was created in 14.4 algorithm, then I can tell my server to send it out at that speed. Mix and match files according to your appropriate bandwidth.

■ RealAudio plug-in feature: The RealAudio Player now includes a plug-in (for browsers that support the plug-in feature, which include all the popular Web browsers) that enables you to visit Web sites that are using this neat RealAudio/plug-in enhancement. This feature enables Web authors to embed player controls found on the player itself into the Web page. You can embed volume controls, rewind, start/stop buttons, and more into your Web page, and your users can click them.

This plug-in does not replace the RealAudio Player. If this HTML feature is not used, the Player launches as a normal helper application via your Web browser. To see how easy it is to add this feature, here's a bit of code to include a Play button from the RealAudio Player in your Web page. When users click this button, they hear a song titled `mysong.rpm`:

```
<EMBED SRC="audio/mysong.rpm" ALIGN BASELINE WIDTH=40 HEIGHT=20
CONTROLS=Playbutton CONSOLE="mysong">
```

You can use many other tricks to spice up your Web page with RealAudio controls. Visit the RealAudio site to check them out.

Automatic Install

The RealAudio Player works with your browser and is launched as a helper application. When I installed my 2.0 player, the setup program automatically installed and configured both my Netscape and Microsoft browsers to use the RealAudio Player. By default, the RealAudio Player sends a 16-bit, 8KHz sound to your sound card. Unfortunately, some sound cards don't support 8KHz audio.

While the RealAudio Player is being installed, the installer program can talk to your sound card and change the preferences automatically.

Manually Installing the Player

First, locate the Options or Preferences settings menu in your Web browser. Look for the Helper Applications and then look for audio/x-pn-realaudio in the file type list. It is not alphabetized, so scroll down to see audio. If you see it, look at the extensions it supports and the application it launches. You should see file extensions of .RA, ram, and Raplayer.exe to launch the RealAudio RA or RAM files. If not, do the following:

1. Click NEW for Type.
2. Enter audio as the new MIME type.
3. Enter x-pn-realaudio as the MIME subtype.
4. Click OK.
5. Enter ra,ram in your EXTENSIONS field.
6. Make sure the word launch is checked. For the application to launch, browse and find the directory where your RealAudio Player exists.
7. Select Raplayer.exe as the application to launch. You're finished!

Where To Find Hot Audio Content

I am amazed at how much RealAudio sound is available on the Internet. Doing a search using www.yahoo.com with the search string REALAUDIO, I found everything from underground bands to full-length songs to famous speeches—all there at the click of my mouse. Most of these sites have directories, like a TV guide, listing live upcoming events.

I visited one site that gave me a host of whole songs on demand, including many live "Internet radio stations." A single word sums up this experience, "Cool!"

Check out the next site for a nice list of music. I found KDGE 94.5 in Texas there. You can actually type messages to the DJs—live on the Internet!

http://ww2.audionet.com/pub/edge/edge.htm

Do you want to check out an entire CD jukebox of sound files? Try Audio Net for one of the largest collections, if not the largest, that has all types of audio in one place. For sports, radio stations, live events, music of all types, and a cool CD jukebox of every type of music you want to hear, point your browser to

http://204.58.152.70/

RealAudio Encoder

Although you can find plenty of sites for using your RealAudio Player, if you want to make your own RealAudio files for others to hear, you must create them using the Encoder program. This requirement doesn't mean that you can't use another audio program or editor to prerecord your own sound. In fact, programs that come with SoundBlaster and other multimedia packages, even the Microsoft Sound Recorder included with Windows 95, do a good job. The RealAudio Encoder accepts au, wav, and raw pcm formats as its source file, and it even accepts external audio sources that come from a CD player, mixing console, microphone, or digital audio tape.

The RealAudio Encoder is quite easy to set up and use. Select a Source file or Live Stream (like a microphone or mixing board) and then a Destination file. (For live broadcasting, select a RealAudio Server.) I took a small wav file, named it Matthew.wav, and as soon as I finished typing the filename in the Encoder, it went to work and automatically encoded audio clip into a RealAudio RA file titled Matthew.ra. The Encoder also automatically recognizes the audio type of your source file. In my experiment, I had a microphone connected to my SoundBlaster input jack. If the Encoder can't recognize the file type, it asks you to select the Sampling Rate and Resolution (8-bit or 16-bit) formats of the source file. The Encoder also supports drag-and-drop encoding.

Figure 36.4 shows the RealAudio Encoder in action.

FIGURE 36.4.

The RealAudio Encoder in action.

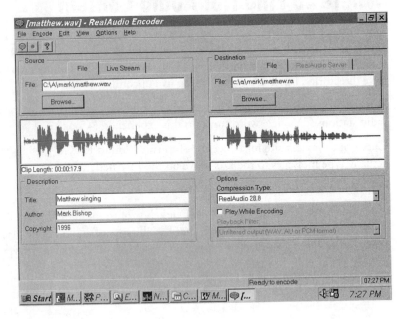

As mentioned before, the RealAudio Encoder compresses the RA sound file. For example, the original size of a wav file recorded at 22KHz, 16 bit, for one minute was 2.6MB. After using the Encoder, the size dropped to 113KB. How does the Encoder compression scheme work? RealAudio Encoder identifies the important parts of the audio file and tosses nonessential sections. File compression enables you to use your bandwidth to its fullest dimensions, stuffing the audio signal and packet all the way!

Accordingly, you can understand the need to use decent audio recording equipment. If you want to become a serious RealAudio provider, buy professional tools from the sound card to the microphone to the recording software. Fortunately, you won't go bankrupt buying good equipment at affordable prices.

The Making of a Good RealAudio Sound File

Even if you aren't a sound-recording expert, you can make high-quality RA files by following a number of common-sense steps.

Source

Make sure you use a high-quality original source such as an audio CD or that you use a quality microphone. If you want to take that box of old cassettes and make RA files, expect plenty of hiss and distortion once the tapes are encoded into an RA format. Progressive Networks recommends encoding from a 16-bit sound file and digitizing at a 22,050Hz sample rate. Even the Microsoft Sound Recorder offers a recording of CD quality with a 44,100Hz, 16-bit, stereo, 172Kbps sampling. After the file was encoded, it sounded quite good. Obviously, preprocessing your original sound file makes a large and noticeable difference in the RA results. To find good recording software to use to prepare your sound file for encoding, check www.yahoo.com for the names of shareware programs.

http://www.yahoo.com/Entertainment/Music/Genres/Computer_Generated/Music_Software

Volume Control

Do you remember the days before stereos came with built-in equalizers? Remember how many slide controls you had to adjust to get quality sound? Once the dials were set, you rarely had to readjust them. The same is true when you make RA files. Although you want to be rather conservative in the sound's volume (not to spike above that red line, whatever that might be), you also want an input level that uses your maximum amplitude. Look for the word *Normalize* on your sound editor; you can use this function to maximize your input level automatically. Most good sound editors/programs have this feature.

Key Audio Words To Live By

Other audio recording considerations include words such as *equalization* or *EQ* that change the tone of the incoming signal. As with stereo equalizers from yesterday, you can adjust the RealAudio Encoder by turning up or turning down certain frequencies. In a way, you are saying, "Yes, I want this sound, but no, I don't want that one." In short, you keep only the good sound. Nevertheless, the Encoder still discards lots of the high-end or treble sound, making your sound file sound flat.

To compensate for this effect, experts suggest increasing the middle frequencies, commonly known as the midrange. This feature also makes the sound file sound better! You should boost this level to about 2.5KHz.

Noise gating, also known as *expansion*, gets rid of undesired background noise and usually reacts when flat empty spots occur in a recording—for example, when you record from a microphone and do not say anything. Noise gating usually occurs automatically so that the beginning of any sound is not removed entirely. Some sound editors have a range control for this setting, and you should set it at 5 to 10dB.

The term *compression* is not related to the file size, as you might think of compressing a file, but rather it means the reduction between the loudest and quietest sections of the sound signal. Compression is important because the RealAudio Encoder creates sounds that weren't present before the encoding process. Some call these extraneous foreign sounds "artifacts."

You can avoid artifacts by using a louder incoming signal to mask these sounds. However, you are also limited by the loudest section of the signal. Compression enables you to quiet the loud section and thus turn up the overall volume. The process sounds complicated, but it works.

The best advice here is for the one doing the encoding. When you're recording speeches, a higher compression (4:1 to 10:1 ratio) makes the audio signal loud enough to cover the quieter artifact noises. With RealAudio's 28.8 format under Compression Type on the Encoder program, the dynamic range is increased so that the artifacts are almost nonexistent.

The RealAudio Encoder also comes bundled with two other command-line utility programs that enable you to edit your RealAudio files: RACUT.EXE and RAPASTE.EXE. The first program makes a copy of your RA file (use the status bar on your player to guide you to what portions of the clip you want to save), whereas RAPASTE.EXE enables you to create a new RA file from two or more other RA files.

Can You Hear Me?

When users listen to a RealAudio file for the first time, the sound quality might be worthless. The first thing to explain to the listener is that the quality is similar to AM radio for RealAudio Players 1.0 and similar to FM mono for the 2.0 version. If, however, the sound is choppy or garbled, then consider some of the following hints:

1. Check your installation. When you originally installed your RealAudio Player, the file Setup is complete should have played by default. Do you recall hearing it? If not, there could be a conflict with the sound card.

2. Visit other Web sites that have RealAudio files to play. If one site sounds better than others, go to the View section of your player and use the Statistics option to check whether any packets are lost or late. Perhaps the problem is with a particular site.

3. Check your modem connection. Look for the high-speed HS light on an external modem. Perhaps you assumed that your connection is 14.4 or 28.8, but it's not.

4. Adjust your modem's port speed. If you have an older serial card with an 8650 UART chip, lower your COM port speed and see if it helps. I recommend buying one of the newer standard high-speed serial cards with a 16650 UART chip. They are actually very inexpensive. If you have the 16650 serial card, increase your COM port speed two to three times higher than your maximum modem speed. (Windows 95 users can use the Control Panel.) Also make sure that for Flow Control, you select Hardware in the Advanced Settings section in the Modem Properties dialog box.

5. Try closing the RealAudio Player. Then clear your Web browser's "disk" cache. In Netscape Navigator, it is under the "Options and Network" preferences. Then, click the Reload button and try listening again.

After all is said and done, having good equipment and a quiet environment in which to record is essential. Test your sound card by making several recordings that use different input levels and settings to get the maximum amplitude. You might even want to consider hiring a professional announcer to develop your RealAudio content.

RealAudio Server

RealAudio Server is the winner of a number of honored Internet and computer-related awards. It streams RealAudio files in real time over modem connections or networks without any download delays. The process is immediate and fast.

Earlier, I told you to think of a stream as the delivery of a RealAudio file to one person. If you want simultaneous connections, you need the appropriate RealAudio Server and license key.

Progressive Networks' prices for the RealAudio Server vary according to how many streams you want—from a five-stream version (list $495.00) to a 20-stream version ($1,895.00) to 100 streams ($8,495.00). I bet that last one made you gasp! Larger stream packages are available upon request.

A visit to the RealAudio Web site is also worthwhile because Progressive Networks does offer very good support and its Web site offers lots of good help. You can also purchase modestly priced upgrade and support options that include up to 100 hours of free technical help, free upgrades for 12 months, and significant discounts on other items. Even without this upgrade, you still get 90 days of free technical help. I was also impressed with Progressive's Academic pricing, which gives faculty, staff, and students from accredited colleges a 25 percent discount on the RealAudio Server, upgrades, and support.

The Evaluation Program

Progressive Networks also has an evaluation program that gives you a five-stream RealAudio Server to use for up to 30 days. Give it a test drive to see if you want to purchase it. The evaluation package is a real version—not crippleware. You can contact Progressive Networks and apply for the evaluation program at

```
http://www.realaudio.com/products/server/2.0eval/program.html
```

The Easy Start Program

Progressive Networks put together a decently priced RealAudio package so that you can start to offer cool sounds on your Web site. You, too, can display real-time audio on your Web pages—no more delays for your users and no more waiting to download an audio file. For about $495, you can get a five-stream RealAudio 2.0 Server, the 2.0 Encoder, a 70 percent discount on upgrades and other support, and a 30-day money-back guarantee. For more information, visit the RealAudio Web site at `http://www.realaudio.com/`.

The Personal Server

You don't have to be a major enterprise with big bucks to enjoy a scaled-down version of the RealAudio Server. You can evaluate your own Personal RealAudio Server that runs on your own PC under Windows 95, Windows NT, or Mac OS. (You need a Pentium computer system and at least a 56K or T1 line to support simultaneous connections.) The Personal Server includes two live streams and one local stream. After the beta period, the retail cost is around $99. Visit the following site for additional information because it's still free:

```
http://christie.prognet.com/persserv/
```

Installing RealAudio Server

My RealAudio Server came on a CD. The license key is generally included with your invoice, or Progressive Networks sends it to you by e-mail. The installation process was fairly simple, even though an install program would be nice. Using my Windows NT 3.51 File Manager, I simply dragged the required directory contents (E:\SERVER\INTEL_NT\BIN) onto my C:\PNSERVER directory. As I said, all of this is done manually.

All the other components such as the RealAudio Player, Encoder, and utility programs come bundled on the CD. Even all the other available operating platforms such as UNIX are included. To install the RealAudio Server and make it operational, you cut and paste your license key into an ASCII SERVER.CFG file that already exists.

Using Administrative Privileges, you then run the program CRTSVC.EXE from the directory where you installed the server. Here's how my setup looked:

```
crtsvc c:\pnserver\bin\pnserv20.exe c:\pnserver\server.cfg
```

This setup places the required entries into your Windows NT Registry. To determine if the setup was successful, you must check the Services menu from the Control Panel.

My original install went fine. In fact, it took only a few minutes to copy the files, change the server.cfg file, and get the player working. If your installation goes bad, you must uninstall and redo. The RealAudio *Administrator's Guide* is very helpful and worth reading. You can test your install by using a RealAudio Player from a workstation or other computer and typing in the server's IP address.

```
pnm://IP-address-of-your-RA-Server-Here>/sound1.ra
```

Select Open Location from the player's File menu and enter the preceding information. If things go well, the player will connect to your RealAudio Server and play the file. If not, you have a problem. At this point I suggest that you call Progressive Networks and get it fixed fast.

The Server software itself works nicely and is supported on many platforms. It uses little of your CPU's processing speed (on a 90MHz Pentium, it uses less than 30 percent of the CPU cycles), and the software itself takes less than 2MB of your hard drive space minus your RealAudio RA files, which are small anyway.

The RealAudio Server does require at least 10Kbps for a 14.4 format and 22Kbps for a 28.8 format for each user connected to your system through the Internet. In short, if you have a 56K line, you are pushing it to the limit with just five simultaneous users accessing RealAudio files in real time. However on a T1, you could support up to 100 simultaneous 14.4 connections—a world of difference. You will probably run out of bandwidth before you run out of computer memory!

The RealAudio Server can work with any Web server that supports configurable MIME types. Some of the platforms tested are Webstar and Webstar PS, Mac HTTP, HTTPD4Mac, Netscape Netsite, EMWAC HTTPS 0.96, NCSA HTTPD, CERN HTTP, O'Reilly Website NT, and Microsoft's IIS. I installed my RealAudio Server onto my Purveyor 1.2, and surprisingly, the folks at Progressive Networks had not yet tested this award-winning Web server with their RealAudio Server. Progressive Networks audio products work with just about any Web server platform. Check the RealAudio Web site to get the latest information on what Web servers its products have been tested on.

Cool Features

The various configuration options of the Server give you a lot of flexibility. For example, RealAudio on a single UNIX machine can run as multiple processes, which enables incoming streams to be balanced on the server's processes. This makes the server more efficient in utilizing its system resources. You can even "cluster" your RealAudio servers and link them together, which provides support for large-stream situations. The previously mentioned *Bandwidth negotiation* feature enables you to organize your files according to their bandwidth usage. In short, arranging your audio content in a certain order (see Chapter 3 of the *Administrator's Guide*) enables the RealAudio Server to check first with the end user's player to determine the correct RA file to send.

The client's RealAudio Player contains information about the quality of the connection and other factors and shares this information with the Server. The RealAudio Server then knows whether to send the 14.4 file or the 28.8 file, thus making the best use of the line.

The RealAudio Server comes with a neat MONITOR.EXE program called the System Manager. This program supports remote monitoring of multiple RealAudio Servers and is password controlled. You can use it to graphically monitor performance issues by remotely connecting to your various RealAudio Servers.

Creating a Hot RealAudio Web Site

Without question, sound adds a positive dimension to your Web pages and Web site. I've visited some excellent sites, and I must confess that Progressive Networks made a big leap forward with its 2.0 RealAudio family of products. What do you do after you make your audio files and get your RealAudio Server up and running? Good question.

The Web sites I enjoyed visiting that offered RealAudio files on demand seemed to follow design guidelines that not only entertained me but also made me want to return. The following sections discuss some ways to make a great Web site.

Combine Hot Graphics with Hot Sound

Combine graphics and sound to keep your visitors' eyes and ears busy. Create pictures that talk back to them. You'll receive more hits and returns if you make your graphics interesting and fun. Use the synchronized presentation feature.

Provide Decent Sound

Make sure your RealAudio files sound decent. Who wants to hear junk? Follow the guidelines given earlier in the chapter for making a good quality RA file. Remember to use a good original source, have a good sound card, and record in a good quiet environment.

Change, Change, and Change

Change your audio files often. Change your site and keep your sound files and content fresh and learn to advertise your site. Tell everyone you have on-demand audio—no waits, no hassles. And when you change or update your sound files, tell others. Especially let people know you have RealAudio with RealAudio icons and banners.

Link to the RealAudio Library

Tell people how to get and use the free RealAudio Player. Those neat sites I visited had a single button click that linked to the RealAudio library at the following URL:

```
http://www.realaudio.com/products/ra2.0/index.html
```

Stereo Sound? No Way!

Progressive Networks has beta released its RealAudio 3.0, which brings broadcast-quality audio to the Internet delivering it to your computer and speakers in stereo sound. You need at least a 28.8 bps modem, and with an ISDN or LAN connection you can get near-CD quality sound. RealAudio now builds onto the famous Dolby Net technology along with many other improvements in its software.

When I listened to the differences of the RealAudio Player 2.0 and 3.0 I was totally amazed at the improved quality. My speakers were blasting sound in real stereo! You can hear the differences between the two versions by first getting your 3.0 player and then visiting the comparison page at

```
http://www.realaudio.com/hpproducts/ra3.0/bettersound.html#stereo
```

The RealAudio Player 3.0 and RealAudio Player Plus 3.0 (a software program that looks and performs like a real radio on your screen) beta versions are currently available for Microsoft Windows 95 and NT and also the Macintosh PowerPC. Visit the RealAudio Web site to learn more about these products.

Summary: RealAudio Only?

Although RealAudio is a superior product for sound on demand, some upcoming companies might eventually put it to the test. One of those companies is the DSP Group, a world leader in digital speech products. TrueSpeech for Windows is a DSP program.

TrueSpeech is similar to RealAudio in that it has a server version and it plays its own encoded sound files on your Web server. However, these files are TrueSpeech's WAV format of files—a common sound file format, indeed. In fact, TrueSpeech 8.5 is built into Microsoft Windows 95 and Windows NT operating systems, and industry leaders such as Intel and Creative Labs have licensed DSP's technology. Even VocalTec, the largest producer of Internet telephone software (such as Internet Phone), is using TrueSpeech's technology.

Although RealAudio is still the superior product, watching the race will be very interesting. Stepping up to the mound after the home runs of RealAudio and TrueSpeech are some other quality programs such as Internet Wave and WHAM. Keep your eye on the ball!

I
INDEX

Symbols

A

D

-d option, 135
daemons, 45, 299
Data Encryption Standard,
  see DES
data mirroring, 103
data objects, 272
data streams (plug-ins),
  859-861
data structure stack
  (memory), 138
data transfer process, 19
data types
  arrays, 351, 377, 396
  Booleans, 584
  bytes, 584
  date (time), 585
  double, 585
  empty, 586
  error, 585
  functions (arguments), 514
  hashes
    %INC, 351
    assigning values, 343
  integers, 584
    Java, 194
  long, 584
  null, 586
  object, 585
  Perl, 339-340
  scalars (modifying
    arguments), 396
  single, 585
  single character, 123
  string, 585
data-caching (WinInet API),
  466
database records, 45
databases (dbm), 324
date (time) data type, 585
date function (VBScript),
  602
Date object, 523-524
dates, formatting, 66

day function (VBScript),
  602-603
dbm databases, 324
DCOM (Distributed COM),
  268, 272, 288
debuggers
  JDK (Java Developer's
    Kit), 139
  Perl, 326
debugging
  Borland debugger,
    153-154
  Cafe, 143
  graphical debuggers, 153
  Java workshop
    debugger, 162
declarations
  check boxes, 245
  Perl, 352
  functions (VBScript), 614
  variables (JavaScript), 503
decoding
  forms, CGI (Common
    Gateway Interface),
    306, 317
  URL-encoded text, Perl,
    323-324
decrement unary operators
  (—), 507
decremental operators
  (Java), 202-203
defaultStatus property, 536
defined function (Perl), 365
defining
  arrays, 518-519
  methods, 516
  objects, 118
definition of objects
  .class file format, 277
  .tlb (type library) file, 277
delete function (Perl), 365
deleting
  menu bars, 259
  URLs (Freehand), 808
delimiting string
  literals, 341

delItem( ) method, 250
delivering graphics based
  on connection speed
  listing, 662
demodulation, 454
demos
  Cafe, 145
  JDK, 133
DES (Data Encryption
  Standard), 83
deselect( ) method, 250
design considerations, 45
designing
  applications, 47-55
    client/server, 92-93
    *public interface
      components, 48*
    *sys devpment methodol-
      ogy, 47-48*
  Web pages, 109-110
destroy( ) method, 220
detecting transactions,
  53-54
development environments,
  131
development files, 174
dial-up connections, 44
dialog boxes
  Alert, 546
  Confirm, 544
  IE3 options, 460
  Prompt, 546
  property page, 822
  Security, 802
die LIST function (Perl), 365
digital certificates, 84
digital code signing
  tools, 459
digital signatures, 75, 82,
  458-459
digital videos, 783
Dim keyword, 580
Director
  bandwidth considerations,
    784-785
  defined, 766

HTML in 10 seconds!*

No kidding.
In the time it takes for a good slurp of coffee, *HTML Transit* generated this Web page.

Say hello to the template.

HTML Transit takes a new approach to online publishing, using a high-speed production template. It's fast and easy. You can turn a 50-page word processing file into multiple, linked HTML pages—complete with graphics and tables—in less than 10 mouse clicks. From scratch.

Customize your template—formatting, backgrounds, navigation buttons, thumbnails—and save even more time. Now in just 4 clicks, you can crank out an entire library of custom Web pages with no manual authoring.

Take a free test drive.

Stop working so hard. Download an evaluation copy of *HTML Transit* from our Web site:

http://www.infoaccess.com

Your download code is **MCML46**. (It can save you money when you order *HTML Transit*.)

Buy HTML Transit risk free.

HTML Transit is just $495, and is backed by a 30-day satisfaction guarantee. To order, call us toll-free at **800-344-9737**.

▶ **Automatic HTML from native word processor formats**
▶ **Creates HTML tables, tables of contents & indexes**
▶ **Graphics convert to GIF or JPEG, with thumbnails**
▶ **Template control over appearance and behavior**
▶ **For use with Microsoft® Windows®**

InfoAccess, Inc.
(206) 747-3203
FAX: (206) 641-9367
Email: info@infoaccess.com

HTML Transit is a trademark of InfoAccess, Inc. Microsoft and Windows are registered trademarks of Microsoft Corporation.
*Single-page Microsoft Word document with graphics and tables, running on 75MHz Pentium. Conversion speed depends on document length, complexity and PC configuration.

Teach Yourself Java in 21 Days, Professional Reference Edition

—Laura Lemay and Michael Morrison

Introducing the first, best, and most detailed guide to developing applications with the hot new Java language from Sun Microsystems. This book provides detailed coverage of the hottest new technology on the World Wide Web and shows you how to develop applications using the Java language. It includes coverage of how to browse Java applications with Netscape and other popular Web browsers. The CD-ROM includes the Java Developers Kit.

Price: $59.99 USA/$84.95 CDN   *User level: Casual–Accomplished–Expert*
ISBN: 1-57521-183-1   *900 pages*

JavaScript Unleashed

—Richard Wagner, et al.

Programming JavaScript is much simpler than programming for Java, because JavaScript code can be embedded directly into an HTML document. *JavaScript Unleashed* unveils the mysteries of this new code, enabling programmers to exploit its full potential in their Web applications. The book covers Netscape LiveWire server system, Netscape Navigator Gold, and more. The CD-ROM includes source code from the book, sample applications, and third-party utilities.

Price: $49.99 USA/$70.95 CDN   *User level: Casual–Accomplished–Expert*
ISBN: 1-57521-118-1   *900 pages*

Laura Lemay's Web Workshop: JavaScript

—Laura Lemay and Michael Moncur

This book provides a clear, hands-on guide to creating sophisticated Web pages. Readers will learn to use JavaScript to create interactive forms and image maps as well as to incorporate Java applets into their Web pages. Customizing JavaScript for ActiveX and Microsoft Internet Explorer is also covered. The CD-ROM includes the complete book in HTML format, publishing tools, templates, graphics, backgrounds, and more.

Price: $39.99 USA/$56.95 CDN   *User level: Casual–Accomplished*
ISBN: 1-57521-141-6   *400 pages*

HTML 3.2 & CGI Unleashed, Professional Reference Edition

—John December and Mark Ginsburg

In this book, readers learn the logistics of how to create compelling, information-rich Web pages that grab readers' attention and keep users returning for more. This comprehensive professional instruction and reference guide for World Wide Web covers all aspects of the development processes, implementation, tools, and programming. The CD-ROM features coverage of planning, analysis, design, HTML implementation, and gateway programming.

Price: $59.99 USA/$84.95 CDN   *User level: Accomplished–Expert*
ISBN: 1-57521-177-7   *900 pages*

Perl 5 Unleashed

—Kamran Husain, et al.

Perl 5 Unleashed is for the programmer who wants to get the most out of Perl. This comprehensive book provides in-depth coverage on all Perl programming topics, including using Perl in Web pages. This is the reference Perl programmers will turn to for the best coverage of Perl. The book includes coverage of these and other Perl topics: Scalar values, lists and array variables, reading and writing files, subroutines, control structures, Internet scripting, system functions, debugging, and many, many more.

Price: $49.99 USA/$70.95 CDN   *User level: Intermediate–Advanced*
ISBN: 0-672-30891-6   *800 pages*

Web Programming with Java

—Harris & Jones

This book gets readers on the road to developing robust, real-world Java applications. Various cutting-edge applications are presented, enabling the reader to quickly learn all aspects of programming Java for the Internet. Readers will be able to create live, interactive Web pages. The CD-ROM contains source code and powerful utilities.

Price: $39.99 USA/$56.95 CDN   *User level: Accomplished–Expert*
ISBN: 1-57521-113-0   *500 pages*

Web Programming with Visual Basic

—Craig Eddy & Brad Haasch

This book is a reference that quickly and efficiently shows the experienced developer how to develop Web applications using the 32-bit power of Visual Basic 4. It includes an introduction and overview of Web programming, then quickly delves into the specifics, teaching readers how to incorporate animation, sound, and more into their Web applications. The CD-ROM contains all the examples from the book, plus additional Visual Basic programs.

Price: $39.99 USA/$56.95 CDN   *User level: Accomplished–Expert*
ISBN: 1-57521-106-8   *400 pages*

Teach Yourself VBScript in 21 Days

—Keith Brophy and Tim Koets

With *Teach Yourself VBScript in 21 Days*, you learn how to use VBScript to create living, interactive Web pages. This unique scripting language from Microsoft is taught with clarity and precision, providing the reader with the best and latest information on this popular language. This book teaches you advanced OLE object techniques and explores VBScript's animation, interaction, and mathematical capabilities. The CD-ROM contains all the source code from the book and examples of third-party software.

Price: $39.99 USA/$56.95 CDN   *User level: New–Casual*
ISBN: 1-57521-120-3   *720 pages*

Add to Your Sams.net Library Today
with the Best Books for Internet Technologies

ISBN	Quantity	Description of Item	Unit Cost	Total Cost
1-57521-183-1		Teach Yourself Java in 21 Days Professional Reference Edition (Book/CD-ROM)	$59.99	
1-57521-118-1		JavaScript Unleashed (Book/CD-ROM)	$49.99	
1-57521-141-6		Laura Lemay's Web Workshop: JavaScript (Book/CD-ROM)	$39.99	
1-57521-177-7		HTML 3.2 & CGI Unleashed, Professional Reference Edition (Book/CD-ROM)	$59.99	
0-672-30891-6		Perl 5 Unleashed (Book/CD-ROM)	$49.99	
1-57521-113-0		Web Programming with Java (Book/CD-ROM)	$39.99	
1-57521-106-8		Web Programming with Visual Basic (Book/CD-ROM)	$39.99	
1-57521-120-3		Teach Yourself VBScript in 21 Days (Book/CD-ROM)	$39.99	
		Shipping and Handling: See information below.		
		TOTAL		

Shipping and Handling: $4.00 for the first book, and $1.75 for each additional book. If you need to have it NOW, we can ship product to you in 24 hours for an additional charge of approximately $18.00, and you will receive your item overnight or in two days. Overseas shipping and handling adds $2.00. Prices subject to change. Call between 9:00 a.m. and 5:00 p.m. EST for availability and pricing information on latest editions.

201 W. 103rd Street, Indianapolis, Indiana 46290

1-800-428-5331 — Orders   1-800-835-3202 — Fax   1-800-858-7674 — Customer Service

Book ISBN 1-57521-117-3

What's On the CD-ROM?

- Visual J++™ Publisher's Edition from Microsoft®
- Freeloader Off-line Web Browser software from FreeLoader
- HTML Transit Demo Version from InfoAccess Software
- Spider—Web Editor from Incontext Systems
- Jpad from Modelworks Software
- JDesigner Pro from Bulletproof Software
- C libraries for CGI programs
- C++ libraries for CGI programs
- Perl libraries for CGI programs
- ScriptEase: WebServer Edition from Nombas Software
- NetFerret from Vironix (All Ferrets)
- WebForms Form generator for HTML from Q&D
- Nico Mak's WinZip for Windows 95/NT
- Internet Explorer 3.0 From Microsoft®
- ActiveX Control Pad From Microsoft®
- All flavors of Perl 5.0
- Source code from the authors
- HTML version of *Web Programming with Visual Basic* from Sams.net
- HTML version of *Web Programming with Java* from Sams.net

Windows 95/NT 4 Installation Instructions

1. Insert the CD-ROM disc into your CD-ROM drive.
2. From the Windows desktop, double-click the My Computer icon.
3. Double-click the icon representing your CD-ROM drive.
4. Double-click the icon titled SETUP.EXE to run the installation program.
5. Installation creates a program group named Web Prog Unleashed. This group will contain icons to browse the CD-ROM.

> **NOTE**
>
> If Windows 95 or NT is installed on your computer and you have the AutoPlay feature enabled, the SETUP.EXE program starts automatically whenever you insert the disc into your CD-ROM drive.

Windows 3.1 Installation Instructions

1. Insert the CD-ROM into your CD-ROM drive.
2. From File Manager or Program Manager, choose Run from the File menu.

3. Type `<drive>\SETUP.EXE` and press Enter, where `<drive>` corresponds to the drive letter of your CD-ROM. For example, if your CD-ROM is drive D:, type `D:\SETUP.EXE` and press Enter.
4. Installation creates a program group named Web Prog Unleashed. This group will contain icons to browse the CD-ROM.

DOS or UNIX (ISO9660) Installation Instructions

Look in the individual directories for software and associated documentation. Read `info.txt` available in the root directory of the CD-ROM for program descriptions.

6. **REDISTRIBUTABLE COMPONENTS.**

   a. **Redistributable Files.** In addition to the license granted in Section 1, Microsoft grants you a nonexclusive, royalty-free right to reproduce and distribute the object code version of those portions of the SOFTWARE designated in the SOFTWARE as: (I) the files identified in the REDISTRB.WRI file located in the \MSDev\Redist subdirectory on the "Microsoft Visual J++ version 1.00" CD-ROM (collectively, "REDISTRIBUTABLES"), provided you comply with Section 6.b.

   b. **Redistribution Requirements.** If you redistribute the REDISTRIBUTABLES, you agree to: (I) distribute the REDISTRIBUTABLES in object code form only in conjunction with and as a part of your software application product which adds significant and primary functionality and which is designed, developed, and tested to operate in the Microsoft Windows and/or Windows NT environments; (ii) not use Microsoft's name, logo, or trademarks to market your software application product; (iii) include a valid copyright notice on your software product; (iv) indemnify, hold harmless, and defend Microsoft from and against any claims or lawsuits, including attorney's fees, that arise or result from the use or distribution of your software application product; and (v) not permit further distribution of the REDISTRIBUTABLES by your end user.Contact Microsoft for the applicable royalties due and other licensing terms for all other uses and/or distribution of the REDISTRIBUTABLES.

7. **U.S. GOVERNMENT RESTRICTED RIGHTS.** The SOFTWARE PRODUCT and documentation are provided with RESTRICTED RIGHTS. Use, duplication, or disclosure by the Government is subject to restrictions as set forth in subparagraph (c)(1)(ii) of the Rights in Technical Data and Computer Software clause at DFARS 252.227-7013 or subparagraphs (c)(1) and (2) of the Commercial Computer Software—Restricted Rights at 48 CFR 52.227-19, as applicable. Manufacturer is Microsoft Corporation/One Microsoft Way/Redmond, WA 98052-6399.

8. **EXPORT RESTRICTIONS.**

   You agree that you will not export or re-export the SOFTWARE PRODUCT to any country, person, entity or end user subject to U.S.A. export restrictions. Restricted countries currently include, but are not necessarily limited to Cuba, Iran, Iraq, Libya, North Korea, Syria, and the Federal Republic of Yugoslavia (Serbia and Montenegro, U.N. Protected Areas and areas of Republic of Bosnia and Herzegovina under the control of Bosnian Serb forces). You warrant and represent that neither the U.S.A. Bureau of Export Administration nor any other federal agency has suspended, revoked or denied your export privileges.

9. **NOTE ON JAVA SUPPORT.** THE SOFTWARE PRODUCT CONTAINS SUPPORT FOR PROGRAMS WRITTEN IN JAVA. JAVA TECHNOLOGY IS NOT FAULT TOLERANT AND IS NOT DESIGNED, MANUFACTURED OR INTENDED FOR USE OR RESALE AS ONLINE CONTROL EQUIPMENT IN HAZARDOUS ENVIRONMENTS REQUIRING FAIL-SAFE PERFORMANCE, SUCH AS IN THE OPERATION OF NUCLEAR FACILITIES, AIRCRAFT NAVIGATION OR COMMUNI-CATIONS SYSTEMS, AIR TRAFFIC CONTROL, DIRECT LIFE SUPPORT MACHINES, OR WEAPONS SYSTEMS, IN WHICH THE FAILURE OF JAVA TECHNOLOGY COULD LEAD DIRECTLY TO DEATH, PERSONAL INJURY, OR SEVERE PHYSICAL OR ENVIRONMENTAL DAMAGE.

MISCELLANEOUS

If you acquired this product in the United States, this EULA is governed by the laws of the State of Washington.

If you acquired this product in Canada, this EULA is governed by the laws of the Province of Ontario, Canada. Each of the parties hereto irrevocably attorns to the jurisdiction of the courts of the Province of Ontario and further agrees to commence any litigation which may arise hereunder in the courts located in the Judicial District of York, Province of Ontario.

If this product was acquired outside the United States, then local law may apply.

Should you have any questions concerning this EULA, or if you desire to contact Microsoft for any reason, please contact the Microsoft subsidiary serving your country, or write: Microsoft Sales Information Center/One Microsoft Way/Redmond, WA 98052-6399.

LIMITED WARRANTY

LIMITED WARRANTY. Except with respect to Microsoft Internet Explorer and the REDISTRIBUTABLES, which are provided "as is," without warranty of any kind, Microsoft warrants that (a) the SOFTWARE PRODUCT will perform substantially in accordance with the accompanying written materials for a period of ninety (90) days from the date of receipt, and (b) any hardware accompanying the SOFTWARE PRODUCT will be free from defects in materials and workmanship under normal use and service for a period of one (1) year from the date of receipt. Some states and jurisdictions do not allow limitations on duration of an implied warranty, so the above limitation may not apply to you. To the extent allowed by applicable law, implied warranties on the SOFTWARE PRODUCT and hardware, if any, are limited to ninety (90) days and one year, respectively.

CUSTOMER REMEDIES. Microsoft's and its suppliers' entire liability and your exclusive remedy shall be, at Microsoft's option, either (a) return of the price paid, or (b) repair or replacement of the SOFTWARE PRODUCT or hardware that does not meet Microsoft's Limited Warranty and which is returned to Microsoft with a copy of your receipt. This Limited Warranty is void if failure of the SOFTWARE PRODUCT or hardware has resulted from accident, abuse, or misapplication. Any replacement SOFTWARE PRODUCT or hardware will be warranted for the remainder of the original warranty period or thirty (30) days, whichever is longer. **Outside the United States, neither these remedies nor any product support services offered by Microsoft are available without proof of purchase from an authorized international source.**

NO OTHER WARRANTIES. TO THE MAXIMUM EXTENT PERMITTED BY APPLICABLE LAW, MICROSOFT AND ITS SUPPLIERS DISCLAIM ALL OTHER WARRANTIES, EITHER EXPRESS OR IMPLIED, INCLUDING, BUT NOT LIMITED TO, IMPLIED WARRANTIES OF MERCHANTABILITY AND FITNESS FOR A PARTICULAR PURPOSE, WITH REGARD TO THE SOFTWARE PRODUCT, AND ANY ACCOMPANYING HARDWARE. THIS LIMITED WARRANTY GIVES YOU SPECIFIC LEGAL RIGHTS. YOU MAY HAVE OTHERS, WHICH VARY FROM STATE/JURISDICTION TO STATE/JURISDICTION.

NO LIABILITY FOR CONSEQUENTIAL DAMAGES. TO THE MAXIMUM EXTENT PERMITTED BY APPLICABLE LAW, IN NO EVENT SHALL MICROSOFT OR ITS SUPPLIERS BE LIABLE FOR ANY SPECIAL, INCIDENTAL, INDIRECT, OR CONSEQUENTIAL DAMAGES WHATSOEVER (INCLUDING, WITHOUT LIMITATION, DAMAGES FOR LOSS OF BUSINESS PROFITS, BUSINESS INTERRUPTION, LOSS OF BUSINESS INFORMATION, OR ANY OTHER PECUNIARY LOSS) ARISING OUT OF THE USE OF OR INABILITY TO USE THE SOFTWARE PRODUCT, EVEN IF MICROSOFT HAS BEEN ADVISED OF THE POSSIBILITY OF SUCH DAMAGES. BECAUSE SOME STATES AND JURISDICTIONS DO NOT ALLOW THE EXCLUSION OR LIMITATION OF LIABILITY FOR CONSEQUENTIAL OR INCIDENTAL DAMAGES, THE ABOVE LIMITATION MAY NOT APPLY TO YOU.

END-USER LICENSE AGREEMENT FOR MICROSOFT SOFTWARE

MICROSOFT VISUAL J++, Publisher's Edition

IMPORTANT—READ CAREFULLY: This Microsoft End-User License Agreement ("EULA") is a legal agreement between you (either an individual or a single entity) and Microsoft Corporation for the Microsoft software product identified above and Microsoft Internet Explorer, which include computer software and associated media and printed materials, and may include "online" or electronic documentation (together, the "SOFTWARE PRODUCT" or "SOFTWARE"). By installing, copying, or otherwise using the SOFTWARE PRODUCT, you agree to be bound by the terms of this EULA. If you do not agree to the terms of this EULA, promptly return the unused SOFTWARE PRODUCT to the place from which you obtained it for a full refund.

SOFTWARE PRODUCT LICENSE

The SOFTWARE PRODUCT is protected by copyright laws and international copyright treaties, as well as other intellectual property laws and treaties. The SOFTWARE PRODUCT is licensed, not sold.

1. **GRANT OF LICENSE.** This EULA grants you the following rights:

   a. You may use one copy of the Microsoft Software Product identified above on a single computer. The SOFTWARE is in "use" on a computer when it is loaded into temporary memory (i.e., RAM) or installed into permanent memory (e.g., hard disk, CD-ROM, or other storage device) of that computer. However, installation on a network server for the sole purpose of internal distribution to one or more other computer(s) shall not constitute "use" for which a separate license is required, provided you have a separate license for each computer to which the SOFTWARE is distributed.

   b. You may only use copies of the Microsoft Internet Explorer software only in conjunction with a validly licensed copy of Microsoft operating system products (e.g., Windows® 95 or Windows NT®). You may make copies of the SOFT-WARE PRODUCT for use on all computers for which you have licensed Microsoft operating system products.

   c. Solely with respect to electronic documents included with the SOFTWARE, you may make an unlimited number of copies (either in hardcopy or electronic form), provided that such copies shall be used only for internal purposes and are not republished or distributed to any third party.

2. **UPGRADES.** If the SOFTWARE is an upgrade, whether from Microsoft or another supplier, you may use or transfer the SOFTWARE only in conjunction with upgraded product. If the SOFTWARE is an upgrade from a Microsoft product, you may now use that upgraded product only in accordance with this EULA.

3. **SUBSCRIPTION UPDATES.** If you have acquired the SOFTWARE PRODUCT as part of a subscription package, then you must treat as an upgrade any subsequent versions of SOFTWARE PRODUCT received as an update to your subscription package.

4. **COPYRIGHT.** All title and copyrights in and to the SOFTWARE PRODUCT (including but not limited to any images, photographs, animations, video, audio, music, text, and "applets" incorporated into the SOFTWARE PRODUCT), the accompanying printed materials, and any copies of the SOFTWARE PRODUCT are owned by Microsoft or its suppliers. The SOFTWARE PRODUCT is protected by copyright laws and international treaty provisions. Therefore, you must treat the SOFTWARE PRODUCT like any other copyrighted material except that you may either (a) make one copy of the SOFTWARE PRODUCT solely for backup or archival purposes or (b) install the SOFTWARE PRODUCT on a single computer provided you keep the original solely for backup or archival purposes. You may not copy the printed materials accompanying the SOFTWARE PRODUCT.

5. **DESCRIPTION OF OTHER RIGHTS AND LIMITATIONS.**

   a. **Limitations on Reverse Engineering, Decompilation, and Disassembly.** You may not reverse engineer, decompile, or disassemble the SOFTWARE PRODUCT, except and only to the extent that such activity is expressly permitted by applicable law notwithstanding this limitation.

   b. **No Separation of Components.** The SOFTWARE PRODUCT is licensed as a single product and neither the software programs making up the SOFTWARE PRODUCT nor any UPDATE may be separated for use by more than one user at a time.

   c. **Rental.** You may not rent or lease the SOFTWARE PRODUCT.

   d. **Software Transfer.** You may permanently transfer all of your rights under this EULA, provided that you retain no copies, you transfer all of the SOFTWARE PRODUCT (including all component parts, the media and printed materials, any upgrades, this EULA, and, if applicable, the Certificate of Authenticity), and the recipient agrees to the terms of this EULA. If the SOFTWARE PRODUCT is an upgrade, any transfer must include all prior versions of the SOFTWARE PRODUCT. Notwithstanding the foregoing, you may permanently transfer all your rights under this EULA that pertain to the Microsoft Internet Explorer only in conjunction with a permanent transfer of your validly licensed copy of a Microsoft operating system product.

   e. **Termination.** Without prejudice to any other rights, Microsoft may terminate this EULA if you fail to comply with the terms and conditions of this EULA. In such event, you must destroy all copies of the SOFTWARE PRODUCT. In addition, your rights under this EULA that pertain to the Microsoft Internet Explorer software shall terminate upon termination of your Microsoft operating system product EULA.

continues on preceding page